User's Guide

Microsoft® Excel

Version 5.0

Microsoft Corporation

Document No. XL57926-0394
Printed in the United States of America.

Contents

Part 2   Essential Skills

Appendixes

Microsoft Support Services

The Microsoft® Support Network

The Microsoft Support Network offers you a wide range of choices and access to high-quality, responsive technical support. Microsoft recognizes that support needs vary from user to user; the Microsoft Support Network allows you to choose the type of support that best meets your needs, with options ranging from electronic bulletin boards to annual support programs.

If you have a question about your Microsoft product, first look in the printed documentation or consult online Help. You can also find late-breaking updates and technical information by double-clicking the Microsoft Excel Readme icon in the Microsoft Excel program group or folder.

If you cannot find the answer, use one of the Microsoft Support Network options. Outside the United States, contact the Microsoft subsidiary office that serves your area. For information about Microsoft subsidiary offices, see "Product Support Worldwide" later in this section.

Services vary outside the United States and Canada. In other locations, contact a local Microsoft subsidiary for information. The Microsoft Support Network is subject to Microsoft's then-current prices, terms, and conditions, and is subject to change without notice.

Product Support Within the United States and Canada

Use the System Info feature to view information about your system

The System Info feature examines your computer and displays information about Microsoft Excel and your operating system, including fonts, printing, proofing tools, graphics filters, text converters, OLE applications, and screen display. This information may be useful to the technical support technician, should you need to call for assistance.

In the United States and Canada, the following support services are available through the Microsoft Support Network.

▶ **To see information with the System Info feature**

1. From the Help menu, choose About Microsoft Excel.

2. Choose the System Info button.

3. In the Choose A Category box, select the type of information you want.

You can also save or print information and run programs from the System Info dialog box.

Electronic Services

These services are available 24 hours a day, seven days a week, including holidays.

Microsoft FastTips   Receive automated answers to common questions, and access a library of technical notes, all delivered by recording or fax.

■ For FastTips for Microsoft Excel, call (800) 936-4100.

You can use the following keys on your touch-tone telephone after you reach FastTips:

To	Press
Advance to the next message	*
Repeat the current message	7
Return to the beginning of FastTips	#

CompuServe®   Interact with other users and Microsoft support engineers, or access the Microsoft Knowledge Base to get product information. At any ! prompt, type **go microsoft** to access Microsoft forums, or type **go mskb** to access the Microsoft Knowledge Base. For an introductory CompuServe membership kit, call (800) 848-8199, operator 519.

Microsoft Download Service   Access the Driver Library and the most current technical notes via modem (1200, 2400, or 9600 baud; no parity; 8 data bits; 1 stop bit). Modem number: In the United States, call (206) 936-6735. In Canada, call (905) 507-3022.

Internet   Access the Driver Library and the Microsoft Knowledge Base. The Microsoft Internet FTP archive host, ftp.microsoft.com, supports anonymous logon. When logging on as anonymous, you should type your complete electronic mail name as your password.

Standard Support

In the United States, no-charge support from Microsoft support engineers is available via a toll call between 6:00 A.M. and 6:00 P.M. Pacific time, Monday through Friday, excluding holidays.

- For technical support for Microsoft Excel for Windows™, call (206) 635-7070.
- For technical support for Microsoft Excel for the Macintosh®, call (206) 635-7080.

In Canada, support engineers are available via a toll call between 8.00 A.M. and 8.00 P.M. Eastern time, Monday through Friday, excluding holidays. Call (905) 568-3503.

When you call, you should be at your computer and have the appropriate product documentation at hand. Be prepared to give the following information:

- The version number of Microsoft Excel you are using
- The type of hardware you are using, including network hardware, if applicable
- The operating system that you are using
- The exact wording of any messages that appeared on your screen
- What happened and what you were doing when the problem occurred
- How you tried to solve the problem

Priority Support

The Microsoft Support Network offers priority telephone access to Microsoft support engineers 24 hours a day, seven days a week, except holidays.

- In the United States, call (900) 555-2000; $2 per minute, $25 maximum. Charges appear on your telephone bill. Not available in Canada.
- In the United States, call (800) 936-5700; $25 per incident, billed to your VISA card, MasterCard, or American Express Card. In Canada, call (800) 668-7975; $30 per incident, billed to your VISA card, MasterCard or American Express Card.

Text Telephone

Microsoft text telephone (TT/TDD) services are available for the deaf or hard-of-hearing. In the United States, using a TT/TDD modem, dial (206) 635-4948 between 6:00 A.M. and 6:00 P.M. Pacific time, Monday through Friday, excluding holidays. In Canada, using a TT/TDD modem, dial (905) 568-9641 between 8.00 A.M. and 8.00 P.M. Eastern time, Monday through Friday, excluding holidays.

Other Support Options

The Microsoft Support Network offers annual support plans. For information, contact Microsoft Support Network at (800) 936-3500 between 6:00 A.M. and 6:00 P.M. Pacific time, Monday through Friday, excluding holidays.

Product Training and Consultation

Microsoft Solution Providers are independent organizations that provide consulting, integration, customization, development, technical support, training, and other services for Microsoft products. These companies are called Solution Providers because they apply technology and provide services to help solve real-world problems.

In the United States, for more information about the Microsoft Solution Providers program or the Microsoft Solution Provider nearest to you, please call (800) 227-4679 between 6:30 A.M. and 5:30 P.M. Pacific time, Monday through Friday, excluding holidays. In Canada, call (800) 668-7975 between 8.00 A.M. and 8.00 P.M. Eastern time, Monday through Friday, excluding holidays.

Product Support Worldwide

If you are outside the United States and have a question about Microsoft Excel, first:

- Consult the Microsoft Excel documentation and other printed information included with Microsoft Excel.
- Check online Help.

- Check the Microsoft Excel Readme Help file that came with your Microsoft Excel disks. This file provides general information that became available after the books in the Microsoft Excel package were published.

- Consult electronic options such as CompuServe forums or bulletin boards, if available.

If you cannot find a solution, you can receive information on how to obtain Microsoft Excel support by contacting the Microsoft subsidiary office that serves your country.

The Microsoft Support Network

The Microsoft Support Network, where available, offers you a wide range of choices and access to high-quality, responsive technical support. Microsoft recognizes that support needs vary from user to user; the Microsoft Support Network allows you to choose the type of support that best meets your needs, with options ranging from electronic bulletin boards to annual support programs.

The Microsoft Support Network is subject to Microsoft's then-current prices, terms, and conditions in place in each country at the time the services are used and is subject to change without notice.

Calling a Microsoft Subsidiary Office

When you call, you should be at your computer and have the Microsoft Excel documentation at hand. Be prepared to give the following information:

- The version number of Microsoft Excel that you are using

- The type of hardware that you are using, including network hardware, if applicable

- The operating system that you are using

- The exact wording of any messages that appeared on your screen

- A description of what happened and what you were doing when the problem occurred

- A description of how you tried to solve the problem

Microsoft subsidiary offices and the countries they serve are listed on the following pages. If there is no Microsoft office in your country, please contact the establishment from which you purchased your Microsoft product.

Area	Telephone numbers
Argentina	Microsoft de Argentina S.A. Customer Service: (54) (1) 814-5105, (54) (1) 814-4807, (54) (1) 814-4808, (54) (1) 814-7199 Technical Support: (54) (1) 815-1521 Fax: (54) (1) 814-0372
Australia	Microsoft Pty. Ltd. Installation Support: (61) (02) 870-2870 Fax: (61) (02) 805-0519 Bulletin Board Service: (61) (02) 870-5200 Technical Support: (61) (02) 870-2131 Sales Information Centre: (61) (02) 870-2100
Austria	Microsoft Ges.m.b.H. Phone: 0222 - 68 76 07 Fax: 0222 - 68 16 2710 Information: 0660 - 6520 Prices, updates, etc.: 0660 - 6520 CompuServe: GO MSEURO (Microsoft Central Europe) Technical Support: Microsoft Excel for Windows: 0660 - 6511 Microsoft Software für den Apple Macintosh: 0660 - 6518
Belgium	Microsoft NV Phone: 02-7303911 Customer Service: 02-7303922 CompuServe: 02-2150530 (GO MSBEN) Bulletin Board: 02-7350045 (1200/2400/9600 bd, 8N1, ANSI) (Dutch-speaking) Technical Support: 02-5133274 (English-speaking) Technical Support: 02-5023432 (French-speaking) Technical Support: 02-5132268
Bolivia	See Argentina
Brazil	Microsoft Informatica Ltda. Phone: (55) (11) 530-4455 Fax: (55) (11) 240-2205 Technical Support Phone: (55) (11) 533-2922 Technical Support Fax: (55) (11) 241-1157 Technical Support Bulletin Board Service: (55) (11) 872-4106
Canada	Microsoft Canada Inc. Head Office Phone: 1 (905) 568-0434 Customer Support Centre: 1 (800) 563-9048 Microsoft Support Network: Standard Technical Support Phone: 1 (905) 568-3503 Priority Support Information: 1 (800) 668-7975 Technical Support Bulletin Board Service: 1 (905) 507-3022 Text Telephone (TT/TDD) 1 (905) 568-9641

Area	Telephone numbers
Caribbean	Microsoft Caribbean, Inc. Tel: (809) 273-2600 Fax: (809) 273-3636 Technical Support: (214) 714-9100
Chile	Microsoft Chile S.A. Tel: 56 2 218 5771, 56 2 218 5711, 56 2 218 7524 Fax: 56 2 218 5747
Colombia	Microsoft Colombia Tel: (571) 618 2245 Soporte Tecnico: (571) 618 2255 Fax: (571) 618 2269
Denmark	Microsoft Denmark AS Phone: (45) (44) 89 01 00 Technical Support: (45) (44) 89 01 11 Microsoft Sales Support: (45) (44) 89 01 90 Microsoft BBS: (45) (44) 66 90 46 (Document 303030 in FaxSvar contains detailed instructions) Microsoft FaxSvar: (45) (44) 89 01 44
Dubai	Microsoft Middle East Phone: (971) 4 513 888 Fax: (971) 4 527 444
England	See United Kingdom
Finland	Microsoft OY For technical support, please contact your local dealer. Phone: (358) (9) 0 525 501 Microsoft BBS: (46) (0) 8 750 47 42 (Information in Swedish and English) Microsoft FaxSvar: (46) (0) 8 752 29 00 (Information in Swedish and English)
France	Microsoft France Phone: (33) (1) 69-86-46-46 Telex: MSPARIS 604322F Fax: (33) (1) 64-46-06-60 Technical Support Phone: (33) (1) 69-86-10-20 Technical Support Fax: (33) (1) 69-28-00-28 Fax Information Service: (33) (1) 69-29-11-55
French Polynesia	See France
Germany	Microsoft GmbH Phone: 089 - 3176-0 Telex: (17) 89 83 28 MS GMBH D Fax: 089 - 3176-1000 Information: 089 - 3176 1199 Prices, updates, etc.: 089 - 3176 1199 Bulletin board, device drivers, tech notes: Btx: microsoft# or *610808000# CompuServe: GO MSEURO (Microsoft Central Europe) Technical Support: Microsoft Excel for Windows: 089/3176-1120 Microsoft Software für den Apple Macintosh: 089/3176-1160

Area	Telephone numbers
Greece	Microsoft Hellas, S.A. Phone: (30) (1) 6893 631 through (30) 6893 635 Fax: (30) (1) 6893 636
Hong Kong	Microsoft Hong Kong Limited Technical Support: (852) 804-4222 Fax: (852) 560-2217
Ireland	See United Kingdom
Israel	Microsoft Israel Ltd. Phone: 972-3-575-7034 Fax: 972-3-575-7065
Italy	Microsoft SpA Phone: (39) (2) 269121 Telex: 340321 I Fax: (39) (2) 21072020 Customer Service (Prices, new product info, product literature): (39) (2) 26901359 Bulletin Board: (39) (2) 21072051 Technical Support: (39) (2) 26901351

Japan	Microsoft Company Ltd.
	Tokyo, Japan
	Phone: (81) (3) 5454-8025 Fax: (81) (3) 5454-7972
	Technical Support:
	    Microsoft Excel for Windows: (81) (3) 5454-2320
	    Microsoft Excel for the Macintosh: (81) (3) 5454-2340
	    Technical Support Fax: (81) (3) 5454-7955
	Customer Service (Version upgrade/Registration):
	    Phone: (81) (3) 5454-2305
	    Fax: (81) (3) 5454-7952
	Channel Marketing (Pre-sales Product Support) Information Center:
	    Phone: (81) (3) 5454-2300
	    Fax: (81) (3) 5454-7951

Korea	Microsoft CH Phone: (82) (2) 531-4500 Fax: (82) (2) 555-1724 Technical Support: (82) (2) 531-4800 Technical Support Fax: (82) (2) 563-5194 Technical Support Bulletin Board Service: (82) (2) 538-3256
Liechtenstein	See Switzerland (German-speaking)
Luxembourg	Microsoft NV Phone: (32) 2-7303911 Customer Service: (32) 2-7303922 CompuServe: (32) 2-2150530 (GO MSBEN) Bulletin Board: (32) 2-7350045 (1200/2400/9600 baud, 8 bits, no parity, 1 stop bit, ANSI terminal emulation) Technical Support: (32) 2-5133274 (Dutch-speaking) (32) 2-5023432 (English-speaking) (32) 2-5132268 (French-speaking)

Area	Telephone numbers
Mexico	Microsoft México, S.A. de C.V. Phone: (52) (5) 325-0910 Customer Service: (52) (5) 325-0911 Bulletin Board: (52) (5) 590-5988 (1200/2400 baud, 8 bits, no parity, 1 stop bit, ANSI terminal emulation) Fax: (52) (5) 280-7940 Desktop & O.S.: (52) (5) 325-0912 Developers & Advanced Systems: (52) (5) 237-4800
Netherlands	Microsoft BV Phone: 02503-89189 Customer Service: 02503-77700 CompuServe: 020-6880085 (GO MSBEN) Bulletin Board: 02503-34221 (1200/2400/9600 baud, 8 bits, no parity, 1 stop bit, ANSI terminal emulation) Technical Support: 02503-77877 (Dutch-speaking) 02503-77853 (English-speaking)
New Zealand	Microsoft New Zealand Ltd Phone: 64 (9) 358-3724 Fax: 64 (9) 358-3726 Technology Link Centre (Technical Support): Phone: 64 (9) 357-5575 Fax: 64 (9) 358-0092
Northern Ireland	See United Kingdom
Norway	Microsoft Norway AS Phone: (47) (22) 02 25 00 Technical Support: (47) (22) 02 25 50 Microsoft Sales Support: (47) 22 02 25 80 Microsoft BBS: (47) 22 1822 09 (Document 404040 in FaxSvar contains detailed instructions) Microsoft FaxSvar: (47) 22 02 25 70
Papua New Guinea	See Australia
Paraguay	See Argentina
Portugal	MSFT, Lda. Phone: (351) 1 4412205 Fax: (351) 1 4412101
Republic of China	Microsoft Taiwan Corp. Phone: (886) (2) 504-3122 Fax: (886) (2) 504-3121 Technical Support: (886) (2) 508-9501
Republic of Ireland	See United Kingdom
Scotland	See United Kingdom

Area	Telephone numbers
South Africa	Microsoft South Africa: Phone: (27) 11 444 0520 Fax: (27) 11 444 0536
Spain	Microsoft Iberica SRL Phone: (34) (1) 804-0000 Fax: (34) (1) 803-8310 Technical Support: (34) (1) 803-9960
Sweden	Microsoft AB Phone: (46) (8) 752 56 00 Information on Technical Support: (46) (8) 752 09 29 Sales Support: (46) (8) 752 56 30 Microsoft BBS: (46) (8) 750 47 42 (Document 202020 in FaxSvar contains detailed instructions) Microsoft FaxSvar: (46) (8) 752 29 00
Switzerland	Microsoft AG Phone: 01 - 839 61 11 Fax: 01 - 831 08 69 Documentation: Phone: 155 59 00 Fax: 064 - 224294, Microsoft Info-Service, Postfach, 8099 Zürich Prices, updates, etc.: 01/839 61 11 CompuServe: GO MSEURO (Microsoft Central Europe) Technical Support: (German-speaking) Microsoft Excel for Windows: 01 - 342 - 4082 Microsoft Software für den Apple Macintosh: 01 - 342 - 4081 Technical Support: (French-speaking) 022 - 738 96 88
Turkey	Microsoft Turkey Phone: (90) 212 2585998 Fax: (90) 212 2585954
United Kingdom	Microsoft Limited Phone: (44) (734) 270000 Fax: (44) (734) 270002 Upgrades & Registration: (44) (81) 614 8000 Technical Support: Bulletin Board Service: (44) (734) 270065 (2400 Baud) (44) (734) 270060 (9600 Baud) Fax Information Service: (44) (734) 270080 Phone: (47) (734) 271000
Uruguay	See Argentina
Venezuela	Corporation MS 90 de Venezuela S.A. Technical Support: 58.2.910046, 58.2.910510 Other Information: 58.2.910008, 58.2.914739, 58.2.913342 Fax: 58.2.923835
Wales	See United Kingdom

PART 1

Getting Started

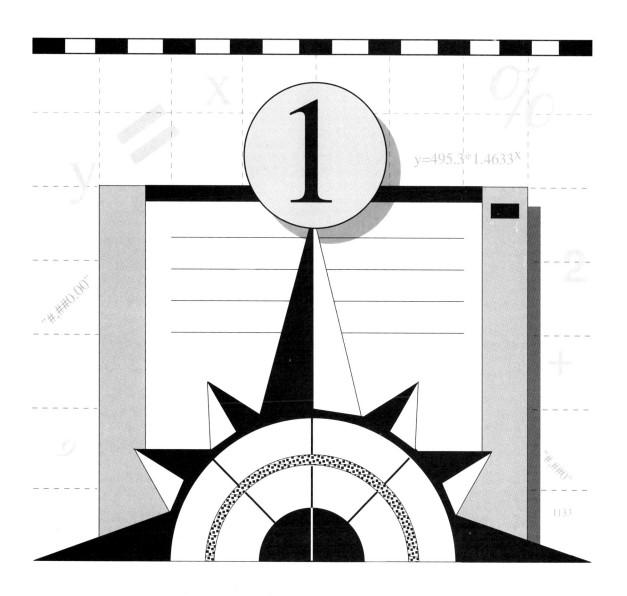

$y = 495.3 * 1.4633^{x}$

CHAPTER 1

Installing and Starting Microsoft Excel

For command, keyboard, and toolbar button information, see online Help.

In This Chapter

What You Need to Use Microsoft Excel

System Requirements for Microsoft Excel for Windows

To use Microsoft Excel for Windows, you need:

- Any IBM®-compatible machine with an 80286 processor or higher.
- A 3.5-inch or 5.25-inch floppy disk drive.
- A hard disk.
- A graphics display compatible with Microsoft Windows version 3.1 or later, such as EGA or VGA.
- At least 4 megabytes of memory.
- MS-DOS® version 3.1 or later, and Microsoft Windows version 3.1 or later in standard or enhanced mode.

A printer is optional; a Microsoft Mouse or compatible pointing device is recommended.

System Requirements for Microsoft Excel for the Macintosh

To use Microsoft Excel for the Macintosh, you need:

- A Macintosh computer with one 800K floppy disk drive and a hard disk drive.
- At least 4 megabytes of memory.
- Macintosh System 7.0 or later.

A printer is optional.

Using Microsoft Excel with Other Operating Systems

If you are using Microsoft Excel with Microsoft Windows NT™ or another operating system not listed above, you'll find information specific to your operating system on Disk 1 - Setup, in the Microsoft Excel Readme file.

Installing Microsoft Excel

Before you install Microsoft Excel, you may want to create a backup copy of the installation disks. The Microsoft Excel license agreement allows you to make one backup copy. The license agreement also allows you to install Microsoft Excel on another computer, such as a laptop computer, provided that you are the computer's primary user and that you use only one copy of Microsoft Excel at a time. For more information, see your Microsoft Excel license agreement.

If you are upgrading from a previous version of Microsoft Excel, you can replace your previous version with version 5.0, or you can install version 5.0 to another location. You may want to install version 5.0 to another location and keep your previous version until you are comfortable working in version 5.0.

Important   If you use a virus protection program on your computer, override it or turn it off before you run the Microsoft Excel Setup program. Microsoft Excel Setup may not run properly with virus protection turned on. After running Setup, be sure to restart your virus protection program.

▶ **To install Microsoft Excel for Windows**

1. Start Microsoft Windows in standard or enhanced mode.
2. Insert the disk labeled "Disk 1-Setup" in drive A.
3. From the File menu in Program Manager, choose Run.
4. Type **a:setup**
5. Press ENTER.
6. Follow the Setup instructions on the screen.

▶ **To install Microsoft Excel for the Macintosh**

1. Insert the disk labeled "Disk 1-Setup" in the disk drive.
2. Double-click the Microsoft Excel Setup icon.
3. Follow the Setup instructions on the screen.

Important   While Setup is running, fill out your Microsoft Excel registration card and return it to Microsoft. This will ensure that you are notified of future product updates, have access to Microsoft product support services, and qualify for the Microsoft product repair and replacement plan.

Installing Components of Microsoft Excel

Once you've installed Microsoft Excel, you can run Setup again at any time to add supplementary applications or files, such as the examples and demos, add-in files, or other options. Installing a component of Microsoft Excel is generally much quicker than the initial installation.

Installing Microsoft Excel on a Network

Instructions for installing and administering Microsoft Excel on a network are located on Disk 1 - Setup.

System	Network instructions are in this file
Windows	NETWORK.TXT
Macintosh	README--NETWORK

If you've already installed Microsoft Excel, you'll also find the network instruction files in your Microsoft Excel directory or folder.

Step By Step

For step-by-step instructions and related information, double-click the ⬛⁇ button to display the Search dialog box in Help, and then:

Type this keyword and choose Show Topics	Select a topic and choose Go To
components of Microsoft Excel	Installing components of Microsoft Excel

Starting and Quitting Microsoft Excel

Starting Microsoft Excel

▶ **To start Microsoft Excel**

1. In Microsoft Excel for Windows, open the program group in which you installed Microsoft Excel.

   In Microsoft Excel for the Macintosh, open the folder in which you installed Microsoft Excel.

2. Double-click the Microsoft Excel program icon.

Microsoft
Excel

For information about using your computer's operating system or the mouse, see your Windows or Macintosh system documentation.

Once you've started Microsoft Excel for Windows, the Quick Preview online tutorial may appear. For information about Quick Preview and the other online tutorials included in Microsoft Excel, see "Where Do I Find It?" in Chapter 5.

The primary Microsoft Excel document is the workbook. When Microsoft Excel starts, it displays a new workbook. For information about opening and closing workbook files, see "Creating or Opening Workbooks" and "Saving and Closing Workbooks" in Chapter 6.

Quitting Microsoft Excel

System	From the File menu, choose
Windows	Exit
Macintosh	Quit

You are prompted to save any unsaved work.

Step By Step

For step-by-step instructions and related information, double-click the ▶? button to display the Search dialog box in Help, and then:

Type this keyword and choose Show Topics	Select a topic and choose Go To
Microsoft Excel, quitting	Quitting Microsoft Excel
Microsoft Excel, starting	Starting Microsoft Excel

CHAPTER 2

If You're New to Microsoft Excel

For command, keyboard, and toolbar button information, see online Help.

In This Chapter

Where to Start?

Welcome to Microsoft Excel, the spreadsheet application for Microsoft Windows and the Apple® Macintosh. This chapter gives you a quick tour of Microsoft Excel, introducing you to the most important concepts and features along the way.

In this chapter, you'll create the following worksheet.

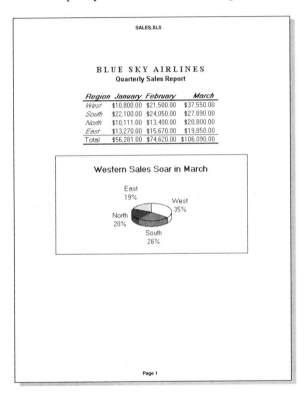

As you complete the steps in this chapter, you'll see cross-references directing you to other chapters in this book. To find out more about a specific feature, follow the "You can also" cross-reference to the chapters' tables of contents.

If You're New to Microsoft Excel

If you are new to Microsoft Excel, the online Quick Preview lesson "Getting Started" is a great place to start. This is a hands-on, interactive lesson. Once you complete that lesson, you can return to this chapter for more information. In Microsoft Excel for Windows, the Quick Preview may start automatically when you start Microsoft Excel.

Note   To use the Getting Started lesson and the online examples and demos, you need to have installed the Tutorial option when you ran Microsoft Excel Setup. This was installed for you if you chose the Typical option during setup. If you cannot complete the steps below, rerun the Setup program and install the Tutorial option. For more information, see Chapter 1, "Installing and Starting Microsoft Excel."

▶ **To start the "Getting Started" lesson in Microsoft Excel for Windows**

1. Start Microsoft Excel.

   If you need help, see the following section, "Starting Microsoft Excel."

2. From the Help menu, choose Quick Preview.

3. Choose Getting Started, and then follow the instructions on your screen.

Once you've completed the lesson, return to this chapter.

▶ **To start the "Getting Started" lesson in Microsoft Excel for the Macintosh**

1. Open the Microsoft Excel folder.

2. Double-click the Quick Preview icon.

   The Quick Preview is a HyperCard™ stack.

3. Choose Getting Started, and then follow the instructions on your screen.

Once you've completed the lesson, return to this chapter.

If You're Upgrading to Microsoft Excel from Another Spreadsheet Application

Microsoft Excel includes several features that help you put your spreadsheet knowledge to work right away. For more information, see Chapter 3, "If You're Switching from Another Spreadsheet," and the Quick Preview lesson "For Lotus 1-2-3 Users . . ." (Microsoft Excel for Windows only).

If You're Updating from a Previous Version of Microsoft Excel

Microsoft Excel version 5.0 has been redesigned to make your work easier to do. For more information, see Chapter 4, "What's New in Microsoft Excel Version 5.0," and the Quick Preview lesson "What's New?"

Starting Microsoft Excel

Microsoft
Excel

▶ **To start Microsoft Excel for Windows**

- Double-click the Microsoft Excel icon in the Program Manager.

The Microsoft Excel window appears. If necessary, enlarge the window by clicking the Maximize button in the upper-right corner of the window.

Microsoft
Excel

▶ **To start Microsoft Excel for the Macintosh**

- Double-click the Microsoft Excel icon in the Finder.

The Microsoft Excel window appears. If necessary, enlarge the window by clicking the zoom box in the upper-right corner of the window.

When Microsoft Excel starts, it creates a new, empty workbook. You'll learn more about workbooks in the following section.

You can also	For more information, see
Automatically open workbooks when you start Microsoft Excel by saving them in your startup directory or folder.	Chapter 35, "Controlling What Happens When You Start Microsoft Excel"

Opening a Workbook

The *workbook* is the normal document or file type in Microsoft Excel. A workbook is the electronic equivalent of a three-ring binder. Inside workbooks you'll find *sheets,* such as worksheets and chart sheets. Each sheet's name appears on a tab at the bottom of the workbook. You can move or copy sheets between workbooks, and you can rearrange sheets within a workbook.

In this tour, you'll use the Blue Sky sales report workbook.

Open

▶ **To open the Blue Sky sales report in Microsoft Excel for Windows**

1. Click the Open button.

   Clicking the Open button is equivalent to choosing the Open command from the File menu. Many of the commands on the menu bar have equivalent toolbar buttons. You can use either the command or the button, depending on your preference.

2. In the Directories box, double-click the EXAMPLES directory.

3. In the File Name box, select SALES.XLS.

4. In the lower-right corner of the dialog box, select the Read Only check box.

   This will preserve the original file so that you or others can use it later.

5. Choose the OK button.

Open

▶ **To open the Blue Sky sales report in Microsoft Excel for the Macintosh**

1. Click the Open button.

   Clicking the Open button is equivalent to choosing the Open command from the File menu. Many of the commands on the menu bar have equivalent toolbar buttons. You can use either the command or the button, depending on your preference.

2. Double-click the EXAMPLES folder.

3. Select BLUE SKY SALES.

4. Select the Read Only check box.

   This will preserve the original file so that you or others can use it later.

5. Choose the Open button.

You can also	For more information, see
Open workbooks by double-clicking them in the File Manager or Finder, even if you have not yet started Microsoft Excel.	Your operating system documentation
Open files in other formats, such as Lotus 1-2-3.	Chapter 3, "If You're Switching from Another Spreadsheet," and Chapter 42, "Importing and Exporting Documents"
Create new workbooks in Microsoft Excel.	Chapter 6, "Managing Workbook Files"
Search your drive for a specific workbook, even if you don't know its name.	Chapter 6, "Managing Workbook Files"
Create template workbooks you can use over and over.	Chapter 36, "Using Templates to Create Your Own Default Workbooks"

What's on the Screen

When you create or open a workbook, Microsoft Excel displays it in a *window*. You can have several workbook windows open at the same time. Your screen should look like the following illustration. In Microsoft Excel for the Macintosh, the screen is slightly different.

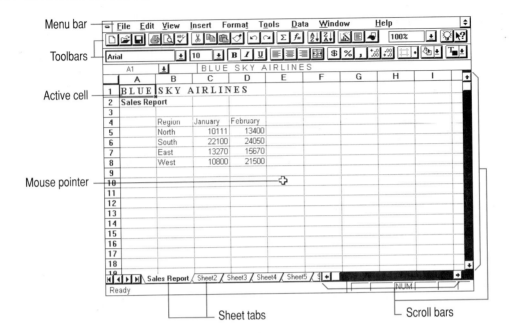

Menu bar
Toolbars
Active cell
Mouse pointer

Sheet tabs
Scroll bars

Most of the work you do in Microsoft Excel will be on a *worksheet.* A worksheet is a grid of rows and columns. Each *cell* is the intersection of a row and a column and has a unique address, or *reference.* For example, the cell where column B and row 5 intersect is cell B5. You use cell references when you write formulas or refer to cells.

Generally, you first *select* the cell or cells you want to work with, and then you enter data or choose a command. Selected cells appear highlighted on your screen. The *active cell* is the cell in which data is entered when you start typing. Only one cell is active at a time. The active cell is shown by a heavy border. In the preceding illustration, cell A1 is the active cell.

▶ **To change the active cell**

• Move the mouse pointer into cell B4 and click.

Notice that the cell's reference ("B4") and its value ("Region") appear in the formula bar.

▶ **To scroll through the worksheet**

1. Move the pointer to the down arrow in the vertical scroll bar on the right edge of the window, and then click.

   The worksheet scrolls down one row.

2. Click the scroll bar area below the scroll box.

   The worksheet scrolls down one screen.

3. Move the pointer into the scroll box. Hold the mouse button down, move the pointer back to the top of the vertical scroll bar, and then release the mouse button. This is called *dragging*.

   The worksheet scrolls back up to the first row.

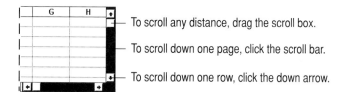

— To scroll any distance, drag the scroll box.

— To scroll down one page, click the scroll bar.

— To scroll down one row, click the down arrow.

You can also	For more information, see
Change the magnification of your view of the workbook to see more or less data.	Chapter 32, "Changing How You View Your Worksheet"
Switch to a full-screen view of your worksheet.	Chapter 32, "Changing How You View Your Worksheet"
Move the toolbars around on your screen, or display other toolbars.	Chapter 34, "Customizing Your Workspace"

Entering and Editing Data

Now you'll enter the March sales data and change the sales report title.

▶ **To enter the March column title**

1. Select the February label in cell D4.

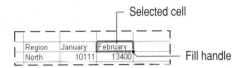

Selected cell

Fill handle

2. Drag the fill handle through E4. As you drag, notice that "March" appears in the formula bar.

Microsoft Excel fills in the March label based on your initial selection. This is called *AutoFill*, and it works with several types of data. For example, you can fill the days of the week, series of numbers, and more.

▶ **To enter the March sales data**

1. Select the cells where you will enter the data by dragging the pointer through the cell *range* E5:E8.

   This is the abbreviated way of saying "E5 through E8." Microsoft Excel uses this form of abbreviation whenever it refers to a range of cells.

2. Type the values shown in the following illustration. Press ENTER to move to the next cell in the selection.

▶ **To enter the "Total" label**

1. Select cell B9.

2. Type **Total** and press ENTER.

   In the next section, you'll enter the total values of the columns.

▶ **To edit the sales report title**

1. Double-click cell A2.

   A flashing insertion point appears in the cell.

2. Click to the left of the word "Sales."

3. Type **Quarterly** followed by a space, and then press ENTER.

Your worksheet should look like the following illustration.

	A	B	C	D	E	F
1	BLUE SKY AIRLINES					
2	Quarterly Sales Report					
3						
4		Region	January	February	March	
5		North	10111	13400	20800	
6		South	22100	24050	27890	
7		East	13270	15670	19850	
8		West	10800	21500	37550	
9		Total				
10						

You can also	For more information, see
Enter series of data such as numbers, days, or your own custom lists with AutoFill.	Chapter 9, "Entering Data"
Move data around on the worksheet by dragging it, or by using the Cut, Copy, and Paste commands on the Edit menu.	Chapter 11, "Editing a Worksheet"

Building Formulas to Calculate Values

So far, you've entered data in a worksheet. To really make that data useful, you'll write *formulas*. Formulas can do simple things, such as adding the values in two cells, or they can do much more complex things. Here's how Microsoft Excel uses the SUM worksheet function to add two values together.

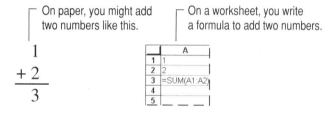

You can always identify a formula in Microsoft Excel because it starts with an equal sign (=). You normally see the formula itself only when you're editing the cell that contains the formula. Otherwise, you see the value produced by the formula.

Now you'll create a formula that adds the sales amounts in the January column, and then you'll copy that formula to the other columns.

▶ **To total the January column**

1. Select cell C9.

AutoSum

2. Click the AutoSum button.

    Microsoft Excel looks at the data around C9 and guesses that you want to add the column of numbers above this cell. It writes the formula, suggesting the range of numbers to sum.

3. Press ENTER to accept the proposed formula.

    You can also click the AutoSum button again.

If you select cell C9 again you'll notice that the formula appears in the formula bar, but the value of the formula appears in the cell.

▶ **To copy the formula to the other columns**

- Drag the fill handle from C9 through D9 and E9.

Microsoft Excel copies the formula to the other cells and, in each column, adjusts the formula's references so that the formula refers to the numbers in that column.

After you copy the formula from C9 to D9:E9 by dragging the fill handle,
Microsoft Excel automatically adjusts the references in the new formulas.

	A	B	C	D	E	F
1	BLUE SKY AIRLINES					
2	Quarterly Sales Report					
3						
4		Region	January	February	March	
5		North	10111	13400	20800	
6		South	22100	24050	27890	
7		East	13270	15670	19850	
8		West	10800	21500	37550	
9		Total	56281	74620	106090	
10						
11						

=SUM(C5:C8)   =SUM(E5:E8)

=SUM(D5:D8)

You can also	For more information, see
Use the Function Wizard to simplify your formula writing.	Chapter 10, "Creating Formulas and Links"
Name cell references or ranges to create more understandable formulas.	Chapter 10, "Creating Formulas and Links"

Managing Lists of Data

Most of the data people keep in a spreadsheet is a list of some sort. An employee directory, a telephone log book, and a sales report are all lists. Microsoft Excel includes several features that make it easy to manipulate data in lists.

Now you'll sort the regions by March sales amounts, listing the region with the largest sales first.

▶ **To sort the regions by March sales amounts**

1. Select cells B5:E8.

2. From the Data menu, choose Sort.

   Microsoft Excel examines the data in the list and then proposes a sorting order in the Sort dialog box.

3. In the Sort By box, select March.

4. Select the Descending option button.

This will put the largest amount at the top of the list.

5. Choose the OK button.

Microsoft Excel sorts the regions by their March sales amounts.

	A	B	C	D	E	F
1	BLUE SKY AIRLINES					
2	Quarterly Sales Report					
3						
4		Region	January	February	March	
5		West	10800	21500	37550	
6		South	22100	24050	27890	
7		North	10111	13400	20800	
8		East	13270	15670	19850	
9		Total	56281	74620	106090	
10						
11						

You can also	For more information, see
Maintain a list within a dialog box.	Chapter 20, Using a List to Organize Data"
Sort outlined data or use a custom sort order.	Chapter 21, "Sorting and Filtering Data in a List"
Quickly display a subset of a list by using criteria you specify.	Chapter 21, "Sorting and Filtering Data in a List"
Automatically insert subtotals and add an outline structure to a list.	Chapter 22, "Summarizing Data in a List"
Create interactive summary tables from data in a list.	Chapter 24, "Creating a Pivot Table"

Formatting Data

There are many formatting tools you can use to highlight your data and make it more readable. Worksheet formatting includes number formats, borders, fonts, patterns, and other options.

In this section you'll apply *autoformats* to the sales data. Autoformats are built-in combinations of formats that you can quickly select and apply to a range of data. You'll also format the sales amounts as currency and change the alignment of the title.

▶ **To format the sales amounts as currency**

1. Select the range C5:E9.

Currency Style

2. Click the Currency Style button.

Microsoft Excel applies a currency number format to the selected range. As you can see, the cells display number signs (###) instead of values. That's because the columns are too narrow to display the full numbers in the new format.

▶ **To widen the columns**

1. Drag through the column headings for columns C, D, and E to select the columns.

2. Move the pointer between the C and D column headings until it changes to a double arrow, and then double-click.

┌ Double-click to adjust column widths.

Column headings ───

Microsoft Excel adjusts the column widths to fit the widest value in each column.

▶ **To format the quarterly sales table**

1. Select any cell within the quarterly sales table; for example, select D7.

2. From the Format menu, choose AutoFormat.

   Microsoft Excel selects the contiguous range of values around D7 and then displays the AutoFormat dialog box. As you can see, Microsoft Excel has several built-in autoformats.

3. In the Table Format box, select Colorful 2.

   You may have to scroll the list to select the Colorful 2 autoformat.

4. Choose the OK button.

Microsoft Excel applies the Colorful 2 autoformat to the selected range.

▶ **To align the title across columns**

1. Select the range A1:F2.

2. Click the Center Across Columns button.

Center Across
Columns

Microsoft Excel displays the values in cells A1 and A2 centered across the selected range.

You can also	For more information, see
Apply manual formatting to cells, ranges, or individual characters within a cell.	Chapter 12, "Formatting a Worksheet"
Create styles similar to word processor styles and apply them to worksheet data.	Chapter 12, "Formatting a Worksheet"
Copy a format from one cell to other cells.	Chapter 12, "Formatting a Worksheet"

Creating a Chart

Charts are visual representations of worksheet data. Microsoft Excel includes several chart types, such as bar, line, and pie charts. You can use charts to clarify trends or relationships that might not be apparent in the worksheet data alone.

A chart is either embedded directly on a worksheet, or it appears on its own chart sheet in the workbook. Microsoft Excel automatically updates a chart if the worksheet data it's based on changes.

Now you'll create a pie chart of the March regional sales amounts and embed it directly on the worksheet. To do this, you'll use the *ChartWizard,* an interactive charting assistant.

▶ **To chart the sales data**

1. Select the range B5:B8.

    This range contains the labels for the chart data. Next you'll select the range containing the data you want to chart.

2. In Microsoft Excel for Windows, hold down CTRL while you select the range E5:E8.

    In Microsoft Excel for the Macintosh, hold down COMMAND while you select the range E5:E8.

ChartWizard

3. Click the ChartWizard button.

4. Drag the pointer from cell A11 to F22. This is where Microsoft Excel will place the finished chart.

    The ChartWizard dialog box appears.

5. You've already selected the range you want to chart, so choose the Next button.

6. Select the 3-D Pie type, and then choose the Next button.

7. Choose the Next button to accept the proposed chart format—a pie chart with slice labels and percentages.

    The ChartWizard displays a sample pie chart using your data.

8. Choose the Next button to continue.

9. Under Add A Legend, select the No option button.

10. In the Chart Title box, type **Western Sales Soar in March** and then choose the Finish button.

Microsoft Excel creates the chart on the worksheet and displays the Chart toolbar. You can hide the Chart toolbar or drag it out of your way.

You can also	For more information, see
Create a chart on its own chart sheet in the workbook.	Chapter 15, "Creating a Chart"
Use chart autoformats to quickly change the chart type and other formatting of your chart.	Chapter 16, "Working with Chart Types and Autoformats"
Change the formatting of embedded charts and chart sheets.	Chapter 18, "Formatting a Chart"

Printing

When you're ready to print your work, you can select from several options to control how your work looks on the page. In this section, you'll change the print options of the worksheet and then preview what will print.

▶ **To center the worksheet data on the page**

1. From the File menu, choose Page Setup.

2. In the Page Setup dialog box, select the Margins tab.

3. Under Center On Page, select the Horizontally check box.

Don't choose the OK button yet; you're not done with the Page Setup dialog box.

▶ **To hide the gridlines when printing**

1. Select the Sheet tab.

2. Under Print, clear the Gridlines check box.

▶ **To print the color formatting as black-and-white**

1. Under Print, select the Black And White check box.

   This will prevent your printer from substituting patterns for colors when you print, while keeping the color formatting visible on your screen.

2. Choose the OK button.

▶ **To preview what will print**

Print Preview

1. Click the Print Preview button.

2. Click the mouse button to magnify the area around the pointer.

   Click again to view the full page.

3. If your computer is connected to a printer, choose the Print button.

   If you don't want to print the worksheet, choose the Close button.

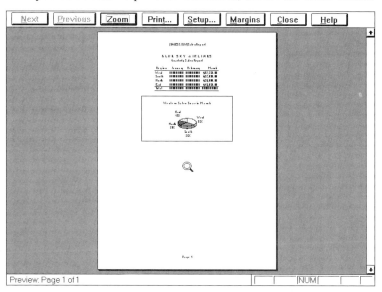

It's a good idea to always preview before you print so that you can make any adjustments before printing and save yourself repeated trips to the printer. You can then print directly from the preview window.

You can also	For more information, see
Adjust margins, change page orientation, and set other options.	Chapter 14, "Printing"
Create custom headers and footers.	Chapter 14, "Printing"
Fit your work onto a specified number of pages.	Chapter 14, "Printing"
Create custom reports made up of named views and scenarios.	Chapter 14, "Printing"
Share your work with others in your workgroup by using electronic mail.	Chapter 40, "Routing Workbooks with Electronic Mail"

Saving a Workbook

You should save your work frequently. If you have a power outage or some other problem, you can start work again on your last saved version of a workbook.

In this section, you'll save the sales report workbook with a different filename. This will preserve the original file for others who may want to complete this lesson.

▶ **To save your work with a different filename**

1. From the File menu, choose Save As.

2. Type the filename you want to use; for example, type **mywork**

3. In Microsoft Excel for Windows, choose the OK button.

   In Microsoft Excel for the Macintosh, choose the Save button.

Once you've saved the workbook, you should save it again frequently.

Save

▶ **To save your work**

- Click the Save button.

▶ **To quit Microsoft Excel for Windows**

- From the File menu, choose Exit.

▶ **To quit Microsoft Excel for the Macintosh**

- From the File menu, choose Quit.

You can also	For more information, see
Save a workbook in another file format, such as Lotus 1-2-3.	Chapter 3, "If You're Switching from Another Spreadsheet," and Chapter 42, "Importing and Exporting Documents"
Set up Microsoft Excel to automatically create a backup file each time you save your work.	Chapter 6, "Managing Workbook Files"
Set up Microsoft Excel to automatically save your work at regular time intervals.	Chapter 6, "Managing Workbook Files"
Add password protection to your workbook.	Chapter 39, "Protecting a Workbook"

What's Next?

Now that you've finished this tour of Microsoft Excel, what should you do next? Here are some ideas.

- To take advantage of the learning features in Microsoft Excel, see Chapter 5, "Getting Information While You Work." It shows you how to best use the books and online Help to find information quickly.

- For hands-on, interactive practice with Microsoft Excel, take a look at the online examples and demos.

System	Do this
Windows	From the Help menu, choose Examples And Demos.
Macintosh	From the Help menu, choose Microsoft Excel Help (if your screen is smaller than 13 inches, choose Help from the Window menu), and then click Examples And Demos in the Help Contents.

CHAPTER 3

If You're Switching from Another Spreadsheet

For command, keyboard, and toolbar button information, see online Help.

In This Chapter

Starting To Make the Switch

Before you start reading this chapter, you should:

- Install Microsoft Excel by following the instructions in Chapter 1, "Installing and Starting Microsoft Excel."

- Read Chapter 2, "If You're New to Microsoft Excel," to become familiar with the parts of the Microsoft Excel window, choosing commands, selecting options in dialog boxes, and using Help.

- If you are switching from Lotus 1-2-3 to Microsoft Excel for Windows, choose the Quick Preview command from the Help menu and select "For Lotus 1-2-3 Users." If you are switching to Microsoft Excel for the Macintosh, start Quick Preview in your Microsoft Excel folder and select "Getting Started."

These interactive lessons show you how easy it is to switch to Microsoft Excel. Each lesson takes approximately 10 minutes to complete.

Some Basics You Need to Know

Before you start using Microsoft Excel, it might be useful to learn some basic concepts and terms. Some of these concepts and terms are just different ways of referring to familiar spreadsheet items or actions. Others might be new to you, especially if you've never used Microsoft Windows or the Apple Macintosh.

- **Select a range, and then choose a command**   In some spreadsheets, you choose a command before specifying the cell or range that the command affects. In Microsoft Excel, you first select the cell, range, or object you want to work with, and then you choose a command or perform an action. After you select a range, you can choose several commands in a row without having to specify a range each time.

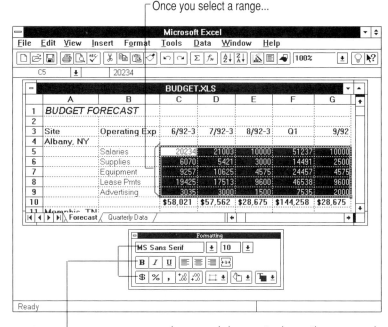

Once you select a range...

...you can use several commands in a row to change the range, such as changing the font, adding the currency style, and applying bold formatting.

- **Entering formulas**   The guidelines for entering formulas in Microsoft Excel are different from those in some other spreadsheets:

  - In Microsoft Excel, you start a formula with an equal sign (=).

  - You can also start a formula with a plus sign (+), as you would in 1-2-3.

  - Although it is not required, you can type an @ sign before Microsoft Excel functions.

  - Microsoft Excel uses a colon (:) to denote a range of cells, instead of the periods (..) used in 1-2-3. You can, however, continue using periods and Microsoft Excel will convert them to a colon.

  - Three-dimensional references in Lotus 1-2-3 use the syntax *sheet:cell..sheet:cell,* such as A:A1..F:C5. In Microsoft Excel, 3-D references use the syntax *sheet:sheet!cell:cell,* for example, SHEET1:SHEET5!A1:F5. You can refer to areas on multiple sheets using 3-D references.

- **Terminology**   Microsoft Excel uses different terms for some spreadsheet items and actions. For example, 1-2-3 refers to words in cells as "labels"; Microsoft Excel uses the term "text." For a list that compares terms from Lotus 1-2-3 and Microsoft Excel, see the Step By Step table at the end of this section.

- **Date systems**   Microsoft Excel supports two different date systems— the 1900 and the 1904 date systems. Microsoft Excel for Windows defaults to the 1900 date system, which is the same date system used by Lotus 1-2-3. However, Microsoft Excel for the Macintosh uses the 1904 date system, which is different from Lotus 1-2-3.

- **Using a mouse**   If you are used to MS-DOS–based spreadsheets, using a mouse may be new to you. Microsoft Excel takes advantage of the mouse to provide easy, intuitive shortcuts to many Microsoft Excel features.

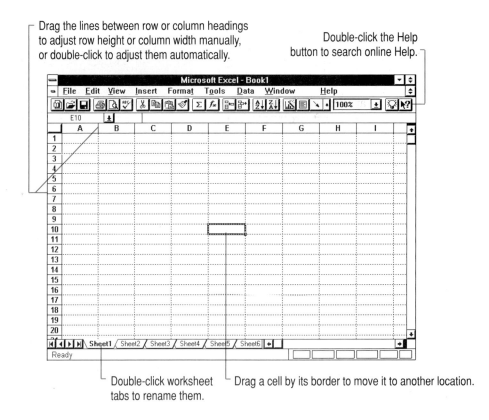

Drag the lines between row or column headings to adjust row height or column width manually, or double-click to adjust them automatically.

Double-click the Help button to search online Help.

Double-click worksheet tabs to rename them.

Drag a cell by its border to move it to another location.

Step By Step

For step-by-step instructions and related information, double-click the 💡 button to display the Search dialog box in Help, and then:

Type this keyword and choose Show Topics	Select a topic and choose Go To
choosing cells	Overview of Selecting Cells and Moving Within a Worksheet
numbers, entering	Overview of Entering Numbers, Dates, and Times
selecting	Overview of Choosing Commands

If you need more information about using Help, see Chapter 5, "Getting Information While You Work."

Opening and Saving Files from Other Spreadsheets

Microsoft Excel can open and save files in many different formats from several applications, including Lotus 1-2-3, Quattro® Pro for MS-DOS, and dBASE®. With Microsoft Excel for Windows, you can open, but not save, files from Microsoft Works and Microsoft Multiplan®.

To specify the type of file you want to open or save, choose Open or Save As from the File menu, and then select a file format from the Open or Save As dialog box.

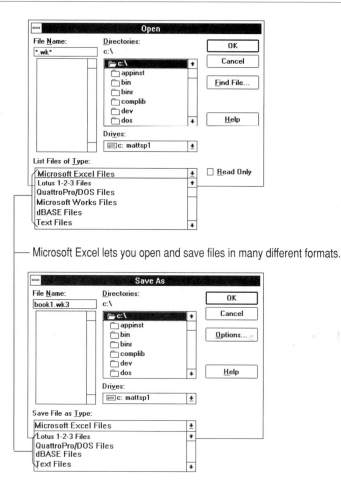

Microsoft Excel lets you open and save files in many different formats.

When opening a file in another application's format, Microsoft Excel preserves as much of the original document as possible, including formatting and macros. If Microsoft Excel cannot accept a formula when opening a file from another application, it substitutes the value calculated by the formula.

Important   When you save a file from another application after working on it in Microsoft Excel, be sure to specify which file format you want it saved in. Normally, Microsoft Excel saves a file in the same format the file was stored in when you opened it. In particular, if you are working on a Lotus 1-2-3 file and you use features that are available only in Microsoft Excel, you must explicitly specify that you want to save the file in Microsoft Excel format. By default, Microsoft Excel saves this file in Lotus 1-2-3 format, which discards all of your Microsoft Excel-specific work.

Step By Step

For step-by-step instructions and related information, double-click the ▶? button to display the Search dialog box in Help, and then:

Type this keyword and choose Show Topics	Select a topic and choose Go To
file formats, changing	Overview of Opening and Saving Documents in Different File Formats
opening workbooks	Open Command (File Menu)
	Overview of Creating or Opening Workbooks

Microsoft Excel Shows You How to Switch

Both Microsoft Excel for Windows and Microsoft Excel for the Macintosh provide online Help and tutorials that show you how to use your knowledge of other spreadsheets to learn the many powerful features of Microsoft Excel.

Help Can Teach You Microsoft Excel for Windows

You can use your knowledge of 1-2-3 to learn Microsoft Excel. Press the SLASH key (/), or choose the Lotus 1-2-3 command from the Help menu to start putting your knowledge of 1-2-3 to work. In the Help for Lotus 1-2-3 Users dialog box, you can type a 1-2-3 command and then see either instructions or an interactive demonstration of the equivalent Microsoft Excel command. If you select the Instructions option button, you can have Microsoft Excel paste the instructions for the task on your sheet so that you can view them conveniently while you finish the task.

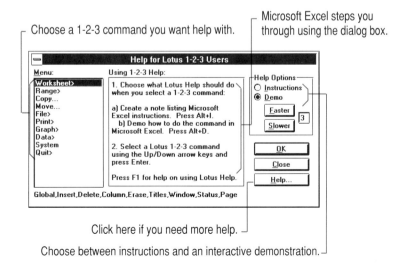

If you are an experienced user of Microsoft Multiplan, you can use your experience to help you learn Microsoft Excel. Choose the Multiplan command from the Help menu, and then type a Multiplan command. Microsoft Excel displays instructions for accomplishing the same command with Microsoft Excel.

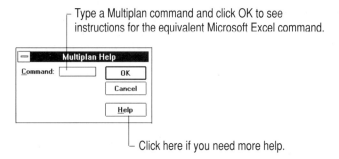

Type a Multiplan command and click OK to see instructions for the equivalent Microsoft Excel command.

Click here if you need more help.

Tutorials Help You Learn Microsoft Excel for Windows

Microsoft Excel for Windows includes extensive online tutorials to make your switch easier. Choose the Quick Preview command from the Help menu to view four in-depth lessons, including the lesson "For 1-2-3 Users." Choose the Examples and Demos command from the Help menu to view short interactive practices and demonstrations that focus on a single task.

Help Can Teach You Microsoft Excel for the Macintosh

If you are an experienced user of Lotus 1-2-3, you can use that experience to help you learn Microsoft Excel. Choose the Help for Lotus 1-2-3 Users command from the Help menu; if the Help menu is not available, you'll find the command on the Window menu. Type a 1-2-3 command, and Microsoft Excel displays the instructions for accomplishing the same task in Microsoft Excel. The dialog box for this command is similar to the Multiplan Help dialog box in Microsoft Excel for Windows, shown earlier in this section.

Tutorials Help You Learn Microsoft Excel for the Macintosh

Microsoft Excel for the Macintosh includes extensive online tutorials to make your switch easier. Choose the Quick Preview command from the Help menu to view three in-depth lessons. Choose the Examples and Demos command from the Help menu to view short interactive practices and demonstrations that focus on a single task. To run these tutorials, you need HyperCard version 2.0 or later installed on your computer. You must allocate at least 1 megabyte of memory to HyperCard.

Step By Step

For step-by-step instructions and related information, double-click the [k?] button to display the Search dialog box in Help, and then:

Type this keyword and choose Show Topics	Select a topic and choose Go To
Lotus 1-2-3, Help for users	Help for Lotus 1-2-3 Users
switching to Microsoft Excel	Switching from Borland Quattro Pro for MS-DOS
	Switching from Lotus 1-2-3
	Switching from Microsoft Works
	Switching from Multiplan

Making Your Transition from Lotus 1-2-3 Easier

Some Microsoft Excel basic spreadsheet operations such as calculating formulas, using the keyboard, and entering dates work differently from those in other spreadsheet applications. Fortunately, Microsoft Excel lets you decide how you want these features to work. You can select either the standard Microsoft Excel operation or the operation that matches 1-2-3 and other spreadsheet applications.

To specify how you want Microsoft Excel to operate, choose the Options command from the Tools menu and select the Transition tab. This tab contains options to help you in your transition to Microsoft Excel.

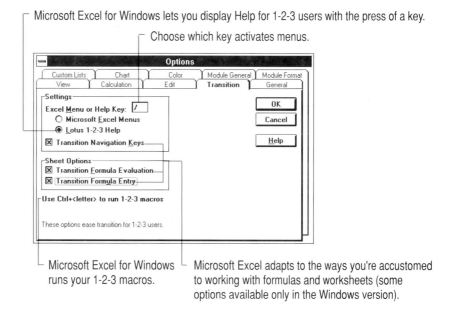

Microsoft Excel for Windows lets you display Help for 1-2-3 users with the press of a key.

Choose which key activates menus.

Microsoft Excel for Windows runs your 1-2-3 macros.

Microsoft Excel adapts to the ways you're accustomed to working with formulas and worksheets (some options available only in the Windows version).

Microsoft Excel also provides a utility called CNF2INI for converting your configuration settings from Lotus 1-2-3. For more information about this utility and how to use it, see the Step By Step table at the end of this section.

Step By Step

For step-by-step instructions and related information, double-click the [?] button to display the Search dialog box in Help, and then:

Type this keyword and choose Show Topics	Select a topic and choose Go To
1-2-3 worksheets	Specifying Settings When Working with 1-2-3 Files in Microsoft Excel
column width	Adjusting column width
defaults, changing	Overview of Changing Defaults and Settings
row height	Adjusting row height

Linking Documents from Other Spreadsheets with Microsoft Excel Workbooks

You can use data from a 1-2-3 worksheet without exporting the worksheet to Microsoft Excel. Instead, you can link 1-2-3 worksheets to Microsoft Excel sheets. Open the 1-2-3 sheet and Microsoft Excel sheet you want to link together; then copy values from the 1-2-3 sheet and paste them in the Microsoft Excel sheet.

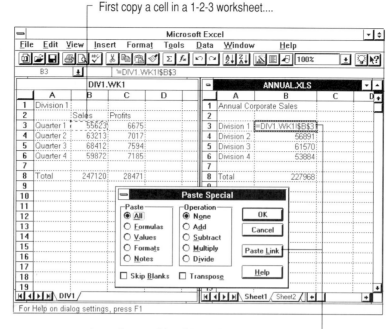

First copy a cell in a 1-2-3 worksheet....

...then select a cell in a Microsoft Excel workbook and use the Paste Link button to link the two documents.

If you have a file in a format that Microsoft Excel can open, you can use that file for any task that involves copying, moving, or linking data between sheets, such as consolidation, copying, and pasting.

Step By Step

For step-by-step instructions and related information, double-click the [?] button to display the Search dialog box in Help, and then:

Type this keyword and choose Show Topics	Select a topic and choose Go To
consolidating data	Overview of Consolidating Data
copying, cells	Overview of Copying and Moving Cells
workbooks, linking	Creating links between workbooks

Microsoft Excel for Windows Runs 1-2-3 Macros

Using the Macro Interpreter for Lotus 1-2-3 Users, you can open your 1-2-3 worksheet and run the macros contained on that worksheet. You can open any 1-2-3 file format (WKS, WK1, or WK3) in Microsoft Excel, and you can run macros that contain menu commands, functions, keywords, and advanced macro commands that are compatible with Lotus 1-2-3 Release 2.01. In addition, Microsoft Excel supports some Release 2.2 functionality.

Even if you save a 1-2-3 worksheet with macros as a Microsoft Excel workbook, you can still use your 1-2-3 macros. You can run any macro that is assigned a macro name consisting of a backslash (\) followed by a single letter. When you open a 1-2-3 worksheet in Microsoft Excel for Windows, the name you assigned to your macro in 1-2-3, such as \a, is defined in Microsoft Excel as a 1-2-3 macro name. Microsoft Excel assigns a lowercase letter to each macro name.

In Microsoft Excel, you cannot create range macro names that begin with a backslash (\). Therefore, you can run only your existing 1-2-3 macros and cannot create new Lotus 1-2-3 macros in Microsoft Excel.

Macros in Quattro Pro for MS-DOS are a superset of macros in Lotus 1-2-3. In Microsoft Excel for Windows, you can run any Quattro Pro for MS-DOS macro that you can run in Lotus 1-2-3 Release 2.01. You can run such macros by opening the document containing them in Microsoft Excel for Windows and pressing CTRL plus the letter assigned to the macro.

Calling Microsoft Excel Macros from a 1-2-3 Macro

You can call or branch to a Microsoft Excel macro from within a 1-2-3 macro by using the command names {XLCALL macro_name} and {XLBRANCH macro_name}. XLCALL and XLBRANCH are provided to simplify your transition from using 1-2-3 macros to using Microsoft Excel macros. These two commands help you translate your 1-2-3 macros in a modular fashion.

For example, if you created a procedure or macro named PagePrint on a module or macro sheet named PRINT, you can call the Microsoft Excel macro by inserting the command {XLCALL PagePrint} within your 1-2-3 macro. As with any subroutine, after the Microsoft Excel macro runs, control of the macro returns to the 1-2-3 macro. If you use XLBRANCH, control branches to Microsoft Excel and does not return to the 1-2-3 macro. You cannot call a 1-2-3 macro from within a Microsoft Excel macro.

Release 2.2 Functionality Supported by Microsoft Excel

Microsoft Excel can run macros that contain any Lotus 1-2-3 Release 2.2 advanced macro commands, such as {BORDERSON}, {BORDERSOFF}, {FRAMEON}, {FRAMEOFF}, {GRAPHON}, {GRAPHOFF}, and {HELP}. Microsoft Excel is also flexible when parsing macro expressions such as the statement

```
{let @cellpointer("address"),5}~
```

which is not valid in 1-2-3 Release 2.01 but is valid in Release 2.2. Microsoft Excel also allows file linking in formulas and macros that enter linking formulas, such as

```
`+<<EXPENSES.WK1>>A1~
```

Do not use macro statements that enter only the value of the linking formula, such as

```
{let A10, <<EXPENSES.WK1>>A1}~
```

However, Microsoft Excel cannot run macros that contain menu commands specific to 1-2-3 Release 2.2 and later, such as the /File Admin or /Add-in menu commands.

Translating 1-2-3 Macros in Microsoft Excel

You can use the Macro Translation Assistant included with Microsoft Excel for Windows to import 1-2-3 macros as Microsoft Excel macros. The Macro Translation Assistant cannot export Microsoft Excel macros to 1-2-3. Normally, you do not need to translate your 1-2-3 macros because Microsoft Excel can run 1-2-3 macros that are compatible with Lotus 1-2-3 Release 2.01.

▶ **To translate a 1-2-3 macro**

1. From File Manager, switch to the directory that contains Microsoft Excel.

2. Start TRANS.EXE by double-clicking the icon or by selecting the icon and choosing Run from the File menu.

   The Macro Translation Assistant window appears.

3. From the Translate menu, choose Lotus 1-2-3.

4. In the Select Source Sheet box, select the 1-2-3 worksheet that contains the macros you want to translate.

5. Choose the OK button.

6. In the Select Macro(s) To Translate box, select the macro you want to translate.

7. Choose the OK button.

If the Macro Translation Assistant cannot translate a function, it inserts a message that describes what action the function performed. To find a Microsoft Excel function that performs the same action, see Microsoft Excel Macro Functions Help.

▶ **To run a translated 1-2-3 macro**

1. From the File menu, choose Open.

2. In the File Name box, type or select the filename of the workbook that contains the macro you want to run.

3. Choose the OK button.

4. From the Tools menu, choose Macro.

5. In the Macro Name/Reference box, select the macro you want to run.

6. Choose the Run button.

Step By Step

For step-by-step instructions and related information, double-click the [?] button to display the Search dialog box in Help, and then:

Type this keyword and choose Show Topics	Select a topic and choose Go To
Lotus 1-2-3, macro conversion	Macro Interpreter for Lotus 1-2-3 Users
Lotus 1-2-3, Macro Translation Assistant	Starting Macro Translation Assistant — Lotus 1-2-3

What's Next?

Now that you're acquainted with how Microsoft Excel version 5.0 differs from spreadsheet applications you already know, it's time to learn more. For information about accomplishing specific tasks with Microsoft Excel version 5.0, see the following chapters and topics in the Microsoft Excel documentation.

For information about	See this part or chapter later in this book
Opening, editing, formatting, and printing workbooks	Part 2, "Essential Skills"
Plotting your data in charts	Part 3, "Creating Charts from Worksheet Data"
Organizing and storing data in lists	Part 4, "Organizing and Managing Data in a List"
Analyzing and consolidating lists of data	Part 5, "Retrieving and Analyzing Data from Lists and Tables"
Solving problems by analyzing your data	Part 6, "Solving Problems by Analyzing Data"
Using Help	Chapter 5, "Getting Information While You Work"

CHAPTER 4

What's New in Microsoft Excel Version 5.0

For command, keyboard, and toolbar button information, see online Help.

In This Chapter

What Happens When I Open My Old Microsoft Excel Files in Version 5.0?

When you open a file in Microsoft Excel version 5.0 that was created in Microsoft Excel version 4.0 or earlier, it is converted to a new file format. After working in the file in version 5.0, you can save the file either in the file format for version 4.0 or earlier, or you can save it in version 5.0 format.

Once you save your work in version 5.0 format, you cannot open it in earlier versions of Microsoft Excel. If you work in version 5.0 and then save the file in version 4.0 or earlier format, portions of your work may not be retained in the version 4.0 file format.

Old Microsoft Excel File Type	Converted to Microsoft Excel 5.0 file type	For more information, see
Add-in	Add-in.	Chapter 37, "Installing Add-in Features"
Chart	Workbook with a single chart sheet.	Chapter 7, "Working in Workbooks," and Chapter 15, "Creating a Chart"
Macro sheet	Workbook with a single Microsoft Excel 4.0 macro sheet.	Appendix B, "Switching From the Microsoft Excel 4.0 Macro Language," in the *Microsoft Excel Visual Basic User's Guide*
Template	Workbook template.	Chapter 36, "Using Templates to Create Your Own Default Workbooks"
Workbook	Workbook. Bound sheets stay in the new workbook. Unbound sheets become new workbooks.	Chapter 6, "Managing Workbook Files," and Chapter 7, "Working in Workbooks"
Worksheet	Workbook with a single worksheet.	Chapter 7, "Working in Workbooks"
Workspace	Workspace.	Chapter 34, "Customizing Your Workspace"

Menu Command Changes in Version 5.0

To make Microsoft Excel simpler to use and more consistent with other applications, such as Microsoft Word, the menu and command structure has been reorganized. Online Help includes a comprehensive list of Microsoft Excel version 4.0 commands and their locations in Microsoft Excel version 5.0. For more information, search Help for "menu commands."

Switching Between Version 4.0 and Version 5.0 Menus

To ease your transition to Microsoft Excel version 5.0, you can switch Microsoft Excel to the version 4.0 menus. You can then switch back to the version 5.0 menus at any time.

To switch to the version 4.0 menus, choose Options from the Tools menu, select the General tab, and then select the Microsoft Excel 4.0 Menus check box.

When you select a version 4.0 menu command, Microsoft Excel performs the equivalent version 5.0 functionality. Not all of the functionality of Microsoft Excel version 5.0 is available when you view the version 4.0 menus.

To switch back to the version 5.0 menus, choose New Menus from the Options menu.

New Features for Everyday Tasks

New feature	For more information, see
Use the TipWizard™ assistant to learn shortcuts for the way you work.	Chapter 5, "Getting Information While You Work"
Display ToolTips to see button names (Microsoft Excel for Windows only).	Chapter 5, "Getting Information While You Work"
All files are workbooks for simpler data management.	Chapter 6, "Managing Workbook Files"
Use the Find File command on the File menu to search for a workbook, even if you don't know its name.	Chapter 6, "Managing Workbook Files"
Create custom AutoFill series.	Chapter 9, "Entering Data"
Enter and edit data directly in cells, or in the formula bar.	Chapter 9, "Entering Data"
Create named ranges in the Name box on the formula bar.	Chapter 10, "Creating Formulas and Links"
Use the interactive Function Wizard to create formulas with worksheet functions.	Chapter 10, "Creating Formulas and Links"
Create 3-D formulas and 3-D names for powerful workbook models.	Chapter 10, "Creating Formulas and Links"
Automatically create grand totals with AutoSum™.	Chapter 10, "Creating Formulas and Links"
Use one spelling dictionary for both Microsoft Excel and Microsoft Word.	Chapter 11, "Editing a Worksheet"
Use single and double underline formats.	Chapter 12, "Formatting a Worksheet"

New feature	For more information, see
Format individual characters in cells containing text.	Chapter 12, "Formatting a Worksheet"
Use tear-off palettes of borders, colors, patterns, and font colors on your worksheet.	Chapter 34, "Customizing Your Workspace"
Use the Format Painter button to quickly copy formats between cells and between objects.	Chapter 12, "Formatting a Worksheet"
Select from a larger group of built-in headers and footers.	Chapter 14, "Printing"
Easily change the default font and font size.	Chapter 35, "Controlling What Happens When You Start Microsoft Excel"
Enlarge the working area on your screen by using the Full Screen command on the View menu.	Chapter 32, "Changing How You View Your Worksheet"

New Features for Creating and Formatting Charts

New feature	For more information, see
Draw graphic objects directly on charts.	Chapter 13, "Creating Graphic Objects on Worksheets and Charts"
Use chart autoformats to instantly change chart type and formatting options, and create your own autoformats.	Chapter 16, "Working with Chart Types and Autoformats"
Drag data directly onto a chart to add a data series or data points.	Chapter 17, "Changing Data in a Chart"
Get better scaling of charts on chart sheets.	Chapter 18, "Formatting a Chart"
Position chart items, such as titles, anywhere you want them.	Chapter 18, "Formatting a Chart"
Add trendlines and error bars to your data series.	Chapter 19, "Using Charts to Analyze Data"

New Features for Organizing and Managing Data in Lists

New feature	For more information, see
Use AutoFilter to temporarily hide data and display only rows that meet your criteria.	Chapter 21, "Sorting and Filtering Data in a List"
Sort by using column labels from your list.	Chapter 21, "Sorting and Filtering Data in a List"

New feature	For more information, see
Create custom sort orders, such as High, Med, and Low.	Chapter 21, "Sorting and Filtering Data in a List"
Automatically add subtotals and grand totals.	Chapter 22, "Summarizing Data in a List"

New Features for Retrieving and Analyzing Data from Lists and Tables

New feature	For more information, see
Add trendlines and error bars to your data series when charting.	Chapter 19, "Using Charts to Analyze Data"
Access external databases with Microsoft Query.	Chapter 23, "Retrieving Data with Microsoft Query"
Use the interactive PivotTable Wizard to cross-tabulate and summarize data from an existing list or table, and then rearrange and instantly recalculate the result.	Chapter 24, "Creating a Pivot Table"

New Features for Solving Problems by Analyzing Data

New feature	For more information, see
Use the new Scenario Manager to quickly create and manage scenarios, protect or merge scenarios, and track changes to scenarios.	Chapter 28, "Managing What-If Scenarios"

New Features for Customizing Microsoft Excel

New feature	For more information, see
Save your list of open workbooks as a workspace file.	Chapter 34, "Customizing Your Workspace"
Use or customize any of the built-in toolbars, or create your own.	Chapter 34, "Customizing Your Workspace"

New feature	For more information, see
Change the images on toolbar buttons.	Chapter 34, "Customizing Your Workspace"
Use autotemplates to create new default workbooks and sheets.	Chapter 36, "Using Templates to Create Your Own Default Workbooks"
Use the new Visual Basic® Programming System, Applications Edition, to create custom solutions in Microsoft Excel.	"Introduction," *Microsoft Excel Visual Basic User's Guide.*

New Features for Reviewing and Sharing Workbooks

New feature	For more information, see
Use the Find File command on the File menu to search for a workbook, even if you don't know its name.	Chapter 6, "Managing Workbook Files"
Click the Toggle File Status button to toggle file status between read-write and read-only.	Chapter 6, "Managing Workbook Files"
Display the precedent, dependent, and error tracers directly on your worksheet to locate problems in formulas.	Chapter 38, "Troubleshooting and Annotating a Worksheet"
Mail and route workbooks within a workgroup.	Chapter 40, "Routing Workbooks with Electronic Mail"

New Features for Exchanging Data with Other Applications

New feature	For more information, see
Microsoft Excel supports OLE 2.0: activate and edit embedded objects without leaving Microsoft Excel; drag and drop data between applications to cut, copy, and paste.	Chapter 41, "Sharing Data and Graphics with Other Applications"
Use the TextWizard to parse data files when you import them.	Chapter 42, "Importing and Exporting Documents"
Open files in Multiplan and Microsoft Works format.	Chapter 42, "Importing and Exporting Documents"

New Features for Programming with Microsoft Excel

New feature	For more information, see
Use the new Visual Basic Programming System, Applications Edition.	Appendix B, "Switching from the Microsoft Excel 4.0 Macro Language," in the *Microsoft Excel Visual Basic User's Guide*
Create custom dialog boxes on a dialog sheet.	Chapter 11, "Controls and Dialog Boxes," in the *Microsoft Excel Visual Basic User's Guide*

New Function Wizard and Help for Worksheet Functions

Microsoft Excel version 5.0 includes two ways to learn about and use worksheet functions:

- **The Function Wizard**   The Function Wizard includes descriptions of all worksheet functions. Use it to select a function, assemble the arguments correctly and insert the function into your formula. To see more information about a function, select it in the Function Wizard and choose the Help button. For more information, see "Using the Function Wizard" in Chapter 10.

- **Online Help**   Online Help includes complete worksheet function descriptions. To see the worksheet function descriptions or a list of new and changed functions, listed by category, search Help for "worksheet functions."

  A complete reference to the Microsoft Excel worksheet functions is available in online Help. This reference is also available in book form *(Microsoft Excel Worksheet Function Reference)* and can be purchased in book and software stores or ordered directly from Microsoft Press. To place a credit card order, call 615-793-5090, or toll-free 800-MS-PRESS. Be sure to have the reference code FXL ready for faster order processing.

CHAPTER 5

Getting Information While You Work

For command, keyboard, and toolbar button information, see online Help.

In This Chapter

Where Do I Find It?

This book is only one part of the documentation for Microsoft Excel—documentation designed for the way you work. Some information is included in the books that come with Microsoft Excel; other information is online. All of the online and printed documentation is designed to work together to help you get your job done quickly and efficiently. The following sections are tailored for your system. If you are using a Macintosh, skip to the "If You Are Using Microsoft Excel for the Macintosh" section now.

If You Are Using Microsoft Excel for Windows

Introductory Lessons: Quick Preview

Use the *Quick Preview* interactive lessons to help you get started—learn about important concepts and features, find out what's new in Microsoft Excel version 5.0, switch over from another spreadsheet program, and find out where to look online to find the information you need. The *Quick Preview* opens automatically the first time you start Microsoft Excel. You can also view it at any time by choosing the Quick Preview command from the Help menu.

Online Information

- **Online Help**   Detailed step-by-step instructions and reference information for all tasks and features including commands, toolbar buttons, functions, and the Visual Basic language. Open Help using commands on the Help menu. For more details about Help and how it works, take a look at the "Guide to Online Help" section later in this chapter.

- **Examples and Demos**   Short, interactive lessons that focus on a single task. You can jump directly to specific examples and demos by clicking the Examples And Demos button included in many of the Help topics. You can browse a complete list of them by choosing the Examples And Demos command from the Help menu.

- **Sample Files**   Examples you can open in Microsoft Excel and use to create and enhance your own work. Most sample files are in the EXAMPLES subdirectory of the directory where Microsoft Excel is installed. Sample files for Microsoft Query are in the MSAPPS\MSQUERY subdirectory of the directory where Windows is installed.

- **Worksheet Functions**   Descriptions of all worksheet functions and their arguments appear in the Function Wizard. Click the Function Wizard button on the Standard toolbar to select a function, assemble the arguments correctly, and insert the function into your formula.

  For more information about the Function Wizard, see "Using the Function Wizard" in Chapter 10. Detailed descriptions and examples of worksheet functions are included in online Help.

Printed Information

- *Microsoft Excel User's Guide*   Explains how to do tasks, often with examples and graphics. Includes cross-references to the comprehensive information in Help. Contains a quick tutorial that introduces important Microsoft Excel concepts and features.

- *Microsoft Excel Visual Basic User's Guide*   Complete guide to automating, customizing, and programming Microsoft Excel.

- *Microsoft Excel Visual Basic Reference*   A complete reference to the Visual Basic language is available in online Help. This reference is also available in book form and can be purchased in book and software stores or ordered directly from Microsoft Press. To place a credit card order, call 615-793-5090, or toll-free 800-MS-PRESS. Be sure to have your reference code FXL ready for faster order processing.

- *Microsoft Query User's Guide*   Guide to accessing and retrieving data from databases.

If You Are Using Microsoft Excel for the Macintosh

Introductory Lessons: Quick Preview

Use the *Quick Preview* interactive lessons to help you get started—learn about important concepts and features, and find out what's new in Microsoft Excel version 5.0 and where to look online to find the information you need. To view the *Quick Preview,* choose the Quick Preview command from the Help menu. If your screen is smaller than 13 inches, the Quick Preview command is on the Window menu.

Online Information

- **Online Help**   Detailed step-by-step instructions and reference information for all tasks and features including commands, toolbar buttons, functions, and the Visual Basic language. Open Help using commands on the Help menu. If your screen is smaller than 13 inches, the Help commands will appear on the Window menu. For more details about Help and how it works, take a look at the "Guide to Online Help" section later in this chapter.

- **Examples and Demos**   Short, interactive lessons that focus on a single task. You can browse a complete list of examples and demos by choosing the Examples and Demos command from the Help menu. If your screen is smaller than 13 inches, the Examples and Demos command is on theWindow menu.

- **Sample Files**   Actual examples you can open in Microsoft Excel and use to create and enhance your own work. The sample files are in the MICROSOFT EXCEL:EXAMPLES folder.

- **Worksheet Functions**   Descriptions of all worksheet functions and their arguments appear in the Function Wizard. Click the Function Wizard button on the Standard toolbar to select a function, assemble the arguments correctly, and insert the function into your formula.

  For more information about the Function Wizard, see "Using the Function Wizard" in Chapter 10. Detailed descriptions and examples of worksheet functions are included in online Help.

Printed Information

- *Microsoft Excel User's Guide*   Explains how to do tasks, often with examples and graphics. Includes cross-references to the comprehensive information in Help. Contains a quick tutorial that introduces important Microsoft Excel concepts and features.

- *Microsoft Excel Visual Basic User's Guide*   Complete guide to automating, customizing, and programming Microsoft Excel.

- *Microsoft Excel Visual Basic Reference*   A complete reference to the Visual Basic language is available in online Help. This reference is also available in book form and can be purchased in book and software stores or ordered directly from Microsoft Press. To place a credit card order, call 615-793-5090, or toll-free 800-MS-PRESS. Be sure to have your reference code FXL ready for faster order processing.

- *Microsoft Query User's Guide*   Guide to accessing and retrieving data from databases. If Microsoft Query did not come with your copy of Microsoft Excel, use the fulfillment coupon in the box to obtain a copy.

Information at Your Fingertips

Microsoft Excel gives you tips for how to work more efficiently and provides detailed instructions and reference information right on your screen. The information you need is never far away. The following sections in this chapter give details on how to use this information.

Click to display the TipWizard for tips about quick and efficient ways to use Microsoft Excel. The light bulb lights up whenever there is a new tip.

See the status bar for a description of the selected command.

Click here for Help, and then choose a command or click a screen element to get detailed information. Double-click here to search for information in Help.

As you move the mouse pointer over the buttons on a toolbar, a description of what the button does appears in the status bar. In Windows, the name of the button appears near the button if you leave the mouse pointer over it. On the Macintosh, you can get information on a button by using Balloon Help™.

Help is also available from every dialog box and alert message.

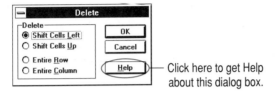

Click here to get Help about this dialog box.

Step By Step

For step-by-step instructions and related information, double-click the ⬛? button to display the Search dialog box in Help, and then:

Type this keyword and choose Show Topics	Select a topic and choose Go To
commands, Help on	Getting help on the command or screen element you choose
Help, searching	Searching Help for a particular topic
TipWizard	Using the TipWizard

Is There a Quicker Way?

When there is a quicker or more efficient way of performing the action you've just performed, the TipWizard will let you know. Click the TipWizard button to display the TipWizard.

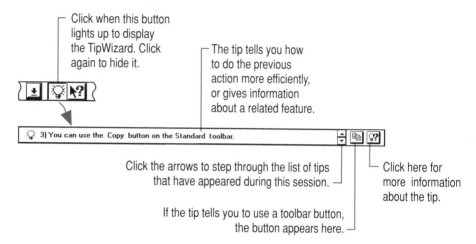

If you want to add a button that appears in the TipWizard to a toolbar, choose the Toolbars command from the View menu and then drag the button from the TipWizard to a toolbar.

Step By Step

For step-by-step instructions and related information, double-click the button to display the Search dialog box in Help, and then:

Type this keyword and choose Show Topics	Select a topic and choose Go To
TipWizard	Using the TipWizard

Searching for the Information You Need

Help

Double-click the Help button on the Standard toolbar to search Help for the exact information you need.

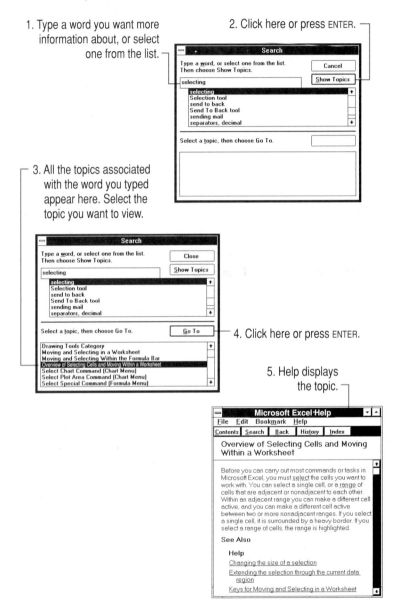

You can also click the Search button in the Help window to display the Search dialog box.

If you want to return to a topic you have previously viewed, you can choose either the Back or the History button in the Help window. The Back button steps you back through the topics in reverse order. The History button displays a list of the topics you've seen. Double-click the topic you want.

Step By Step

For step-by-step instructions and related information, double-click the ▶? button to display the Search dialog box in Help, and then:

Type this keyword and choose Show Topics	Select a topic and choose Go To
Help, searching	Searching Help for a particular topic

Guide to Online Help

You can open Help using commands on the Microsoft Excel menus.

System	Where to find Help commands
Windows	Help menu
Macintosh	Help menu (Window menu if your screen is smaller than 13 inches)

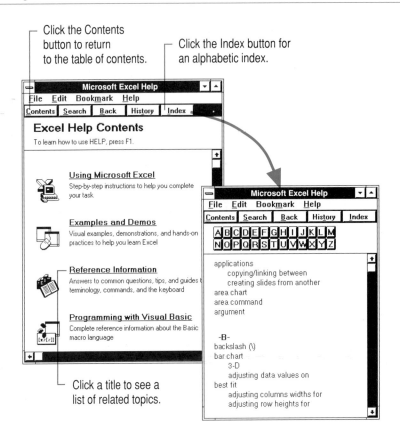

Click the Contents button to return to the table of contents.

Click the Index button for an alphabetic index.

Click a title to see a list of related topics.

Help in Microsoft Windows

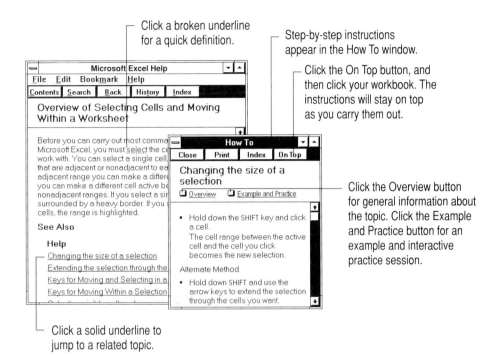

Click a broken underline for a quick definition.

Step-by-step instructions appear in the How To window.

Click the On Top button, and then click your workbook. The instructions will stay on top as you carry them out.

Click the Overview button for general information about the topic. Click the Example and Practice button for an example and interactive practice session.

Click a solid underline to jump to a related topic.

Help on the Macintosh

Click a broken underline for a quick definition.

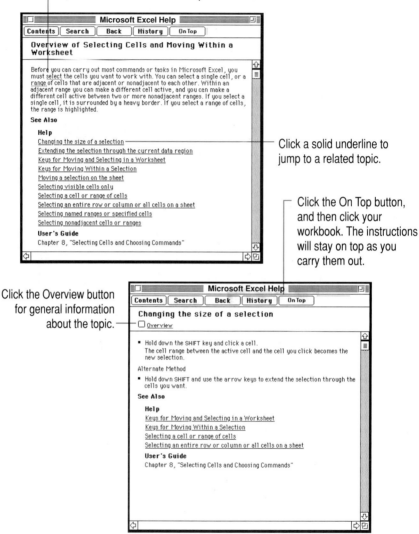

Click a solid underline to jump to a related topic.

Click the On Top button, and then click your workbook. The instructions will stay on top as you carry them out.

Click the Overview button for general information about the topic.

Step By Step

For step-by-step instructions and related information, double-click the ⟦?⟧ button to display the Search dialog box in Help, and then:

Type this keyword and choose Show Topics	Select a topic and choose Go To
Help, overview	Overview of Using Help to Find the Information You Need

PART 2

Essential Skills

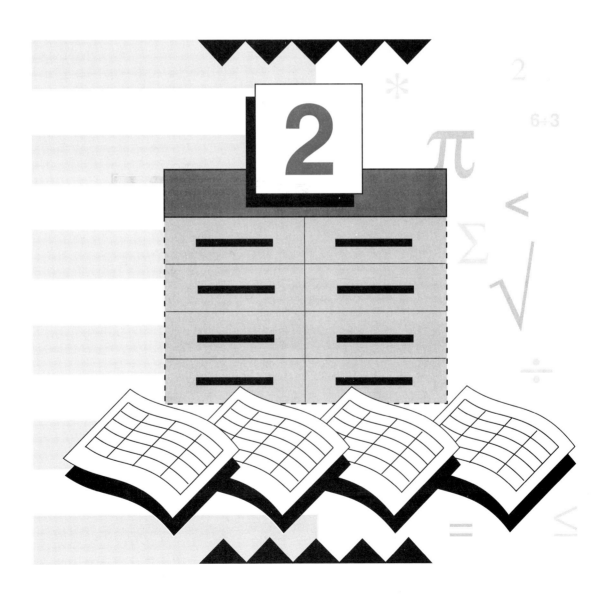

CHAPTER 6

Managing Workbook Files

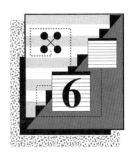

For command, keyboard, and toolbar button information, see online Help.

In This Chapter

Creating or Opening Workbooks

A *workbook* is a Microsoft Excel version 5.0 file in which you work. Workbooks contain sheets, such as worksheets, chart sheets, and macro sheets. This chapter describes how to open, close, save, and search for workbook files. For information about working within a workbook, see Chapter 7, "Working in Workbooks."

Creating a New Workbook

New Workbook

When you start Microsoft Excel, a new workbook opens. To begin working, just start typing. If you want to create a new workbook at any time, click the New Workbook button.

You can also choose the New command from the File menu. If you have templates in your startup directory or startup folder, Microsoft Excel will display a list of templates that you can use as a basis for new workbooks. For general-purpose workbooks, select the Workbook template. For information about templates, see Chapter 36, "Using Templates to Create Your Own Default Workbooks."

Opening an Existing Workbook

You can open a workbook you recently worked on by choosing it from the list at the bottom of the File menu.

If the list of recently opened workbooks does not appear on the File menu, you can display it. Choose the Options command from the Tools menu, select the General tab, and then select the Recently Used File List check box.

Note   If you are using a small Macintosh monitor, the list of recently opened workbooks is not available.

Open

You can open any workbook by choosing the Open command from the File menu or by clicking the Open button. When the Open dialog box appears, select a workbook filename. You may need to select a different drive, directory, or folder to see the workbook you want. If you can't find a particular workbook, choose the Find File button in the Open dialog box to search for it. For information about searching for workbooks, see "Finding Workbooks" later in this chapter.

Tip   You can specify a default directory or folder for Microsoft Excel to use every time you select the Open or Save As commands on the File menu. For information about how to change the default directory or folder, see "Setting the Working Directory or Folder" in Chapter 35.

Sharing Workbooks on a Network

You can share your Microsoft Excel work in many ways. If your group uses a local area network, Windows for Workgroups, Macintosh System 7 File Sharing, or another network system, you can share workbooks with others.

Depending on your network system, you may see a Network button in the Open and Save As dialog boxes in Microsoft Excel for Windows. If so, follow the instructions below. If not, refer to your network documentation for information about sharing files.

To open or save a workbook on a network, connect to a network drive and then select the network drive in the Open or Save As dialog box.

System	To connect to a network drive
Windows	Choose the Network button in either the Open or Save As dialog box to display the File Manager Connect Network Drive dialog box, and then connect to the network drive in the usual way. (If you are not connected to a network, the Network button will not appear in the Open or Save As dialog box.)
Macintosh	Use the Chooser.

If you open a workbook from a network, others who try to open the workbook are notified that the workbook is in use. They are given the option of opening a read-only copy of the workbook, or of being notified when the workbook is available.

Tip When working with workbooks you've opened from a network drive, you should close the workbook as soon as you are done with it so that others can have read-write access to it.

Notes If you select the Read Only check box in the Open dialog box when you open a workbook from a network, the workbook can still be opened as read-write by another user.

If you want to save changes to a workbook that you opened as read-only, you must use the Save As command on the File menu and save the workbook with a new name. The original workbook remains unchanged.

Step By Step

For step-by-step instructions and related information, double-click the [?] button to display the Search dialog box in Help, and then:

Type this keyword and choose Show Topics	Select a topic and choose Go To
workbooks, automatic starting	Starting Microsoft Excel and opening a workbook automatically
workbooks, creating	Creating a new workbook
workbooks, list of recently opened	Hiding the list of recently opened workbooks on the File menu
workbooks, opening	Opening a recently opened workbook
	Opening a workbook
	Opening several workbooks at one time (Windows)

Saving and Closing Workbooks

Saving a Workbook

Save File

To save the active workbook, choose the Save command from the File menu, or click the Save button.

If you haven't saved the workbook previously, or if you opened it as read-only, the Save As dialog box appears so that you can type a name for the workbook. You can select the drive, directory, or folder where you want to save the workbook.

Saving Summary Information

You can enter *summary information* about a workbook by choosing the Summary Info command from the File menu. The summary information includes the workbook's title, subject, author, keywords, and comments. Microsoft Excel uses this information when you search for workbooks. For information about searching for workbooks, see "Finding Workbooks" later in this chapter.

Tip If you want to display the Summary Info dialog box each time you save a new workbook, choose the Options command from the Tools menu and select the General tab. Then select the Prompt For Summary Info check box.

Automatically Saving Changes

Microsoft Excel can automatically save the active workbook or all open workbooks at a specified time interval. To set up Microsoft Excel so that it automatically saves your work, choose the AutoSave command from the Tools menu. Then specify how often you want your work saved, what to save, and whether you should be prompted before saving.

Note The AutoSave command is an *add-in*. If the AutoSave command appears on the Tools menu, it is already installed. If the AutoSave command doesn't appear, choose the Add-Ins command from the Tools menu to see the list of add-ins currently available. If AutoSave appears there, make sure that its adjacent check box is selected. If AutoSave does not appear, you need to run the Microsoft Excel Setup program to install the AutoSave add-in. For more information, see Chapter 1, "Installing and Starting Microsoft Excel," or the Step By Step table at the end of this section.

Making Backup Copies and Restoring Lost Work

Microsoft Excel can save the previous version of a workbook as a backup copy every time you save the workbook. To save a backup copy of a workbook, choose the Save As command from the File menu and select the Options button. Then select the Always Create Backup check box. Now whenever you save the workbook, Microsoft Excel will create a backup copy in the same directory or folder as the original workbook.

System	Backup copy filename
Windows	Same name as original workbook, but with the extension .BAK. For example, if the original workbook is named Q1SALES.XLS, the backup copy is named Q1SALES.BAK.
Macintosh	BACKUP OF *workbook filename*. For example, if the original workbook is named FIRST QUARTER SALES, the backup copy is named BACKUP OF FIRST QUARTER SALES. If necessary, Microsoft Excel will shorten the filename to prevent the backup name from exceeding 31 characters.

In case of a power failure or some other problem, you can restore the workbook to its previously saved state by opening the backup copy.

Saving a Workbook in Another File Format

If you share workbooks with others who use different spreadsheet applications, you can save a Microsoft Excel workbook in another file format, such as Lotus 1-2-3.

System	To select a different file format
Windows	From the File menu, choose Save As. Select a format in the Save File As Type box.
Macintosh	From the File menu, choose Save As. Select a format in the Save File As Type box.

For more information, see "Opening and Saving Documents in Different File Formats" in Chapter 42.

Closing a Workbook and Quitting Microsoft Excel

To	Do this
Close the active workbook	From the File menu, choose Close.
Close all open workbooks	Hold down SHIFT and choose Close All from the File menu.
Close all open workbooks and quit Microsoft Excel	From the File menu, choose Exit (Windows) or Quit (Macintosh).

If the workbook has changes that you have not saved, Microsoft Excel asks if you want to save the changes before closing. If you choose the Yes button but have not named the workbook, the Save As dialog box is displayed.

If you're working on a network, closing a workbook makes it available as a read-write file for other users on the network.

Step By Step

For step-by-step instructions and related information, double-click the  button to display the Search dialog box in Help, and then:

Type this keyword and choose Show Topics	Select a topic and choose Go To
add-ins	Installing or removing an add-in
automatic saving	Saving your work automatically
summary information	Entering and editing summary information
workbooks, closing	Closing a workbook
	Closing all workbooks
workbooks, saving	Saving a workbook
	Saving a workbook using a different name or file format

Finding Workbooks

You can locate a workbook or other file using almost any information about it. For example, Microsoft Excel can find a workbook based on its filename or disk, or directory or folder location. If you included summary information when you saved a workbook, you can also search for that workbook based on its author, title, or keywords. For example, you can search for all workbooks that contain the word "sales" in their titles. For more information about summary information, see "Saving and Closing Workbooks" earlier in this chapter.

The information you use to search for workbooks is called *search criteria,* which you can save and reuse.

Searching for Workbooks

To look for a workbook, choose the Find File command from the File menu. You can also choose the Open command from the File menu and then choose the Find File button.

Once you complete a search, Microsoft Excel displays a list of files that meet the search criteria in the Find File dialog box.

Note   Microsoft Excel periodically updates the information in the Find File dialog box so that a current list is displayed.

Specifying Search Criteria

Search criteria can include such items as filenames and directory or folder locations, the contents and modification dates of workbooks, and summary information. The first time you choose Find File, the Search dialog box appears so that you can specify the search criteria you want to use. Thereafter, Microsoft Excel uses the last search criteria you specified. Microsoft Excel always lists only those files that meet the current search criteria.

To specify search criteria, choose the Search button in the Find File dialog box, and then select the search options you want in the Search dialog box.

To	Do this
Search for a full or partial filename	In the File Name box, type the filename you want to search for, or select a file type. You can use an asterisk (*) wildcard character if you don't know the full filename.
Search another disk	Select the drive in the Location box.
Save your search criteria to use again later	Choose the Save Search As button, then name the search.
Specify more advanced search criteria	Choose the Advanced Search button.

Once you have defined a set of criteria, you can save it with a name and reuse it. For more information, see "Saving and Reusing Search Criteria" later in this section.

Searching with Advanced Search Criteria

If you want to specify additional criteria such as multiple directories or folders, modification dates, or summary information, choose the Advanced Search button in the Search dialog box, and then select the criteria you want in the Advanced Search dialog box.

To	Select this tab, and then enter the search options you want
Search by location, including filename, directory or folder, or disk	Location tab
Search by summary information entered with the Summary Info command on the File menu	Summary Info tab
Search for the date a file was last saved, or by the author's name	Timestamp tab

Note   The only criteria you can use to search for a password-protected Microsoft Excel workbook are the filename, location, and modification dates. You cannot search summary information.

Fine-tuning Searches

In some kinds of search criteria, you can use special characters called *wildcards* to search for workbooks. You can substitute an asterisk (*) or a question mark (?) for any text. To control a search, you can use *search operators*. For example, with the ampersand operator (&), you can find two values of a single criterion. Using search operators, particularly when searching for text contained in a workbook, saves you time because it helps to narrow down the list of files Microsoft Excel finds.

In Microsoft Excel for Windows, you can also specify more than one filename extension in any File Name box if you separate each extension with a semicolon. For example, typing ***.xls;*.xlw** finds files with either of those filename extensions.

A list of wildcard characters and search operators you can use is included in online Help. For more information, see the Step By Step table at the end of this section.

Spaces and Punctuation in Criteria

If the text you type in an advanced search includes spaces or punctuation, enclose the text in quotation marks. For example, to find the phrase *fiscal year* in workbooks, type **"fiscal year"** in the Containing Text box on the Summary tab.

Pinpointing a Workbook

The more criteria you specify, the more exact Microsoft Excel will be in finding particular files. If you specify a single criterion, such as a particular author, the search will quickly yield a list of workbooks.

Saving and Reusing Search Criteria

Once you've specified a set of search criteria, you can name and save it. Then you can reuse the criteria by selecting the name in the Search dialog box. To save a set of search criteria, choose the Save Search As button, and then name the search.

Finding Files with Saved Search Criteria

Once you've saved a set of search criteria and given it a name, you can reuse it by selecting it in the Saved Searches box in the Search dialog box. When you choose the OK button, Microsoft Excel finds the appropriate files and displays them in the Find File dialog box. The name of the current set of search criteria is displayed above the list.

Modifying and Deleting Saved Search Criteria

You can modify saved search criteria instead of creating new criteria. To modify a set of saved search criteria, select the name of the search you want to modify in the Saved Searches box, and choose the Advanced Search button. Then modify the search criteria, and save the new search.

To delete a saved search, select the name of the search you want to delete in the Saved Searches box, and then choose the Delete Search button.

Step By Step

For step-by-step instructions and related information, double-click the 🕵? button to display the Search dialog box in Help, and then:

Type this keyword and choose Show Topics	Select a topic and choose Go To
finding, workbooks	Modifying saved searches
	Saving search criteria
	Searching for workbooks
	Searching with advanced search criteria
	Using special characters in a search

Previewing Workbooks and Viewing Summary Information

You can see the upper-left corner of the leftmost sheet in a workbook before you open the workbook. If you enter information such as the workbook's title, purpose, and author in the upper-left corner of the leftmost sheet, seeing the preview can help you quickly select the workbook you want before you open it. You can also view information about a workbook, such as its file size and its summary information. To see these views, choose the Find File command from the File menu, and use the information in the following table.

To	Select the file in the Find File dialog box, and then do this
See a thumbnail view of the workbook	Select Preview in the View box.
See title, size, author, and other information about the workbook	Select File Info or Summary in the View box.

You can also preview other file formats, if they support the thumbnail view.

Sorting Listed Files and Displaying Document Titles

In the Find File dialog box, Microsoft Excel displays the files that meet the current search criteria. Microsoft Excel lists the files according to their location on a disk, starting with those that are stored in the root directory or folder and working down the directory or folder hierarchy. You can sort files within each directory or folder by choosing the Commands button and then choosing the Sorting command from the menu. Use the options under Sort Files By to select the way you want to sort the files.

Previewing Workbooks and Browsing Directories or Folders

In the Find File dialog box, the files and directories or folders that meet the current search criteria are displayed as a directory or folder hierarchy. A closed folder icon is displayed with a plus sign (+), and an open folder icon is displayed with a minus sign (–). To open or close a folder, double-click the folder icon.

Note   You cannot see the preview or summary information of a password-protected workbook. For more information about password protection, see "Protecting Workbooks, Sheets, and Their Contents" in Chapter 39.

Viewing File Information

To view basic information about a workbook, select File Info in the View box in the Find File dialog box.

Note   The information that Microsoft Excel displays about a workbook depends on how you sort the list. If you sort the list by using the Last Saved By option, the Author column changes to Last Saved By. If you sort the list by creation date, the Last Saved Date column becomes Created Date.

Viewing Summary Information

You can view summary information for a workbook in two ways:

- If the workbook is open, choose the Summary Info command from the File menu.

- In the Find File dialog box, select the workbook you want, and then select Summary in the View box.

If you haven't supplied summary information for the workbook, some of the spaces will be blank.

Step By Step

For step-by-step instructions and related information, double-click the [⯑?] button to display the Search dialog box in Help, and then:

Type this keyword and choose Show Topics	Select a topic and choose Go To
finding, workbooks	Sorting a list of files found with the Find File command
	Viewing and editing summary information for workbooks

Managing Workbooks with Find File

With the Find File feature it's easy for you to open, copy, print, and delete files without leaving Microsoft Excel.

To manage files, choose the Find File command from the File menu and find the files you want to work with by specifying the appropriate search criteria in the Search dialog box. When Microsoft Excel displays the list of files, select the files you want to work with, choose the Commands button, and then choose a command from the menu.

To	Do this
Open the workbook as read-only	Choose the Open Read Only command.
Print the workbook	Choose the Print command and then select the options you want.
View summary information about the workbook	Choose the Summary command.
Delete a file	Choose the Delete command. Microsoft Excel asks you to confirm that you want to delete the file.
Copy a file	Choose the Copy command, then select the location to which you want to copy the file.
Sort files	Choose the Sorting command, and then select the option you want to use to sort the files
Create a new directory or folder	Choose the Copy command, and then choose the New Directory or New Folder button. In the Name box, type the path and name of the directory or folder that you want to create.

Step By Step

For step-by-step instructions and related information, double-click the 📭 button to display the Search dialog box in Help, and then:

Type this keyword and choose Show Topics	Select a topic and choose Go To
finding, files	Managing files with the Find File command
	Selecting multiple files in the Find File dialog box

CHAPTER 7

Working in Workbooks

For command, keyboard, and toolbar button information, see online Help.

In This Chapter

How a Workbook Works

What Is a Workbook?

In Microsoft Excel version 5.0, the file in which you work and store your data is called a *workbook*. Each workbook can contain many sheets. You can also have different types of sheets in one workbook. For example, you could have a year's sales data on a worksheet in a workbook, and also have a chart sheet for the data in the same workbook. Whenever you open, close, or save a file in Microsoft Excel 5.0, you are opening, closing, or saving the workbook file.

The default workbook opens with 16 worksheets, named Sheet1 through Sheet16. The sheet names appear on tabs at the bottom of the workbook window. By clicking on the tabs you can move from sheet to sheet within a workbook. The tab of the active sheet is always bold.

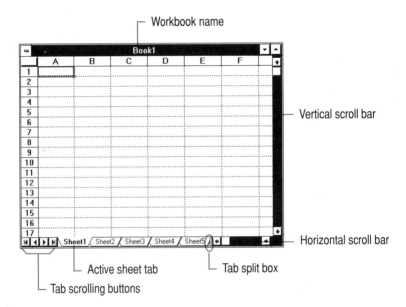

Do any of the following to arrange your workbook the way you want:

- Insert new sheets
- Delete sheets
- Rename sheets
- Move or copy sheets within a workbook or to another workbook
- Hide sheets

For information about hiding sheets, see "Hiding and Unhiding Workbooks and Sheets" in Chapter 39.

Note If you don't see the tabs in your workbook, you may need to select the Sheet Tabs option. Choose the Options command from the Tools menu, select the View tab, and then select the Sheet Tabs check box. If you still don't see the sheet tabs, double-click the tab split box at the far left of the horizontal scroll bar.

Types of Sheets

You can have six different types of sheets in a workbook.

Type of sheet	Used for
Worksheet	Entering and calculating data
Chart sheet	Charts not embedded within a worksheet
Visual Basic module	Microsoft Excel Visual Basic language
Dialog	Microsoft Excel Visual Basic language
Microsoft Excel 4.0 macro sheet	Compatibility with earlier versions of Microsoft Excel
Microsoft Excel 4.0 international macro sheet	Compatibility with earlier versions of Microsoft Excel

Grouping Worksheets for Fast Data Entry, Editing, and Formatting

If you select several sheets, you can perform tasks on all of the selected sheets simultaneously. For example, you could delete several sheets in one operation, or enter the same data onto several worksheets at once.

System	To select adjacent sheets	To select nonadjacent sheets
Windows	Click the first sheet tab, hold down SHIFT, and then click the last sheet tab in the group you want to select.	Click the first sheet tab, hold down CTRL, and then click the other sheet tabs.
Macintosh	Click the first sheet tab, hold down SHIFT, and then click the last sheet tab in the group you want to select.	Click the first sheet tab, hold down COMMAND, and then click the other sheet tabs.

For more information about selecting sheets, see "Selecting Sheets in a Workbook" in Chapter 8.

Shortcut Menus

The sheet tab shortcut menu provides fast access to commands useful for working with sheets.

System	To display the sheet tab shortcut menu, point to a tab and
Windows	Click the right mouse button.
Macintosh	Hold down CTRL and click.

In Windows, you can also display a shortcut menu for the title bar, a workbook icon, or the Microsoft Excel workspace.

Moving Around in a Sheet

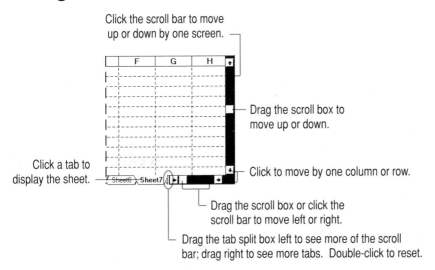

To move with the keyboard	Windows	Macintosh
Up, down, left, right	Arrow keys	Arrow keys
Up or down one window	PAGE UP or PAGE DOWN	PAGE UP or PAGE DOWN
To the beginning of the row	HOME	HOME
To the beginning of the sheet	CTRL+HOME	COMMAND+HOME
To the last cell containing data in the sheet	CTRL+END	COMMAND+END

Going to a Specific Place on a Worksheet

Use the Name box to move to and select a specific location on a worksheet. Type a cell or range address, such as B23 or A20:B25, in the Name box, or click on the arrow and then select a previously defined range name from the list.

Enter a cell or range reference you want to go to and then press ENTER.

```
 =  File  Edit  View  Insert  Format
A10:B15      ±
 Sales        B      C        D
 Totals
 Variables
  10
  11
  12
```

You can also select a previously defined name
to go to that cell or range.

You can also use the Go To command on the Edit menu to move to and select
named ranges, or references that you type.

Tip Use the Name box to quickly define names for selected cells and ranges. For
more information, see "Working with Names" in Chapter 10.

Finding Text and Numbers on a Worksheet

To find specific characters on your worksheet, choose the Find command from the
Edit menu. To find specific types of data, choose the Go To command from the Edit
menu, then choose the Special button. For more information about finding
characters, see "Finding and Replacing Text, Numbers, or Cells" in Chapter 11.
For more information about selecting special types of cell contents, see "Selecting
Cells with Common Types of Contents" in Chapter 38.

Moving Between Split Panes on a Worksheet

To move between split panes on a worksheet, click a cell in the pane you want to
switch to. With the keyboard, press F6 to move between split panes. For more
information about split panes, see "Splitting Worksheets and Freezing Titles" in
Chapter 32.

Tip To get a quick overview of the contents of the entire active sheet, reduce the
magnification of your worksheet view with the Zoom Control box on the toolbar.
Viewing more of your worksheet makes it easier to see the worksheet's overall
structure and to move around quickly. For more information, see "Zooming In or
Out on a Worksheet" in Chapter 32.

Step By Step

For step-by-step instructions and related information, double-click the ⟦▶?⟧ button to
display the Search dialog box in Help, and then:

Type this keyword and choose Show Topics	Select a topic and choose Go To
assigning names	Naming a cell, range, or formula
finding, cells	Going to specific cells or ranges

Type this keyword and choose Show Topics	Select a topic and choose Go To
finding, cells	Selecting cells with common types of contents
finding, text	Finding text or numbers
splitting windows	Splitting a window into panes
zooming	Zooming in or out on a worksheet

Moving Around in a Workbook

You can quickly view and switch between different sheets in a workbook.

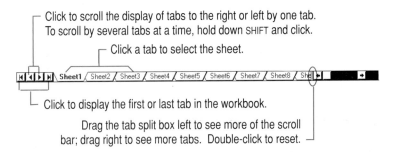

The scrolling buttons only make different tabs visible; you must click on a tab to make a sheet active.

You can also use the keyboard to move from sheet to sheet.

System	To move to the next sheet	To move to the previous sheet
Windows	CTRL+PAGE DOWN	CTRL+PAGE UP
Macintosh	COMMAND+PAGE DOWN	COMMAND+PAGE UP
	–Or–	–Or–
	OPTION+RIGHT ARROW	OPTION+LEFT ARROW

Step By Step

For step-by-step instructions and related information, double-click the ▶? button to display the Search dialog box in Help, and then:

Type this keyword and choose Show Topics	Select a topic and choose Go To
moving, between sheets	Moving between sheets
scrolling	Keys for Scrolling in a Workbook Window
selecting worksheets	Selecting a sheet or sheets

Inserting and Deleting Sheets

A new workbook opens with 16 sheets named Sheet1 through Sheet16. You can easily insert or delete sheets. The maximum number of sheets is limited only by available memory.

Tip You can change the number of sheets in a new workbook by choosing the Options command from the Tools menu. Select the General tab and then change the setting in the Sheets In New Workbook box. The maximum number of sheets in a new workbook is 255.

Inserting Sheets

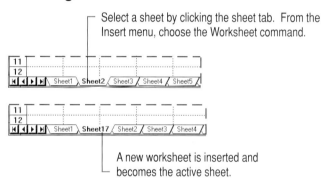

Select a sheet by clicking the sheet tab. From the Insert menu, choose the Worksheet command.

A new worksheet is inserted and becomes the active sheet.

You can insert several worksheets at once by selecting the number of sheets you want to insert, and then choosing Worksheet from the Insert menu.

To insert	From the Insert menu, choose
Worksheet or worksheets	Worksheet. You can also press SHIFT+F11.
Chart sheet	Chart, and then choose As New Sheet. You can also press F11.
Visual Basic module	Macro, and then choose Module.
Dialog	Macro, and then choose Dialog.
Microsoft Excel 4.0 macro sheet	Macro, and then choose MS Excel 4.0 Macro. You can also press CTRL+F11 (Windows) or COMMAND+F11 (Macintosh).

You can also use the Insert command on the sheet tab shortcut menu to insert new sheets.

Deleting Sheets

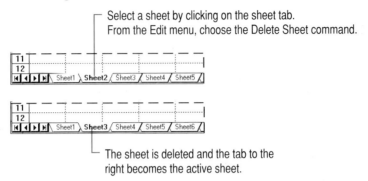

Select a sheet by clicking on the sheet tab.
From the Edit menu, choose the Delete Sheet command.

The sheet is deleted and the tab to the
right becomes the active sheet.

You can delete several sheets at once by selecting the sheets you want to delete, and
then choosing the Delete Sheet command from the Edit menu.

You can also use the Delete command on the sheet tab shortcut menu to delete
sheets.

Step By Step

For step-by-step instructions and related information, double-click the 🔍❓ button to
display the Search dialog box in Help, and then:

Type this keyword and choose Show Topics	Select a topic and choose Go To
deleting, sheets	Deleting sheets
inserting sheets	Inserting sheets

Renaming Sheets

You can change the name of any sheet to a name of up to 31 characters, including
spaces. Once you rename a sheet, the tab for that sheet contains the new name.

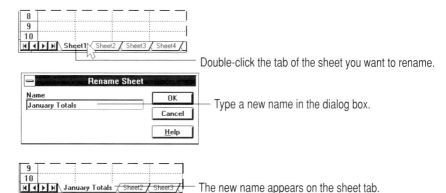

Double-click the tab of the sheet you want to rename.

Type a new name in the dialog box.

The new name appears on the sheet tab.

You can also choose the Sheet command from the Format menu and then choose the Rename command, or choose Rename from the shortcut menu.

Step By Step

For step-by-step instructions and related information, double-click the [?] button to display the Search dialog box in Help, and then:

Type this keyword and choose Show Topics	Select a topic and choose Go To
renaming sheets	Renaming a sheet

Moving and Copying Sheets

You can rearrange sheets in a workbook by moving them. You can also move sheets into another workbook or put them into a new workbook of their own.

You can also easily copy sheets within a workbook, or copy them into another workbook, or a new workbook.

Note   You cannot use the Cut, Copy, and Paste commands to move or copy sheets.

Moving a Sheet Within a Workbook

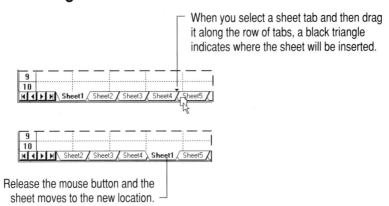

When you select a sheet tab and then drag it along the row of tabs, a black triangle indicates where the sheet will be inserted.

Release the mouse button and the sheet moves to the new location.

You can move more than one sheet by selecting several sheets and then dragging. If the selected sheets are nonadjacent, the moved sheets are inserted together.

Moving a Sheet into Another Workbook

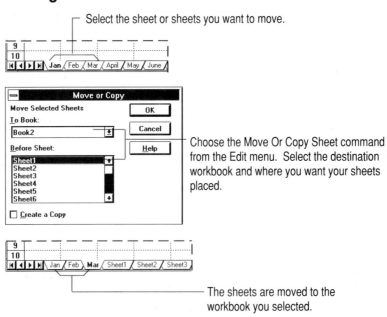

Select the sheet or sheets you want to move.

Choose the Move Or Copy Sheet command from the Edit menu. Select the destination workbook and where you want your sheets placed.

The sheets are moved to the workbook you selected.

Note If a sheet with the same name exists in the destination workbook, the moved sheet will be renamed.

You can also move sheets between workbooks by dragging the sheet tabs across workbook windows. Arrange the workbook windows so that the sheet tabs for both workbooks are visible before dragging.

Moving a Sheet into a New Workbook

You can move sheets into a new workbook by choosing the Move Or Copy Sheet command from the Edit menu, and then selecting New Book as the destination workbook in the To Book box. A new workbook is created; it contains only the sheets you selected. You can also do this by dragging sheets outside a workbook window and releasing the mouse button.

Tip   When dragging sheets to a new workbook, size your workbook window so that there is a place on the Microsoft Excel desktop to drop the selected sheet or sheets.

Copying a Sheet Within a Workbook

You can copy sheets within a workbook. Microsoft Excel renames the copy of your sheet. For example, a copy of Sheet1 becomes Sheet1 (2).

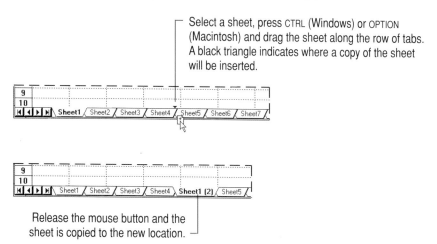

Select a sheet, press CTRL (Windows) or OPTION (Macintosh) and drag the sheet along the row of tabs. A black triangle indicates where a copy of the sheet will be inserted.

Release the mouse button and the sheet is copied to the new location.

You can copy more than one sheet by selecting several sheets at once. If the selected sheets are nonadjacent, the copied sheets are inserted together.

Copying a Sheet to Another Workbook

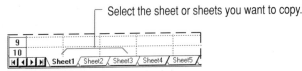

Select the sheet or sheets you want to copy.

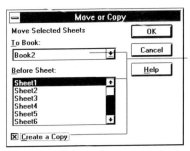

Choose the Move Or Copy Sheet command from the Edit menu. Select the destination workbook and where you want your sheets placed, and then select the Create A Copy check box.

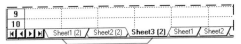

The sheets are copied to the workbook you selected.

If the selected sheets are nonadjacent, the copied sheets are inserted together.

Note If a sheet with the same name exists in the destination workbook, Microsoft Excel renames the copy of the sheet, as shown in the preceding illustration.

You can also copy sheets between workbooks by dragging the sheet tabs across workbook windows. Arrange the workbook windows so that the sheet tabs for both workbooks are visible before dragging.

System	To copy sheets to another workbook, select the sheets and then
Windows	Press CTRL and drag to the other workbook.
Macintosh	Press OPTION and drag to the other workbook.

Copying a Sheet into a New Workbook

You can copy sheets into a new workbook by choosing the Move Or Copy Sheet command from the Edit menu, selecting New Book as the destination workbook in the To Book box, and then selecting the Create A Copy check box. A new workbook is created; it contains only the sheets you selected. You can also do this by holding down CTRL (Windows) or OPTION (Macintosh), dragging the sheets outside the workbook window, and releasing the mouse button.

Tip   When dragging sheets to a new workbook, size your workbook window so that there is a place on the Microsoft Excel desktop to drop copies of the selected sheet or sheets.

Step By Step

For step-by-step instructions and related information, double-click the [?] button to display the Search dialog box in Help, and then:

Type this keyword and choose Show Topics	Select a topic and choose Go To
copying, worksheets	Copying sheets to other workbooks
	Copying sheets within a workbook
sheets, moving	Moving sheets to other workbooks
	Moving sheets within a workbook

Opening, Arranging, and Closing Workbook Windows

Multiple windows make it easy to enter, compare, format, and edit data in:

- Different parts of a sheet
- Different sheets in the same workbook
- Two or more workbooks

Create a new window on a workbook by choosing the New Window command from the Window menu. You can then arrange the windows to see them all at the same time.

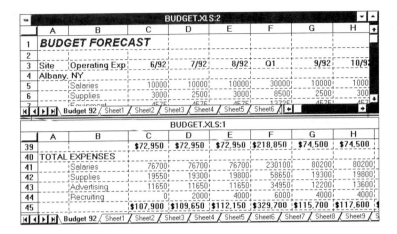

Windows showing different parts of one sheet

Each window on this workbook displays a different sheet.

Windows showing different sheets in the same workbook

These two windows display two
sheets of the same workbook.

This window displays a
sheet in another workbook.

		BUDGET.XLS:2		
	A	B	C	D
1	*BUDGET FORECAST*			
2				
3	Site	Operating Exp	6/93	7/
4	Albany, NY			
5		Salaries	10234	10
6		Supplies	3070	2
7		Equipment	4582	4

Budget 92 \ **Budget 93** / Sheet2 / Sheet3

		SUMMARY.XLS		
	A	B	C	
1	*BUDGET FORECAST*			
2				
3	Site	Operating Exp	6/92-3	
4	Albany, NY			
5		Salaries	20234	
6		Supplies	6070	
7		Equipment	9257	
8		Lease Pmts	19425	
9		Advertising	3035	
10			$58,021	$57
11	Memphis, TN			
12		Salaries	15000	
13		Supplies	4000	
14		Equipment	16000	
15		Lease Pmts	16400	
16		Advertising	5000	
17			$56,400	$56

		BUDGET.XLS:1		
	A	B	C	D
1	*BUDGET FORECAST*			
2				
3	Site	Operating Exp	6/92	7/
4	Albany, NY			
5		Salaries	10000	10
6		Supplies	3000	2
7		Equipment	4575	4

Budget 92 \ Budget 93 / Sheet2 / Sheet3

92-93 Summary / Sheet2

Windows showing different workbooks

To move among the different windows, click a window or choose its name from the
Window menu.

A window can be closed or hidden when you no longer need to see it. In Microsoft
Excel for Windows, you can also minimize a window.

Arranging, Minimizing, and Hiding Windows

Arrange multiple windows so that you can see them all by choosing the Arrange
command from the Window menu. To arrange only the windows of the active
workbook, select the Windows Of Active Workbook check box in the Arrange
dialog box.

You can also hide windows by switching to the window you want to hide and
choosing the Hide command from the Window menu. Hidden windows remain
open. Unhide windows by choosing the Unhide command from the Window menu
and selecting the windows you want to unhide in the dialog box.

In Microsoft Excel for Windows, you can minimize windows so that they appear as
a workbook icon in the Microsoft Excel workspace. These icons can be arranged on
the screen, or restored by double-clicking.

Closing Windows

When you no longer need a window you have created, you can close it without
closing the workbook file.

System	To close a window
Windows	Double-click the workbook Control-menu box, or choose the Close command from the workbook Control menu.
Macintosh	Click the close box in the title bar.

If the window is the only window of the workbook, the workbook will be closed when you close the window. If changes have been made since the workbook was last saved, a message asks if you want to save changes.

Step By Step

For step-by-step instructions and related information, double-click the [?] button to display the Search dialog box in Help, and then:

Type this keyword and choose Show Topics	Select a topic and choose Go To
arranging icons	Arranging icons (Windows only)
hiding sheets	Hiding and unhiding a sheet
minimizing windows	Minimizing and restoring windows (Windows only)
workbook windows	Arranging workbook windows
	Displaying and closing new windows of a workbook

CHAPTER 8

Selecting Cells and Choosing Commands

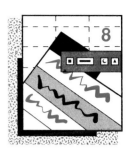

For command, keyboard, and toolbar button information, see online Help.

In This Chapter

Selecting Cells and Moving Within a Selection

Before you can enter data or use most commands in Microsoft Excel, you must select the cells or objects you want to work with.

Selecting Cells

Selections are always rectangular blocks of cells.

	A	B	C	D	E
1	*NORTHWIND TRADERS SALES*				
2		Jan	Feb	Mar	
3	Mike Jones				
4	Greenville	$7,128	$8,135	$12,200	
5	Hempton	$5,675	$5,919	$6,295	
6	S. Minton	$7,750	$13,982	$17,055	
7	Mike's Totals	$20,553	$28,036	$35,550	
8	Pam Coburn				
9	Metro Area	$7,005	$8,106	$7,877	
10	East End	$2,172	$2,124	$2,103	
11	Pam's Totals	$9,177	$10,230	$9,980	
12					
13	TOTALS	$29,730	$38,266	$45,530	
14					
15					

To select a single cell, click it.

To select a range of cells, drag diagonally from the first cell to the last cell.

	A	B	C	D	E
1	*NORTHWIND TRADERS SALES*				
2		Jan	Feb	Mar	
3	Mike Jones				
4	Greenville	$7,128	$8,135	$12,200	
5	Hempton	$5,675	$5,919	$6,295	
6	S. Minton	$7,750	$13,982	$17,055	
7	Mike's Totals	$20,553	$28,036	$35,550	
8	Pam Coburn				
9	Metro Area	$7,005	$8,106	$7,877	
10	East End	$2,172	$2,124	$2,103	
11	Pam's Totals	$9,177	$10,230	$9,980	
12					
13	TOTALS	$29,730	$38,266	$45,530	
14					
15					

	A	B	C	D	E
1	*NORTHWIND TRADERS SALES*				
2		Jan	Feb	Mar	
3	Mike Jones				
4	Greenville	$7,128	$8,135	$12,200	
5	Hempton	$5,675	$5,919	$6,295	
6	S. Minton	$7,750	$13,982	$17,055	
7	Mike's Totals	$20,553	$28,036	$35,550	
8	Pam Coburn				
9	Metro Area	$7,005	$8,106	$7,877	
10	East End	$2,172	$2,124	$2,103	
11	Pam's Totals	$9,177	$10,230	$9,980	
12					
13	TOTALS	$29,730	$38,266	$45,530	
14					
15					

To select nonadjacent cells or ranges, hold down CTRL (Windows) or COMMAND (Macintosh) as you click or drag through additional cells.

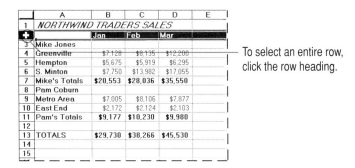

To select an entire row, click the row heading.

To select an entire column, click the column heading.

To select all cells on the sheet, click the Select All button.

Selecting all cells on the worksheet is most useful for global formatting—for example, changing the font of all text on the worksheet.

Moving Within a Selection

Press ENTER or TAB to move down or right within a selection, and SHIFT+ENTER or SHIFT+TAB to reverse direction.

Step By Step

For step-by-step instructions and related information, double-click the 📖 button to display the Search dialog box in Help, and then:

Type this keyword and choose Show Topics	Select a topic and choose Go To
selecting cells	Changing the size of a selection
	Extending the selection through the current data region
	Moving a selection on the sheet (Macintosh only)
	Selecting a cell or range of cells
	Selecting an entire row or column or all cells on a sheet
	Selecting named ranges or specified cells
	Selecting nonadjacent cells or ranges
	Selecting visible cells only

Selecting Sheets in a Workbook

You can enter data on, edit, and format a single worksheet or multiple worksheets in a workbook. Normally you work with one *active sheet* at a time. The active sheet is the sheet currently displayed in the workbook. The tab of the active sheet is white with bold type.

You can also work with multiple worksheets in a workbook simultaneously by making them part of a *group selection.* Some of the things you can do with a group selection include:

- Entering common column titles and formulas in several sheets.
- Formatting cells and ranges on several sheets.
- Hiding or deleting several sheets at once.

Note   You must have a mouse to select a group of sheets.

Selecting a Single Sheet

You can make any sheet in a workbook the active sheet by clicking its tab. You can also use the keyboard to make the next or previous sheet the active sheet.

System	To make the next or previous sheet the active sheet
Windows	Hold down CTRL and press PAGE DOWN or PAGE UP.
Macintosh	Hold down COMMAND and press PAGE DOWN or PAGE UP, or hold down OPTION and press RIGHT ARROW or LEFT ARROW.

Selecting Two or More Sheets

You can select a group of sheets that are next to one another by clicking the tab for the first sheet you want to select, holding down the SHIFT key, and then clicking the tab for the last sheet you want to select.

You can also select nonadjacent sheets.

System	To select nonadjacent sheets, click the tab for the first sheet you want to select, and then
Windows	Hold down CTRL and click the other tabs.
Macintosh	Hold down COMMAND and click the other tabs.

After you have selected a group, the word "[Group]" appears in the title bar of the active window and selected tabs are shown in white.

To cancel the selection, choose the Ungroup Sheets command from the sheet tab shortcut menu.

Selecting All Sheets

Selecting all sheets is useful for operations like spell checking, and finding and replacing data that occurs throughout a workbook.

To select all of the sheets in the workbook, choose the Select All Sheets command from the sheet tab shortcut menu.

To cancel the selection, click the tab of any sheet.

Step By Step

For step-by-step instructions and related information, double-click the ⌨️? button to display the Search dialog box in Help, and then:

Type this keyword and choose Show Topics	Select a topic and choose Go To
selecting worksheets	Cancelling a group selection
	Selecting a sheet or sheets
	Selecting all sheets

Choosing Commands

Choose commands to tell Microsoft Excel what to do next. There are usually
several methods to achieve the same result in Microsoft Excel. For example, there
are several equivalent ways to copy data. Choose the method that suits you best.

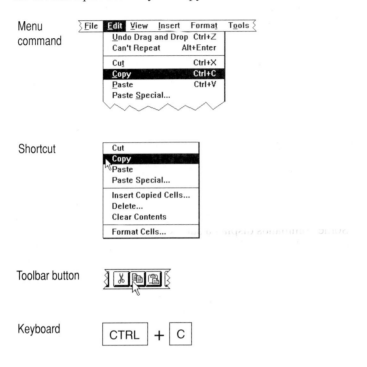

Menu command

Shortcut

Toolbar button

Keyboard

Important   Remember, you must select the cells or objects you want to work with
before choosing most commands.

Menu Commands

Menu commands are grouped into menus across the menu bar. Equivalent
commands are also available in shortcut menus and as toolbar buttons. Many
commands also have keyboard equivalents.

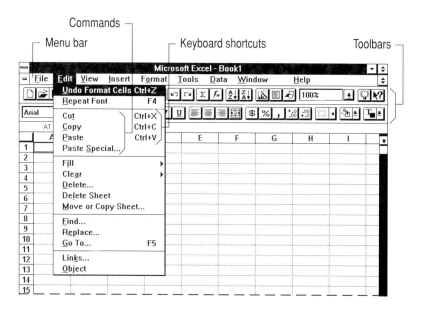

Some commands display a submenu. Submenus are indicated by a ▶ following the command name. Submenus contain additional, related commands.

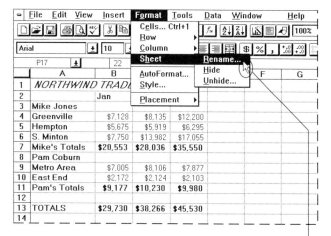

To display a submenu, choose a command that is followed by a ▶. The submenu appears to the side of the command name.

Shortcut Menus

Shortcut menus contain the most useful commands for the cell or object you have selected.

System	To display a shortcut menu
Windows	Click the right mouse button.
Macintosh	Hold down CTRL and click the mouse button.

For example, you can select a range of data, display the shortcut menu for the selected range, and then choose the command you want from the menu.

Shortcut menus appear
at the mouse pointer.

	A	B	C	D	E	F
1	*NORTHWIND TRADERS SALES*					
2		Jan	Feb	Mar		
3	Mike Jones				Cut	
4	Greenville	$7,128	$8,135	$12,2	Copy	
5	Hempton	$5,675	$5,919	$6,2	Paste	
6	S. Minton	$7,750	$13,982	$17,0	Paste Special...	
7	Mike's Totals	$20,553	$28,036	$35,5!		
8	Pam Coburn				Insert...	
9	Metro Area	$7,005	$8,106	$7,8	Delete...	
10	East End	$2,172	$2,124	$2,1	Clear Contents	
11	Pam's Totals	$9,177	$10,230	$9,9!	Format Cells...	
12						
13	TOTALS	$29,730	$38,266	$45,530		
14						

Toolbar Buttons

To choose a toolbar button, click it. Using buttons requires a mouse. For information about displaying and customizing toolbars, see "Customizing Toolbars" in Chapter 34.

Keyboard Shortcuts

You can complete nearly all tasks in Microsoft Excel with the keyboard. For information about using the keyboard, see "Using the Keyboard with Microsoft Excel" later in this chapter. You'll also find keyboard shortcuts throughout online Help.

Step By Step

For step-by-step instructions and related information, double-click the [**k?**] button to display the Search dialog box in Help, and then:

Type this keyword and choose Show Topics	Select a topic and choose Go To
choosing buttons	Choosing a toolbar button
choosing commands	Choosing a menu bar command
	Choosing a shortcut menu command
showing toolbars	Displaying or hiding toolbars

Undoing and Repeating Commands

Undo

When you change your mind or make a mistake, you can reverse your last command or other action by choosing the Undo command from the Edit menu, or clicking the Undo button. The Undo command changes to show the most recent command or action. If Undo doesn't apply, the words "Can't Undo" appear dimmed on the menu. Remember, you can undo only the last command you chose or the last cell entry you typed.

Caution   You cannot undo the results of all commands in Microsoft Excel. For example, you cannot undo the Delete command on the sheet tab shortcut menu. When you choose a command that cannot be undone and will change your data, Microsoft Excel will warn you before it carries out the command.

Repeat

To repeat the last command you chose, including any options you changed in a dialog box, choose the Repeat command on the Edit menu, or click the Repeat button. When a command cannot be repeated, the words "Can't Repeat" appear dimmed on the menu.

Step By Step

For step-by-step instructions and related information, double-click the button to display the Search dialog box in Help, and then:

Type this keyword and choose Show Topics	Select a topic and choose Go To
undoing, commands	Undoing or repeating a command

Working in Dialog Boxes

Some commands display a dialog box. You select options in the dialog box to control how Microsoft Excel carries out the command.

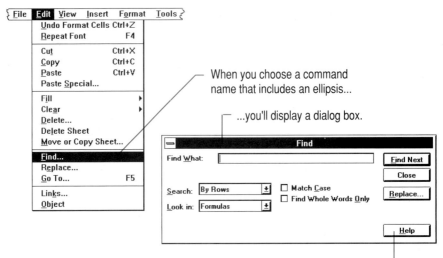

When you choose a command name that includes an ellipsis...

...you'll display a dialog box.

Need help with dialog box options? Choose the Help button.

Some dialog boxes are made up of tabs, each with its own name. To see the options on each tab, select the tab name.

To display another tab in the dialog box, click the tab.

Step By Step

For step-by-step instructions and related information, double-click the 〔?〕 button to display the Search dialog box in Help, and then:

Type this keyword and choose Show Topics	Select a topic and choose Go To
dialog boxes	Choosing dialog box options

Using the Keyboard with Microsoft Excel

You can use the keyboard for nearly all functionality in Microsoft Excel.

Keyboard Conventions

- In documentation, key names match the names shown on most keyboards and appear in small capital letters. For example, the Shift key appears as SHIFT.

- The RETURN key and the ENTER key usually perform the same action in Microsoft Excel for the Macintosh. "Press ENTER" means that you can press either ENTER or RETURN on the Macintosh, unless specifically stated otherwise.

- The following conventions apply in all keyboard instructions in the Microsoft Excel documentation set.

Convention	Example	How to do it
Plus sign (+) between key names means to press the keys at the same time	Select current row: SHIFT+SPACEBAR	Press SHIFT and hold it down while you press SPACEBAR
Comma (,) between key names means to press the keys sequentially	(Windows) Open command on the File menu: ALT, F, O	Press ALT and release it, press F and release it, and then press O and release it.
	(Macintosh) Open command on the File menu: SLASH(/), F, O	Press SLASH (/) and release it, press F and release it, and then press O and release it.

Using Keyboard Shortcuts

The following table summarizes the general patterns in keyboard shortcuts. The complete list of keyboard shortcuts is available in online Help.

Windows key	Macintosh key	Action
ENTER	ENTER or RETURN	Confirms or carries out an action
ESC	COMMAND+PERIOD or ESC	Cancels an action
Function keys (F1, F2, and so on)	Function keys (F1, F2, and so on)	Used as shortcuts for common commands and actions
INSERT, DELETE, and BACKSPACE	INSERT, DEL, and DELETE	Used for editing
TAB, the arrow keys, HOME, END, PAGE UP, and PAGE DOWN	TAB, the arrow keys, HOME, END, PAGE UP, and PAGE DOWN	Move, select, or scroll

Windows key	Macintosh key	Action
ALT	COMMAND or ALT	Generally used for actions related to application windows, such as choosing commands and dialog box options
SHIFT	SHIFT	Usually used to extend the selection, perform the opposite action, or go in the opposite direction
CTRL	COMMAND or CTRL	Used with several keyboard shortcuts to apply options in dialog boxes

Step By Step

For step-by-step instructions and related information, double-click the k? button to display the Search dialog box in Help, and then:

Type this keyword and choose Show Topics	Select a topic and choose Go To
Keyboard Guide	Keyboard Guide

C H A P T E R   9

Entering Data

For command, keyboard, and toolbar button information, see online Help.

In This Chapter

Note You can enter data on multiple worksheets in a workbook simultaneously by making them part of a group selection. For more information, see "Selecting Sheets in a Workbook" in Chapter 8.

Data Entry Techniques

With Microsoft Excel, you can enter worksheet data quickly and efficiently.

Entering Data into a Cell

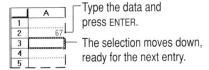

Type the data and press ENTER.

The selection moves down, ready for the next entry.

Note If the selection does not move down when you press ENTER, choose the Options command from the Tools menu, select the Edit tab, and then select the Move Selection After Enter check box.

Entering Data into a Range of Cells

Select a range of cells. You can then enter data into successive cells in the range.

To enter data within a selection	Press
Top to bottom	ENTER
Bottom to top	SHIFT+ENTER
Left to right	TAB
Right to left	SHIFT+TAB

You can also make nonadjacent selections and then enter data successively into the selected cells.

Tip You can type the same entry into several cells at once. Select the cells you want to enter the data into, type the entry into one cell, and then press CTRL+ENTER.

Canceling an Entry

To cancel an entry before you have pressed ENTER, press the ESC key. On the Macintosh you can also press COMMAND+PERIOD.

If you have already pressed ENTER, choose the Undo Entry command on the Edit menu.

Step By Step

For step-by-step instructions and related information, double-click the ⟨▶?⟩ button to display the Search dialog box in Help, and then:

Type this keyword and choose Show Topics	Select a topic and choose Go To
entries, cancelling	Canceling or undoing an entry
cells, entering data in	Data entry techniques
	Entering numbers in cells
	Entering text in cells

How Microsoft Excel Interprets What You Enter

You can enter two types of data in a worksheet:

- **A constant value** is data that you type directly into a cell; it can be a numeric value, including a date, time, currency, percentage, fraction, or scientific notation, or it can be text. Constant values do not change unless you select the cell and edit the value yourself.

- **A formula** is a sequence of values, cell references, names, functions, or operators that produces a new value from existing values. Formulas always begin with an equal sign (=). A value that is produced as the result of a formula can change when other values in the worksheet change. For more information about creating formulas, see "Use Formulas to Analyze Your Data" in Chapter 10.

International Note

Microsoft Excel uses the country settings defined in your operating system to determine default settings such as currency sign, date format, and decimal separators. For example, if your operating system is configured for Sweden, Microsoft Excel uses "kr" as the currency sign, year-month-day as the date format, and comma (,) as the decimal separator.

For information about country settings, see your operating system documentation.

Numbers

When you create a new worksheet, all cells are formatted with the General number format. The General format displays numbers as precisely as possible, using integer format (789), decimal fraction format (7.89), or, if the number is longer than the width of the cell, scientific notation (7.89E+08).

When it can, Microsoft Excel automatically assigns the correct number format to your entry. For example, when you enter a number that contains a dollar sign before the number or a percent sign after the number, Microsoft Excel automatically changes the cell's format to a currency format or a percentage format, respectively. When you enter numbers, they align to the right of the cell.

When You See ####   If a number is too long to be displayed in a cell, Microsoft Excel displays a series of number signs (####) in the cell. If you widen the column enough to accommodate the width of the number, the number is displayed in the cell.

Tip   An easy way to widen a column to fit the selection is to double-click the right border of the column heading.

Changing the Way a Number Is Displayed   You can change the number format Microsoft Excel assigns and you can create and assign custom number formats of your own. For more information see "Applying Number Formats" and "Creating Custom Number Formats" in Chapter 12.

You may also want to enter a number as text by applying the Text format to the cells before entering your data. For example, you might want to enter a list of part numbers. To do this, select the cells, choose the Cells command from the Format menu, select the Number tab, and then select the Text category and the @ format code. You can also enter a number as text by preceding it with an apostrophe.

Displayed Value vs. Stored Value

The number you see in a cell is based on the cell number format and may differ from the number Microsoft Excel stores. For example, if a cell is formatted to display only two decimal places and you type 26.006 in that cell, Microsoft Excel displays 26.01. Microsoft Excel stores numbers with 15 digits of accuracy. In calculations, Microsoft Excel uses the stored number, no matter how it is displayed on the screen.

If you want Microsoft Excel to calculate on the basis of displayed values only, choose the Options command from the Tools menu, select the Calculation tab, and then select the Precision As Displayed check box. Selecting this check box permanently changes constant values to their displayed values. Clearing this check box does not restore the original values.

Dates and Times

Although you can display dates and times in several standard formats, Microsoft Excel stores all dates as serial numbers and all times as decimal fractions. Because dates and times are seen as numbers, they can be added, subtracted, and included in other calculations. You can view a formatted date or time as a serial number or decimal fraction by changing the cell's format to General.

Microsoft Excel supports two date systems: the 1900 and 1904 date systems. The default date system for Microsoft Excel for Windows is 1900. Microsoft Excel for the Macintosh uses the 1904 date system. To change the date system, choose the Options command from the Tools menu, select the Calculation tab, and select the Date System check box.

Text

Text can be characters or any combination of numbers and characters. Any set of characters entered into a cell that Microsoft Excel does not interpret as a number, formula, date, time, logical value, or error value is interpreted as text. When you enter text, the characters align to the left of the cell.

Logical and Error Values

Usually, logical values result from formulas that contain a logical function or an equation. The valid logical values are TRUE and FALSE. Error values are displayed when a formula cannot be properly calculated for a cell. Error values always begin with the number sign (#). The error values are: #N/A, #VALUE!, #REF!, #NULL!, #DIV/0!, #NUM!, and #NAME?. Generally, you do not enter logical or error values as data in your worksheet. For more information about logical and error values, see "Use Formulas to Analyze Your Data" in Chapter 10.

Entering Numbers

To enter a number as a constant value, select a cell and type the number. Numbers can include numeric characters (0 through 9) and any of the following special characters:

+ − ( ) , / $ % . E e

Use the following guidelines when entering numbers:

- You can include commas in numbers, such as 1,000,000.
- A single period in a numeric entry is treated as a decimal point.
- Plus signs entered before numbers are ignored.
- Precede negative numbers with a minus sign or enclose them within parentheses.

If you type	Microsoft Excel displays	Using the
1.0	1	General format
−1.1230	−1.123	
1,581	1,581	Number format #,##0
1.1%	1.10%	Percentage format 0.00%
1.112%	1.11%	
10e2	1.00E+03	Scientific format 0.00E+00
0 1/2	1/2	Fraction format # ?/?
3 3/5	3 3/5	
3/4	4-Mar	Date format d-mmm
$4.50	$4.50	Currency format
−$78.91	($78.91)	$#,##0.00_; [Red]($#,##0.00)

You can change the assigned number format or create a custom number format of your own. For more information, see "Applying Number Formats" and "Creating Custom Number Formats" in Chapter 12.

Tips Enter all fractions as mixed (0 1/2) to avoid entering a date format.

You can quickly format a number as text by preceding it with an apostrophe. Text aligns to the left in a cell and numbers align to the right.

Fixed Decimal Places

You can enter decimal points automatically. To do this, choose Options from the Tools menu, select the Edit tab, and then select the Fixed Decimal check box and specify the number of decimal places you want. Then you can quickly enter numbers using the numeric keypad. Press NUM LOCK to use the keypad.

If you are entering currencies, you can format the cells by clicking the Currency Style toolbar button before or after entering your data.

Entering Numbers in Formulas

To include a number in a formula, just type the number. In a formula, you cannot use parentheses to indicate a negative number, a comma to separate thousands, or a dollar sign ($) before the number. If you type a percent sign (%) after a number, Microsoft Excel interprets it as the percentage operator and stores it as part of the formula. The percentage operator acts on the preceding number when the formula is calculated. For information about creating formulas, see "Use Formulas to Analyze Your Data" in Chapter 10.

Step By Step

For step-by-step instructions and related information, double-click the 🅺? button to display the Search dialog box in Help, and then:

Type this keyword and choose Show Topics	Select a topic and choose Go To
assigning formats	Assigning a number, date, or time format
cells, entering data in	Data entry techniques
	Entering numbers in cells
custom number formats	Creating and deleting custom number formats
fixed decimal places	Entering numbers with fixed decimal places

Entering Dates or Times

When you enter a date or time that Microsoft Excel recognizes, the cell's format automatically changes from General to the appropriate date or time format.

Use the following guidelines when entering dates or times:

- Microsoft Excel ignores capitalization.

- If you want to display time using the 12-hour clock, type **am** or **pm;** for example, 3:00 PM. You can also type **a** or **p** instead of **am** or **pm;** you must include a space between the time and the letter. Unless you type **am** or **pm,** Microsoft Excel automatically displays time using the 24-hour clock; for example, 15:00.

- You can type a date and time in the same cell. Just separate the date and time by a space.

- To enter dates, use either a slash (/) or a hyphen (-).

If you type	Microsoft Excel uses this format
3/4/94	m/d/yy
4-Mar-94	d-mmm-yy
3/4 or Mar-4	d-mmm
Mar-94	mmm-yy
8:50 PM	h:mm AM/PM
8:50:35 PM	h:mm:ss AM/PM
20:50	h:mm
20:50:35	h:mm:ss
3/4/94 20:50	m/d/yy h:mm

System	To enter today's date, press
Windows	CTRL+;
Macintosh	COMMAND+HYPHEN

System	To enter the current time, press
Windows	CTRL+SHIFT+:
Macintosh	COMMAND+;

You can also create your own date or time formats. Microsoft Excel allows you to enter hours greater than 24 and minutes or seconds greater than 60 by using custom number formats. For more information, see "Creating Custom Number Formats" in Chapter 12.

Entering Dates and Times in Formulas

You cannot enter numbers in date or time formats directly in a formula; you must enter the date or time as text enclosed in double quotation marks (" "). Microsoft Excel converts it to the corresponding number when calculating the formula. For example, the formula ="5/12/94"–"3/5/94" would display a difference of 68.

If Microsoft Excel does not recognize a date or time format you type, it stores the date or time as text instead of as a serial number. If you try to use the date or time in calculations that expect a number, Microsoft Excel returns the #VALUE! error value. For this reason, you should either use a built-in format or create a custom format when using dates or times in calculations.

Step By Step

For step-by-step instructions and related information, double-click the [?] button to display the Search dialog box in Help, and then:

Type this keyword and choose Show Topics	Select a topic and choose Go To
assigning formats	Assigning a number, date, or time format
custom number formats	Creating and deleting custom number formats
entering, data	Data entry techniques
entering, dates	Entering a date or a time

Entering Text

To enter text, select a cell and type the text. A cell can hold up to 255 characters. You can format the characters within a cell individually.

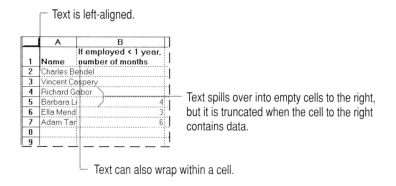

Text is left-aligned.

Text spills over into empty cells to the right, but it is truncated when the cell to the right contains data.

Text can also wrap within a cell.

You can create text entries that include numbers and text or just numbers.

You might want to enter a number as text; for example, you might want to enter a list of postal codes. You can do this by first applying the text format to the blank cells. Choose the Cells command from the Format menu, select the Number tab, and then select the Text category and the @ format code. Another way to enter a number as text is to precede the entry with an apostrophe.

If you want to enter an airline flight number such as TWA395, you need only type the entry. If an entry contains characters that are not numerical, Microsoft Excel interprets it as text.

Text Wrapping

Instead of letting long strings of text overflow into adjacent cells, you can display the text on multiple lines within a cell. This is called text wrapping. Before wrapping text, adjust your column to the desired width. Choose the Cells command from the Format menu, select the Alignment tab, and then select the Wrap Text check box.

Entering Text in Formulas, Charts, and Text Boxes

To enter text in formulas, enclose the characters in double quotation marks. For example, the formula ="Totals for "&1994 would display the text "Totals for 1994."

The labels displayed on charts are treated as text. For information about entering text in charts, see "Changing Chart Text" in Chapter 17.

Text boxes are graphic objects that contain text. For information about creating text boxes, see "Text Boxes" in Chapter 13.

Step By Step

For step-by-step instructions and related information, double-click the [?] button to display the Search dialog box in Help, and then:

Type this keyword and choose Show Topics	Select a topic and choose Go To
cell contents, editing	Editing cell contents
characters, formatting	Overview of Formatting Characters in Cells
entering, data	Data entry techniques
entering, text	Entering text in cells
text boxes	Creating and deleting text boxes

Filling Adjacent Cells and Creating Series

You can copy the contents of cells into other cells by dragging the fill handle or by using the Fill command on the Edit menu.

You can also create a series by incrementing the value in the active cell into a range you drag through using the fill handle. For example, you can extend a series such as 1,2,3 to include 4,5,6... or create series such as Period 1, Profit, Loss, Period 2, Profit, Loss,... and so on.

The fill handle copies and fills data, and creates series using the AutoFill feature. You drag the fill handle to the left, right, up, or down to fill data.

Dragging to Fill a Range

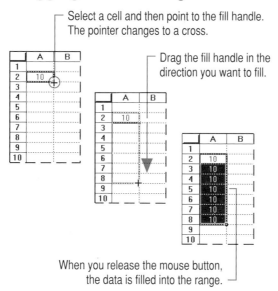

Select a cell and then point to the fill handle. The pointer changes to a cross.

Drag the fill handle in the direction you want to fill.

When you release the mouse button, the data is filled into the range.

Tip You can quickly enter data in a range by selecting the range, typing data into a cell and pressing CTRL+ENTER.

Caution If you drag the fill handle up or to the left of a selection and stop in the selected cells without going past the first column or the top row, you will erase the data within the selection.

Double-Clicking to Fill a Range

You can fill a range adjacent to a range of data by double-clicking the fill handle.

	A	B	C	D	E
1	Northwind Traders				
2	Employee Sales, 1st Quarter 1993			Sale Amount	@ $1.56 per £
3	Country	Salesperson	Order ID	in US Dollars	in Br. Pounds
4	UK	Buchanan, B. L.	10869	$1,630	£1,045
5	UK	Buchanan, B. L.	10872	$2,058	
204	UK	Dodsworth, Annabella	10953	$4,441	
205	USA	Peacock, Phyllis	11026	$1,030	
206	USA	Peacock, Phyllis	11044	$592	
207					
208					

	A	B	C	D	E
1	Northwind Traders				
2	Employee Sales, 1st Quarter 1993			Sale Amount	@ $1.56 per £
3	Country	Salesperson	Order ID	in US Dollars	in Br. Pounds
4	UK	Buchanan, B. L.	10869	$1,630	£1,045
5	UK	Buchanan, B. L.	10872	$2,058	£1,320
204	UK	Dodsworth, Annabella	10953	$4,441	£2,847
205	USA	Peacock, Phyllis	11026	$1,030	£660
206	USA	Peacock, Phyllis	11044	$592	£379
207					
208					

Double-clicking the fill handle extends the selection from the current cell to the row at the end of the adjacent range and fills data into the selection.

Incrementing a Series of Numbers or Dates

When you drag the fill handle in a cell or range of cells that contain values that Microsoft Excel recognizes as a series of sequential numbers, the series is incremented in the range you drag through. Some examples of data types and their sequences are listed in the following table.

Data type	Initial selection	Extended series
Numbers	10, 15	20,25,30,35,...
Months and dates	Jan	Feb, Mar, Apr, May,...
	1/12/94	1/13/94, 1/14/94, 1/15/94,...
Ordinals	1st Period	2nd Period, 3rd Period, 4th Period,...

You can also choose the Fill command from the Edit menu, and then choose the Series command to increment series.

For more information about the types of series that Microsoft Excel increments, see the Step By Step table at the end of this section.

Creating a Series Based on a Single Value

Select the cell or range you want to
increment, and then point to the fill
handle. The pointer changes to a cross.

When you drag the fill handle, the months, days,
and numerals in text strings are incremented.

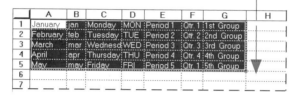

Creating a Series Based on Multiple Values

Select the range you want to increment, and then point
to the fill handle. The pointer changes to a cross.

When you drag the fill handle, a series is
created from the first two rows of the selection.
For example, in column G the series of every
seventh day in the first two rows is extended.

Controlling How Values Are Incremented

You can use CTRL both to create a series from simple values and to suppress series
that Microsoft Excel normally increments. If the active cell contains a simple value,
such as 40, the value is copied into the range you drag through. To increment a
simple value through a range, for example to increment 40 to 41, 42, 43 and so on,

hold down CTRL and then drag the fill handle. To prevent values that Microsoft Excel automatically increments, such as "Jan" and "Qtr1," from incrementing, hold down CTRL and then drag the fill handle.

Creating a Series That Decreases in Value

Just as you can create a series that incrementally increases in value in one direction, you can create a series that decreases in value in the other direction. You do this by dragging the fill handle up or to the left. For example, if you have a series such as 0,1,2 that extends right, you could extend the series left for $-3,-2,-1,0,1,2$.

Caution If you drag the fill handle up or to the left of a selection and stop in the selected cells without going past the first column or the top row, you will erase the data within the selection.

Filling Cells, Values, and Formats Using the Shortcut Menu

You can choose commands for filling data from the AutoFill shortcut menu after dragging the fill handle.

System	To display the shortcut menu, drag the fill handle while holding down
Windows	Right mouse button
Macintosh	CTRL

You can also use the Fill command on the Edit menu to fill data into adjacent cells in a selection.

The shortcut menu also includes commands for creating simple linear trend and growth trend series. For more information, see the following section, "Creating Simple Forecasts and Trends."

Step By Step

For step-by-step instructions and related information, double-click the ⟨k?⟩ button to display the Search dialog box in Help, and then:

Type this keyword and choose Show Topics	Select a topic and choose Go To
creating, forecasts	Creating simple forecasts and trends
filling	Filling a range of adjacent cells
	Turning AutoFill on or off
series	Types of Series
values, incrementing	Incrementing a series of numbers or dates

Creating Simple Forecasts and Trends

You can create simple growth trend and linear trend series by dragging the fill handle and choosing commands from the AutoFill shortcut menu, or by choosing the Fill command from the Edit menu and then choosing the Series command.

Important   Creating linear trend and growth trend series by dragging is a simple way to create trends based on data you've already entered. You should not use this technique to extend complex or nonlinear data. For more flexibility and precision in creating trends, use the TREND, GROWTH, LINEST and LOGEST worksheet functions. For more information about these functions, see the *Microsoft Excel Worksheet Function Reference*.

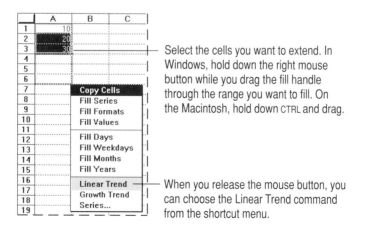

Select the cells you want to extend. In Windows, hold down the right mouse button while you drag the fill handle through the range you want to fill. On the Macintosh, hold down CTRL and drag.

When you release the mouse button, you can choose the Linear Trend command from the shortcut menu.

— A linear trend is filled in the range you drag through.

You can also create a growth trend using the shortcut menu.

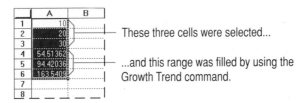

— These three cells were selected...

...and this range was filled by using the Growth Trend command.

The Linear Trend command creates a simple least-squares linear extension similar to the TREND function. The Growth Trend command uses a similar method to create a growth trend based on the selected data.

System	To display the shortcut menu, drag the fill handle while holding down
Windows	Right mouse button
Macintosh	CTRL

Step By Step

For step-by-step instructions and related information, double-click the 🕮 button to display the Search dialog box in Help, and then:

Type this keyword and choose Show Topics	Select a topic and choose Go To
creating, forecasts	Creating simple forecasts and trends
filling	Turning AutoFill on or off
series	Types of Series
values, incrementing	Incrementing a series of numbers or dates

Customizing AutoFill

If you frequently use special series of data, such as product lists or names, you can use AutoFill to automatically enter that data on your worksheets.

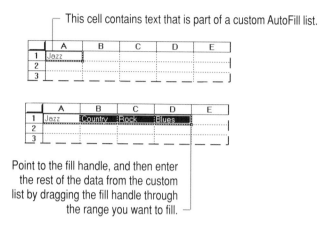

This cell contains text that is part of a custom AutoFill list.

Point to the fill handle, and then enter the rest of the data from the custom list by dragging the fill handle through the range you want to fill.

Creating a Custom AutoFill List

Create a custom AutoFill list using the Options command on the Tools menu either by selecting a list you've already entered on a worksheet or by typing it directly into the Custom Lists tab in the dialog box.

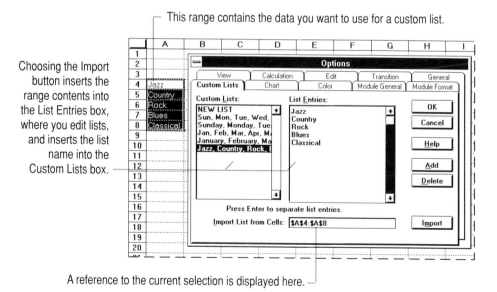

This range contains the data you want to use for a custom list.

Choosing the Import button inserts the range contents into the List Entries box, where you edit lists, and inserts the list name into the Custom Lists box.

A reference to the current selection is displayed here.

You can also type a list directly into the List Entries box and choose the Add button to save the list.

You can import multiple custom lists by selecting them on a worksheet and choosing the Import button. If the current selection contains more than one column and more than one row, a message appears asking if you want to import lists from the rows or the columns in the current selection.

Guidelines for Creating Custom Lists

- Start lists with any character except a number.
- Error values and formulas are ignored when creating lists.
- Individual list entries can contain up to 80 characters.
- Each custom list can contain up to 2000 characters.

Custom lists can be used to define custom sort orders. For example, using a custom list, you can sort a list containing the entries "High," "Medium," and "Low" in priority order rather than alphabetic order. For more information about custom sort orders, see "Sorting Data in a List" in Chapter 21.

Editing or Deleting a Custom AutoFill List

To edit or delete a custom AutoFill list, choose Options from the Tools menu, and then select the Custom Lists tab.

- To edit an item in a list, select it in the Custom Lists box and type your changes in the List Entries box.
- To delete an item in a list, use the following table.

System	Press
Windows	BACKSPACE
Macintosh	DELETE

- To delete an entire custom list, select the list in the Custom Lists box and choose the Delete button.

Note   You can't edit or delete the built-in lists.

Sharing Custom AutoFill Lists with Other Users

You can share custom AutoFill lists with other Microsoft Excel users by sharing a copy of the toolbar file. To merge a custom list from another user, open a copy of their toolbar file by choosing the Open command from the File menu. When the file is opened, its custom lists are merged with the custom lists in the current toolbar file. For more information, see "Customizing Toolbars" in Chapter 34.

System	Toolbar filename and location
Windows	EXCEL5.XLB in the same directory as Microsoft Windows
Macintosh	EXCEL TOOLBARS (5) in the PREFERENCES folder in the SYSTEM folder

Caution   Built-in toolbars are replaced by those in the toolbar file you are merging. Custom tools and toolbars are merged.

Step By Step

For step-by-step instructions and related information, double-click the 🗘 button to display the Search dialog box in Help, and then:

Type this keyword and choose Show Topics	Select a topic and choose Go To
AutoFill	Customizing AutoFill
	Entering a custom AutoFill list on a worksheet
creating, forecasts	Creating simple forecasts and trends
custom AutoFill lists	Editing or deleting a custom AutoFill list

C H A P T E R   1 0

Creating Formulas and Links

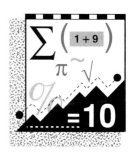

For command, keyboard, and toolbar button information, see online Help.

In This Chapter

Use Formulas to Analyze Your Data

Using a formula can help you analyze data on a worksheet. With a formula you can perform operations, such as addition, multiplication, and comparison on worksheet values. Use a formula when you want to enter calculated values on a worksheet.

- A Microsoft Excel formula always begins with an equal sign (=).
- A *constant* is a numeric or text value that you type directly into a cell.

A simple formula combines constant values with operators, such as a plus sign or minus sign, in a cell to produce a new value from existing values. In Microsoft Excel, formulas can assume many additional forms using references, functions, text, and names to perform various tasks. Think of a formula as one side of an equation whose result is shown in the cell.

The following are examples of formulas, showing some of the elements you can include.

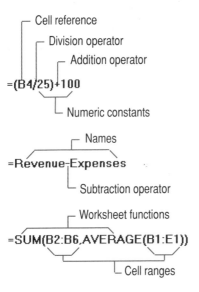

To enter a formula in a worksheet cell, you use a combination of these elements. Each one is covered later in this chapter. For more information about entering data, see Chapter 9, "Entering Data."

The Formula Bar

When the formula bar is active, or when editing directly in cells, you can type a formula, insert worksheet functions and names into a formula, and insert references into a formula by selecting cells. Click the mouse in the entry area or begin typing to activate the formula bar.

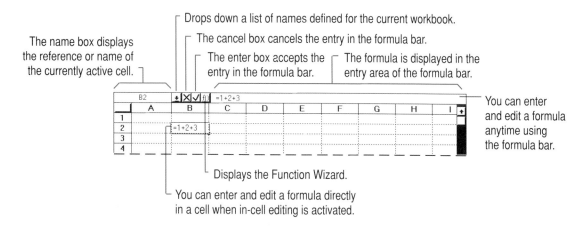

The name box displays the reference or name of the currently active cell.

Drops down a list of names defined for the current workbook.

The cancel box cancels the entry in the formula bar.

The enter box accepts the entry in the formula bar.

The formula is displayed in the entry area of the formula bar.

You can enter and edit a formula anytime using the formula bar.

Displays the Function Wizard.

You can enter and edit a formula directly in a cell when in-cell editing is activated.

For information about editing directly in cells, see "Editing Within a Cell" in Chapter 11. For information about the Function Wizard, see "Using the Function Wizard" later in this chapter.

Understanding Operators

You use *operators* to specify the operation, such as addition, subtraction, or multiplication, to perform on elements of a formula.

Arithmetic Operators   Perform basic mathematical operations; combine numeric values and produce numeric results.

+   Addition

−   Subtraction (or *negation* when placed *before* a value, as in −1)

/   Division

*   Multiplication

%   Percent (placed *after* a value, as in 20%)

^   Exponentiation

For example, the formula =20^2*15% raises 20 to the power of 2 and multiplies the result by 0.15 to produce a result of 60.

Some operators act on two values; others act on one. The formula =5+2 contains the addition operator, which requires two or more values, whereas the formula =3% uses the percentage operator, which requires only one; the percentage operator divides 3 by 100 to produce the value 0.03.

Comparison Operators Compare two values and produce the logical value TRUE or FALSE.

=	Equal
>	Greater than
<	Less than
>=	Greater than or equal to
<=	Less than or equal to
<>	Not equal to

For example, the formula =A1<25 produces the logical value TRUE if cell A1 contains a value less than 25; otherwise, the formula produces the logical value FALSE. For information about how logical values are calculated, see "Controlling Calculation" later in this chapter.

Text Operator Joins two or more text values into a single combined text value.

& Connects, or *concatenates*, two text values to produce one continuous text value. If one of the values is a cell reference and the referenced cell contains a formula, this operator joins the value produced by the formula in the referenced cell as a text value.

For example, if cell A1 contains the text "First Quarter 1994," the formula ="Total Sales for "&A1 produces the text value "Total Sales for First Quarter 1994."

Microsoft Excel also uses *reference operators,* which are discussed in the section "References Make Formulas More Powerful" later in this chapter.

Order of Evaluation of Operators

If you combine several operators in a single formula, Microsoft Excel performs the operations in the order shown in the following table. (Note that reference operators are evaluated before any of the following operators.)

Operator	Description
–	Negation (as in −10)
%	Percent
^	Exponentiation
* and /	Multiplication and division
+ and −	Addition and subtraction
&	Text joining
= < > <= >= <>	Comparison

Combine Expressions with Parentheses

If a formula contains operators with the same priority, Microsoft Excel evaluates the operators from left to right. If you want to alter the order of evaluation, use parentheses to group expressions in your formula.

Note   Do not use parentheses to indicate negative numbers within a formula. Precede the number with a minus sign instead. For example, =5*–10 produces the value –50.

Microsoft Excel first calculates the expressions in parentheses and then uses those results to calculate the formula, as shown in the following table.

This formula	Produces this value
=2+4*5	22
=(2+4)*5	30

Tip   Microsoft Excel emphasizes the matching left parenthesis in bold when you type a right parenthesis in the formula bar. That way, you can make sure you have the correct number of parentheses in a formula. When you use the keyboard to type or move the insertion point past a parenthesis, Microsoft Excel temporarily displays the parenthesis and its matching parenthesis in bold.

Displaying Formulas on the Worksheet

A cell containing a formula normally displays the formula's resulting value on the worksheet. When you select a cell containing a formula, the formula is always displayed in the formula bar. You can also set up the worksheet to display formulas instead of resulting values.

Normally, only the values produced by formulas are displayed.

You can change the display to show the underlying formulas.

System	To switch between displaying formulas and values, press
Windows	CTRL+` (left single quotation mark—to the left of the 1 key on the alphanumeric keyboard)
Macintosh	COMMAND+` (left single quotation mark)

You can also control how formulas are displayed using the Options command on the Tools menu, clicking the View tab, and selecting Formulas in the Window Options box.

Either method of displaying formulas applies only to the selected sheet. For more information about customizing your display, see Chapter 34 "Customizing Your Workspace."

Note   Besides using the equal sign, you can begin entering a formula by typing a plus sign (+), a minus sign (–) or a Lotus 1-2-3 @ function. Microsoft Excel automatically converts a plus or minus sign into an equal sign when you finish entering the formula. Lotus @ functions are converted into the equivalent Microsoft Excel functions. For more information about built-in features to assist you in switching from another spreadsheet program, see Chapter 3, "If You're Switching from Another Spreadsheet."

How Microsoft Excel Converts Values

When you enter a formula, Microsoft Excel expects certain types of values for each operator. If you enter something that is different from what Microsoft Excel expects, Microsoft Excel converts the value, if possible. This feature gives you more flexibility when using formulas. It is rarely necessary to use special functions to convert between types of values. The following table gives some examples of how Microsoft Excel converts values.

The formula	Produces	Explanation
="1"+"2"	3	The plus sign causes Microsoft Excel to expect numbers. Even though the quotation marks mean that 1 and 2 are text values, the text values are automatically converted to numbers.
=1+"$4.00"	5	When a number is expected, text is converted if it is in a format that would normally be accepted for a number.
=SQRT("Sunday")	#VALUE!	Microsoft Excel cannot convert the text to a number because it is not in an acceptable format for a number constant.
="6/1/92"–"5/1/92"	31	Because the dates are in one of the Microsoft Excel date formats, they are converted to serial numbers.
="A="&TRUE	A=TRUE	When text is expected, numbers and logical values are converted to text.
=IF(0,"yes","no")	no	When a logical value is expected, the number 0 is converted to FALSE, and other numbers are converted to TRUE.
=IF("true","yes","no")	yes	The value "true" is converted to a logical TRUE.

The formula	Produces	Explanation
=IF("OK","yes","no")	#VALUE!	When expecting a logical value, Microsoft Excel produces the #VALUE! error when it encounters any text other than "true" or "false" because "OK" cannot be converted to a logical value.

Note If transition formula evaluation is turned on, formulas are evaluated using Lotus 1-2-3 rules. To activate transition formula evaluation, choose Options from the Tools menu, click the Transition tab, and select the Transition Formula Evaluation check box. For more information to assist you in switching from another spreadsheet program, see Chapter 3, "If You're Switching from Another Spreadsheet."

Formulas That Produce Error Values

Microsoft Excel displays an error value in a cell when it cannot calculate the formula for that cell properly. Error values always begin with a number sign (#).

This error value	Means that a formula
#DIV/0!	Is trying to divide by zero.
#N/A	Refers to a value that is not available.
#NAME?	Uses a name that Microsoft Excel doesn't recognize.
#NULL!	Specifies an invalid intersection of two areas.
#NUM!	Uses a number incorrectly.
#REF!	Refers to a cell that is not valid.
#VALUE!	Uses an incorrect argument or operand.
#####	Produces a result that is too long to fit in the cell. Also occurs when a constant numeric value is too long. This is not actually an error value, but an indicator that the column needs to be wider.

If a formula includes a reference to a cell that contains an error value, that formula also produces an error value (unless you are using the special worksheet functions ISERR, ISERROR, ISNA, or ERROR.TYPE that look for error values). You might have to trace the references back through a series of cells to discover the source of the error.

Tip For more information about using the Microsoft Excel auditing tools to trace error values and check the internal consistency and accuracy of a worksheet, see Chapter 38, "Troubleshooting and Annotating a Worksheet."

For information about functions, click the Function Wizard button on the Standard toolbar or see Online Help.

Step By Step

For step-by-step instructions and related information, double-click the 🕮 button to display the Search dialog box in Help, and then:

Type this keyword and choose Show Topics	Select a topic and choose Go To
formulas, entering	Entering formulas
formulas, errors in	Overview of Error Values

References Make Formulas More Powerful

With references, you can use data located in different areas in one formula and use one cell's value in several formulas.

- References identify cells or groups of cells on a worksheet.
- References tell Microsoft Excel which cells to look in to find the values to be used in a formula.
- References are based on the column and row headings in a worksheet.

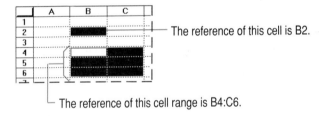

The reference of this cell is B2.

The reference of this cell range is B4:C6.

When you first start Microsoft Excel, columns are labeled with letters (A through IV, for a total of 256 columns) and rows are labeled with numbers (1 through 16384). This is known as A1 reference style. The reference of the active cell is displayed in the name box at the far left of the formula bar.

Understanding References

There are three types of references: *relative references, absolute references,* and *mixed references.*

Relative References A reference such as A1 tells Microsoft Excel how to find another cell, starting from the cell containing the formula. Using a relative reference is like giving someone directions that explain where to go from where that person started—"go up two blocks and over one."

Absolute References   A reference such as $A$1 tells Microsoft Excel how to find a cell based on the exact location of that cell in the worksheet. An absolute reference is designated by adding a dollar sign ($) before the column letter and the row number. Using an absolute reference is like giving someone a street address— "3812 Atlantic Street."

Mixed References   A reference such as A$1 or $A1 tells Microsoft Excel how to find another cell by combining a reference of an exact column or row with a relative row or column. A mixed reference is designated by adding a dollar sign ($) before either the column letter or the row number. For example, in the mixed reference $A2, the column reference ($A) is absolute and the row reference (2) is relative. Besides typing mixed references directly, you can select the reference in the formula or place the insertion point within the reference and press the reference key.

System	To change the reference type, press
Windows	F4
Macintosh	COMMAND+T

Each time you press the reference key, the reference type changes in the following order: relative (A1), absolute ($A$1), mixed (A$1), mixed ($A1).

Note   Do not use dollar signs before numbers to indicate currency within a formula. Instead, use number formatting to determine the way resulting values are displayed. For more information about number formats, see "Applying Number Formats" in Chapter 12.

Understanding Reference Operators

There are three types of reference operators:

- **Range (colon)**   Produces one reference to all the cells between and including the two references.

- **Union (comma)**   Produces one reference that includes the two references.

- **Intersection (space)**   Produces one reference to cells common to the two references.

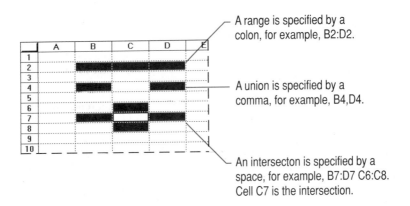

A range is specified by a colon, for example, B2:D2.

A union is specified by a comma, for example, B4,D4.

An intersecton is specified by a space, for example, B7:D7 C6:C8. Cell C7 is the intersection.

When using a range reference operator to refer to entire columns, rows, or a range of entire columns or rows, use the following abbreviated forms of the references.

To refer to	Type
All of column A	A:A
All of row 1	1:1
All of rows 1 through 3	1:3
Entire worksheet	A:IV or 1:16384

Note In addition to the Microsoft Excel range operator (:), you can also use Lotus 1-2-3 range syntax (..) to indicate a reference to cells between and including two references. When you enter a reference using 1-2-3 syntax (A2..A4), it is automatically converted into Microsoft Excel syntax (A2:A4). For more information about built-in features to assist you in switching from another spreadsheet program, see Chapter 3, "If You're Switching from Another Spreadsheet."

Entering References

You can always enter references in formulas by typing them. However, the easiest way is to select the cell or range directly on the worksheet. After typing an equal sign or an operator (for example, +, −, <, or a comma), just click the cell or drag through the cell range you want to reference. The selection is surrounded by a dotted line called the *moving border,* and the reference to the cell or range appears in the formula.

You can enter references in formulas when the cells are on the same worksheet as the formula or when they are on a separate worksheet. You can also select cells contained in separate workbooks to enter external references. For more information, see "Linking Microsoft Excel Workbooks" later in this chapter.

Note If Microsoft Excel does not convert a reference to uppercase letters when you enter the formula, the reference is not valid, and you should check for typing errors.

Referring to Other Sheets in a Workbook

Just as you can use references to cells located elsewhere on a sheet, you can also use references to cells located on other sheets in the same workbook. You can even refer to a range of cells three-dimensionally through a range of sheets in a workbook.

The following illustration shows the syntax for creating a reference to another sheet in a workbook.

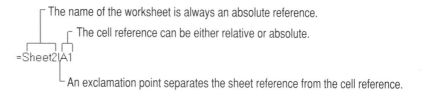

You can always enter a reference to another sheet by typing it in the proper syntax. However, an easier way is to select cells directly on the other sheet. After you type an equal sign or an operator in a formula, click the sheet tab to activate the sheet. Then click or drag through the cells you want to reference.

Note If your sheet names include spaces, you must enclose the entire sheet reference in single quotation marks, for example ='January Sales'!$A$1. If you enter references by selecting cells directly, Microsoft Excel adds the quotation marks automatically if they are needed.

Understanding 3-D References

A 3-D reference is a range that spans two or more sheets in a workbook. The following illustration shows a formula using a reference to a range of cells on a range of sheets in a workbook.

A sheet range is specified with a colon between
the names of the beginning and ending sheets.

=SUM(Sheet2:Sheet6!$A$2:$C$5)

This formula adds the values contained in the range $A$2:$C$5 in each of the sheets between and including Sheet2 and Sheet6.

Note With Microsoft Excel, you can also refer to cells in other workbooks and data in other applications. References to cells in other workbooks are called *external references*. References to data in other applications are called *remote references*. For information about external references, see "Linking Microsoft Excel Workbooks" later in this chapter. For information about remote references, see Chapter 41, "Sharing Data and Graphics with Other Applications."

For more information about workbooks, see Chapter 7, "Working in Workbooks."

Entering 3-D References

To enter a reference to a range of worksheets into a formula, you can type the reference directly, or you can select the worksheet tabs that indicate the beginning and ending sheets from which you want to include references. For example, suppose you want to enter the reference Sheet2:Sheet6!B6:F6 into a formula on Sheet1. The following illustration shows how to enter this reference using the mouse.

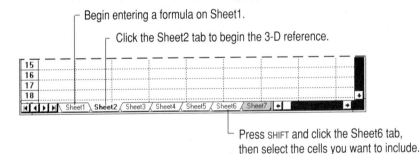

Begin entering a formula on Sheet1.

Click the Sheet2 tab to begin the 3-D reference.

Press SHIFT and click the Sheet6 tab, then select the cells you want to include.

The resulting 3-D reference includes the indicated cell range on all sheets between and including Sheet2 and Sheet6. A formula using the completed 3-D reference uses the same cell or range on each sheet in the sheet range you specify.

For example, you can create a consolidation model in a workbook using 3-D references. Start by creating a separate, but identically laid out sheet for each month's sales totals and one extra for the year-to-date consolidated sales. Then create the formulas.

You can use 3-D references to refer to cells on other sheets, to define names, and to create formulas using the following worksheet functions.

SUM	MIN	VAR
COUNTA	PRODUCT	VARP
AVERAGE	STDEV	COUNT
MAX	STDEVP	

Note You cannot use 3-D references with array formulas, with the intersection operator, or in formulas using implicit intersection. For information about arrays, see "Working With Arrays" later in this chapter. For information about implicit intersection, see "Referring to Intersecting Ranges" in the "Names Make References Easier to Use" section later in this chapter.

For more information about worksheet functions, see "Worksheet Functions Simplify Formulas" later in this chapter. For more information about names, see "Names Make References Easier to Use" later in this chapter.

Understanding R1C1 Reference Style

The R1C1 reference style, in which both rows and columns are numbered, is an alternative to the A1 reference style. This style is useful for showing relative references.

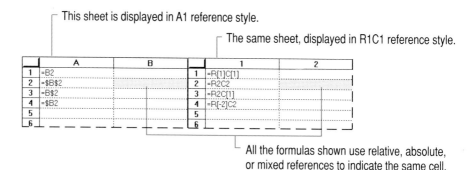

In the preceding illustration, the references in row 1 are relative, those in row 2 are absolute, and those in rows 3 and 4 are mixed. When you select a reference style, all references in the workbook are changed automatically.

In R1C1 style, a cell's location is indicated by an R followed by a row number and a C followed by a column number. For example, the absolute reference R1C1 is equivalent to the absolute reference $A$1 in A1 reference style. If the active cell is A1, the relative reference R[1]C[1] refers to the cell one row down and one column to the right, or cell B2 in A1 reference style.

To change the reference style to R1C1, choose the Options command from the Tools menu and click the General tab. In the Reference Style box, select the R1C1 option button.

Note Changing the reference style affects all worksheets in a workbook.

The following table shows examples of references in R1C1 style.

This reference	Indicates
R[-2]C	The cell two rows up, same column
RC[-2]	The cell in the same row, two columns to the left
R[2]C[2]	The cell two rows down, two columns to the right
R2C2	Absolute reference to the cell in the second row, second column
R[-2]C2	Mixed relative and absolute reference to the cell two rows up in the second column
R[-1]	The entire row above the active cell
R	The current row
C	The current column

Step By Step

For step-by-step instructions and related information, double-click the [?] button to display the Search dialog box in Help, and then:

Type this keyword and choose Show Topics	Select a topic and choose Go To
cell references	Changing a cell's reference type
references, 3-D	Defining a name with a 3-D reference
worksheet references	Entering a reference to a range of sheets in a workbook
	Entering a reference to another sheet in a workbook

Moving and Copying Formulas and References

The Microsoft Excel basic editing techniques offer time-saving advantages when moving and copying formulas and references. For general information about editing, see Chapter 11, "Editing a Worksheet."

For example, the following figure shows three formulas that use the values in row 2, before and after row 2 is deleted.

After deleting row 2, this formula produces an error because a direct reference to cell A2 (in row 2) appeared in the original formula.

Notice that the SUM formulas adjust to the deleted row, even though the original formula in column C contains a range reference that specifies a cell in row 2. Therefore, it is a good idea to use range references whenever appropriate in your formulas, rather than specifying individual cells, as the formula shown in column A does.

How Inserting and Deleting Sheets Affect 3-D References

The following are guidelines for moving, inserting, and deleting sheets that are included in a 3-D reference. The formula =SUM(Sheet2:Sheet6!A2:A5) is used as an example.

- If you insert sheets between Sheet2 and Sheet6 (the *endpoint* sheets in this example), the values in the referenced cell range (A2:A5) in the inserted sheets are included in the calculation.

- If you delete sheets between Sheet2 and Sheet6 in the workbook, their values are removed from the calculation.

- If you move sheets from between Sheet2 and Sheet6 to a location outside the referenced sheet range, their values are removed from the calculation.

- If you move either Sheet2 or Sheet6 to another location in the workbook, the calculation adjusts to accommodate the new range of sheets between them.

Note If you move one endpoint sheet past the other endpoint sheet, the results might not be what you expected. For example, if you move Sheet6 *before* Sheet2 in a workbook, a formula containing the reference Sheet2:Sheet6!A1 would change to Sheet2:Sheet5!A1.

Names Make References Easier to Use

A name is an easy-to-remember identifier you create to refer to a cell, a group of cells, a value, or a formula. Using names has the following advantages:

- Each workbook can share a single set of names. The names you create to refer to cells on a worksheet can be used throughout the workbook, eliminating the need to re-create names for each new worksheet or to type worksheet references in formulas. Sets of related worksheets can be kept together to take advantage of this feature.

- You can also create special names that are specific to a particular sheet. This allows you to use common names such as "Sales" to define related cells on different sheets in the same workbook.

- You can use a named reference almost anywhere you might use a regular reference, including formulas and dialog boxes.

- Formulas that use names are easier to read and remember than formulas using cell references. For example, the formula =Assets−Liabilities is easier to read than the formula =F6−D6.

- If you change the structure of your worksheet, you can update the reference in one place, and all formulas using that name are automatically updated.

- You can paste names into formulas quickly and easily using the name box in the formula bar.

- You can have Microsoft Excel automatically create names for cells based on row or column titles on your worksheet, or you can enter names for cells or formulas yourself.

To define names, use the Name command on the Insert menu or the name box in the formula bar. The following illustration shows possible ways to define names that refer to cells on a worksheet.

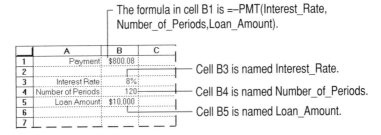

The following illustration shows how you might define names that refer to ranges of data entered on a worksheet.

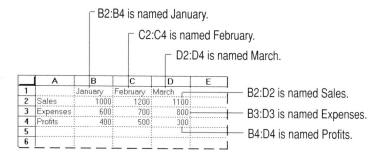

After you define a name for a cell or range, you can:

- Replace references with that name in all or part of your worksheet by applying the name. For example, if you define the name Margin as =$F$12, you can replace all references to cell $F$12 with the name Margin.

- Redefine a name by editing its reference or formula, thereby updating all formulas that use that name.

The Name Box

You can use the name box in the formula bar to:

- Define a name
- Select a named cell or range
- Insert a name into a formula

Once you define a name, it appears in the name box. To open the name box, click the arrow. For example, the names defined for the preceding illustration appear in the name box, as shown in the following illustration.

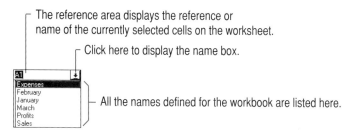

If the currently selected cell or range has been previously named, its name appears in the reference area; otherwise, the reference of the active cell appears (A1 in the preceding illustration).

When you select a name from the name box:

- The named cell or range is selected if the formula bar is not active.
- The selected name is inserted into the formula if the formula bar is active.

When you type a name into the reference area:

- If the name has not been defined, it is defined as the currently selected cell or range and added to the list in the name box.
- If the name has been defined, the named cell or range is selected.

3-D Names

A name can also be defined by a 3-D reference. For example, the name YTD_Sales might be defined as =Sheet2:Sheet13!F2:F11, where F2:F11 contains monthly sales data on each sheet in the workbook between and including Sheet2 and Sheet13. The same rules for 3-D references apply for 3-D names.

For more information about 3-D references, see "References Make Formulas More Powerful" earlier in this chapter.

Book-Level and Sheet-Level Names

Normally, once you define a name on any sheet in a workbook, you can use that name on any other sheet in the workbook, but duplicate names are not allowed. For example, if you define the name Sales on Sheet1 and then attempt to define a different range using the same name on Sheet2, the name Sales is redefined with the new reference.

You can also create sheet-level names that are useful if you want to use a common name such as Sales on several sheets in the same workbook. To create a sheet-level name, use the Name command on the Insert menu, and then choose Define. Precede the text of the name you want to create with the name of the sheet, followed by an exclamation point.

Name type	Location in Define Name dialog box	Syntax example
Book-level	Names in Workbook box	Sales
	Refers To box	=Sheet1!$A$10:$D$10
Sheet-level	Names in Workbook box	Sheet1!Sales
	Refers To box	=Sheet1!$A$10:$D$10

For example, to create the sheet-level name Sales on Sheet2, type **Sheet2!Sales** as the name, and enter the name definition normally. When you use a sheet-level name in a formula on the sheet where the name is defined, you do not type the sheet name and exclamation point, nor do they appear in the name box in the formula bar.

Using the preceding example, if you enter a formula on Sheet2 and insert the name Sales using the name box in the formula bar, the sheet-level name (Sheet2!Sales) is used, even if the book-level name Sales exists in the current workbook. Sheet-level names override book-level names when used on the sheet where they are defined.

You can also refer to sheet-level names from other sheets. In this case, you must use the full name, as defined. For example, you would enter a formula on Sheet3 that uses the sheet-level name Sheet2!Sales by including the sheet name and exclamation point along with the name in the formula, as in =SUM(Sheet2!Sales). However, a sheet-level name does not appear in the Define Name dialog box unless the sheet where the name is defined is the active sheet.

Rules for Names

Follow these guidelines for defining a name:

- **Valid characters**   The first character must be a letter or an underscore character; other characters can be letters, numbers, periods, and underscore characters. The name cannot look like a reference (such as A$1 or R1C1).

- **Separators**   Spaces are not allowed. An underscore character or a period works well as a word separator, for example, Interest.Rate or Interest_Rate.

- **Length**   A name can be up to 255 characters long.

- **Capitalization**   You can use uppercase or lowercase letters. Microsoft Excel records the name exactly as entered. However, it does not distinguish between uppercase and lowercase letters when reading names in formulas.

Tip If you define your names with mixed uppercase and lowercase letters, you can use this as a way to check them later. For example, when entering a name in a formula, use lowercase only. If Microsoft Excel recognizes the name, it is automatically converted to the proper uppercase and lowercase form. If this does not happen, you probably misspelled the name.

Referring to Intersecting Ranges

The intersection operator, a space, is used to refer to a cell that two intersecting cell ranges share in common. Names make this feature easy to apply.

In the following illustration, names are used in three formulas, each using intersection differently.

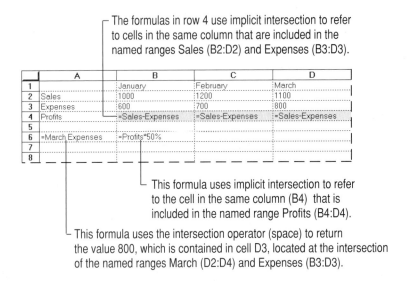

The formulas in row 4 use implicit intersection to refer to cells in the same column that are included in the named ranges Sales (B2:D2) and Expenses (B3:D3).

	A	B	C	D
1		January	February	March
2	Sales	1000	1200	1100
3	Expenses	600	700	800
4	Profits	=Sales-Expenses	=Sales-Expenses	=Sales-Expenses
5				
6	=March Expenses	=Profits*50%		
7				
8				

This formula uses implicit intersection to refer to the cell in the same column (B4) that is included in the named range Profits (B4:D4).

This formula uses the intersection operator (space) to return the value 800, which is contained in cell D3, located at the intersection of the named ranges March (D2:D4) and Expenses (B3:D3).

Implicit Intersection   If you specify a reference to a row or column of cells that should be a reference to a single cell, Microsoft Excel chooses just one cell from that reference on which to perform the operation.

In the preceding illustration, cell B6 contains the formula =Profits*50%. Microsoft Excel looks for a cell in the same row or column that fits the description given in the formula. In this case, the named range Profits (B4:D4) includes a cell in column B, the same column as the formula. Therefore, the cell used in the formula is B4. Moreover, a complete intersection statement like the one in the formula in cell A6 is not necessary. If you copy the formula to the right, each new formula uses a cell in the range Profits that is in the same column as the copied formula.

Note   You cannot use either implicit or explicit intersection with 3-D names.

For more information about the intersection operator, see "References Make Formulas More Powerful" earlier in this chapter.

Named Formulas and Constants

You can also name a formula without putting that formula into a cell using the Name command on the Insert Menu and then choosing Define. Define a name for a formula when it appears in many places throughout a workbook. In the following illustration, the name Rate is already defined as cell B3 on Sheet1 of the workbook. The named formula Monthly_Rate does not exist on a sheet but can be referred to by other formulas.

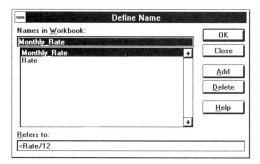

A named constant is similar to a named formula, except that the name is defined by a fixed value rather than by a formula. For example, the name Interest can be defined as =8.5%.

Editing Named References

Once defined, you can insert or delete cells or entire rows and columns within a named cell reference, and the name definition adjusts accordingly. For example, you define the name Divisions as $A$1:$A$10. If you select row 3 and insert a new row, the name Divisions is redefined as $A$1:$A$11. If you then delete rows 10 and 11, the name Divisions is again redefined as $A$1:$A$9.

If you move an entire named reference, the name is redefined to reflect the new reference. For example, if you select the entire Divisions cell range ($A$1:$A$9) and move it to $B$1:$B$9, the definition changes to match the new location. Moving any subset of the named reference to a new location does not affect the name definition. However, the values contained in the moved cells are outside the named area and are no longer included in any calculations that use that name.

Naming Relative References

Microsoft Excel normally uses absolute references (such as =$A$1) to define names. This ensures that the name entered in a cell refers to a specific range of cells and does not change if you move or copy the cell containing the name. If you want to use names that always refer to cells relative to the cell containing the name, change the references to relative references (such as =A1) in the Define Name dialog box by deleting the dollar signs in the reference. You should use relative references with caution, however, because the actual cells referred to change when a formula using the name is moved or copied.

Note   You can have Microsoft Excel for Windows treat range names as Lotus 1-2-3 does. Choose the Options command on the Tools menu. On the Transition tab, select the Transition Formula Entry check box to use range names according to 1-2-3 rules. For information, see Chapter 3, "If You're Switching from Another Spreadsheet."

The #NAME? Error Value

Formulas return the #NAME? error value when a specified name cannot be found. If you receive the #NAME? error value, be sure that you:

- Typed the name in the formula correctly.

- Typed the names of the functions in your formula correctly.

- Created the name you are trying to use or have not deleted the name from the current workbook.

- Did not enclose the name in quotation marks. Microsoft Excel interprets only nonquoted text as a name.

- Did not omit a colon in a range reference. If you type A1D10 instead of A1:D10, Microsoft Excel interprets it as a name.

Working with Names

Inserting a Name into a Formula

As you enter a formula, you can insert an existing name using the name box on the formula bar. After typing an operator or an equal sign, select the name from the name box.

You can also enter a name in a formula by typing the name directly.

Defining a Name

Use the Name command on the Insert menu, and then choose Define to define names using the Define Name dialog box. An even faster method is to use the name box in the formula bar, as shown in the following illustration.

To define a name for the current selection, type a new name in the reference area of the formula bar. If the name you type already exists, the range it defines is selected.

Notice that the names listed in the name box or in the Define Name dialog box include all names defined in the current workbook. In addition, the name box lists any sheet-level names defined on the current sheet.

Note If you use the same name to define both a sheet-level name and a book-level name, the sheet-level name takes precedence on the sheet where it is defined.

The same set of workbook-level names can be used on any sheet in a workbook.

Caution If you type in the name box an existing name that is defined as a formula or constant, the name definition is replaced by the reference of the selected range.

Creating and Applying Names

In the following illustration, the Create Names dialog box is used to define names based on the selected range. To display this dialog box, use the Name command on the Insert menu, and then choose Create.

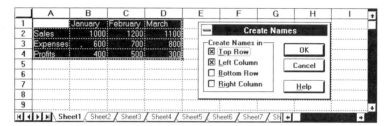

Microsoft Excel then creates the following names.

Name	Is defined as
Sales	=Sheet1!$B$2:$D$2
Expenses	=Sheet1!$B$3:$D$3
Profits	=Sheet1!$B$4:$D$4
January	=Sheet1!$B$2:$B$4
February	=Sheet1!$C$2:$C$4
March	=Sheet1!$D$2:$D$4

If you create the formula =January Profits, the value 400 in cell B4(the cell at the intersection of the two named ranges)is returned.

In the preceding illustration, the Sales and Expenses rows contain constant values. The Profits row contains formulas. The names just created can now be applied to the existing formulas on the worksheet. For example, cell B4 contains the formula =B2−B3. After applying names, the formula becomes =Sales−Expenses because the references in the formula correspond to named ranges in the same column.

To display the Apply Names dialog box, choose Name from the Insert menu, and then choose Apply. All the names defined in the workbook are displayed in the Apply Names box, as shown in the following illustration.

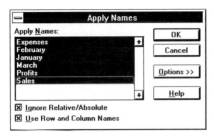

Select the names you want to apply, and choose the OK button.

When you apply names:

- They are substituted in formulas for any cell references that match name definitions.

- They are applied to the entire sheet or only to the selected cells if more than one cell is selected.

Replacing Types of References with Names

When the Ignore Relative/Absolute check box is selected in the Apply Names dialog box, Microsoft Excel replaces references with names regardless of the reference type of either the names or the references. If you clear this check box, Microsoft Excel replaces a reference only if it is the same reference type as the name you are applying. If the name refers to an absolute reference, only absolute references are replaced. Likewise, relative reference names replace only relative references, and mixed reference names replace only mixed references. For information about relative and absolute references, see "References Make Formulas More Powerful" earlier in this chapter.

Using Names on Other Workbooks

You can also refer to a name you defined on another workbook. When you refer to a name on another workbook, you create a link to the other workbook. For information about linking, see "Linking Microsoft Excel Workbooks" later in this chapter.

Copying Named Ranges Between Workbooks

If you copy a formula to another workbook that contains a name that is already defined on the destination workbook, Microsoft Excel displays a message asking if you want to use the existing definition of the name. To use the definition that already exists on the destination workbook, choose the Yes button. To use the definition of the name as copied from the source workbook, choose the No button. If you choose the No button, Microsoft Excel asks you to create a different name for the definition being copied.

Step By Step

For step-by-step instructions and related information, double-click the [?] button to display the Search dialog box in Help, and then:

Type this keyword and choose Show Topics	Select a topic and choose Go To
cell references	Replacing cell references with a defined name
names, changing	Changing a name
names, creating	Naming a cell, range, or formula
names, displaying in Info window	Displaying names in the Info window
names, list of, pasting	Pasting a list of all defined names
names, pasting into formulas	Pasting a name into a formula
names, reference of	Checking the reference of a name
	Editing a name's reference or formula
names, using row, column titles	Creating names based on row and column titles
ranges, intersecting, referring to	Referring to intersecting cell ranges
references, 3-D	Defining a name with a 3-D reference

Worksheet Functions Simplify Formulas

A *function* is a special prewritten formula that takes a value or values, performs an operation, and returns a value or values. Functions can be used alone or as building blocks in larger formulas. Using functions simplifies and shortens formulas in your worksheets, especially those that perform lengthy or complex calculations.

You use the Microsoft Excel built-in worksheet functions to perform standard calculations. The values that you give to a function to perform operations on are called *arguments*. For information about inserting functions into your formulas, see "Using the Function Wizard" later in this chapter.

For example, instead of typing the formula

=A1+A2+A3+A4

you can use the SUM function to build the formula

=SUM(A1:A4)

For more information about specific Microsoft Excel functions, click the Function Wizard on the Standard toolbar or see online Help.

You use functions by entering them in formulas. The sequence of characters used to enter a valid function is called the *syntax*. All functions have the same basic syntax. You use parentheses to enclose all the arguments, and commas to separate individual arguments within the parentheses. If you do not follow this syntax, Microsoft Excel displays a message indicating that there is an error in the formula.

The illustration that follows is an example of a function and its syntax.

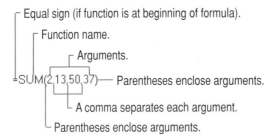

Note Although commas are widely used, the argument separator can be different, depending on the country settings used in your operating system. For more information about country settings, see your operating system documentation.

Guidelines for Using Functions

- Parentheses tell Microsoft Excel where the arguments begin and end. Remember to include both parentheses with no preceding or following spaces.

- Do not use commas to separate thousands for numeric values. Instead, use number formatting to determine the way resulting values are displayed. For more information about number formats, see "Applying Number Formats" in Chapter 12.

- You specify arguments within the parentheses of a function. Arguments can consist of numbers, references, text, logical values, arrays, or error values. Some functions accept optional arguments that are not required for the function to perform its calculations.

- A function's arguments can be constant values or formulas. If you use a formula as an argument, it can contain other functions. When an argument to a function is itself a function, it is said to be *nested*. In Microsoft Excel, you can nest up to seven levels of functions in a formula.

Note If Microsoft Excel does not convert a function name to uppercase letters when you enter the formula, the function is not valid, and you should check for typing errors.

Using Microsoft Excel's Built-in Functions

Although you can type a function directly into a formula, the easiest method of inserting functions is to use the Function Wizard. For more information, see "Using the Function Wizard" later in this chapter.

Note   When transition formula entry is turned on, Microsoft Excel for Windows automatically translates a Lotus 1-2-3 style function into a Microsoft Excel function when you press ENTER. For example, if you enter the formula @AVG(A1..A5), Microsoft Excel changes it to =AVERAGE(A1:A5). From the Tools menu, choose the Options command, click the Transition tab, and select the Transition Formula Entry check box. For more information about built-in features to assist you in switching from another spreadsheet program, see Chapter 3, "If You're Switching from Another Spreadsheet."

Creating Your Own Functions

You can create your own functions for specialized calculations you perform often. These are called *user-defined functions.* For information about user-defined functions, see Chapter 3 of the *Microsoft Excel Visual Basic User's Guide.*

Error Messages

If Microsoft Excel displays a message indicating there is an error in your function or formula, make sure that:

- All your parentheses match.
- All the required arguments are included in the required order and data types. If you omit an argument, type a comma as a placeholder.

Using the AutoSum Button

The SUM function is the most frequently used of all worksheet functions. With it, you can transform a complex formula such as =A2+A3+A4+A5+A6 into the more concise form =SUM(A2:A6). Even more convenient is the AutoSum button on the Standard toolbar. When you use the AutoSum button, Microsoft Excel types the function for you and even suggests the range of cells you want to add.

Entering a Sum Formula with the AutoSum Button

Σ
AutoSum

To enter a sum formula, select a cell adjacent to a row or column of numbers you want to add, and click the AutoSum button.

The following illustration shows the result of clicking the AutoSum button with cell B4 selected.

	A	B	C	D	E	F
1	Division A	Product 1	Product 2	Product 3	Total	
2	East	30	70	110		
3	West	40	80	120		
4	Total	=SUM(B2:B3)				
5						
6						

Microsoft Excel enters an equal sign and a SUM function, suggests B2:B3 as the range to sum, and highlights the reference in the formula bar.

=SUM(B2:B3)

If the suggested range is incorrect, or if Microsoft Excel cannot determine a range to suggest, you can drag through the correct range and press ENTER to accept the completed formula.

Entering Multiple Sum Formulas with the AutoSum Button

When you select a range of cells adjacent to rows or columns of values and click the AutoSum button, sum formulas are inserted into all the selected cells simultaneously, as shown in the following illustration.

	A	B	C	D	E	F
1	Division A	Product 1	Product 2	Product 3	Total	
2	East	30	70	110		
3	West	40	80	120		
4	Total	70	150	230		
5						
6						

Select this range, and click the AutoSum button to
add a sum formula to each selected cell simultaneously.

You can also select the values you want to add before clicking the AutoSum button. Microsoft Excel adds sum formulas to the first empty row below the selected range.

	A	B	C	D	E	F
1	Division A	Product 1	Product 2	Product 3	Total	
2	East	30.00	70.00	110.00		
3	West	40.00	80.00	120.00		
4	Total					
5						

Select this range, and click the AutoSum
button to add sum formulas in row 4.

	A	B	C	D	E	F
1	Division A	Product 1	Product 2	Product 3	Total	
2	East	30.00	70.00	110.00		
3	West	40.00	80.00	120.00		
4	Total	70.00	150.00	230.00		
5						
6						

To add AutoSum formulas to both rows and columns at the same time, select a range of cells that includes the values you want to sum and empty cells where you want the sum formulas to appear.

	A	B	C	D	E	F
1	Division A	Product 1	Product 2	Product 3	Total	
2	East	30.00	70.00	110.00		
3	West	40.00	80.00	120.00		
4	Total					
5						
6						

Select this range, and click the AutoSum button to add sum formulas in column E and row 4 simultaneously.

	A	B	C	D	E	F
1	Division A	Product 1	Product 2	Product 3	Total	
2	East	30.00	70.00	110.00	210.00	
3	West	40.00	80.00	120.00	240.00	
4	Total	70.00	150.00	230.00	450.00	
5						
6						

Entering Grand Totals with the AutoSum Button

You can sum subtotal rows and columns into grand total rows and columns using the AutoSum button. Microsoft Excel assumes that you want to add the subtotals and ignore the values, as shown in the following illustration.

	A	B	C	D	E	F
1	Division A	Product 1	Product 2	Product 3	Total	
2	East	30.00	70.00	110.00		
3	West	40.00	80.00	120.00		
4	Total	70.00	150.00	230.00		
5	Division B					
6	East	30.00	70.00	110.00		
7	West	40.00	80.00	120.00		
8	Total	70.00	150.00	230.00		
9	Grand Total					
10						
11						

Select this range, and click the AutoSum button to add totals in column E and grand totals in row 9 automatically.

The grand total formula in cell B9 is =SUM(B4,B8).

	A	B	C	D	E	F
1	Division A	Product 1	Product 2	Product 3	Total	
2	East	30.00	70.00	110.00	210.00	
3	West	40.00	80.00	120.00	240.00	
4	Total	70.00	150.00	230.00	450.00	
5	Division B					
6	East	30.00	70.00	110.00	210.00	
7	West	40.00	80.00	120.00	240.00	
8	Total	70.00	150.00	230.00	450.00	
9	Grand Total	140.00	300.00	460.00	900.00	
10						
11						

Step By Step

For step-by-step instructions and related information, double-click the 𝖭? button to display the Search dialog box in Help, and then:

Type this keyword and choose Show Topics	Select a topic and choose Go To
AutoSum button	Entering a single sum formula with the AutoSum button
	Entering grand totals with the AutoSum button
	Entering multiple sum formulas with the AutoSum button

Using the Function Wizard

Function Wizard

Whenever you want to use a built-in Microsoft Excel function or a custom function, you can use the Function Wizard to help you select a function, assemble the arguments correctly, and insert the function into your formula. The formula bar shows the changes you make as you build your formula.

To add a function to a formula, activate the Function Wizard by clicking the Function Wizard button.

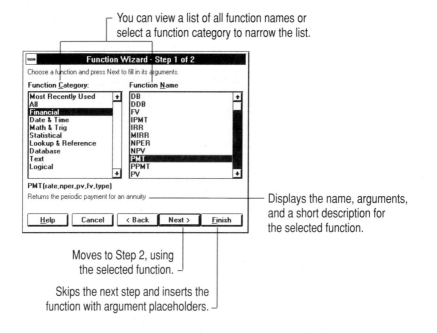

You can view a list of all function names or select a function category to narrow the list.

Displays the name, arguments, and a short description for the selected function.

Moves to Step 2, using the selected function.

Skips the next step and inserts the function with argument placeholders.

Tip For quick access to the last 10 functions used, choose the function category named Most Recently Used.

When you click the Finish button in the Step 1 dialog box, the selected function is inserted into your formula with the argument names inserted as placeholders. For example, clicking the Finish button in the previous illustration inserts PMT(rate,nper,pv,fv,type) into the formula. You can then replace the argument text with the values necessary to complete the function.

From the Step 1 dialog box, click the Next button to display the Step 2 dialog box. When it appears, you can enter numbers, references, names, formulas, text, or other functions into the argument edit boxes. After you have entered valid values for each required argument, the calculated value for the function appears in the Value box at the top of the Step 2 dialog box. Click the Finish button to insert the completed function into your formula.

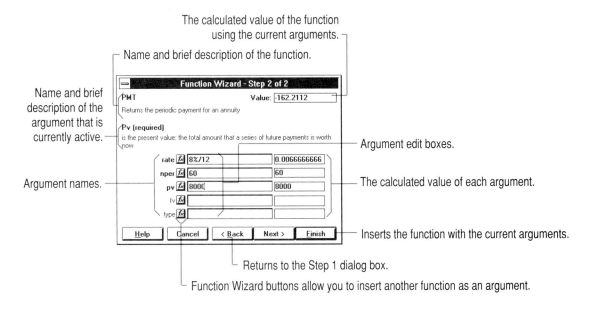

While typing a formula, you can quickly display the Function Wizard Step 2 dialog box to assist in entering the arguments.

System	Type a valid function name, then press
Windows	CTRL+A
Macintosh	CONTROL+A

You can also paste the argument names directly into a formula without activating the Function Wizard.

System	Type a valid function name, then press
Windows	CTRL+SHIFT+A
Macintosh	CONTROL+SHIFT+A

Entering Nested Functions

You might want to enter functions as arguments to other functions, as in the formula =ABS(AVERAGE(B4,SUM(D4:D12))). This formula is said to have two levels of *nested* functions. The SUM function is entered as an argument to the AVERAGE function, which is itself an argument to the ABS function. To nest a function, click the small Function Wizard button in the appropriate argument edit box in the Function Wizard Step 2 dialog box. When you click this button, another Function Wizard dialog box appears, allowing you to nest another function as an argument. You can nest up to seven levels of functions in this manner.

Entering Names as Arguments

If you have defined names for your workbook, you can type or insert them as arguments in the Function Wizard Step 2 dialog box. To insert a name, select the name in the name box in the formula bar. For more information about the name box, see "Names Make References Easier to Use" earlier in this chapter.

Editing Functions in an Existing Formula

When you select a cell containing an existing formula that includes functions, you can choose the Function Wizard button. The first function in the formula is opened in the Function Wizard Editing mode, allowing you to modify the arguments. This is a good way to debug a function.

For example, if you click the Function Wizard button while a cell containing the formula =SUM(ABS(B2),C2,D2) is selected, the following dialog box appears.

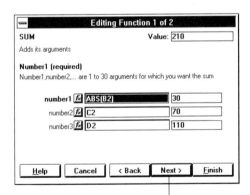

Clicking the Next button moves you to the next function in the selected formula and displays it in the Editing Function dialog box.

The Function Wizard opens the first function in the formula in the editing version of the Step 2 dialog box so you can edit the arguments. Notice that the dialog box title is Editing Function 1 of 2. If you click the Next button, your edits are entered for the current function, and the second function in the formula, the ABS function, is opened for editing.

Step By Step

For step-by-step instructions and related information, double-click the [?] button to display the Search dialog box in Help, and then:

Type this keyword and choose Show Topics	Select a topic and choose Go To
Function Wizard	Editing formulas containing functions with Function Wizard
	Inserting a worksheet function into a formula with Function Wizard

Linking Microsoft Excel Workbooks

You can dynamically link a formula in a workbook to source data located in another workbook so that any changes you make to the source data are immediately reflected in the linked formula. The following terms apply to linking workbooks:

External Reference A reference to a cell or range on a sheet in another Microsoft Excel workbook or a reference to a defined name in another workbook.

Dependent Workbook A workbook that contains a link to another workbook and thereby depends on information in another workbook.

Source Workbook A workbook that is the source of the information referred to in an external reference formula.

The following illustration shows a formula linking two Microsoft Excel for Windows workbooks. The link tells Microsoft Excel to update the value in the formula in the dependent workbook Q4SUM.XLS whenever the source value in the source workbook Q4SALES.XLS changes.

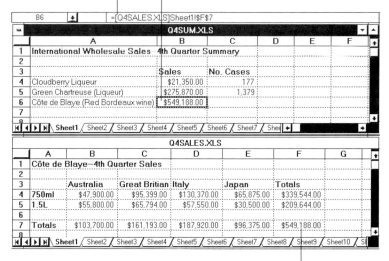

The external reference formula links cell B6 in Q4SUM.XLS to cell F7 in Q4SALES.XLS.

Cell B6 in the dependent workbook contains an external reference formula.

Cell F7 in the source workbook provides the value used by the external reference formula.

Notice that the workbook filename is included at the start of the external reference and is enclosed in brackets. For more information about creating and using workbooks, see Chapter 6, "Managing Workbook Files."

When to Link Workbooks

Linking is especially useful for working with large worksheet models or systems of worksheets where it would be impractical to keep them together in the same workbook. The following are a few ways you can use linking most effectively:

Merging Data from Several Workbooks For example, you can link workbooks from several users or departments and integrate the pertinent data into a summary workbook. The original workbooks can still be edited separately from the summary workbook.

Creating Different "Views" of Your Data You can enter all your data and formulas in one or more source workbooks and then create a "report" workbook that contains links to only the pertinent data in the source workbooks.

Streamlining Large, Complex Models By breaking down a complicated model into a series of interdependent workbooks, you save memory because you can work on the model without opening all its related sheets at the same time. Smaller workbooks are easier to edit and faster to open, save, and calculate.

Linking is not restricted to links between two workbooks. You can also construct hierarchies of linked workbooks. The following illustration shows an income and expenses reporting system based on workbooks linked this way.

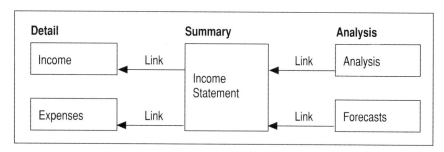

The Detail workbooks are sources, the Summary workbook is dependent on Detail and is the source for the Analysis workbooks, which depend on the Summary workbook.

Working with Links

The following illustration shows the parts of an external reference formula; it uses a path and filename for Microsoft Excel for Windows.

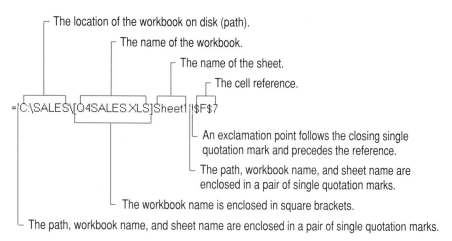

A similar link in Microsoft Excel for the Macintosh might be:

='Hard Disk:Sales:[Q4 Sales]Sheet1'!$F$7

If the worksheet referred to by the external reference formula is in the same
directory or folder as the worksheet containing the external reference formula,
typing the path is not necessary.

When to Type Single Quotation Marks in a Reference

If you include the disk path, or if the workbook or sheet name includes space
characters (as is common on the Macintosh), you must enclose the path,
filename, and sheet name in single quotation marks. Type the exclamation
point following the closing single quotation mark. For example:

Windows   ='C:\EXCEL\[BOOK1.XLS]SHEET1'!$A$1

Macintosh   ='Hard Disk:Excel:[Workbook1]Sheet1'!$A$1

If you are unsure whether to type single quotation marks, do so anyway. If
the reference does not need quotation marks, Microsoft Excel ignores them
when you press ENTER. If you enter references by selecting cells directly,
Microsoft Excel adds the quotation marks automatically if they are needed.

Entering External References by Selecting

Creating a formula that links two workbooks is just as easy as creating a formula
with references to the same workbook because you can use the mouse to select the
cells on a sheet in another workbook to which you want the formula to refer. For
example, after you type an equal sign to start a formula, select the cells in the
external workbook that you want to use.

Note To make it easy to move between documents, choose the Arrange command
from the Window menu. In the Arrange Windows dialog box, select the Tiled,
Horizontal, or Vertical option button to display all windows at the same time.

How External References Are Displayed

If the source workbook is closed, the external reference is displayed in the formula
bar with the full path—drive, directory name or folder name—plus book name,
sheet name, and cell reference, as shown in the preceding illustration. If the source
workbook is open, the external reference is displayed without the path, for example:

System	External reference syntax
Windows	'[Q4SALES.XLS]Sheet1'!$F$7
Macintosh	'[Q4 Sales]Sheet1'!$F$7

Using Names in Linking Formulas

You can create an external reference formula using a defined name that refers to the cell or cells you want to use. For example, the following external reference formulas refer to the name Totals.

System	External reference syntax using names
Windows	='C:\EXCEL\JANSALES.XLS'!Totals
Macintosh	='Hard Disk:Excel:January Sales'!Totals

Notice that the preceding formulas do not include brackets around the workbook name. This form is used when referring to book-level names. You can also create external references to sheet-level names. For example, the following external reference formulas refer to the name Totals that is defined as a sheet-level name on Sheet2.

System	External reference syntax using names
Windows	='C:\EXCEL\[JANSALES.XLS]Sheet2'!Totals
Macintosh	='Hard Disk:Excel:[January Sales]Sheet2'!Totals

For information about names, see "Names Make References Easier to Use" earlier in this chapter.

Saving Linked Workbooks

In general, you should always save source workbooks before saving the dependent workbook linked to them. This ensures that formulas in a source workbook have been calculated and that workbook and sheet names in external references are current. If you name or rename a source workbook with the Save or Save As command, the dependent workbook must be open for the name to be updated automatically in the external reference.

If you change the name of a source workbook while the dependent workbook is closed, or if you move linked workbooks to different directories or folders, you must change the links in the dependent workbook to include the new name or full path of the source workbooks. Use the Links command on the Edit menu, and choose the Change Source button in the dialog box that appears.

Note If you move a dependent workbook and none of its external references are to workbooks in the original directory or folder or any of its subdirectories or subfolders, you don't need to change any of the links. If you try to save a dependent workbook that contains a reference to an unnamed Microsoft Excel source workbook, Microsoft Excel displays a message.

Opening, Updating, and Changing Links

Use the Links command on the Edit menu to manage source data for the active workbook. When you choose the Links command, the Links dialog box lists the workbook and sheet name for each external reference used in the active workbook. When you select a filename from the list, you can:

- Open the source workbook by choosing the Open button.

- Update the data, if necessary, by choosing the Update Now button. The source workbook remains closed. The Update Now button is unavailable if the data is current.

- Change the source workbook, if necessary, by choosing the Change button. The Change Source dialog box appears, allowing you to locate and open a different workbook.

Removing Links Between Workbooks

If an external reference consists of an entire formula, you can replace the formula with its current value. Copy the cell containing the formula, choose the Paste Special command from the Edit menu, and select the Values option button. Only the current value of the copied formula is pasted.

If an external reference is part of a larger formula, you can calculate the reference alone to change it to a value while preserving the rest of the formula. This is called freezing the value of an external reference. First, select the entire external reference in the formula.

System	To calculate the value of an external reference, press
Windows	F9 or CTRL+=
Macintosh	F9 or COMMAND+=

Managing Linked Workbooks in Different Locations

Whenever possible, you should try to save linked workbooks in the same directory or folder. However, you might find it more efficient to set up certain models with linked workbooks in different directories or folders. Follow these guidelines when you work with linked workbooks in different directories or folders:

- To maintain links correctly, save the source workbooks before saving the dependent workbook.

- If you move Microsoft Excel workbooks between directories or folders, also move all linked workbooks stored in the same directory or folder or subdirectories or subfolders.

If you don't follow these guidelines, your links can become disconnected. When you try to open a dependent workbook, Microsoft Excel displays a message indicating that it can't find the source workbook. If this happens, use the Links command on the Edit menu to change the links for the dependent or source workbooks you've moved to different directories.

Saving a Workbook That Contains Links to a Large Workbook

If a workbook with several links to another workbook requires an unusually large amount of disk space, choose the Options command from the Tools menu, and click the Calculation tab. Then clear the Save External Link Values check box. This prevents Microsoft Excel from saving copies of the values contained in the source workbook along with your workbook.

Step By Step

For step-by-step instructions and related information, double-click the [?] button to display the Search dialog box in Help, and then:

Type this keyword and choose Show Topics	Select a topic and choose Go To
external references	Entering an external reference in a formula
links, workbook, creating	Creating links between workbooks
links, workbook, removing	Removing links between workbooks
saving workbooks	Renaming a stand-alone or a dependent workbook
	Saving unnamed linked workbooks
source documents	Viewing a list of source documents for a dependent workbook
	Viewing the source data for a link
source workbooks	Opening source workbooks
	Redirecting links for source workbooks
	Replacing a source workbook with another workbook
	Updating data from a source workbook

Controlling Calculation

Calculation is the process of computing formulas and then displaying the results as values in the cells containing the formulas.

- Whenever possible, Microsoft Excel updates only those cells affected by values you change, thus avoiding unnecessary calculations.

- Microsoft Excel calculates on the basis of the underlying stored values in cells, rather than the values as you have formatted them for display. This means that you can change the appearance of a value on a worksheet without affecting the value itself.

- While Microsoft Excel is calculating, you can choose commands or perform actions, such as entering numbers or formulas. Microsoft Excel temporarily interrupts calculation to carry out the other commands or actions and then resumes calculation.

Using Manual Calculation

Each time you enter or edit a formula, Microsoft Excel automatically recalculates all the formulas contained in the current workbook. If you are entering or editing many formulas on a complex worksheet, you can speed up the response time considerably by changing from automatic to manual calculation.

Automatic calculation is the default. To switch to manual calculation, choose the Options command from the Tools menu, click the Calculation tab, and select the Manual option button.

Values Stored vs. Values Displayed

Normally, Microsoft Excel stores values with 15 digits of accuracy. This is called *full precision*. However, numbers are displayed according to the format of the cells containing them, so the number you see in a cell may differ from the underlying stored value.

The formula bar displays the actual stored value of the active cell.

No matter how the value is formatted for display, Microsoft Excel uses the stored value in calculations. For more information about cell formatting, see Chapter 12, "Formatting a Worksheet."

Calculating Using Displayed Values By default, all calculations use the entire stored value, no matter how the values are formatted and displayed. If you display numbers with less precision than their stored values, the displayed numbers are rounded. This may cause some formulas to display results that appear to be incorrect, although the underlying values are correct. For example, if two cells each contain the value 3.006, and you add them in a third cell, the result is 6.012. If all three cells are formatted to display only two decimal places, the result is 3.01+3.01=6.01, which appears to be wrong. On the other hand, if you calculate using the displayed values, the result is 3.01+3.01=6.02.

You can set Microsoft Excel to calculate on the basis of displayed values only. This is useful for calculating figures based on monetary amounts. To do so, choose the Options command from the Tools menu, click the Calculation tab, and select the Precision As Displayed check box.

Calculating with precision as displayed:

- Affects all worksheets in the active workbook.
- Does not affect numbers in the General format, which are always calculated with full precision.
- Slows calculation because Microsoft Excel must round off the numbers as it calculates.

Caution Selecting the Precision As Displayed check box for a workbook permanently changes stored constant values to their displayed values. If you later want to return to full precision, the original full precision values are not restored.

Replacing a Formula with Its Calculated Value

To replace a formula with its resulting value, copy the cell containing the formula. Then use Paste Special on the Edit menu, and choose the Values option button. When you press ENTER, the formula is replaced by its resulting value.

You can also replace a portion of a formula with its resulting value. When you make a selection in the formula bar, only the selected part of the formula is calculated when you press the Calculate key.

System	To calculate the selected portion of a formula, press
Windows	F9 or CTRL+=
Macintosh	F9 or COMMAND+=

=1+`2+3+4+5`+6

In the formula bar, select a portion of a formula, and press the
Calculate key to replace the selection with its resulting value.

=1+`14`+6

Caution Replacing a formula with its value permanently removes the formula. If
you inadvertently replace a formula with a value and want to restore the formula,
choose the Undo Entry command from the Edit menu immediately after entering or
pasting the value. If the formula bar is still active, you can also press ESC in
Microsoft Excel for Windows or COMMAND+PERIOD in Microsoft Excel for the
Macintosh to restore the previous entry.

Windows vs. Macintosh Date Systems

Microsoft Excel stores dates as serial numbers. The serial number that corresponds
to a date differs depending on the date system that was in effect when you entered
the dates.

Microsoft Excel provides two date systems—the 1900 date system and the 1904
date system. The 1900 date system is the default used by Microsoft Excel for
Windows and by Lotus 1-2-3. In the 1900 date system, the serial number 1
corresponds to the date January 1, 1900, the serial number 2 corresponds to January
2, 1900, and so on. The 1904 date system is the default used by Microsoft Excel for
the Macintosh. In the 1904 date system, the date serial number 1 corresponds to the
date January 2, 1904, the date serial number 2 corresponds to January 3, 1904, and
so on.

For example, the date 12/31/93 is stored in Microsoft Excel for Windows as the
date serial number 34344, using the 1900 date system. In Microsoft Excel for the
Macintosh, the same date is stored as the serial number 32872, using the 1904 date
system.

If you create a file in Microsoft Excel for the Macintosh and then open it in Microsoft Excel for Windows, Microsoft Excel recognizes the file format and changes to the 1900 date system for you. Similarly, if you create a file in Microsoft Excel for Windows and then open it in Microsoft Excel for the Macintosh, Microsoft Excel recognizes the file format and changes to the 1904 date system for you.

Important Changing the date system affects only the active workbook and any new dates that are entered. Dates that have already been entered are not converted when you change date systems; the date serial numbers for previously entered dates remain the same. However, those date serial numbers produce different dates after you change date systems. Therefore, you should always choose the date system you want to use for a workbook before entering any dates in the workbook.

Updating References to Data from Other Applications

If you want Microsoft Excel to automatically update formulas with remote references to data in documents created by applications other than Microsoft Excel, use the Options command on the Tools Menu, click the Calculation tab, and select the Update Remote References check box. If this check box is cleared, Microsoft Excel calculates using the last values received from the other application. This option affects only the active workbook. For more information, see Chapter 41, "Sharing Data and Graphics With Other Applications."

Note Microsoft Excel and Lotus 1-2-3 evaluate certain formulas and expressions differently. To calculate formulas and database criteria according to 1-2-3 rules, choose the Options command from the Tools menu, click the Transition tab, and select the Transition Formula Evaluation check box. For more information, see Chapter 3, "If You're Switching from Another Spreadsheet."

How Logical Values Are Calculated

Microsoft Excel recognizes the logical values TRUE and FALSE and evaluates them as the numeric values 1 and 0, respectively. For example, suppose cell A1 contains the value 6. The formula =A1>5 in cell B1 produces the logical value TRUE, and the formula =100+B1 produces the value 101 because the logical value TRUE evaluates to the numeric value 1.

Step By Step

For step-by-step instructions and related information, double-click the ▶️? button to display the Search dialog box in Help, and then:

Type this keyword and choose Show Topics	Select a topic and choose Go To
calculating formulas	Calculating a portion of a formula
calculating with displayed precision	Calculating with precision as displayed
calculating worksheets	Calculating all open documents when calculation is set to manual
	Calculating only the active worksheet
calculation, preventing	Freezing the values in a range of cells
	Replacing an entire formula with its calculated value
	Switching between manual and automatic calculation
	Turning off calculation before saving
date systems	Date system differences for Microsoft Windows and Macintosh

Solving Circular Reference Formulas Using Iteration

When a formula refers back to its own cell, either directly or indirectly, it is called a *circular reference.* Sometimes this is an error, but it is also possible to use circular references to solve certain types of problems. When you want to do this, Microsoft Excel must use *iteration,* which is the repeated calculation of the worksheet until a specific numeric condition is met.

If two formulas depend on each other for their results and, therefore, contain references to each other, Microsoft Excel displays a message that it cannot resolve the circular reference. For formulas where a circular reference is required, use the Options command on the Tools menu, click the Calculation tab, and select the Iteration check box. Unless you change the default settings, Microsoft Excel stops calculating after 100 iterations or after all values in the model change by less than 0.001 between iterations.

For example, suppose you need to compute an employee bonus that is 10 percent of net profit, while the net profit depends on the amount of the bonus. Your gross profit is $1000, your net profit equals the gross profit minus the bonus, and the bonus is 10 percent of the net profit. The following illustration shows the formulas to calculate the bonus and net profit.

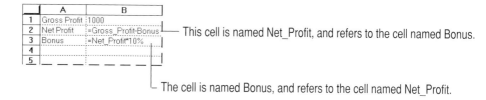

	A	B
1	Gross Profit	1000
2	Net Profit	=Gross_Profit-Bonus
3	Bonus	=Net_Profit*10%
4		
5		

This cell is named Net_Profit, and refers to the cell named Bonus.

The cell is named Bonus, and refers to the cell named Net_Profit.

The formulas in cells B2 and B3 create a circular reference because each formula refers to the other. When you use iteration to calculate formulas, Microsoft Excel calculates each cell involved in the circular reference once using the results of the previous iteration.

Note   Circular references can also occur due to faulty logic on the worksheet or incorrect cell references in formulas. You can use the Microsoft Excel troubleshooting features to find errors that are causing the circular reference. For information, see Chapter 38, "Troubleshooting and Annotating a Worksheet."

Step By Step

For step-by-step instructions and related information, double-click the 🔡 button to display the Search dialog box in Help, and then:

Type this keyword and choose Show Topics	Select a topic and choose Go To
iterations, controlling	Controlling iteration

Working with Arrays

Array formulas can be described as multiple-value formulas. These differ from single-value formulas because they can produce more than one result.

- One array formula can occupy several cells.
- Arrays of up to approximately 6500 elements are permitted.

Understanding Arrays

To understand how an array formula works, first consider how an ordinary, single-value formula works. A single-value formula produces a single result from one or more arguments or values. For example, the formula =A1+B1 produces a single result—the sum of the values in cells A1 and B1. However, the array formula {=A1:A3+B1:B3} produces a set of three results—the sum of the values in cells A1 and B1, the sum of the values in cells A2 and B2, and the sum of the values in cells A3 and B3.

Because array formulas can produce multiple results, you can use array formulas to reduce the amount of time you spend entering repetitive formulas. For example, you can enter five single-value formulas in five cells, as shown on the left in the following illustration, or you can enter one array formula in five cells—called an *array range*—as shown on the right.

Note In Microsoft Excel 5.0, an array formula uses more memory than the equivalent ordinary formulas.

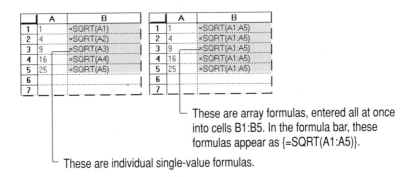

These are array formulas, entered all at once into cells B1:B5. In the formula bar, these formulas appear as {=SQRT(A1:A5)}.

These are individual single-value formulas.

You can recognize an array formula by the braces ({ }) enclosing it in the formula bar. You don't type the braces yourself. Microsoft Excel automatically puts the braces around a formula when you enter it as an array, using the following shortcut keys:

System	To enter an array formula, press
Windows	CTRL+SHIFT+ENTER
Macintosh	COMMAND+RETURN

- If you select any cell in a range containing an array formula, the same array formula is displayed in the formula bar.

- You cannot change or delete individual cells in the array range because all the cells share a single formula.

You can also use array formulas to simplify some worksheet models. For some calculations, you can replace several different formulas with a single array formula that consolidates all of the calculations into one result. The following illustrations show how a worksheet can be simplified using an array formula.

The stock values are produced by three separate
formulas: =B2*B3, =C2*C3, and =D2*D3.

	A	B	C	D
1		Acme	Apex	Apogee
2	Shares	500	300	150
3	Price	$10	$15	$50
4	Value	$5,000	$4,500	$7,500
5				
6	Total	$17,000		
7				
8				

The formula =SUM(B4:D4) computes the sum of the three stock values in B4:D4.

Instead of having to enter four formulas as in the preceding model, you can compute the total with one array formula, as shown in the following illustration.

	A	B	C	D
1		Acme	Apex	Apogee
2	Shares	500	300	150
3	Price	$10	$15	$50
4				
5	Total	$17,000		
6				
7				

The array formula {=SUM(B2:D2*B3:D3)} computes the
array of stock values and then sums the values in the array.

Editing Arrays

Because an array range shares one formula, you edit an array range differently from ordinary cells. When you edit an array range, you edit the entire range at once as if it were a single cell. You cannot perform any operation that modifies only a portion of the array range, such as:

- Changing the contents of cells that are a part of an array.

- Clearing, moving, or deleting cells that are a part of an array.

- Inserting cells into an array range.

If you attempt any of these operations, Microsoft Excel displays a message that tells you the operation cannot be done for an array. If you want to edit an entire array, choose the Go To command on the Edit menu, click the Special button, and select the Current Array option to select the array containing the active cell. For information about editing cell contents, see Chapter 11, "Editing a Worksheet."

You can, however, format individual cells in an array range. You can also copy and paste a cell or range of cells from an array range to another part of the worksheet. Microsoft Excel adjusts the relative references in the copied formula just as it does with ordinary formulas. For information about formatting, see Chapter 12, "Formatting a Worksheet."

Step By Step

For step-by-step instructions and related information, double-click the ⟨k?⟩ button to display the Search dialog box in Help, and then:

Type this keyword and choose Show Topics	Select a topic and choose Go To
array formulas	Editing an array formula
	Entering an array formula
array ranges	Clearing an array range
	Converting an array range to constant values
	Selecting an array range

What Is an Array Constant?

In an ordinary formula, you can either enter a reference to a cell containing a value, or type the value itself into the formula. Similarly, in any array formula where you use a reference to a range of cells, you can type the array of values contained in the range of cells. The array of values you type is called an *array constant*. Generally, you use array constants in place of references when you don't want to enter each constant value in a separate cell on your worksheet.

To enter an array constant:

- Type the values directly into the formula, and enclose them in braces ({ }).
- Use commas to separate values in different columns.
- Use semicolons to separate values in different rows.

For example, to use the following array in a formula:

1 2 3
4 5 6

type: **{1,2,3;4,5,6}**, including the braces. This is a 2-by-3 array because it consists of 2 rows of 3 values each, or 2 rows and 3 columns. If this array constant is also part of an array formula, you would enter it as an array formula.

System	To enter an array formula, press
Windows	CTRL+SHIFT+ENTER
Macintosh	COMMAND+RETURN

You can use an array constant in place of a cell range reference in any formula that uses multiple components or arguments. For example, consider the example in the following illustration.

	A	B	C
1	Length in Feet	Price/Foot	Price/Unit
2	3	$4.00	$12.00
3	6	$3.75	$22.50
4	9	$3.25	$29.25
5	12	$2.50	$30.00
6			
7			

This range contains the array formula {=A2:A5*B2:B5}.

You could replace the reference to cells B2:B5 in the array formula with an array constant and delete the Price/Foot column as shown in the following illustration.

	A	B
1	Length in Feet	Price/Unit
2	3	$12.00
3	6	$22.50
4	9	$29.25
5	12	$30.00
6		
7		

This range contains the array formula {=A2:A5*{4;3.75;3.25;2.5}}.

Caution   You can successfully enter an array constant or range into an ordinary formula. However, if you do, the formula might produce a different result from when it is entered as an array formula. In an ordinary formula, only the first item in an array constant is used and produces only a single result. For example, if you enter the formula ={1,2,3}+{2,3,4} as an ordinary formula, Microsoft Excel adds the first value in each array and produces the single result 3. If you enter the formula as an array formula, it produces three results: 3, 5, and 7.

What Does an Array Constant Contain?

- Array constants can contain numbers, text, logical values, or error values.
- Numbers in array constants can be in integer, decimal, or scientific format.
- Text must be enclosed in double quotation marks.
- You can include different types of values in the same array constant.
- The values in an array constant must be constants, not formulas.
- Array constants cannot contain dollar signs, parentheses, or percent signs.
- You cannot enter array constants that have columns or rows of unequal length.

The following are some examples of array constants.

Type	To get this
{10,20,30,40}	1-by-4 array: 10 20 30 40
{100;200;300}	3-by-1 array: 100 200 300
{7,8,9;"x","y","z"}	2-by-3 array: 7 8 9 x y z
{1,2;TRUE,FALSE}	2-by-2 array: 1 2 TRUE FALSE

Microsoft Excel does not allow you to list cell references or names in an array formula the same way that you list constants. For example, you could not use {A1,B1,C1} to represent the array containing the values in cells A1, B1, and C1. Instead, you must use the cell range reference A1:C1 or enter the values of those cells directly in the array as constants, for example, {10,20,30}.

How Microsoft Excel Expands Array Formulas

When you use an array constant in a formula or function, the other components or arguments should have the same dimensions as the first array. If necessary, Microsoft Excel expands the necessary components to the required dimensions. Each component must have the same number of rows as the component with the greatest number of rows, and the same number of columns as the component with the greatest number of columns.

For example, in the formula =SUM({1,2,3}*4), one component is a 1-by-3 array and the other is a single value. In evaluating this formula, Microsoft Excel automatically expands the second component to a 1-by-3 array and evaluates the formula as =SUM({1,2,3}*{4,4,4}). The formula's result equals 24, which is the sum of 1*4, 2*4, and 3*4.

The following table shows how array components or arguments are expanded.

In this formula	The arguments are evaluated as	Explanation
=1+{1,2;3,4}	{1,1;1,1}+{1,2;3,4}	The constant 1 is expanded to match the array.
={1,2,3}*{2;3}	{1,2,3;1,2,3}*{2,2,2;3,3,3}	Each array is expanded to accommodate the dimensions of the other.
={1,2}+{1,2,3;4,5,6}	{1,2,#N/A;1,2,#N/A}+{1,2,3;4,5,6}	Each array is expanded, but no value exists in the first array to add to the third column values in the second array.
=MOD({5,6,7},4)	MOD({5,6,7},{4,4,4})	The constant 4 is expanded to match the array.

You should enter an array formula in a range of cells with the same dimensions as the resulting array produced by the formula. Microsoft Excel can then place each value in the resulting array into one cell of the array range.

- If an array formula produces an array smaller than the selected array range, Microsoft Excel expands the resulting array to fill the range.

- If Microsoft Excel expands an array to fill a range larger than the array formula, #N/A error values appear in cells for which no valid expandable value is available.

- If an array formula produces an array larger than the selected array range, the excess values do not appear on the worksheet.

For example, the formula ={1,2,3}*{2,3,4} produces the 1-by-3 array {2,6,12}. If you enter this formula into a 2-by-3 array range, Microsoft Excel expands the result to {2,6,12;2,6,12}. If you enter the same formula into a 1-by-4 array range, Microsoft Excel expands the result to {2,6,12,#N/A}. If you enter the same formula into a 1-by-2 array range, the result is {2,6}.

Special Functions Help You Work with Arrays

Microsoft Excel includes some worksheet functions that return arrays of values or require either array constants or references to cell ranges as arguments.

For example, you want to compute the trend of your monthly sales over the last six months. That trend is described not by one value, but by six—the trend values corresponding to the sales in each of the last six months. Microsoft Excel provides a worksheet function, TREND, that performs this computation for you and produces the six values. You enter the trend formula as shown in the following illustration.

	A	B	C	D	E	F	G
1		Jan	Feb	Mar	Apr	May	Jun
2	Actual Sales	$3,100	$4,500	$4,400	$5,400	$7,500	$8,100
3	Trend of Sales	$3,000	$4,000	$5,000	$6,000	$7,000	$8,000
4							
5							

The array formula {TREND(B2:G2)} is entered in the array range B3:G3.

The Microsoft Excel functions that work with arrays are included in the following table.

Function name	Array usage
COLUMN	Returns an array when the argument is a range
COLUMNS	Requires an array or cell range as an argument
GROWTH	Requires arrays or cell ranges as arguments and can return an array
HLOOKUP	Requires an array or cell range as an argument
INDEX (array form)	Requires an array as an argument and can return an array
LINEST	Always returns an array
LOGEST	Always returns an array
LOOKUP (array form)	Requires an array or cell range as an argument
MATCH	Requires an array or cell range as an argument
MDETERM	Requires an array as an argument
MINVERSE	Always returns an array
MMULT	Always returns an array
ROW	Returns an array when the argument is a range
ROWS	Requires an array or cell range as an argument
SUMPRODUCT	Requires arrays, cell ranges, or values as arguments
TRANSPOSE	Always returns an array
TREND	Requires arrays or cell ranges as arguments and can return an array
VLOOKUP	Requires an array or cell range as an argument

There are also other functions that can take either single-value arguments or array arguments. These functions return different results when used with array arguments. For more information about functions, click the Function Wizard button on the Standard toolbar or see online Help.

Caution Before you enter a function on a worksheet, you need to know what the function returns. For example, the MINVERSE (matrix inverse) function returns an array the same size as its argument. Another function, TRANSPOSE, returns an array with the opposite dimensions of its argument. Make sure you allow space on your worksheet for the resulting array.

For more information about using functions, see "Worksheet Functions Simplify Formulas" and "Using the Function Wizard" earlier in this chapter.

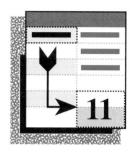

CHAPTER 11

Editing a Worksheet

For command, keyboard, and toolbar button information, see online Help.

In This Chapter

Note You can edit multiple worksheets in a workbook simultaneously by making them part of a group selection. For more information, see "Selecting Sheets in a Workbook" in Chapter 8.

Editing Within a Cell

You can edit a cell on your worksheet by typing a new entry over an existing one or by editing part of the information within the cell. To edit within a cell, double-click the cell. When you edit a cell containing a formula, the formula is displayed and the value is hidden.

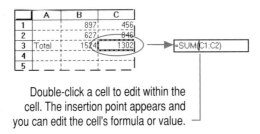

Double-click a cell to edit within the cell. The insertion point appears and you can edit the cell's formula or value.

You can also edit cell contents in the formula bar. You use the same techniques to edit within a cell and in the formula bar. For information about the formula bar, see "Use Formulas to Analyze Your Data" in Chapter 10.

Note If you prefer to edit only in the formula bar, choose the Options command from the Tools menu, select the Edit tab, and then clear the Edit Directly In Cell check box.

Moving and Selecting Within a Cell

To	Do this
Position the insertion point in the cell	Point and double-click
Select characters in the cell	Drag through the characters you want to select
Select a word in the cell	Double-click the word you want

Editing Cell Contents

To edit cell contents, choose commands from the Edit menu or the shortcut menu, or use the Cut, Copy, and Paste buttons.

Cut

- **Cut**   Removes the selected characters from the cell and places them on the Clipboard.

Copy

- **Copy**   Makes a copy of the selected characters and places them on the Clipboard.

Paste

- **Paste**   Places the contents of the Clipboard in a cell at the insertion point.
- **Clear**   Clears the selected characters from the cell. The characters are not stored on the Clipboard. You can also press the DEL key to clear selected characters.

In addition to pasting the contents of the Clipboard at the insertion point in a cell, you can paste them into a blank cell, into a formula in another cell, or in place of selected text.

Note   You can undo or repeat most editing actions and commands by clicking the Undo or Repeat toolbar button immediately after performing an action or choosing a command.

Step By Step

For step-by-step instructions and related information, double-click the 🅺 button to display the Search dialog box in Help, and then:

Type this keyword and choose Show Topics	Select a topic and choose Go To
cell contents, copying	Copying or moving characters within a cell
cell contents, editing	Editing cell contents
shortcut keys	Keys for Working in Cells or the Formula bar

Copying and Moving Cells

You can change the location of cells on a worksheet by copying or moving cells to a different part of the same worksheet, to another worksheet within a workbook, or to another application.

There are two ways to copy and move cells:

- By using Cut, Copy, and Paste
- By dragging with the mouse

What Happens When You Copy or Move Cells?

When you copy a cell, you duplicate the cell contents and paste it into a new location. When you move cells, you remove the cell contents and paste them into a new location. You can insert the cells you are copying or moving between existing cells, or you can paste cells over existing cells. When you paste cells over existing cells, you overwrite the existing cell contents.

When you copy cells, references in the original cells are not affected. Microsoft Excel adjusts relative references of formulas that are pasted into a new location.

When you move cells, Microsoft Excel adjusts relative references to the moved cells to reflect their new locations.

For more information about how copying and moving affect formulas and references, see "Moving and Copying Formulas and References" in Chapter 10.

Copying and Moving Cells with Cut, Copy, and Paste

Use the Cut, Copy, and Paste commands, toolbar buttons, or shortcut keys if you are copying or moving cells long distances within a large worksheet, to a different worksheet within a workbook, or to another window or application.

Copying Cells

When you copy cells, they are duplicated in another location.

Select the cells you want to copy and choose the Copy command from the Edit menu or shortcut menu. The copy area is marked with a moving border.

Select a destination cell.

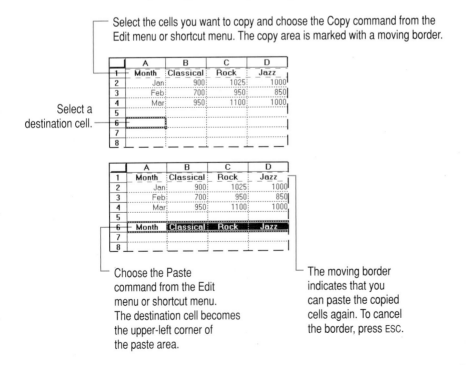

Choose the Paste command from the Edit menu or shortcut menu. The destination cell becomes the upper-left corner of the paste area.

The moving border indicates that you can paste the copied cells again. To cancel the border, press ESC.

Moving Cells

When you move cells, they are cut and transferred to another location.

Select the cells you want to move and choose the Cut command from the Edit menu or shortcut menu. The cut area is marked with a moving border.

	A	B	C	D
1	Month	Classical	Rock	Jazz
2	Jan	900	1025	1000
3	Feb	700	950	850
4	Mar	950	1100	1000
5				
6	Totals	2550	3075	2850
7				
8				
9				
10				

Select a destination cell.

	A	B	C	D
1	Month	Classical	Rock	Jazz
2	Jan	900	1025	1000
3	Feb	700	950	850
4	Mar	950	1100	1000
5				
6				
7				
8	Totals	2550	3075	2850
9				
10				

Choose the Paste command from the Edit menu or shortcut menu. The destination cell becomes the upper-left corner of the paste area.

The cut area is cleared.

In addition to using menu commands to copy and move cells, you can use the toolbar buttons and shortcut keys.

To	Click this button	Or press these keys
Cut		CTRL+X (Windows) COMMAND+X (Macintosh)
Copy		CTRL+C (Windows) COMMAND+C (Macintosh)
Paste		CTRL+V or ENTER (Windows) COMMAND+V (Macintosh)

Tip When pasting, select only the cell that you want to become the upper-left corner of the paste area.

Inserting Cells Between Existing Cells

To insert copied or cut cells between existing cells, copy or cut the cells you want, select a destination cell, and then choose the Copied Cells or Cut Cells command from the Insert menu or the Insert Cut Cells or Insert Copied Cells command from the shortcut menu.

Note You can insert cells only once after each copy. To insert cells again, repeat the procedure.

Pasting Multiple Copies

You can paste copied cells in many areas of the worksheet by selecting the upper-left cell of the paste area, pasting the cells, and repeating these steps to make multiple copies.

You can also paste multiple copies of a cell or range on a worksheet using one paste operation.

The copy area is marked
with a moving border.

	A	B	C	D
1	Month	Classical	Rock	Jazz
2	Jan	900	1025	1000
3	Feb	700	950	850
4	Mar	950	1100	1000
5				
6	Month	Classical	Rock	Jazz
7				
8				
9				
10				
11	Month	Classical	Rock	Jazz
12				
13				

The paste area contains
nonadjacent selections.

To paste multiple copies in nonadjacent areas on your worksheet, copy a selection, select the upper-left cells of the paste areas, and paste the copied cells.

System	To make nonadjacent selections, hold down this key as you make additional selections
Windows	CTRL
Macintosh	COMMAND

Copying and Moving Cells by Dragging

Using the mouse is a quick way to copy and move cells a short distance on a worksheet.

Note If you are unable to use the mouse to copy and move, you need to select the Cell Drag And Drop option. To select this option, choose the Options command from the Tools menu, select the Edit tab, and then select the Allow Cell Drag And Drop check box.

Copying Cells by Dragging

Position the mouse pointer over the border of a selection. Hold down CTRL (Windows) or OPTION (Macintosh) and drag the border to a new location.

	A	B	C	D
1	Month	Classical	Rock	Jazz
2	Jan	900	1025	1000
3	Feb	700	950	850
4	Mar	950	1100	1000
5				
6				
7				
8				

	A	B	C	D
1	Month	Classical	Rock	Jazz
2	Jan	900	1025	1000
3	Feb	700	950	850
4	Mar	950	1100	1000
5				
6	Month	Classical	Rock	Jazz
7				
8				

Release the mouse button, and then the key. The cell contents are copied to their new location.

When you copy over cells that contain data, the old cells are replaced with the copied cells.

Moving Cells by Dragging

Position the mouse pointer
over the border of a selection and
drag the border to a new location.

	A	B	C	D
1	Month	Classical	Rock	Jazz
2	Jan	900	1025	1000
3	Feb	700	950	850
4	Mar	950	1100	1000
5				
6	Totals	2550	3075	2850
7				
8				
9				
10				

	A	B	C	D
1	Month	Classical	Rock	Jazz
2	Jan	900	1025	1000
3	Feb	700	950	850
4	Mar	950	1100	1000
5				
6				
7				
8	Totals	2550	3075	2850
9				
10				

When you release the mouse button
the cells are moved to their new location.

When you move over cells that contain data, the old cells are replaced with the moved cells.

Inserting Cells by Dragging

Position the mouse pointer over the border of the selection. Hold down SHIFT and drag the border to a new location.

	A	B	C	D	E
1	Month	Classical	Rock	Jazz	Folk
2	Jan	900	1025	1000	500
3	Feb	700	950	850	450
4	Mar	950	1100	1000	400
5					
6	Totals	2550	3075	2850	1350
7					
8					

	A	B	C	D	E
1	Month	Rock	Classical	Jazz	Folk
2	Jan	1025	900	1000	500
3	Feb	950	700	850	450
4	Mar	1100	950	1000	400
5					
6	Totals	3075	2550	2850	1350
7					
8					

Release the mouse button, and then the key. The cells are moved and inserted between existing cells.

System	To insert copies of cells, press these keys and then drag the border
Windows	CTRL+SHIFT
Macintosh	OPTION+SHIFT

Using the Shortcut Menu When Dragging

Position the mouse pointer over the border of a selection. In Windows, hold down the right mouse button and drag the border. On the Macintosh, hold down CTRL and drag the border.

	A	B	C	D	E	F
1	Month	Classical	Rock	Jazz	Folk	Total Sales
2	Jan	900	1025	1000	500	3425
3	Feb	700	950	850	450	2950
4	Mar	950	1100	1000	400	3450
5						
6	Totals	2550	307			9825
7						
8						
9						
10						
11						
12						
13						

Copy
Move
Copy Formats
Copy Values
Shift Down and Copy
Shift Right and Copy
Shift Down and Move
Shift Right and Move

When you release the mouse button, a shortcut menu with a variety of copying and moving commands is displayed.

Copying to Adjacent Cells by Dragging

Make a selection and then position the mouse pointer over the fill handle. The pointer changes to a black cross.

Drag the fill handle in the direction you want to copy.

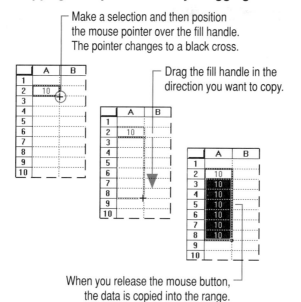

When you release the mouse button, the data is copied into the range.

Note If Microsoft Excel finds a series in your initial selection, it extends that series in the direction you drag the fill handle. For more information, see "Filling Adjacent Cells and Creating Series" in Chapter 9.

Step By Step

For step-by-step instructions and related information, double-click the [?] button to display the Search dialog box in Help, and then:

Type this keyword and choose Show Topics	Select a topic and choose Go To
copying, cells	Copying and moving with the shortcut menu
	Copying cells
	Inserting cut or copied cells
cells, moving	Moving cells
pasting multiple copies	Pasting multiple copies

Copying and Pasting Cells for Special Results

After you have copied cells using the Copy command, toolbar button, or shortcut keys, you can choose the Paste Special command from the Edit menu to select several options for pasting the copied cells. The Paste Special command is not available when pasting cut cells.

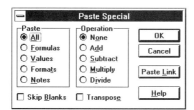

You can perform the following operations using the Paste Special dialog box:

- Paste only a cell's formula, value, format, or note by selecting an option button under Paste.

- Combine the contents of the copy and paste areas by selecting the Formulas or Values option button under Paste and then, under Operation, selecting the operation you want to use to combine each copied cell and its paste area. If you select the Subtract option button, the copied formula or value will be subtracted from the paste area formula or value.

  For example, if you want to increase a range of numbers by a certain percentage, you would multiply the value of a single cell containing the percentage and paste it to a range.

- Transpose the copied rows and columns in the paste area by selecting the paste area and then selecting the Transpose check box. For example, if the data in the copy area is arranged in columns, the data will be pasted in rows.

- Avoid overwriting the destination cell when the copy area is a blank cell by selecting the Skip Blanks check box.

Format Painter

Tips Use the Format Painter button to copy only the cell formats of the cells you have selected. If you double-click the button, you can do multiple pastes until you click the button again.

A quick way to copy only formats or values with the mouse is to use the shortcut menu while dragging. For more information, see "Copying and Moving Cells by Dragging" earlier in this chapter.

When copying charts, the Paste Special dialog box includes different options. When copying graphic objects, you have the choice of copying or moving either the graphic object or a picture of the object.

You can copy data and create a link as you paste. For more information, see "Linking Microsoft Excel Workbooks" in Chapter 10. When you are working with other applications, you can link pasted data to its source document. For more information, see Chapter 41, "Sharing Data and Graphics with Other Applications."

Step By Step

For step-by-step instructions and related information, double-click the [k?] button to display the Search dialog box in Help, and then:

Type this keyword and choose Show Topics	Select a topic and choose Go To
copying, cells	Copying cells
copying, formats	Copying only the cell format
copying, formulas	Copying only the cell formula
copying, nonblank cells	Copying only visible or nonblank cells
copying, using shortcut menu	Copying and moving with the shortcut menu
copying, values	Copying only the cell value
pasting combined values, formulas	Calculating as you paste
pasting multiple copies	Pasting multiple copies
transposing	Transposing rows and columns as you paste

Inserting, Deleting, and Clearing Cells, Rows, and Columns

You can insert, delete, or clear cells, rows, or columns to change the structure of data on a worksheet.

You can insert blank cells or entire blank rows and columns anywhere on a worksheet. When you insert cells, the other cells on the worksheet are shifted to make room for the new cells. When you delete cells, the surrounding cells shift to fill in the space. When you clear cells, only the cell contents are removed; the empty cells remain.

For information about inserting data between existing cells, see "Copying and Moving Cells" earlier in this chapter.

Inserting Rows or Columns

When you insert a row or column, Microsoft Excel creates a new blank row or column and shifts the existing rows and columns to make room for the inserted cells. Microsoft Excel adjusts references to the shifted cells to reflect their new locations.

Select the number of rows you want to shift to open space for new rows.

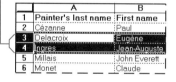

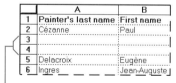

When you choose the Rows command from the Insert menu, new blank rows are inserted above the selection.

You can also choose the Insert command from the shortcut menu to insert rows.

Follow the same steps to insert columns. Select the number of columns you want to shift to open space for new columns, and then choose the Columns command from the Insert menu or the Insert command from the shortcut menu. When you insert columns, the new blank columns are placed to the left of the selected columns.

Inserting Blank Cells

Select a range of cells the same
size as the new cells you want to insert.

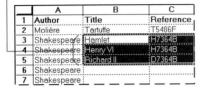

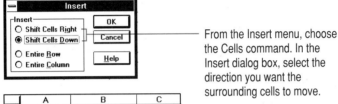

From the Insert menu, choose
the Cells command. In the
Insert dialog box, select the
direction you want the
surrounding cells to move.

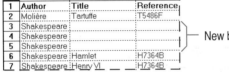

New blank cells are inserted.

You can also choose the Insert command from the shortcut menu to insert blank
cells.

Deleting Cells vs. Clearing Cells

When you delete cells, they are removed from the worksheet and the surrounding
cells shift to fill in the space.

When you clear cells, you clear the contents, formats, or notes but leave the cells on
the worksheet.

Deleting and clearing cells produce different results for formulas that reference
those cells. If a cell's contents are cleared, its value is zero; a formula referring to
that cell will get a value of zero from that cell. If a cell is deleted, it no longer
exists; a formula referring to the deleted cell will not be able to find it and will
return the #REF! error value.

Deleting Cells

When you delete cells, the cells are removed and the surrounding cells shift to fill in the space.

Select the range of cells you want to delete.

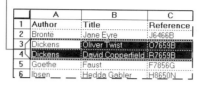

	A	B	C
1	Author	Title	Reference
2	Brontë	Jane Eyre	J6466B
3	Dickens	Oliver Twist	O7659B
4	Dickens	David Copperfield	R7659B
5	Goethe	Faust	F7856G
6	Ibsen	Hedda Gabler	H8650N

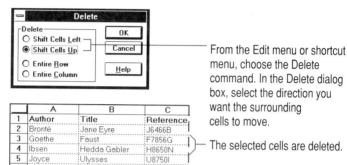

From the Edit menu or shortcut menu, choose the Delete command. In the Delete dialog box, select the direction you want the surrounding cells to move.

	A	B	C
1	Author	Title	Reference
2	Brontë	Jane Eyre	J6466B
3	Goethe	Faust	F7856G
4	Ibsen	Hedda Gabler	H8650N
5	Joyce	Ulysses	U8750I
6	Molière	Tartuffe	T5486F

The selected cells are deleted.

Clearing Cells

When you clear cells, you remove the cell contents, but the cells remain on the worksheet.

Select the cells you want to clear.

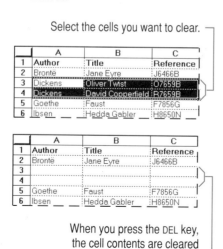

	A	B	C
1	Author	Title	Reference
2	Brontë	Jane Eyre	J6466B
3	Dickens	Oliver Twist	O7659B
4	Dickens	David Copperfield	R7659B
5	Goethe	Faust	F7856G
6	Ibsen	Hedda Gabler	H8650N

	A	B	C
1	Author	Title	Reference
2	Brontë	Jane Eyre	J6466B
3			
4			
5	Goethe	Faust	F7856G
6	Ibsen	Hedda Gabler	H8650N

When you press the DEL key, the cell contents are cleared and the cells remain.

You can also clear cells by selecting them, choosing the Clear command from the Edit menu or the shortcut menu, and then selecting All, Contents, Formats, or Notes. Clearing the contents clears any formulas or data from a cell.

Step By Step

For step-by-step instructions and related information, double-click the 　button to display the Search dialog box in Help, and then:

Type this keyword and choose Show Topics	Select a topic and choose Go To
blank cells	Inserting blank cells
cells, clearing	Clearing cells
cells, deleting	Deleting cells
cells, inserting	Inserting cut or copied cells
columns, inserting	Inserting rows and columns
rows, clearing	Clearing rows and columns
rows, deleting	Deleting rows and columns
transposing	Transposing rows and columns as you paste

Finding and Replacing Text, Numbers, or Cells

You can find cells that contain specific characters on a worksheet by choosing the Find command from the Edit menu. To find and replace sequences of characters in cells, choose the Replace command from the Edit menu. These commands can be used on all sheets except Visual Basic modules.

Tip To find and replace characters on more than one sheet in a workbook, select a group of sheets and then choose the Replace command from the Edit menu. To find and replace data on all worksheets in a workbook, choose the Select All Sheets command from the sheet tab shortcut menu. Then choose the Replace command from the Edit menu.

For information about finding and viewing a subset of data in a Microsoft Excel database or list, see "How Sorting and Filtering Work" in Chapter 21.

Finding Variations on a Sequence of Characters

Use the question mark (?) and asterisk (*) in the Find What box in the Find and Replace dialog boxes to find variations on a sequence of characters. The question mark (?) represents any single character in the same position as the question mark. The asterisk (*) represents any number of characters in that same position. Precede asterisks and question marks with a tilde (~) to find actual asterisks and question marks.

Finding Cells with Specific Types of Contents

You can use the Go To Special dialog box to find and select cells with specific types of contents, such as constant values, formulas, notes, or blanks.

To find and select cells with specific types of contents, choose the Go To command from the Edit menu, choose the Special button, and then select the option you want.

System	Press these keys to move through selected cells	Press these keys to move between areas of a nonadjacent selection
Windows	TAB and SHIFT+TAB	CTRL+ALT+RIGHT ARROW and CTRL+ALT+LEFT ARROW
Macintosh	TAB and SHIFT+TAB	CTRL+OPTION+RIGHT ARROW and CTRL+OPTION +LEFT ARROW

For more information about finding and selecting special cells, such as cells that refer to other cells or cells that differ from the contents of another cell, see Chapter 38, "Troubleshooting and Annotating a Worksheet."

Step By Step

For step-by-step instructions and related information, double-click the ⬚ button to display the Search dialog box in Help, and then:

Type this keyword and choose Show Topics	Select a topic and choose Go To
finding, cells	Selecting cells with common types of contents
finding, numbers	Finding text or numbers
replacing	Finding and replacing text or numbers

Checking Spelling

Spelling

You can correct the spelling of worksheets and charts using the Spelling command on the Tools menu or the Spelling button. When you spell check an entire sheet, all items on the sheet, including text in charts, text boxes, buttons, headers and footers, and cell notes, are spell checked.

To check the spelling of	Select this and click the Spelling button
A cell	The contents of the cell
A range of cells	A range of cells
An entire worksheet	A single cell
A chart	The chart (an embedded chart or a separate chart sheet)

Tip To check the spelling of all sheets in a workbook, choose the Select All Sheets command from the sheet tab shortcut menu, and then click the Spelling button.

Creating a Custom Dictionary

If you frequently use specialized terms such as names, acronyms, and abbreviations, you can add them to a custom dictionary so that they won't be questioned during spelling checks. You can create multiple custom dictionaries, but you can only use one at a time.

To create a custom dictionary, choose the Spelling command from the Tools menu, type a name for the new dictionary in the Add Words To box, and then choose the Add button.

Step By Step

For step-by-step instructions and related information, double-click the [?] button to display the Search dialog box in Help, and then:

Type this keyword and choose Show Topics	Select a topic and choose Go To
dictionaries, custom	Creating a custom dictionary
spelling checking	Checking spelling
	Checking spelling in a chart

C H A P T E R   1 2

Formatting a Worksheet

For command, keyboard, and toolbar button information, see online Help.

In This Chapter

Note You can format multiple worksheets in a workbook simultaneously by making them part of a group selection. For more information, see "Selecting Sheets in a Workbook" in Chapter 8.

Format Your Data for the Look You Want

Use the many formatting options in Microsoft Excel to add emphasis to your data, or to make your worksheets easier to read and more visually appealing.

You can format worksheet cells before or after you enter your data. For example, you can enter data into a range of cells and then format the range to be bold. Or, if you apply the bold format to the range of cells, any data you enter in those cells will be bold as you enter it.

A cell's formats are separate from the data contained in the cell. Cell formats can be copied between cells, and changed or cleared separately from the data contained in the cells.

Formatting Examples

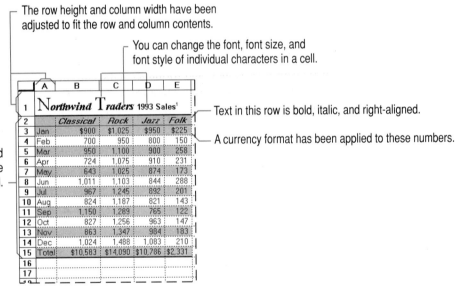

The row height and column width have been adjusted to fit the row and column contents.

You can change the font, font size, and font style of individual characters in a cell.

Text in this row is bold, italic, and right-aligned.

A currency format has been applied to these numbers.

Pattern, color, and border formats make the list easy to read.

	A	B	C	D	E
1	Northwind Traders 1993 Sales[1]				
2		Classical	Rock	Jazz	Folk
3	Jan	$900	$1,025	$950	$225
4	Feb	700	950	800	150
5	Mar	950	1,100	900	258
6	Apr	724	1,075	910	231
7	May	643	1,025	874	173
8	Jun	1,011	1,103	844	288
9	Jul	967	1,245	892	201
10	Aug	824	1,187	821	143
11	Sep	1,150	1,289	765	122
12	Oct	827	1,256	963	147
13	Nov	863	1,347	984	183
14	Dec	1,024	1,488	1,083	210
15	Total	$10,583	$14,090	$10,786	$2,331
16					
17					

Applying Formats

Apply cell formats by choosing the Cells command from the Format menu, or the Format Cells command from the shortcut menu. The most frequently used formats are also available as buttons on the Formatting toolbar, shown in the following illustration.

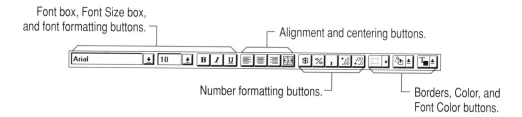

Font box, Font Size box, and font formatting buttons.

Alignment and centering buttons.

Number formatting buttons.

Borders, Color, and Font Color buttons.

Autoformats and styles make it easy to apply combinations of formats.

- **Autoformats** Apply combinations of built-in formats to ranges of data with the AutoFormat command on the Format menu. The AutoFormat command recognizes text, values, and formulas in the current range, and applies formats accordingly. For more information, see "Applying Formats Automatically" later in this chapter.

- **Styles** Use styles to save combinations of cell formats and apply them to other cells and ranges. When you change the formats for a cell style, all cells using that style are updated to reflect the change. For more information, see "Using Styles to Save and Apply Format Combinations" later in this chapter.

Copying Formats

Format Painter

You can use the Format Painter button to quickly copy formats from a cell and apply that cell's formats to another cell or range of cells. Click the cell containing the formats you want to copy, and then click the Format Painter button and drag through the range where you want to apply the formats. For more information, see "Copying Formats Quickly" later in this chapter.

Changing Column Widths and Row Heights

You can adjust both the column width and the row height as needed. Rows automatically adjust to accommodate wrapped text or the largest font entered into the row.

In a new worksheet all the columns are set to the standard width. You can change the standard width setting to adjust all columns on the sheet, or you can adjust only the columns you want to change.

Adjusting Column Width

	A	B	C	D
1		Animal Food Consumption		
2		Average Weight (Kg)	Average daily food consumption (Kg)	Daily food consumption (% of body weight)
3	Wolf	44	9	20%
4	Camel	465	3.6	1%
5	Horse	475	6.4	1%
6	Lion	169.5	34	20%
7	Elephan	5,400	140	3%
8	Human	69	1.5	2%
9	Hummin	0.02	0.04	200%
10				
11				

Adjust column width by dragging or double-clicking the right column heading border.

	A	B	C	D
1		Animal Food Consumption		
2		Average Weight (Kg)	Average daily food consumption (Kg)	Daily food consumption (% of body weight)
3	Wolf	44	9	20%
4	Camel	465	3.6	1%
5	Horse	475	6.4	1%
6	Lion	169.5	34	20%
7	Elephant	5,400	140	3%
8	Human	69	1.5	2%
9	Hummingbird	0.02	0.04	200%
10				
11				

When you double-click, the column adjusts to fit the longest entry.

You can adjust several columns at once by first selecting columns and then adjusting the width on any one of the selected columns.

Note If the pointer changes to a split double arrow, dragging will unhide hidden columns. To avoid this, keep the pointer directly over the right column border. For more information about hidden columns, see "Hiding and Unhiding Rows and Columns" in Chapter 32.

You can also choose the Column command from the Format menu, and then choose a command to:

- Set a numeric column width (Width command)
- Adjust the column to automatically fit the longest entry (AutoFit Selection command)
- Hide or unhide columns (Hide or Unhide command)
- Set the selected column to the standard width, or change the standard column width for the worksheet (Standard Width command)

With a column selected, you can also use commands on the shortcut menu to adjust column widths.

Adjusting Row Height

Adjust row height by dragging the bottom border of the row heading.

When you double-click the bottom border of a row heading, the row height adjusts to fit the tallest entry in the row. You can adjust several rows at once by first selecting rows and then adjusting the height on any one of the selected rows.

The row has been widened.

Note If the pointer changes to a split double arrow, dragging will unhide hidden rows. To avoid this, keep the pointer directly over the bottom row border. For more information about unhiding rows, see "Hiding and Unhiding Rows and Columns" in Chapter 32.

You can also choose the Row command from the Format menu, and then choose a command to:

- Set a numeric row height (Height command)
- Automatically fit the row to the largest font in the row (AutoFit command)
- Hide or unhide rows (Hide or Unhide command)

When you have a row selected, you can also use the commands on the shortcut menu to adjust row height.

Step By Step

For step-by-step instructions and related information, double-click the ?? button to display the Search dialog box in Help, and then:

Type this keyword and choose Show Topics	Select a topic and choose Go To
column width	Adjusting column width
row height	Adjusting row height
rows, hiding and unhiding	Hiding and unhiding a row or column

Aligning Worksheet Data

Select the alignment you want for the numbers or characters in worksheet cells.

The following illustration shows examples of cell alignments.

Centered across columns
and centered vertically

Centered —

Oriented sideways

	A	B	C	D	E
1			FY 1993		
2	Region	Q1	Q2	Q3	Q4
3	Pennsylvania	97.5	103.5	98.5	93.5
4	New York	53.9	59.9	54.9	49.9
5	New Jersey	71.3	77.3	72.3	67.3
6	Connecticut	52.1	58.1	53.1	48.1
7	Ohio	66.5	72.5	67.5	62.5
8	West Virginia	64.5	70.5	65.5	60.5
9					
10					

Left-aligned

Right-aligned

Unless you change the alignment, all cells initially have the General format, which automatically aligns numbers to the right, text to the left, and logical and error values centered.

The easiest way to align the contents of cells is to use the buttons on the Formatting toolbar.

Center Align button

Left Align button —

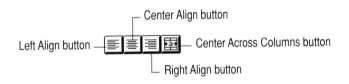

Center Across Columns button

Right Align button

To center a cell's contents across a selection of blank cells, select the cell containing the data as the leftmost cell, and then extend the selection to include adjacent blank cells to the right. Click the Center Across Columns button, and the contents of the leftmost cell are displayed centered across the selection of blank cells. The cell contents remain in the leftmost cell.

For alignments other than left, right, centered, and centered across columns, use the Cells command on the Format menu, or the Format Cells command on the shortcut menu. Select the Alignment tab, and then choose the alignment options you want.

Wrapping and Justifying Text in Cells

Text can be aligned to the left, right, or centered just like other data. You can also *wrap* text in a cell so that lines of text are broken and stacked to fit within the current column width. When you wrap text, the row height adjusts automatically. You can also *justify* text so that it is aligned both left and right within the cell.

- **Wrapping Text**   To wrap text within a cell, adjust the column to the width you want, select the cells that contain the text you want to wrap, and choose the Cells command from the Format menu. Then, select the Alignment tab, and select the Wrap Text check box.

- **Justifying Text**   To justify text, select the Justify option button on the Alignment tab. This option automatically wraps the text. You must have more than one line of wrapped text to see the justification.

Tip If you adjust the column width after wrapping or justifying text you can quickly readjust the row height by double-clicking on the bottom border of the row heading.

Text can also be entered into text boxes and then manipulated as a graphic object. For more information about text boxes, see "Text Boxes" in Chapter 13.

Step By Step

For step-by-step instructions and related information, double-click the ⓚ button to display the Search dialog box in Help, and then:

Type this keyword and choose Show Topics	Select a topic and choose Go To
cell contents, alignment	Aligning data within cells
	Justifying text in cells
centering	Centering cell entries across columns
wrapping text	Wrapping text in cells

Formatting Fonts

You can format the font characteristics of cells to change the appearance of data entered into the cells.

	A	B	C	D	E	F
1	Blue Sky Airlines					
2	1993 Sales Summary					
3		Qtr 1	Qtr 2	Qtr 3	Qtr 4	Total
4	Europe	40	49	64	57	210
5	S. America	41	34	32	38	145
6	Far East	47	58	54	50	209
7	Total	128	141	150	145	564
8						
9						

These cells use bold formatting.

These cells are formatted with a different font.

In cells containing text, you can also apply different font formats to individual characters or words.

To format individual characters in a cell, select the characters...

...and then click formatting buttons, or choose the Cells command from the Format menu.

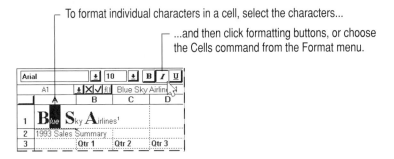

Applying Font Formats to Cells

You can apply font formats to cells and ranges of cells so that all of the characters within the cell—whether they are text, values, or formulas—have the same font characteristics. Select the cell or range you want to format and use the Font and Font Size boxes, and the Bold, Italic, and Underline buttons on the Formatting toolbar to change font formats. You can also choose the Cells command from the Format menu, or the Format Cells command from the shortcut menu, select the Font tab, and then select the format options you want.

Formatting Characters Within a Cell

In cells containing text, individual characters can use different font formats. In cells containing formulas and values, all characters use the same font formats.

To format characters within a cell, double-click the cell, or click in the formula bar, and select characters, whole words, or groups of words. Then use buttons on the Formatting toolbar to format selected characters. You can also choose the Cells command from the Format menu, and then select the format options you want. For information about moving, selecting, and editing in cells, see "Editing Within a Cell" in Chapter 11.

Copying the Formatting of Cells with Individual Cell Formatting When copying the formats of a cell to another cell with the Format Painter button or the Paste Special command on the Edit menu, the formatting of the first character in the copied cell is pasted into the destination cells.

Step By Step

For step-by-step instructions and related information, double-click the [▶?] button to display the Search dialog box in Help, and then:

Type this keyword and choose Show Topics	Select a topic and choose Go To
cell contents, editing	Editing cell contents
cell contents, formatting	Changing the font, size, and color of characters
cell contents, underlining	Underlining cell contents
cell contents, wrapping	Wrapping text in cells
superscripts	Using superscripts and subscripts

Adding Borders, Patterns, and Colors

Microsoft Excel offers a wide variety of border types and widths, patterns, and colors that you can use to create more attractive and effective worksheets.

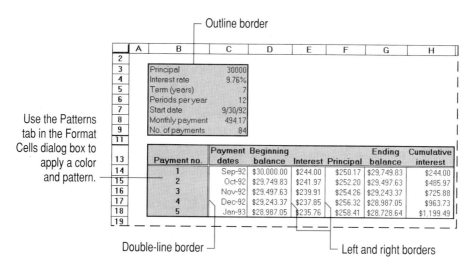

Use the Patterns tab in the Format Cells dialog box to apply a color and pattern.

Outline border

Double-line border

Left and right borders

To apply borders, patterns, or colors, select the cells you want to change and then use the buttons in the following list.

Button	Name	Location
	Borders button	Formatting toolbar
	Color button	Formatting toolbar
	Pattern button	Drawing toolbar

You can also choose the Cells command from the Format menu, or the Format Cells command from the shortcut menu. Then select the options you want on the Border or Patterns tab.

Note Adjoining cells appear to share borders. For example, putting a bottom border on one cell produces the same effect as putting a top border on the cell below it. The border does not appear, however, when you print just the cell below. When you print a sheet, borders are printed for a cell only if they are actually applied to that cell.

Hiding and Printing Gridlines

By hiding gridlines on a sheet, you can make formats such as borders, double underlining and shading stand out. To hide gridlines when you display or print a sheet, choose Options from the Tools menu, then select the View tab and clear the Gridlines check box. To prevent gridlines from printing only when you print a sheet, choose Page Setup from the File menu and clear the Gridlines check box on the Sheet tab.

Step By Step

For step-by-step instructions and related information, double-click the ⟨↖?⟩ button to display the Search dialog box in Help, and then:

Type this keyword and choose Show Topics	Select a topic and choose Go To
borders	Adding borders
cells, shading	Shading cells with patterns and colors
colors	Customizing colors in a color palette

Applying Number Formats

The default number format for all cells on a new worksheet is the General format. In the General format, Microsoft Excel displays numbers as integers (789), decimal fractions (7.89), or scientific notation (7.89E+08) if the number is longer than the width of the cell. The General format displays up to 11 digits.

When you type data into a cell that has the General format, Microsoft Excel checks whether one of the other built-in number formats would be appropriate for the data and, if so, assigns another built-in format based on what you type. For example, when you enter a number that starts with a dollar sign or ends with a percent sign, Microsoft Excel changes the cell's number format from General to a currency format or a percentage format, respectively.

At any time, you can change the number format of a cell to another of the built-in formats, or you can create your own custom number format and apply it.

Using the Toolbar Buttons to Apply Number Formats

You can use the buttons on the Formatting toolbar to apply number formats.

To	Click	Sample of format
Apply the Currency style	$	12345 becomes $12,345.00
Apply the Percent style	%	.12 becomes 12%
Apply the Comma style	,	12345 becomes 12,345.00
Increase decimal places	+.0 .00	12,345.00 becomes 12,345.000
Decrease decimal places	.00 +.0	12,345.00 becomes 12,345.0

Applying the Currency, Percent, or Comma style automatically applies the number format currently defined for that style. For information about redefining a style, see "Using Styles to Save and Apply Format Combinations" later in this chapter.

Applying Number Formats from the Number Tab

To change the number format of a cell to another built-in number format, choose the Cells command from the Format menu, or the Format Cells command from the shortcut menu, and then select the Number tab.

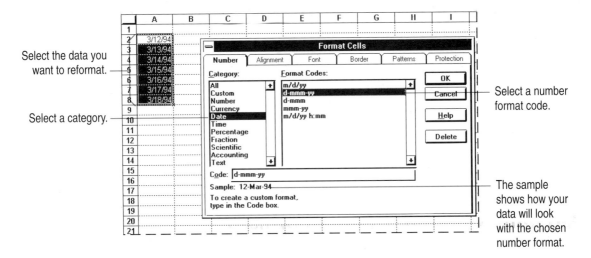

Select the data you want to reformat.

Select a category.

Select a number format code.

The sample shows how your data will look with the chosen number format.

Note   To see a sample on the Number tab, be sure the active cell on your worksheet contains some relevant data.

You may want to format numbers as text. For example, you may want to enter 1-2, but you don't want Microsoft Excel to interpret it as a date, 2-Jan. First, format the cells using the @ number code in the Text category on the Number tab. Then enter your data. You can also enter a number as text by preceding it with an apostrophe.

For a detailed description of the number format codes, see "Number Format Codes" later in this chapter.

Applying the Accounting Number Formats

Microsoft Excel comes with four built-in accounting formats. The accounting formats keep the dollar sign to the left of the cell, show negative values in parentheses, and show zero values as hyphens.

The accounting formats can be used with the Single Accounting and Double Accounting underlining. To use underlining, choose the Cells command from the Format menu and select the Font tab. Then select Single Accounting or Double Accounting from the Underline box.

Step By Step

For step-by-step instructions and related information, double-click the [?] button to display the Search dialog box in Help, and then:

Type this keyword and choose Show Topics	Select a topic and choose Go To
assigning formats	Assigning a number, date, or time format
cells, entering data in	Entering numbers in cells
dates	Entering a date or a time
number formats, applying using buttons	Formatting numbers with toolbar buttons
number formats, codes for	Number Format Codes
number formats, text	Formatting numbers as text
underlining	Underlining cell contents

Creating Custom Number Formats

You can create your own number formats for a workbook. When you create a number format, it is available on all sheets whenever you open the workbook. In a new workbook, only the built-in number formats are initially available.

Number Format Categories

Custom number formats are automatically stored in the appropriate category. If you create a new percentage number format, you will find it in the Percentage category on the Number tab in the Format Cells dialog box. You will also find it in the Custom category and at the bottom of the All category.

Number Format Codes Explained

Each format you create can have up to three number sections and a fourth section for text. The sections are separated by semicolons.

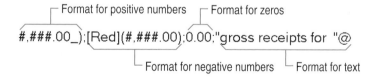

If you applied the number format shown in the preceding illustration to blank cells, your entries would look like this:

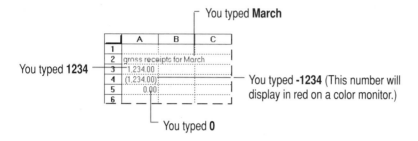

You typed **March**

You typed **1234**

You typed **-1234** (This number will display in red on a color monitor.)

You typed **0**

The number of sections you include determines the format for positive numbers, negative numbers, zeros, and text, in that order. If you include only two number sections, the first one is used for both positive numbers and zeros, and the second one for negative numbers. If you have only one number section, all numbers use that format.

Including a Text Section

A text format section, if included, is always the last section in the number format. Include within double quotation marks any text that you want to always be displayed. When you include the @ character, any text entered into the cell replaces the @ character. If the format does not have a text section, text you enter is not affected by the format.

If you have a text section, it changes how the number sections are applied. For example, if a format has three sections and the last section is a text format, Microsoft Excel applies the format of the first section if the number is positive or a zero, the second section if the number is negative, or the third section if the cell contains text.

How to Create a Custom Number Format

To create your own number format, Choose the Cells command from the Format menu, or the Format Cells command from the shortcut menu, and then select the Number tab. Select a built-in format and modify it in the Code box to create a new format. When you choose the OK button, the new number format is saved and will be applied to your selection. The next time you select the Number tab, your custom number format will appear in the appropriate categories.

Note   The built-in number formats always remain available, along with the custom formats you create. Modifying a built-in format to create a new custom format does not eliminate the built-in format.

Guidelines for Creating Number Formats

Follow these guidelines when creating new number formats:

- **Digit Placeholders**   Microsoft Excel uses the 0 and the # as digit placeholders. If you use the 0, then the digit is always displayed, even if it is a zero. The # suppresses the display of nonsignificant zeros.

- **Aligning Characters**   An underscore followed by any character creates a space the width of the character. For example, an underscore followed by a right parenthesis allows positive numbers to line up correctly with negative numbers that are enclosed in parentheses.

- **Setting Color**   To set the color for a section of the format, type the name of the color in square brackets in the section.

- **Displaying Commas**   To display commas, add them to your format. Commas not surrounded by digit placeholders can be used to scale numbers by thousands. For example the format   #,   would display the number 120000 as 120.

- **Preventing Display**   To prevent any of the number types — positive, negative, or zero — from being displayed, omit the code for the corresponding section. For example, the number format   0.00;–0.00;;"Error"   will prevent zeros from being displayed because the third section is blank.

Sample Custom Number Formats

The following table shows some examples of number formats you can create.

With this format	This number	Appears this way
#.##	1234.568	1234.57
	0.1	.1
#.0#	1234.568	1234.57
	12	12.0
X=0.0;X=−0.0	1234.568	X=1234.6
	−12.34	X=−12.3
#.00 "Cr";#,##.00 "Deb";0.0	1234.568	1234.57 Cr
	−12.34	−12.34 Deb
	0	0.0
#,	12,000	12
0.00,,	12,200,000	12.20

With this format	This number	Appears this way
$* #,##0.00;$* −#,##0.00	1234.568	$ 1,234.57
	−12.34	$ −12.34
000−00−0000	215527825	215−52−7825
"Acct. No." 0000	8978	Acct. No. 8978
"Done"	Any entry number or text	Done
;;;	Any entry number or text	Hides cell contents

For a detailed description of number format codes, see "Number Format Codes" later in this chapter.

Custom Time and Date Formats

Although Microsoft Excel provides several built-in time and date formats, you can create your own formats.

You can create time formats that allow for hours that are greater than 24, or minutes or seconds greater than 60. To do this, use square brackets around the first code letters in the time format. You can also create time codes that display fractions of a second.

Microsoft Excel stores all dates as serial numbers and all times as decimal fractions. Because dates and times are seen as numbers, they can be added, subtracted, and included in other calculations. You can view a formatted date or time as a serial number or decimal fraction by changing the cell's format to General.

Tip Always use a built-in format or create a custom format when using dates or times in calculations.

The following table shows some examples of time and date formats you can create.

With this format	This entry	Appears this way
mmmm d, yyyy	2/10/94	February 10, 1994
d mmmm yy	2/10/94	10 February 94
mmm d, yyyy	2/10/94	Feb 10, 1994
hh:mm AM/PM	13:45	01:45 PM
[h]:mm	25:02	25:02
[mm]:ss	1:03:46	63:46

For a detailed description of number format codes, see "Number Format Codes" later in this chapter.

Conditional Custom Number Formats

By enclosing a conditional value within square brackets, you can set your own criteria for the number format sections. For example, in the format

[>1000][BLUE]#,##0;[<–1000] [RED]#,##0;[GREEN]#,##0

the first section is the number format for entries greater than a thousand, the second section is for entries less than – 1000, and the third section is for all other entries not covered by the first and second sections. If you have a format with only two sections and a conditional value only in the first section, the second section formats all entries not formatted by the first section.

You can use any of the symbols <, >, =, >=, <=, and <>, combined with any number.

Step By Step

For step-by-step instructions and related information, double-click the [?] button to display the Search dialog box in Help, and then:

Type this keyword and choose Show Topics	Select a topic and choose Go To
cell contents, hiding	Hiding data in cells
currency formats	Creating international currency formats
custom number formats	Creating and deleting custom number formats
number formats, assigning	Assigning a number, date, or time format
number formats, codes for	Number Format Codes

Number Format Codes

Microsoft Excel uses these symbols in its built-in formats. You can use these symbols to create your own custom number formats.

Format Symbol	Meaning
General	Displays the number in General format.
#	Digit placeholder. If the number has more digits to the right of the decimal point than there are #'s to the right in the format, Microsoft Excel rounds the number to as many decimal places as there are #'s to the right. If the number has more digits to the left of the decimal point than there are #'s to the left in the format, Microsoft Excel displays the extra digits.

Format Symbol	Meaning
0 (zero)	Digit placeholder. Follows the same rules as the # placeholder, except that if the number has fewer digits than there are zeros in the format, Microsoft Excel displays the extra zeros. For example, if you want the number 8.9 to appear as 8.90, type **#.00** for the format.
?	Digit placeholder. Follows the same rules as for 0 preceding, except that Microsoft Excel places a space for insignificant zeros on either side of the decimal point so that decimal points align. You can also use this symbol for fractions that have varying numbers of digits.
period (.)	Decimal point. This symbol determines how many digits (0's or #'s) Microsoft Excel displays to the right and left of the decimal point. If the format contains only #'s to the left of this symbol, Microsoft Excel begins numbers less than 1 with a decimal point. To avoid this, use 0 as the first digit placeholder to the left of the decimal point instead of #. You can also use the decimal point to create time formats that display fractions of a second.
%	Percentage. Microsoft Excel multiplies by 100 and adds the % character.
comma (,)	Thousands separator. Microsoft Excel separates thousands by commas if the format contains a comma surrounded by #'s or 0's. A comma following a placeholder scales the number by a thousand. For example, the format #, would scale the number by a thousand and the format #,, would scale the number by a million. The format 0.0,, would display the number 12,200,000 as 12.2.
E− E+ e− e+	Scientific format. If a format contains a 0 or # to the right of an E−, E+, e−, or e+, Microsoft Excel displays the number in scientific format and inserts an E or e. The number of 0's or #'s to the right determines the exponent's number of digits. E− or e− places a minus sign by negative exponents. E+ or e+ places a minus sign by negative exponents and a plus sign by positive exponents.
$ − + / ( ) : space	Displays that character. To display a character other than one of these, precede the character with a backslash (\) or enclose the character in double quotation marks(" "). You can also use the slash (/) character for fraction formats.

Format Symbol	Meaning
\\	Displays the next character in the format. Microsoft Excel does not display the backslash. This is the same as enclosing the next character in double quotation marks. If you enter any of the following symbols, Microsoft Excel provides the backslash for you: ! ^ & ' (left single quotation mark) ' (right single quotation mark) ~ { } = < >
*	Repeats the next character in the format enough times to fill the column width. You cannot have more than one asterisk in one section of a format.
_ (underline)	Skips the width of the next character. For example, you could type _) at the end of a format section for positive numbers to have Microsoft Excel skip the width of the parenthesis characters, so positive numbers align with negative numbers that contain parentheses.
"*text*"	Displays whatever text is inside the double quotation marks.
@	Text placeholder. If there is text entered in the cell, the text from the cell is placed in the format where the @ character appears.
m	Displays the month as a number without leading zeros (1–12). If you use m immediately after the h or hh symbol, Microsoft Excel displays the minute rather than the month.
mm	Displays the month as a number with leading zeros (01–12). If you use mm immediately after the h or hh symbol, Microsoft Excel displays the minute rather than the month.
mmm	Displays the month as an abbreviation (Jan–Dec).
mmmm	Displays the month as a full name (January–December).
d	Displays the day as a number without leading zeros (1–31).
dd	Displays the day as a number with leading zeros (01–31).
ddd	Displays the day as an abbreviation (Sun–Sat).
dddd	Displays the day as a full name (Sunday–Saturday).
yy or yyyy	Displays the year as a two-digit number (00–99), or as a four-digit number (1900–2078).
h or hh	Displays the hour as a number without leading zeros (0–23), or as a number with leading zeros (00–23). If the format contains an AM or PM indicator, the hour is based on the 12-hour clock. Otherwise, the hour is based on the 24-hour clock.
m or mm	Displays the minute as a number without leading zeros (0–59), or as a number with leading zeros (00–59). The m or mm must appear immediately after the h or hh symbol, or Microsoft Excel displays the month rather than the minute.

Format Symbol	Meaning
s or ss	Displays the second as a number without leading zeros (0–59), or as a number with leading zeros (00–59).
[]	Displays hours greater than 24, or minutes or seconds greater than 60. Place the brackets around the leftmost part of the time code; for example, the time code [h]:mm:ss would allow the display of hours greater than 24.
AM/am/A/a PM/pm/P/p	Displays the hour using a 12-hour clock. Microsoft Excel displays AM, am, A, or a for times from midnight until noon, and PM, pm, P, or p for times from noon until midnight. If no AM/PM indicator is used, the hour is based on the 24-hour clock.
[BLACK]	Displays the characters in the cell in black.
[BLUE]	Displays the characters in the cell in blue.
[CYAN]	Displays the characters in the cell in cyan.
[GREEN]	Displays the characters in the cell in green.
[MAGENTA]	Displays the characters in the cell in magenta.
[RED]	Displays the characters in the cell in red.
[WHITE]	Displays the characters in the cell in white.
[YELLOW]	Displays the characters in the cell in yellow.
[COLOR *n*]	Displays the corresponding color in the color palette, where *n* is a number from 0 to 56. For more information about the color palette, see "Creating a Custom Color Palette" in Chapter 34.
[*condition value*]	Where *condition* may be < , >, =, >=, <=, <>, and *value* may be any number. With the [*condition value*] symbol, you can set your own criteria for each section of a number format.

Step By Step

For step-by-step instructions and related information, double-click the [?] button to display the Search dialog box in Help, and then:

Type this keyword and choose Show Topics	Select a topic and choose Go To
assigning formats	Assigning a number, date, or time format
currency formats	Creating international currency formats
custom number formats	Creating and deleting custom number formats

Copying Formats Quickly

You can easily copy formats between cells with the Format Painter button.

Format Painter

Select the cell that has the formats you want to copy.

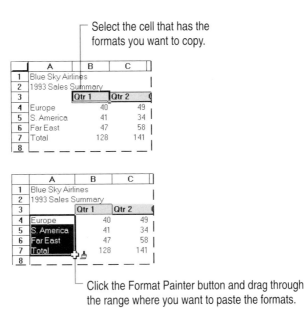

Click the Format Painter button and drag through the range where you want to paste the formats.

The formats are pasted into the cells you dragged through.

You can format more than one range with the Format Painter button by double-clicking on the button and selecting the ranges you want to format. The Format Painter cursor stays active until you click the Format Painter button again.

Note If a cell containing multiple text formats is selected when you click the Format Painter button, only the formatting of the first character will be pasted into the cells you select with the Format Painter cursor.

With the Format Painter button, you can also transfer various types of formatting from one cell range—such as a table that has been formatted with the AutoFormat command on the Format menu—to similar ranges of data.

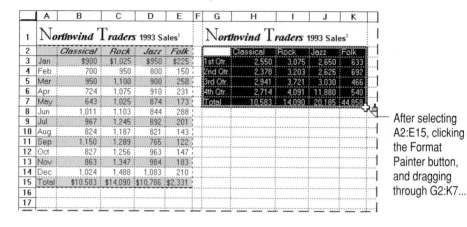

After selecting A2:E15, clicking the Format Painter button, and dragging through G2:K7...

...the formats from A2:E15 are applied to G2:K7 .

You can also use the Format Painter button to transfer formatting between objects.

Step By Step

For step-by-step instructions and related information, double-click the [k?] button to display the Search dialog box in Help, and then:

Type this keyword and choose Show Topics	Select a topic and choose Go To
autoformats, applying	Applying an autoformat to a range
formats, copying	Copying formats using the Format Painter button
styles	Applying a style

Using Styles to Save and Apply Format Combinations

You can define and save a combination of formats and then apply all of the formats at the same time. This combination of formats is called a *style*. If you redefine the style by changing the formats included, all cells that have that style applied to them change to reflect the new definition.

In a new workbook, only the built-in styles are initially available. You can create new styles, or copy styles you have created in another workbook. Styles in a workbook are available on all sheets in the workbook.

Creating a Style

To create a style, select a cell that has the formats you want to use, choose the Style command from the Format menu, and type in the Style Name box the name you want to use for the style. If you want to specify that some of the cell formats (such as the number or pattern format for the cell) not be part of the style, clear the appropriate check boxes in the dialog box.

Note If you select multiple cells with conflicting formats and create a style with the Style command, the style includes only the formats that the selected cells have in common. For example, if all the cells you selected have only their number formats exactly the same, the proposed style would include only the number format.

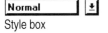

Style box

You can also use the Style box to create and apply styles. The Style box is in the Formatting category. To create a style with the Style box, select a cell that has the formats you want to use, type in the Style box the name you want to use for the style, and press ENTER. For information about adding the Style box to a toolbar, see the Step By Step table at the end of this section, and "Customizing Toolbars" in Chapter 34.

Applying a Style

To apply a style to the current selection, choose the Style command from the Format menu, and select the style you want to apply from the Style Name box. If you've added the Style box to a toolbar, you can apply a style by selecting it from the Style box.

Tip You can quickly copy formatting between cells with the Format Painter button. For more information about the Format Painter button, see "Copying Formats Quickly" earlier in this chapter.

When you apply a style to a cell, the style overrides any individual formats previously applied to the cell. You can change the formatting of cells to which you have applied styles without affecting the definition of the style.

Copying Styles Between Workbooks

To copy styles from one workbook to another, open both workbooks, switch to the workbook that you want to copy styles into, and then choose the Style command from the Format menu. Choose the Merge button, and select the workbook that contains the styles you want to copy. When you choose the OK button, the styles in the workbook you selected are copied into the active workbook.

Caution If the active workbook contains any styles that have the same name as styles you are copying, Microsoft Excel asks if you want to merge the styles that have the same names. You can choose to replace the existing styles in the active workbook with the styles you are merging, keep the existing styles in the active workbook, or cancel the copying procedure. You receive this warning only once, regardless of the number of conflicting style names.

Redefining a Style

You can change the definition of existing styles, including the built-in styles such as the Normal style. When you change the formats that are part of a style, all of the cells and ranges in the active workbook that use that style are updated to reflect the new definition.

To redefine a style based on the formats of a cell, select a cell that has the formats you want, choose the Style command from the Format menu, and type the name of the style you want to redefine.

You can also choose the Style command, select the style you want to change in the Style Name box, and choose the Modify button. Microsoft Excel displays the Format Cells dialog box, where you can select the formatting options you want for the style. After you choose the OK button to close the Format Cells dialog, clear any of the check boxes for formats that you don't want included in the style.

To change the standard combination of formats that Microsoft uses to format data you enter into a worksheet, you can redefine the Normal style.

About the Normal Style

All cells in all of the sheets in a new workbook are initially formatted with the Normal style. The Normal style controls the look of data you enter into a cell until you change the formatting. You can change the format of the Normal style just as you can for any style. If you change the Normal style for a workbook, the Normal style for other workbooks is unaffected.

The Normal style consists of the following combination of formats:

For this format	The setting in the Normal style is
Number	General
Font	Arial 10 (Windows)
	Geneva 10 (Macintosh)
Alignment	General, bottom aligned
Border	None
Patterns	None
Protection	Locked

Tip You can change the standard font for all new workbooks by choosing the Options command on the Tools menu, and then selecting the General tab. Then, in the Standard Font box and the Size box, select the font and font size you want.

Deleting a Style

Delete a style by choosing the Style command from the Format menu, selecting the style you want to delete in the Style Name box, and choosing the Delete button. When you delete a style, cells formatted with that style revert to the Normal style. If you added any formats to a cell after the style was applied, those formats remain after the style is deleted.

Note You cannot delete the Normal style.

Step By Step

For step-by-step instructions and related information, double-click the [?] button to display the Search dialog box in Help, and then:

Type this keyword and choose Show Topics	Select a topic and choose Go To
buttons, adding to toolbar	Adding or deleting a toolbar button
styles	Applying a style
	Copying styles from another workbook
	Creating and deleting a style
	Redefining a style

Applying Formats Automatically

You can quickly apply various built-in combinations of formats—such as patterns, font formatting, and borders—to a range of cells with the AutoFormat command on the Format menu. When you apply an *autoformat,* Microsoft Excel selects the current range, determines the levels of summary and detail, checks for text, values, and formulas, and then applies formats accordingly.

	A	B	C	D	E	F
1						
2	Blue Sky Airlines					
3	1993 Sales Summary					
4		Qtr 1	Qtr 2	Qtr 3	Qtr 4	Total
5	Europe	40	49	64	57	210
6	S. America	41	34	32	38	145
7	Far East	47	58	54	50	209
8	Total	128	141	150	145	564
9						
10						

Select any cell in the range of data you want Microsoft Excel to format for you. Then choose the AutoFormat command from the Format menu and select a format.

	A	B	C	D	E	F
1						
2	Blue Sky Airlines					
3	1993 Sales Summary					
4		Qtr 1	Qtr 2	Qtr 3	Qtr 4	Total
5	Europe	$40.00	$49.00	$64.00	$57.00	$210.00
6	S. America	41.00	34.00	32.00	38.00	145.00
7	Far East	47.00	58.00	54.00	50.00	209.00
8	Total	$128.00	$141.00	$150.00	$419.00	$564.00
9						
10						

The AutoFormat command recognizes row and column titles, values, and formulas, and then applies formats accordingly.

	A	B	C	D	E	F
1						
2	Blue Sky Airlines					
3	1993 Sales Summary					
4		Qtr 1	Qtr 2	Qtr 3	Qtr 4	Total
5	Europe	$40.00	$49.00	$64.00	$57.00	$210.00
6	S. America	41.00	34.00	32.00	38.00	145.00
7	Far East	47.00	58.00	54.00	50.00	209.00
8	Total	$128.00	$141.00	$150.00	$419.00	$564.00
9						

You can use the AutoFormat command to switch easily from one autoformat to another.

Autoformats are combinations of the following types of formats:

- Number
- Alignment

- Font (including size, type, color, bold, italic, and effects)
- Borders
- Patterns
- Column widths and row heights

Applying an Autoformat

Apply an autoformat by selecting a cell in a range, or by selecting the entire range you want to format, and choosing the AutoFormat command from the Format menu. In the Table Format box, select the autoformat you want to apply. The Sample box shows what the different autoformats look like. After applying an autoformat, you can continue to apply other individual formats.

If you want to use an autoformat but don't want to lose certain formats you've already applied, select the autoformat you want to use, choose the Options button in the AutoFormat dialog box, and clear the check boxes for the formats that you don't want the autoformat to change.

For example, to preserve the number formats you applied to a range, you would choose the Options button and clear the Number check box. The number formats you already applied will remain after you apply the autoformat.

Clearing an Autoformat

You can remove an autoformat by choosing the Undo AutoFormat command from the Edit menu immediately after you apply the autoformat. To remove an autoformat at a later time, select a cell within the formatted range, choose the AutoFormat command from the Format menu, and then choose the None option in the Table Format box.

Step By Step

For step-by-step instructions and related information, double-click the 🅺? button to display the Search dialog box in Help, and then:

Type this keyword and choose Show Topics	Select a topic and choose Go To
autoformats, applying	Applying an autoformat to a range
	Applying only some of the formats of an autoformat
autoformats, clearing	Clearing an autoformat

CHAPTER 13

Creating Graphic Objects on Worksheets and Charts

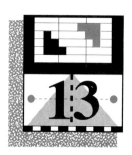

For command, keyboard, and toolbar button information, see online Help.

In This Chapter

Graphic Objects on Worksheets and Charts

You can put graphic objects on worksheets, charts, and dialog sheets. The graphic objects are not actually part of the worksheet or chart. They are inserted on a transparent layer laid over the worksheet or chart and can be moved, sized, and formatted independently of the data or chart underneath. In this sense, an embedded chart is like a graphic object.

Drawing

You can draw graphic objects by using buttons on the Drawing toolbar. You must have a mouse to use the Drawing toolbar. Click the Drawing button to display the Drawing toolbar.

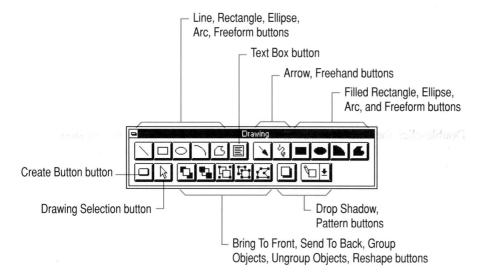

The information in this chapter also applies to another kind of object called a *control.* You can use controls to make your worksheet interactive without writing macros or programs. For information about controls and using graphics objects on dialog sheets, see Chapter 11, "Controls and Dialog Boxes," in the *Microsoft Excel Visual Basic User's Guide.*

For information about embedded charts, see "Creating an Embedded Chart on a Worksheet" in Chapter 15.

For information about copying graphics to and from other applications, see Chapter 41, "Sharing Data and Graphics with Other Applications."

For information about assigning macros to graphic objects and custom buttons, see Chapter 1, "Automating Repeated Tasks," in the *Microsoft Excel Visual Basic User's Guide.*

For information about using graphic objects on dialog sheets, see Chapter 11, "Controls and Dialog Boxes," in the *Microsoft Excel Visual Basic User's Guide.*

Lines, Arrows, Rectangles, Ellipses, and Arcs

To draw a simple shape, click one of the buttons on the Drawing toolbar and drag from one corner of the area where you want the shape to appear to the diagonally opposite corner.

 Line, Arrow, Freehand buttons

 Rectangle, Ellipse, Arc buttons

 Filled Rectangle, Ellipse, Arc buttons

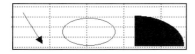

Some objects drawn on a worksheet: arrow, ellipse, filled arc

Double-click the button to draw more than one shape in succession. To stop drawing shapes, click the button again.

To delete a graphic object, click it to select it, and then press the DEL key.

You can change the size, position, and formatting of graphic objects you have created. See "Sizing, Moving, and Copying Graphic Objects" and "Formatting a Graphic Object" later in this chapter.

Step By Step

For step-by-step instructions and related information, double-click the [k?] button to display the Search dialog box in Help, and then:

Type this keyword and choose Show Topics	Select a topic and choose Go To
drawing, lines	Drawing a line or an arrow
drawing, shapes	Drawing a rectangle, an ellipse, or an arc
	Drawing multiple arrows, lines, or shapes
graphic objects, formatting	Overview of Formatting a Graphic Object

Polygons

Freeform

Filled Freeform

Use either the Freeform button or the Filled Freeform button to draw a polygon.

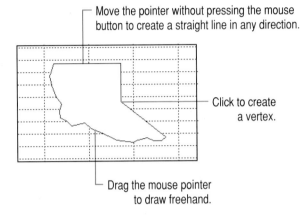

Move the pointer without pressing the mouse button to create a straight line in any direction.

Click to create a vertex.

Drag the mouse pointer to draw freehand.

Reshape

To change the shape of a polygon, select it and then click the Reshape button. A freehand line is made up of small straight lines. Selection handles appear at the beginning and end of each straight line in the polygon.

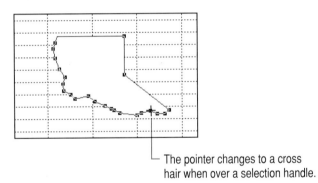

The pointer changes to a cross hair when over a selection handle.

To move a vertex (an intersection of two sides), drag it. To delete a vertex, hold down CTRL (Windows) or OPTION (Macintosh) while you click it. To add a vertex, hold down CTRL (Windows) or OPTION (Macintosh) while you drag a line.

Step By Step

For step-by-step instructions and related information, double-click the ⟦▶?⟧ button to display the Search dialog box in Help, and then:

Type this keyword and choose Show Topics	Select a topic and choose Go To
graphic objects, formatting	Overview of Formatting a Graphic Object
polygons, drawing	Drawing a polygon
polygons, editing	Editing a polygon

Text Boxes

A text box is a rectangle with text in it. Text boxes are useful for highlighting specific data on a worksheet or chart, especially when they're used with lines or arrows. The text wraps within the text box. You can rotate the text, format it, and change the border and fill patterns of the box. You can paste text copied from the formula bar into a text box, and you can assign a macro to a text box so that the macro will run whenever you click the text box. You can also lock a text box by using the Object command on the Format menu (on a worksheet) or the Selected Object command on the Format menu (on a chart).

Text Box

To add a text box, click the Text Box button, drag from one corner to the diagonally opposite corner, and then type the text.

To change text, click the text box to select it, select the text you want to change, and then edit it the same way you edit text in cells. For more information, see "Editing Within a Cell" in Chapter 11.

You can link the text in a text box to a cell on a sheet by selecting the text box, clicking the formula bar, typing an equal sign (=), clicking the cell you want to link to, and then pressing ENTER.

Format text the same way you format text in a cell: select the text you want to format, and then choose the Object command from the Format menu (on a worksheet) or choose the Selected Object command from the Format menu (on a chart). The dialog box shows all of the formats you can apply to the selected characters.

To format the text box itself, select it (click outside the text box, then click the text box once) and then choose the Object command from the Format menu (on a worksheet) or choose the Selected Object command from the Format menu (on a chart). The dialog box shows all of the formats you can apply to the text box itself.

For information about changing the text in chart and axis titles, data and tick-mark labels, and the legend, see Chapter 17, "Changing Data in a Chart."

For information about checking spelling in a text box, see "Checking Spelling" in Chapter 11.

For information about protecting text boxes, see Chapter 39, "Protecting a Workbook."

For information about assigning macros to graphic objects, see Chapter 1, "Automating Repeated Tasks," in the *Visual Basic User's Guide*.

Step By Step

For step-by-step instructions and related information, double-click the 🏷 button to display the Search dialog box in Help, and then:

Type this keyword and choose Show Topics	Select a topic and choose Go To
graphic objects, formatting	Overview of Formatting a Graphic Object
text boxes	Creating and deleting text boxes
	Editing the text in a text box
	Formatting the text in a text box

Selecting, Grouping, and Overlapping Graphic Objects

To change the format, size, or position of an object, or to copy or delete an object, you must first select it.

You can group several objects into one. This maintains the relationship of the objects while you move, copy, or format the entire group at once.

You can also control which object is on top when two or more objects overlap. This is useful for putting a picture or object behind a chart to enhance the visual effect.

Selecting Graphic Objects

Drawing Selection

You can select an object just by clicking it. However, it is often better to first click the Drawing Selection button. This changes the mouse pointer to an arrow, which means that:

- Only objects can be selected, not cells.

- If there is a macro assigned to an object, clicking it will select the object without running the macro.

- You can select a group of graphic objects by dragging to draw a rectangle around the objects you want to select.

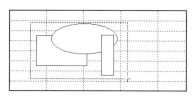 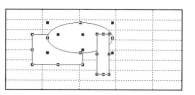

Click the Drawing Selection button, and then drag to surround the objects you want to select.

Small black selection handles surround each selected object.

Note If the object has no fill pattern (that is, it is transparent), or if the object is a text box or a custom button and text within it is selected, you must click the object's border to select the object. If the object is invisible, drag to draw a rectangle around the object to select it.

Grouping and Ungrouping Graphic Objects

Group Objects

You group objects by selecting two or more objects and then clicking the Group Objects button.

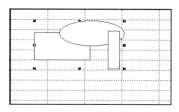

One set of selection handles surrounds the group of objects.

Ungroup Objects

Now you can format the group and move, size, copy, or delete it as if it were a single object. The Ungroup Objects button separates the group into individual objects again.

Overlapping Graphic Objects

Bring To Front

You can place an object in front of or behind another object by selecting the object and then clicking the Bring To Front or Send To Back button.

Send To Back

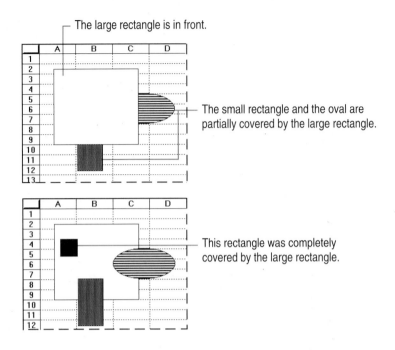

The large rectangle is in front.

The small rectangle and the oval are partially covered by the large rectangle.

This rectangle was completely covered by the large rectangle.

Note If an object has a fill pattern (that is, it is not transparent), you will not be able to use the mouse to select cells that are completely covered by the object. Use the arrow keys to move through and select covered cells. If you want to select a range of cells that includes cells covered by an object, you can drag through the covered cells as long as you begin dragging from an uncovered cell.

Step By Step

For step-by-step instructions and related information, double-click the ⟦k?⟧ button to display the Search dialog box in Help, and then:

Type this keyword and choose Show Topics	Select a topic and choose Go To
grouping	Grouping and ungrouping graphic objects
overlapped graphic objects	Reordering overlapped graphic objects

Sizing, Moving, and Copying Graphic Objects

Resizing an Object

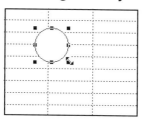 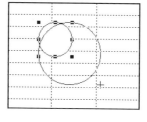 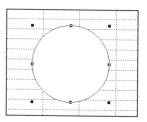

Select the object and position the mouse pointer over a selection handle.

Drag to the new size.

Release the mouse button.

Moving an Object

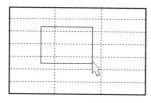

Position the mouse pointer over the object so that it changes to an arrow.

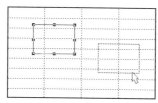

Drag to the new position.

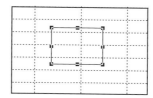

Release the mouse button.

System	To copy an object, hold down this key as you drag
Windows	CTRL
Macintosh	OPTION

Controlling the Way a Graphic Object Is Moved or Sized

Objects on worksheets are initially formatted to move or change size when the width or height of the cells under the objects changes, when those cells are moved with the mouse, or when the move is the result of inserting and deleting cells from the worksheet.

You can change this behavior for an individual object by selecting the object, choosing the Object command from the Format menu, and then changing the Object Positioning option on the Properties tab. You can change this for all objects in all Microsoft Excel documents by choosing the Options command from the Tools menu and then clearing the Cut, Copy, And Sort Objects With Cells check box on the Edit tab.

Rectangle on worksheet

	Acme	Apex	Apogee	
Shares	500	300	150	
Price	10	15	50	
Value	5000	4500	7500	
Total	17000			

	Acme	Apex	Apogee	
Shares	500	300	150	
Price	10	15	50	
Value	5000	4500	7500	
Total	17000			

	Acme	Apex	Apogee	
Shares	500	300	150	
Price	10	15	50	
Value	5000	4500	7500	
Total	17000			

Formatted to move and size with cells, the rectangle moves when a column is inserted.

Formatted not to move or size with cells, the rectangle does not move when a column is inserted.

For information about how objects are moved and sized on charts, see Chapter 18, "Formatting a Chart."

Objects do not move or size when you use the Copy command or the Cut command on the Edit menu because both of these commands operate on the contents of the cells, not on the cells themselves.

Imported pictures move but do not change size with cells.

For information about sorting graphic objects along with the data in cells, see "Sorting a List That Contains Graphic Objects" in Chapter 21.

Step By Step

For step-by-step instructions and related information, double-click the [▶?] button to display the Search dialog box in Help, and then:

Type this keyword and choose Show Topics	Select a topic and choose Go To
graphic objects, copying	Copying a graphic object
graphic objects, detaching	Detaching a graphic object from underlying cells
graphic objects, moving	Moving a graphic object
graphic objects, sizing	Resizing a graphic object
graphic objects, sorting	Including graphic objects when sorting
gridlines, aligning objects with	Aligning objects with gridlines

Formatting a Graphic Object

Formatting is changing an object's looks: its color, pattern, border, and so on. For information about changing an object's size or position, see the preceding section. For information about formatting charts, see Chapter 18, "Formatting a Chart."

You format an object by selecting it and then choosing the Object command from the Format menu. The dialog box displays the tabs and options relevant to the object selected. You can also double-click any object other than a text box to display the dialog box.

For some individual formats, you can also use the buttons in the following list.

Button	Name	Location
[▢]	Drop Shadow	Drawing toolbar
[🎨▼]	Color	Formatting toolbar
[🖊▼]	Pattern	Drawing toolbar

Step By Step

For step-by-step instructions and related information, double-click the [▶?] button to display the Search dialog box in Help, and then:

Type this keyword and choose Show Topics	Select a topic and choose Go To
borders	Formatting an object's border and fill pattern
lines	Formatting a line or an arrow

Hiding and Printing Graphic Objects

You can hide all objects or display placeholders for embedded charts and pictures to speed up scrolling. Choose the Options command from the Tools menu, and then select one of the three options under Objects on the View tab.

System	To cycle through the three options without choosing the command, press
Windows	CTRL+6
Macintosh	COMMAND+6

On a worksheet, you can set each object so that it will print or not print when you print your document. Select the object, choose the Object command from the Format menu, and then select or clear the Print Object check box on the Properties tab. All objects on a chart print with the chart.

Step By Step

For step-by-step instructions and related information, double-click the [?] button to display the Search dialog box in Help, and then:

Type this keyword and choose Show Topics	Select a topic and choose Go To
graphic objects, hiding	Hiding and unhiding graphic objects
graphic objects, printing	Printing graphic objects

Pictures of Charts and Worksheets

You can create pictures of embedded charts or cells, and you can copy graphics from another application into Microsoft Excel. You can put a picture on a different sheet, in a different part of the same sheet, or into a document created in another application.

Select the cells or embedded chart you want to make a picture of, and then hold down SHIFT while you choose the Copy Picture command from the Edit menu. Next, click where you want to put the picture, and then choose the Paste command from the Edit menu.

In Microsoft Excel for Windows, you can choose between two formats for the copy: Bitmap or Picture. In most cases, choose Picture. This format scales pictures proportionately when you size them, and they can be displayed on screens of varying resolutions. Bitmaps can be displayed correctly only on a screen of the same type and resolution as the screen they were copied from.

You can also link a picture of cells to the original cells. Choose the Copy command from the Edit menu and then hold down SHIFT and choose the Paste Picture Link command from the Edit menu. You can also use the Camera button. Changes in the original cells will be reflected in the picture. If you have pasted the picture into another document, double-clicking the picture will open the original document.

Note   When you change the size of a picture, the scaling proportion appears in the reference area to the left of the formula bar; 100 percent is the size when you first pasted the picture.

If you are using Microsoft Excel for Windows, see Chapter 41, "Sharing Data and Graphics with Other Applications," for information about inserting graphics directly from files on your disk.

Step By Step

For step-by-step instructions and related information, double-click the [▶?] button to display the Search dialog box in Help, and then:

Type this keyword and choose Show Topics	Select a topic and choose Go To
Camera button	Camera Button
graphic objects, copying	Copying a chart, cells, or a graphic object as a picture
linked pictures	Copying a linked picture of cells
	Updating a linked cell picture

CHAPTER 14

Printing

For command, keyboard, and toolbar button information, see online Help.

In This Chapter

Setting Up What You Want to Print

Selecting a Printer

Before you can print, you must select a printer.

System	To select a printer
Windows	From the File menu, choose Print. Click the Printer button, and then select the printer you want to use.
Macintosh	From the Apple menu, choose Chooser. Then select the printer you want to use.

If no printer is available, you must install one. For information about installing a printer, see your printer and system documentation.

Setting Up the Page

You can control the appearance of your printed sheets by changing the options in the Page Setup dialog box. Here are some of the options you can change.

Adjust all margins, including header and footer margins.

Add custom headers and footers.

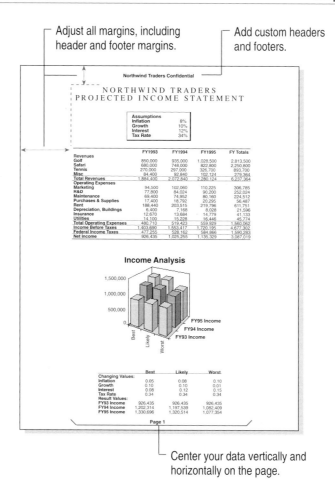

Center your data vertically and horizontally on the page.

To	From the File menu, choose Page Setup and then
Set margins	Select the Margins tab. In the Top, Bottom, Left, Right, Header and Footer boxes, enter the measurements for the margins you want.
Set vertical and horizontal alignment on the page	Select the Margins tab. Under Center On Page, select the option you want.
Add or edit headers and footers	Select the Header/Footer tab. In the Header and Footer boxes, select the headers and footers you want.
Set page orientation	Select the Page tab. Under Orientation, select the option you want.

Choosing What to Print

You can control what part of your sheet is printed, and whether gridlines, cell notes, or row and column headings are printed. You can also specify rows or columns that will appear as titles on every page.

Print row or column titles from the first page on all pages.

Northwind Traders Confidential

Country	Salesperson	Shipped Date	Order ID	Sale Amount
UK	Suyama, Michael	8-Jan-93	10867	$98.40
UK	Suyama, Michael	15-Jan-93	10885	$1,209.00
UK	Suyama, Michael	24-Jan-93	10907	$108.50
UK	Suyama, Michael	27-Jan-93	10914	$537.50
UK	Suyama, Michael	6-Feb-93	10929	$1,174.75
UK	Suyama, Michael	7-Feb-93	10944	$1,025.33
UK	Suyama, Michael	10-Feb-93	10933	$920.60
UK	Suyama, Michael	14-Feb-93	10956	$677.00
UK	Suyama, Michael	17-Feb-93	10959	$131.75
UK	Suyama, Michael	21-Feb-93	10973	$291.55
UK	Suyama, Micha			
UK	Suyama, Micha			
UK	Suyama, Micha			
UK	Suyama, Micha			
USA	Callahan, Linda			
USA	Callahan, Linda			
USA	Callahan, Linda			
USA	Callahan, Linda			
USA	Callahan, Linda			
USA	Callahan, Linda			
USA	Callahan, Linda			
USA	Callahan, Linda			
USA	Callahan, Linda			
USA	Callahan, Linda			
USA	Callahan, Linda			
USA	Callahan, Linda			
USA	Callahan, Linda			
USA	Callahan, Linda			
USA	Callahan, Linda			
USA	Callahan, Linda			
USA	Callahan, Linda			
USA	Callahan, Linda			
USA	Davolio, Nancy			
USA	Davolio, Nancy			
USA	Davolio, Nancy			
USA	Davolio, Nancy			
USA	Davolio, Nancy			
USA	Davolio, Nancy			

Northwind Traders Confidential

Northwind Traders
Employee Sales, 1st Quarter 1993

Country	Salesperson	Shipped Date	Order ID	Sale Amount
UK	Buchanan, B. L.	6-Jan-93	10869	$1,630.00
UK	Buchanan, B. L.	6-Jan-93	10872	$2,058.46
UK	Buchanan, B. L.	8-Jan-93	10874	$310.00
UK	Buchanan, B. L.	9-Jan-93	10866	$1,096.20
UK	Buchanan, B. L.	10-Jan-93	10870	$160.00
UK	Buchanan, B. L.	23-Jan-93	10899	$122.40
UK	Buchanan, B. L.	30-Jan-93	10922	$742.50
UK	Buchanan, B. L.	14-Feb-93	10954	$1,659.53
UK	Buchanan, B. L.	25-Mar-93	11043	$210.00
UK	Dodsworth, Annabella	1-Jan-93	10828	$932.00
UK	Dodsworth, Annabella	7-Jan-93	10871	$1,979.23
UK	Dodsworth, Annabella	17-Jan-93	10893	$5,502.11
UK	Dodsworth, Annabella	20-Jan-93	10889	$11,380.00
UK	Dodsworth, Annabella	31-Jan-93	10905	$342.00
UK	Dodsworth, Annabella	12-Feb-93	10942	$560.00
UK	Dodsworth, Annabella	19-Feb-93	10953	$4,441.25
UK	Dodsworth, Annabella	20-Feb-93	10963	$57.80
UK	Dodsworth, Annabella	3-Mar-93	10951	$458.75
UK	Dodsworth, Annabella	9-Mar-93	11016	$491.50
UK	Dodsworth, Annabella	16-Mar-93	11017	$6,750.00
UK	Dodsworth, Annabella	19-Mar-93	10978	$1,303.19
UK	Dodsworth, Annabella	20-Mar-93	10970	$224.00
			11022	$1,402.00
			10876	$917.00
			10880	$1,500.00
			10890	$860.10
			10891	$368.93
			10868	$1,920.60
			10896	$750.50
			10923	$748.80
			10937	$644.80
			10941	$4,011.75
			10958	$781.00
			10993	$4,895.44
			11033	$3,232.80
			11030	$12,615.05
			11037	$60.00
			11048	$525.00
			11047	$817.88
			11066	$928.75
			11055	$1,727.50
			10826	$730.00

	A	B	C	D	E	F
1	Data Entry Instructions:					
2		1. Obtain daily sales reports from individual salespeople.				
3		2. Enter the sales figures.				
4		3. After entering figures, sort list by country.				
5	Northwind Traders					
6	Employee Sales, 1st Quarter 1993					
7						
8	Country	Salesperson	Shipped Date	Order ID	Sale Amount	
9	UK	Buchanan, B. L.	6-Jan-93	10869	$1,630.00	
10	UK	Buchanan, B. L.	6-Jan-93	10872	$2,058.46	
11	UK	Buchanan, B. L.	8-Jan-93	10874	$310.00	
12	UK	Buchanan, B. L.	9-Jan-93	10866	$1,096.20	
13	UK	Buchanan, B. L.	10-Jan-93	10870	$160.00	
14	UK	Buchanan, B. L.	23-Jan-93	10899	$122.40	
15	UK	Buchanan, B. L.	30-Jan-93	10922	$742.50	
16	UK	Buchanan, B. L.	14-Feb-93	10954	$1,659.53	
17	UK	Buchanan, B. L.	25-Mar-93	11043	$210.00	
18	UK	Dodsworth, Annabella	1-Jan-93	10828	$932.00	
19	UK	Dodsworth, Annabella	7-Jan-93	10871	$1,979.23	

Define a range of data as a print area. Then print only that data.

To	From the File menu, choose Page Setup and then
Specify a worksheet range to print	Select the Sheet tab. In the Print Area box, enter the range to print.
Print row or column titles on multiple pages	Select the Sheet tab. Under Print Titles, enter the row or column ranges that you want to be printed as titles.
Control whether gridlines, cell notes, or row and column headings are printed	Select the Sheet tab. Under Print, select the check boxes for the items you want to print.

Step By Step

For step-by-step instructions and related information, double-click the 🔖 button to display the Search dialog box in Help, and then:

Type this keyword and choose Show Topics	Select a topic and choose Go To
headers and footers	Creating headers and footers
page margins	Setting margins and alignment
page size	Setting page orientation and size
print area	Specifying an area of a worksheet to print
printing cell notes	Printing cell notes with a worksheet
printing gridlines	Printing gridlines and row and column headings
printing titles on multiple pages	Printing titles on multiple pages
selecting printers	Selecting a printer

Printing Your Work

Previewing What Will Print

By previewing your sheet, you can see each page exactly as it will print, with the correct margins and page breaks, and the headers and footers in place. Previewing a sheet can save you time and trips to the printer.

Print Preview

To preview your sheet, click the Print Preview toolbar button. When working in the Page Setup dialog box, you can also choose the Print Preview button in the dialog box.

Drag the handles to adjust the page margins, header and footer margins, and column widths.

Click to magnify a portion of the page. Click again to display the whole page.

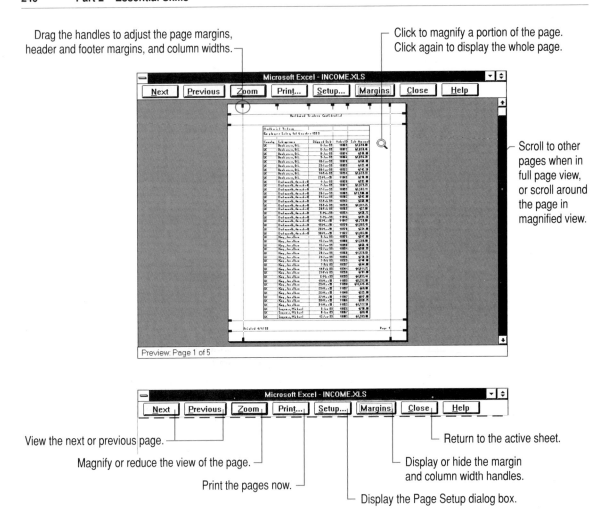

Scroll to other pages when in full page view, or scroll around the page in magnified view.

View the next or previous page.

Magnify or reduce the view of the page.

Print the pages now.

Return to the active sheet.

Display or hide the margin and column width handles.

Display the Page Setup dialog box.

Printing Sheets

There are several ways to print your work.

Print

To print from the	Do this
Workbook window	Click the Print button on the Standard Toolbar.
Print preview window	Choose the Print button in the Print Preview window.
Page Setup dialog box	Choose the Print button in the dialog box.

Note Clicking the Print toolbar button in the workbook window prints your work immediately. Microsoft Excel uses the current settings in the Page Setup and Print dialog boxes. To display the Print dialog box before you print, choose the Print command from the File menu. You can then select the print range and number of copies in the Print dialog box.

Creating Forms with Microsoft Excel

You can use the formatting features in Microsoft Excel to create all kinds of forms for printing. For example, you can create time sheets, job applications, and other forms you intend to fill out by hand.

In addition to creating forms to print, you can create your forms in Microsoft Excel, then distribute them through electronic mail. For information about using Microsoft Excel and an electronic mail program, see Chapter 40, "Routing Workbooks with Electronic Mail."

Fitting Your Work to the Page

Your work may not fit exactly on the number of printed pages you want. You can scale your printed work to fit more or fewer pages than it would at normal size, or you can specify a certain number of pages for your printed work.

At normal scaling, the printed data spills onto a second page.

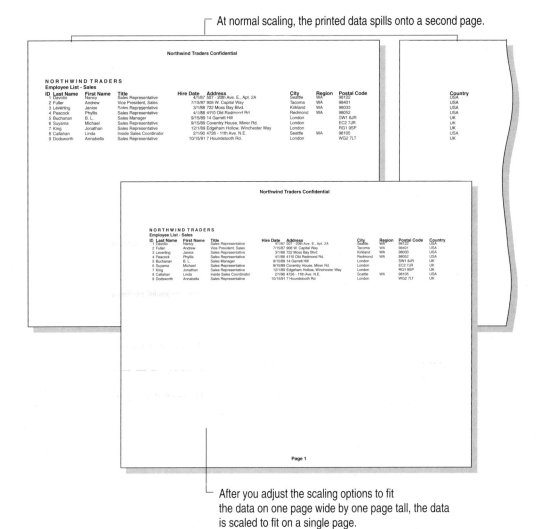

After you adjust the scaling options to fit
the data on one page wide by one page tall, the data
is scaled to fit on a single page.

To	From the File menu, choose Page Setup and then
Enlarge or reduce your printed data	Select the Page tab. Select the Adjust To option button, and then type or select the scaling percentage you want.
Reduce your data so that it fits on the number of pages you specify	Select the Page tab. Select the Fit To option button, and then type or select the number of pages you want.

Controlling Page Breaks, Page Numbers, and Printing Order

If a sheet is larger than one page, Microsoft Excel divides it into pages for printing by inserting automatic page breaks. These page breaks are based on the paper size, margin settings, and scaling options in the Page Setup dialog box.

You can also create manual page breaks. When you set a manual page break, Microsoft Excel adjusts the automatic page breaks in the rest of the sheet.

After you manually place a page break at cell G8, that cell becomes the upper-left corner of a new page.

	C	D	E	F	G	H	I	J
1	Jan	Feb	Mar	Qtr 1	Apr	May	Jun	Qtr 2
2								
3	31,735.00	11,566.00	71,639.00	114,940.00	44,132.00	16,276.00	65,668.00	126,076.00
4	63,074.00	20,519.00	12,828.00	96,421.00	83,793.00	16,039.00	52,379.00	152,211.00
5	45,696.00	77,739.00	76,476.00	199,911.00	22,164.00	67,842.00	88,076.00	178,082.00
6	140,505.00	109,824.00	160,943.00	411,272.00	150,089.00	100,157.00	206,123.00	456,369.00
7								
8	90,196.00	85,310.00	24,513.00	200,019.00	27,491.00	70,941.00	29,808.00	128,240.00
9	80,260.00	18,206.00	66,115.00	164,581.00	62,070.00	46,504.00	16,572.00	125,146.00
10	63,075.00	82,701.00	51,812.00	197,588.00	77,758.00	60,902.00	29,935.00	168,595.00
11	233,531.00	186,217.00	142,440.00	562,188.00	167,319.00	178,347.00	76,315.00	421,981.00
12								
13	374,036.00	296,041.00	303,383.00	973,460.00	317,408.00	278,504.00	282,438.00	878,350.00
14								
15								

The dashed lines indicate page breaks.

Microsoft Excel numbers and prints pages in one of the following ways.

- **Down, Then Across**   Numbering and printing proceed from the first page to the pages below, and then move to the right and continue printing down the sheet.

- **Across, Then Down**   Numbering and printing proceed from the first page to the pages to the right, and then move down and continue printing across the sheet.

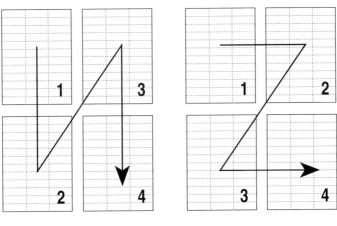

Down, then across   Across, then down

When printing more than one sheet at a time, Microsoft Excel numbers all of the pages in one continuous sequence. For each sheet, you can also specify the number at which you want page numbering to start.

To	Do this
Display page breaks on the screen	From the Tools menu, choose Options. Select the View tab, and then select the Automatic Page Breaks check box.
Set a manual page break (both vertical and horizontal)	Select the cell where you want to start a new page, and then choose Page Break from the Insert menu.
Set a manual page break (vertical only)	Select the column where you want to start the left edge of the new page, and then choose Page Break from the Insert menu.
Set a manual page break (horizontal only)	Select the row where you want to start the top edge of the new page, and then choose Page Break from the Insert menu.
Set page printing order	From the File menu, choose Page Setup, and then select the Sheet tab. Under Page Order, select the printing order you want.
Begin numbering pages at a specified page number	From the File menu, choose Page Setup, and then select the Page tab. In the First Page Number box, type the starting page number you want.

Sizing and Printing Charts

You can embed your charts on a worksheet, or keep them on separate chart sheets. When the chart is embedded on a worksheet, it prints as it appears on the worksheet. When it is on a chart sheet, however, you can choose how to scale it when printed.

To adjust scaling and printing options for a chart sheet, choose Page Setup from the File menu. Select the Chart tab, and then select the scaling and printing options you want. For more information, see "Changing the Look of a Chart" in Chapter 18.

Tip To print more than one chart per page, embed the charts on a worksheet. Show page breaks, and then size the charts so that they fit on the number of pages you want.

Step By Step

For step-by-step instructions and related information, double-click the ⬚? button to display the Search dialog box in Help, and then:

Type this keyword and choose Show Topics	Select a topic and choose Go To
page breaks	Inserting or removing page breaks
print area	Reducing or enlarging what you want to print
print preview	Previewing what will print
printing selected ranges	Printing a range of pages
	Printing a sheet, selected range, or entire workbook
sizing chart sheets	Choosing how to size a chart sheet

Creating and Printing Custom Reports

What Is a Report?

A report is a unique set of sheet, named view, and/or scenario options set up for printing. A report is made up of one or more sections. Each section can consist of:

- One sheet
- One named view (optional)
- One scenario (optional)

Use reports to:

- **Print Sheets in Any Order**   Using the normal printing options in Microsoft Excel, you can print your sheets only in sequential order. In a report, however, you can create sections that contain workbook sheets. By changing the order of the sections, you can create a report that prints your sheets in the order you want.

- **Print Views Using Different Display Options**   A view is a set of display and print options you can apply to a worksheet. For example, in one report you could print a detail view and a summary view of the same worksheet. For information about views, see "Creating Different Views of a Worksheet" in Chapter 32.

- **Print Worksheet Models with Scenario Input Values**   A scenario is a set of input values you can apply to worksheet formulas. For example, a report for a budget forecast worksheet could present best case, worst case, and likely case scenarios. For information about scenarios, see "Keep Track of What-if Assumptions Using Scenarios" in Chapter 28.

This report is set up
with three sections.
Each section of the
report starts on a
new page.

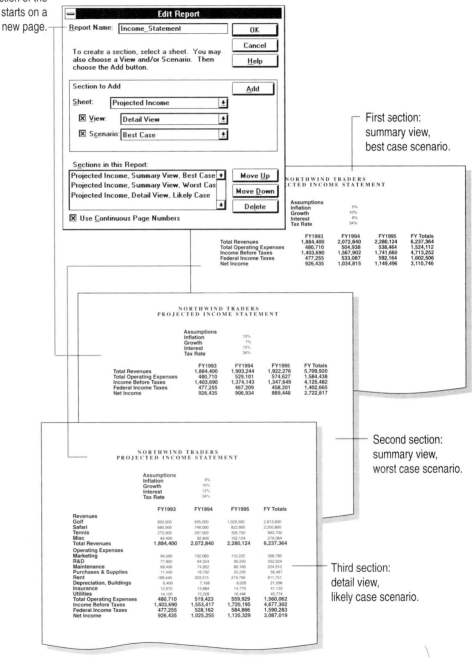

First section:
summary view,
best case scenario.

Second section:
summary view,
worst case scenario.

Third section:
detail view,
likely case scenario.

You can create multiple reports for each workbook. Reports are saved with the workbook file.

Creating and Printing Reports

When you're ready to create a report, choose Print Report from the File menu. Choose the Add button to display the Add Report dialog box.

The Print Report command is an add-in. If the Print Report command appears on the File menu, it is already installed. If the Print Report command doesn't appear, choose the Add-ins command from the Tools menu to see the list of add-ins currently available. If Report Manager appears there, make sure that its adjacent check box is selected. If Report Manager does not appear, you need to run the Microsoft Excel Setup program to install the Report Manager add-in. For more information, see Chapter 1, "Installing and Starting Microsoft Excel," or the Step By Step table at the end of this section.

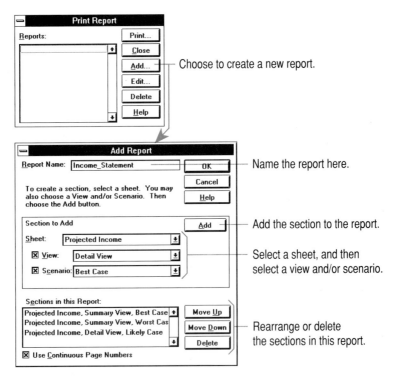

To print a report, choose Print Report from the File menu, select the report to print, and then choose the Print button. Microsoft Excel prints the report, starting each section of the report on a new page.

Step By Step

For step-by-step instructions and related information, double-click the ⬚?⬚ button to display the Search dialog box in Help, and then:

Type this keyword and choose Show Topics	Select a topic and choose Go To
add-ins	Installing or removing an add-in
reports, creating	Creating a report
reports, editing	Editing a report
reports, printing	Printing a report

PART 3

Creating Charts from Worksheet Data

C H A P T E R   1 5

Creating a Chart

For command,
keyboard, and
toolbar button
information, see
online Help.

In This Chapter

What Is a Chart?

A chart is a graphic representation of worksheet data. Values from worksheet cells, or *data points,* are displayed as bars, lines, columns, pie slices, or other shapes in the chart. Data points are grouped into *data series,* which are distinguished by different colors or patterns.

Showing your data in a chart can make it clearer, more interesting, and easier to read. Charts can also help you evaluate your data and make comparisons between different worksheet values.

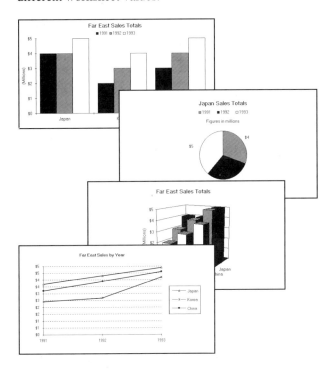

The ChartWizard

ChartWizard

The ChartWizard is a series of dialog boxes that simplifies creating a chart. The ChartWizard guides you through the process step by step: you verify your data selection, select a chart type, and decide whether to add items such as titles and a legend. A sample of the chart you are creating is displayed so that you can make changes before you finish working in the ChartWizard.

For more information about creating charts, see "Creating an Embedded Chart on a Worksheet" and "Creating a Chart Sheet in a Workbook" later in this chapter.

Embedded Charts and Chart Sheets

You can create an *embedded chart* as an object on a worksheet when you want to display a chart along with its associated data. For example, you can use embedded charts for reports and other documents in which it's best to display a chart within the context of the worksheet data.

You can create a *chart sheet* as a separate sheet in a workbook when you want to display a chart apart from its associated data. You might do this when you want to show overhead projections of your charts as part of a presentation.

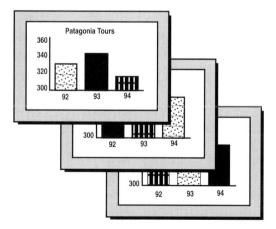

Whether you create an embedded chart or a chart sheet, your chart data is automatically linked to the worksheet you created it from. When you change the data on your worksheet, the chart is updated to reflect these changes.

How a Worksheet Range Translates into a Chart

The following illustration shows one way worksheet data can be displayed in a chart—with the data series in worksheet rows.

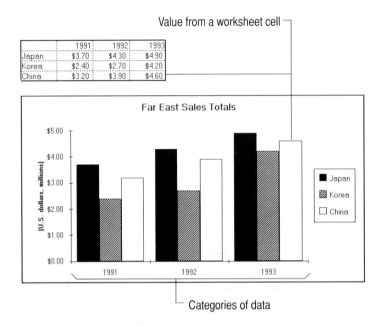

Value from a worksheet cell

	1991	1992	1993
Japan	$3.70	$4.30	$4.90
Korea	$2.40	$2.70	$4.20
China	$3.20	$3.90	$4.60

Categories of data

Plotting Data Series in Rows or Columns   When you create a chart, you specify the *orientation* of the data—that is, whether the data series are in worksheet rows or worksheet columns. You can also use the ChartWizard to change the orientation of the data in an existing chart.

For information about the available chart types, see Chapter 16, "Working with Chart Types and Autoformats." For more information about changing the orientation of data in an existing chart, see Chapter 17, "Changing Data in a Chart."

Plotting Nonadjacent Selections   Sometimes the data you are plotting is in rows or columns separated by other data, or by blank rows or columns. You can make *nonadjacent selections* (sometimes called "discontiguous" selections) and use them to create the chart.

These nonadjacent selections...

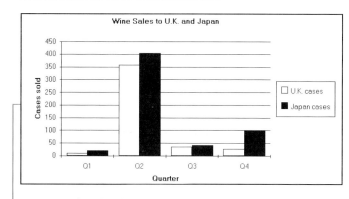

...create a chart showing cases sold, but not dollar sales.

Tip   Nonadjacent selections must be a rectangular shape. In cases such as the preceding illustration, in which some cells contain text for series and category names, the blank cell in the upper-left corner of the rectangle must be selected to create the chart correctly.

To make nonadjacent selections, begin by selecting cells in the first row or column.

System	To make nonadjacent selections, hold down this key as you make additional selections
Windows	CTRL
Macintosh	COMMAND

For information about selecting cells on a worksheet, see Chapter 8, "Selecting Cells and Choosing Commands."

You can also hide rows and columns you don't want to include in your chart, or you can create an outline and collapse the levels you want to exclude. For more information, see "Charting Visible Worksheet Data" in Chapter 19.

Multicategory 3-D Charts When your data has two classifications associated with one set of values, you can create a multicategory 3-D chart. In the following illustration, the number of units sold is shown in relation to both the number of mailed pamphlets and the number of minutes advertised on television.

		Mailed Pamphlets (K=thousand)				
		2-5K	6-10K	11-15K	16-20K	21-30K
TV Advertising	2-5 min.	1112	1245	1395	1562	1750
(in minutes)	6-10 min.	1699	1903	2131	2387	2673
	11-15 min.	2670	2990	3349	3751	4201
	16-20 min.	4140	4637	5193	5816	6300
	20-30 min.	6418	7188	8051	8540	9800

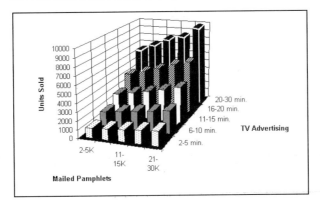

For more information about 3-D charts, see Chapter 16, "Working with Chart Types and Autoformats."

The Default Chart Format

When you create a new chart, by default it is a column chart with a legend displayed and some standard formatting applied. You can change these attributes either as you're creating the chart or later, using the commands on the Format menu. You can also add items to your chart, using the commands on the Insert menu.

However, if you want most or all of the charts you create to be a type other than column, or to have different formatting, you can change the default format. Changing the default format does not affect existing charts, but all charts you subsequently create will have the new characteristics you specify.

Changing the Default Chart To change the default chart, choose Options from the Tools menu. Select the Chart tab, and then under Default Chart Format, select the format you want. To reset the default to the original Microsoft Excel format, select Built-In.

For information about creating custom chart formats, see Chapter 16, "Working with Chart Types and Autoformats." For information about changing the formatting in a chart without changing the default format, see Chapter 18, "Formatting a Chart."

Step By Step

For step-by-step instructions and related information, double-click the [k?] button to display the Search dialog box in Help, and then:

Type this keyword and choose Show Topics	Select a topic and choose Go To
chart format, default	Changing the default chart format
chart sheets, creating	Creating a chart sheet in a workbook
embedded charts, creating	Creating an embedded chart on a worksheet

Creating an Embedded Chart on a Worksheet

When you create an embedded chart, the chart is saved as an object on the worksheet when you save the workbook.

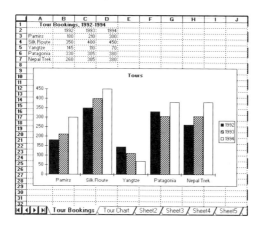

The embedded chart is always available when the worksheet is active, and the chart is printed with the data when you print the worksheet. The chart data is still linked to the source data and is automatically updated when the worksheet data changes.

Creating an Embedded Chart

ChartWizard

Select the worksheet data you want to display in the chart, and then click the ChartWizard button. The mouse pointer changes to a cross hair with a chart symbol. You can either click anywhere on the worksheet to have the chart placed automatically, or place the cross hair and drag where you want the chart to appear. Follow the instructions in the ChartWizard; the chart is added to the worksheet.

Tip To move from step to step in the ChartWizard, choose the Next and Back buttons. To have Microsoft Excel finish creating the chart from any step in the ChartWizard, choose the Finish button.

Another way to create an embedded chart is to select your worksheet data, choose Chart from the Insert menu, and then choose On This Sheet.

Moving and Sizing an Embedded Chart To move the chart on the worksheet, select it by clicking anywhere in the chart and then drag it where you want it. If the chart is active, you can move it by dragging its border.

To change the size of the chart, select it by clicking anywhere in the chart and then point to one of its corners. When the pointer changes to a double-headed arrow, drag the chart to resize it.

For more information about activating or selecting a chart, see "Activating a Chart to Modify It" later in this chapter.

Deleting an Embedded Chart You can delete an embedded chart from a worksheet by selecting the chart and then pressing DEL. You can also choose Clear from the Edit menu and then choose All.

For more information about working with existing charts, see Chapter 16, "Working with Chart Types and Autoformats"; Chapter 17, "Changing Data in a Chart"; and Chapter 18, "Formatting a Chart."

Step By Step

For step-by-step instructions and related information, double-click the [↖?] button to display the Search dialog box in Help, and then:

Type this keyword and choose Show Topics	Select a topic and choose Go To
ChartWizard Button	ChartWizard Button
embedded charts, creating	Creating an embedded chart on a worksheet

Creating a Chart Sheet in a Workbook

When you create a chart sheet in a workbook, the chart sheet is saved along with the other sheets when you save the workbook.

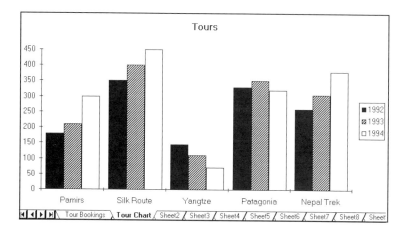

The chart data is still linked to the source data and is automatically updated when the worksheet data changes. You can print the chart sheet independently of the other sheets in the workbook.

Creating a Chart Sheet

To create a chart sheet, select the worksheet data you want to display in the chart, choose Chart from the Insert menu, and then choose As New Sheet.

Follow the instructions in the ChartWizard. The new chart sheet is added to the active workbook, to the left of the worksheet containing the associated data. The chart sheets you create in a workbook are named Chart1, Chart2, and so on by default. You can rename them if you want to by using the Rename command (Format menu, Sheet submenu).

Tip   To move from step to step in the ChartWizard, choose the Next and Back buttons. To have Microsoft Excel finish creating the chart from any step in the ChartWizard, choose the Finish button.

Shortcut to Creating a Chart Sheet   You can create a chart sheet quickly by pressing F11 after selecting the worksheet data. The ChartWizard is displayed if Microsoft Excel needs more information to correctly interpret and plot your data.

For example, you might want to create the chart and then apply a custom chart format you have created. To apply a custom format, choose AutoFormat from the Format menu and then select the format you want.

For more information about working with existing charts, see Chapter 16, "Working with Chart Types and Autoformats"; Chapter 17, "Changing Data in a Chart"; and Chapter 18, "Formatting a Chart." For information about working with workbooks, see Chapter 6, "Managing Workbook Files."

Step By Step

For step-by-step instructions and related information, double-click the [?] button to display the Search dialog box in Help, and then:

Type this keyword and choose Show Topics	Select a topic and choose Go To
chart sheets, creating	Creating a chart sheet in a workbook
ChartWizard Button	ChartWizard Button
sheets, deleting	Deleting sheets
sheets, inserting	Inserting sheets

Activating a Chart to Modify It

To make changes to a chart, you must activate it. When a chart is active, the chart commands are available, and you can select items within the chart and make the changes you want. For example, you can add items—such as a legend to identify the data series—by using the commands on the Insert menu. You can also format items—such as columns, lines, or pie slices—by using the commands on the Format menu.

To move, size, or delete an embedded chart on a worksheet, you select the chart just as you would select any object on the worksheet, without activating the chart.

Activating an Embedded Chart

To activate the chart, double-click the chart on the worksheet. The chart border changes from a thin line to a thicker gray border, indicating that the chart is active.

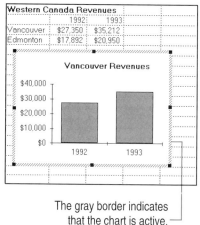

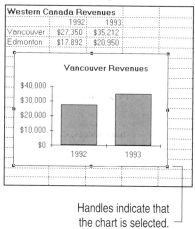

The gray border indicates
that the chart is active.

Handles indicate that
the chart is selected.

Selecting an Embedded Chart To move, size, or delete an embedded chart, select it by clicking anywhere in the chart on the worksheet. The chart is not active, though —that is, you cannot make changes to it, and the chart commands are not available.

If the embedded chart is active and you want to select it to move, size or delete it, click anywhere outside the chart, and then click anywhere inside the chart to select it.

Activating a Chart Sheet

With the appropriate workbook open, select the tab for the chart sheet you want.

Step By Step

For step-by-step instructions and related information, double-click the ⟨▶?⟩ button to display the Search dialog box in Help, and then:

Type this keyword and choose Show Topics	Select a topic and choose Go To
charts, activating	Activating a chart

Selecting Items in a Chart

To change an item in a chart, begin by selecting the item. For example, you might want to select slices in a pie chart and then change the way they are formatted.

In some cases, a command is not available until you've selected an item that command can act on. For example, to add error bars to a data series, you must select the series before you can choose Error Bars from the Insert menu.

The Parts of a Chart

The following illustration shows the parts of a 2-D chart.

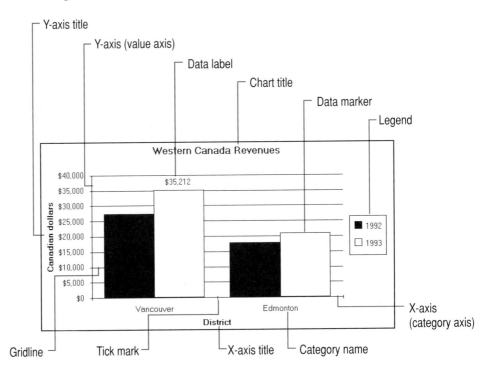

The following illustration shows parts specific to a 3-D chart.

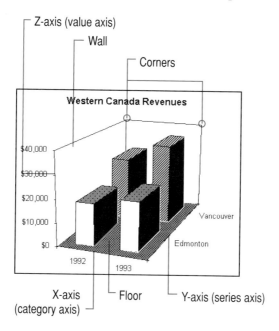

The Chart Area and the Plot Area   You can select the entire chart (the *chart area*) if, for example, you want to copy the chart to another sheet. The chart area contains all of the data series and the axes, along with the chart title, the axis titles, and the legend.

You can also select the *plot area* to change its size or formatting. In a 2-D chart, the plot area is bounded by the axes. In a 3-D chart, the plot area includes the category names, tick-mark labels, and axis titles. The following illustration shows the difference between the chart area and the plot area.

The chart area is selected.

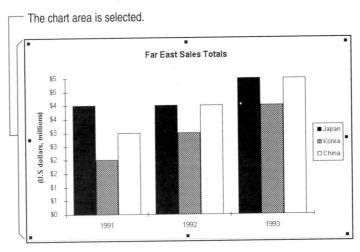

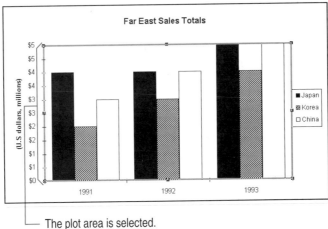

The plot area is selected.

Other Chart Items You Can Select Depending on the chart type, there are other items that you can select and format. The following illustration shows several of these items.

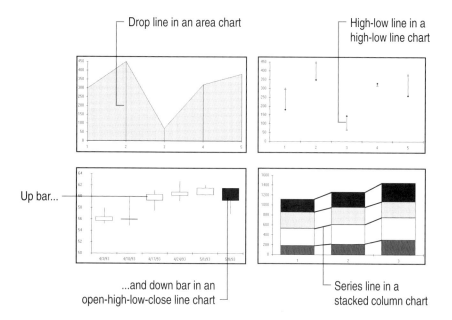

You can also select and change trendlines and error bars, and graphic objects such as text boxes, arrows, ovals, and rectangles. For information about adding trendlines and error bars to data series, see Chapter 19, "Using Charts to Analyze Data." For information about working with graphic objects, see Chapter 13, "Creating Graphic Objects on Worksheets and Charts."

Tip When an item is selected, its name is displayed at the left end of the formula bar.

Selecting Items with the Mouse

Before you select the chart area or an item within it, activate the chart. To select the chart area, click in the chart, but not on any specific item. Then click any items you want to select.

Selecting a Data Series or a Data Point   When you click a data marker, you select the data series containing that data point. Changes you make, such as inserting data labels, apply to all of the data points in the selected series. To select and change only one data marker, click the marker again after selecting the series.

Click a data marker once to select the data series.

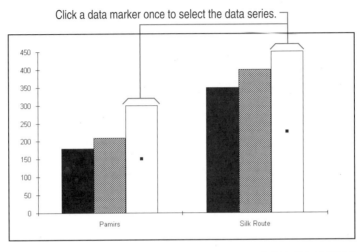

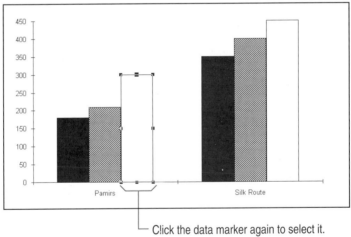

Click the data marker again to select it.

Selecting a Legend, a Legend Entry, or a Legend Key To select any part of a legend, begin by clicking the legend itself. Then you can make changes that affect the entire legend, such as moving it, sizing it, or adding a border to it. To change only one legend entry or legend key, click the entry or key a second time.

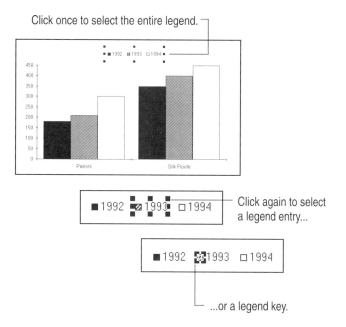

Selecting Items with the Keyboard

Instead of using the mouse, you can use the keyboard to make selections after you've activated a chart.

- Use the arrow keys to select chart items and graphic objects. The selection moves from item to item as you press the UP ARROW and DOWN ARROW keys. The selection moves between items within a group as you press the RIGHT ARROW and LEFT ARROW keys.

- After clicking to select a graphic object, press TAB to move between graphic objects. The selection moves to the next graphic object each time you press TAB.

For information about formatting a chart and individual items in a chart, see Chapter 18, "Formatting a Chart." For information about changing the information in a chart, see Chapter 17, "Changing Data in a Chart."

Canceling a Selection

To undo the selection of a chart or a chart item, press ESC.

Step By Step

For step-by-step instructions and related information, double-click the ⬛ button to display the Search dialog box in Help, and then:

Type this keyword and choose Show Topics	Select a topic and choose Go To
chart items, selecting	Selecting items in a chart with the keyboard
	Selecting items in a chart with the mouse

Adding Data Labels, Titles, and Other Items to a Chart

A simple chart cannot always convey information as clearly or completely as you would like. You can add information, increase visual interest, and enhance readability by adding elements such as data labels, titles, a legend, gridlines, or a combination of these.

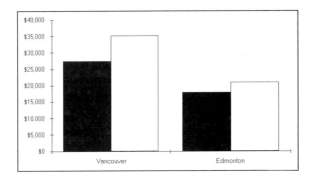

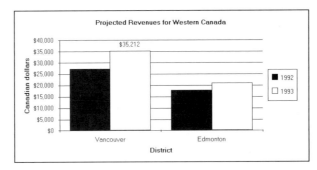

Adding Data Labels

To add data labels to a data point or a data series, select the point or the series and then choose the Data Labels command from the Insert menu. In the dialog box, specify what kind of data labels you want displayed.

If you have not selected a data point or a data series before choosing the command, data labels are added to all points in the chart.

Adding a Chart Title and Axis Titles

To add a chart title, axis titles, or both, choose the Titles command from the Insert menu and then specify which titles you want. You can then select each title and type the text you want.

Adding a Legend

Legend

To add a legend that identifies the data series or categories in your chart, choose the Legend command from the Insert menu, or click the Legend button on the Chart toolbar.

Adding Gridlines

Horizontal Gridlines

To add gridlines, which extend from the tick marks on an axis across the plot area, choose the Gridlines command from the Insert menu. Specify which gridlines you want: major, minor, horizontal, vertical, or any combination of these. You can also add major horizontal gridlines by clicking the Horizontal Gridlines button on the Chart toolbar.

Other Items That Can Be Added to a Chart

You can add text boxes, arrows, and other graphic objects to charts. For more information, see Chapter 13, "Creating Graphic Objects on Worksheets and Charts."

You can also add a secondary axis and specify which axis a data series is associated with. For more information, see "Formatting Axes, Gridlines, and Tick Marks" in Chapter 18.

Trendlines and error bars can provide additional information about the data in a chart. For more information about adding trendlines and error bars, see Chapter 19, "Using Charts to Analyze Data."

For information about formatting all the parts of a chart, see Chapter 18, "Formatting a Chart."

Step By Step

For step-by-step instructions and related information, double-click the ⟨k?⟩ button to display the Search dialog box in Help, and then:

Type this keyword and choose Show Topics	Select a topic and choose Go To
chart titles	Adding a chart title and axis titles
data labels	Adding data labels
deleting, chart items	Deleting data labels, titles, legends, or gridlines
gridlines, adding	Adding gridlines
legends, adding	Adding a legend

CHAPTER 16

Working with Chart Types and Autoformats

For command, keyboard, and toolbar button information, see online Help.

In This Chapter

Chart Types and Autoformats

When you create a chart from worksheet data, you'll want to choose the chart type that presents that particular data most clearly and effectively. Microsoft Excel offers 14 different chart types for you to choose from.

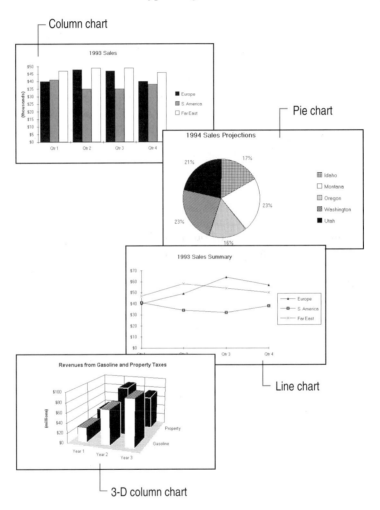

Column chart

Pie chart

Line chart

3-D column chart

For information about the 14 chart types, see "What's the Best Chart Type for Your Data?" later in this chapter.

You can choose a chart type for the entire chart, or you can assign a chart type to one or more data series. For example, you might want to show revenues for several corporate divisions in columns, and revenue totals as a line. For more information, see "Combining Multiple Chart Types in a Chart" later in this chapter.

Chart Subtypes

Each chart type has at least one *subtype,* or variation, which you can choose to show your data somewhat differently. You can use subtypes and chart types in combinations to create a variety of looks.

Column chart

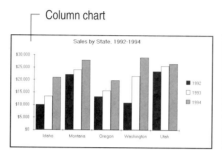
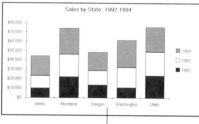

Stacked column chart subtype

Chart Autoformats

Once you create a chart, you can move, size, and change the look of many chart items. Or, instead of selecting and formatting individual items, you can apply an *autoformat* to your chart.

This area chart autoformat has drop lines.

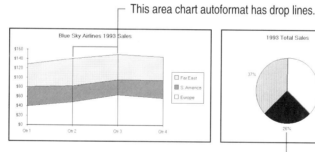
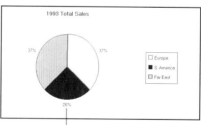

This pie chart autoformat has percent data labels.

Autoformats are similar to templates or styles. When you apply an autoformat to the active chart, it changes the entire look of the chart but does not affect your data. You can create custom autoformats and apply them to other charts whenever you want.

For more information about using autoformats, see "Working with Built-in and Custom Chart Autoformats" later in this chapter. For information about creating a chart, see Chapter 15, "Creating a Chart." If you need to change the data or text in your chart, see Chapter 17, "Changing Data in a Chart." For information about formatting the items in a chart, see Chapter 18, "Formatting a Chart."

Changing the Chart Type

Sometimes you want to change the chart type for all data series. In the following illustration, the data series are shown first as a column chart and then as a line chart.

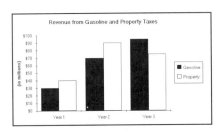
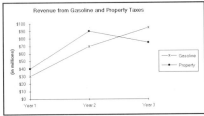

To change the chart type, first activate the chart. Then choose the Chart Type command from the Format menu, and select the chart type you want.

In the dialog box, you can specify whether you are changing the type for the whole chart, the selected data series, or a *chart type group*—several data series of the same type. If you select a data series before choosing the command, the chart type changes for that series only, unless you specify otherwise.

Chart Type

Instead of choosing the Chart Type command, you can click the arrow next to the Chart Type button on the Chart toolbar and select the type you want from the palette.

For information about the chart types you can choose from, see "What's the Best Chart Type for Your Data?" later in this chapter. For information about chart type groups and combining different chart types in one chart, see "Combining Multiple Chart Types in a Chart" later in this chapter. For information about activating a chart and selecting a data series, see Chapter 15, "Creating a Chart."

Step By Step

For step-by-step instructions and related information, double-click the [?] button to display the Search dialog box in Help, and then:

Type this keyword and choose Show Topics	Select a topic and choose Go To
autoformats, applying	Applying an autoformat to a chart
chart types	Changing the chart type of an entire chart

Combining Multiple Chart Types in a Chart

Sometimes it's helpful to display data in more than one way in the same chart. For example, you might want to show several data series as columns, but show another data series as a line to set it off visually from the others. By combining different chart types, you can create an overlay effect.

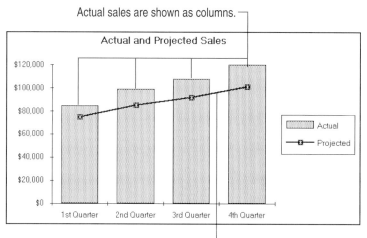

Actual sales are shown as columns.

Projected sales are shown as a line.

When you format one or more data series as one chart type, you are creating a chart type group, which is then listed on the Format menu. The preceding illustration shows a column chart group and a line chart group. You can select the group and make changes, such as changing the chart subtype or plotting the group along a secondary axis. The changes you make apply only to the data series included in the group.

Using Autoformats to Combine Chart Types   You can quickly combine chart types by choosing a combination autoformat instead of changing the chart type for individual series. You can do this when you create a chart or when you're working with an existing chart. But be careful with existing charts: any custom formatting you have applied will be lost if you apply any autoformat.

Autoformats are grouped by chart type and can be applied by using the AutoFormats command on the Format menu. For more information, see "Working with Built-in and Custom Chart Autoformats" later in this chapter.

Displaying Data Series as Different Chart Types

To assign a chart type to a data series, first select the data series, and then choose the Chart Type command from the Format menu. To make other changes, such as changing the subtype or the series order, choose the Options button after changing the chart type.

Chart Type

After selecting the data series, you can click the arrow next to the Chart Type button on the Chart toolbar and select the type you want from the palette. This is an alternative method to choosing the Chart Type command.

For information about chart types and their variations, see "What's the Best Chart Type for Your Data?" later in this chapter.

Plotting Data Along Different Axes

When the average values for different data series vary widely, or you have mixed types of data such as price and volume, you can plot one or more data series along a secondary value axis instead of along the primary axis. The scale of the secondary axis reflects the values for the associated series.

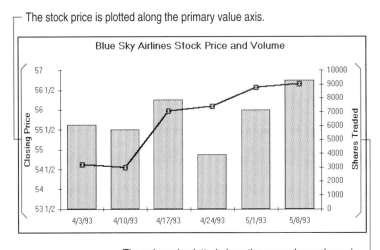

The stock price is plotted along the primary value axis.

The volume is plotted along the secondary value axis.

Plotting One Data Series Along a Secondary Axis Select the series and then choose the Selected Series command from the Format menu. Select the Axis tab and then select the Secondary Axis option button.

Plotting a Group of Data Series Along a Secondary Axis Choose the chart type group—for example, Column Group or Line Group—from the Format menu. Select the Axis tab and then select the Secondary Axis option.

Tip To display or hide axes, choose the Axes command from the Insert menu.

Guidelines for Combining Chart Types and Assigning Series to Axes

Because different chart types use axes differently, there are some limitations on how you can combine chart types. The following are guidelines for combining 2-D chart types:

- You can create any combination of area, column, line, and xy (scatter) charts.

- You can have one group assigned as a bar, pie, doughnut, or radar chart, along with any combination of area, column, line, and xy (scatter) charts. A bar chart group must have secondary axes assigned because the axes are rotated; that is, the category axis is vertical and the value axis is horizontal.

Note   You cannot combine chart types when using 3-D charts.

Step By Step

For step-by-step instructions and related information, double-click the 🕮 button to display the Search dialog box in Help, and then:

Type this keyword and choose Show Topics	Select a topic and choose Go To
chart types	Changing the chart type of a data series
plotting data	Plotting data along a secondary axis

Working with Built-in and Custom Chart Autoformats

Applying an *autoformat,* instead of formatting items individually, can save time and give your charts a consistent look. You can use built-in autoformats or create your own custom (user-defined) autoformats.

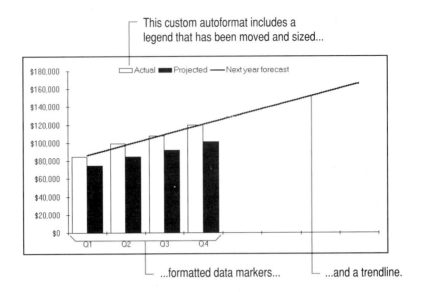

This custom autoformat includes a legend that has been moved and sized...

...formatted data markers... ...and a trendline.

Autoformats work much like templates or styles. Each autoformat is based on a chart type. An autoformat can also include a subtype, legend, gridlines, data labels, colors, patterns, and the placement of various items. When you apply an autoformat to an active chart, it changes the entire look of the chart but does not affect your data. You cannot modify autoformats, but you can add or delete custom autoformats.

If you've applied custom formatting that you don't want to lose, but you want to use a different chart type, do not apply an autoformat. Instead, change the chart type using the Chart Type command on the Format menu or the Chart Type button.

Applying a Built-in or Custom Autoformat to a Chart

To apply an autoformat, choose the AutoFormat command from the Format menu. Select User-Defined for custom autoformats or Built-in, depending on which kind of format you want to apply, and then select the format you want.

Tip You can add autoformat buttons to a toolbar by choosing the Toolbars command from the View menu, and then choosing the Customize button. If you don't like the last autoformat you applied, you can use the Undo command on the Edit menu to clear the autoformat from the chart.

Adding a Custom Autoformat to the Formats List

To add a custom autoformat to the Formats list, you can activate a chart you have created that has the characteristics you want to include. Or you can create a new chart and apply the formatting you want.

When all the formatting is the way you want it, choose the AutoFormat command from the Format menu. Select the User-Defined option button and then choose the Customize button.

In the User-Defined AutoFormats dialog box, choose the Add button. Give the custom autoformat a name and a description. The autoformat is added to the Formats list, and you can apply it to other charts whenever you want.

Deleting a Custom Autoformat   To delete a custom autoformat, choose the AutoFormat command from the Format menu. Select the User-Defined option button and then choose the Customize button. Select the autoformat you want to delete from the Formats list and choose the Delete button.

Sharing Custom Autoformats with Other Microsoft Excel Users

You can share your custom autoformats with other Microsoft Excel users. You can do this in two ways: copy individual chart files and then manually add them to the other user's list of custom autoformats; or copy the workbook in which all your custom autoformats are stored. The following table lists the filename and location of this workbook.

System	Filename and location of custom autoformats
Windows	XL5GALRY.XLS in the XLSTART directory in the directory where you installed Microsoft Excel
Macintosh	EXCEL CHART AUTOFORMATS (5) in the EXCEL STARTUP FOLDER (5), which is in the PREFERENCES folder within the SYSTEM FOLDER

These workbooks are transferable between Windows and Macintosh systems. For more information, see "Moving Microsoft Excel Files Between Windows and the Macintosh" in Chapter 42.

Note   When you change the chart format that is applied automatically to new charts —that is, the default chart format—you designate one of the built-in or custom autoformats as the new default chart format. You can change the default chart format setting in the Chart tab of the Options dialog box, which is available from the Tools menu. For more information, see "What is a Chart?" in Chapter 15.

Step By Step

For step-by-step instructions and related information, double-click the 『**?** button to display the Search dialog box in Help, and then:

Type this keyword and choose Show Topics	Select a topic and choose Go To
custom autoformats	Adding a custom autoformat to the Formats list
	Applying an autoformat to a chart
	Deleting a custom autoformat from the Formats list

What's the Best Chart Type for Your Data?

You can choose from 14 chart types to present your data clearly and effectively. Each chart type has several subtypes, or variations. The pages that follow describe and illustrate each chart type.

For information about creating charts, see Chapter 15, "Creating a Chart." For information about the ways you can format all the items in your charts, see Chapter 18, "Formatting a Chart." For information about creating combination charts with more than one chart type, see "Combining Multiple Chart Types in a Chart" earlier in this chapter.

Tip You can add trendlines and error bars to provide more information about the data series in your charts. For information about trendlines and error bars, see Chapter 19, "Using Charts to Analyze Data."

Area Chart Type

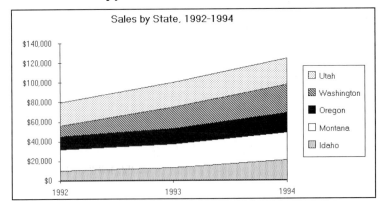

Shows the relative importance of values over a period of time. Although similar to a line chart, an area chart emphasizes the amount of change (magnitude of values) rather than time and the rate of change.

Bar Chart Type

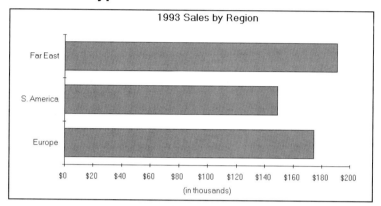

Shows individual figures at a specific time or illustrates comparisons between items. The stacked and 100% stacked subtypes show relationships to a whole. The categories on a bar chart are organized vertically, the values horizontally, placing more emphasis on comparisons and less emphasis on time.

Column Chart Type

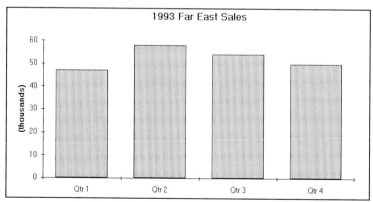

Shows variation over a period of time or illustrates comparisons between items. The stacked and 100% stacked subtypes show relationships to a whole. Although similar to a bar chart, a column chart's categories are organized horizontally, its values vertically.

Line Chart Type

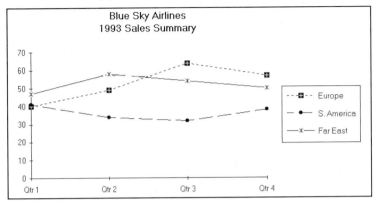

Shows trends or changes in data over a period of time, at even intervals. Although similar to an area chart, a line chart emphasizes time flow and rate of change, rather than the amount of change.

When you need to show trends or changes in data at uneven or clustered intervals, an xy (scatter) chart is usually more appropriate than a line chart. For more information, see "XY (Scatter) Chart Type" later in this section.

High-Low-Close and Open-High-Low-Close Charts The high-low-close and open-high-low-close subtypes are often used for stock prices; the open-high-low-close subtype is sometimes called a "candlestick" chart.

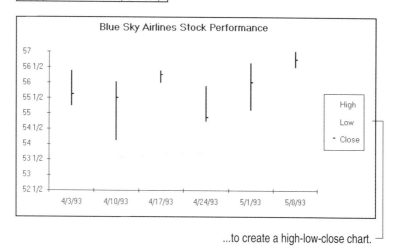

Arrange your data in this order...

Date	High	Low	Close
4/3/93	56 3/8	55 1/4	55 5/8
4/10/93	56	54 1/8	55 1/2
4/17/93	56 3/8	56	56 1/4
4/24/93	55 7/8	54 3/4	54 7/8
5/1/93	56 5/8	55 1/8	56
5/8/93	57	56 1/2	56 3/4

...to create a high-low-close chart.

Important You must organize your data series in the correct order to create these charts. That is, the order of the data in worksheet rows or columns must be the high values followed by the low and close values, or the open values followed by the high, low, and close values.

The high-low-close chart subtype can also be used for scientific data—for example, to indicate temperature changes.

For information about adding error bars to data series to show the plus-or-minus factor for your data, see Chapter 19, "Using Charts to Analyze Data."

Pie Chart Type

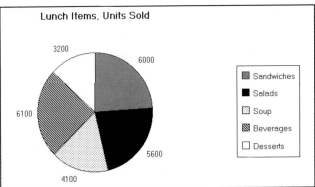

Shows the relationship or proportions of parts to a whole; this chart type is useful for emphasizing a significant element. A pie chart always contains one data series—if you have more than one data series selected, only one will be displayed in your chart.

Tip If you want to show more than one data series in a round chart, you can use the doughnut chart type.

Doughnut Chart Type

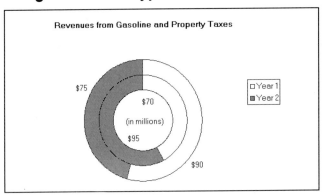

Similar to the pie chart. The main difference, other than the "doughnut hole," is that it can show more than one data series, unlike the pie chart. The doughnut chart is widely used in the Far East.

Radar Chart Type

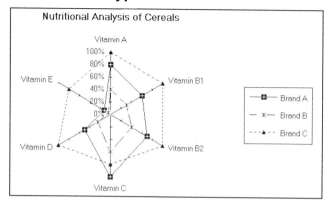

Shows changes or frequencies of data series relative to a center point and to one another. Each category has its own value axis radiating from the center point. Lines connect all the data markers in the same series. The radar chart is widely used in the Far East.

XY (Scatter) Chart Type

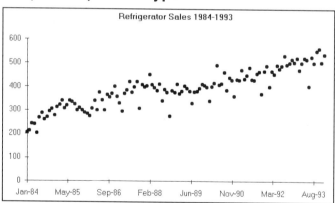

Shows the relationship or degree of relationship between the numeric values in several chart data series, or plots two groups of numbers as one series of xy coordinates. The xy (scatter) chart shows uneven intervals, or clusters, of data. It is commonly used for scientific data.

Tip You can connect the points in a xy (scatter) chart with a line by selecting the appropriate autoformat when you create the chart. If you want to connect the points in an existing xy (scatter) chart, double-click the data series to display the Format Data Series dialog box, and specify a line in the Patterns tab.

Arranging Your Data for an XY (Scatter) Chart When you create an xy (scatter) chart, you generally arrange your data with x values in one row or column and with one or more corresponding y values in the adjacent rows or columns.

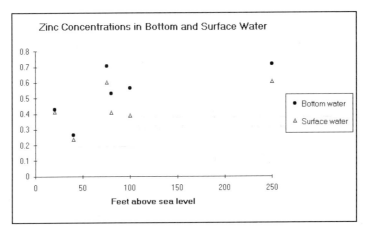

Zinc Concentrations in Bottom and Surface Water			
Stream altitude	Bottom water	Surface water	
20	0.43	0.415	
40	0.266	0.238	
100	0.567	0.39	
80	0.531	0.41	
75	0.707	0.605	
250	0.716	0.609	

X Values

Y Values

Tip You can also create an xy (scatter) chart with different x values for each set of y values. Arrange your data as shown above and then change the x value for the data series. Double-click a data series, select the X Values tab in the Format Selected Series dialog box, and change the worksheet reference.

Or you can plot multiple xy pairs from your worksheet by making nonadjacent selections. For information about plotting nonadjacent selections, see "What Is a Chart?" in Chapter 15.

3-D Area Chart Type

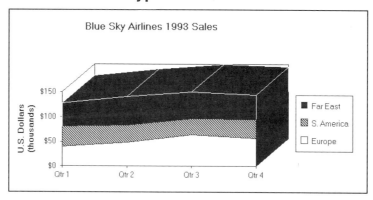

Shows a 3-D view of an area chart, which emphasizes the sum of plotted values and separates chart data series into distinct rows to show differences between the data series.

3-D Bar Chart Type

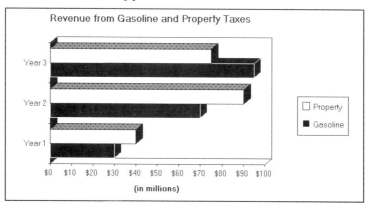

Shows a 3-D view of a bar chart, which emphasizes the values of individual items at a specific time or draws comparisons between items. The stacked and 100% stacked subtypes show relationships to a whole.

3-D Column Chart Type

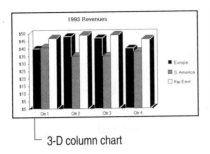
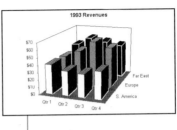

3-D column chart

3-D perspective column chart

Shows a 3-D view of a column chart in one of two variations: The simple 3-D column chart displays 3-D column markers along the x (category) axis. The 3-D perspective column chart compares data points along two axes—the x (category) axis and the y (series) axis. In both variations, the data values are plotted along the z axis. This chart type allows you to compare data within a data series more easily and still view the data by category.

3-D Line Chart Type

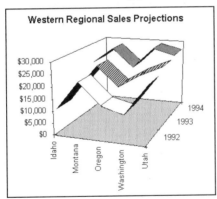

Shows lines in a line chart as 3-D ribbons. This chart type is often used to display data attractively for presentations.

3-D Pie Chart Type

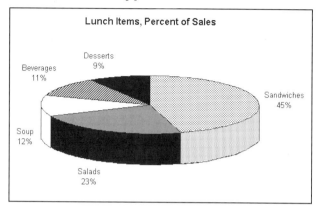

Shows a 3-D view of a pie chart, which emphasizes the data values in the front wedges. You can show one data series in a pie chart; if you want to show more than one series in a round chart shape, you can use the 2-D doughnut chart type.

3-D Surface Chart Type

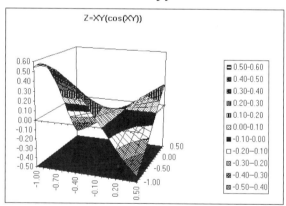

Shows what appears to be a rubber sheet stretched over a 3-D column chart. A 3-D surface chart is useful for finding the best combinations between two sets of data. This chart may show relationships between large amounts of data that otherwise would be difficult to see. As in a topographic map, colors or patterns indicate areas that are at the same value. Color does not mark the data series.

The "wire frame" format shows the data without color. The contour chart formats provide 2-D views of these charts from above, like 2-D topographic maps.

CHAPTER 17

Changing Data in a Chart

For command, keyboard, and toolbar button information, see online Help.

In This Chapter

Adding and Deleting Chart Data

Once you have created a chart, you sometimes need to update it by adding or deleting data series or data points. In some cases, you might want to change the range of worksheet data the chart is based on.

Adding Data Series and Data Points

There are two ways you can add data to an embedded chart on a worksheet:

- Select the data on the worksheet and drag it onto the chart. This is the faster way; it's equivalent to using the Copy and Paste commands.

- Use the New Data command on the Insert menu for charts.

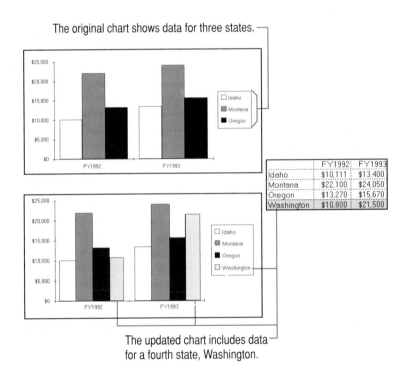

The original chart shows data for three states.

	FY1992	FY1993
Idaho	$10,111	$13,400
Montana	$22,100	$24,050
Oregon	$13,270	$15,670
Washington	$10,800	$21,500

The updated chart includes data for a fourth state, Washington.

When you are adding data points to a data series, you can add the category name along with the data by including it in the selection that you add to the chart.

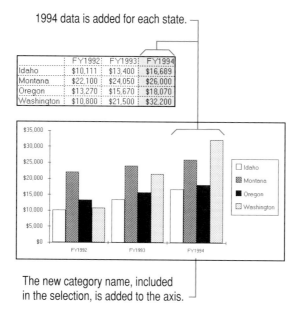

1994 data is added for each state.

	FY1992	FY1993	FY1994
Idaho	$10,111	$13,400	$16,689
Montana	$22,100	$24,050	$26,000
Oregon	$13,270	$15,670	$18,070
Washington	$10,800	$21,500	$32,200

The new category name, included
in the selection, is added to the axis.

When you drag data or choose the New Data command, Microsoft Excel examines your selection and compares it to the existing data in the chart. Based on how the existing data is plotted, the new data is placed in the chart.

In cases where placement and orientation of the data are uncertain, the Paste Special dialog box is displayed so that you can specify whether the new data is series or points.

When you are adding data to a chart sheet, select the worksheet data you want to add, choose the Copy command from the Edit menu, switch to the chart sheet, and then choose the Paste command. For more information about moving, copying, and pasting worksheet data, see Chapter 11, "Editing a Worksheet."

Deleting a Data Series from a Chart

You can delete a data series by selecting it and pressing the DEL key. You can also choose the Clear command from the Edit menu, and then choose Series.

If you have added data points or series incorrectly, you can remove them by choosing the Undo command from the Edit menu if you do so before taking another action.

To delete individual data points from a data series, delete the data on the worksheet or change the range plotted in the chart, as described in the following section.

Changing the Range of Data Plotted in a Chart

If you want a chart to display different data than was originally plotted, you can change the worksheet range the chart is based on.

ChartWizard

To change the range, select the embedded chart on your worksheet or switch to the chart sheet in your workbook. Then click the ChartWizard button. In step 1, specify the new range to be plotted in the chart.

The original range and
corresponding chart

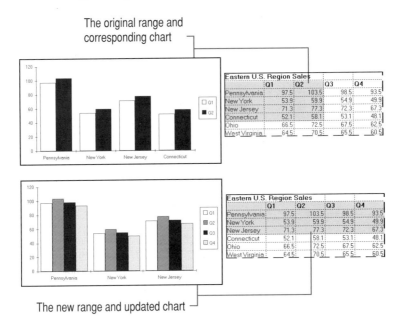

The new range and updated chart

For information about creating a chart and working with the ChartWizard, see Chapter 15, "Creating a Chart."

Changing the Range for a Chart Based on a Pivot Table   You can create a chart from a pivot table, which is an interactive table that allows you to create different views of your data. Whether you can change the range your chart is based on depends on the layout of your pivot table. In some cases, the chart may need to be created from the entire pivot table, and you cannot change the range.

For more information about creating a pivot table, see "Creating a Chart from a Pivot Table" in Chapter 24.

Step By Step

For step-by-step instructions and related information, double-click the [?] button to display the Search dialog box in Help, and then:

Type this keyword and choose Show Topics	Select a topic and choose Go To
updating, charts	Adding data series or data points to a chart sheet
	Adding data series or data points to an embedded chart
	Changing the worksheet range plotted in a chart
	Deleting a data series

Changing Chart Values

Once you have created a chart, the data points are automatically linked to the worksheet values they represent. If you need to change a value in an existing chart, it is easiest to change the worksheet contents directly. The chart is updated accordingly.

For many chart types, you can also change a value in both the chart and the worksheet by dragging the data marker on the chart. The illustration below shows the North column being adjusted by dragging.

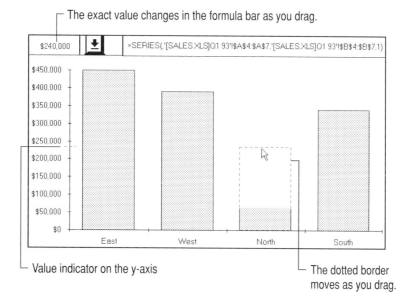

The exact value changes in the formula bar as you drag.

Value indicator on the y-axis

The dotted border moves as you drag.

You can drag the data markers on 2-D bar, 2-D column, 2-D line, 2-D stacked, 2-D pie, doughnut, and xy (scatter) charts.

Changing Values in Formulas

If the data marker you drag is associated with a formula, the Goal Seek dialog box is displayed. You can then enter a cell reference for a value in the formula that needs to be adjusted to achieve the result you want for the selected data point.

In the example shown in the following illustration, goal seeking can determine what value for University is needed to increase the Total value to 1,000.

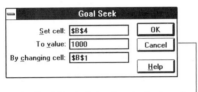

— When the value is generated by a formula...

...the Goal Seek dialog box is displayed. ⌐

For information about selecting items in a chart, see Chapter 15, "Creating a Chart." For information about working with goal seeking, see Chapter 27, "Solving What-If Problems." For information about the GOAL.SEEK function, click the Function Wizard button on the Standard toolbar or see online Help.

Step By Step

For step-by-step instructions and related information, double-click the [▶?] button to display the Search dialog box in Help, and then:

Type this keyword and choose Show Topics	Select a topic and choose Go To
changing, charts	Changing the value of a chart data point
editing, cell contents	Editing cell contents

Changing Chart Text

When you create a chart, the data labels, legend entries, and axis tick-mark labels are created from and automatically linked to the worksheet selection the chart is based on. It is usually easiest to make changes to this text by editing cells on the worksheet. You can edit data labels directly in the chart, although this breaks the automatic link.

If you have added a chart title, axis titles, or text boxes ("floating text") to your chart, you can select this text and type new text to replace it, or place the insertion point and edit it directly in the chart. Vertically aligned text is displayed horizontally until you are finished editing it.

You can also link titles and text boxes to worksheet cells, so that the text is updated automatically when the cell contents change.

When you are working with the chart, you can make changes to the kinds of text shown in the following illustration.

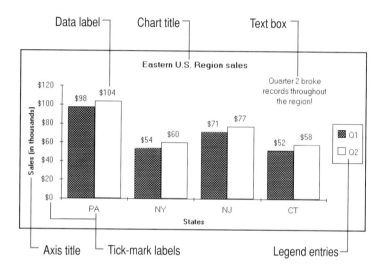

To change	Use this method
Chart title	Select and edit in place
Axis title	Select and edit in place
Text box	Select and edit in place
Data label contents	Select and edit in place
Data label type	Double-click the data series or data point and select the Data Labels tab
Category or series tick-mark labels	Double-click the first data series and select the X Values tab
Value tick-mark labels	Double-click the axis and select the Scale tab

To change	Use this method
Legend entries (data series names)	Double-click the data series and select the Name and Values tab

Tip You can restore the automatic links to worksheet data for data labels that have been edited. Double-click the data series, or select and double-click a single data point. On the Data Labels tab, select the Automatic Text check box.

For information about adding data labels, titles, and a legend to a chart, see Chapter 15, "Creating a Chart." For information about adding text boxes to a chart, see Chapter 13, "Creating Graphic Objects on Worksheets and Charts."

Linking Chart Text to a Worksheet Cell

To link a chart title, axis title, or text box to a worksheet cell, select the title or text box. In the formula bar, type an equal sign (=) and then select the worksheet cell. You can also type the cell reference following the equal sign. Once you have established a link, if you want to edit the text, you must do so in the formula bar.

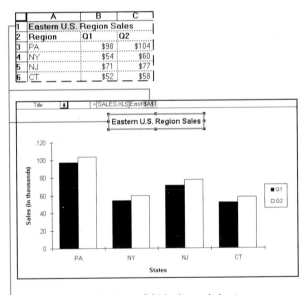

The chart title is linked to cell A1 in the worksheet.

Checking the Spelling of Chart Text

Spelling

To ensure that your chart text is spelled correctly, activate the chart and choose Spelling from the Tools menu. You can also click the Spelling button.

Step By Step

For step-by-step instructions and related information, double-click the [?] button to display the Search dialog box in Help, and then:

Type this keyword and choose Show Topics	Select a topic and choose Go To
chart labels	Adding data labels
	Changing data labels
	Changing tick-mark labels
chart legends	Changing legend entries
chart text	Changing the font and alignment of chart text
chart text boxes	Linking chart text to a worksheet cell
chart values	Changing number formats for chart values
checking spelling	Checking spelling in a chart
text boxes	Creating and deleting text boxes
	Editing titles and text boxes

Changing the Way Your Data Is Plotted

You can change the way your data is plotted in three ways. You can change whether the data series are plotted in worksheet rows or columns; reverse the plotting order of categories or values; or change the order in which series are plotted.

Plotting Data Series in Rows or Columns

You can change the orientation of your data—that is, define your data series in worksheet rows instead of columns, or vice versa, by using the ChartWizard.

ChartWizard

Select the embedded chart or switch to the chart sheet. Then click the ChartWizard button, go to step 2, and specify the orientation you want.

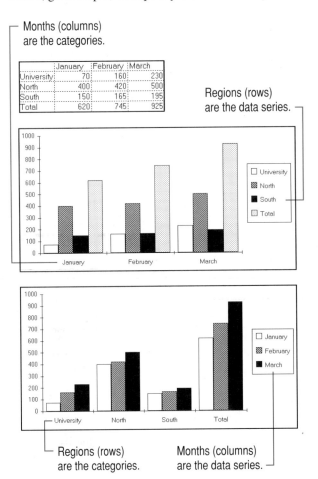

Months (columns)
are the categories.

	January	February	March
University	70	160	230
North	400	420	500
South	150	165	195
Total	620	745	925

Regions (rows)
are the data series.

Regions (rows)
are the categories.

Months (columns)
are the data series.

For more information about plotting data from worksheet rows and columns, see "What Is a Chart?" in Chapter 15.

Reversing the Plot Order of Categories or Values

You can display categories or values in reverse order along a chart axis. Double-click the axis and select the Scale tab; then select the Categories In Reverse Order check box or the Values In Reverse Order check box.

The orginal order of categories on the x-axis

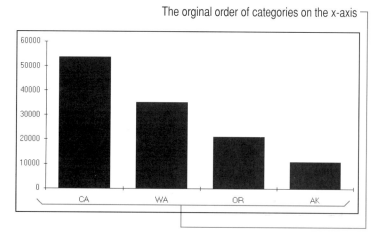

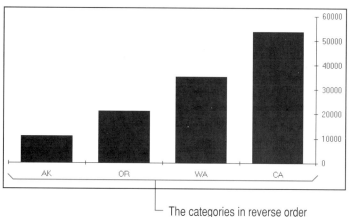

The categories in reverse order

Changing the Plot Order of Data Series

For data series within the same chart type group (other than radar charts), you can change the order in which the series are plotted. Choose the selected chart type from the Format menu (for example, 4 Column Chart) and select the Series Order tab. Specify the order you want by moving the series up and down in the list box.

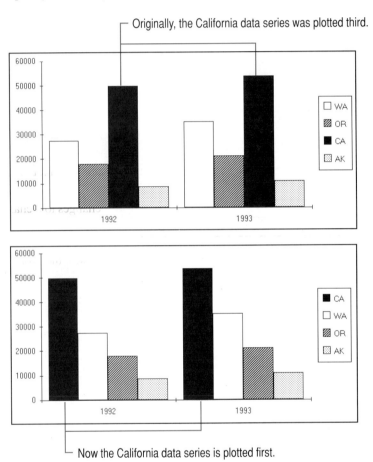

Originally, the California data series was plotted third.

Now the California data series is plotted first.

For information about using multiple chart types in a chart, see "Combining Multiple Chart Types in a Chart" in Chapter 16.

Step By Step

For step-by-step instructions and related information, double-click the ⬛️ button to display the Search dialog box in Help, and then:

Type this keyword and choose Show Topics	Select a topic and choose Go To
plotting charts	Changing the plot order of data series
	Plotting data series from rows or columns
	Reversing the plot order of categories, values, or series

How You Can Prevent Changes to a Chart

You can protect a chart's contents and formatting from accidental or unauthorized changes. You protect an embedded chart as you would any graphic object on a worksheet. You protect a chart sheet individually or with the workbook it resides in.

Tip   If you are trying unsuccessfully to make changes to a chart, check to see if the chart has been protected.

To protect embedded charts and chart sheets, choose the Protection command from the Tools menu.

For more information about protecting workbooks, worksheets, charts, and graphic objects, see Chapter 39, "Protecting a Workbook."

CHAPTER 18

Formatting a Chart

For command, keyboard, and toolbar button information, see online Help.

In This Chapter

Changing the Look of a Chart

You can change the look of a chart in many ways to get the final effect you want. These changes might include adjusting its overall size and color scheme, and sizing, arranging, and formatting items within the chart. For example, you can give the columns, lines, or pie slices different colors and patterns, and display text with different fonts and styles. Finally, you can set the way you want the chart to print and view it before printing.

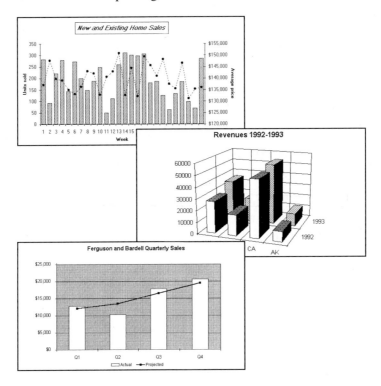

In addition to formatting your chart, you can add items such as titles and a legend by choosing commands from the Insert menu. For more information, see Chapter 15, "Creating a Chart."

If you want to change the chart type—for example, to display lines instead of columns—see Chapter 16, "Working with Chart Types and Autoformats."

Arranging and Sizing Chart Items

After activating the chart, you can move chart items such as titles, data labels, and pie and doughnut slices by selecting and dragging them. You can move and resize the plot area, the legend, and any graphic objects, such as text boxes and arrows, that you have created.

The legend has been moved and resized.

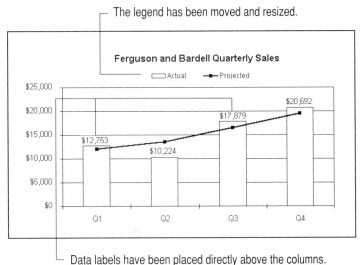

Data labels have been placed directly above the columns.

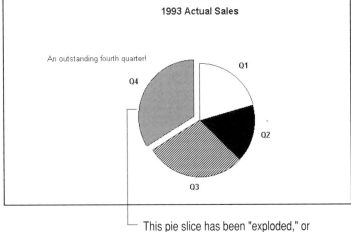

This pie slice has been "exploded," or pulled away from the rest of the pie.

Important   When you drag data markers, you change the corresponding values on the source worksheet. For more information, see "Changing Chart Values" in Chapter 17.

---

316   Part 3   Creating Charts from Worksheet Data

For information about selecting chart items, see "Selecting Items in a Chart" in Chapter 15. For information about creating text boxes, arrows, and other graphic objects, see Chapter 13, "Creating Graphic Objects on Worksheets and Charts."

You can also adjust the elevation, rotation, and perspective in 3-D charts. For more information, see "Changing the 3-D Chart View" later in this chapter.

Sizing a Chart for Printing By default, a chart sheet prints in landscape orientation, sized to fit the full page. However, you can change the orientation and the printing option, and then, if necessary, resize the chart area and move the chart on the page to achieve the final effect you want.

You can also move and size an embedded chart on the worksheet where it resides. For more information, see "Preparing a Chart for Printing" later in this chapter.

Tip To get close-up views of chart details, choose the Zoom command from the View menu, or click the Zoom Control Box, and specify how large or small you want the view. For more information, see "Zooming In or Out on a Worksheet" in Chapter 32.

Formatting the Chart Area and the Plot Area

For presentation purposes, you might want to apply a color or pattern to the entire chart area or the whole plot area. When formatting the chart area, you can also change the default text formatting for the chart.

The formatted chart area

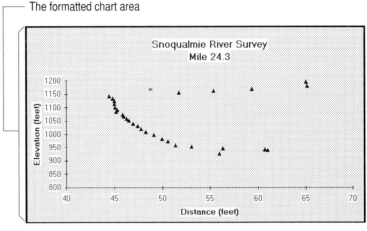

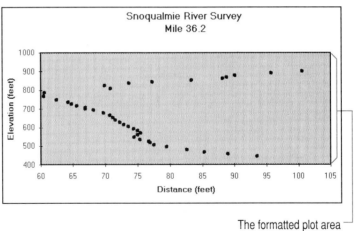

The formatted plot area

Formatting the Chart Area   Double-click outside the plot area to display the Format Chart Area dialog box. Make the changes you want to the area and border in the Patterns tab. To format the text, select the Font tab and make the changes you want to the font, style, size, and other characteristics.

Formatting the Plot Area   Double-click the plot area to display the Format Plot Area dialog box, and change the color, pattern, and border in the Patterns tab.

Changing the Color Palette for Charts in a Workbook

The colors available for formatting chart items depend on the color settings for the workbook in which your embedded chart or chart sheet resides. If you want a different set of colors to choose from in the Patterns tab, you can customize colors or use a customized color palette. These colors will then apply to all new and current charts and sheets in the workbook.

To modify the color settings, choose the Options command from the Tools menu and select the Color tab. To customize one or more colors, select a color in the Chart Lines and Chart Fills boxes, and then edit it by choosing the Edit button and making the changes you want in the Color Picker. Other changes in this tab apply to the worksheets in your workbook. For more information, see "Using Custom Color Palettes" in Chapter 34.

You can also copy custom palettes between workbooks. Select the file you want in the Copy Colors From list box. For information about sharing custom color palettes between Windows and Macintosh systems, see "Moving Microsoft Excel Files Between Windows and the Macintosh" in Chapter 42.

Step By Step

For step-by-step instructions and related information, double-click the ⬚ button to display the Search dialog box in Help, and then:

Type this keyword and choose Show Topics	Select a topic and choose Go To
chart items, moving	Moving and sizing chart items
charts, embedded	Moving and sizing an embedded chart
color palettes	Copying color palettes between workbooks
	Customizing colors in a color palette
sizing chart sheets	Sizing a chart sheet with the window

Formatting Chart Items: Colors, Patterns, Text, and Numbers

To change the appearance of the items in your chart and make your chart effective and attractive, you can:

- Apply colors and patterns to data markers such as columns, lines, and pie slices.

- Change the shapes of markers in line, radar, and xy (scatter) charts.

- Create borders around titles, legends, and text boxes, and apply a color to the area within the borders.

- Change the font, size, style, and alignment of text in titles, data labels, and category labels.

- Format numbers in data labels, tick-mark labels, and category labels.

- Change the line style and color of gridlines.

- Display lines with markers in line and radar charts, and add connecting lines to xy (scatter) charts.

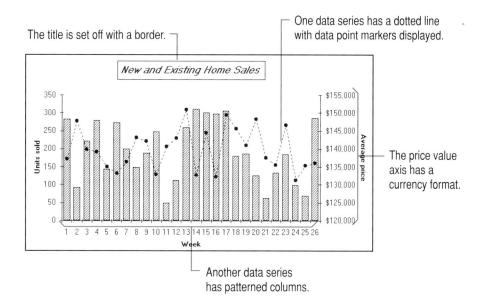

The title is set off with a border.

One data series has a dotted line with data point markers displayed.

The price value axis has a currency format.

Another data series has patterned columns.

Selecting a Chart Item and Displaying the Format Dialog Box

If necessary, activate the chart. To format a chart item, first double-click it or select it. When you double-click, the formatting dialog box for that item is displayed. When you select the item, a command with its name, indicating that it is selected, appears on the Format menu. For example, if you select the legend, you then choose the Selected Legend command, and the Format Legend dialog box is displayed. For more information about selecting chart items, see "Selecting Items in a Chart" in Chapter 15.

Note Text boxes you might have created are the exception to these instructions. When you double-click a text box, it is activated so that you can edit or format the text inside. To display the dialog box, choose the Selected Object command from the Format menu.

Applying Colors, Patterns, and Borders to Chart Items

To apply colors, patterns, or borders to a chart item, double-click it to display the appropriate dialog box. Then select the Patterns tab and make the changes you want. The options available vary depending on the item selected.

Changing the Font, Style, and Alignment of Chart Text

You can change the default font for text in your chart by double-clicking the chart area to display the Format Chart Area dialog box. In the Font tab, make the font and style changes you want. These changes apply to all the chart text.

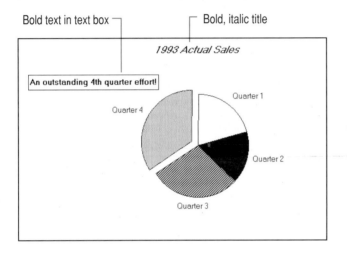

To format text in a chart item, double-click the item and make the changes in the Font tab. To format category labels, select the category axis. To format data labels, select all labels for a data series or an individual label.

To change the way text is aligned—for example, to place the y axis title vertically instead of horizontally—double-click the item to display the dialog box, select the Alignment tab, and make the changes you want.

You can also use the buttons on the Formatting toolbar to change chart text — for example, to make it bold.

Note If chart text, such as a title or a text box, is linked to a worksheet cell, you cannot apply different formatting to individual characters in the text. For example, you can make a linked chart title bold, but you cannot make part of the title bold and another part italic. For information about linking chart text to a worksheet cell, see "Changing Chart Text" in Chapter 17.

Changing Number Formats for Chart Values

You can apply different number formats, such as currency, time, data, or decimals, to numbered tick-mark labels, category labels, data labels, and trendline labels. Some values, such as tick-mark labels, can be formatted only as a group.

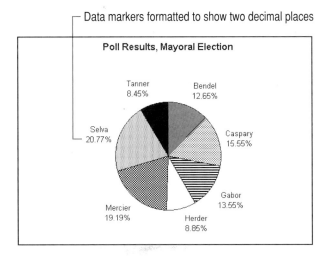

— Data markers formatted to show two decimal places

Poll Results, Mayoral Election

Double-click the item and specify the number format you want in the Number tab. For tick-mark labels, double-click the appropriate axis.

Clearing Formatting from Chart Items

Select the item whose formatting you want to clear, choose the Clear command from the Edit menu, and then choose Formats.

Important Be careful when clearing formats from the chart area; this will also delete the legend, titles, and other items you have added.

Formatting Graphic Objects on Your Charts You can also format any rectangles, arrows, or other graphic objects you've added to your chart. Double-click the graphic object and make the changes you want as described for other items in this section. For more information about working with graphic objects, see Chapter 13, "Creating Graphic Objects on Worksheets and Charts." For information about adding controls such as push buttons or edit boxes to charts, see Chapter 11, "Controls and Dialog Boxes," in the *Microsoft Excel Visual Basic User's Guide*.

Note If you need to change the text or values in your chart instead of just the formatting, see Chapter 17, "Changing Data in a Chart."

Step By Step

For step-by-step instructions and related information, double-click the ![?] button to display the Search dialog box in Help, and then:

Type this keyword and choose Show Topics	Select a topic and choose Go To
chart items, formatting	Applying colors, patterns, and borders to chart items
formats, number	Changing number formats for chart values
formatting, chart text	Changing the font and alignment of chart text

Formatting Data Series and Chart Type Groups

For some charts, you can add useful information and enhance your data by adding certain types of lines and bars. When you have added any of these items, you can then select and format them, as described below.

Formatting Trendlines and Error Bars

A trendline shows the trend, or direction, of data in a series. Error bars indicate the degree of uncertainty—the "plus or minus" range—for data.

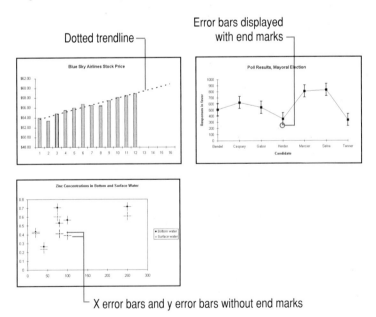

Formatting a Trendline Double-click the trendline (be sure it is the trendline, not the data series), select the Patterns tab, and format the line the way you want it. If you want to modify other trendline settings, select the Type tab or the Options tab and make the changes you want.

Formatting a Trendline Label If you have displayed a label with the equation and the R-squared value for a regression trendline, you can move and format the label as you can any other data label. Double-click the label and make the changes you want in the Font tab and the Number tab.

Formatting Error Bars Double-click an error bar, and make the changes you want in the Patterns tab. Be aware that any changes you make apply to all error bars for that data series. If you want to modify other error bar settings, select the Y Error Bars tab. For xy (scatter) charts, you can also make changes in the X Error Bars tab.

For more information about adding and working with trendlines and error bars, see Chapter 19, "Using Charts to Analyze Data."

Adding and Formatting Drop Lines, High-Low Lines, Up Bars, Down Bars, and Series Lines

You can add drop lines to area charts and line charts, high-low lines or up bars and down bars to line charts, and series lines to stacked column and stacked bar charts. Adding or formatting these lines and bars clarifies the information displayed in the chart.

Adding Lines and Bars From the Format menu, choose the command for the chart type group for which you want to add lines or bars. For example, to add drop lines to an area chart, choose the Area Type Group command from the Format menu. In the Options tab, select the appropriate check box.

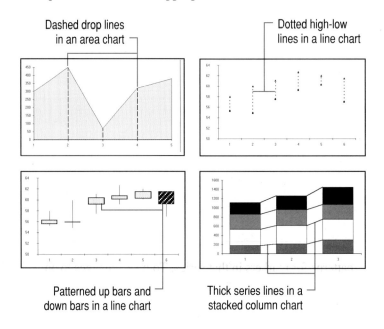

Dashed drop lines in an area chart

Dotted high-low lines in a line chart

Patterned up bars and down bars in a line chart

Thick series lines in a stacked column chart

Another way you can add these lines and bars is by selecting the appropriate autoformat; to do this, choose the AutoFormat command from the Format menu. However, if you have applied custom formatting to your chart, changing the autoformat will undo your formatting.

Formatting Lines and Bars To change the appearance of these lines and bars, double-click the item and make changes in the Patterns tab. The changes apply to all the lines or bars for the chart type group.

For more information about chart types and autoformats, see Chapter 16, "Working with Chart Types and Autoformats."

Step By Step

For step-by-step instructions and related information, double-click the [?] button to display the Search dialog box in Help, and then:

Type this keyword and choose Show Topics	Select a topic and choose Go To
chart data	Using special lines and bars to emphasize data
trendlines	Formatting a trendline

Formatting Data Markers and Data Labels

In addition to changing colors and patterns, you can change the spacing between column and bar data markers, "explode" one or more slices in a pie chart or a doughnut chart, smooth the angles in line and xy (scatter) charts, format data labels, and use pictures in place of data markers for some chart types.

Formatting Data Markers

If necessary, activate the chart. Double-click a data series to change colors and patterns for markers in that series. To make changes to only one data marker, click once to select the series and then click a second time to select the marker. You can also add markers to lines, or add a line to connect points in an xy (scatter) chart. You make these changes in the Patterns tab of the Format Data Series dialog box.

Formatted pie slices ...

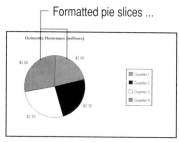

... columns ...

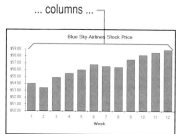

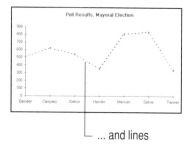

... and lines

For pie charts and doughnut charts, you can "explode" a slice by selecting it and dragging it out from the pie. You can set the angle of the first slice by choosing the Pie Group command or the Doughnut Group command from the Format menu. Select the Options tab and specify the angle you want. For doughnut charts, you can also adjust the size of the doughnut hole in the Options tab.

In a single-series chart, you can give each data marker a different color by choosing the chart type group command (for example, Column Group) from the Format menu and selecting the Vary Colors By Point check box in the Options tab. For pie charts only, the slices are formatted with different colors automatically when the chart is created.

Note For line, xy (scatter), and radar charts, Microsoft Excel version 5.0 applies by default a different marker shape to each data series. This can make these charts easier to read when printed in black and white, and may reduce the need for custom formatting. If you are working with a line, xy (scatter), or radar chart that you created using Microsoft Excel version 4.0, exercise caution when applying an autoformat. Once you do, the original chart formatting is lost.

Changing the Spacing Between Column or Bar Data Markers You can expand or reduce the spaces between clusters of columns or bars. You can also display columns or bars overlapped. The higher the gap width value, the larger the space between clusters of data markers. The higher the overlap value, the more the data markers are overlapped.

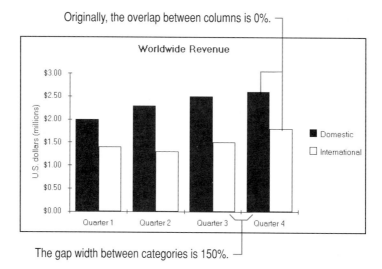

Originally, the overlap between columns is 0%.

The gap width between categories is 150%.

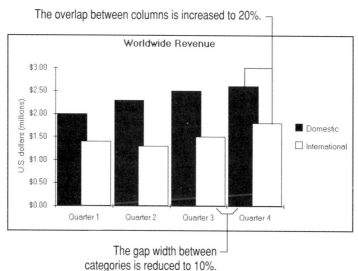

The overlap between columns is increased to 20%.

The gap width between categories is reduced to 10%.

Choose the Bar Group command or the Column Group command from the Format menu. In the Options tab, change the spacing and the overlap. You can check the sample in the dialog box as you make adjustments.

For more information about setting the gap width for 3-D charts, see "Changing the 3-D Chart View" later in this chapter.

Smoothing the Angles in Line and XY (Scatter) Charts If you want smooth curves instead of angular lines in line and xy (scatter) charts, double-click the data series, and select the Smoothed Line check box in the Patterns tab.

The original line chart with sharp angles ⌐

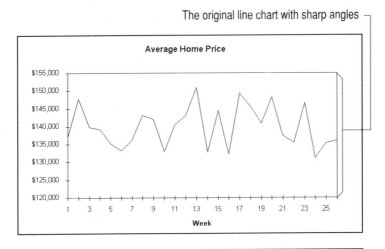

The same chart with smoothed lines ⌐

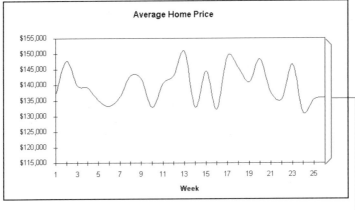

Unless you have applied custom formatting that you don't want to lose, you can also select a built-in autoformat with smoothed lines for line and xy (scatter) charts. You can do this in the ChartWizard or by choosing the AutoFormat command from the Format menu. For more information, see "Working with Built-in and Custom Chart Autoformats" in Chapter 16.

Formatting the Levels in a 3-D Surface Chart   Although you cannot select the levels in a 3-D surface chart, you can format them. Select the corresponding keys in the legend and change the colors and patterns. The formatting you apply to the legend keys is also applied to the corresponding levels; this is the case for all chart types.

Formatting Data Labels

You can format all data labels for a data series, or just one label. Double-click the label or labels you want to change. In the Format Data Labels dialog box, make the changes you want to text or values in the Patterns, Font, Number, and Alignment tabs.

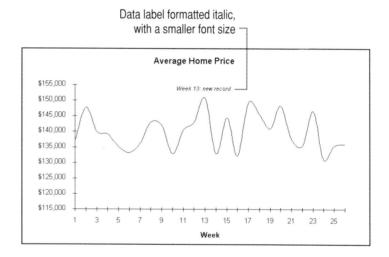

Data label formatted italic, with a smaller font size

Data labels are linked by default to worksheet cells. As long as the link is intact, you can apply text formatting to whole labels, but you cannot apply different formatting to individual characters. If editing the label text breaks the link, you can then apply individual character formatting.

For information about adding data labels to your chart, see "Adding Data Labels, Titles, and Other Items to a Chart" in Chapter 15. For information about changing text and values in your chart, see Chapter 17, "Changing Data in a Chart."

Creating Picture Markers in a Chart

To add visual interest to your chart, you can use pictures in place of plain data markers. You can copy existing pictures, or you can create graphic objects using Microsoft Excel's drawing tools or another application, and use these as picture markers.

You can add picture markers to data series or individual data points in bar, column, line, xy (scatter), and radar charts. In bar and column charts, the picture markers can be stretched, shrunk, or stacked to show different values or quantities of units.

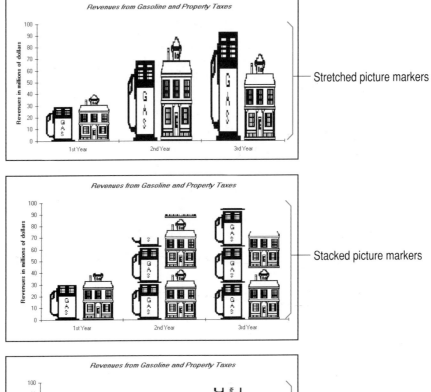

Stretched picture markers

Stacked picture markers

Stacked and scaled picture markers

Creating Picture Markers   To create picture markers, copy the picture or the graphic object, select the data marker or data series where you want to place the image, and choose the Paste command from the Edit menu.

Tip   To add pictures to xy (scatter), line, and radar charts, be sure that the data series are formatted with data markers displayed.

For information about creating graphic objects, see Chapter 13, "Creating Graphic Objects on Worksheets and Charts."

Stacking or Stretching Picture Markers After pasting picture markers into a chart, double-click the data series or individual marker you want to format. In the Format Data Series (or Data Point) dialog box, select the Patterns tab and then select the options you want. If you select Stack And Scale To, type the number of units each picture should represent.

Clearing Pictures from Data Markers Select the data marker or data series whose picture markers you want to clear. Choose Clear from the Edit menu, and then choose Formats. If you selected a data series, its original format is restored. If you selected one data marker, it is formatted to match the other markers in the same data series.

Note You can combine an embedded chart with a picture object on a worksheet by layering the objects. For example, you might want to display a picture behind the plot area. For more information, see Chapter 13, "Creating Graphic Objects on Worksheets and Charts."

Step By Step

For step-by-step instructions and related information, double-click the ? button to display the Search dialog box in Help, and then:

Type this keyword and choose Show Topics	Select a topic and choose Go To
data markers	Arranging and spacing data markers in bar and column charts
	Clearing formatting from data markers
	Creating and formatting picture markers
	Formatting data markers
	Formatting data markers in line, radar, and xy (scatter) charts
formatting, charts	Formatting 3-D surface chart levels
	Formatting pie and doughnut slices

Formatting the Legend

You can change the look of the legend in a chart by moving it, resizing it, and formatting the text entries and keys. You can also add a border to the legend, and you can format the area inside the border with a color or fill pattern.

The legend is formatted with a border, fill color, and italic text.

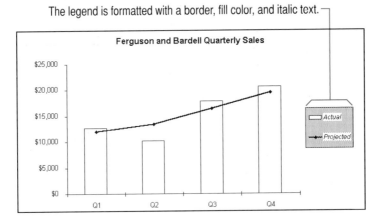

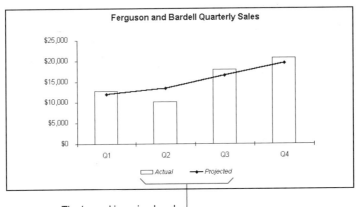

The legend is resized and moved below the chart.

Moving and Sizing the Legend

You can select the legend and move or resize it by dragging. A dotted border shows the shape, size, and grid as you drag.

Instead of moving the legend by dragging, you can place it at the top, bottom, right, left, or corner of the chart. You do this by double-clicking the legend, selecting the Placement tab in the Format Legend dialog box, and then indicating the location you want. When you position the legend this way, the plot area is resized as needed to accommodate the legend, and the legend size is set to the default. If you want to resize the legend, it's best to position it first.

Formatting the Legend Border and Area

To specify colors and patterns for the legend border and area, double-click the legend to display the Format Legend dialog box, and make the changes you want in the Patterns tab.

Formatting Legend Entries and Keys

To change the size, style, and color of legend entry text, double-click an entry and make the changes you want in the Font tab in the Format Legend Entry dialog box. To change all legend entries at once, double-click the legend rather than an individual entry, and make the changes you want in the Font and Patterns tabs.

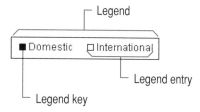

Legend keys can only be formatted individually. To change the border and area color or pattern for a legend key, double-click the key to display the Format Legend Key dialog box, and make the changes you want in the Patterns tabs. Remember that changing the legend key will change the data markers for the associated data series; if you have applied custom colors, they will be changed to the new colors. To clear custom formatting and restore default formatting, select the Automatic option button.

Formatting the Levels in a 3-D Surface Chart   To change the colors or patterns of the levels in a 3-D surface chart, you must double-click the legend key for each level and make changes in the Patterns tab in the Format Legend Key dialog box. You cannot select data markers within the 3-D surface chart as you can with other chart types. When you change the formatting of the legend key, the corresponding level in the chart is changed accordingly.

Step By Step

For step-by-step instructions and related information, double-click the 🅝? button to display the Search dialog box in Help, and then:

Type this keyword and choose Show Topics	Select a topic and choose Go To
chart legends	Formatting legend entries and keys
	Moving and sizing the legend

Formatting Axes, Gridlines, and Tick Marks

When you create a chart, the axes automatically appear. You can hide the primary or secondary axes, change the patterns and colors of all displayed axes, and format the tick marks and tick-mark labels.

Gridlines are extensions of the tick marks that can make it easier to see the values associated with the data markers. By default, black gridlines are displayed, but you can turn them off or format them as you do other lines, with colors and patterns.

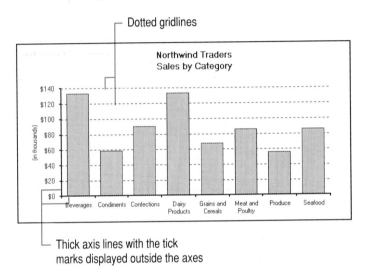

You can also change the *scale* of an axis, which means adjusting the range of values displayed and the intervals between values. This can be useful for controlling where data points are placed in your chart.

Hiding and Displaying Axes

You can turn the display of axes on and off by choosing the Axes command from the Insert menu. If some data series have been assigned to secondary axes, you have the option of hiding and displaying them also. For information about assigning data series to axes, see "Combining Multiple Chart Types in a Chart" in Chapter 16.

Formatting an Axis

To format an axis, double-click it, or select it and choose the Selected Axis command from the Format menu. Change line color, weight, and style in the Patterns tab, change number formatting in the Number tab, and change text in the Font and Alignment tabs.

Formatting Gridlines

To format gridlines, double-click the gridlines and make the changes you want in the Patterns tab. To restore the original formatting, select the Automatic option button.

Formatting Tick Marks and Tick-Mark Labels

The category axis displays category names if they were included in the worksheet selection. The value axis has labels based on the range of values plotted in the chart. In 3-D perspective charts, the series axis lists the data series in the chart.

To format tick marks and their labels, double-click the axis. In the Patterns tab, under Tick Mark Type, select the options you want. If you have adjusted the point at which axes cross, select the Next To Axis option to keep the tick-mark labels adjacent to the selected axis.

For information about formatting an axis title, see "Formatting Chart Items: Colors, Patterns, Text, and Numbers" earlier in this chapter.

Changing the Axis Scale

For the category axis, you can change how the tick marks and tick-mark labels are displayed, and where the category axis crosses the value axis.

For the value axis, you can change the range of values displayed—that is, broaden or narrow the range of values, or set a different range of values. You can also change the interval between values along the axis, change the point at which the value axis crosses the category axis, or set the scale to logarithmic if your data requires.

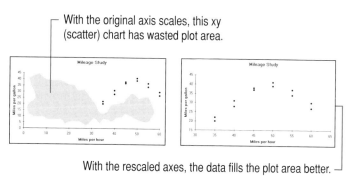

With the original axis scales, this xy (scatter) chart has wasted plot area.

With the rescaled axes, the data fills the plot area better.

In an xy (scatter) chart, both the x axis and the y axis are value axes, and you can adjust the range of values and interval for each, as described above. To change the axis scale, double-click the axis. In the Scale tab, make the changes you want.

You can also change or reverse the order in which data series are plotted in your chart. For more information, see "Changing the Way Your Data Is Plotted" in Chapter 17. For information about assigning data series to axes, see "Combining Multiple Chart Types in a Chart" in Chapter 16.

Step By Step

For step-by-step instructions and related information, double-click the [?] button to display the Search dialog box in Help, and then:

Type this keyword and choose Show Topics	Select a topic and choose Go To
axes, scale	Changing the category or series axis scale
	Changing the value axis scale
chart axes	Displaying or hiding axes
	Formatting axes, tick marks, and gridlines
formatting, charts	Formatting 3-D surface chart levels
tick mark labels	Formatting and arranging tick-mark labels

Changing the 3-D Chart View

In 3-D charts, you can format the walls, floor, elevation, perspective, and rotation.

There are three kinds of 3-D charts. A simple 3-D chart has three-dimensional markers arranged along the x (category) axis. A 3-D *perspective* chart has a third axis, the *series axis,* which displays three-dimensional markers representing the data series from front to back. In both of these variations, values are plotted along the z axis. The third kind, a 3-D pie chart, has no axes, walls, or floor. You can format its data markers and change its rotation, elevation, and height.

Tip Once you have formatted and adjusted a 3-D chart, you can save your custom formatting as a user-defined autoformat and apply it to other charts. For more information, see "Working with Built-in and Custom Autoformats" in Chapter 16.

Formatting the Walls and Floor

Double-click a wall or the floor of your 3-D chart. In the Format Walls or Format Floor dialog box, change the border and area in the Patterns tab.

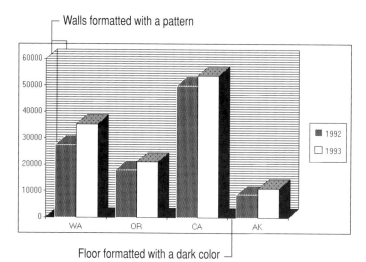

You can format the gridlines as you would for 2-D charts, by double-clicking a gridline and selecting the line style, color, and weight you want.

Tip For an interesting presentation effect in some 3-D charts, you can format gridlines to extend from the x (category) axis and the z (value) axis in the foreground of the chart, overlaid on the background of the chart depth. To do this, select the Right Angle Axes check box in the Format 3-D View dialog box. Then choose the Gridlines command from the Insert menu, and select the 2-D Walls And Gridlines check box. This effect is not available for 3-D perspective charts that contain a series axis.

Changing the 3-D Look

To change the elevation, rotation, and perspective, you can drag a corner of the plot area, or change the settings in the Format 3-D View dialog box. To display and drag the corners, click a wall and then a corner. Check the reference at the left of the formula bar for the word "Corners" to confirm that you've selected correctly.

A 3-D perspective column chart with the default 3-D view settings

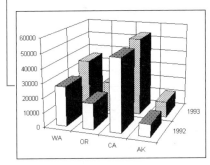
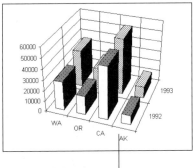

The same chart with increased elevation ...

... with a different rotation setting ...

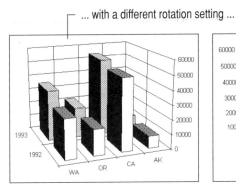
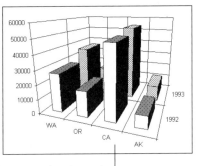

... and with the perspective changed

The following table describes the settings available in the Format 3-D View dialog box.

Option	Effect	Available Range	Additional Information
Elevation	Sets the height from which you view chart data.	10 to 80 degrees for pie charts. 0 to 44 degrees for 3-D bar charts. −90 to 90 degrees for all other chart types.	
Rotation	Rotates the chart sideways.	0 to 360 degrees. Specifying 180 degrees turns your chart around and displays it from the back.	
Perspective	Specifies the ratio of the width of the front to the back, or how distant the rear data markers appear to be.	0 to 100. The higher the number, the greater the perspective.	Not available when the Right Angle Axes check box is selected.
Auto Scaling	When selected, automatically sets the chart height to fill the window with the chart.	None.	Clear this check box to set the height manually.
Right Angle Axes	Locks axes at 90-degree angles.	None.	Clear this check box to set the perspective.
Height Of Base	Sets the chart height in relation to the length of the x (category) axis.	5 to 500%.	Not available when the Auto Scaling check box is selected.

Tip When dragging, you see a "wire frame" version of the chart without the data markers. If you want to see the whole chart with the data markers while dragging, hold down the CTRL key in Microsoft Excel for Windows, or the CMD key or the CTRL key in Microsoft Excel for the Macintosh.

Whenever you want to, you can restore the default 3-D formatting to undo changes you have made to the elevation, rotation, perspective, and height. Choose the Default button in the Format 3-D View dialog box.

Other Ways to Adjust the 3-D Look   There are several other changes you can make, including adjusting the chart depth and the spacing of data markers. You can make these changes by choosing the chart type group command (for example, 3-D Column Group) from the Format menu, selecting the Options tab, and adjusting the settings described in the following table.

Option	Description	Available Range
Chart Depth	Determines the shape of the chart base (floor).	20 to 2000. The larger the number, the deeper the 3-D floor and the chart.
Gap Depth	Determines the depth between 3-D columns.	0 to 500.
Gap Width	Determines the spacing between 3-D columns.	20 to 2000. The larger the gap, the narrower the columns.

Tip   If you have graphic objects on a 3-D chart, they are not sized, scaled, or rotated proportionally when you change the elevation, proportion, and rotation as described above. This is because graphic objects are sized and scaled in two dimensions rather than three. Be aware that graphic objects might not remain where you have placed them on the chart when you change the 3-D view.

For information about all the available chart types, see "What's the Best Chart Type for Your Data?" in Chapter 16.

Step By Step

For step-by-step instructions and related information, double-click the 🔡 button to display the Search dialog box in Help, and then:

Type this keyword and choose Show Topics	Select a topic and choose Go To
3-D charts	Changing a 3-D chart's depth and width
	Rotating and elevating a 3-D chart
	Setting a 3-D chart's height and perspective
3-D charts, formatting	Formatting a 3-D chart's walls and floor

Preparing a Chart for Printing

After creating, editing, and formatting your chart, you'll want to know what you will get when you print it, without wasting time and paper. If it's an embedded chart, you can size and place it on the worksheet and view it in Print Preview. If it's a chart sheet, you can size and scale it the way you want, specify how it should be placed on the paper you'll be printing on, and view it in the window to see how it will look before you send it to the printer.

If you want to resize and rearrange individual items in the chart, see "Changing the Look of a Chart" earlier in this chapter.

Sizing an Embedded Chart

You size an embedded chart as you do any object on a worksheet—by selecting it and dragging. The chart prints with the size, proportions, and position you've given it on the worksheet. Note that the text is sized independently of the chart. In some cases, you might want to adjust the font size after resizing the chart.

To get a full-page view of the chart on the worksheet, choose the Print Preview command from the File menu. For information about selecting an embedded chart, see "Selecting Items in a Chart" in Chapter 15.

Note The remaining information in this section applies to chart sheets only. For information about printing a worksheet with an embedded chart, see Chapter 14, "Printing."

Sizing and Setting Up a Chart Sheet for Printing

To prepare your chart sheet for printing, you can begin by choosing the Print Preview command from the File menu. By default, the chart is set to print in landscape orientation, filling the entire page.

If you are not satisfied with the chart size relative to the page, choose the Setup button in the Print Preview window, or choose the Page Setup command from the File menu. On the Chart tab, select the Custom option, and then you can select the chart area and drag to change its size and shape until it looks the way you want it to print.

The three options available on the Chart tab in the Page Setup dialog box are shown in the following illustration.

Use Full
Page

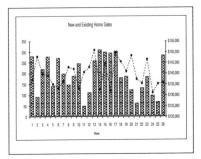

Scale To
Fit Page

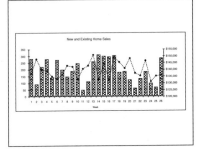

Custom

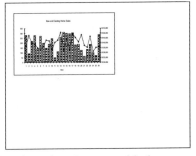

Use Full Page The chart size changes with the paper size. The proportions are adjusted as needed to use the full page, minus the margins. For example, if you are printing on 8.5-by-11-inch paper, with landscape orientation, your chart sheet will be scaled to print 9 inches wide by 6.5 inches high (with 1-inch margins on all sides). You cannot move and resize the chart area when this option is selected, because by definition the chart area fills the page.

Scale To Fit Page The chart is scaled to fit the page, keeping the same proportions as the ones you see on the screen. For example, if the chart width is twice the chart height on screen, on 8.5-by-11-inch paper it will print 9 inches wide (filling the width of the page) by 4.5 inches high (with 1-inch margins).

Custom The chart size is independent of the paper size. It is printed as you have sized it on screen, with the same proportions, and with the same relative position on the page as you have placed it on-screen. When this option is selected, you can place the chart area anywhere on the page.

Tip If you are having difficulty sizing an item within the chart—for example, the plot area—you can set the Custom printing option and enlarge the chart area to allow more space. The selected chart area has a thick gray border making it easier to size and move. Any objects you move partially outside the chart area will be cropped, or cut off, when you print the chart.

Sizing the Chart with the Window   You can also turn on the Sized With Window option to have the chart sized automatically to fit the window in which it appears. Choose the Sized With Window command from the View menu. When this option is on, you cannot size and move the chart area. The chart is automatically resized to fit the window. This may affect the printed result, depending on the Page Setup option you have selected.

Chart sheet sized with the window

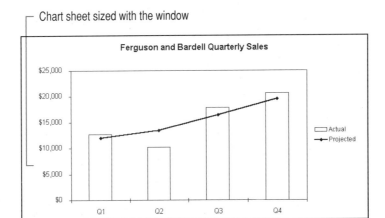

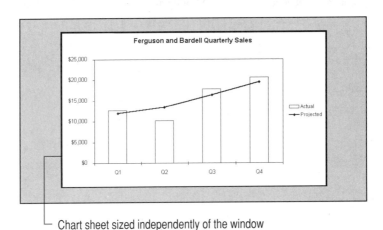

Chart sheet sized independently of the window

Tip   When you are printing charts for a presentation and you want to remove the headers and footers, choose the Page Setup command from the File menu and select the Header/Footer tab. Specify None under both Header and Footer in the tab.

Printing a Chart with Colors

By default, Microsoft Excel charts are printed with the screen colors translated to shades of gray. But if you have a color printer, you can print your chart with colors. The results depend on the printer you are using.

To print with color, choose the Page Setup command from the File menu. Select the Chart tab and then clear the Print In Black And White check box. Microsoft Excel sends the color formatting information to the printer, which matches the screen colors as closely as possible.

For more information about printing charts and other Microsoft Excel sheets, see Chapter 14, "Printing."

Step By Step

For step-by-step instructions and related information, double-click the [?] button to display the Search dialog box in Help, and then:

Type this keyword and choose Show Topics	Select a topic and choose Go To
chart sheets, printing	Selecting the print size for a chart sheet
charts, embedded	Moving and sizing an embedded chart
printing charts	Printing charts with colors
sizing chart sheets	Sizing a chart sheet with the window

C H A P T E R   1 9

Using Charts to Analyze Data

For command, keyboard, and toolbar button information, see online Help.

In This Chapter

Adding a Trendline to a Data Series

You can add a trendline to a data series in a chart to show the trend, or the direction, of the data in the series. Trendlines are commonly used to study problems of prediction, also called *regression analysis.* They are also frequently used to show *moving averages,* which smooth fluctuations in data to show the pattern or trend more clearly.

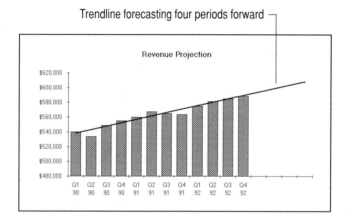

You can add trendlines to data series that are formatted as area, bar, column, line, and xy (scatter) charts. You cannot add trendlines to 3-D, pie, doughnut, or radar chart types. If you add a trendline to a series and later change the format to one of the latter chart types, the trendline will be permanently deleted. For more information about chart types, see Chapter 16, "Working with Chart Types and Autoformats."

After you have added a trendline to a data series, the trendline remains associated with that series. If you move the series, for example, by changing the plot order, the trendline moves with it. If you change data in the series, the trendline's values are recalculated and its shape is adjusted accordingly.

Creating a Trendline

The first step in creating a trendline is to select the data series that you want the trendline associated with. Then you choose the Trendline command from the Insert menu. On the Type tab, select the type of trendline you want. On the Options tab, you can give the trendline a name and specify other options, as described later in this section.

Regression Trendlines

The following are the five types of regression trendlines you can choose from.

Type		Description
	Linear	Creates the trendline using the linear equation $y = mx+b$
		This example shows revenue data. Selecting this type is equivalent to using the LINEST function.
	Logarithmic	Creates the trendline using the logarithmic equation $y = c\ln x+b$
		This example shows data for a population estimate.
	Polynomial	Creates the trendline using the polynomial equation $y = b+c_1x+c_2x^2+...+c_6x^6$
		This example displays data for a mileage experiment. Polynomial regression is also called curvilinear regression.
	Power	Creates the trendline using the power equation $y = cx^b$
		This example shows data for an acceleration experiment. You cannot create a power trendline if your data contains negative values.
	Exponential	Creates the trendline using the exponential equation $y = ce^{bx}$
		This example shows half-life data for a radioactive substance. You cannot create an exponential trendline if your data contains negative values.

You can use the regression trendline to forecast forward, backward, or both, for the number of periods that you specify. For xy (scatter) charts, you specify units. You can also display more information on the chart, including the regression equation and the R-squared value.

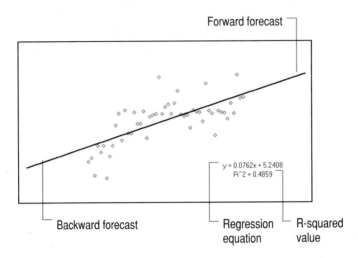

$y = 0.0762x + 5.2408$
$R^2 = 0.4859$

Forward forecast

Backward forecast   Regression   R-squared
                             equation   value

You can move and format the regression equation and the R-squared value as you do other data labels. For more information, see Chapter 18, "Formatting a Chart."

Displaying the R-squared Value   You can use the R-squared value to evaluate the reliability of a trendline. Note that the R-squared value you can display is not an adjusted R-squared value. For logarithmic, power, and exponential trendlines, Microsoft Excel uses a transformed regression model, in which the R-squared value refers to estimated rather than actual values.

Setting the Y-Intercept   Another option you have is to set the Y-intercept to a specific value instead of allowing Microsoft Excel to automatically calculate it based on your data.

Moving Average

A moving average indicates a sequence of averages that are computed from parts of the data series. When you create the moving average, you specify the number of periods that the moving average will be based on. For example, a period of 50 was specified to create the 50-day moving average in the following illustration.

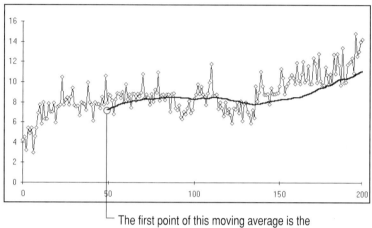

The first point of this moving average is the
average of the first 50 values in the data series.

When you add a moving average to an xy (scatter) chart, the moving average is based on the order of the x values plotted in the chart. To get the result you want, you might need to sort the x values before adding the moving average.

Note   Forecasting, displaying an equation or R-squared value, and setting the Y-intercept as described earlier are not available for moving averages.

For the equations Microsoft Excel uses to calculate trendlines and the R-squared value, see "Equations for Calculating Trendlines" later in this chapter. For more information about using Microsoft Excel for statistical analysis, see Chapter 31, "Statistical Analysis of Data."

Formatting a Trendline

After creating a trendline, you can change its color, style, and weight by double-clicking the trendline to display the Format Trendline dialog box.

Step By Step

For step-by-step instructions and related information, double-click the [▶?] button to display the Search dialog box in Help, and then:

Type this keyword and choose Show Topics	Select a topic and choose Go To
trendlines	Adding a trendline to a data series
	Deleting a trendline
	Formatting a trendline
	Modifying trendline settings

Equations for Calculating Trendlines

The following are the equations Microsoft Excel uses to calculate regression trendlines, the R-squared value for regression trendlines, and moving average trendlines.

Regression

Linear: Calculates the least squares fit for a line represented by the equation:

$$y = mx + b$$

where m is the slope and b is the intercept. Selecting this type of regression is equivalent to using the LINEST() function.

Polynomial: Calculates the least squares fit through points using the equation:

$$y = b + c_1 x + c_2 x^2 + c_3 x^3 + \ldots + c_6 x^6$$

where b and $c_1 \ldots c_6$ are constants.

Logarithmic: Calculates the least squares fit through points using the equation:

$$y = c \ln x + b$$

where c and b are constants, and ln is the natural logarithm function.

Exponential: Calculates the least squares fit through points using the equation:

$$y = ce^{bx}$$

where c and b are constants, and e is the base of the natural logarithm.

Power: Calculates the least squares fit through points using the equation:

$$y = cx^b$$

where c and b are constants.

R-squared Value

$$R^2 = 1 - \frac{SSE}{SST}$$

where

$$SSE = \sum \left(Y_i - \hat{Y}_i \right)^2$$

and

$$SST = \left(\sum Y_i^2 \right) - \frac{\left(\sum Y_i \right)^2}{n}$$

Note The R-squared value that you can display with a trendline is not an adjusted R-squared value. For logarithmic, power, and exponential trendlines, Microsoft Excel uses a transformed regression model.

Moving Average

$$F_t = \frac{A_t + A_{t-1} + \ldots A_{t-n+1}}{n}$$

Note The number of points in a moving average trendline equals the total number of points in the series less the number you specify for the period.

For information about the GROWTH(), LINEST(), LOGEST(), TREND(), and STEYX() functions, click the Function Wizard button on the Standard toolbar or see online Help.

Adding Error Bars to a Data Series

You can add error bars to a data series in a chart to indicate the degree of uncertainty—the "plus or minus range"—for the data in the series. Commonly used for engineering and statistical data, error bars express the error factor visually, showing the error amount relative to the data marker.

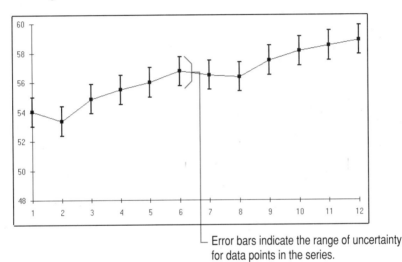

└─ Error bars indicate the range of uncertainty for data points in the series.

After you have added error bars to a data series, they remain associated with that series. If you move the series, for example, by changing the plot order, the error bars move with it. If you change data in the series, the error bars are recalculated and adjusted accordingly.

Which Chart Types Can Include Error Bars?

You can add error bars to data series formatted as area, bar, column, line, and xy (scatter) charts. You cannot add them to 3-D, pie, doughnut, or radar chart types. If you add error bars to a series and later change the format to one of the latter chart types, the error bars will be permanently deleted.

In xy (scatter) charts, you can display both x and y error bars, corresponding to the values on both axes. For more information about chart types, see Chapter 16, "Working with Chart Types and Autoformats."

Creating Error Bars for a Data Series

The first step in creating error bars is to select the data series that you want them associated with. Then you choose the Error Bars command from the Insert menu, select the display you want, and specify how the error amount should be calculated or obtained.

Tip You can show different error amounts for plus and minus, or different error amounts for each data point, by using Custom error amounts.

How Microsoft Excel Obtains the Error Amount

You can choose from the following options when specifying the error amount.

Error amount		Description
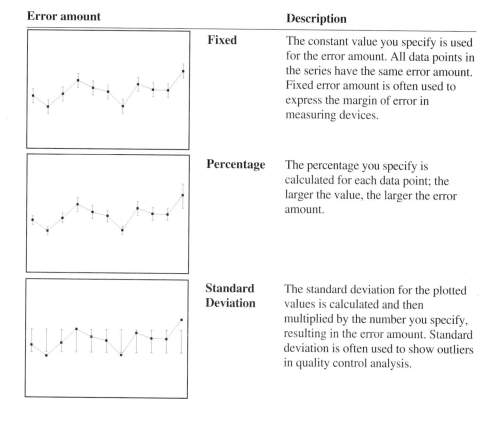	**Fixed**	The constant value you specify is used for the error amount. All data points in the series have the same error amount. Fixed error amount is often used to express the margin of error in measuring devices.
	Percentage	The percentage you specify is calculated for each data point; the larger the value, the larger the error amount.
	Standard Deviation	The standard deviation for the plotted values is calculated and then multiplied by the number you specify, resulting in the error amount. Standard deviation is often used to show outliers in quality control analysis.

Error amount		Description
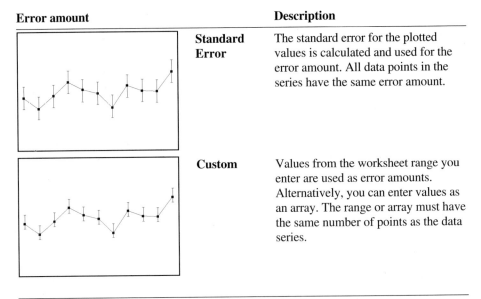	**Standard Error**	The standard error for the plotted values is calculated and used for the error amount. All data points in the series have the same error amount.
	Custom	Values from the worksheet range you enter are used as error amounts. Alternatively, you can enter values as an array. The range or array must have the same number of points as the data series.

Important When you specify standard deviation, Microsoft Excel calculates the error amount using the mean of values actually plotted in the data series. Other associated worksheet data is not included in the calculation. You can use the Custom option to refer to data on the worksheet if you want to use that data for the error amounts.

For the equations Microsoft Excel uses to calculate the standard deviation and the standard error, see "Equations for Calculating the Error Amount" later in this chapter. For more information about using Microsoft Excel for statistical analysis, see Chapter 31, "Statistical Analysis of Data."

Formatting Error Bars

After creating error bars, you can change their color, style, and weight by double-clicking one error bar to display the Format Error Bars dialog box. Your formatting changes will be applied to all the error bars for that data series.

Step By Step

For step-by-step instructions and related information, double-click the 🔃 button to display the Search dialog box in Help, and then:

Type this keyword and choose Show Topics	Select a topic and choose Go To
array formulas	Entering an array formula
error bars	Adding error bars to a data series
	Deleting error bars

Type this keyword and choose Show Topics	Select a topic and choose Go To
error bars	Formatting error bars
	Modifying error bar settings

Equations for Calculating the Error Amount

The following are the equations Microsoft Excel uses to calculate standard deviation and standard error for chart error bars.

Standard Deviation

$$S.D. = \sqrt{\frac{\sum\limits_{s=1}^{m}\sum\limits_{i=1}^{n}(y_{is} - M)^2}{(n_y - 1)}}$$

$$M = \frac{\sum\limits_{s=1}^{m}\sum\limits_{i=1}^{n} y_{is}}{n_y}$$

where:

s = series number

i = point number in series s

m = number of series for point y in chart

n = number of points in each series

y_{is} = data value of series s and the ith point

n_y = total number of data values in all series

M = arithmetic mean

Standard Error

$$S.E. = \sqrt{\frac{\sum\limits_{s=1}^{m}\sum\limits_{i=1}^{n} y_{is}{}^2}{(n_y - 1)(n_y)}}$$

For information about the LINEST() and STDEV() functions, click the Function Wizard button on the Standard toolbar or see online Help.

Displaying Multilevel Categories and Series in a Chart

When your worksheet has multiple levels of categories or series, or both, you can create a chart that displays these levels. These are also known as *hierarchical* categories or series.

When you select a worksheet range containing multilevel categories and series and then click the ChartWizard button, Microsoft Excel examines the organization of the data and assigns chart category and series names accordingly. The following example illustrates one way category and series names can be plotted.

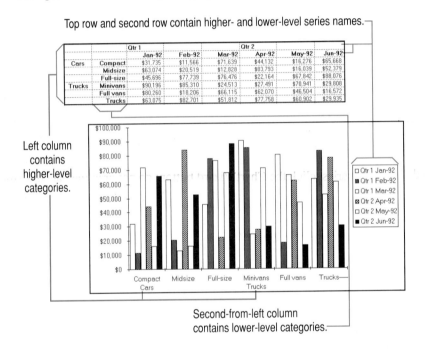

Top row and second row contain higher- and lower-level series names.

Left column contains higher-level categories.

Second-from-left column contains lower-level categories.

As you are creating your chart with the ChartWizard, step 4 indicates how many rows or columns will be used as category names (category levels) and as legend text (series levels).

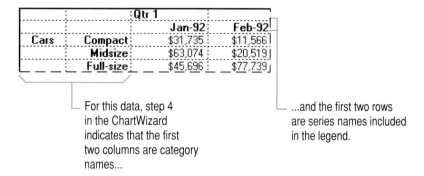

For this data, step 4 in the ChartWizard indicates that the first two columns are category names...

...and the first two rows are series names included in the legend.

If the number of rows and columns indicated is incorrect, adjust the numbers in step 4 of the ChartWizard. Or you may need to rearrange some of your data so that Microsoft Excel can evaluate the levels correctly.

ChartWizard

Important When you want to add data to a chart that has multilevel categories or series, click the ChartWizard button; do not drag the data onto the chart, or choose the Paste Special command or the New Data command. Using the ChartWizard ensures that your category and series levels will remain intact.

For information about creating a chart, see Chapter 15, "Creating a Chart." For information about entering and editing data, see Chapter 9, "Entering Data," and Chapter 11, "Editing a Worksheet."

Charting Data from a Pivot Table

A pivot table is an interactive table that allows you to create different views of your data. You can create a chart that displays a pivot table's multilevel categories and series. The currently displayed values, but not the underlying associated values, are displayed in the chart. When plotted data changes in the pivot table, the chart is updated accordingly.

You create a chart from a pivot table in the same way described earlier in this section. For information about creating a pivot table, see Chapter 24, "Creating a Pivot Table."

Step By Step

For step-by-step instructions and related information, double-click the [?] button to display the Search dialog box in Help, and then:

Type this keyword and choose Show Topics	Select a topic and choose Go To
charts, creating	Creating a chart from a pivot table
	Creating an embedded chart on a worksheet
deleting, cells	Overview of Inserting, Deleting, and Clearing Cells, Rows, and Columns
pivot tables, creating	Creating a pivot table

Charting Visible Worksheet Data

When you are working with outlined data, or data that has hidden rows or columns, you can create a chart that displays only the data currently visible in the worksheet range. The following illustration shows a collapsed outline with a corresponding chart.

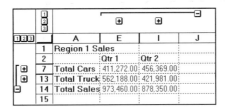

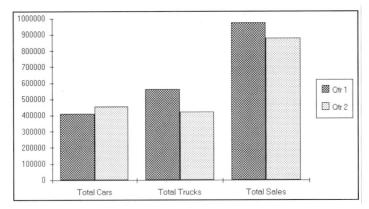

The data displayed in the chart is automatically updated whenever you expand or collapse levels in your outline, or when you hide or unhide data. The expanded outline and the updated chart are shown in the following illustration.

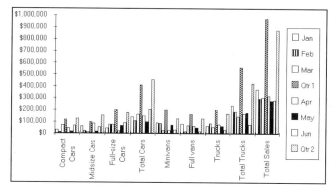

Creating a Chart from Visible Worksheet Data

ChartWizard

To chart visible worksheet data, select the data and click the ChartWizard button.

To turn off automatic updating, choose the Options command from the Tools menu. Then clear the Plot Visible Cells Only check box on the Chart tab. When you do, the original data used to plot the chart is displayed.

To plot only the visible data and prevent the chart from being updated when the worksheet display changes, click the Select Visible Cells button before you create the chart. For information about adding this button to a toolbar, see the Step By Step table at the end of this section, and "Customizing Toolbars" in Chapter 34.

For more information about creating a chart, see Chapter 15, "Creating a Chart." For information about creating an outline in a worksheet, see Chapter 33, "Outlining a Worksheet." For information about hiding and displaying worksheet data, see "Hiding and Unhiding Rows and Columns" in Chapter 32.

Step By Step

For step-by-step instructions and related information, double-click the [k?] button to display the Search dialog box in Help, and then:

Type this keyword and choose Show Topics	Select a topic and choose Go To
buttons, adding to toolbar	Adding or deleting a toolbar button
charts, creating	Creating a chart from a pivot table
	Creating a chart from visible worksheet data
	Creating an embedded chart on a worksheet
outlines, creating	Creating an outline automatically
pivot tables, creating	Creating a pivot table
rows, hiding and unhiding	Hiding and unhiding a row or column
toolbars	Displaying or hiding toolbars

Organizing and Managing Data in a List

C H A P T E R   2 0

Using a List to Organize Data

For command, keyboard, and toolbar button information, see online Help.

In This Chapter

What Is a List?

One way to store data on a worksheet is in a *list*. A list is a labeled series of rows that contain similar data. For example, a list can be a listing of clients and their phone numbers, or a database of invoices. Microsoft Excel lists have some common features.

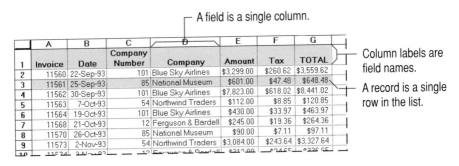

Cells in the same column contain like data.

The first row contains column labels.

Rows in a list contain similar sets of data.

A List Can Be Used as a Database

You can think of a list as a simple database, where rows are *records* and columns are *fields*.

A field is a single column.

Column labels are field names.

A record is a single row in the list.

You don't need to do anything special to your list to make it a database. When performing most database tasks—such as finding, sorting, or subtotaling data—Microsoft Excel automatically recognizes your list as a database. For information about sorting and finding data, see Chapter 21, "Sorting and Filtering Data in a List." For information about subtotaling data, see Chapter 22, "Summarizing Data in a List."

Guidelines for Creating a List on a Worksheet

Microsoft Excel has a number of automatic features that make it easy to manage and analyze data in a list. To take full advantage of these features, enter rows and columns in a list according to the following guidelines.

List Size and Location

- Avoid having more than one list on a worksheet, because some list management features—such as *filtering*—can be used on only one list at a time on a worksheet.

- Leave at least one blank column and one blank row between your list and other data on the worksheet. This helps Microsoft Excel automatically select your list when you sort, filter, or insert automatic subtotals.

- For best results, avoid storing other critical data to the left or right of the list, because it might be hidden when you filter the list.

- A list can be as large as an entire worksheet: 16,384 rows by 256 columns.

Column Labels

- Create column labels in the first row of your list. Microsoft Excel uses these labels to create reports and find and organize data.

- Use a font, data type, alignment, format, pattern, border, or capitalization style for column labels that is different from the format you assign to the data in your list.

- Use cell borders to insert lines below the labels, if you want to separate the labels from the data. Don't use blank rows or dashed lines. For more information about formatting, see "Adding Borders, Patterns, and Colors" in Chapter 12.

- Column labels, like other cells, can contain a maximum of 255 characters.

Tip If a column label is wider than the data in the column, you can wrap the text. Select the label, and choose the Cells command from the Format menu. Then select the Alignment tab, and select the Wrap Text check box.

Row and Column Contents

- Design your list so that all the rows have similar items in the same column.

- Don't insert extra spaces at the beginning of a cell; extra spaces affect sorting and searching.

- Use the same format for all the cells in a column. To apply a cell format, use the Cells command on the Format menu.

Naming the List If you will be using the list in a larger worksheet model, you might want to name it using the Name box in the formula bar or the Name command on the Insert menu. Then, whenever Microsoft Excel requests a reference to the list, you can use this name. However, you don't need to name your list to use any of the list management features provided by Microsoft Excel.

If you name your list Database, Microsoft Excel always identifies the first row as labels or field names. For information about naming a range, see "Names Make References Easier to Use" in Chapter 10.

Capitalization You can use either uppercase or lowercase characters when you type data in a list. Microsoft Excel distinguishes between uppercase and lowercase characters only when you sort, and then only when you select the Case Sensitive sort option. For more information about sorting, see "Sorting Data in a List" in Chapter 21.

Formulas You can use formulas to calculate values in columns, just as you do in any other worksheet cell. When you sort or search for values in a list, Microsoft Excel uses the values produced by the formulas, rather than using the formulas themselves.

Step By Step

For step-by-step instructions and related information, double-click the [?] button to display the Search dialog box in Help, and then:

Type this keyword and choose Show Topics	Select a topic and choose Go To
aligning text	Wrapping text in cells
assigning formats	Assigning a number, date, or time format
automatic subtotals	Displaying automatic subtotals in a list
borders	Adding borders
formulas, entering	Entering formulas
lists, filtering	Filtering a list using AutoFilter
	Filtering a list using complex criteria
lists, sorting	Sorting a list from top to bottom
naming	Naming a cell, range, or formula

List Management Made Easy

If your worksheet data is stored as a list, Microsoft Excel makes it easy for you to organize the list, edit it, and create reports from it.

Maintain a List by Using a Dialog Box

You can use a type of dialog box called a *data form* to display, edit, and delete one record at a time. For more information, see "Maintaining a List by Using a Data Form" later in this chapter.

Organize Data

You can sort your list alphabetically, numerically, or chronologically according to the contents of a specified column or columns. You can also sort using a custom sort order that you define. For more information see "Sorting Data in a List" in Chapter 21.

Find and Display a Subset of Data

To edit, print, format, subtotal, or create a chart from a subset of your list, you can *filter* the list. Filtering temporarily hides all rows that don't meet specified search criteria. Using AutoFilter, with a click of the mouse you can find rows that contain selected items. Using Advanced Filter, you can create custom search criteria using formulas and multiple criteria. For more information, see "Filtering a List Using AutoFilter" and "Filtering a List Using Complex Criteria" in Chapter 21.

Create Summary Reports

With Microsoft Excel, you can insert automatic subtotals for columns you choose. You can also create interactive summary tables called *pivot tables,* which cross-tabulate data in a list. Pivot tables help you compare and analyze data using a layout and calculation you choose. For more information about subtotals, see "Displaying Automatic Subtotals in a List" in Chapter 22. For more information about pivot tables, see Chapter 24, "Creating a Pivot Table," and Chapter 25, "Customizing a Pivot Table."

Step By Step

For step-by-step instructions and related information, double-click the ? button to display the Search dialog box in Help, and then:

Type this keyword and choose Show Topics	Select a topic and choose Go To
automatic subtotals	Displaying automatic subtotals in a list
data forms	Overview of Maintaining a List by Using a Data Form
lists, filtered	Working with a Filtered List
lists, filtering	Filtering a list using AutoFilter
	Filtering a list using complex criteria
lists, sorting	Sorting a list from top to bottom
pivot tables, creating	Creating a pivot table

Maintaining a List by Using a Data Form

Once you create a list, you can add, find, edit, or delete records by using a data form. A data form is a dialog box that displays one complete record at a time.

To use a data form, your list needs to have column labels. Before you type your first record in the data form, you have to type the column labels on the worksheet. For information about column labels, see "What Is a List?" earlier in this chapter.

Note You don't have to use a data form to edit or find data in a list. You can edit cells directly in a list or database.

How a Data Form Works

You can use a data form with a Microsoft Excel list or database, or with any range of data organized in labeled columns. When you select a single cell in your list and choose the Form command from the Data menu, Microsoft Excel displays a dialog box that contains the first record in your list. When you type or edit data in the data form, the corresponding cells on the worksheet reflect the changes you make.

Elements of the Data Form

The data form dialog box consists primarily of a title, data form fields, edit boxes, and command buttons.

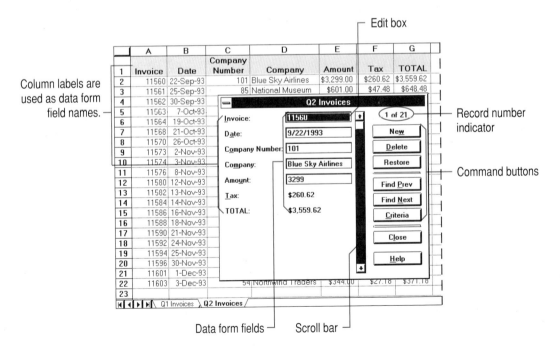

Edit box

Column labels are used as data form field names.

Record number indicator

Command buttons

Data form fields — Scroll bar

Data Form Title   The title bar at the top of the dialog box displays the name of the worksheet that contains the list.

Data Form Fields   The fields that make up a record are stored as a single row in a list. The data form dialog box displays fields in one of two ways:

- Fields containing constant values, which you can edit, appear in an edit box.

- Computed fields, which can't be edited, do not appear in an edit box. These fields contain the results of formulas. For example, the Tax and TOTAL fields in the example are computed fields.

Fields appear in the data form in the order in which they appear from left to right on the worksheet. The width of the widest column in the list determines the length of the edit boxes for fields in the data form dialog box.

Field Names   Field names are created from the column labels as they appear in your list. To change a field name in the data form, you have to change the associated column label on the worksheet.

Scroll Bar   The scroll bar to the right of the data form fields shows you the approximate location of the displayed record in the list and enables you to browse through the records.

Record Number Indicator   In the upper-right corner of the dialog box, the record number indicator shows which record is displayed and how many records are in the list. When you first display the data form, Microsoft Excel displays the first record in the list.

Command Buttons   Use the command buttons to:

- Add a new record.
- Delete a displayed record.
- Undo changes to the displayed record.
- Move between adjacent records.
- Find records based on criteria you specify.

Note   You can display up to 32 fields in the data form.

Entering a Record

Switch to the worksheet that contains your list, and choose the Form command from the Data menu. Then choose the New button, and fill in the fields you want. Use the TAB key to move between fields. When you finish, press ENTER in Microsoft Excel for Windows, or press RETURN in Microsoft Excel for the Macintosh. Microsoft Excel adds the record to the end of your list.

Note If Microsoft Excel detects data in the row beneath the last row, it displays a message. For best results, don't store data directly below your list.

Finding a Record

There are three ways to find a record using the data form:

- Browse through records in your list using the Find Prev and Find Next buttons in the data form dialog box.

- Browse using the scroll bar in the data form dialog box.

- Use the Criteria button to find a subset of records based on criteria you specify.

Finding Records by Using Criteria When you choose the Criteria button in the data form dialog box, Microsoft Excel changes the data form so that data you type in the fields is interpreted as search conditions called *comparison criteria.* Comparison criteria can be a series of characters you want matched, such as "Northwind Traders," or an expression, such as ">300". You can also specify criteria for computed fields.

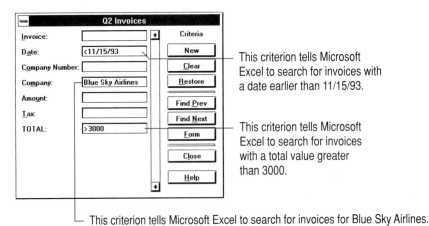

This criterion tells Microsoft Excel to search for invoices with a date earlier than 11/15/93.

This criterion tells Microsoft Excel to search for invoices with a total value greater than 3000.

This criterion tells Microsoft Excel to search for invoices for Blue Sky Airlines.

When you specify search criteria in the data form dialog box, Microsoft Excel searches for records that meet all the specified criteria.

To display the next record that meets the criteria, choose the Find Next button. To display the previous record that meets the criteria, choose the Find Prev button. When you specify criteria using the Criteria button, the Find Prev and Find Next buttons move you only between records that meet all the specified criteria. To regain access to the entire list, choose the Criteria button and then choose the Clear button.

For details about specifying comparison criteria, choose the Help button in the data form dialog box.

Note   To display an entire subset of records at the same time, choose the Filter command from the Data menu, and then choose the AutoFilter command to find the records. The AutoFilter command displays all the records that meet the specified criteria, so you can edit, print, format, or delete them at the same time. For more information, see "Filtering a List Using AutoFilter" in Chapter 21.

Editing a Record

You can use the data form to edit any field except a protected or computed field. If a field can be edited, the data for that field is displayed in an edit box.

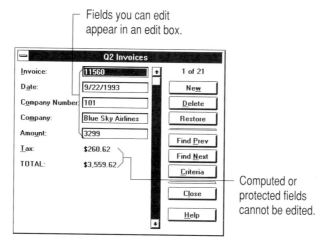

Display the record in the data form, and then make the changes in the edit boxes. When you press ENTER in Microsoft Excel for Windows, or RETURN in Microsoft Excel for the Macintosh, Microsoft Excel reflects your edits in the list. To cancel changes to the displayed record before you move to another record or choose the Close button, choose the Restore button.

Preventing Fields from Being Edited If you don't want a field to be edited, you can *protect* it. To protect a field, you have to enable worksheet protection using the Protection command on the Tools menu. Microsoft Excel protects all cells except those that have been unlocked. For information about locking and unlocking cells and about using the Protection command, see Chapter 39, "Protecting a Workbook."

Note If you enable worksheet protection, you can't type data for new records in the locked fields until you unprotect the worksheet or unlock specific cells.

Deleting a Record

Display the record you want to delete, and then choose the Delete button.

Caution Microsoft Excel permanently removes the row containing the record from the list and then shifts all the rows below it up one position.

Creating a Custom Data Form in Microsoft Excel Version 5.0

You can create a custom data form dialog box in Microsoft Excel by using Visual Basic. Use Visual Basic to create dialog box *controls*—such as command buttons, scroll bars, and data form fields—and to build *macros* to attach to those controls. For more information about using Visual Basic, see the *Microsoft Excel Visual Basic User's Guide.*

Using a Custom Data Form Created in Microsoft Excel Version 4.0

You can use a custom data form created with the Microsoft Excel version 4.0 Dialog Editor. Open the Microsoft Excel version 4.0 worksheet or macro sheet that contains the dialog box definition for the data form. From the Data menu, choose the Form command. Microsoft Excel displays the custom data form.

Using the Microsoft Excel Version 4.0 Dialog Editor with Microsoft Excel Version 5.0

First, start the Microsoft version 4.0 Dialog Editor.

System	Procedure
Windows	Double-click the Dialog Editor icon in the Microsoft Excel version 4.0 Group window in your Windows Program Manager.
Macintosh	Double-click the Dialog Editor icon in the folder containing Microsoft Excel version 4.0.

Then create the data form dialog box definition. Paste the dialog box definition into a Microsoft Excel version 5.0 macro sheet, and then name it Data_form. For information about using the Dialog Editor, see your Microsoft Excel version 4.0 documentation.

Step By Step

For step-by-step instructions and related information, double-click the 🕮? button to display the Search dialog box in Help, and then:

Type this keyword and choose Show Topics	Select a topic and choose Go To
data forms	Adding a record by using a data form
	Deleting a record by using a data form
	Editing a record by using a data form
	Using a data form to find records that meet search criteria
	Using a Microsoft Excel version 4.0 customized data form
lists, filtering	Filtering a list using AutoFilter
protecting cell ranges	Locking and unlocking individual cell ranges on a worksheet
workbooks, protecting	Protecting and unprotecting a sheet

Using Functions to Look Up Values in a List

One way to use a list is as a *lookup table*. In a lookup table, you can use a worksheet formula to find one item of data that is associated with another item of data in the same list. For example, you can find the product name and unit price of an item in the following list if you know the product ID.

	A	B	C	D	E	F	G
1	Product ID	Product Name	Unit Price				
2	17	Alice Springs Lamb	$39.00				
3	14	Bean Curd	$23.25		Product ID:	3	
4	11	Cabrales Cheese	$21.00		Product Name:	Licorice Syrup	
5	1	Dharamsala Tea	$18.00		Unit Price:	$10.00	
6	48	Dutch Chocolate	$12.75				
7	10	Fish Roe	$31.00				
8	33	Goat Cheese	$2.50				
9	31	Gorgonzola Telino	$12.50				
10	13	Kelp Seaweed	$6.00				
11	3	Licorice Syrup	$10.00				
12	32	Mascarpone Fabioli	$32.00				
13	9	Mishi Kobe Beef	$97.00				
14	28	Rössle Sauerkraut	$45.60				
15	34	Sasquatch Ale	$14.00				
16	27	Schoggi Chocolate	$43.90				
17	21	Sir Rodney's Scones	$10.00				
18	35	Steeleye Stout	$18.00				
19	29	Thüringer Sausage	$123.79				
20	23	Thin Bread	$9.00				
21	2	Tibetan Barley Beer	$19.00				
22	47	Zaanse Cookies	$9.50				
23							

Entering the product ID...

...returns the associated product name and unit price from the list.

The item of data you use to find another item of data is called a *search value*. Once you type the search value in a cell on a worksheet, you can use the VLOOKUP function to find other values in the list.

	A	B	C	D	E	F	G
1	Product ID	Product Name	Unit Price				
2	17	Alice Springs Lamb	$39.00				
3	14	Bean Curd	$23.25		Product ID:	3	
4	11	Cabrales Cheese	$21.00		Product Name:	Licorice Syrup	
5	1	Dharamsala Tea	$18.00		Unit Price:	$10.00	
6	48	Dutch Chocolate	$12.75				
7	10	Fish Roe	$31.00				
8	33	Goat Cheese	$2.50				
9	31	Gorgonzola Telino	$12.50				
10	13	Kelp Seaweed	$6.00				
11	3	Licorice Syrup	$10.00				
12	32	Mascarpone Fabioli	$32.00				
13	9	Mishi Kobe Beef	$97.00				

Cell F4 contains the formula =VLOOKUP($F$3, Product_List,2, FALSE), which uses the search value in cell F3 to find the product name.

Cell F5 contains the formula =VLOOKUP($F$3,Product_List,3,FALSE), which uses the search value in cell F3 to find the unit price.

The VLOOKUP function compares the search value with the first column in the list and then returns an associated value in the same row. To use the VLOOKUP function, type a formula that uses the following syntax in a blank cell on your worksheet:

=VLOOKUP(*lookup_value,table_array,col_index_num,range_lookup*)

- The *lookup_value* argument specifies the search value you want to compare with the first column in the list. In the preceding example, this value is $F$3, which is the *absolute reference* to the cell where the search value is located. Using a cell reference enables you to quickly change what value you want to use as a search value.

- The *table_array* argument specifies the range containing the entire list. In the example, this is Product_List, the name assigned to range A1:C22.

- The *col_index* argument identifies the column containing the value you want returned. In the example formula in cell F4, this is 2 for the Product Name column, which is the second column in the list (cells B2:B22). In cell F5, this is 3 for the Unit Price column, which is the third column in the list (cells C2:C22).

- The *range_lookup* argument tells Microsoft Excel how to compare the search value with the first column. Entering FALSE tells Microsoft Excel to find an exact match for the search value.

For more information about using references and constructing formulas, see Chapter 10, "Creating Formulas and Links."

Note   If your lookup table is set up so that the lookup values are in the first row rather than the first column, you can use the HLOOKUP function instead of the VLOOKUP function. For more information about the HLOOKUP function, click the Function Wizard button on the Standard toolbar or see online Help.

When the Lookup Column Isn't the First Column in Your List   The VLOOKUP function requires the lookup column—the column you want to compare your search value with—to be the first column in your list. You have to use other functions if you want to find a search value in a column other than the first column. For example, use the MATCH and INDEX functions together to locate a value where the search value exactly matches a value in the lookup column. Use the MATCH function to find the position of the search value. Use the array form of the INDEX function to find the related item of data by using that position number.

For example, if you want to find the unit price for a product using the product ID, and the Product ID column is not the first column in the list, type the following formulas on the worksheet:

- The formula =MATCH($F$3,Product_ID,0) compares the search value in cell F3 to the Product ID column and returns the search value's position number in the list.

- The formula =INDEX(Unit_Price,$F$4) uses the position number returned by the MATCH function in cell F4 to find the unit price in the Unit Price column in the list.

For more information about the arguments for the MATCH and INDEX functions, click the Function Wizard button on the Standard toolbar or see online Help.

Note To use column labels with the MATCH and INDEX functions, you first have to name your columns by using either the Name box in the formula bar or by choosing the Name command from the Insert menu, and then choosing the Create Names command. For more information, see "Names Make References Easier to Use" in Chapter 10.

Entering Functions Using the Function Wizard

You can use the *Function Wizard* to guide you through the steps of entering the VLOOKUP, MATCH, and INDEX functions instead of typing the formulas yourself. To use the Function Wizard, click the Function Wizard button and select the function you want to use from the Function Name box. For more information, see "Using the Function Wizard" in Chapter 10.

Finding a Value by Searching a Range of Values

You can also use the VLOOKUP function to find a value that is assigned to a range of values. For example, you can use the VLOOKUP function with the following list to determine what percentage of discount to give to a customer if you know the amount on that customer's invoice.

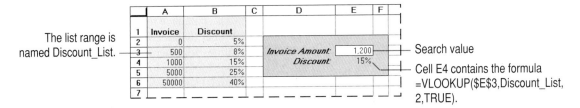

The list range is named Discount_List.

Search value

Cell E4 contains the formula =VLOOKUP($E$3,Discount_List, 2,TRUE).

The VLOOKUP function in cell E4 compares the search value in cell E3 to the first column in the list (range A1:B6, named Discount_List) to find the associated discount in the Discount column (column 2). VLOOKUP returns the value 15% because the search value 1200 falls between 1000 and 5000 in the list.

To use the VLOOKUP function this way, assign to the fourth argument (*range_lookup*) the value TRUE, which tells Microsoft Excel to find an approximate match and return the associated value.

Setting Up a List for a Range Lookup   Because Microsoft Excel looks for an approximate match for the search value, you have to arrange your list so that the values you want to compare your search value with—the *compare values*—appear in ascending order. This is because Microsoft Excel finds the first value that is greater than your search value, backs up one position, and then returns the associated value.

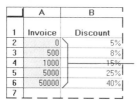

Enter compare values in ascending order.

Tip   If you are using an existing list, an easy way to arrange the values in ascending order is to sort the list by the column containing the compare values. Use the Sort command on the Data menu. For more information, see "Sorting Data in a List" in Chapter 21.

What Is Ascending Order?

Ascending order for numbers goes from the smallest negative number to the greatest positive number (such as −99 to 99). For text values, this is normal alphabetic order (A to Z). For dates and times, ascending order is from the earliest date or time to the latest (1/1/93 to 12/31/93, for example).

When the Lookup Column Isn't the First Column in Your List   If you want to do a range lookup and the lookup column is not the first column in the list, use the vector form of the LOOKUP function instead of the VLOOKUP function. For example, if the Invoice column in the preceding example is the second column instead of the first, entering the formula =LOOKUP($E$3, Invoice, Discount) enables you to find the discount for the search value in cell E3. The LOOKUP function compares the search value to the Invoice column and then returns the associated value in the Discount column, regardless of the order of columns in the list.

For information about the arguments for the LOOKUP function, click the Function Wizard button on the Standard toolbar or see online Help. For more information about constructing formulas, see Chapter 10, "Creating Formulas and Links."

Note To use column labels as arguments with the LOOKUP function, you first have to name your columns by using either the Name box in the formula bar or by choosing the Name command from the Insert menu and then choosing the Create Names command. For more information, see "Names Make References Easier to Use" in Chapter 10.

Step By Step

For step-by-step instructions and related information, double-click the [?] button to display the Search dialog box in Help, and then:

Type this keyword and choose Show Topics	Select a topic and choose Go To
formulas, entering	Overview of Entering a Formula
HLOOKUP function	HLOOKUP
INDEX function	INDEX
LOOKUP function	LOOKUP
MATCH function	MATCH
naming	Naming a cell, range, or formula
VLOOKUP function	VLOOKUP

CHAPTER 21

Sorting and Filtering Data in a List

For command, keyboard, and toolbar button information, see online Help.

In This Chapter

How Sorting and Filtering Work

Microsoft Excel makes it easy for you to organize, find, and create reports from data stored in a list:

- *Sort* to organize data in a list alphabetically, numerically, or chronologically.
- *Filter* to quickly find and work with a subset of your data without moving or sorting it.

A list is data organized by rows or records on a worksheet. For information about creating a list, see "What is a List?" in Chapter 20.

How Sorting Works

When you sort a list, Microsoft Excel rearranges rows according to the contents of one or more columns. For example, rows in the following list are sorted according to the contents of the Sales column, from the smallest sales amount to the largest sales amount.

Sales column

	A	B	C	D	E	
1	Month	Salesperson	Type	Units	Sales	
2	Mar	Buchanan	Beverage	4,997	$656	
3	Mar	Davolio	Meat	6,740	$699	
4	Jan	Davolio	Meat	7,832	$1,441	
5	Mar	Davolio	Produce	7,549	$1,500	
6	Jan	Suyama	Produce	744	$2,666	
7	Jan	Buchanan	Beverage	587	$3,522	
8	Jan	Buchanan	Meat	5,889	$4,953	
9	Mar	Suyama	Produce	2,449	$5,971	
10	Mar	Suyama	Meat	9,435	$6,040	
11	Feb	Suyama	Meat	8,953	$6,127	
12	Feb	Davolio	Beverage	767	$6,711	
13	Mar	Buchanan	Produce	2,652	$6,715	
14	Jan	Davolio	Produce	9,888	$7,047	
15	Jan	Suyama	Beverage	2,898	$7,538	
16	Feb	Buchanan	Meat	5,847	$8,179	
17	Jan	Davolio	Beverage	8,207	$8,461	
18	Feb	Buchanan	Produce	340	$8,751	
19	Feb	Suyama	Beverage	690	$9,862	
20						

Whole rows sorted according to the contents of the Sales column

If a column in your list contains a limited set of items, such as department numbers or product names, sorting places rows with identical items together. For example, the following list is sorted in alphabetic order by the Salesperson column, so that rows with Buchanan in the Salesperson column appear together, rows with Davolio appear together, and so on.

Salesperson column

	A	B	C	D	E
1	Month	Salesperson	Type	Units	Sales
2	Mar	Buchanan	Beverage	4,997	$656
3	Jan	Buchanan	Beverage	587	$3,522
4	Jan	Buchanan	Meat	5,889	$4,953
5	Mar	Buchanan	Produce	2,652	$6,715
6	Feb	Buchanan	Meat	5,847	$8,179
7	Feb	Buchanan	Produce	340	$8,751
8	Mar	Davolio	Meat	6,740	$699
9	Jan	Davolio	Meat	7,832	$1,441
10	Mar	Davolio	Produce	7,549	$1,500
11	Feb	Davolio	Beverage	767	$6,711
12	Jan	Davolio	Produce	9,888	$7,047
13	Jan	Davolio	Beverage	8,207	$8,461
14	Jan	Suyama	Produce	744	$2,666
15	Mar	Suyama	Produce	2,449	$5,971
16	Mar	Suyama	Meat	9,435	$6,040
17	Feb	Suyama	Meat	8,953	$6,127
18	Jan	Suyama	Beverage	2,898	$7,538
19	Feb	Suyama	Beverage	690	$9,862
20					

Whole rows sorted according to the contents of the Salesperson column

Use this type of sorting to prepare a list for automatic subtotals. For more information about inserting automatic subtotals, see Chapter 22, "Summarizing Data in a List."

You can also sort data in an outline or a single row or column, or you can sort a list that has been filtered.

How Filtering Works

Filtering is a quick and easy way to find and work with a subset of data in a list. When you filter a list, Microsoft Excel displays only those rows that contain a certain value, or that meet a set of search conditions called *criteria*.

Unlike sorting, filtering does not rearrange a list. Filtering temporarily hides rows you do not want displayed. For example, all rows in the following list are hidden except those containing Produce in the Type column and Davolio in the Salesperson column.

An unfiltered list

The same list, filtered
so that only rows
containing Davolio's
produce sales
are displayed

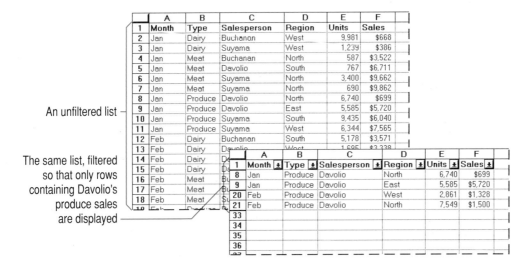

There are two ways to filter a list in Microsoft Excel:

- Use AutoFilter to filter your list quickly by matching cell contents or using simple comparison criteria, such as "display rows where Sales are greater than 2000." For more information, see "Filtering a List Using AutoFilter" later in this chapter.

- Use Advanced Filter to filter data based on complex or computed criteria. You can also use Advanced Filter to automatically copy data that meets specified criteria to another location. For more information, see "Filtering a List Using Complex Criteria" later in this chapter.

When Microsoft Excel filters rows, your worksheet is placed in *Filter mode.* When you are in Filter mode, you can edit, format, chart, and print your list subset without rearranging or moving it.

Note   You can also find rows or records in a list using a *data form.* With a data form, you can display one record at a time in a dialog box, for easy viewing and editing. For more information, see "Maintaining a List by Using a Data Form" in Chapter 20.

Sorting Data in a List

When you sort a list, Microsoft Excel rearranges rows according to the contents of a column you choose—the Sort By column. You can also sort selected rows or data in a single column.

You also choose an ascending or descending *sort order.* The sort order is the way you want the data arranged. For example, when you use an ascending sort order, numbers are sorted from 1 to 9, text is sorted from A to Z, and dates are sorted from earliest to latest. When you use a descending sort order, numbers are sorted from 9 to 1, text is sorted from Z to A, and dates are sorted from latest to earliest.

Performing a Simple Sort

To sort your entire list, just select a single cell in the list and choose the Sort command from the Data menu. Microsoft Excel automatically selects the whole list for you. If your list has column labels in the first row, Microsoft Excel excludes them from the sort and uses them to help you choose the Sort By column.

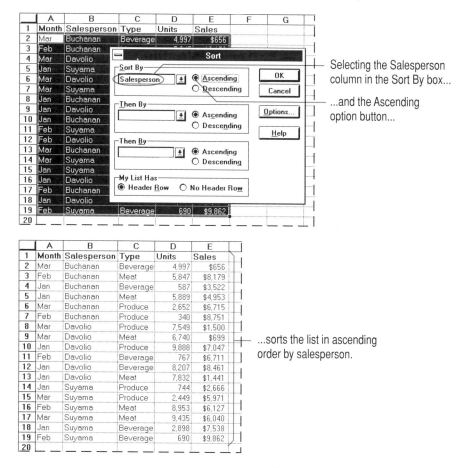

Selecting the Salesperson column in the Sort By box...

...and the Ascending option button...

...sorts the list in ascending order by salesperson.

If Microsoft Excel does not automatically select the data you want to sort, manually select the data and choose the Sort command again.

Rows that contain duplicate items in the Sort By column appear together in the sorted list in their original order. If you want to sort these duplicate rows further, you can specify a second column to sort by in the first Then By box. If there are duplicate items in this second column, you can specify a third column to sort by in the second Then By box. You can sort by up to three columns at a time.

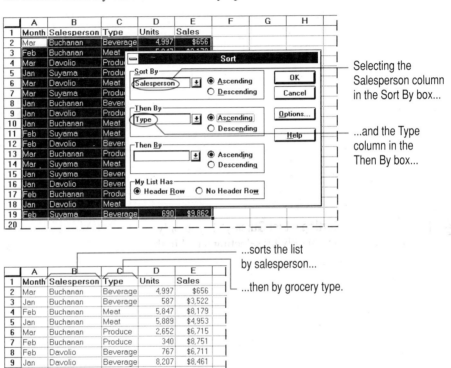

Selecting the Salesperson column in the Sort By box...

...and the Type column in the Then By box...

...sorts the list by salesperson...

...then by grocery type.

Microsoft Excel saves the sort options you select in the Sort dialog box and Sort Options dialog box—such as the Sort By column, sort order (ascending or descending), and sort orientation (top to bottom or left to right)—and displays them each time you choose the Sort command until you change the options or sort another list.

Note Hidden rows or columns are not moved when you sort, unless they are part of an outline. For more information about sorting rows or columns in an outline, see "Sorting Data in an Outline" later in this chapter.

Undoing a Sort If you do not like the results of a sort, you can undo it by immediately choosing the Undo Sort command from the Edit menu.

Tip To be able to return your list to its original unsorted state after sorting several times, you can number the rows before you sort. Insert and label a column in your list and fill it with sequential numbers using the AutoFill handle or the Fill command on the Edit menu. Then, when you want to return your list to its original order, sort the list by this column. For information about using AutoFill, see "Filling Adjacent Cells and Creating Series" in Chapter 9.

Sort Ascending

Sorting a List Quickly If you only need to sort by a single column, you can sort a list quickly by selecting a cell in the column you want to sort by and then clicking the Sort Ascending button. Microsoft Excel sorts all rows in the list, except column labels, in ascending order by the contents of the selected column.

Sort Descending

To sort the list in descending order, click the Sort Descending button.

The Sort Ascending and Sort Descending buttons use the options—such as a custom sort order or the case-sensitive option—currently specified in the Sort Options dialog box.

Sorting by a Column That Contains Numbers or Text and Numbers

If the Sort By column contains numbers, make sure the numbers are all in a numeric format, or are all formatted as text. For information about entering numbers as text, see "Entering Text" in Chapter 9. For information about formatting existing numbers, see "Applying Number Formats" in Chapter 12.

Note If the column you want to sort by contains both numbers and numbers that include text characters (such as 100, 100a, 200, 200a), format them all as text if you want to sort them together. If you do not, Microsoft Excel will sort the numbers first, then the numbers that include text (100, 200, 100a, 200a). To format a number as text, precede the number with an apostrophe (').

Sort Orders

You can sort a list in ascending order, descending order, or using a custom sort order you define. Content and data type determine how a value is sorted.

Ascending Sort Order

- Numbers, from the smallest negative number to the largest positive number; dates and times, from earliest to latest.
- Text values, sorting numbers entered as text first, then regular text.
- Logical values, FALSE then TRUE
- Error values, such as #VALUE! or #NAME?, in the order in which they are found.
- Blanks

Descending Sort Order

When you select a descending sort order, Microsoft Excel sorts values in the order opposite from the ascending order, except for blank cells, which are always sorted last.

How Microsoft Excel Identifies Column Labels

Microsoft Excel identifies column labels by comparing the formatting in the top rows of your list. If there is a difference between the rows—such as data type, capitalization, font, alignment, or pattern—Microsoft Excel identifies the first row as column labels and excludes it from the sort by automatically selecting the Header Row option button under My List Has in the Sort dialog box. Microsoft Excel can identify up to two rows of column labels.

Sorting a List That Does Not Have Column Labels If there are no differences in data type, capitalization, font, alignment, or pattern between the first rows and rows that follow, Microsoft Excel does not identify column labels. Microsoft Excel automatically selects the No Header Row option button under My List Has in the Sort dialog box. If for some reason Microsoft Excel identifies your first row as column labels but you want to include the row in the sort, manually select the No Header Row option button. You can then select a column to sort by using the generic column headings (Column A, Column B, and so on).

Sorting Columns Left to Right in a List

With the Sort command, you can sort columns instead of rows. Choose the Options button in the Sort dialog box. In the Sort Options dialog box, select the Sort Left To Right option button, and then choose the OK button. Then select the rows you want to sort by (Row 1, Row 2, and so on) in the Sort By and Then By boxes.

Sorting Items in a Pivot Table

When you choose the Sort command after selecting a cell in a pivot table, Microsoft Excel displays a special Sort dialog box for you. For information about using this dialog box to sort items in a pivot table, see "Sorting Items in a Pivot Table Field" in Chapter 25.

Sorting a List That Includes Graphic Objects

If the list you want to sort contains graphic objects such as buttons, text boxes, or drawings, Microsoft Excel sorts them with the associated row. If you do not want an object to be sorted with your list, select the object and choose the Object command from the Format menu. Then select the Properties tab and select the Don't Move Or Size With Cells option button under Object Positioning.

Sorting Selected Data

To sort only a subset of rows, or to sort the data in a single column of a list, first select the rows or columns you want to sort before you choose the Sort command.

If you select data in a single column or row, Microsoft Excel displays a message asking you to confirm that you want to sort only the selected cells. If you select the Continue With The Current Selection option button and complete the sort, Microsoft Excel sorts only the selected data, leaving the surrounding data in place.

Caution   Sorting selected data does not move data in adjacent columns or rows.

Sorting by Four or More Columns

Although a list can have up to 256 columns, you can sort by only three columns at a time. If you want to sort by four columns or more, sort the list two or more times.

First, sort by the three least important columns. Then choose the Sort command again to sort the remaining columns in the order of their importance.

For example, suppose you want to sort a list by Type, then by Salesperson, Region, and Sales. First, sort the list by specifying Salesperson in the Sort By box and Region and Sales in the Then By boxes. Then choose the Sort command again. Sort the list again by selecting Type in the Sort By box and None in the Then By boxes.

First sort by Salesperson,
Region, and Sales...

...then sort
again by Type.

	A	B	C	D	E	F
1	Month	Type	Salesperson	Region	Units	Sales
2	Mar	Dairy	Buchanan	East	3,326	$1,132
3	Feb	Dairy	Buchanan	South	5,178	$3,571
4	Jan	Dairy	Buchanan	West	9,981	$668
5	Feb	Dairy	Davolio	East	3,260	$6,805
6	Feb	Dairy	Davolio	North	6,890	$8,725
7	Mar	Dairy	Davolio	South	3,796	$7,669
8	Feb	Dairy	Davolio	West	1,695	$3,338
9	Mar	Dairy	Suyama	East	5,636	$4,356
10	Mar	Dairy	Suyama	North	8,404	$6,239
11	Jan	Dairy	Suyama	West	1,239	$386
12	Mar	Dairy	Suyama	West	8,578	$5,477
13	Feb	Meat	Buchanan	East	3,389	$8,012
14	Jan	Meat	Buchanan	North	587	$3,522
15	Mar	Meat	Buchanan	South	4,997	$656
16	Feb	Meat	Buchanan	West	5,847	$8,179
17	Mar	Meat	Davolio	East	7,832	$1,441
18	Mar	Meat	Davolio	South	5,735	$3,316
19	Jan	Meat	Davolio	South	767	$6,711
20	Feb	Meat	Suyama	East	410	$265

Using a Custom Sort Order

Instead of choosing a simple ascending or descending order, you can specify a custom sort order for the Sort By column. A custom sort order does not use the usual alphabetic or numeric sort rules. For example, the following list is sorted by month in calendar order using the custom sort order "Jan, Feb, Mar."

A custom sort order applied to the Month column...

	A	B	C	D	E
1	Month	Salesperson	Type	Units	Sales
2	Jan	Buchanan	Beverages	587	$3,522
3	Jan	Buchanan	Meat	5,889	$4,953
4	Jan	Davolio	Meat	7,832	$1,441
5	Jan	Davolio	Produce	9,888	$7,047
6	Jan	Davolio	Beverages	8,207	$8,461
7	Jan	Suyama	Produce	744	$2,666
8	Jan	Suyama	Beverages	2,898	$7,538
9	Feb	Buchanan	Meat	5,847	$8,179
10	Feb	Buchanan	Produce	340	$8,751
11	Feb	Davolio	Beverages	767	$6,711
12	Feb	Suyama	Meat	8,953	$6,127
13	Feb	Suyama	Beverages	690	$9,862
14	Mar	Buchanan	Beverages	4,997	$656
15	Mar	Buchanan	Produce	2,652	$6,715
16	Mar	Davolio	Meat	6,740	$699
17	Mar	Davolio	Produce	7,549	$1,500
18	Mar	Suyama	Produce	2,449	$5,971
19	Mar	Suyama	Meat	9,435	$6,040
20					

...sorts rows by month
in calendar order.

To use a custom sort order, choose the Options button in the Sort dialog box, then select a custom sort order in the First Key Sort Order box. If the Sort By column contains items that are not recognized by the custom sort order, those items are sorted last in the standard alphabetic or numeric order.

The Ascending and Descending sort order options you select for the Sort By column in the Sort dialog box apply to the custom sort order. For example, a descending sort order for "Jan, Feb, Mar" would be "Dec, Nov, Oct" and so on.

Microsoft Excel uses the custom sort order until you select another custom sort order or sort another list.

For basic information about sort orders, see "Sort Orders" earlier in this section.

Note   The Custom Sort order applies only to the column you specify in the Sort By box of the Sort dialog box. You cannot apply a custom sort order to columns in the Then By boxes.

Creating a Custom Sort Order   You can create your own custom sort order, such as "Low, Medium, High," using the Custom Lists Tab of the Options dialog box. To display the Options dialog box and the Custom Lists tab, choose the Options command from the Tools menu. In the List Entries box, type each unique item in your Sort By column. Type the items in the order you want them to appear when you sort the list in ascending order. Your new custom sort order becomes an option you can select when you choose the Sort command.

Step By Step

For step-by-step instructions and related information, double-click the [?] button to display the Search dialog box in Help, and then:

Type this keyword and choose Show Topics	Select a topic and choose Go To
columns, sorting by	Sorting by four or more columns
custom sort order	Creating a custom sort order
	Using a custom sort order
date series	Incrementing a series of numbers or dates
default sort orders	Default Sort Orders
graphic objects, detaching	Detaching a graphic object from underlying cells
sorting lists	Sorting a list from left to right
	Sorting a list from top to bottom
sorting pivot table items	Sorting pivot table items by labels
	Sorting pivot table items by values in the data area
text	Formatting numbers as text

Sorting Data in an Outline

When you sort rows that are part of a worksheet outline, the highest-level groups (level 1 groups) are sorted so that rows or columns that are grouped together stay together. For example, the groups in the following outline (Eastern, Southern, and Western) are sorted in ascending order according to values in the Jan-92 column.

These outline groups...

	A	B	C	D	E	F	G	H
1			Jan-92	Feb-92	Mar-92	Qtr 1-92	Apr-92	May
2	Eastern	Windsurfing	$29,608	$71,941	$29,823	$131,372	$12,519	$41
3		Golf	$27,164	$16,868	$16,572	$60,604	$16,276	$65
4		Tennis	$60,902	$43,831	$29,935	$134,668	$16,039	$52
5	Eastern Total		$117,674	$132,640	$76,330	$326,644	$44,834	$159.
6	Southern	Golf	$18,557	$21,535	$24,513	$64,605	$27,491	$70
7		Safari	$50,260	$18,206	$66,115	$134,581	$62,070	$46
8		Tennis	$63,075	$82,701	$51,812	$197,588	$77,758	$60
9	Southern Total		$131,892	$122,442	$142,440	$396,774	$167,319	$178.
10	Western	Golf	$31,735	$11,566	$71,639	$114,940	$44,132	$16
11		Safari	$63,074	$20,519	$12,828	$96,421	$83,793	$16
12		Tennis	$45,696	$77,739	$76,476	$199,911	$22,164	$67
13	Western Total		$140,505	$109,824	$160,943	$411,272	$150,089	$100.
14								

...are sorted by values in the Jan-92 column.

Microsoft Excel evaluated only the Jan-92 value for the highest-level row in each group (rows 5, 9, and 13) to determine the order of the groups. All rows grouped with row 5 (rows 2, 3, and 4) are moved with row 5, all rows grouped with row 9 are moved with row 9, and so on, even if the detail rows are hidden.

To sort rows in a worksheet outline, select a single cell in the outlined data and choose the Sort command from the Data menu. If Microsoft Excel does not select what you expect, select the rows manually and choose the Sort command again. To sort the columns left to right in your list instead of sorting rows, choose the Options button in the Sort dialog box and select the Left To Right option button under Sort Orientation.

For information about creating and using a worksheet outline, see Chapter 33, "Outlining a Worksheet."

Note   If level 1 of your outline consists of a single group, Microsoft Excel sorts groups in level 2.

For information about creating a worksheet outline, see Chapter 33, "Outlining a Worksheet."

Sorting a List that has Automatic Subtotals   If your outline was created by inserting automatic subtotals, you need to hide detail rows before you sort. For more information, see "Sorting a Subtotaled List" in Chapter 22.

Step By Step

For step-by-step instructions and related information, double-click the [k?] button to display the Search dialog box in Help, and then:

Type this keyword and choose Show Topics	Select a topic and choose Go To
outlines, creating	Overview of Creating and Removing an Outline
showing detail data	Hiding and showing detail data in a subtotaled list
sorting lists	Sorting a list from left to right
	Sorting a list from top to bottom

Filtering a List Using AutoFilter

AutoFilter enables you to display a subset of your list with a click of a mouse button. When you choose the Filter command from the Data menu and then choose AutoFilter, Microsoft Excel places drop-down arrows directly on the column labels of your list. Clicking an arrow displays a list of all the unique items in the column. By selecting an item from a list for a specific column, you can instantly hide all rows except those rows that contain the selected value.

	A	B	C	D	E	F
1	Month	Type	Salesperson	Region	Units	Sales
2	Jan	Meat	(All)	North	3,400	$9,662
3	Jan	Dairy	(Custom...)	West	1,239	$386
4	Jan	Meat	Buchanan / Davolio	North	690	$9,862
5	Jan	Produce	Suyama	East	5,585	$5,720
6	Jan	Produce	(Blanks) / (NonBlanks)	South	9,435	$6,040
7	Jan	Meat	Davolio	South	767	$6,711
8	Jan	Meat	Buchanan	North	587	$3,522
9	Jan	Produce	Davolio	North	6,740	$699
10	Jan	Produce	Suyama	West	6,344	$7,565
11	Jan	Dairy	Buchanan	West	9,981	$668
12	Feb	Produce	Buchanan	West	234	$1,450
13	Feb	Meat	Suyama	East	4,105	$265
14	Feb	Dairy	Davolio	West	605	$2,330

When you select Buchanan from the Salesperson drop-down list...

	A	B	C	D	E	F
1	Month	Type	Salesperson	Region	Units	Sales
8	Jan	Meat	Buchanan	North	587	$3,522
11	Jan	Dairy	Buchanan	West	9,981	$668
12	Feb	Produce	Buchanan	West	234	$1,450
16	Feb	Meat	Buchanan	West	5,847	$8,179
17	Feb	Meat	Buchanan	East	3,389	$8,012
20	Feb	Dairy	Buchanan	South	5,178	$3,571
22	Mar	Dairy	Buchanan	East	3,326	$1,132
26	Mar	Produce	Buchanan	South	2,652	$6,715
28	Mar	Produce	Buchanan	West	5,943	$9,411
30	Mar	Meat	Buchanan	South	4,997	$656
33						

...all rows that do not contain Buchanan are hidden.

The item you select in a column drop-down list is called the *filter criterion.* You can filter your list further by choosing another criterion from another column. For example, selecting West from the Region drop-down list hides all rows except those that contain Buchanan and West.

	A	B	C	D	E	F
1	Month ±	Type ±	Salesperson ±	Region ±	Units ±	Sales ±
11	Jan	Dairy	Buchanan	West	9,981	$668
12	Feb	Produce	Buchanan	West	234	$1,450
16	Feb	Meat	Buchanan	West	5,847	$8,179
28	Mar	Produce	Buchanan	West	5,943	$9,411
33						

Tip   If the list of items is long, you can quickly move to an item by selecting the arrow, then typing the first letters of the item.

When you hide rows using criteria, you are applying a filter to a list. Microsoft Excel helps you recognize the filter status of a list by providing some visual cues.

Arrows for columns with filter criterion selected appear blue on your worksheet.

Row headings appear blue on your worksheet.

	A	B	C	D	E	F
1	Month ±	Type ±	Salesperson ±	Region ±	Units ±	Sales ±
11	Jan	Dairy	Buchanan	West	9,981	$668
12	Feb	Produce	Buchanan	West	234	$1,450
16	Feb	Meat	Buchanan	West	5,847	$8,179
28	Mar	Produce	Buchanan	West	5,943	$9,411
33						
34						
35						
36						
37						
38						

The status bar displays the number of rows that meet the criteria, or the text "Filter Mode."

Filter Mode

Note   You can filter only one list at a time on a worksheet.

Applying AutoFilter to Selected Columns   If you select a single cell before choosing the AutoFilter command, arrows are applied to all column labels in the list. If you want to filter a list using selected columns, select the labels for those columns before you choose the AutoFilter command. Microsoft Excel applies the arrows only to those columns. To apply arrows to a single column, select the label and the cell below it.

Finding Rows with Empty Cells or Fields   To find rows with blank cells in a column, select Blanks from the drop-down list for that column. For example, if you have a list of potential clients and you want to find all customer records without a date in the Sales Call column, select the Blanks option from the Sales Call drop-down list.

Finding Rows with Nonblank Cells To display all rows that contain data in a specified column, select the NonBlanks option from the drop-down list for that column.

Removing a Filter To remove filter criteria for a single column, select All from the column's drop-down list. To show all hidden rows in the list, choose the Filter command from the Data menu, then choose Show All. To display all hidden rows and remove the AutoFilter arrows, choose the Filter command, and then clear the AutoFilter command.

Filtering a Subtotaled List Because Microsoft Excel does not recalculate automatic subtotals when you filter, you should sort and filter your list before you insert automatic subtotals. For information about sorting a filtered list, see "Working with a Filtered List" later in this chapter. For information about inserting automatic subtotals in a filtered list, see "Displaying Automatic Subtotals in a List" in Chapter 22.

Using Custom Criteria with AutoFilter

With AutoFilter, you can specify *custom criteria* for each column. This is useful when you want to:

- Display rows that contain either of two items in a text field, such as rows that contain "Buchanan" and rows that contain "Davolio" in the Salesperson column.

- Display rows that contain values that fall within a range of values, such as rows that contain sales values greater than 7000 and less than 10,000.

To specify custom criteria for a column, select the Custom option from the drop-down list for the column. Then type the criteria you want applied to the column in the Custom AutoFilter dialog box. For example, if you select the Custom option from the Sales drop-down list in the following worksheet list, you can specify criteria that hide all rows except those with sales values greater than 5000 and less than 7000.

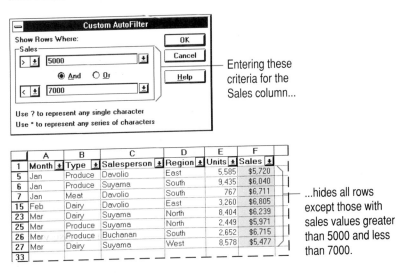

Entering these criteria for the Sales column...

...hides all rows except those with sales values greater than 5000 and less than 7000.

Tip   Instead of typing values to compare in the Custom AutoFilter dialog box, you can click the arrow and select an item from the drop-down list that appears. This list contains all unique items that appear in the column.

When you specify custom criteria, you select the *comparison operator* you want to use, such as "greater than" (>) or "equal to" (=). If you specify two custom criteria, choose how you want Microsoft Excel to apply the criteria.

To display rows	Select this option	Example
That meet both specified criteria	the And option button	>3000 And <4500 Displays all rows with values that fall between 3000 and 4500.
That meet either one or the other of the specified criteria	the Or option button	<3000 Or >4500 Displays all rows with values that are either less than 3000 or greater than 4500.

You can also use *wildcard characters* (* or ?) to find approximate values. For information about using wildcard characters, choose the Help button in the Custom AutoFilter dialog box.

Step By Step

For step-by-step instructions and related information, double-click the [?] button to display the Search dialog box in Help, and then:

Type this keyword and choose Show Topics	Select a topic and choose Go To
AutoFilter	Creating a custom AutoFilter
filters, removing	Removing a filter from a list
lists, filtering	Filtering a list using AutoFilter
	Filtering a list using complex criteria
subtotals, automatic	Displaying automatic subtotals in a list

Filtering a List Using Complex Criteria

To filter a list using more complex criteria than you use with AutoFilter, use the Advanced Filter (Data menu, Filter submenu).

The Advanced Filter command filters your list in place, as AutoFilter does, but it does not display drop-down lists for columns. Instead, you type criteria in a *criteria range* on your worksheet.

	A	B	C	D	E	F
1	Salesperson	Region				
2	Davolio					
3		North				
4						
5	Month	Type	Salesperson	Region	Units	Sales
6	Jan	Meat	Davolio	South	767	$6,711
8	Jan	Produce	Davolio	East	5,585	$5,720
9	Jan	Meat	Buchanan	North	587	$3,522
10	Jan	Meat	Suyama	North	690	$9,862
12	Jan	Produce	Davolio	North	6,740	$699
13	Jan	Meat	Suyama	North	3,400	$9,662
17	Feb	Produce	Davolio	North	7,549	$1,500
18	Feb	Dairy	Davolio	North	6,890	$8,725
20	Feb	Dairy	Davolio	West	1,695	$3,338
24	Feb	Dairy	Davolio	East	3,260	$6,805
25	Feb	Produce	Davolio	West	2,861	$1,328
26	Mar	Dairy	Davolio	South	3,796	$7,669
28	Mar	Produce	Suyama	North	2,449	$5,971
29	Mar	Dairy	Suyama	North	8,404	$6,239
32	Mar	Meat	Davolio	East	7,832	$1,441
36	Mar	Meat	Davolio	South	5,735	$3,316
37						

Using this criteria range with the Advanced Filter command...

...hides all rows except those containing Salesperson Davolio or Region North.

To use the Advanced Filter command, first create the criteria range using the guidelines outlined later in this section. For best results, place the criteria range above or below the list, so it won't be hidden when the list is filtered. Then select a single cell in the list, choose the Filter command from the Data menu, and then choose the Advanced Filter command. When the Advanced Filter dialog box appears, specify:

- The range that contains the list you want filtered. If you selected a single cell in the list, Microsoft Excel enters the reference to the whole list for you.

- The range that contains your criteria. Make sure you include the criteria labels.

Make sure the Filter The List, In-place option button under Action is selected. When you choose the OK button, Microsoft Excel temporarily hides all rows that do not meet the specified criteria.

You can filter one list at a time on a worksheet.

Note You cannot complete successive filters using the Advanced Filter command. If you change the data in the criteria range and filter again, Microsoft Excel applies the criteria to both hidden and displayed rows in the list.

What Are Complex Criteria?

A criteria range enables you to filter data using two kinds of complex criteria: multiple *comparison criteria* and *computed criteria.*

- Comparison criteria enable you to display rows that contain specified values, or that contain values that fall within limits you specify. Comparison criteria can be a series of characters you want matched, such as "South," or an expression, such as ">=6000."

- Computed criteria evaluate a selected column in your list against values not contained in the list. For example, to display only rows where the sales value is greater than the quarterly average, you can type "=Sales>$F$2" as the criteria, where Sales is the column containing sales data and $F$2 is the *absolute cell reference* of the cell that contains the average sales value for the quarter. Only rows for which the formula evaluates to TRUE are displayed.

Note If you want to specify only one or two comparison criteria, such as "display rows whose Sales value is greater than 1000," use the Custom option in the AutoFilter command. For more information, see "Filtering a List Using AutoFilter" earlier in this chapter.

Types of Comparison Criteria

You can use the following types of comparison criteria in a criteria range:

A Series of Characters You Want Matched   To find records that contain an exact value, type the text, number, date, or logical value in the cell below the criteria label. For example, if you type 98133 below a Postal Code label in the criteria range, Microsoft Excel displays only rows that contain the postal code value 98133.

When you use text as criteria, Microsoft Excel finds all items that begin with that text. For example, if you type the text "Dav" as a criterion, Microsoft Excel finds Davolio, David, and Davis. To match only the specified text, type the formula

="=*text*"

where *text* is the text you want to match.

Wildcard Characters   To find text values that share some characters but not others, use a wildcard character. A wildcard character represents one or more unspecified characters.

Use this character	To find	Example
? (question mark)	Any single character in the same position as the question mark	**sm?th** finds "smith" and "smyth"
* (asterisk)	Any number of characters in the same position as the asterisk	***east** finds "Northeast" and "Southeast"
~ (tilde) followed by ?, *, or ~	An actual question mark, asterisk, or tilde	**fy91~?** finds "fy91?"

A Quantity You Want Compared   To display only rows that fall within certain limits, type a comparison operator, followed by a value, in the cell below the criteria label. For example, to find rows whose unit values are greater than or equal to 1000, type ">=1000" under the Units criteria label in the criteria range.

Comparison operator	Meaning
=	Equal to
>	Greater than
<	Less than
>=	Greater than or equal to

Comparison operator	Meaning
<=	Less than or equal to
<>	Not equal to

Note You can use either uppercase or lowercase characters in your comparison criteria. Microsoft Excel does not distinguish between uppercase and lowercase characters when evaluating data.

Using Comparison Criteria in a Criteria Range

Comparison criteria enable you to *query by example*—specify criteria that match or approximate the values you want to find in your list. To create a criteria range using comparison criteria, use one row of criteria labels and at least one row of criteria. Criteria labels must be identical to the labels for the columns you want evaluated.

Tip An easy way to make sure criteria labels match the column labels in the list is to copy and paste the column labels.

Comparison criteria labels have to be identical to the column labels in the list.

	A	B	C	D	E	F
1	Type	Region				
2	Dairy					
3		North				
4						
5	Month	Type	Salesperson	Region	Units	Sales
6	Jan	Meat	Suyama	North	690	$9,862
7	Jan	Produce	Davolio	East	5,585	$5,720
8	Jan	Produce	Davolio	North	6,740	$699
9	Jan	Dairy	Buchanan	West	9,981	$668
10	Jan	Meat	Suyama	North	3,400	$9,662

The column labels Type and Region in a criteria range tell Microsoft Excel to evaluate the Type and Region columns in the list using the criteria in range A1:B3.

Follow these guidelines when typing comparison criteria:

- Type all your criteria in the same row to find records that meet all criteria in that row. For example, the following criteria range finds all rows that contain Davolio *and* sales values greater than 1000.

	A	B
1	Salesperson	Sales
2	Davolio	>1000
3		

- Use a column label more than once if you want to find records that meet more than one criterion for the same column. For example, this criteria range finds all rows with sales values greater than 1000 *and* less than 1500.

	A	B
1	Sales	Sales
2	>1000	<1500
3		

- Type criteria in different rows to find records that meet all criteria in the first row *or* the second row. For example, the following criteria range finds all rows that contain Buchanan and sales values greater than 1500, *or* rows that contain Davolio and sales values greater than 1000.

	A	B
1	Salesperson	Sales
2	Buchanan	>1500
3	Davolio	>1000
4		

Note   When you choose the Advanced Filter command (Data menu, Filter submenu) and type or select the reference for the criteria range, make sure you include the criteria labels.

Using Computed Criteria in a Criteria Range

You can also use a worksheet formula to specify criteria. A formula enables you to specify criteria computed with values external to your list. You can use computed criteria alone, or you can combine computed and comparison criteria in the same criteria range. For example, to find February sales records greater than the average January sales, the criteria range in the following list includes both comparison criteria and computed criteria. The computed criterion formula in cell B2 compares each cell in the Sales column (column F) to the January sales average, which is calculated using the AVERAGE function.

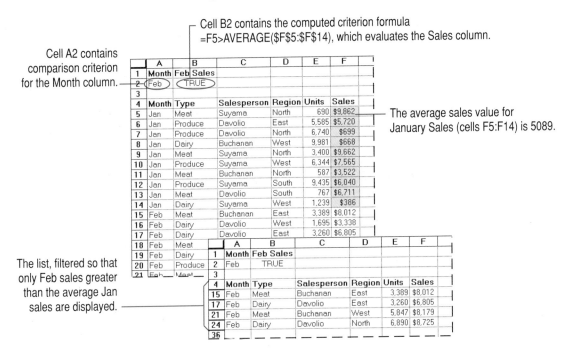

Cell B2 contains the computed criterion formula
=F5>AVERAGE($F$5:$F$14), which evaluates the Sales column.

Cell A2 contains comparison criterion for the Month column.

The average sales value for January Sales (cells F5:F14) is 5089.

The list, filtered so that only Feb sales greater than the average Jan sales are displayed.

Use the following guidelines when typing computed criteria in a criteria range.

- The formula has to produce the logical value TRUE or FALSE. Only rows containing values that produce TRUE are displayed when the list is filtered. In the previous example, only rows for February whose sales value (the value in column F) is greater than the average January sales are displayed. TRUE is displayed in the criteria range because the formula is TRUE for the first row.

- The formula has to refer to at least one column in the list. Type the *relative cell reference* to the cell in the first row of your list for that column. Using a relative cell reference tells Microsoft Excel to adjust the formula for each cell in the column it is evaluating. In the previous example, the relative cell reference F5 in the formula tells Microsoft Excel to evaluate the formula against each cell in the Sales column (column F).

- If you label the computed criterion formula, use text other than an existing column label as a criterion label. Otherwise, Microsoft Excel uses the result of the computed criterion formula as comparison criteria, which can produce unexpected or inaccurate results.

When you specify the criteria range for computed criteria in the Advanced Filter dialog box, include both the cell containing the formula and the criteria label above it. If you did not label the formula, make sure you include the cell above the formula anyway.

For information about formulas and using relative cell references, see Chapter 9, "Entering Data."

When to Use Relative or Absolute Cell References in Computed Criteria

When you use a relative cell reference in a computed criteria formula, Microsoft Excel adjusts that reference for each cell in the column it is evaluating. Use relative cell references to designate the first cell in the column you want evaluated. Use absolute cell references when you compare a column to a cell whose location does not change. To designate an absolute cell reference, type it with dollar signs, for example, $A$1.

Using Names in Computed Criteria   Instead of using a relative cell reference in a computed criteria formula, you can use the column label when referring to the column you want evaluated. For example, instead of using the relative cell reference F5 in the previous example, you can use the column label Sales. For best results, name the columns before you use them in a formula. To name columns in your list, use the Name box on the formula bar or the Create Names command (Insert menu, Name submenu).

Note   You can use column labels in formulas even if you don't name the columns using the Create Names command. Microsoft Excel filters the list, but displays the error #NAME? in the cell that contains the computed criterion formula. You can ignore this error, as it does not affect how the list is filtered.

For information about creating names, see "Names Make References Easier to Use" in Chapter 10.

Removing an Advanced Filter

To display rows hidden using the Advanced Filter command, choose the Filter command from the Data menu, then choose Show All.

Filtering Duplicate Rows or Records

You can use the Advanced Filter command to hide duplicate rows or records in a list. First, set up a criteria range. Then, when you choose the Advanced Filter command (Data menu, Filter submenu), select the Unique Records Only check box before choosing the OK button.

Tip   To filter all duplicate records, choose the Advanced Filter command, clear the Criteria Range box, and select the Unique Records Only check box. Microsoft Excel hides all duplicate rows in the list.

Using Microsoft Excel Version 4.0 Databases with Advanced Filter

If you open a worksheet that contains a database created in Microsoft Excel version 4.0, Microsoft Excel version 5.0 recognizes the database, criteria, and extract ranges you defined. When you select a cell in the database range and choose the Advanced Filter command, Microsoft Excel automatically enters the references to the database and criteria ranges in the Advanced Filter dialog box. If you select the Copy To Another Location option button, Microsoft Excel automatically displays the reference to the existing extract range.

Step By Step

For step-by-step instructions and related information, double-click the ▶? button to display the Search dialog box in Help, and then:

Type this keyword and choose Show Topics	Select a topic and choose Go To
criteria ranges	Setting up a criteria range
filtered data, copying	Copying filtered data that meets complex criteria
lists, filtering	Filtering a list using AutoFilter
	Filtering a list using complex criteria
formulas, entering	Entering formulas
titles, row and column	Creating names based on row and column titles

Copying Filtered Data to Another Location

You can use the Advanced Filter command to automatically copy rows that meet complex criteria to another worksheet location. First create the criteria range. Then select a single cell in the list and choose the Advanced Filter command. Select the Copy To Another Location option button under Action. In the Copy To box, specify the worksheet location to which you want to copy rows that meet the criteria. Microsoft Excel displays the filtered list in the specified location; the original list remains as it was.

Note If you are filtering a list using simple criteria, you might find it easier to filter the list using the AutoFilter command, then copy the data using the Copy command on the Edit menu. When you are in Filter mode, the Copy command copies only displayed data.

Setting Up the Copy To Range

When Microsoft Excel copies the rows that meet the criteria, it examines the contents of the Copy To range to determine what data to copy from the list.

- If you specify a single blank cell as the Copy To range, Microsoft Excel copies all rows that meet the criteria into a range starting with that cell, including all column labels from the list.

Caution If you specify a single cell, make sure there is enough room to paste the data below and to the right of the cell. Existing data in the destination range will be overwritten without warning.

- If you specify a range of cells as the Copy To range, Microsoft Excel copies as many rows as will fit in the range. If there is not enough room for all rows that meet the criteria, Microsoft Excel displays a message asking you if you want to paste the remaining rows.

- If you specify a Copy To range that consists of a limited set of column labels from the list, Microsoft Excel copies only those columns that match the column labels. This is useful if you have a large list and do not need to see all columns. You can arrange the column labels in the Copy To range in any order you choose.

	A	B	C	D	E	F
1	Month	Feb Sales				
2	Feb	TRUE				
3						
4	Month	Type	Salesperson	Region	Units	Sales
5	Jan	Meat	Suyama	North	690	$9,862
6	Jan	Produce	Davolio	East	5,585	$5,720
7	Jan	Produce	Davolio	North	6,740	$699
8	Jan	Dairy	Buchanan	West	9,981	$668
9	Jan	Meat	Suyama	North	3,400	$9,662
10	Jan	Produce	Suyama	West	6,344	$7,565
11						
32	Mar	Dairy	Suyama	West	8,878	$9,477
33	Mar	Meat	Davolio	East	7,832	$1,441
34	Mar	Meat	Buchanan	South	4,997	$656
35	Mar	Dairy	Suyama	North	8,404	$6,239
36						
37	Month	Saleperson	Sales			
38	Feb	Buchanan	$8,012			
39	Feb	Davolio	$6,805			
40	Feb	Buchanan	$8,179			
41	Feb	Davolio	$8,725			
42						

— Copy To range

— Subset of data copied from the list in range A4:F35 using the Advanced Filter command

When you specify only a subset of labels as the Copy To range, Microsoft Excel copies only a subset of columns from the list.

Copying Data in a List to Another Worksheet

You can only specify a range on the current worksheet in the Copy To Range box in the Advanced Filter dialog box. If you want to copy data to another worksheet, use one of the following methods.

The easiest way to copy data to another worksheet is to filter the list in place using either the AutoFilter or Advanced Filter command on the Data menu. Then copy the filtered data to another worksheet using the Copy command on the Edit menu.

If you still want to use the Copy To Another Location option in the Advanced Filter dialog box, first switch to the worksheet you want to copy to, then choose the Advanced Filter command. You can then specify the list range and criteria ranges by including the sheet reference. For example, if you want to copy to Sheet2 and your list is on Sheet1, choose the Advanced Filter command from Sheet2. Then, in the List Range box, type the reference to the list on Sheet1 using the following syntax:

Sheet1!*range*

where Sheet1 is the worksheet name, and *range* is the range that contains the list.

Step By Step

For step-by-step instructions and related information, double-click the 🕐 button to display the Search dialog box in Help, and then:

Type this keyword and choose Show Topics	Select a topic and choose Go To
copying, cells	Copying cells
criteria ranges	Setting up a criteria range
filtered data, copying	Copying filtered data that meets complex criteria
lists, filtering	Filtering a list using complex criteria

Working with a Filtered List

Filtering enables you to perform operations such as editing, printing, sorting, and charting on a subset of your list.

When you use the AutoFilter and Advanced Filter commands to hide rows, you are in Filter mode. While you are in Filter mode, many Microsoft Excel commands and features operate only on the displayed rows. This enables you to exclude those rows you don't want to work with. You can tell you are in Filter mode because the row headings of your list are blue, and the status bar displays "Filter Mode."

To cancel Filter mode, display all hidden rows in the filtered list using the Show All command (Data menu, Filter submenu).

Printing a Filtered List

When you print a filtered list using the Print command on the File menu, Microsoft Excel prints only displayed data. For information about printing a worksheet, see "Printing Your Work" in Chapter 14.

Note   The Print command does not print the AutoFilter arrows.

Editing and Formatting Cells in a Filtered List

The following table lists some typical editing and formatting features you might want to use with a filtered list, and the result when used in Filter mode.

This Microsoft Excel feature	Does this in Filter mode
AutoFill feature	Enters the value of the active cell in visible cells only. You cannot fill series using the AutoFill feature when your worksheet is in Filter mode.
Cells command (Format menu)	Formats only visible cells in the selection.
Clear command (Edit menu)	Clears only visible cells in the selection.
Copy command (Edit menu)	Copies only visible cells in the selection.
Delete command (Edit menu)	Becomes Delete Row command. Deletes only visible rows. You can delete only whole rows on a worksheet that contains a filtered list.
Insert command (shortcut menu)	Becomes Insert Row command. Inserts whole rows. You can insert only whole rows on a worksheet that contains a filtered list.
Insert Copied Cells (shortcut menu)	Becomes Insert Paste Row command. Pastes copied data in complete rows. You can paste only whole rows on a worksheet that contains a filtered list.

Note If you are copying to another application, make sure you do not choose the Show All command (Data menu, Filter submenu), before pasting the copied data in the target location.

Using the AutoSum Button with a Filtered List

If you use the AutoSum button to total a range of data in a filtered list, Microsoft Excel displays a total value for only the displayed data. If you change the filter or choose the Show All command, Microsoft Excel adjusts the total accordingly. For information on using the AutoSum button, see "Using the AutoSum Button" in Chapter 10.

Creating a Chart from a Filtered List

ChartWizard

When you create a chart from a filtered list, Microsoft Excel plots only the displayed data. Select the range you want to plot, then click the ChartWizard button. Then click once on the worksheet, or drag the pointer to anchor the chart. This starts the ChartWizard, which you use to select a chart type and add a title or legend.

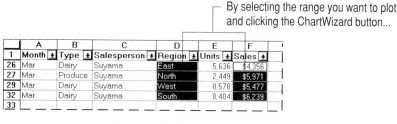

By selecting the range you want to plot and clicking the ChartWizard button...

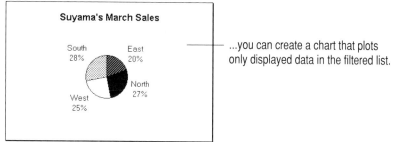

...you can create a chart that plots only displayed data in the filtered list.

This chart uses *nonadjacent selections* from the list, because the columns to be plotted are not next to each other. For more information about selecting nonadjacent ranges to create a chart, see "What Is a Chart?" in Chapter 15.

A chart maintains a link to the source data in the list, so if you change the filter or use the Show All command, your chart changes to include all displayed data.

Note   You can also hide columns using the Column command on the Format menu before selecting the ranges to plot. For more information, see "Charting Visible Worksheet Data" in Chapter 19.

Select Visible Cells

Preventing a Chart from Updating When You Change a Filter   If you do not want a chart that you create from a filtered list to change when you show all rows or apply another filter, you must select only visible cells before you create the chart. To select visible cells, click the Select Visible Cells button before you select a range in the filtered list. To use the Select Visible Cells button, you must add it to an existing toolbar from the Utility button category using the Toolbars command on the View menu. For information about adding buttons to toolbars, see "Customizing Toolbars" in Chapter 34.

Subtotaling Data Before You Plot a Chart   If you want to subtotal multiple items before you create a chart, you can insert automatic subtotals in your filtered list. For more information, see "Displaying Automatic Subtotals in a List" in Chapter 22. For information about charting a subtotaled list, see "Preparing a Subtotaled List as a Report" in Chapter 22.

Sorting a Filtered List

Sorting a filtered list is useful if you want to organize the displayed rows for a report, or if you want to insert automatic subtotals. When you sort a filtered list, only the displayed rows are rearranged. Hidden rows are not moved from their original positions.

Type column

	Month	Type	Salesperson	Region	Units	Sales
3	Feb	Dairy	Davolio	West	1,695	$3,338
4	Feb	Dairy	Davolio	East	3,260	$6,805
10	Feb	Dairy	Davolio	North	6,890	$8,725
13	Mar	Dairy	Davolio	South	3,796	$7,669
14	Jan	Meat	Davolio	South	767	$6,711
17	Mar	Meat	Davolio	South	5,735	$3,316
19	Mar	Meat	Davolio	East	7,832	$1,441
21	Jan	Produce	Davolio	East	5,585	$5,720
22	Jan	Produce	Davolio	North	6,740	$699
24	Feb	Produce	Davolio	West	2,861	$1,328
30	Feb	Produce	Davolio	North	7,549	$1,500
33						

A filtered list, sorted by the Type column

As with any sorting process, you sort a filtered list by selecting a cell in the list and choosing the Sort command from the Data menu. Then select the column you want to sort by and the sort order you want to use. For more information, see "Sorting Data in a List" earlier in this chapter.

For information about inserting automatic subtotals in a filtered and sorted list, see "Displaying Automatic Subtotals in a List" in Chapter 22.

Step By Step

For step-by-step instructions and related information, double-click the [?] button to display the Search dialog box in Help, and then:

Type this keyword and choose Show Topics	Select a topic and choose Go To
AutoSum button	Entering a single sum formula with the AutoSum button
cells, clearing	Clearing cells
cells, deleting	Deleting cells

Type this keyword and choose Show Topics	**Select a topic and choose Go To**
charts, creating	About Creating Charts from Nonadjacent Selections
	Creating a chart from visible worksheet data
	Creating an embedded chart on a worksheet
copying, cells	Copying cells
date series	Incrementing a series of numbers or dates
formatting, cells	Overview of Formatting Cells with Borders, Patterns, and Color
pasting cut cells	Inserting cut or copied cells
sorting lists	Sorting a list from top to bottom
subtotals, automatic	Displaying automatic subtotals in a list
workbooks, printing	Printing a sheet, selected range, or entire workbook

C H A P T E R   2 2

Summarizing Data in a List

For command, keyboard, and toolbar button information, see online Help.

In This Chapter

How Automatic Subtotals Work

Inserting automatic subtotals is a quick way to summarize data in a Microsoft Excel list or database. You do not need to enter formulas on the worksheet to use automatic subtotals. Using the groups of data you choose, Microsoft Excel automatically calculates subtotal and grand total values, inserts and labels the total rows, and outlines the list for you.

	A	B	C	D
1	Salesperson	Type	Units	Sales
2	Buchanan	Beverages	4,997	$656
3	Buchanan	Meat	5,889	$4,953
4	Buchanan	Produce	340	$8,751
5	Buchanan	Meat	5,847	$8,179
6	Buchanan	Beverages	587	$3,522
7	Buchanan	Produce	2,652	$6,715
8	Davolio	Produce	7,549	$1,500
9	Davolio	Meat	7,832	$1,441
10	Davolio	Beverages	8,207	$8,461
11	Davolio	Produce	9,888	$7,047
12	Davolio	Meat	6,740	$699
13	Davolio	Beverages	767	$6,711
14	Suyama	Beverages	690	$9,862
15	Suyama	Meat	9,435	$6,040
16	Suyama	Produce	2,449	$5,971
17	Suyama	Beverages	2,898	$7,538
18	Suyama	Produce	744	$2,666
19	Suyama	Meat	8,953	$6,127
20				

A typical list, grouped by Salesperson

Automatic subtotals insert subtotal and Grand Total rows...

...and outline the list.

	A	B	C	D
1	Salesperson	Type	Units	Sales
2	Buchanan	Beverages	4,997	$656
3	Buchanan	Meat	5,889	$4,953
4	Buchanan	Produce	340	$8,751
5	Buchanan	Meat	5,847	$8,179
6	Buchanan	Beverages	587	$3,522
7	Buchanan	Produce	2,652	$6,715
8	Buchanan Total		20,312	$32,776
9	Davolio	Produce	7,549	$1,500
10	Davolio	Meat	7,832	$1,441
11	Davolio	Beverages	8,207	$8,461
12	Davolio	Produce	9,888	$7,047
13	Davolio	Meat	6,740	$699
14	Davolio	Beverages	767	$6,711
15	Davolio Total		40,983	$25,859
16	Suyama	Beverages	690	$9,862
17	Suyama	Meat	9,435	$6,040
18	Suyama	Produce	2,449	$5,971
19	Suyama	Beverages	2,898	$7,538
20	Suyama	Produce	744	$2,666
21	Suyama	Meat	8,953	$6,127
22	Suyama Total		25,169	$38,204
23	Grand Total		86,464	$96,839
24				

Using the outline symbols, you can hide detail data to display only summary data.

Outline symbols

	A	B	C	D
1	Salesperson	Type	Units	Sales
8	Buchanan Total		20,312	$32,776
15	Davolio Total		40,983	$25,859
22	Suyama Total		25,169	$38,204
23	Grand Total		86,464	$96,839
24				

Once you display the level of summary data you want, you can format it quickly and print it—or create a chart—to provide a report.

Tip If you just want to add up the data in a single column, use the AutoSum button. For more information, see "Using the AutoSum Button" in Chapter 10.

How Subtotal and Grand Total Values Are Calculated

Microsoft Excel calculates subtotal values using a *summary function,* such as Sum or Average, that you choose. You can display subtotals for more than one type of calculation at a time.

Grand total values are always derived from the original detail data, not from the subtotal rows. For example, if you use the summary function Average, the Grand Total row displays an average of all detail data in the list, not an average of the subtotal values. Grand total values are calculated using the same summary function you choose for the subtotals.

Subtotal and grand total values are automatically recalculated as you edit detail rows. Microsoft Excel automatically displays hidden rows when you insert automatic subtotals, unless you filter your list first using the Filter command on the Data menu. For more information about filtering a list, see Chapter 21, "Sorting and Filtering Data in a List."

Advanced Totals

Microsoft Excel provides two advanced features for summarizing data:

- Database and selected math functions enable you to total rows or cells that meet criteria you specify. Because functions are used in formulas, you can place them anywhere on your worksheet. For more information, see "Creating Advanced Totals Using Functions" later in this chapter.

- *Pivot tables* enable you to create interactive summary tables from your list. For more information, see Chapter 24, "Creating a Pivot Table" and Chapter 25, "Customizing a Pivot Table."

Displaying Automatic Subtotals in a List

To use automatic subtotals, your data must be organized in labeled columns. For example, a list of sales records might include a column labeled Salesperson, which contains text names; a column labeled Type, which contains merchandise categories; and a column labeled Sales, which contains dollar amounts. When you use the Subtotals command, you choose:

- The items you want subtotals for, such as for each salesperson in the Salesperson column.

- The values for the items to be summarized, such as Sales.

- The summary function—such as Sum or Average—to use on the values.

Note When you insert automatic subtotals, Microsoft Excel outlines your list. Because you can hide rows using the outline symbols, any data positioned to the left or right of the list might be hidden. If you want this data displayed at all times, put it above or below your list. For best results, always leave at least one blank row or column between your list and other data on the worksheet.

Preparing a List for Automatic Subtotals

Before you insert automatic subtotals, arrange the rows so that the items to subtotal are grouped together. An easy way to do this is to sort the list using the Sort command on the Data menu.

First sort the list by Salesperson and Type...

	A	B	C	D
1	Salesperson	Type	Units	Sales
2	Buchanan	Beverages	4,997	$656
3	Buchanan	Beverages	587	$3,522
4	Buchanan	Meat	5,889	$4,953
5	Buchanan	Meat	5,847	$8,179
6	Buchanan	Produce	340	$8,751
7	Buchanan	Produce	2,652	$6,715
8	Davolio	Beverages	8,207	$8,461
9	Davolio	Beverages	767	$6,711
10	Davolio	Meat		
11	Davolio	Meat		
12	Davolio	Produce		
13	Davolio	Produce		
14	Suyama	Beverages		
15	Suyama	Beverages		
16	Suyama	Meat		
17	Suyama	Meat		
18	Suyama	Produce		
19	Suyama	Produce		
20				

...to display subtotals for each salesperson and each grocery type for each salesperson.

	A	B	C	D
1	Salesperson	Type	Units	Sales
4		Beverages Total	5,584	$4,178
7		Meat Total	11,736	$13,132
10		Produce Total	2,992	$15,466
11	Buchanan Total		20,312	$32,776
14		Beverages Total	8,974	$15,172
17		Meat Total	14,572	$2,140
20		Produce Total	17,437	$8,547
21	Davolio Total		40,983	$25,859
24		Beverages Total	3,588	$17,400
27		Meat Total	18,388	$12,167
30		Produce Total	3,193	$8,637
31	Suyama Total		25,169	$38,204
32	Grand Total		86,464	$96,839
33				

In the preceding illustration, the Salesperson column was selected as the first column to sort by, and the Type column was selected as the second column to sort by. To choose columns you want to sort by, select column names in the Sort By box and the Then By box in the Sort dialog box.

You can sort a list by up to three columns. You can also sort a list using a custom sort order. For information about sorting a list, see "Sorting Data in a List" in Chapter 21.

Displaying Subtotal Rows

Once your list is organized, you display automatic subtotals by selecting a single cell in the list and choosing the Subtotals command from the Data menu. Microsoft Excel uses the column labels to help you identify the items you want grouped and the values you want summarized.

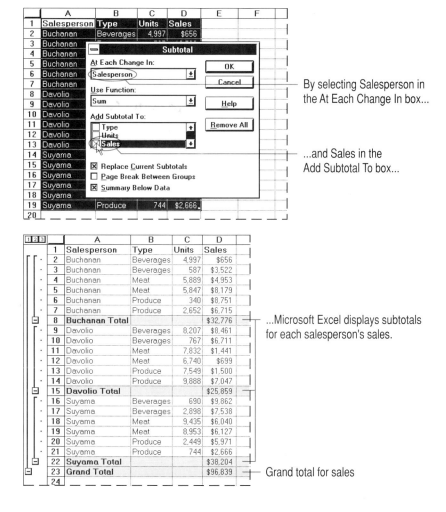

By selecting Salesperson in the At Each Change In box...

...and Sales in the Add Subtotal To box...

...Microsoft Excel displays subtotals for each salesperson's sales.

Grand total for sales

Choosing the Items You Want Subtotals For   When you first choose the Subtotals command from the Data menu, the At Each Change In box automatically displays the label of the left-most column. You can make that your selection or select any other column label from your list. When you choose the OK button, Microsoft Excel inserts a subtotal row for each group of identical items in the selected column. The next time you choose the Subtotals command for that list, the At Each Change In box displays the label of the last column you selected.

Choosing a Summary Function   The first time you use the Subtotals command for a list, Microsoft Excel suggests a summary function based on the type of data in the column you select in the Add Subtotal To box.

- If the column contains numbers, Microsoft Excel proposes using the Sum function to summarize the data.
- If the column contains text items, such as "Department 101" or "South," Microsoft Excel proposes using the Count function to provide a count of the items.

Choose a different calculation, such as Average, by selecting a different summary function in the Use Function box in the Subtotal dialog box.

Choosing the Values to Summarize   The first time you use the Subtotals command, the Add Subtotal To box displays the label of the right-most column. You can leave that label as your selection, or you can select the label of any other column in the list. The next time you use the Subtotals command, Microsoft Excel displays the label of the last column you selected.

Displaying Subtotal Rows Above the Detail Data   If you want your subtotal rows to appear above their associated detail data, and if you want the Grand Total row to appear at the top of the list, clear the Summary Below Data check box in the Subtotal dialog box. This is useful if you have a large list and you do not want to scroll to the end of the list to see grand total data.

Choosing More Than One Column to Summarize

You can display subtotals for more than one column in the same subtotal row. For example, you can provide subtotal values for both the Units and the Sales columns.

	A	B	C	D
1	Salesperson	Type	Units	Sales
2	Buchanan	Beverages	4,997	$656
3	Buchanan	Beverages	587	$3,522
4	Buchanan	Meat	5,889	$4,953
5	Buchanan	Meat	5,847	$8,179
6	Buchanan	Produce	340	$8,751
7	Buchanan	Produce	2,652	$6,715
8	Buchanan Total		20,312	$32,776
9	Davolio	Beverages	8,207	$8,461
10	Davolio	Beverages	767	$6,711
11	Davolio	Meat	7,832	$1,441
12	Davolio	Meat	6,740	$699
13	Davolio	Produce	7,549	$1,500
14	Davolio	Produce	9,888	$7,047
15	Davolio Total		40,983	$25,859
16	Suyama	Beverages	690	$9,862
17	Suyama	Beverages	2,898	$7,538
18	Suyama	Meat	9,435	$6,040
19	Suyama	Meat	8,953	$6,127
20	Suyama	Produce	2,449	$5,971
21	Suyama	Produce	744	$2,666
22	Suyama Total		25,169	$38,204
23	Grand Total		86,464	$96,839
24				

Selecting more than one column label in the Add Subtotal To box inserts a subtotal for each column.

Displaying Nested Subtotals

You can insert subtotals for smaller groups within existing subtotal groups. For example, you can insert subtotals for each grocery type in a list that already has subtotals for each salesperson.

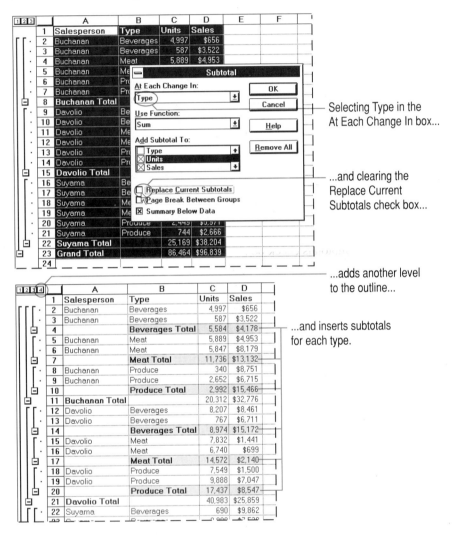

Selecting Type in the
At Each Change In box...

...and clearing the
Replace Current
Subtotals check box...

...adds another level
to the outline...

...and inserts subtotals
for each type.

Before subtotals were inserted, this list was sorted first by Salesperson and then by Type. Because the grocery types are grouped under each salesperson, the Type subtotals are at a lower level in the outline.

Choosing More Than One Summary Function

You can use more than one summary function to calculate data in the same column.

	A	B	C	D
1	Salesperson	Type	Units	Sales
2	Buchanan	Beverage	4,997	$656
3	Buchanan	Beverage	587	$3,522
4	Buchanan	Meat	5,889	$4,953
5	Buchanan	Meat	5,847	$8,179
6	Buchanan	Produce	340	$8,751
7	Buchanan	Produce	2,652	$6,715
8	**Buchanan Total**		20,312	$32,776
9	**Buchanan Average**		3,385	$5,463
10	Davolio	Beverage	8,207	$8,461
11	Davolio	Beverage	767	$6,711
12	Davolio	Meat	7,832	$1,441
13	Davolio	Meat	6,740	$699
14	Davolio	Produce	7,549	$1,500
15	Davolio	Produce	9,888	$7,047
16	**Davolio Total**		40,983	$25,859
17	**Davolio Average**		6,831	$4,310
18	Suyama	Beverage	690	$9,862

When you select both Sum and Average, Microsoft Excel inserts a subtotal row for each.

To use more than one summary function, choose the Subtotals command and select one function in the Use Function box. Choose the OK button, then choose the Subtotals command again. Select another function and clear the Replace Current Subtotals check box.

Counting Rows in a List or Cells in a Column

You can use the Subtotals command to count identical items in a list or single column. For example, if you sort the following list so that identical items in the Type column appear together, you can display a count of records for each grocery type.

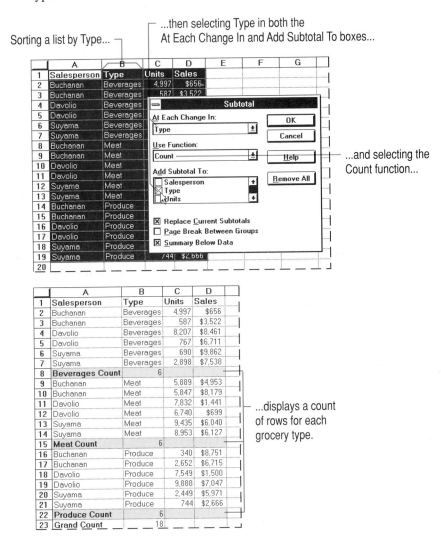

Sorting a list by Type...

...then selecting Type in both the At Each Change In and Add Subtotal To boxes...

...and selecting the Count function...

...displays a count of rows for each grocery type.

	A	B	C	D
1	Salesperson	Type	Units	Sales
2	Buchanan	Beverages	4,997	$656
3	Buchanan	Beverages	587	$3,522
4	Davolio	Beverages	8,207	$8,461
5	Davolio	Beverages	767	$6,711
6	Suyama	Beverages	690	$9,862
7	Suyama	Beverages	2,898	$7,538
8	**Beverages Count**		6	
9	Buchanan	Meat	5,889	$4,953
10	Buchanan	Meat	5,847	$8,179
11	Davolio	Meat	7,832	$1,441
12	Davolio	Meat	6,740	$699
13	Suyama	Meat	9,435	$6,040
14	Suyama	Meat	8,953	$6,127
15	**Meat Count**		6	
16	Buchanan	Produce	340	$8,751
17	Buchanan	Produce	2,652	$6,715
18	Davolio	Produce	7,549	$1,500
19	Davolio	Produce	9,888	$7,047
20	Suyama	Produce	2,449	$5,971
21	Suyama	Produce	744	$2,666
22	**Produce Count**		6	
23	Grand Count		18	

Displaying Automatic Subtotals in a Filtered List

To subtotal only a subset of the rows, you can *filter* your list first using the Filter command on the Data menu. Filtering hides all rows except those that meet criteria you choose. When you insert automatic subtotals in a filtered list, Microsoft Excel summarizes only the visible data. As with an unfiltered list, sort the rows before you choose the Subtotals command.

For more information about filtering a list, see Chapter 21, "Sorting and Filtering Data in a List."

Removing Subtotals

There are three ways to remove subtotals.

To	Use this procedure
Remove subtotals you have just inserted	Choose the Undo Subtotals command from the Edit menu.
Replace existing subtotals with new subtotals	Choose the Subtotals command from the Data menu. Select the Replace Current Subtotals check box, and choose the OK button.
Remove all subtotals from the list	Choose the Subtotals command from the Data menu. Then choose the Remove All button in the Subtotal dialog box.

Step By Step

For step-by-step instructions and related information, double-click the [?] button to display the Search dialog box in Help, and then:

Type this keyword and choose Show Topics	Select a topic and choose Go To
AutoFilter	Filtering a list using AutoFilter
automatic subtotals	Displaying automatic subtotals in a list
	Displaying nested automatic subtotals
	Removing or replacing automatic subtotals
sorting lists	Sorting a list from top to bottom

Hiding and Showing Detail Data in a Subtotaled List

When you display automatic subtotals, Microsoft Excel automatically outlines the
list by grouping detail rows with each associated subtotal row, and subtotal rows
with the Grand Total row. As with other worksheet outlining, Microsoft Excel
displays the outline symbols so you can see the organization of the list and so you
can quickly hide and show detail data.

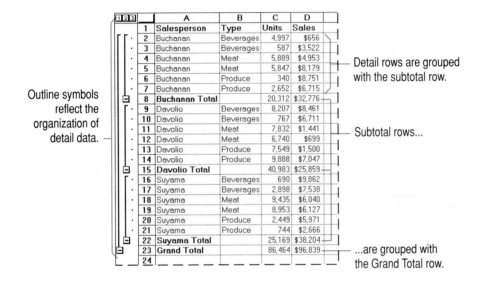

Outline symbols reflect the organization of detail data.

Detail rows are grouped with the subtotal row.

Subtotal rows...

...are grouped with the Grand Total row.

You can hide details for all subtotal groups using the row level symbols.

Clicking the row
level 2 symbol...

	A	B	C	D
1	Salesperson	Type	Units	Sales
2	Buchanan	Beverages	4,997	$656
3	Buchanan	Beverages	587	$3,522
4	Buchanan	Meat	5,889	$4,953
5	Buchanan	Meat	5,847	$8,179
6	Buchanan	Produce	340	$8,751
7	Buchanan	Produce	2,652	$6,715
8	Buchanan Total		20,312	$32,776
9	Davolio	Beverages	8,207	$8,461
10	Davolio	Beverages	767	$6,711
11	Davolio	Meat	7,832	$1,441
12	Davolio	Meat	6,740	$699
13	Davolio	Produce	7,549	$1,500
14	Davolio	Produce	9,888	$7,047
15	Davolio Total		40,983	$25,859
16	Suyama	Beverages	690	$9,862
17	Suyama	Beverages	2,898	$7,538
18	Suyama	Meat	9,435	$6,040
19	Suyama	Meat	8,953	$6,127
20	Suyama	Produce	2,449	$5,971
21	Suyama	Produce	744	$2,666
22	Suyama Total		25,169	$38,204
23	Grand Total		86,464	$96,839
24				

...hides all rows except
the subtotal rows and
the Grand Total row.

	A	B	C	D
1	Salesperson	Type	Units	Sales
8	Buchanan Total		20,312	$32,776
15	Davolio Total		40,983	$25,859
22	Suyama Total		25,169	$38,204
23	Grand Total		86,464	$96,839
24				

To hide the detail rows for a single subtotal group, click the hide detail symbol (⊟).

Clicking the hide
detail symbol...

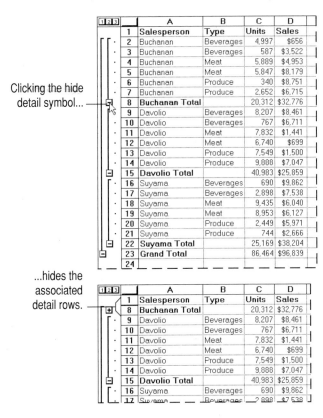

...hides the
associated
detail rows.

To redisplay the hidden rows, click the show detail symbol (⊞).

For more information about using the outline symbols, see "Showing and Hiding Details in an Outline" in Chapter 33.

Note   You can also use the Hide Detail and Show Detail commands on the Data menu, Outline submenu.

Step By Step

For step-by-step instructions and related information, double-click the [▶?] button to display the Search dialog box in Help, and then:

Type this keyword and choose Show Topics	Select a topic and choose Go To
showing detail data	Hiding and showing detail data in a subtotaled list
showing outline symbols	Displaying or hiding the outline symbols

Sorting a Subtotaled List

You can quickly organize your subtotal groups by sorting them. As with any sorting process, you sort subtotal groups by values in a column you choose. For example, the following subtotal rows are sorted in ascending order by values in the Sales column.

		A	B	C	D
	1	Salesperson	Type	Units	Sales
	8	Davolio Total		40,983	$25,859
	15	Buchanan Total		20,312	$32,776
	22	Suyama Total		25,169	$38,204
	23	Grand Total		86,464	$96,839
	24				

To sort subtotal groups, first hide their detail rows using the row level symbols (1 2 3). Then use the Sort command on the Data menu. When you sort a list with detail rows hidden, the hidden rows are sorted with their associated subtotal rows.

For information about sorting and sorting options, see "Sorting Data in a List" in Chapter 21.

Note If you choose the Sort command with all detail rows displayed, Microsoft Excel removes the subtotals and sorts all rows in the list.

Step By Step

For step-by-step instructions and related information, double-click the 🅺❓ button to display the Search dialog box in Help, and then:

Type this keyword and choose Show Topics	Select a topic and choose Go To
sorting lists	Overview of Sorting a List
	Sorting a list from top to bottom

Preparing a Subtotaled List as a Report

With automatic subtotals, you can quickly format and print your list as a report. You can also create a chart using only subtotal values, if you first use the row level symbols to display only the level of detail you want.

Formatting a Subtotaled List Automatically

One way to format a list quickly is to apply an *autoformat.* An autoformat applies special cell formatting to the subtotal and Grand Total rows so that they are easier to see.

	A	B	C	D
1	Salesperson	Type	*Units*	*Sales*
2	Buchanan	Beverages	587	$3,522
3	Buchanan	Beverages	4,997	$656
4	Buchanan	Meat	5,847	$8,179
5	Buchanan	Meat	5,889	$4,953
6	Buchanan	Produce	340	$8,751
7	Buchanan	Produce	2,652	$6,715
8	Buchanan Total		20,312	$32,776
9	Davolio	Beverages	8,207	$8,461
10	Davolio	Beverages	767	$6,711
11	Davolio	Meat	7,832	$1,441
12	Davolio	Meat	6,740	$699
13	Davolio	Produce	7,549	$1,500
14	Davolio	Produce	9,888	$7,047
15	Davolio Total		40,983	$25,859
16	Suyama	Beverages	690	$9,862
17	Suyama	Beverages	2,898	$7,538
18	Suyama	Meat	9,435	$6,040
19	Suyama	Meat	8,953	$6,127
20	Suyama	Produce	744	$2,666
21	Suyama	Produce	2,449	$5,971
22	Suyama Total		25,169	$38,204
23	*Grand Total*		86,464	$96,839
24				

A subtotaled list with the autoformat Classic 1 applied

Use the AutoFormat command on the Format menu to apply an autoformat. For more information about applying autoformats, see "Applying Formats Automatically" in Chapter 12.

Printing a Subtotaled List

Microsoft Excel makes it easy to print a subtotaled list.

To	Follow this procedure
Insert page breaks between highest level groups so that each group is printed on its own page.	Select the Page Break Between Groups check box in the Subtotal dialog box.
Use column labels as titles at the top of each printed page.	Type the range reference for the column labels in the Rows To Repeat At Top box on the Sheet tab of the Page Setup dialog box. To display the Page Setup dialog box, choose the Page Setup command from the File menu.
Use row labels as titles on the left side of each printed page.	Type the range reference for the row labels in the Columns To Repeat At Left box in the Sheet tab of the Page Setup dialog box. To display the Page Setup dialog box, choose the Page Setup command from the File menu.

To print a list after selecting these options, use the Print command on the File menu. For information about printing a worksheet, see "Printing Your Work" in Chapter 14.

Tip If your list has a large number of columns, and you do not need to display all of the columns in the printed report, you can hide the columns you don't need by using the Column command on the Format menu. Hidden columns are not printed. For more information, see "Hiding and Unhiding Rows and Columns" in Chapter 32.

Creating a Chart from a Subtotaled List

ChartWizard

To create a chart from a subtotaled list, first hide all detail rows using the row level symbols ([1][2][3]) in the left margin of the list. Then select the ranges to plot, excluding the Grand Total row, and click the ChartWizard button. Then click the worksheet or drag the pointer to anchor the chart. This starts the ChartWizard, which you use to select a chart type and add a title or legend.

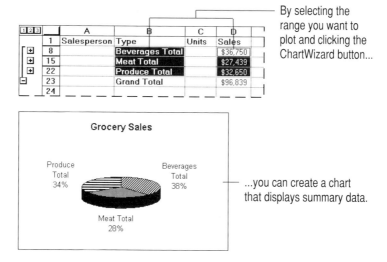

By selecting the range you want to plot and clicking the ChartWizard button...

...you can create a chart that displays summary data.

This chart was created using *nonadjacent selections* from the list, because the column containing the Type subtotal labels is not next to the Sales column, which is the column being summarized. For more information about selecting nonadjacent ranges to create a chart, see "What Is a Chart?" in Chapter 15.

Note You can also hide columns using the Column command on the Format menu before selecting the ranges to plot. For more information, see "Charting Visible Worksheet Data" in Chapter 19.

Step By Step

For step-by-step instructions and related information, double-click the [?] button to display the Search dialog box in Help, and then:

Type this keyword and choose Show Topics	Select a topic and choose Go To
autoformats, applying	Applying an autoformat to a range
charts, creating	Creating a chart from visible worksheet data
	Creating an embedded chart on a worksheet
hidden rows or columns	Hiding and unhiding a row or column
printing titles on multiple pages	Printing titles on multiple pages
workbooks, printing	Printing a sheet, selected range, or entire workbook

Creating Advanced Totals Using Functions

Automatic subtotals provide totals for all rows in a list. To display summary values only for rows or cells that meet certain criteria, you can use worksheet functions. Because you use functions by entering a formula, you can display totals in any worksheet location you choose.

For more information about entering formulas, see "Worksheet Functions Simplify Formulas" in Chapter 10.

Adding Up Values That Meet a Single Criterion

To derive the sum of only those values that meet a single criterion, such as "only loan amounts with interest rates greater than 9%," use the following function:

=SUMIF(*range,criteria,sum_range*)

where *range* is the range to evaluate, *criteria* is the criterion to apply to *range,* and *sum_range* is the range containing the values you want summarized.

For example, to calculate total sales for only those rows in the following list with a unit value less than 1000, type the formula =SUMIF(C2:C19,"<1000",D2:D19) in a blank cell on the worksheet.

Cell F2 contains the formula
=SUMIF(C2:C19,"<1000",D2:D19)

	A	B	C	D	E	F
1	Salesperson	Type	Units	Sales		Total Sales for Units<1000
2	Buchanan	Beverages	587	$3,522		$31,512
3	Buchanan	Beverages	4,997	$656		
4	Buchanan	Meat	5,847	$8,179		
5	Buchanan	Meat	5,889	$4,953		
6	Buchanan	Produce	340	$8,751		
7	Buchanan	Produce	2,652	$6,715		
8	Davolio	Beverages	8,207	$8,461		
9	Davolio	Beverages	767	$6,711		
10	Davolio	Meat	7,832	$1,441		
11	Davolio	Meat	6,740	$699		
12	Davolio	Produce	7,549	$1,500		
13	Davolio	Produce	9,888	$7,047		
14	Suyama	Beverages	690	$9,862		
15	Suyama	Beverages	2,898	$7,538		
16	Suyama	Meat	9,435	$6,040		
17	Suyama	Meat	8,953	$6,127		
18	Suyama	Produce	744	$2,666		
19	Suyama	Produce	2,449	$5,971		
20						

Values that meet the criterion

The range C2:C19 specifies the Units column as the column to be evaluated. The expression "<1000" is the criterion to be applied to the Units column, and range D2:D19 is the column to be summarized—in this case, the Sales column.

Tip   You can make specifying ranges easier by naming each column using the Name command on the Insert menu. For more information about naming ranges, see "Names Make References Easier to Use" in Chapter 10.

Counting Values That Meet a Single Criterion

To count those cells or rows that meet a single criterion, enter the following formula in a blank cell on the worksheet:

=COUNTIF(*range,criteria*)

where *range* is the column or range to evaluate, and *criteria* is the criterion to apply to the range. For example, to provide a count of all records in the list above with a unit value greater than 1000, type the following formula in a blank cell on your worksheet:

=COUNTIF(C2:C19,">1000")

where the range C2:C19 is the Units column.

Counting Blank Cells or Fields   Use the COUNTBLANK function to count all cells that are blank or that contain formulas that return an empty text string. For example, if you have a list of service order records and you want to report how many have not been resolved, use the COUNTBLANK function to count rows that do not have an entry in the Resolve Date column. To use the COUNTBLANK function, specify the range you want examined. For example, to count all blank cells in the range A1:A54, type the following formula:

=COUNTBLANK(A1:A54)

Specifying the Criterion for the SUMIF and COUNTIF Functions

You can specify the criterion for the SUMIF and COUNTIF functions using a number, an expression such as ">500", or text such as "Davolio". The following table shows the operators to use if you use an expression as a criterion.

Operator	Meaning
=	Equal to
>	Greater than
<	Less than
>=	Greater than or equal to
<=	Less than or equal to
<>	Not equal to

Entering Functions Using the Function Wizard

You can use the *Function Wizard* to guide you through the steps of entering the SUMIF, COUNTIF, and Database functions instead of typing the formulas yourself. To use the Function Wizard, click the Function Wizard button and select the function you want to use from the Function Name box. For more information, see "Using the Function Wizard" in Chapter 10.

Summarizing Values That Meet Complex Criteria

To summarize only values that meet complex criteria, such as "provide a count of rows or records where sales are greater than 1000 but less than 2500," use a *database function*. To use a database function, you must create a *criteria range*. For example, the formula on the following worksheet uses a criteria range to find the average sales for records containing the grocery type "Meat" and unit values greater than 7000.

Criteria range — Cell F4 contains the formula =DAVERAGE(A3:D21,"Sales",A1:B2).

	A	B	C	D	E	F
1	Type	Units				
2	Meat	>7000				
3	Salesperson	Type	Units	Sales		Average for Meat Sales with >7000 Units
4	Buchanan	Beverages	587	$3,522		$4,536
5	Buchanan	Beverages	4,997	$656		
6	Buchanan	Meat	5,847	$8,179		
7	Buchanan	Meat	5,889	$4,953		
8	Buchanan	Produce	340	$8,751		
9	Buchanan	Produce	2,652	$6,715		
10	Davolio	Beverages	8,207	$8,461		
11	Davolio	Beverages	767	$6,711		
12	Davolio	Meat	7,832	$1,441		
13	Davolio	Meat	6,740	$699		
14	Davolio	Produce	7,549	$1,500		
15	Davolio	Produce	9,888	$7,047		
16	Suyama	Beverages	690	$9,862		
17	Suyama	Beverages	2,898	$7,538		
18	Suyama	Meat	9,435	$6,040		
19	Suyama	Meat	8,953	$6,127		
20	Suyama	Produce	744	$2,666		
21	Suyama	Produce	2,449	$5,971		
22						

Values that meet the criteria

Specify three arguments when using a database function:

- The range that contains your list. Remember to include the row that contains the column labels or field names. In the previous example, A3:D21 is the list range.

- The label for the column to be summarized. In the previous example, Sales is the column containing the values to be averaged.

- The range that contains the criteria. In the example, A1:B2 is the criteria range.

For more information about creating a criteria range or about specifying complex or computed criteria, see "Filtering A List Using Complex Criteria" in Chapter 21.

Database Functions The following table lists the database functions you can use with a criteria range.

For more information about these functions, click the Function Wizard button on the Standard toolbar or see online Help.

To	Use
Average numbers	DAVERAGE
Count numbers	DCOUNT
Count nonblank cells	DCOUNTA
Extract a single value	DGET
Find a maximum value	DMAX
Find a minimum value	DMIN
Multiply numbers	DPRODUCT
Calculate standard deviation	DSTDEV or DSTDEVP
Add numbers	DSUM
Calculate variance	DVAR or DVARP

Step By Step

For step-by-step instructions and related information, double-click the [?] button to display the Search dialog box in Help, and then:

Type this keyword and choose Show Topics	Select a topic and choose Go To
database functions	Database Functions
formulas, entering	Entering formulas
setting up criteria ranges	Setting up a criteria range

PART 5

Retrieving and Analyzing Data from Lists and Tables

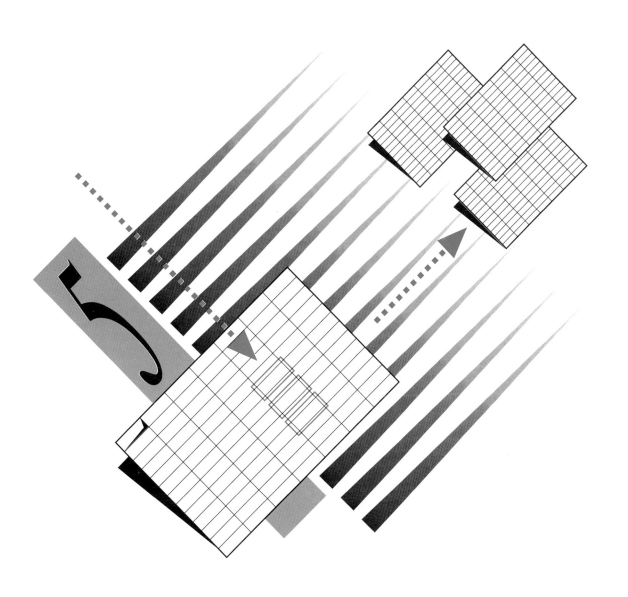

CHAPTER 23

Retrieving Data with Microsoft Query

For command,
keyboard, and
toolbar button
information, see
online Help.

Note to Apple Macintosh Users If Microsoft Query did not come with your copy of
Microsoft Excel, use the fulfillment coupon in the box to obtain a copy.

In This Chapter

Note This chapter documents using Microsoft Query with Microsoft Excel. For
information about using Microsoft Query, see the *Microsoft Query User's Guide.*

Retrieving External Data with Microsoft Excel

There are four ways to retrieve external data using Microsoft Excel:

- Use Microsoft Query to create a query and return the results to Microsoft Excel. Use this method if you want to display and manipulate data before you bring it into Microsoft Excel.

- Use the Visual Basic and Microsoft Excel version 4.0 Macro Language functions in the Microsoft ODBC Add-in for Microsoft Excel to create custom Microsoft Excel applications. Use these functions to interact directly with database drivers without using Microsoft Query.

- Use the Microsoft Excel command equivalents in the Microsoft Query Add-in for Microsoft Excel to create custom applications. Use the command equivalents to use Microsoft Query to access external data.

- Use the PivotTable Wizard to access external data and create a pivot table with the results.

Data Access Components Available with Microsoft Excel Version 5.0

Component	Description
Microsoft Query	Graphical application used to retrieve and organize data from a variety of data sources. Use Microsoft Query by itself, or use it to return data to Microsoft Excel or other applications.
Microsoft Query Add-in for Microsoft Excel	An add-in macro you can use to access Query from within Microsoft Excel. Provides the commands and buttons that access Microsoft Query, and the command-equivalent Microsoft Excel version 4.0 macro language and Visual Basic functions.
Microsoft ODBC Add-in for Microsoft Excel	ODBC Visual Basic Language Extensions and ODBC Macro Language Extensions for Microsoft Excel used to retrieve data directly from external data sources using Microsoft ODBC.
ODBC drivers	DLLs used by applications such as Microsoft Excel to gain access to specific data sources.
ODBC Driver Manager	A DLL that provides access to ODBC drivers.
Control Panel ODBC utility (Windows)	A utility you can use to install drivers and define data sources.

Component	Description
ODBC Setup (Macintosh)	A utility you can use to install drivers and define data sources.
Northwind Sample Database (NWIND) (Windows)	A set of sample files in FoxPro format for use with Microsoft Query and Microsoft Excel.
Data Access Macro (Macintosh)	An add-in macro that enables you to use macros you created with the Data Access Macro from Microsoft Excel version 4.0. The Data Access Macro enables data access via DAL Client Software independent of Microsoft Query and ODBC.

What You Can Do with Microsoft Query

Microsoft Query is a self-contained, ODBC-supported data access application. You can use it alone or with other applications that support dynamic data exchange (DDE). Use Query with Microsoft Excel to:

- Bring data from remote database files and tables into your worksheet for analysis, reporting, and charting.

- Retrieve data from other Microsoft Excel workbooks. (This functionality is available only in Microsoft Excel version 5.0 for Windows.)

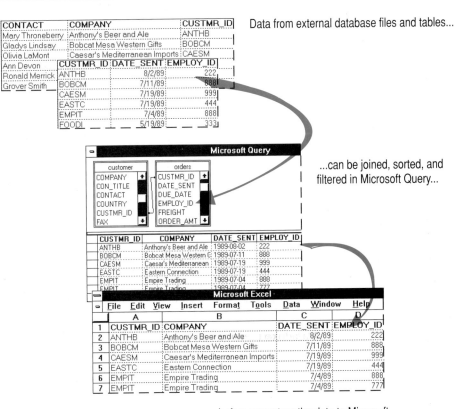

Data from external database files and tables...

...can be joined, sorted, and filtered in Microsoft Query...

...before you return the data to Microsoft Excel for analysis and reporting.

Microsoft Query does more than retrieve data. With Microsoft Query, you can:

- Retrieve records from multiple external data sources using search criteria you specify.
- Select the fields you want to display.
- Display, edit, and organize the results before you return them to Microsoft Excel.
- Compute totals for records within the *result set.*

To access Microsoft Query from within Microsoft Excel, you use tools and commands provided by the Microsoft Query Add-in. For information about installing Microsoft Query and the Microsoft Query Add-in, see "Before You Begin to Retrieve Data" later in this chapter.

The Types of Data You Can Retrieve

The types of data you can retrieve depend on the *open database connectivity (ODBC) drivers* you installed to work with Microsoft Query and Microsoft Excel. An ODBC driver is a system *dynamic-link library (DLL)* that allows ODBC-enabled applications such as Microsoft Query and Microsoft Excel to access specified data sources and retrieve data created in another format, such as dBASE.

Note If an ODBC driver you want is not available when you run the Microsoft Excel Setup program, you'll find a fulfillment coupon and directions for ordering the driver in the Microsoft Excel box.

The following drivers are available for and supported by Microsoft Excel version 5.0 for Windows:

- Microsoft FoxPro® (versions 2.0 and 2.5)
- Microsoft Access® (versions 1.0 and 1.1)
- Paradox® (versions 3.0 and 3.5)
- dBASE® (versions 3.0 and 4.0)
- SQL Server (versions 1.1, 4.2, and NT, and Synbase 4.x)
- Microsoft Excel (XLS) (versions 3.0, 4.0, and 5.0)
- Btrieve® (version 5.1)
- ORACLE® Server (version 6.0)
- ODBC ODS Gateway
- Text

A variety of drivers are available for and supported by Microsoft Excel version 5.0 for the Apple Macintosh. For information about which drivers are available, see the Readme file for Microsoft Excel version 5.0, or contact your database vendor.

You can also use other full-conformance-level ODBC drivers. For more information about the Microsoft Query driver requirements, see Appendix B, "ODBC Drivers: Requirements, Installation, and Adding Data Sources," in the *Microsoft Query User's Guide.* For information about the setup and conformance level for a specific driver, see the documentation for that driver.

If You Want to Create Macros to Access Data

Programmers using the Microsoft Visual Basic Programming System, Applications Edition, can write macros or custom data access applications in Microsoft Excel to access remote data sources without using Query.

You can also write macros or custom database applications that use Query. Use the Visual Basic command equivalents in the Microsoft Query Add-in.

To add data access commands to the macros already created in the Microsoft Excel version 4.0 macro language, use the Microsoft ODBC Add-in for Microsoft Excel. With these macros you can access external data sources without using Microsoft Query. Use the Microsoft Query command-equivalent functions available in the Microsoft Query Add-in to access external data with Microsoft Query.

If You Use Q+E® for Microsoft Excel for Windows

Because Microsoft Query provides better integration than Q+E for Microsoft Excel for Windows, you will want to use it for all your data access needs. However, you can still use macros created using Q+E with Microsoft Query. For more information, see "Before You Begin to Retrieve Data" and "Switching from Q+E to Microsoft Query and Microsoft Excel for Windows" later in this chapter.

If You Use the Data Access Macro with Microsoft Excel for the Macintosh

Because Microsoft Query provides more flexibility and better integration than the Data Access Macro for Microsoft Excel for the Macintosh, you will want to use it for all your data access needs. However, if you want to continue using macros created with the Data Access Macro command-equivalent functions from Microsoft Excel version 4.0, you will need to use the new Data Access Macro. For information about the components you need to install to use Microsoft Query or the Data Access Macro, see "Before You Begin to Retrieve Data" later in this chapter. For information about switching to Microsoft Query, see "Changing to Microsoft Query from the Data Access Macro for Microsoft Excel for the Macintosh."

How Microsoft Excel Retrieves Data Using Microsoft Query and Open Database Connectivity

Microsoft Excel communicates with Microsoft Query using *dynamic data exchange (DDE).* If you are a macro programmer and you want more information about the DDE functions and Visual Basic procedures, see "Using DDE" in Chapter 10 of the *Microsoft Excel Visual Basic User's Guide,* or see the *Microsoft Excel Development Kit.*

To learn more about the DDE commands supported by Query, see Chapter 9, "Using Dynamic Data Exchange with Microsoft Query," in the *Microsoft Query User's Guide,* and "DDE Commands" in Microsoft Query Help.

Microsoft Query accesses remote data using ODBC, which consists of a Driver Manager and a set of ODBC drivers. These ODBC drivers enable applications to use *Structured Query Language (SQL)* as a standard language to access data created and stored in another format, such as FoxPro. The ODBC Driver Manager is a DLL that provides access to the ODBC drivers.

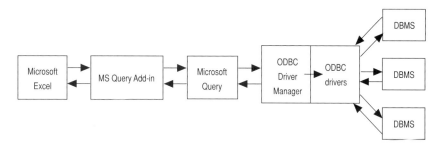

Microsoft Excel data access components that use Microsoft Query to retrieve data from an external data source

Each *database management system* (DBMS) you want to access, such as SQL Server or FoxPro, requires a different ODBC driver. For information about obtaining and setting up drivers so that Microsoft Excel can work with Microsoft Query and ODBC, see "Before You Begin to Retrieve Data" later in this chapter.

Important   System requirements vary depending on the data you want to access. For example, if you are using Microsoft Excel for the Macintosh and want to access data from a Data Access Language (DAL) server, you must install a DAL ODBC driver and DAL Client software. For information about specific requirements, see the documentation that comes with the driver.

If you are a macro programmer, use the Microsoft ODBC Add-in for Microsoft Excel to create macros that interact directly with ODBC through the ODBC Driver Manager. For information about installing the Microsoft ODBC Add-in and making it available to Microsoft Excel, see "Before You Begin to Retrieve Data" later in this chapter.

The Microsoft ODBC Add-in for Microsoft Excel contains functions in Visual Basic and the Microsoft Excel version 4.0 macro language.

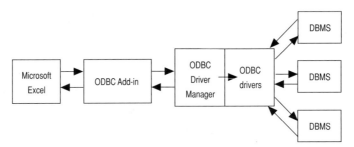

Microsoft Excel data access components that interact directly with the ODBC Driver Manager to retrieve data from an external data source

ODBC Visual Basic Language Extensions and ODBC Macro Extensions Available to the Programmer

The Microsoft ODBC Add-in for Microsoft Excel contains the following eight macros and one worksheet function in both the Visual Basic and Microsoft Excel version 4.0 macro languages.

ODBC Visual Basic Language Extensions	**Microsoft Excel ODBC Macro Language Extensions**	**Description**
SQLBind	SQL.BIND	Specifies storage for a result column.
SQLClose	SQL.CLOSE	Closes a data source connection.
SQLError	SQL.ERROR	Returns detailed error information.
SQLExec	SQL.EXEC.QUERY	Sends a query to a data source.
SQLGetSchema	SQL.GET.SCHEMA	Gets information about a connected data source.
SQLOpen	SQL.OPEN	Establishes a connection with a data source.
SQLRetrieve	SQL.RETRIEVE	Retrieves query results.
SQLRetrieveToFile	SQL.RETRIEVE.TO.FILE	Retrieves query results and places them in a file.
SQLRequest (a worksheet function)	SQL.REQUEST (a worksheet function)	Connects with an external data source, performs the query, and returns the result set.

The Microsoft Query Add-in has the following three Visual Basic and Microsoft Excel version 4.0 macro language command equivalents.

ODBC Visual Basic command-equivalent functions	**Microsoft Excel version 4.0 macro language command-equivalent functions**	**Description**
QueryRefresh	QUERY.REFRESH	Updates the query containing the active cell.
QueryGetData	QUERY.GET.DATA	Executes a new query.
QueryGetDataDlg	QUERY.GET.DATA?	Executes a new query and opens the Get External Data dialog box.

Before You Begin to Retrieve Data

The method you use to access external data determines whether you need to install all or some of the data access components included with Microsoft Excel.

The Files You Need to Install

To use Microsoft Query with Microsoft Excel, you need to install Microsoft Query, the Microsoft Query Add-in, the drivers for the types of data you want to retrieve, and the necessary ODBC files. If you have not yet installed Microsoft Excel, you install these files by selecting the Complete/Custom option when you run Setup, making sure the Data Access check box is selected. If you do not want to install all the drivers provided with Microsoft Excel, select the Data Access option, choose the Change Option button, and then clear the check boxes for the drivers you do not need. Remember, however, that you need to install at least one driver to use Microsoft Query. Also make sure that you do not clear the check box for Microsoft Query, as this option installs Microsoft Query, the Microsoft Query Add-in, and all the ODBC files you need.

If you did not install Microsoft Query or the drivers you need during your initial Microsoft Excel setup, run the Setup program again. To install additional external drivers, or to install drivers not included with Microsoft Excel, open your Control Panel and use one of the following utilities.

System	Utility
Windows	Control Panel ODBC utility
Macintosh	ODBC Setup

For more information about the Microsoft Excel Setup program, see Chapter 1, "Installing and Starting Microsoft Excel."

Important If you use Microsoft Excel for the Macintosh and want to access data from a Data Access Language (DAL) server, you must install an ODBC DAL driver and DAL Client software version 1.3.4 or later. For information about obtaining the ODBC DAL driver and the most recent version of the DAL Client software, see the Microsoft Excel Readme file.

The Installation You Need for ODBC Programming If you want to write macros that interact directly with ODBC, you can obtain all the files you need by following the installation instructions outlined above. If you do not want to install Microsoft Query, you must install at least one driver provided in Microsoft Excel Setup to obtain the Microsoft ODBC Add-in and the other ODBC files. If you intend to use a driver that is not provided in Setup, you must select the Microsoft Query check box in Setup in order to install the Microsoft ODBC Add-In and required ODBC files.

Switching from Q+E for Microsoft Excel for Windows If you already have macros that work with Q+E, you will want to modify them using the Microsoft Query Add-in functions or the Microsoft ODBC Add-in. If you want to continue to use QE.XLA command-equivalent macros with Microsoft Query, use the Q+E Add-in (QE.XLA) replacement. When you install Microsoft Query using Microsoft Excel Setup, the Q+E Add-in replacement is automatically installed in the same directory as your existing QE.XLA, as long as the existing QE.XLA is located in either the QE directory or the XLSTART directory in the directory in which you installed the previous version of Microsoft Excel. The name of your existing QE.XLA is then changed to QEOLD.XLA.

If your existing QE.XLA is not located in either the QE or XLSTART directory, the new copy of the QE.XLA is not installed. To install the new QE.XLA, copy your old one to one of these directories and run Setup again. To use the Q+E Add-in, first make it available to Microsoft Excel by using the Add-ins command on the Tools menu.

Installing the Data Access Macro for Microsoft Excel for the Macintosh   If you created macros in Microsoft Excel for the Macintosh version 4.0 that use the Data Access Macro and you want to continue using these macros, you need to install the new version of the Data Access Macro. First rename the old Data Access Macro file. Then, when you run Microsoft Excel setup, select the Complete/Custom installation option and make sure the Data Access Macro option is selected under Data Access. To use the Data Access Macro after installation, activate it using the Add-Ins command on the Tools menu.

Defining Data Sources

In addition to installing the correct drivers, you need to define data sources. A data source includes the data you want to access and the information needed to get to that data. An example of a data source is a set of dBASE files and the directory that contains them. An SQL Server database, the server on which it resides, and the network used to access that server are all elements of a data source, too.

When you define a data source, you assign it a name, which Microsoft Query then uses to locate data.

You can choose among the following three methods to define data sources:

- From the Microsoft Excel Setup program, follow the instructions.

- From Microsoft Query, choose the Other button in the Select Data Source dialog box and then choose the New button in the ODBC Data Sources dialog box. Then select the driver you want to use for the data source. Provide the specific information requested by each ODBC driver.

- From the Control Panel, use one of the following ODBC driver installation utilities:

System	ODBC driver installation utility
Windows	Control Panel ODBC utility
Macintosh	ODBC Setup

For more information, see Appendix B, "ODBC Drivers: Requirements, Installation, and Adding Data Sources," in the *Microsoft Query User's Guide.*

Making the Microsoft Query Add-in or the Microsoft ODBC Add-in Available After Installation

After you install the Microsoft Query Add-in file, you need to make it available to Microsoft Excel before you can access Microsoft Query. To see the list of add-ins currently available, choose the Add-ins command from the Tools menu. If the Microsoft Query Add-in appears in the Add-ins dialog box, make sure that its check box is selected. If it does not appear, choose the Browse button to find it. Look for one of the following files.

System	Add-in filename
Windows	XLQUERY.XLA
Macintosh	XLQUERY

If you want to use the Microsoft ODBC Add-in, and it does not appear in the Add-ins dialog box, choose the Browse button and look for one of the following files.

System	Add-in filename
Windows	XLODBC.XLA
Macintosh	XLODBC

If you cannot find the add-in file on your hard disk, run the Microsoft Excel Setup program to install it.

For more information about making add-ins available, see Chapter 37, "Installing Add-in Features."

Get External Data

When the Microsoft Query Add-in is available, the Get External Data command is added to the Data menu, and the Get External Data button is added to the Query And Pivot toolbar. The Refresh Data command on the Data menu and the Refresh Data button on the Query And Pivot toolbar are modified to update a query if the active cell is in the result set.

Refresh Data

Note To display the Query And Pivot toolbar, choose Toolbars from the View menu. Select the Query And Pivot toolbar, and then choose the Show button.

Retrieving Data from Lists and External Databases Using Microsoft Query

You retrieve data by building a *query definition* with Microsoft Query. A query definition:

- Contains the information that Microsoft Query uses to connect to a data source.
- Contains the information that Microsoft Query uses to determine which data to retrieve from the data source.
- Is sent to the data source in the form of an SQL statement for execution.
- Can include table names, field names, and criteria.

To retrieve data, choose the Get External Data command from the Microsoft Excel Data menu. The Get External Data command starts Microsoft Query.

Building a Query

As part of building a query in Microsoft Query, you need to specify the data source you want to use and the tables or files from the data source you want to access. Then use Microsoft Query to display, sort, filter, or join data from the selected tables. You can display some or all of the fields from selected records.

For more information about specifying data sources, adding tables, or using Microsoft Query, see the *Microsoft Query User's Guide*.

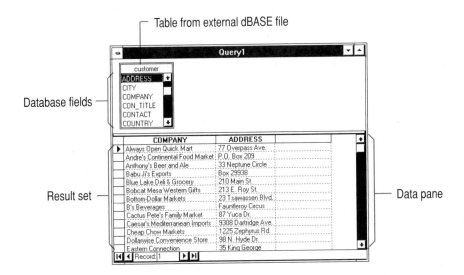

Table from external dBASE file

Database fields

Result set

Data pane

Returning the Result Set to Microsoft Excel

When you finish building a query, return the result set to your Microsoft Excel worksheet.

Choose the Return
Data To Microsoft
Excel command in
Microsoft Query...

...to return data...

...to your Microsoft
Excel worksheet.

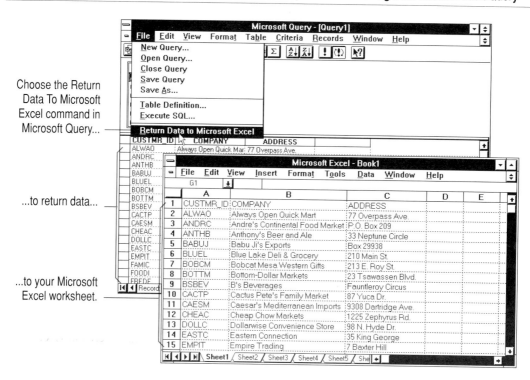

Note The Return Data command and button appear in Microsoft Query only if you
started Microsoft Query from within Microsoft Excel.

When you return data to Microsoft Excel, you confirm or change the destination on
the worksheet where you want to place the result set. If you do not change the
destination, Microsoft Excel uses the active cell as the destination.

The worksheet area that contains the pasted data is called a data range. The cell you
specify as the destination is the upper-left cell of the range where the data will
appear.

Saving the Query Definition

You also need to indicate whether you want to save the query definition with the
result set. A query definition is the information Microsoft Query uses to connect to
a data source and decide which data to retrieve from it. A query definition can
include a table name, field names, and criteria.

If you want to update or modify the result set later with new data from the data
source, save the query definition with your result set.

When to Save a Query Definition

When you retrieve data with Microsoft Query, you can save the query definition along with the result set on your worksheet.

Save a query definition if:

- You want to update the result set later with changes made in the source file or table.

- You want the option to change the existing result set by editing the existing query definition.

- You are going to create a chart or pivot table using the result set, and you want to update the result set when the source data changes.

Do not save a query definition if:

- You are going to format, sort, or filter the result set in Microsoft Excel, and you have no need to update with changes in the source file.

- You only want to take a snapshot of the data in the database for report purposes.

Closing Microsoft Query

When you return data to Microsoft Excel, Microsoft Query stays open. Unless you have other applications that are also using Microsoft Query, closing Microsoft Excel closes Microsoft Query as well.

If you switch from Microsoft Excel to Microsoft Query, you can also use one of the following commands to close Microsoft Query.

System	Command on File menu
Windows	Exit
Macintosh	Quit

Important If you close the Microsoft Query window before using the Return Data To Microsoft Excel command, you get a blank result set in Microsoft Excel. Double-click any cell in the blank result set in Microsoft Excel to open the query definition in Microsoft Query. Then return the data to Microsoft Excel again.

Closing Microsoft Query does not close Microsoft Excel.

What Happens When Data Is Retrieved Using Microsoft Query

When you return data to the Microsoft Excel worksheet, the result set appears in the format applied to the destination cells in Microsoft Excel, not the format from Microsoft Query.

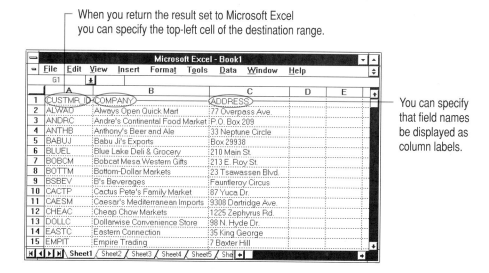

When you return the result set to Microsoft Excel you can specify the top-left cell of the destination range.

You can specify that field names be displayed as column labels.

Updating Query Results

You can update results if you saved the query definition before closing Microsoft Query.

To update your result set, select a cell in the result set and choose the Get External Data command.

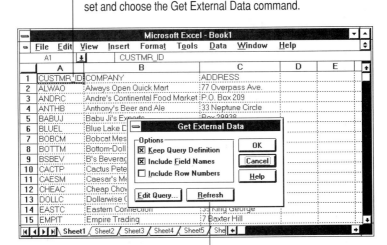

Then, choose the Refresh button.

Important Updating data replaces your extracted result set and all changes—including sorting and formatting—you might have made. If you want to save changes and formatting to a result set, copy the result set to another sheet in the workbook. If you want to maintain a sort order, do the sorting in Microsoft Query before you bring the data into Microsoft Excel.

You can also click the Refresh Data button on the Query And Pivot toolbar or choose the Refresh Data command from the Data menu.

Retrieving Data from Other Microsoft Excel Workbooks with Microsoft Query (Windows Only)

You can use Microsoft Query to retrieve data from Microsoft Excel lists in other workbooks if you have the Microsoft Excel driver. Install the Microsoft Excel driver, and then specify Microsoft Excel data sources.

To extract Microsoft Excel data from only one worksheet, the Filter command is usually sufficient.

How to Choose Between Microsoft Query and Microsoft Excel to Filter Data

When you want to	Use
Filter data that fits on a worksheet in Microsoft Excel	Microsoft Excel
Join two or more separate tables of data based on specific criteria	Microsoft Query
Retain the order of the data after updating your result	Microsoft Query
Set up complex criteria	Microsoft Query
Set up user-defined columns	Microsoft Query
Use simple criteria	Microsoft Excel

For more information about filtering, see Chapter 21, "Sorting and Filtering Data in a List."

Retrieving Data for a Pivot Table

Use Microsoft Query to retrieve external data for use in a pivot table. For information about creating a pivot table using data retrieved with Microsoft Query, see "Using External Data to Create a Pivot Table" in Chapter 24.

Moving Data and the Query Definition to Another Worksheet or Workbook

To use Microsoft Query to copy data to another workbook, first save the file in Microsoft Query and return it to Microsoft Excel. From a new workbook in Microsoft Excel, use the Get External Data command on the Data menu or the Get External Data button on the Query And Pivot toolbar to open the file in Microsoft Query. Then return the data to the new Microsoft Excel workbook or worksheet.

You can also copy data to another worksheet in the same workbook. First, copy the data using the Copy command on the Edit menu. Then use the Paste command on the Edit menu to paste the data onto the new worksheet.

Step By Step

For step-by-step instructions and related information, double-click the [?] button to display the Search dialog box in Help, and then:

Type this keyword and choose Show Topics	Select a topic and choose Go To
add-ins	Installing or removing an add-in
AutoFilter	Filtering a list using AutoFilter

Type this keyword and choose Show Topics	Select a topic and choose Go To
moving, query definitions	Moving data and the query definition to another workbook
query results updating	Updating query results
retrieving data	Retrieving data from lists and external databases
showing toolbars	Displaying or hiding toolbars

Editing an Existing Result Set

To change your result set in Microsoft Excel, edit the query in Microsoft Query. The result set in Microsoft Excel is a copy of the data; it is not actively linked to the data source. Any changes in the source data are not reflected in the result set in Microsoft Excel unless you update the data using the Refresh Data command on the Data menu or the Refresh Data button on the Query And Pivot toolbar.

Important You need to save a query definition before you can edit it. Otherwise, you have to create the query again in Microsoft Query and return the result set to Microsoft Excel.

To edit a query without displaying the Get External Data dialog box, double-click a cell in the result set in Microsoft Excel to display the query in Microsoft Query.

Modify the query in Microsoft Query. Then, from the Microsoft Query File menu, choose the Return Data To Microsoft Excel command, to return the new result set to Microsoft Excel.

To change the options in the Get External Data dialog box as well as edit the query definition, choose the Get External Data command from the Data menu in Microsoft Excel. Change the options and then choose the Edit button.

Step By Step

For step-by-step instructions and related information, double-click the 【?】 button to display the Search dialog box in Help, and then:

Type this keyword and choose Show Topics	Select a topic and choose Go To
editing, result sets	Editing an existing query result set in a workbook
query results, updating	Updating query results

Working with Query Results

Once you return a result set to Microsoft Excel, you can use it just as you would use any other list. You can:

- Extract data
- Create reports using subtotals
- Create charts
- Format
- Sort
- Filter

Just remember that anything you do to the result set once it's in Microsoft Excel is undone or replaced when you update using the Refresh Data command. If you want to preserve your Microsoft Excel changes, you can copy your data to another worksheet before you format, sort, or chart the data.

You can create a pivot table directly from external data without moving the result set into Microsoft Excel. For more information, see Chapter 24, "Creating a Pivot Table."

Step By Step

For step-by-step instructions and related information, double-click the 🔃 button to display the Search dialog box in Help, and then:

Type this keyword and choose Show Topics	Select a topic and choose Go To
lists, filtering	Overview of Filtering Data in a List
	Sorting and Filtering Data in a List
lists, sorting	Overview of Sorting a List
removing, query definitions	Removing a query definition from a worksheet
worksheets, formatting	Formatting a Worksheet

Switching from Q+E to Microsoft Query and Microsoft Excel for Windows

Microsoft Excel version 5.0 is designed to take advantage of the flexibility and power of Microsoft Query and ODBC. Switch to Microsoft Query for better integration with Microsoft Excel.

It's best to write all new data access macros using the Visual Basic functions that come with Microsoft Excel. However, you can also use Microsoft Excel version 4.0 macros created for Q+E if you use the following guidelines.

Naming Your Data Sources

To use Microsoft Excel version 4.0 Q+E macros with Microsoft Query, make sure that you name your data sources as you would when using Q+E. For example, if a Q+E query accesses a data source named dBaseFile, make sure that you name that data source dBaseFile when defining it for ODBC.

For more information about defining data sources, see Appendix B, "ODBC Drivers: Requirements, Installation, and Adding Data Sources" in the *Microsoft Query User's Guide,* or see the documentation for your driver.

Converting Microsoft Excel Version 4.0 Macros That Use Q+E for Microsoft Excel

Microsoft Query supports many of the DDE commands, but not the formatting and editing ones. Microsoft Query DDE commands handle such tasks as connecting to data sources, querying data sources, and manipulating data.

For more information about the DDE commands supported by Microsoft Query, see "Using DDE" in Microsoft Query Help.

If Your DDE Macros Contain an INITIATE Call to Q+E   If you want to redirect your DDE macros that contain an INITIATE call from Q+E to Microsoft Query, change the *app_text* argument for any INITIATE function from "qe" to "msquery". For example, change

=INITIATE("QE","SYSTEM")

to

=INITIATE("MSQUERY","SYSTEM")

If Your Macro Contains Q+E Add-in Command-Equivalent Functions   To use macros that are written in the Microsoft Excel version 4.0 macro language and that use the Q+E Add-in command-equivalent functions, use the Q+E Add-in (QE.XLA) replacement. For information about installing the Q+E Add-in replacement, see "Before You Begin to Retrieve Data" earlier in this chapter.

Changing to Microsoft Query from the Data Access Macro for Microsoft Excel for the Macintosh

When you switch to Microsoft Query, you have access to a wider array of data sources than you have with the Microsoft Excel version 4.0 Data Access Macro. You'll also enjoy better integration with Microsoft Excel.

Each external data source you may want to access requires a different ODBC driver. A variety of ODBC drivers are available for and supported by Microsoft Excel version 5.0 and the Apple Macintosh. For information about which drivers are available, see the Readme file for Microsoft Excel version 5.0, or contact your database vendor. For information about installing drivers, see "Before You Begin to Retrieve Data" earlier in this chapter.

Important If you want to use Microsoft Query to access data from a Data Access Language (DAL) server, you must install an ODBC driver and DAL Client software version 1.3.4 or later. For information about obtaining the ODBC DAL driver and the most recent version fo the DAL Client software, see the Microsoft Readme file.

If Your Macro Contains Microsoft Excel Version 4.0 Command-Equivalent Functions

It's best to rewrite your existing data access macros using Micrososft Excel version 5.0 functions or Visual Basic in Microsoft Excel. However, if you do not want to use Microsoft Query and ODBC, you can continue to use Microsoft Excel version 4.0 macros created for the Data Access Macro if you install the new version of the Data Access Macro provided with the Microsoft Excel version 5.0. For information about installing and activating the Data Access Macro, see "Before You Begin to Retrieve Data" earlier in this chapter.Where to Find Additional Information

Microsoft Excel version 5.0, Microsoft Query, and Microsoft ODBC include a full set of user's guides and Help.

About Setting Up and Using Microsoft Query

For information about	See
Step-by-step procedures for using Query with Microsoft Excel	Microsoft Excel Help
Using Microsoft Query	*Microsoft Query User's Guide*
	Microsoft Query Help
	Microsoft Query Cue Cards
Using the Northwind Sample Database (Windows)	*Microsoft Query User's Guide*
Using Microsoft Query with pivot tables	Chapter 24 in the *Microsoft Excel User's Guide*
Using DDE with Microsoft Excel	Chapter 4 and Appendix A in the *Microsoft Excel Software Development Kit*

About ODBC

For information about	See
Defining or adding additional data sources	*Microsoft Query User's Guide*
	Control Panel ODBC utility Help (Windows)
	ODBC Setup documentation (Macintosh)
Installing ODBC drivers	Microsoft Excel Help
	Microsoft Query User's Guide
	Control Panel ODBC utility Help (Windows)
	ODBC Setup documentation (Macintosh)
Specific drivers	ODBC Driver Reference in Microsoft Excel version 5.0 Help
	Documentation that comes with the driver

About Microsoft Excel Version 5.0 Programming Language Options for Data Access

For information about	See
ODBC procedures for Visual Basic	*Microsoft Excel Visual Basic User's Guide*
Data access functions in the Microsoft Excel version 4.0 macro language	"Database & List Management" in Microsoft Excel Macro Functions Help
DDE commands supported in Microsoft Query	Microsoft Query Help
	Microsoft Excel Visual Basic User's Guide
Instructions for programming in Visual Basic in Microsoft Excel	*Microsoft Excel Visual Basic User's Guide*

C H A P T E R   2 4

Creating a Pivot Table

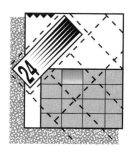

For command, keyboard, and toolbar button information, see online Help.

In This Chapter

What You Can Do with a Pivot Table

A pivot table is an interactive worksheet table that quickly summarizes large amounts of data using a format and calculation methods you choose. It is called a pivot table because you can rotate its row and column headings around the core data area to give you different views of the source data. As source data changes, you can update a pivot table. Because it resides on a worksheet, you can integrate a pivot table into a larger worksheet model using standard formulas.

Analyze Existing Data Quickly

A pivot table provides an easy way for you to display and analyze summary information about data already created in Microsoft Excel or another application. For example, with a Microsoft Excel database that contains sales records for several salespeople, you can create a pivot table that organizes and totals sales data using categories—or *fields*—such as Year, that you choose from the source data.

In the following pivot table, sales data from the displayed Microsoft Excel list is summarized by year and type of grocery item sold.

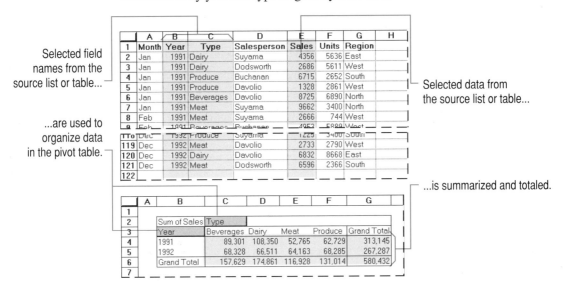

Selected field names from the source list or table...

...are used to organize data in the pivot table.

Selected data from the source list or table...

...is summarized and totaled.

A pivot table summarizes data using calculations—or *summary functions*—you choose, such as Sum or Average. You can also control how subtotals and grand totals are calculated. When you change the source data, you can easily update or recalculate data in the pivot table.

What Data Can I Use?   The data you use for a pivot table can come from:

- A single Microsoft Excel list, database, or any worksheet range that has labeled columns.

- A collection of Microsoft Excel ranges that contain data you want to consolidate. These ranges must have both labeled rows and labeled columns.

- A database file or table created in an external application or database management system such as Microsoft Access, FoxPro, dBASE, ORACLE, or SQL Server.

- Data from an existing pivot table or a Microsoft Excel version 4.0 crosstab table.

Show Only the Details You Want Displayed

You can choose both the level and type of detail to include in a pivot table. For example, the preceding pivot table can be changed to hide all grocery items except Beverages and Dairy and to show sales totals broken out by salesperson.

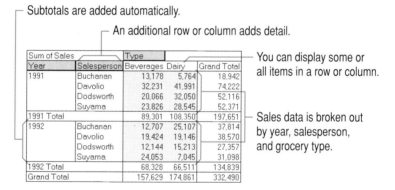

Subtotals are added automatically.

An additional row or column adds detail.

You can display some or all items in a row or column.

Sales data is broken out by year, salesperson, and grocery type.

Sum of Sales		Type		
Year	Salesperson	Beverages	Dairy	Grand Total
1991	Buchanan	13,178	5,764	18,942
	Davolio	32,231	41,991	74,222
	Dodsworth	20,066	32,050	52,116
	Suyama	23,826	28,545	52,371
1991 Total		89,301	108,350	197,651
1992	Buchanan	12,707	25,107	37,814
	Davolio	19,424	19,146	38,570
	Dodsworth	12,144	15,213	27,357
	Suyama	24,053	7,045	31,098
1992 Total		68,328	66,511	134,839
Grand Total		157,629	174,861	332,490

Easily Change Your View of the Data

You can change your view of the data by moving fields and associated data using the mouse. This enables you to arrange categories based on the type of analysis you want to perform.

For example, the preceding pivot table compared the total sales for individual salespeople for two types of grocery items (Beverages and Dairy). To compare sales data for 1991 and 1992 for each type of grocery item, you can move the Year field from a row to a column orientation.

Moving a field...

Sum of Units				
Year	Salesperson	Beverages	Dairy	Grand Total
1991	Buchanan	14,980	22,403	37,383
	Davolio	18,797	29,392	48,189
	Dodsworth	27,244	20,748	47,992
	Suyama	14,262	16,609	30,871
1991 Total		75,283	89,152	164,435
1992	Buchanan	18,104	11,623	29,727
	Davolio	23,617	19,162	42,779
	Dodsworth	18,473	5,065	23,538
	Suyama	17,767	14,206	31,973
1992 Total		77,961	50,056	128,017
Grand Total		153,244	139,208	292,452

...changes how details are displayed.

Sum of Units	Year	Type		1991 Total	1992		1992 Total	Grand Total
	1991				1992			
Salesperson	Beverages	Dairy			Beverages	Dairy		
Buchanan	14,980	22,403		37,383	18,104	11,623	29,727	67,110
Davolio	18,797	29,392		48,189	23,617	19,162	42,779	90,968
Dodsworth	27,244	20,748		47,992	18,473	5,065	23,538	71,530
Suyama	14,262	16,609		30,871	17,767	14,206	31,973	62,844
Grand Total	75,283	89,152		164,435	77,961	50,056	128,017	292,452

Create Charts that Change with the Pivot Table Data

You can create charts that show the multiple levels of detail in a pivot table.

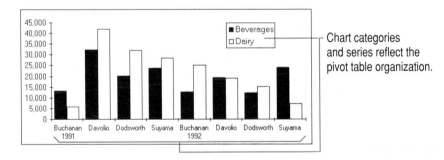

Chart categories and series reflect the pivot table organization.

As you hide and show detail or change the pivot table view, the chart changes automatically. For more information, see "Creating a Chart from a Pivot Table" later in this chapter.

How a Pivot Table Works

Because you create a pivot table from existing data, knowing the organization of the source data and how it is used in a pivot table will help you make the best decisions about how much data to use and how to organize it.

Fields and Items Control How Data Is Organized

You specify what data you want to include and how you want to organize it by choosing from the source table or list the *fields* and *items* you want to appear in the table. A field is a category of data, such as Year, Region, or Sales. An item is a subcategory in a field, such as West, East, South, and North in the Region field, or 1991 and 1992 in the Year field. In a Microsoft Excel list, a field name appears as a column label.

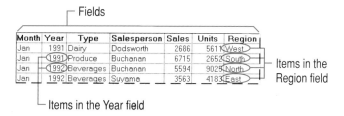

In your pivot table, you can use two types of fields from the source list or table:

- Fields to use as row field, column field, and page field labels in the pivot table. These fields usually contain a limited set of text values, such as North, South, East, and West.

- *Data fields,* which contain the data you want summarized. These fields typically contain numeric data, such as sales amounts, inventory totals, or statistical data, but can also contain text.

You can use as many fields as you want from the source list or table.

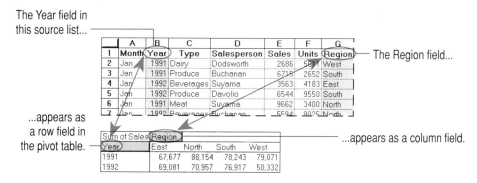

Items from the source list become row or column labels in the resulting pivot table. These labels—or *pivot table items*—are subcategories of a field in a pivot table, just as they are subcategories of the field in the source list. In the following example, the North, South, East, and West items that appear in the Region field of the source list appear as items under the column field Region in the table. The 1991 and 1992 items that appear in the Year field of the source list appear as items under the row field Year in the pivot table.

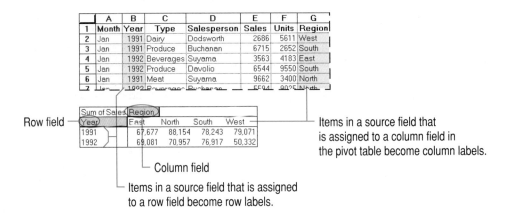

Row field

Items in a source field that
is assigned to a column field in
the pivot table become column labels.

Column field

Items in a source field that is assigned
to a row field become row labels.

Numeric data, and sometimes text data, is summarized in the *data area* in the pivot table. This pivot table summarizes data from the Sales field in the source list.

The Sales field is selected as the data field for the pivot table.

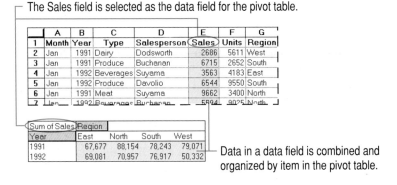

Data in a data field is combined and
organized by item in the pivot table.

The arrangement of fields and items in a pivot table is called a *layout.* You can change this layout using the mouse, and you can rename fields and items.

Fields and Items Control How Data Is Summarized

The fields and items you include in a pivot table determine how data is summarized in the data area. For example, in the following pivot table, the value of the cell at the intersection of the West column and the 1991 row is the sum of all sales data that appears in source rows that contain West as a region and 1991 as a year.

	A	B	C	D	E	F	G
1	Month	Year	Type	Salesperson	Sales	Units	Region
2	Jun	1992	Meat	Davolio	5575	9970	South
3	May	1991	Dairy	Davolio	5477	8578	West
4	Feb	1991	Meat	Suyama	2666	744	West
5	May	1992	Produce	Suyama	5416	677	East
6	Aug	1992	Dairy	Davolio	1647	3515	East
7	Dec	1991	Dairy	Buchanan	668	9981	West
8	Jan	1991	Beverages	Davolio	8725	6890	North
9	Oct	1991	Meat	Buchanan	656	4997	South

Sales data from rows that contain the region West and the year 1991...

Sum of Sales	Region			
Year	East	North	South	West
1991	67,677	88,154	78,243	79,071
1992	69,081	70,957	76,917	50,332

...is summarized in the cell at the intersection of West and 1991 in the pivot table.

Notice that the pivot table data includes sales totals for all salespeople in the source list. By specifying only Year and Region as fields, you are telling Microsoft Excel to summarize all data, limited only by the displayed Year and Region items. When you move and insert additional fields in the pivot table, the data is reorganized and recalculated accordingly.

Data Field Calculation   If the data field you choose from the source list or table contains numeric data, Microsoft Excel uses the Sum function to calculate the values in the data area of the pivot table. If the data field you choose contains text items, Microsoft Excel uses the Count function to provide a count of the source items. You can change this calculation to another function, such as Average, using the PivotTable Field command on the Data menu.

Totals   Subtotals and grand totals are included in the pivot table automatically. You can delete totals, or choose a different calculation for subtotals. For more information, see "Working with Totals in a Pivot Table" in Chapter 25.

Page Fields Filter Your View of the Data

To filter your view of data in a pivot table, you can use a *page field.* A page field breaks the pivot table up into separate *pages,* so that you can see data for one item at a time.

For example, the preceding pivot table contained sales data for all salespeople, displayed by Year and Region. To see the total sales for only one salesperson at a time, assign the Salesperson field from the source list to a page field in the pivot table.

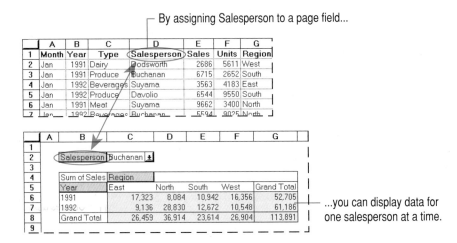

By assigning Salesperson to a page field...

...you can display data for one salesperson at a time.

Only sales data for the salesperson named Buchanan is displayed. To display data for another salesperson, you select the arrow next to the name Buchanan and select a name from the list that appears. For more information about displaying different pages in a pivot table, see "Changing Your View of the Data Using Page Fields" in Chapter 25.

You create page fields when you create the pivot table. You can also move a row or column field to a page orientation after you create the pivot table.

Steps to Creating a Simple Pivot Table

You create a pivot table using the *PivotTable Wizard*. The PivotTable Wizard is an interactive set of dialog boxes that guide you through the steps of choosing the source data and layout you want to use for the pivot table.

Note You can create a pivot table on any worksheet you choose. You can also have more than one pivot table on a worksheet. If you will be changing the pivot table often, you should place it on its own worksheet. To add a new worksheet to your workbook, use the Worksheet command on the Insert menu.

Start the PivotTable Wizard

From the Data menu, choose the PivotTable command. This displays Step 1 of the PivotTable Wizard. To use the PivotTable Wizard, see the instructions in each step, then use the buttons at the bottom of the PivotTable Wizard dialog box to continue.

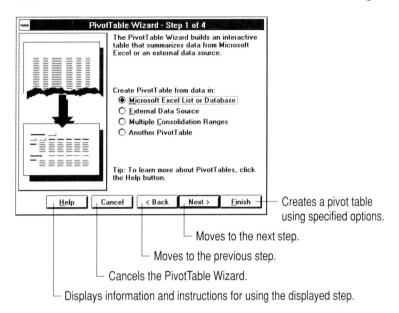

Creates a pivot table using specified options.

Moves to the next step.

Moves to the previous step.

Cancels the PivotTable Wizard.

Displays information and instructions for using the displayed step.

Specify the Type of Source Data

In Step 1 of the PivotTable Wizard, tell Microsoft Excel what type of source data you want to use. The option you choose determines which screen will be displayed next.

Select this option	To
Microsoft Excel List or Database	Summarize data from a multi-column list you created in Microsoft Excel. The list must contain labeled columns.
External Data Source	Query and summarize data from external database files or tables created using external applications or database management systems, such as Microsoft Access, FoxPro, dBASE, ORACLE, or SQL Server.
Multiple Consolidation Ranges	Combine and summarize data from multiple Microsoft Excel worksheet ranges that have row and column labels.
Another Pivot Table	Use data from an existing pivot table in the same workbook.

Specify the Location of the Source Data

In Step 2 of the PivotTable Wizard, identify the location of the source data. For example, if you select the Microsoft Excel List or Database option button, specify the worksheet range you want to use. The PivotTable Wizard dialog boxes and Help provide specific instructions for completing Step 2, regardless of the type of data you specified in Step 1.

Create a Pivot Table Layout

In Step 3, create a layout for the pivot table. You can easily change this layout later using the mouse.

Drag the fields you want to use as row field and column field labels into the Row and Column areas.

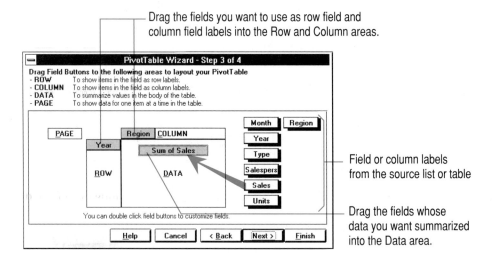

Field or column labels from the source list or table

Drag the fields whose data you want summarized into the Data area.

The more fields you include in an area, the more detail the finished pivot table contains.

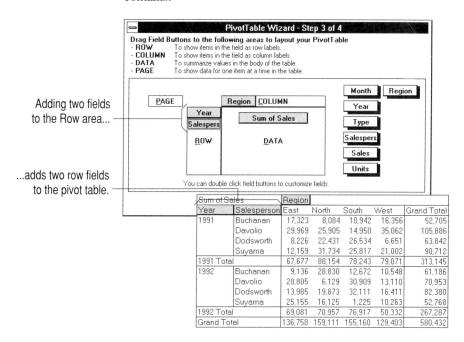

Adding two fields to the Row area...

...adds two row fields to the pivot table.

If you move a field to the Page area, the resulting pivot table displays data for only one item in that field at a time.

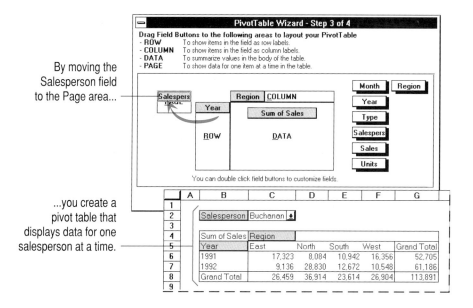

By moving the Salesperson field to the Page area...

...you create a pivot table that displays data for one salesperson at a time.

Select the Worksheet Destination and Display Options

In Step 4 of the PivotTable Wizard, specify where you want the pivot table to appear. You can place a pivot table on any worksheet you choose, in any workbook you choose. If you will be changing the source data or layout of the pivot table often, avoid placing the pivot table where it can overwrite existing data.

You need to type or select the cell reference only for the upper-left cell of the range where you want the pivot table to appear. If the destination worksheet is displayed, you can select the cell on the worksheet to enter the cell reference. If the destination worksheet is not open, type the full path, the workbook name, the sheet name, and the cell reference. To create the pivot table on a new worksheet, leave the PivotTable Starting Cell box blank.

For a description of the other options, choose the Help button in the PivotTable Wizard.

When you choose the Finish button, Microsoft Excel creates the pivot table and displays the Query And Pivot toolbar on the worksheet.

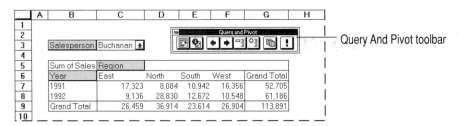

Query And Pivot toolbar

The Query And Pivot toolbar provides buttons to help you quickly customize the pivot table. For more information, see Chapter 25, "Customizing a Pivot Table."

When to Save Data with the Pivot Table Layout   When you create a pivot table, Microsoft Excel stores a copy of the source data as hidden data with the pivot table layout on the worksheet. If you have a large amount of data and you do not want to store a copy of it with the pivot table, clear the Save Data With Table Layout check box in Step 4 of the PivotTable Wizard. The next time you change or refresh the pivot table, the pivot table data is updated automatically from the source data.

Customize the Fields, Data, and Layout

Once you create a basic pivot table, you can customize it in the following ways:

- Insert, delete, or rearrange fields and items in the pivot table.
- Change how data is calculated.
- Display or delete subtotals and block totals.
- Change the names of fields and items.
- Change the format.

- Hide and show detail data.
- Group and sort items.

For detailed information about completing these tasks, see Chapter 25, "Customizing a Pivot Table."

Step By Step

For step-by-step instructions and related information, double-click the [?] button to display the Search dialog box in Help, and then:

Type this keyword and choose Show Topics	Select a topic and choose Go To
creating, pivot tables	Creating a pivot table
pivot tables	How a Pivot Table Works
pivot tables, deleting	Deleting a pivot table

Creating a Pivot Table from a Microsoft Excel List or Database

If the data you want to use is on a Microsoft Excel worksheet as a multiple column range, select the Microsoft Excel List Or Database option button in Step 1 of the PivotTable Wizard. The source list or database must contain column labels.

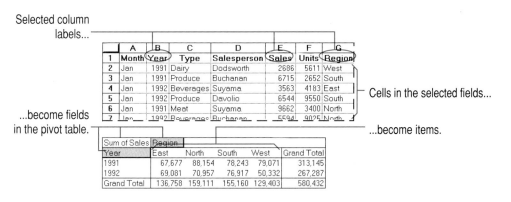

Selected column labels...

...become fields in the pivot table.

Cells in the selected fields...

...become items.

Choose the PivotTable command from the Data menu, then select the Microsoft Excel List or Database option button. Follow the instructions in the PivotTable Wizard. If you need help, choose the Help button in the PivotTable Wizard.

For information about creating a list or database in Microsoft Excel, see "What Is a List?" in Chapter 20.

Using the PivotTable Wizard to Specify the Location of a List When you specify the location of your source list in Step 2 of the PivotTable Wizard, make sure you include the column labels in the cell reference. Microsoft Excel uses the data in the first row of the range you specify for field names.

Tip If the list you want to use is in an open workbook, select a single cell in the list before choosing the PivotTable command. The PivotTable Wizard fills in the reference to the list for you in Step 2.

Using a List that Is Filtered or Contains Automatic Subtotals Microsoft Excel ignores any filters created using the Filter command on the Data menu, so delete them before creating a pivot table. For more information about filters, see Chapter 21, "Sorting and Filtering Data in a List."

Microsoft Excel automatically includes grand totals and subtotals in the pivot table, so remove any subtotals from your list. For information about removing automatic list subtotals, see "Displaying Automatic Subtotals in a List" in Chapter 22.

Step By Step

For step-by-step instructions and related information, double-click the 🞂❓ button to display the Search dialog box in Help, and then:

Type this keyword and choose Show Topics	Select a topic and choose Go To
automatic subtotals	Removing or replacing automatic subtotals
creating, pivot tables	Creating a pivot table
filters, removing	Removing a filter from a list
pivot tables, deleting	Deleting a pivot table

Using External Data to Create a Pivot Table

You can use the PivotTable Wizard to create a pivot table from data created in an application or database management system other than Microsoft Excel. The PivotTable Wizard provides access to Microsoft Query, a data access application that retrieves and displays data stored in external tables before returning the data to Microsoft Excel and the pivot table.

Important   Before you can create a pivot table using external data, you must install Microsoft Query and the appropriate *open database connectivity* (ODBC) drivers, and define the data sources you want to use.

If you use an Apple Macintosh and Microsoft Query did not come with your copy of Microsoft Excel, use the fulfillment coupon in the box to obtain a copy.

For more information about the types of data you can access and about installing and using Microsoft Query with Microsoft Excel, see Chapter 23, "Retrieving Data with Microsoft Query." For detailed information about using Microsoft Query, see the *Microsoft Query User's Guide*.

Using Microsoft Query When Creating a Pivot Table

Select the External Data Source option button in Step 1 of the PivotTable Wizard. Choosing the Get Data button in Step 2 of the PivotTable Wizard starts Microsoft Query.

Using Microsoft Query, you create a *query,* which is a set of search instructions used to retrieve an external data set. To create a query, you must:

- Specify the *data source* you want to use. A data source includes the data you want to access and the information needed to get to that data; for example, a set of dBASE files and the directory that contains them.

- Specify the tables or files from the data source you want to access.

- Display, sort, filter, or join data from the selected tables using Microsoft Query before returning the data to the PivotTable Wizard.

External database tables

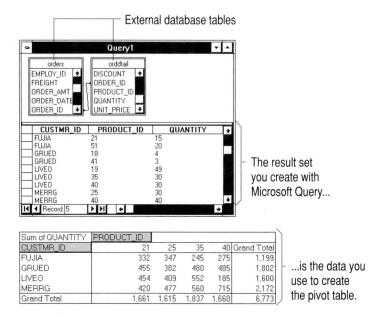

The result set
you create with
Microsoft Query...

...is the data you
use to create
the pivot table.

When you finish working in Microsoft Query, return the result set to Microsoft Excel by choosing the Return Data to Microsoft Excel command from the Microsoft Query File menu. This redisplays Step 2 of the PivotTable Wizard. Choose the Next button to move on to Step 3, which you use to create a layout for the pivot table.

Storing External Data as a List in Microsoft Excel   To examine or edit the source data in Microsoft Excel before you create a pivot table from it, use Microsoft Query to place external data directly on a worksheet as a list with labeled columns. Then you can create a pivot table from the list. For more information about creating a list using external data, see "Retrieving Data from Lists and External Databases Using Microsoft Query" in Chapter 23. For information about using a list as a source for a pivot table, see "Creating a Pivot Table from a Microsoft Excel List or Database" earlier in this chapter.

Changing the Query for a Pivot Table

PivotTable

To retrieve a different set of data for a pivot table, modify the query or edit the result set in Microsoft Query. Select a cell in the pivot table and choose the PivotTable command, or click the PivotTable button on the Query And Pivot toolbar. Click the Back button until Step 2 of the PivotTable Wizard is displayed. Then choose the Get Data button. This displays Microsoft Query and the query definition used to retrieve data for the pivot table. When you finish working in Microsoft Query, choose the Return Data to Microsoft Excel command from the Microsoft Query File menu.

Step By Step

For step-by-step instructions and related information, double-click the 🅺? button to display the Search dialog box in Help, and then:

Type this keyword and choose Show Topics	Select a topic and choose Go To
pivot tables, creating	Creating a pivot table
pivot tables, deleting	Deleting a pivot table
pivot tables, editing queries	Editing a query for a pivot table

Consolidating Data from Multiple Ranges into a Pivot Table

You can use the PivotTable Wizard to consolidate data from multiple worksheet ranges created in Microsoft Excel. This is useful for combining data from budget worksheets or reports that have similar layouts and identical row and column labels.

For example, the following worksheets report 1992 and 1993 sales for the Eastern and Western regions of a tour company. Using the PivotTable Wizard, this data is consolidated into a single pivot table.

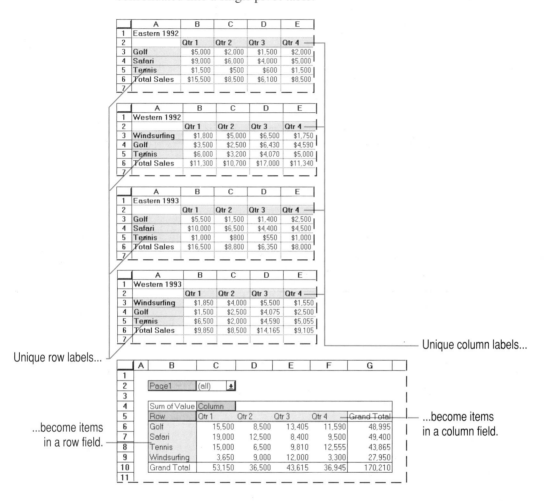

Unique row labels...

Unique column labels...

...become items in a row field.

...become items in a column field.

Notice that Microsoft Excel combines the data using the original row and column labels as a guide. For example, the Golf excursion total for Qtr 1 in cell C6 of the pivot table is the sum of all the Golf excursion totals for Qtr 1 in all the source worksheet ranges.

To create a pivot table from multiple worksheet ranges, choose the PivotTable command from the Data menu, then select the Multiple Consolidation Ranges option button in Step 1. In Step 2 of the PivotTable Wizard, choose how you want to create the page fields.

- If you select the Create A Single Page Field For Me option button, Microsoft Excel creates a page field that enables you to display one page for each source range or one page that consolidates all ranges from the source data.

- If you select the I Will Create the Page Fields option button, you can use the PivotTable Wizard to assign ranges to item names in up to four page fields.

To create your own page fields, see "Creating Your Own Page Fields" later in this section.

Specifying the Location of Worksheet Ranges in the PivotTable Wizard

Follow the instructions in the PivotTable Wizard for specifying the location of the source ranges. In general, you should include only the row labels, column labels, and data.

	A	B	C	D	E
1	Eastern 1992				
2		Qtr 1	Qtr 2	Qtr 3	Qtr 4
3	Golf	$5,000	$2,000	$1,500	$2,000
4	Safari	$9,000	$6,000	$4,000	$5,000
5	Tennis	$1,500	$500	$600	$1,500
6	Total Sales	$15,500	$8,500	$6,100	$8,500
7					

Select only the row labels, column labels, and data when specifying a range.

Tip If you are going to include grand totals in your pivot table, do not include any total rows or columns from your source data when specifying the source worksheet ranges.

Naming Fields and Items in the Finished Pivot Table

When you create a pivot table using multiple consolidation ranges, Microsoft Excel creates temporary row and column field names (Row, Column, and so on). You can rename them by selecting the field in the finished pivot table and typing a new name. For more information, see "Formatting and Editing a Pivot Table" in Chapter 25.

Creating Your Own Page Fields

To create page fields other than the one Microsoft Excel creates for you, create your own items and assign ranges to them in the PivotTable Wizard. For example, to display only 1992 data or only 1993 data, and not both, you can create a page field that contains the items 1992 and 1993.

When assigned to the item 1992 in a page field, these two ranges...

...are combined in this page of the pivot table.

When assigned to the item 1993 in a page field, these two ranges...

...are combined in this page of the pivot table.

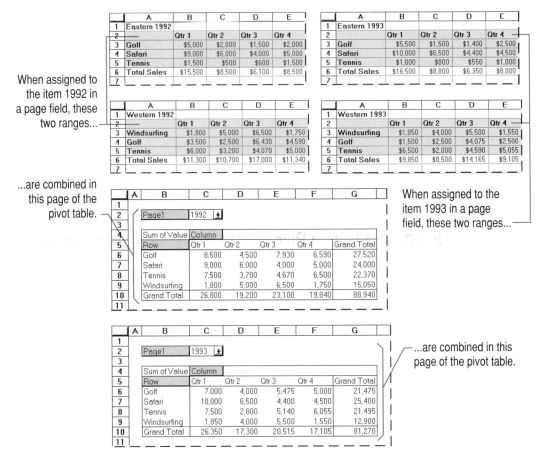

You create your own page fields by selecting the I Will Create The Page Fields option button in Step 2. For information about assigning ranges to page fields and items, choose the Help button in the PivotTable Wizard dialog box.

Step By Step

For step-by-step instructions and related information, double-click the 「?」 button to display the Search dialog box in Help, and then:

Type this keyword and choose Show Topics	Select a topic and choose Go To
pivot tables, changing information	Changing the name of a pivot table field
	Changing the name of a pivot table item
pivot tables, creating	Creating a pivot table
pivot tables, deleting	Deleting a pivot table

Using Data from an Existing Pivot Table

You can create a pivot table using source data in an existing pivot table. This is especially useful if you created a pivot table using external data, and you do not want to create the query again.

Using Data from a Pivot Table in the Same Workbook

When you create a pivot table, a copy of the source data is stored as hidden data with the pivot table on the worksheet. The PivotTable Wizard makes it easy to create another pivot table using the same source data.

Choose the PivotTable command from the Data menu, then select the Another Pivot Table option button in Step 1 of the PivotTable Wizard. Select a pivot table from the list of pivot tables in the current workbook. Then follow the instructions in the PivotTable Wizard.

Caution   When you use the data from an existing pivot table in the same workbook, the pivot tables are linked to the same hidden data set. If you clear the Save Data With Table Layout check box in the PivotTable Wizard for either table, the hidden data usually stored with the pivot tables is deleted for both of them when you close the worksheet. When you refresh one pivot table, the other pivot table is refreshed as well.

Using Data from a Pivot Table in Another Workbook

If the pivot table whose data you want to use is in another workbook, use the Copy and Paste commands on the Edit menu or shortcut menu to copy the first pivot table to the workbook where you want the new pivot table to appear. You can then customize the new copy of the pivot table as much as you want. Pivot tables in different workbooks do not share the same hidden data set, so they can be refreshed separately.

For information about copying ranges from one workbook to another, see "Copying and Moving Cells" in Chapter 11.

Converting a Microsoft Excel Version 4.0 Crosstab Table to a Pivot Table

You can convert a Microsoft Excel version 4.0 crosstab table to a pivot table. Open the Microsoft Excel version 4.0 worksheet that contains the crosstab table you want to convert. Choose the PivotTable command from the Data menu. This displays Step 3 of the PivotTable Wizard, which you use to create a layout. Follow the instructions in the PivotTable Wizard.

Caution This procedure permanently converts the crosstab table to a Microsoft Excel version 5.0 pivot table. If you want to use the crosstab table again in Microsoft Excel version 4.0, make sure you convert only a copy.

Step By Step

For step-by-step instructions and related information, double-click the ![help] button to display the Search dialog box in Help, and then:

Type this keyword and choose Show Topics	Select a topic and choose Go To
crosstab tables	Converting a Microsoft Excel version 4.0 crosstab table to a pivot table
pivot tables, creating	Creating a pivot table
pivot tables, deleting	Deleting a pivot table

Updating a Pivot Table

Refresh Data

If you change data in the source list or table, you can update, or *refresh,* the pivot table without recreating it. Most changes you make to the source data can be quickly displayed in the pivot table using the Refresh Data command on the Data menu or shortcut menu, or by clicking the Refresh Data button on the Query And Pivot toolbar. These include:

- Changes to data in a data field in the source list or table.
- Fields or items deleted from the source list or table.
- New or changed items in existing rows or fields in the source list or table.

New fields do not appear in the pivot table, but are available if you display Step 3 of the PivotTable Wizard.

Caution   Any formatting applied using the Cells command on the Format menu is removed when you use the Refresh Data command or button. If you refresh the pivot table often, use only formats you can apply with the AutoFormat command from the Format menu or the Number button in the PivotTable Field dialog box. For more information, see "Formatting and Editing a Pivot Table" in Chapter 25.

Refreshing a Pivot Table Created from Microsoft Excel Source Data

When you refresh a pivot table created from a Microsoft Excel list, database, or consolidation ranges, Microsoft Excel examines only those cells in the ranges specified in Step 2 of the PivotTable Wizard. If you insert additional rows or columns in the source list or range, you might have to change this reference if you want these changes reflected in the pivot table.

Select a cell in the pivot table, then choose the PivotTable command from the Data Menu, or click the PivotTable button on the Query And Pivot toolbar. Choose the Back button to display the Step 2 dialog box of the PivotTable Wizard. If you created the pivot table using the Microsoft Excel List or Database option, change the range reference in the Range box to include the new rows and columns, or select the range on the worksheet. If you created the pivot table using the Multiple Consolidation Ranges option, change the range references in the All Ranges box.

When you choose the Finish button, Microsoft Excel recreates the pivot table, including any new fields, items, or data.

Tip   If you often insert additional rows or columns in your list and want these changes reflected in the pivot table, name the range containing the list or data before you create the pivot table. For more information about naming a range, see "Names Make References Easier to Use" in Chapter 10.

Refreshing a Pivot Table Created with Microsoft Query

When you refresh data in a pivot table created with external data, Microsoft Excel queries the data source again using the criteria you specified in Microsoft Query when you created the pivot table. For information about changing this query, see "Using External Data to Create a Pivot Table" earlier in this chapter.

Taking a Snapshot of Data in a Pivot Table

If you use a pivot table as a report that you do not plan to change, you can prevent it from being refreshed. Copy the pivot table using the Copy command from the Edit menu or shortcut menu. Then paste the pivot table to a new location by choosing the Paste Special command from the Edit menu, then selecting the Values option button.

Note This creates a copy of the pivot table values only. You cannot use this copy as a real pivot table.

Step By Step

For step-by-step instructions and related information, double-click the ⬛? button to display the Search dialog box in Help, and then:

Type this keyword and choose Show Topics	Select a topic and choose Go To
changing, source data	Changing source data for a pivot table
naming	Naming a cell, range, or formula
pivot tables, updating data in	Updating data in a pivot table
pivot tables, editing queries	Editing a query for a pivot table

Creating a Chart from a Pivot Table

You can create a chart that displays the multiple levels of categories in the pivot table. When you hide and show detail in the pivot table, or when you move fields, these changes are automatically reflected in the chart.

For best results, follow these guidelines when creating a chart from a pivot table:

- The pivot table should have no more than two row fields and two column fields.
- Delete grand totals and subtotals from the pivot table before charting. For more information, see "Working with Totals in a Pivot Table" in Chapter 25.
- You cannot chart page field items as series or categories. You can chart individual pages of a pivot table.

ChartWizard

To create a chart from a pivot table, select the pivot table and choose the ChartWizard button. Then click the worksheet or drag the pointer to anchor the chart. This starts the ChartWizard, which you use to select a chart type and assign pivot table items to categories and series. Microsoft Excel uses item labels as category and series names.

Items in the outermost field become highest-level categories.

Items in the column field become series names.

Items in the inner field become lower-level categories.

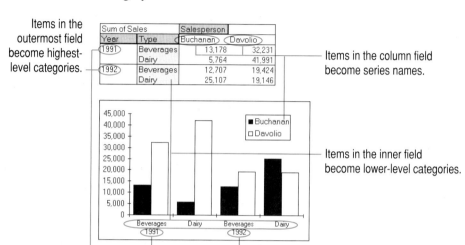

Microsoft Excel automatically assigns the pivot table dimension (row or column dimension) with the largest number of fields to the category (x) axis in the chart. You can change which items are assigned to categories or series by changing the orientation of the data series in Step 4 of the ChartWizard. You can also change the orientation of the row and column fields in the pivot table itself. For example, in the following pivot table, the Salesperson and Type fields are switched to change the data series and category names.

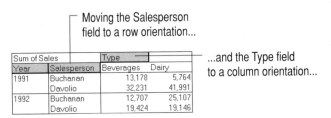

Moving the Salesperson field to a row orientation...

...and the Type field to a column orientation...

Sum of Sales		Type	
Year	Salesperson	Beverages	Dairy
1991	Buchanan	13,178	5,764
	Davolio	32,231	41,991
1992	Buchanan	12,707	25,107
	Davolio	19,424	19,146

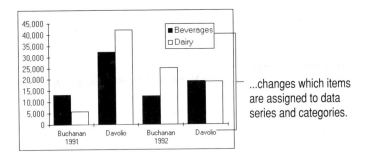

...changes which items are assigned to data series and categories.

A chart created from a pivot table changes when you hide items, hide and show detail, or when you rearrange fields. For more information about changing the orientation of row and column fields, or about hiding and showing detail, see Chapter 25, "Customizing a Pivot Table."

Tip   If the resulting category names are hard to read, try changing the alignment of the text using the Alignment tab in the Format Axis dialog box. To display the Format Axis dialog box, switch to the chart, select the category (x) axis, and choose the Selected Axis command from the Format menu. You can also change the font size of the text using the Font tab in the Format Axis dialog box.

For more information about creating a chart, see Chapter 15, "Creating a Chart." For more information about using the ChartWizard to create multilevel charts, see "Displaying Multilevel Categories and Series in a Chart" in Chapter 19.

Creating a Chart from a Pivot Table with Page Fields

To create a chart from a pivot table that contains page fields, select only the main body of the pivot table before choosing the ChartWizard button.

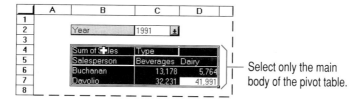

Select only the main body of the pivot table.

As you display each item in the page field, the chart adjusts to display the new data.

Tip   Place the embedded chart near the page field of the pivot table so you can see the chart as you display each page.

Show Pages

To save and print charts for all page fields in a pivot table, copy pages to separate worksheets using the Show Pages button on the Query And Pivot toolbar, then chart them individually. For more information about creating separate worksheets for pages, see "Changing Your View of the Data Using Page Fields" in Chapter 25.

Step By Step

For step-by-step instructions and related information, double-click the [?] button to display the Search dialog box in Help, and then:

Type this keyword and choose Show Topics	Select a topic and choose Go To
charts, creating	Creating a chart
	Creating a chart from a pivot table
	Creating a chart from visible worksheet data
grand totals	Hiding and displaying grand totals in a pivot table
pages, pivot table	Displaying pivot table pages on separate worksheets
removing, subtotals	Removing subtotals for a row or column field

C H A P T E R   2 5

Customizing a Pivot Table

For command, keyboard, and toolbar button information, see online Help.

In This Chapter

Note   This chapter documents the options and tools you use to customize an existing pivot table. If you have not yet created a pivot table, see Chapter 24, "Creating a Pivot Table."

How You Can Customize a Pivot Table

Creating a pivot table is only the first step to making it work for you. You can easily customize a pivot table by changing the portion of the source data it displays. You can also choose how a pivot table is organized, formatted, and calculated by using the Query And Pivot toolbar, the pivot table shortcut menu, and other advanced features.

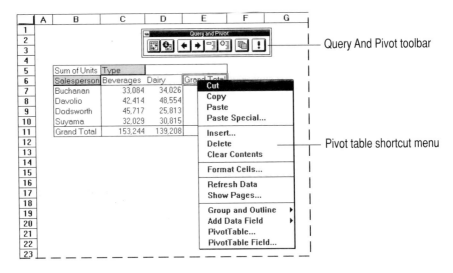

Query And Pivot toolbar

Pivot table shortcut menu

The Query And Pivot toolbar is displayed automatically when you create a pivot table.

To display the pivot table shortcut menu in Microsoft Excel for Windows, click the right mouse button with the pointer inside the pivot table. In Microsoft Excel for the Macintosh, hold down OPTION+COMMAND while you click the mouse button. You can also use the mouse to move fields and items.

You can also perform most pivot table tasks using the PivotTable and PivotTable Field commands on the Data menu.

Adding and Removing Data in a Pivot Table

You can quickly change what portion of the source data appears in a pivot table by adding or removing whole fields or items. To review how fields and items are used in a pivot table, see "How a Pivot Table Works" in Chapter 24.

Note Because a pivot table maintains a link to the source data, you cannot directly edit the data area of a pivot table. To convert a pivot table to a worksheet range that you can edit, copy the pivot table using the Copy command on the Edit menu. Then paste it into a new location using the Paste Special command on the Edit menu. Select the Values option button in the Paste Special dialog box.

Adding a Row, Column, or Page Field

PivotTable

To add detail to existing data in a pivot table, add a row or column field. To display smaller subsets of data, use page fields. To add a row, column, or page field, select a cell in the pivot table, and then click the PivotTable button on the Query And Pivot toolbar. Then add the fields you want using the PivotTable Wizard.

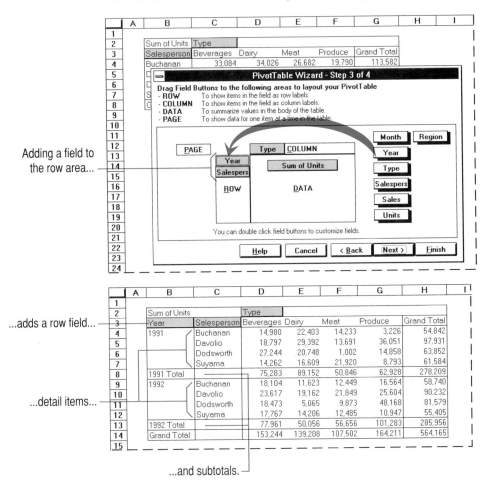

Adding a field to the row area...

...adds a row field...

...detail items...

...and subtotals.

Tip You can also add a detail row or column field by double-clicking an item in the innermost row or column field. Then select from the list the field you want to add. For more information, see "Hiding and Showing Detail in a Pivot Table" later in this chapter.

Removing a Row, Column, or Page Field

Select the row, column or page field you want to remove. Drag it outside the pivot area.

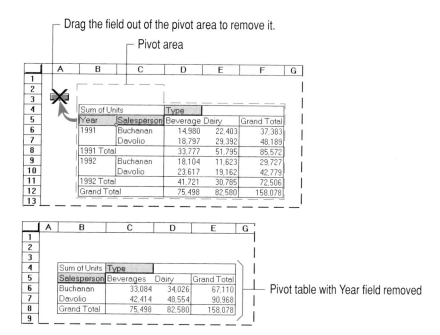

Drag the field out of the pivot area to remove it.

Pivot area

Sum of Units		Type			
Year	Salesperson	Beverage	Dairy		Grand Total
1991	Buchanan	14,980	22,403		37,383
	Davolio	18,797	29,392		48,189
1991 Total		33,777	51,795		85,572
1992	Buchanan	18,104	11,623		29,727
	Davolio	23,617	19,162		42,779
1992 Total		41,721	30,785		72,506
Grand Total		75,498	82,580		158,078

Sum of Units	Type		
Salesperson	Beverages	Dairy	Grand Total
Buchanan	33,084	34,026	67,110
Davolio	42,414	48,554	90,968
Grand Total	75,498	82,580	158,078

Pivot table with Year field removed

Including an Additional Data Field

You can summarize more than one data field from the source list or table in a pivot table. For example, if a source list or table has two numeric fields, such as Units and Sales, you can display summary data for both of them. Select a cell in the pivot table, and then click the PivotTable button on the Query And Pivot toolbar. Then drag the additional data field into the pivot area in Step 3 of the PivotTable Wizard.

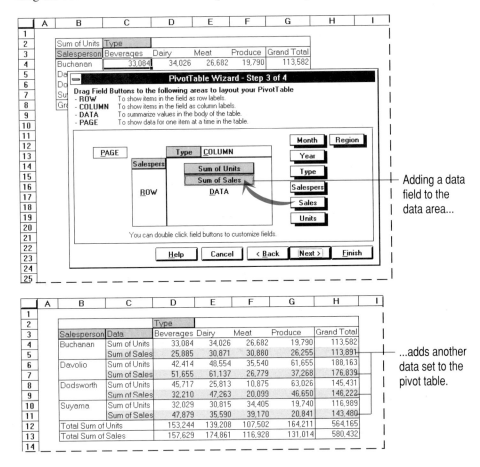

Adding a data field to the data area...

...adds another data set to the pivot table.

You can choose a different *summary function,* such as Sum or Average, for each data field. For more information, see "Changing How Pivot Table Data Is Calculated" later in this chapter.

Displaying the Same Data Field More Than Once If you want to summarize a single data field in more than one way, you can include it more than once in the same pivot table. Then you can change its summary function using the PivotTable Field button on the Query And Pivot toolbar. For example, to show both Sum of Units and Average of Units in an existing pivot table, select any cell in the pivot table and click the PivotTable button on the Query And Pivot toolbar. Then drag the Units field twice into the pivot area in Step 3 of the PivotTable Wizard. Now you can change the summary function to Average for one of the Units fields. For more information about changing the summary function of a data field, see "Changing How Pivot Table Data Is Calculated" later in this chapter.

Removing a Data Field

A pivot table must have at least one data field. To remove a data field from a pivot table that has more than one, select any cell in the pivot table. Then click the PivotTable button on the Query And Pivot toolbar. When the Step 3 dialog box of the PivotTable Wizard appears, drag the data field out of the pivot area.

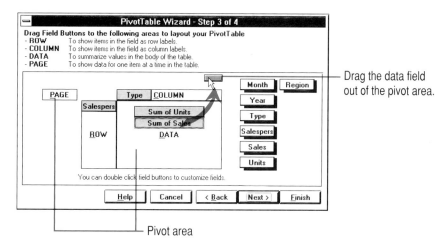

Drag the data field out of the pivot area.

Pivot area

Hiding a Row, Column, or Page Item

PivotTable Field

To remove data from a single row or column in a pivot table, hide the associated item. Double-click the field containing the item you want to hide, or click the PivotTable Field button on the Query And Pivot toolbar. In the Hide Items box in the PivotTable Field dialog box, select the items you want to hide.

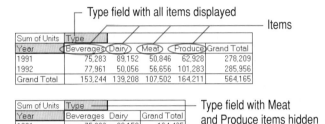

Displaying a Hidden Row, Column, or Page Item

To redisplay a hidden item, clear the item in the Hide Items box in the PivotTable Field dialog box.

Step By Step

For step-by-step instructions and related information, double-click the k? button to display the Search dialog box in Help, and then:

Type this keyword and choose Show Topics	Select a topic and choose Go To
fields, removing	Removing a data field from a pivot table
hiding, items, pivot table field	Hiding or displaying items in a pivot table field
pivot table fields	Adding a field to a pivot table
pivot tables, creating	Creating a pivot table
removing, page fields, from pivot tables	Removing a row, column, or page field from a pivot table

Changing the Layout of a Pivot Table

You can quickly change how data is organized in a pivot table by using the mouse to drag fields from one place to another. You can also move items within a field.

Moving a Field

Move a field by dragging it with the mouse. Move a field from a row to a column orientation, or vice versa, when you want to change how detail data is displayed in the data area.

When you move a field, you move all its associated items. The pointer changes to show the orientation the field and the items will have—row, column, or page—when you release the mouse button.

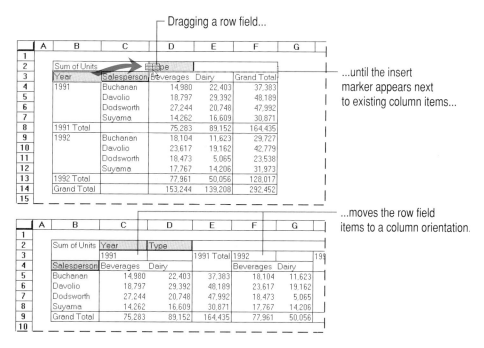

┌ Dragging a row field...

...until the insert marker appears next to existing column items...

...moves the row field items to a column orientation.

Moving a row or column field to a page orientation enables you to see the data for each item in a field separately.

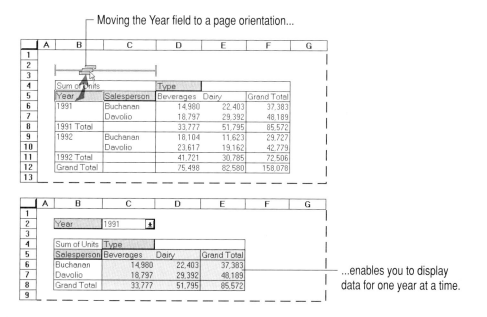

┌ Moving the Year field to a page orientation...

...enables you to display data for one year at a time.

You can also move a field using the PivotTable Wizard, or the PivotTable Field command on the Data menu or the shortcut menu.

Moving an Item

Move items when you want to change which items in a field appear next to each other.

┌ Select the item and move the pointer until it changes to an arrow.

Sum of Units	Type				
Year	Beverages	Dairy	Meat	Produce	Grand Total
1991	75,283	89,152	50,846	62,928	278,209
1992	77,961	50,056	56,656	101,283	285,956
Grand Total	153,244	139,208	107,502	164,211	564,165

┌ Then drag the selection border to the location where you want the item to appear.

Sum of Units	Type				
Year	Beverages	Dairy	Meat	Produce	Grand Total
1991	75,283	89,152	50,846	62,928	278,209
1992	77,961	50,056	56,656	101,283	285,956
Grand Total	153,244	139,208	107,502	164,211	564,165

Note   You can move an item only within the same field.

You can also move items in a field by sorting. For more information, see "Sorting Items in a Pivot Table Field" later in this chapter.

Changing the Orientation of Data in a Pivot Table with Multiple Data Fields

If a pivot table has more than one data field, such as Sales and Units, the data field label changes from a flat heading to a button labeled Data. You can change how the data is displayed by dragging the data field button from one orientation to another.

Data field button in a row orientation

Year	Data	Type		Grand Total
		Beverages	Dairy	
1991	Sum of Units	75,283	89,152	164,435
	Sum of Sales	89,301	108,350	197,651
1992	Sum of Units	77,961	50,056	128,017
	Sum of Sales	68,328	66,511	134,839
Total Sum of Units		153,244	139,208	292,452
Total Sum of Sales		157,629	174,861	332,490

Data field button in a column orientation

	Data	Type	Sum of Sales		Total Sum of Units	Total Sum of Sales
		Sum of Units				
Year	Beverages	Dairy	Beverages	Dairy		
1991	75,283	89,152	89,301	108,350	164,435	197,651
1992	77,961	50,056	68,328	66,511	128,017	134,839
Grand Total	153,244	139,208	157,629	174,861	292,452	332,490

Note   You cannot move a data field button to a page orientation.

Step By Step

For step-by-step instructions and related information, double-click the 🗚? button to display the Search dialog box in Help, and then:

Type this keyword and choose Show Topics	Select a topic and choose Go To
fields, moving	Moving a pivot table field
items in pivot tables, moving	Moving a pivot table item
items in pivot tables, sorting by labels	Sorting pivot table items by labels
items in pivot tables, sorting by values	Sorting pivot table items by values in the data area

Changing Your View of the Data Using Page Fields

Page fields *filter* data in a pivot table. Unlike items in row and column fields, the items and associated data for a page field are displayed one at a time on the worksheet.

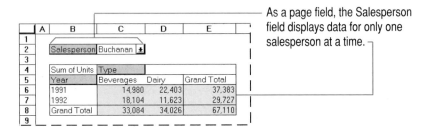

As a page field, the Salesperson field displays data for only one salesperson at a time.

For information about adding page fields, see "Adding and Removing Data in a Pivot Table" earlier in this chapter. For information about moving a row or column field to a page orientation, see "Changing the Layout of a Pivot Table" earlier in this chapter.

Displaying Pages

To display an item in a page field, click the arrow next to the page field. Then select from the list the item you want to display.

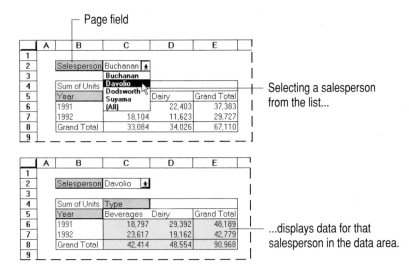

Page field

Selecting a salesperson from the list...

...displays data for that salesperson in the data area.

Showing Combined Data for All Items in a Page Field

You can combine data from all items in a page field by selecting the All item from the list.

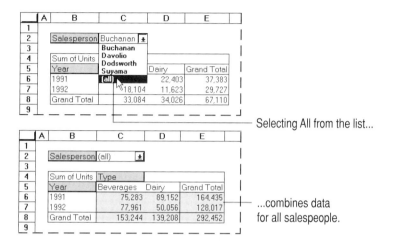

Selecting All from the list...

...combines data for all salespeople.

Note   Choosing the All item combines data for all available items in a page field—even hidden items. For more information about hiding and displaying items, see "Adding and Removing Data in a Pivot Table" earlier in this chapter.

Using More Than One Page Field

The more page fields you have, the more filtered the data is on a page. For example, a pivot table with the single page field Salesperson shows total sales for only one salesperson at a time. Adding the page field Region filters the data even more by displaying total sales data only for the selected region for the selected salesperson.

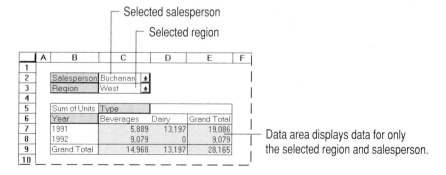

Selected salesperson

Selected region

Data area displays data for only the selected region and salesperson.

For information about adding page fields, see "Adding and Removing Data in a Pivot Table" earlier in this chapter.

Displaying Pages on Separate Worksheets

To print all pages in a pivot table or store them as separate reports, you can copy them to separate worksheets in the same workbook.

Show Pages

Select a cell in the pivot table, and then click the Show Pages button on the Query And Pivot toolbar. Microsoft Excel displays a dialog box so you can select the page field whose items you want displayed.

You can also use the Show Pages command on the shortcut menu.

Tip To print all pages at once, select the tabs for all the worksheets created when you chose the Show Pages button. From the File menu, choose the Print command. In the Print dialog box, select the Selected Sheets option button under Print. Choose the OK button. Microsoft Excel prints each page field worksheet on a separate piece of paper.

Step By Step

For step-by-step instructions and related information, double-click the ⟦?⟧ button to display the Search dialog box in Help, and then:

Type this keyword and choose Show Topics	Select a topic and choose Go To
page fields	Showing combined data for all items in a page field
pages, pivot table	Displaying pivot table pages on separate worksheets
pivot tables, displaying information	Displaying pages in a pivot table
pivot tables fields	Adding a field to a pivot table

Working with Totals in a Pivot Table

Unless you specify otherwise, Microsoft Excel automatically adds subtotal and grand total lines to a pivot table.

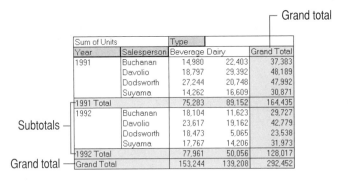

Grand totals provide total values for all cells in the rows and columns of a pivot table. *Subtotals* provide total values for outer items when the pivot table contains more than one row field or column field. You can add and remove grand totals and subtotals.

Values in a grand total row or column are calculated using the same summary function used in the data area of the pivot table. Microsoft Excel creates grand totals by calculating values directly from the source data, excluding data only for hidden items. Grand totals do not use subtotal values. This is important to note when you are using a summary function other than Sum, such as Average.

As with grand totals, subtotals are calculated from values in the source data. Unlike grand totals, however, you can choose different summary functions to calculate subtotal values.

You can display the records or rows used to calculate a value for a grand total or subtotal. For more information, see "Hiding and Showing Detail in a Pivot Table" later in this chapter.

Hiding and Displaying Grand Totals

Grand totals are included when you create a pivot table if you select the grand totals check boxes in Step 4 of the PivotTable Wizard.

Sum of Units	Type				
Year	Beverages	Dairy	Meat	Produce	Grand Total
1991	14,980	22,403	14,233	3,226	54,842
1992	18,104	11,623	12,449	16,564	58,740
Grand Total	33,084	34,026	26,682	19,790	113,582

Grand total for each row

Grand total for each column ⌐   ⌐ Grand total for all data

To display or hide grand totals in a pivot table, click the PivotTable button on the Query And Pivot toolbar, and then choose the Next button to display Step 4 of the PivotTable Wizard. Select or clear one or both of the grand total check boxes.

Grand Totals for Pivot Tables with Multiple Data Fields   When a pivot table has more than one data field, Microsoft Excel provides one grand total row or column for each data field. Each of the grand total rows or columns uses the summary function used for the associated data field.

When you include more than one data field in your pivot table...

Year	Data	Type		Grand Total
		Beverage	Dairy	
1991	Sum of Sales	89,301	108,350	197,651
	Sum of Units	75,283	89,152	164,435
1992	Sum of Sales	68,328	66,511	134,839
	Sum of Units	77,961	50,056	128,017
Total Sum of Sales		157,629	174,861	332,490
Total Sum of Units		153,244	139,208	292,452

....grand totals are displayed for each data field.

You cannot add or remove grand totals for only one data field. For more information about adding multiple data fields, see "Adding and Removing Data in a Pivot Table" earlier in this chapter.

Hiding and Displaying Subtotals for Row or Column Fields

When you include more than one row or column field in a pivot table, subtotals are added automatically to all row and column fields except the innermost ones.

Year field

Sum of Units		Type		
Year	Salesperson	Beverage	Dairy	Grand Total
1991	Buchanan	14,980	22,403	37,383
	Davolio	18,797	29,392	48,189
	Dodsworth	27,244	20,748	47,992
	Suyama	14,262	16,609	30,871
1991 Total		75,283	89,152	164,435
1992	Buchanan	18,104	11,623	29,727
	Davolio	23,617	19,162	42,779
	Dodsworth	18,473	5,065	23,538
	Suyama	17,767	14,206	31,973
1992 Total		77,961	50,056	128,017
Grand Total		153,244	139,208	292,452

Subtotals for the Year field

Type field

Sum of Units	Type		Beverages Total	Dairy		Dairy Total	Grand Total
	Beverages			Dairy			
Salesperson	1991	1992		1991	1992		
Buchanan	14,980	18,104	33,084	22,403	11,623	34,026	67,110
Davolio	18,797	23,617	42,414	29,392	19,162	48,554	90,968
Dodsworth	27,244	18,473	45,717	20,748	5,065	25,813	71,530
Suyama	14,262	17,767	32,029	16,609	14,206	30,815	62,844
Grand Total	75,283	77,961	153,244	89,152	50,056	139,208	292,452

Subtotals for the Type field

To remove subtotals, double-click the field containing the subtotaled items. Under Subtotals, select the None option button. You can also use the PivotTable Field command on the Data menu or the shortcut menu.

To restore subtotals, select the Automatic option button under Subtotals. To use another summary function, select the Custom option button. Then select the functions you want to use.

You can also use the PivotTable Field button on the Query And Pivot toolbar.

PivotTable Field

Displaying Subtotals for the Innermost Row or Column Field To display subtotals for the innermost row or column field, create *block totals*. A block total is a series of total rows or columns added above the row grand totals or to the left of the column grand totals.

Innermost row field

Sum of Sales		Type		
Year	Salesperson	Dairy	Meat	Grand Total
1991	Buchanan	5,764	16,847	22,611
	Davolio	41,991	9,680	51,671
	Dodsworth	32,050	1,433	33,483
	Suyama	28,545	24,805	53,350
1991 Total		108,350	52,765	161,115
1992	Buchanan	25,107	14,033	39,140
	Davolio	19,146	17,099	36,245
	Dodsworth	15,213	18,666	33,879
	Suyama	7,045	14,365	21,410
1992 Total		66,511	64,163	130,674
	Buchanan Sum	30,871	30,880	61,751
	Davolio Sum	61,137	26,779	87,916
	Dodsworth Sum	47,263	20,099	67,362
	Suyama Sum	35,590	39,170	74,760
Grand Total		174,861	116,928	291,789

Block totals for the innermost row field

Double-click the field to which you want to add subtotals. Under Subtotals, select the Custom option button. Then select the summary functions you want to use.

You can also use the PivotTable Field button on the Query And Pivot toolbar.

Note   You can only add block totals for the innermost column or row field.

Changing the Summary Function for a Subtotal

Microsoft Excel automatically calculates the values in subtotal rows and columns using the same function you chose for the associated data field. If the data field contains numeric items, the default summary function is Sum. The default summary function is Count if the data field contains text items.

To subtotal data another way—or if you want two types of subtotals, such as Sum and Average—double-click the field to display the PivotTable Field dialog box. Under Subtotals, select the Custom option button. Then select one or more of the subtotal functions. Microsoft Excel adds one subtotal line for each type you select.

Subtotals using the Sum function total the data.

Sum of Units		Type		
Year	Salesperson	Beverages	Dairy	Grand Total
1991	Buchanan	14,980	22,403	37,383
	Davolio	18,797	29,392	48,189
	Dodsworth	27,244	20,748	47,992
	Suyama	14,262	16,609	30,871
1991 Sum		75,283	89,152	164,435
1991 Average		4,182	4,692	4,444
1992	Buchanan	18,104	11,623	29,727
	Davolio	23,617	19,162	42,779
	Dodsworth	18,473	5,065	23,538
	Suyama	17,767	14,206	31,973
1992 Sum		77,961	50,056	128,017
1992 Average		5,569	3,850	4,741
Grand Total		153,244	139,208	292,452

Subtotals using the Average function display the average value of data.

For a description of the available subtotal functions, choose the Help button in the PivotTable Field dialog box.

Step By Step

For step-by-step instructions and related information, double-click the [?] button to display the Search dialog box in Help, and then:

Type this keyword and choose Show Topics	Select a topic and choose Go To
pivot tables, changing information	Changing the summary function for a subtotal
pivot tables, displaying information	Hiding and displaying grand totals in a pivot table
	Displaying subtotals for row or column fields in a pivot table
subtotals, removing	Removing subtotals for a row or column field

Formatting and Editing a Pivot Table

A pivot table can be recalculated and reorganized frequently without losing its link to the source list or table. Because of this, Microsoft Excel provides special editing and formatting tools that enable you to keep the basic appearance of text and numbers in a pivot table while you reorganize and recalculate the data it contains.

PivotTable Field

- Using the AutoFormat command on the Format menu, you can format an entire pivot table.
- Using the PivotTable Field button or command, you can change the number formatting in the data area.
- You can rename fields and items and still maintain links to the original labels in the source data.

Note If you do need to change the data in the data area of a pivot table, you can copy the data using the Copy command on the Edit menu or the shortcut menu. Then paste it in another location using the Paste Special command on the Edit menu, with the Values option button selected. This converts the pivot table to a worksheet range you can edit. Links to original data are not maintained, because the new range is no longer a pivot table.

Formatting a Pivot Table

Because data is recalculated and reformatted when you reorganize or update a pivot table, you should avoid manually formatting individual cells or ranges. Instead, use the AutoFormat command on the Format menu.

If you select the AutoFormat Table check box in the PivotTable Wizard when you create the pivot table, it is formatted for you. To apply a different autoformat, select a cell in the pivot table, and then choose a format using the AutoFormat command.

	A	B	C	D	E	F	
1							
2		Sum of Units		Type			
3		Year	Salesperson	Beverages	Dairy	Grand Total	
4		1991	Buchanan	14,980	22,403	37,383	
5			Davolio	18,797	29,392	48,189	
6			Dodsworth	27,244	20,748	47,992	
7			Suyama	14,262	16,609	30,871	
8		1991 Sum		75,283	89,152	164,435	
9		1992	Buchanan	18,104	11,623	29,727	
10			Davolio	23,617	19,162	42,779	
11			Dodsworth	18,473	5,065	23,538	
12			Suyama	17,767	14,206	31,973	
13		1992 Sum		77,961	50,056	128,017	
14		Grand Total		153,244	139,208	292,452	
15							

A pivot table with the autoformat Classic 1 applied

Note   Autoformats do not format page fields.

For more information about using autoformats, see "Applying Formats Automatically" in Chapter 12.

Changing the Number Format for the Data Area

When you create a pivot table, Microsoft Excel formats the data area using the number format included in the Normal style for the worksheet. To change the number formatting of the data area, use the Number button in the PivotTable Field dialog box. For example, you can apply a currency format.

Sum of Sales	Type		
Salesperson	Beverages	Dairy	Grand Total
Buchanan	$25,885	$30,871	$56,756
Davolio	$51,655	$61,137	$112,792
Dodsworth	$32,210	$47,263	$79,473
Suyama	$47,879	$35,590	$83,469
Grand Total	$157,629	$174,861	$332,490

Data area with a currency number format applied

PivotTable Field

To display the PivotTable Field dialog box, select a cell in the data area, and then click the PivotTable Field button on the Query And Pivot toolbar.

A number format applied with the Number button is retained when you refresh or reorganize the pivot table.

Changing the Name of a Pivot Table Field or Item

Pivot table field and item names are derived from the source list or table. When you rename them in the pivot table, the new names are retained even when you refresh the pivot table.

To change the name of a field or item, select the cell containing the field or item name, and then type the new name.

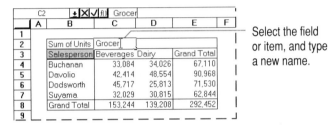

Select the field or item, and type a new name.

You can also use the Name edit box in the PivotTable Field dialog box to change the name of a pivot table field or item. Choose the PivotTable Field command on the Data menu or the shortcut menu.

You cannot change a field name to the same name as another field in the pivot table, even when that other field is not displayed. You cannot change an item name to the same name as another item in the field. If you type a name that exists, Microsoft Excel inserts the item with that name in the cell where you typed the name.

Note If you rename an item in a pivot table, then later rename the same item in the source data, Microsoft Excel does not retain the current name in the pivot table when you update it. If you change the name of the a source field, the pivot table field with the original or customized name is removed when you update the pivot table. You can add the field again using the PivotTable command on the Data menu or the shortcut menu.

Step By Step

For step-by-step instructions and related information, double-click the [k?] button to display the Search dialog box in Help, and then:

Type this keyword and choose Show Topics	Select a topic and choose Go To
pivot tables, changing information	Changing the name of a pivot table field
pivot tables, changing names	Changing the name of a pivot table item
pivot tables, formatting	Formatting a pivot table

Changing How Pivot Table Data Is Calculated

Each cell in the data range of a pivot table contains a value that summarizes data from the source list or table. The default function Microsoft Excel uses to calculate the value for each cell is Sum if the field contains numeric data, and Count if the field contains text.

For more information about how data is summarized, see "How a Pivot Table Works" in Chapter 24.

Changing the Summary Function for a Data Field

Change the summary function when you want Microsoft Excel to return a summary value other than a sum total or count, such as the average of a set of data, or a maximum or minimum value. For example, to display the highest monthly total for Beverage units for each salesperson in 1991 and 1992 in the following pivot table, you use the Max function.

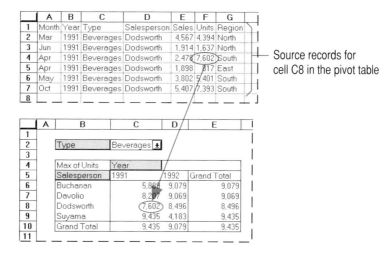

Source records for cell C8 in the pivot table

With the Max function applied, each cell in the data area displays the highest value in the source data for that cell. For example, cell C8 in the pivot table displays 7,602, the highest value for 1991 Beverage unit sales for salesperson Dodsworth.

For each cell in the data area of this pivot table, Microsoft Excel uses the Max function to examine the specified data field in the source data (in this case, the Units field) and returns the item with the highest value.

If a pivot table contains more than one data field, or if you included the same field more than once, you can use a different summary function for each field.

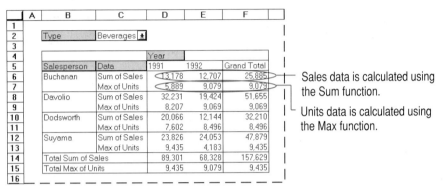

Sales data is calculated using the Sum function.

Units data is calculated using the Max function.

PivotTable Field

To change a summary function, select a cell in the data area, and then click the PivotTable Field button on the Query And Pivot toolbar. Then select a summary function under Summarize By. For a description of the available summary functions, choose the Help button in the PivotTable Field dialog box.

Tip To view the source data that is used to calculate the value of a particular cell in the data area of a pivot table, double-click the cell. For more information, see "Hiding and Showing Detail in a Pivot Table" later in this chapter.

Changing the Calculation Type for a Data Field

Microsoft Excel can calculate the values of cells in the data area based on the values of other cells in the data area. This is called a *custom calculation*. For example, each cell in the data area of the following pivot table is displayed as a percentage of its row.

Sum of Units	Type				
Region	Beverages	Dairy	Meat	Produce	Grand Total
East	24.24%	23.96%	23.74%	28.06%	100.00%
North	30.43%	30.64%	8.83%	30.11%	100.00%
South	26.71%	11.57%	34.26%	27.47%	100.00%
West	27.54%	35.89%	5.21%	31.35%	100.00%
Grand Total	27.16%	24.68%	19.06%	29.11%	100.00%

A pivot table with the % Of Row calculation type applied

To change the calculation type for a data field, select a cell in the data area for that field. Click the PivotTable Field button on the Query And Pivot toolbar, and then choose the Options button. Under Show Data As, select the calculation you want, and then select the fields and items you want to use, if they are required for the calculation. In the preceding example, no field or item is specified because none is required for the % Of Row calculation type.

You can also use the PivotTable Field command on the Data menu or the shortcut menu.

Calculation Types   The following table lists the calculation types you can use in a pivot table.

This calculation type	Has this result in a pivot table
Difference From	Displays all the data in the data area as the difference from a field and item you specify.
% Of	Displays all the data in the data area as a percentage of a field and item you specify.
% Difference From	Displays all the data in the data area using the same method as the Difference From calculation type, but displays the difference as a percentage of the base data.
Running Total In	Displays the data for successive items as a running total. You must select the field whose items will be shown in a running total.
% of Row	Displays the data in each row as a percentage of the row's total.
% of Column	Displays all the data in each column as a percentage of the column's total.
% of Total	Displays the data in the data area as a percentage of the grand total of all the data in the pivot table.
Index	Displays the data using the following algorithm: $[(value\_in\_cell) \text{ x } (Grand\ Total)] \div [(Grand\_Row\_Total) \text{ x } (Grand\_Column\_Total)]$

Step By Step

For step-by-step instructions and related information, double-click the 🔼? button to display the Search dialog box in Help, and then:

Type this keyword and choose Show Topics	Select a topic and choose Go To
pivot tables, changing information	Changing the summary function for a pivot table data field
	Changing the calculation type for a pivot table data field

Hiding and Showing Detail in a Pivot Table

If a pivot table has more than one row or column field or contains grouped items, you can hide detail items to display summary data.

For more information about grouping items in fields, see "Grouping Items in a Pivot Table Field" later in this chapter.

Hiding Detail Rows or Columns

Double-click the item whose detail you want hidden.

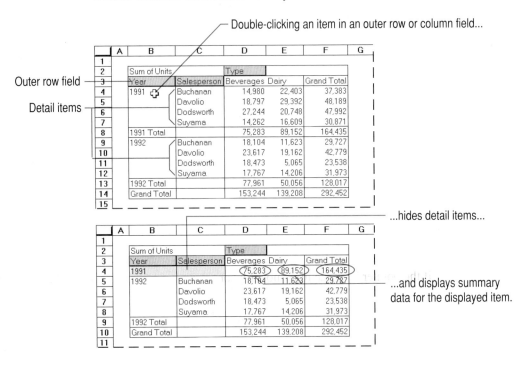

Double-clicking an item in an outer row or column field...

Outer row field

Detail items

...hides detail items...

...and displays summary data for the displayed item.

Note If you select the cell before double-clicking, Microsoft Excel enables cell editing instead of hiding detail rows or columns. To be sure that double-clicking always hides detail rows or columns, clear the Edit Directly In Cell check box under Settings on the Edit tab in the Options dialog box. To display the Options dialog box, choose Options from the Tools menu.

Hide Detail

You can also choose the Group And Outline command from the Data menu or the shortcut menu, and then choose Hide Detail, or, you can click the Hide Detail button on the Query And Pivot toolbar.

Showing Detail Rows or Columns

Double-click the summary item.

Double-clicking the summary item redisplays detail items.

	A	B	C	D	E	F	G
1							
2		Sum of Units		Type			
3		Year	Salesperson	Beverages	Dairy	Grand Total	
4		1991		75,283	89,152	164,435	
5		1992	Buchanan	18,104	11,623	29,727	
6			Davolio	23,617	19,162	42,779	
7			Dodsworth	18,473	5,065	23,538	
8			Suyama	17,767	14,206	31,973	
9		1992 Total		77,961	50,056	128,017	
10		Grand Total		153,244	139,208	292,452	
11							

Show Detail

You can also choose the Group And Outline command from the Data menu or the shortcut menu, and then choose Show Detail, or, you can click the Show Detail button on the Query And Pivot toolbar.

Showing Detail for the Innermost Row or Column

If the pointer is on the innermost row or column when you double-click, Microsoft Excel enables you to add a row or column field. Select the field you want to add from the displayed list. If the field you select is already displayed in another part of the pivot table, Microsoft Excel moves the field to the new position.

Hiding and Showing Detail for All Items in a Field

To hide details for all items in a field, select the field and click the Hide Detail button on the Query And Pivot toolbar or choose the Hide Detail command from the Data menu, Outline submenu.

To display hidden detail for all items in a field, select the field and click the Show Detail button on the Query And Pivot toolbar, or choose the Show Detail command from the Data menu, Outline submenu.

Displaying the Source Data for a Cell in the Data Area

To display a list of the source rows or records used to calculate the value of a cell in the data area, double-click the cell. The list is displayed on a new worksheet.

	A	B	C	D	E	F	G
1							
2		Sum of Units		Type			
3		Year	Salesperson	Beverages	Dairy	Grand Total	
4		1991	Buchanan	14,980	22,403	37,383	
5			Davolio	18,797	29,392	48,189	
6			Dodsworth	27,244	20,748	47,992	
7			Suyama	14,262	16,609	30,871	
8		1991 Total		75,283	89,152	164,435	
9		1992	Buchanan	18,104	11,623	29,727	
10			Davolio	23,617	19,162	42,779	
11			Dodsworth	18,473	5,065	23,538	
12			Suyama	17,767	14,206	31,973	
13		1992 Total		77,961	50,056	128,017	
14		Grand Total		153,244	139,208	292,452	
15							

Double-clicking a cell in the data area...

	A	B	C	D	E	F	G
1	Month	Year	Type	Salesperson	Sales	Units	Region
2	Feb	1991	Beverages	Buchanan	4,953	5,889	West
3	Jul	1991	Beverages	Buchanan	1,132	3,326	East
4	Aug	1991	Beverages	Buchanan	3,522	587	North
5	Feb	1991	Beverages	Buchanan	3,571	5,178	South
6							

...displays a copy of the source data used to calculate the cell.

You can also choose the Group And Outline command from the Data menu or the shortcut menu, and then choose Show Detail, or, you can click the Show Detail button on the Query And Pivot toolbar.

Note The displayed list is only a copy of the source records or rows. No changes you make to this list are reflected in the pivot table or the source list or table.

Step By Step

For step-by-step instructions and related information, double-click the ⟨?⟩ button to display the Search dialog box in Help, and then:

Type this keyword and choose Show Topics	Select a topic and choose Go To
items in a pivot table, grouping, described	Grouping selected items in a pivot table field
items in pivot tables, showing detail	Hiding and showing detail for items in a pivot table
pivot tables, source data	Displaying source data for a cell in the data area of a pivot table

Grouping Items in a Pivot Table Field

To summarize data using higher level categories than those provided by the source data, you can *group* items within pivot table fields. For example, if you are analyzing sales data for 15 salespeople from four regional offices, and the regional office information is not provided in your source records, you can group salespeople by regional office so that their data is summarized together.

There are three ways to group items, depending on the types of items in a pivot table. You can:

- Group selected items into categories you choose.
- Automatically group numeric items, such as inventory or transaction numbers, into ranges.
- Automatically group dates and times into larger time units, such as days, months, quarters, or years.

You can also create groups within groups. For example, you can group dates into months, and then group months into quarters.

Grouping Selected Items

Group

Select the items you want to group and then click the Group button on the Query And Pivot toolbar. You can move the *group field* you create, just as you can move any other field.

Selecting the items you want to group...

...and choosing the Group button...

...adds a group field...

...and a group item to the pivot table.

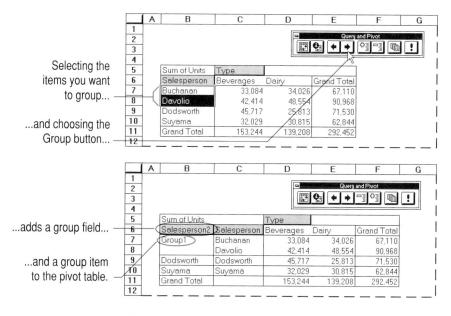

Then choose the next items you want to group.

When you finish grouping items, you can name the items in the group. You can also name the group field.

You can rename the group field...

...and group items.

	Sum of Units		Type		
	Teams	Salesperson	Beverage	Dairy	Grand Total
Team 1	Buchanan		33,084	34,026	67,110
	Davolio		42,414	48,554	90,968
Team 2	Dodsworth		45,717	25,813	71,530
	Suyama		32,029	30,815	62,844
Grand Total			153,244	139,208	292,452

For more information about changing the name of a field or item, see "Formatting and Editing a Pivot Table" earlier in this chapter.

To hide detail and display summary data for the group field, double-click the group item.

Group items, with detail items hidden.

	Sum of Units		Type		
	Teams	Salesperson	Beverage	Dairy	Grand Total
Team 1			75,498	82,580	158,078
Team 2			77,746	56,628	134,374
Grand Total			153,244	139,208	292,452

To remove all the detail items at once, drag the detail field out of the pivot table.

Dragging the original field out of the pivot table...

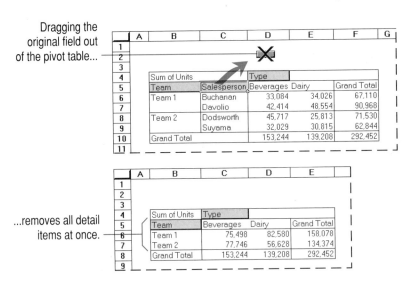

	Sum of Units		Type		
	Team	Salesperson	Beverages	Dairy	Grand Total
Team 1	Buchanan		33,084	34,026	67,110
	Davolio		42,414	48,554	90,968
Team 2	Dodsworth		45,717	25,813	71,530
	Suyama		32,029	30,815	62,844
Grand Total			153,244	139,208	292,452

...removes all detail items at once.

	Sum of Units	Type		
	Team	Beverages	Dairy	Grand Total
Team 1		75,498	82,580	158,078
Team 2		77,746	56,628	134,374
Grand Total		153,244	139,208	292,452

To restore detail fields removed in this way, use the PivotTable command on the Data menu or the shortcut menu.

Ungroup

Ungrouping Items To ungroup a single group, select the group item, and then click the Ungroup button on the Query And Pivot toolbar.

Selecting the
Team 1 item...

...and choosing the
Ungroup button...

...ungroups and
removes the
Team 1 item.

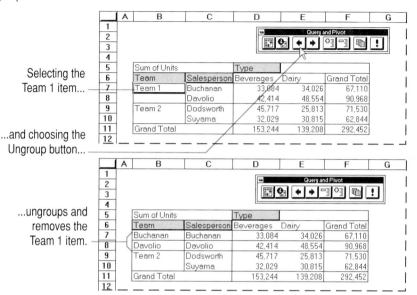

To ungroup all grouped items in a row or column field, select all the grouped items. Then click the Ungroup button on the Query And Pivot toolbar.

You can also choose the Outline command from the Data menu or the shortcut menu, and then choose the Ungroup command.

Grouping Numeric Items into Ranges

You can automatically group numeric items into ranges. For example, you can group a range of product numbers in series of 100s, so that data for all 100-series products is combined, 200-series data is combined, and so on.

	A	B	C	D	E	F	G	H
1								
2		Sum of Units	Region					
3		ProductID	East	North	South	West	Grand Total	
4		101	14,919	7,346	3,951	6,020	32,236	
5		102	7,895	2,820	10,540	7,380	28,635	
6		103	6,727	5,764	7,335	13,312	33,138	
7		104	12,730	3,195	7,340	8,414	31,679	
8		105	8,815	2,277	8,315	12,186	31,593	
9		201	6,606	13,794	1,481	3,913	25,794	
10		202	6,944	6,571	6,236	2,664	22,415	
11		203	6,083	4,512	8,478	2,249	21,322	
12		204	3,587	10,829	4,327	6,033	24,776	
13		205	3,587	5,281	3,324	13,077	25,269	
14		301	1,537	5,864	13,895	4,093	25,389	
15		302	338	12,169	13,710	3,337	29,554	
16		303	9,681	3,450	10,867	341	24,339	
17		304	8,737	4,243	5,400	3,511	21,891	
18		305	6,833	5,152	8,930	4,536	25,451	
19		Grand Total	105,019	93,267	114,129	91,066	403,481	
20								

Numeric items...

	A	B	C	D	E	F	G	H
1								
2		Sum of Units	Region					
3		ProductID	East	North	South	West	Grand Total	
4		100-200	51,086	21,402	37,481	47,312	157,281	
5		200-300	26,807	40,987	23,846	27,936	119,576	
6		300-400	27,126	30,878	52,802	15,818	126,624	
7		Grand Total	105,019	93,267	114,129	91,066	403,481	
8								

...can be grouped into ranges.

Group

Select a single item, and then click the Group button on the Query And Pivot toolbar. Microsoft Excel displays a dialog box that enables you to choose the numbers you want to group and the size of the resulting ranges. You can also choose the Group And Outline command from the Data menu or the shortcut menu, and then choose the Group command.

Ungrouping Numeric Items   To ungroup all grouped items in a numeric row or column field, select the group field. Then click the Ungroup button on the Query And Pivot toolbar.

Select the group field...

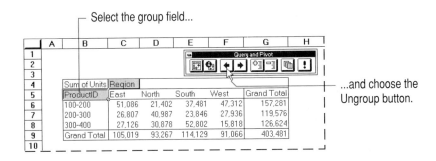

...and choose the Ungroup button.

You can also choose the Outline command from the Data menu or the shortcut menu. Then choose the Ungroup command.

Note   You cannot ungroup a single group in a numeric field. All groups are automatically ungrouped when you click the Ungroup button.

Grouping Dates and Times into Ranges

You can easily group dates—such as 1-Jan, 4/2/92, and so on—into days, months, quarters, or years. For example, the items in the Date field are grouped by month in the following pivot table.

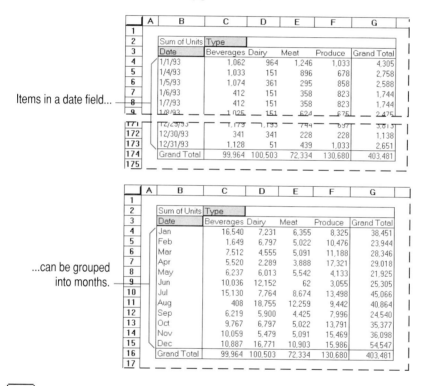

Items in a date field...

...can be grouped into months.

Group

To group dates automatically, select one of the dates, and then click the Group button on the Query And Pivot toolbar. Microsoft Excel displays a dialog box that enables you to select the time period—days, months, quarters, or years—by which you want to group dates. You can also group times—such as 12:33 P.M.—into days, hours, minutes, or seconds.

Note   The dates and times you want to group must be in a date or time format recognized by Microsoft Excel. For a list of valid date and time formats, see "Number Format Codes" in Chapter 12.

Ungrouping Items in a Date Field   To ungroup dates or times, select the group field, and then click the Ungroup button on the Query And Pivot toolbar.

Note You cannot ungroup a single group in a date or time field. All groups are automatically ungrouped when you click the Ungroup button.

Grouping Items in a Page Field

You cannot group items in page fields directly with the Group command. To group page items, move the page field to a row or column orientation, group the items, and then move the group field back to a page orientation.

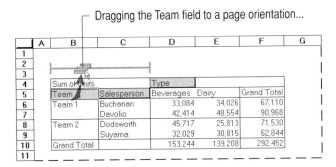

For information about moving fields, see "Changing the Layout of a Pivot Table" earlier in this chapter.

Step By Step

For step-by-step instructions and related information, double-click the ⟨⁇⟩ button to display the Search dialog box in Help, and then:

Type this keyword and choose Show Topics	Select a topic and choose Go To
items in a pivot table	Grouping selected items in a pivot table
pivot tables, grouping information	Grouping numeric items into ranges in a pivot table

Type this keyword and choose Show Topics	Select a topic and choose Go To
items in pivot tables, ungrouping	Ungrouping text items in a pivot table
	Ungrouping numeric items in a pivot table
	Ungrouping date items in a pivot table
page fields	Grouping items in a page field

Sorting Items in a Pivot Table Field

Sorting a pivot table is a quick way to see the rank of items in a row or column field based on values in the data area of the pivot table. You can also sort items by their labels, or you can choose a custom sort order.

When you sort, choose:

- What you want to sort (items in columns or items in rows).
- A sort order—ascending or descending.
- A sort key, which is the item you want to sort by if you are sorting by values.

Microsoft Excel bases its sort on the field you choose. If you select a row field or an item in a row field, Microsoft Excel sorts all items in the selected row field. If you select a column field or an item in a column field, Microsoft Excel sorts all items in the selected column field.

You can change the sort key, sort order, and sort orientation as needed using the Sort command on the Data menu.

Note You cannot sort items in page fields.

You can also rearrange items by dragging them. For more information, see "Changing the Layout of a Pivot Table" earlier in this chapter.

Sorting Items by Labels

When you add a field to a pivot table, its items are automatically sorted for you according to their labels. If you later move or sort the items, you can reset them in their original order by resorting them by their labels.

Sort Ascending

Select the field containing the items you want to sort, and then click the Sort Ascending or Sort Descending button. The following example uses the Sort Ascending button to reorder the Salespeople field alphabetically, by name.

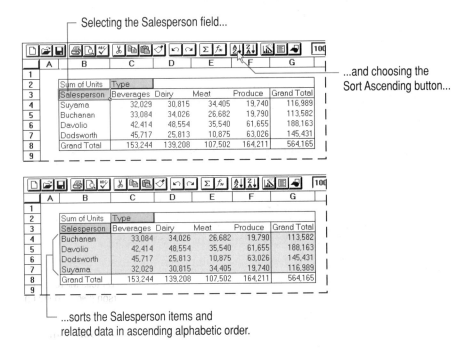

Selecting the Salesperson field...

...and choosing the Sort Ascending button...

...sorts the Salesperson items and related data in ascending alphabetic order.

You can also use the Sort command on the Data menu. If you use the Sort command, make sure the Labels option button in the Sort dialog box is selected.

Note If you hide items before sorting, and then display them again using the PivotTable Field command, they are added as the last items in the field.

Sorting Items by Values in the Data Area

You can order items in a row or column field by a value in the data area. For example, salespeople in the following pivot table are sorted by Dairy sales.

Salespeople...

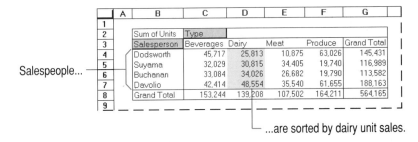

...are sorted by dairy unit sales.

To sort by value, select the field containing the items you want to sort, and then choose the Sort command from the Data menu. In the Sort By box, select a cell in the data area for the item you want to sort by. The Values option button under Sort is selected for you.

Salesperson is the row field containing the items to be sorted.

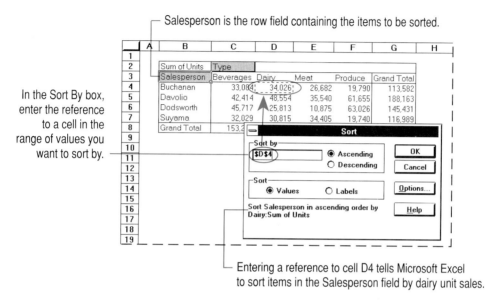

In the Sort By box, enter the reference to a cell in the range of values you want to sort by.

Entering a reference to cell D4 tells Microsoft Excel to sort items in the Salesperson field by dairy unit sales.

If you select a column field before choosing the Sort command, items are sorted left to right. For example, the following pivot table shows grocery types sorted by grand total from left to right.

Items in the Type field...

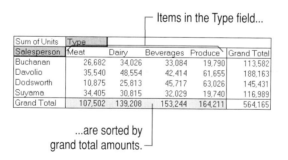

...are sorted by grand total amounts.

Sorting Items in Inner Row or Column Fields   When you sort items in an inner row or column field, the sort order is applied to each group of items. For example, if you sort the Salespeople field by 1991 dairy sales, the order of salespeople in 1992 is changed as well.

The order of salespeople that results from sorting by 1991 dairy unit sales...

...is also applied to the salespeople under the 1992 item.

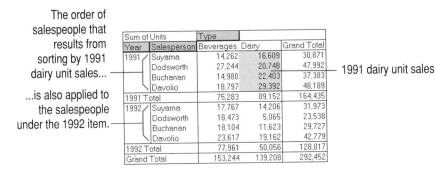

1991 dairy unit sales

Using a Custom Sort Order

When you create a pivot table that contains items—such as Jan, Feb, Mar—that are typically ordered chronologically rather than alphanumerically, Microsoft Excel automatically sorts them in the expected order using a *custom sort order*. If you sort or move items into another order, you must choose this custom sort order to return the items to their original order.

To apply a custom sort order, select a field. Choose the Sort command from the Data menu, and then choose the Options button. Select a sort order under First Key Sort Order.

Creating Your Own Custom Sort Order   To create your own custom sort order, such as Low, Medium, High, use the Custom Lists tab in the Options dialog box. To display the Options dialog box, choose the Options command from the Tools menu. For more information, see "Sorting Data in a List" in Chapter 21.

Step By Step

For step-by-step instructions and related information, double-click the [k?] button to display the Search dialog box in Help, and then:

Type this keyword and choose Show Topics	Select a topic and choose Go To
items in pivot tables, sorting by labels	Sorting pivot table items by labels
items in pivot tables, sorting by values	Sorting pivot table items by values in the data area
pivot tables, sorting	Using a custom sort order in a pivot table

C H A P T E R   2 6

Consolidating Data

For command,
keyboard, and
toolbar button
information, see
online Help.

In This Chapter

Summarizing Data Using Consolidation

When you need to abstract the salient points of one or more big worksheets, using the Consolidate command can be the best method. You can summarize large amounts of data from separate locations on one worksheet.

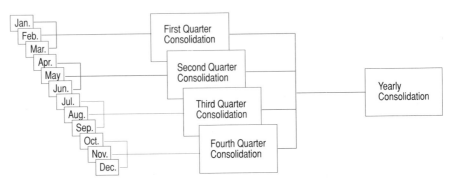

For example, consolidate data from worksheets containing monthly reports into quarterly reports. Then further consolidate the quarterly reports into a yearly report.

Source data can exist in separate workbooks, together in the same workbook, or on the same sheet. You can even consolidate data from Lotus 1-2-3 worksheets. You can include any combination of these sources in a single consolidation.

You can define only one consolidation table at a time on one worksheet. To perform a different consolidation, you must select a different destination area and specify a different set of source areas.

To consolidate data, you specify:

- **A destination area**   The range that will hold the consolidated information
- **Source areas**   The ranges from which you want to consolidate information

Once you specify these ranges, perform the initial consolidation, and save the worksheet, you can easily perform another consolidation later. Microsoft Excel retains the source and destination information you supplied.

Most worksheets contain one or more *categories* of data. For example, each of the four quarterly reports shown above has data categorized by month. Each of the three monthly categories in each quarterly consolidation is identified by a *label*—a row or column heading. You can choose whether to consolidate data according to its categories or according to its relative position on the source worksheets.

Consolidating by Position

Consolidate data by position when similar categories of data—such as the four divisions in the quarterly reports shown below—occupy identical relative positions in each source area. In general, consolidate data by position from a series of identical worksheets, such as worksheets created from the same template.

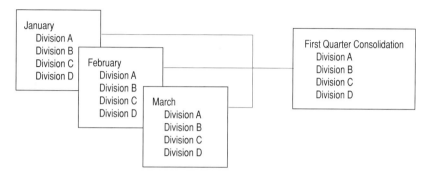

When you consolidate by position, category labels—such as the row headings on the three monthly reports—are ignored, and data from the same position in each of the source areas is consolidated.

Tip You can also use 3-D references to create dynamic consolidations using source areas identically positioned on separate sheets in the same workbook. For more information, see "References Make Formulas More Powerful" in Chapter 10.

Keep the following in mind when you select the destination area for data you want consolidated by position:

- Category labels are not copied to the destination area, even if they are selected in the source areas. When consolidating by position, do not include labels in either the source or destination areas. You can type labels above and to the left of the selected destination area if you want row or column headings.

- All source areas and the destination area must be arranged identically, with identical absolute locations on each worksheet.

Tip If you select a group of sheets in a workbook, you can enter identical text, formulas, and formatting for all selected sheets at once to ensure consistency in your consolidation model. For more information, see "Selecting Sheets in a Workbook" in Chapter 8.

Consolidating by Category

Consolidate data by category when source areas contain:

- Similar data in different relative locations
- Differing numbers of rows or columns of data in each category

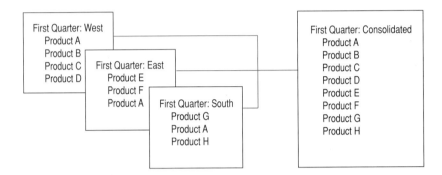

Consolidate by category when you want to collect similar data from source areas that are laid out differently.

Microsoft Excel uses the labels in the source areas to determine the categories, and can actually copy the labels as row or column headings to the destination area during the consolidation. For example, in the preceding illustration, Microsoft Excel consolidates all the ranges labeled "Product A," no matter where they appear in the source areas. For this reason, the labels for similar data must be identical in each source area.

Tip   You can also use pivot tables to create dynamic category-based consolidations. For more information, see "Consolidating Data from Multiple Ranges for a Pivot Table" in Chapter 24.

Linking Consolidated Data

When you consolidate, you can create links so that your destination area is automatically updated if your source data changes. You can accomplish a similar objective by using conventional formulas on a summary worksheet using references to source data. But using either linked or unlinked consolidation offers advantages over conventional linking formulas, particularly if the source data is in several workbooks.

- Using unlinked consolidation, you can collect data from disparate sources without the overhead of actual physical links between workbooks.

- Using unlinked consolidation, you can choose to update your summary information manually at a specific time.

- Using either linked or unlinked consolidation, you can set up your worksheets faster and more easily than when manually typing linking formulas.

You cannot create links to the source data when the source areas are on the same worksheet as the destination area.

Working with Consolidation

About the Destination Area

Before you choose the Consolidate command from the Data menu, select the destination area where you want your consolidation table to appear, using the following guidelines.

Destination area selected	Result
Single cell	Microsoft Excel expands the destination area down and to the right to accommodate all the categories from the source areas.
Range of cells in a single row	Microsoft Excel expands the destination area down to accommodate all the row categories from the source areas, but consolidates only as many column categories as there are columns in your selection.
Range of cells in a single column	Microsoft Excel expands the destination area to the right to accommodate all the column categories from the source areas, but consolidates only as many row categories as there are rows in your selection.
Range of cells including multiple rows and columns	Microsoft Excel consolidates only as many categories as will fit in the range you selected.

Formatting the Destination Area   To format the cells in the destination area, Microsoft Excel uses the number formats in the first source area listed in the All References box in the Consolidate dialog box. Number formats already in the destination area are replaced. Microsoft Excel does not replace other formats in the destination area.

Using Wildcard Characters in Source Area Category Labels When consolidating by category, you use labels in the destination area to control which categories are consolidated. You can use the asterisk (*) and question mark (?) as wildcard characters in the labels you type in the destination area. For example, categories labeled Sales1 and Sales2 are consolidated into a category labeled Sales* in the destination area.

Defining the Consolidation

Specify the details of your consolidation table by choosing the Consolidate command from the Data menu. The Consolidate dialog box appears.

Choosing a Function to Apply to the Consolidation From the Function list box in the Consolidate dialog box, select one of 11 worksheet functions you want Microsoft Excel to apply to your consolidation.

Sum	Min	Var
Count	Product	Varp
Average	StDev	Count Nums
Max	StDevp	

The Sum function is the default. The Count function counts cells that contain any alphanumeric entry, and corresponds to the COUNTA worksheet function. The Count Nums function counts only those cells containing numbers, and corresponds to the COUNT worksheet function. For more information about these functions, click the Function Wizard button on the Standard toolbar or see online Help.

Specifying Source Areas In the Reference text box, type or select each source area. When you choose the Add button, the source area reference is added to the All References list.

- You can specify up to 255 source areas for one consolidation table.

- The workbooks containing the source areas do not have to be open during consolidation.

- Cells that contain text in the source area are treated as blank cells (except for category labels, if you're consolidating by category).

- If you include cells that contain formulas in a source area, Microsoft Excel consolidates only the resulting values and ignores the formulas.

Tip While the Consolidate dialog box is open, you can activate worksheets within a workbook, activate open workbooks by choosing their names from the Window menu, and select cells and ranges directly on a worksheet. When the Reference box is selected and you drag across a cell range, the range reference automatically appears in the Reference box.

Using Named Ranges in the Source Reference   Naming the source areas before consolidating data can ensure that the correct ranges are consolidated, even if you add or delete rows or columns or move the source areas. For more information about naming, see "Names Make References Easier to Use" in Chapter 10.

Using Wildcard Characters in the Source Reference   You can use the asterisk (*) and question mark (?) as wildcard characters in the filename part of the source reference. For example, you can create a group of sales workbooks whose labels all start with Sales, such as Sales1, Sales2, and so on. The first sheet in each workbook contains a summary area named Results. You can consolidate from the same range in all the workbooks in the group by specifying the source area.

System	Type the source area reference
Windows	SALES*.XLS!Results
Macintosh	SALES*!Results

Microsoft Excel displays a message if the source reference is not a valid name or if it cannot find a reference during consolidation.

Note   Using this method, the first sheet in a workbook must contain the source area you want to consolidate.

Referencing a Source Area on a Closed Sheet   If a source area is on a worksheet that is not open, you can use the Browse button in the Consolidate dialog box to enter in the Reference box the path and filename of the worksheet containing the source area. In the Browse dialog box, locate the worksheet and choose the OK button.

If the file you choose in the Browse dialog box is a Microsoft Excel workbook file or a Lotus WK3 file, you can include the sheet name using the following syntax.

System	Syntax
Windows	'C:\EXCEL\[BOOK1.XLS]SHEET1'!A1:C2
Macintosh	'DISK1:EXCEL:[WORKBOOK1]SHEET1'!A1:C2
Lotus WK3 (Windows only)	'C:\LOTUS\[FILE0001.WK3]A'!A1:C2

If you do not include the sheet name in a reference to a Microsoft Excel workbook file or a Lotus WK3 file, Microsoft Excel uses the specified range on the first sheet in the file.

Consolidating Data by Category   Consolidate data by category by selecting either or both of the Use Labels In check boxes in the Consolidate dialog box.

- If you typed category labels in the destination worksheet, include the labels in the destination area selection.

- The category labels in the destination area must match the labels in the source areas exactly. The labels can be inserted in any order in the destination area; Microsoft Excel consolidates the correct values for each corresponding category.

- If you do not include category labels in the destination area selection, Microsoft Excel copies them in the order in which they appear in the source areas.

When selecting the source ranges for your consolidation, be sure to include the category labels you want to use.

Creating Links to Source Data   To link the destination area to the source areas permanently, select the Create Links To Source Data check box before choosing the OK button.

Caution If the worksheet containing your consolidation table also contains an outline, or has been used previously for a linked consolidation, do not create a new linked consolidation without first removing the existing outline and consolidation linking formulas. Microsoft Excel inserts rows or columns in your consolidation table to hold the linking formulas for the consolidated cells, and then it outlines the destination area to hide the linking formulas. Be sure that the rows or columns added to your destination area do not disrupt other parts of your worksheet. You cannot use the Undo command on a consolidation in which you create links. For more information about outlining, see Chapter 33, "Outlining a Worksheet."

To check the consolidation before creating the links, perform an unlinked consolidation first. Then perform the linked consolidation.

Performing the Consolidation

When you choose the OK button in the Consolidate dialog box, Microsoft Excel consolidates the data from the source areas and displays it in the destination area.

You can reverse an unlinked consolidation by choosing the Undo command from the Edit menu immediately after you consolidate. You cannot use the Undo command to reverse a linked consolidation, so be sure to save the workbook first.

Repeating the Consolidation Once you define a set of consolidation source areas, the source references are saved with the worksheet. The next time you open the workbook and switch to the consolidation worksheet, simply choose the Consolidate command and choose the OK button to update the consolidation table.

Troubleshooting Consolidation

If consolidation did not produce the results you expected, be sure that:

- You selected the appropriate function in the Consolidate dialog box.

- You specified a destination area large enough to hold the consolidated data.

- If you are consolidating by position, each source area contains the same number of elements in the same order.

If you are consolidating by category, also be sure that:

- You selected the Top Row, Left Column, or both check boxes in the Consolidate dialog box.

- You included the row or column labels in your source areas and also in your destination areas, if necessary.

- You spelled category labels identically in all source areas.

- Source areas have unique labels for categories you don't want consolidated together, such as "total" labels.

Step By Step

For step-by-step instructions and related information, double-click the ⬚ button to display the Search dialog box in Help, and then:

Type this keyword and choose Show Topics	Select a topic and choose Go To
creating, links	Creating links to source data
data consolidation	Consolidating data by category
	Consolidating data by position
pivot tables, creating	Creating a Pivot Table
references, external	Changing the reference to a source area
	Deleting a reference to a source area
source areas, adding, adjusting	Adding a source area to an existing consolidation

Solving Problems by Analyzing Data

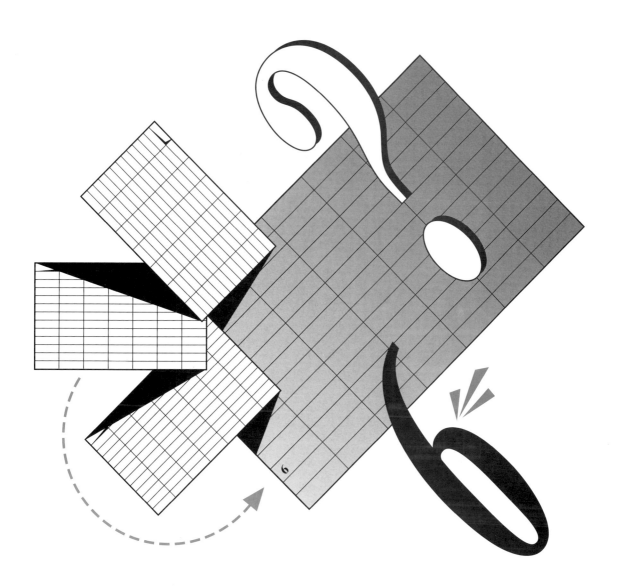

C H A P T E R   2 7

Solving What-If Problems

For command,
keyboard, and
toolbar button
information, see
online Help.

In This Chapter

Seeking a Value That Solves a Formula

Often you know the result you want a formula to return, but you don't know the input value the formula needs to reach that result. To solve such a formula, you can use goal seeking. With goal seeking, Microsoft Excel varies the value in a cell you specify until a formula that's dependent on that cell returns the result you want. Goal seeking saves you from performing time-consuming trial-and-error analysis.

When to Use Goal Seeking

To find a specific value for a particular cell by adjusting the value of only one other cell, use the Goal Seek command on the Tools menu.

To find the optimum value for a particular cell by adjusting the values of one or more cells or to apply specific limitations to one or more values involved in the calculation, use Microsoft Excel Solver. For information about Solver, see Chapter 29, "Using Solver to Analyze Multiple-Variable Problems."

Using the Goal Seek Command

To find a specific value that solves a formula, select the cell containing the formula. Then choose Goal Seek from the Tools menu.

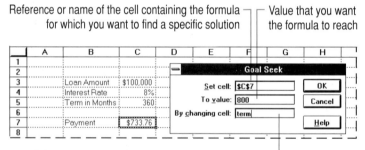

Reference or name of the cell containing the formula ┐ ┌ Value that you want
for which you want to find a specific solution   the formula to reach

Reference or name of the cell containing the variable ┘
that you want adjusted until the goal is reached

Notice that in the preceding illustration, the By Changing Cell box contains a name defined for cell C5. You can enter either cell references or names in the By Changing Cell and Set Cell boxes.

Goal-Seeking Guidelines

- You can enter either cell references or names in the Set Cell and By Changing Cell boxes. For information about names, see Chapter 10, "Creating Formulas and Links."

- A changing cell must contain a value that the formula in the Set Cell box depends on, either directly or indirectly.

- A changing cell cannot contain a formula.

- While goal seeking proceeds, the Goal Seek Status dialog box appears on the screen. To interrupt the operation, choose the Pause button.

- If you want to continue one step at a time after choosing the Pause button, choose the Step button. Choose the Continue button to resume normal operation.

- When goal seeking is complete, Microsoft Excel displays the results on the worksheet and in the Goal Seek Status dialog box. Choose the OK button to keep the solution values on the worksheet; choose the Cancel button to restore the original values.

- If you decide to keep the solution on the worksheet but then change your mind, choose Undo Goal Seek from the Edit menu immediately after goal seeking is complete.

Note You can also perform goal seeking graphically by dragging data points on a chart. For more information about graphical goal seeking, see Chapter 17, "Changing Data in a Chart."

Step By Step

For step-by-step instructions and related information, double-click the ⟦▶?⟧ button to display the Search dialog box in Help, and then:

Type this keyword and choose Show Topics	Select a topic and choose Go To
values, input	Seeking a specific solution to a formula using the Goal Seek command

Projecting Figures Using a Data Table

Once you've entered formulas on your worksheet, you can perform a "what-if" analysis using a *data table* to see how changing certain values in your formulas affects the results of the formulas. A data table is a range of cells that shows the results of substituting different values in one or more formulas. Data tables provide:

- A shortcut for calculating multiple variations in one operation.

- A way to view and compare the results of all of the different variations together on your worksheet.

There are two types of data tables.

One-Input Data Table You enter different values for one variable and see the effect on one or more formulas.

Two-Input Data Table You enter different values for two variables and see the effect on one formula.

Using a One-Input Data Table

To see how changes in one variable affect one or more formulas, use a one-input data table. The data table in the following illustration is set up so that the interest rates entered in column B—the input values—are substituted in cell D5—the input cell. The resulting monthly payments are entered in the cells below the formula in cell C11.

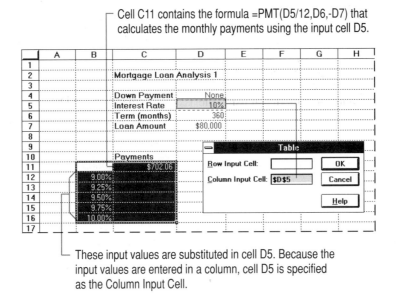

Cell C11 contains the formula =PMT(D5/12,D6,-D7) that calculates the monthly payments using the input cell D5.

These input values are substituted in cell D5. Because the input values are entered in a column, cell D5 is specified as the Column Input Cell.

First, select the rectangular range containing the formula and the input values (B11:C16). When you choose Table from the Data menu, specify cell D5 as the Column Input Cell because the input values are entered in a column. After you choose the OK button, the table looks like the following illustration.

	A	B	C	D	E
1					
2			Mortgage Loan Analysis 1		
3					
4			Down Payment	None	
5			Interest Rate	10%	
6			Term (months)	360	
7			Loan Amount	$80,000	
8					
9					
10			Payments		
11			$702.06		
12		9.00%	$643.70		
13		9.25%	$658.14		
14		9.50%	$672.68		
15		9.75%	$687.32		
16		10.00%	$702.06		

The Table command calculates these values and adds them to your worksheet.

Adding Formulas or Input Values to an Existing Data Table

You can use as many formulas and input values as you need in a one-input data table. However, each formula must directly or indirectly refer to the same input cell. To add additional formulas or input values to a data table, enter them in the blank cells below or to the right of the existing formulas or values. Then select the entire table and modify it using the Table command on the Data menu.

In the preceding illustration, for example, you can also enter a formula in cell D11 that calculates total interest paid on the loan. First, select the rectangular range containing both the formulas and the input values, as shown in the following illustration. Then specify cell D5 as the column input cell. After you choose the OK button, the new values are added to the table under cell D11.

	A	B	C	D	E
1					
2			Mortgage Loan Analysis 1		
3					
4			Down Payment	None	
5			Interest Rate	10%	
6			Term (months)	360	
7			Loan Amount	$80,000	
8					
9					
10			Payments	Total Interest	
11			$702.06	$172,740.61	
12		9.00%	$643.70		
13		9.25%	$658.14		
14		9.50%	$672.68		
15		9.75%	$687.32		
16		10.00%	$702.06		
17					

Cell D11 contains the formula =(C11*D6)-D7, which calculates total interest paid. The formula refers to cell C11, which refers to the input cell D5.

Row Input Values Versus Column Input Values

In addition to entering input values in a column, as shown in the preceding examples, you can also enter input values in a row across the top of the table and enter formulas down the side of the table. With this layout, you specify a Row Input Cell in the Table dialog box.

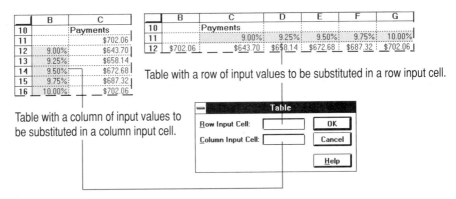

Table with a row of input values to be substituted in a row input cell.

Table with a column of input values to be substituted in a column input cell.

Using a Two-Input Data Table

To see how changes in two variables affect one formula, use a two-input data table. You can include a number of values for each of the two variables, but you can use only one formula in a two-input data table.

In the following illustration, the worksheet is set up so that interest rates entered in column A are substituted in the column input cell—D5. Loan terms entered in row 9 are substituted in the row input cell—D6.

Cell A9 contains the formula =ABS(PMT(D5/12,D6,D7)) that calculates the monthly payments using input cells D5 and D6.

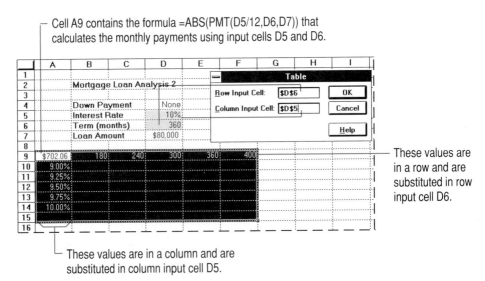

These values are in a row and are substituted in row input cell D6.

These values are in a column and are substituted in column input cell D5.

To set up a two-input data table, first enter a formula that directly or indirectly refers to two input cells. Then enter one set of input values below the formula and a second set of input values to the right of the formula. Select the entire table, choose Table from the Data menu, and then specify the row input cell and the column input cell. After you choose the OK button, the table looks like the following illustration.

	A	B	C	D	E	F
1						
2		Mortgage Loan Analysis 2				
3						
4		Down Payment		None		
5		Interest Rate		10%		
6		Term (months)		360		
7		Loan Amount		$80,000		
8						
9	$702.06	180	240	300	360	400
10	9.00%	$811.41	$719.78	$671.36	$643.70	$631.81
11	9.25%	$823.35	$732.69	$685.11	$658.14	$646.64
12	9.50%	$835.38	$745.70	$698.96	$672.68	$661.56
13	9.75%	$847.49	$758.81	$712.91	$687.32	$676.58
14	10.00%	$859.68	$772.02	$726.96	$702.06	$691.69

— The Table command calculates these values and adds them to your worksheet.

Editing a Data Table

You can edit the input values or formulas in the top row or leftmost column of a data table at any time. However, because the resulting values in a data table are an array, you cannot edit them individually. For more information about arrays, see Chapter 10, "Creating Formulas and Links." Some editing operations require you to select the entire data table; others require you to select only the resulting values. The following illustration shows the difference.

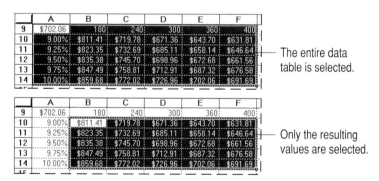

— The entire data table is selected.

— Only the resulting values are selected.

Here are some tips for editing data tables.

- To copy resulting values from a data table, select them and then choose Copy from the Edit menu. When you do this, only the values are copied, not the formulas for those values.

- To modify, move, or delete a table, first select the entire data table.

- To convert the resulting values array into a range of constant values, select the resulting values, copy them, choose Paste Special from the Edit menu, and then select the Values option button. For more information about the Paste Special command, see Chapter 11, "Editing a Worksheet."

- To clear the resulting values array from a data table, select the resulting values and then press the DEL key. You cannot clear individual values; you must clear all the values. Make sure not to select the formulas and input values, unless you want to clear the entire data table.

- To move a data table, select the entire table. Then click the border of the selection, and drag it to the new location.

Speeding Up Calculation of a Worksheet Containing a Data Table

Microsoft Excel calculates all the formulas that depend on the input cell every time it tests a new row or column input value in the cell or whenever you edit one of the formulas used to generate the data table results. Therefore, tables usually require more calculation time than do normal worksheet formulas.

To control when tables are calculated, choose Options from the Tools menu. On the Calculation tab, select the Automatic Except Tables option button. Then, whenever you want to recalculate the table, either choose the Calc Now button on the Calculation tab or press one of the following shortcut keys.

System	To recalculate a table, press
Windows	F9
Macintosh	COMMAND+=

For more information about controlling calculation, see Chapter 10, "Creating Formulas and Links."

Step By Step

For step-by-step instructions and related information, double-click the [?] button to display the Search dialog box in Help, and then:

Type this keyword and choose Show Topics	Select a topic and choose Go To
input, values	Filling in a one-input data table
	Filling in a two-input data table
tables, data, adding to	Adding a formula to an existing data table
	Adding input values to a data table

Type this keyword and choose Show Topics	**Select a topic and choose Go To**
clearing, data tables	Clearing an entire data table
clearing, values from data tables	Clearing the resulting values from a data table
values, converting	Converting resulting data table values to constant values

CHAPTER 28

Managing What-If Scenarios

For command,
keyboard, and
toolbar button
information, see
online Help.

In This Chapter

Keep Track of What-If Assumptions Using Scenarios

In Microsoft Excel, you can create and save sets of input values that produce different results as *scenarios*. A scenario is a group of input values called *changing cells* that is saved with a name you provide. Each set of changing cells represents a set of what-if assumptions that you can apply to a worksheet model to see the effects on other parts of the model. You can define up to 32 changing cells per scenario.

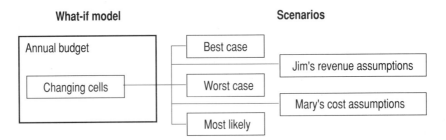

You can use the Scenario Manager to:

- Create multiple scenarios with multiple sets of changing cells.
- View the results of each scenario on your worksheet.
- Create a summary report of all input values and results.
- Merge scenarios from a group into a single scenario model.
- Protect scenarios from modification and hide scenarios.
- Keep track of modifications with an automatic scenario history.

To work with scenarios, use the Scenarios box on the Workgroup toolbar. With the Scenarios box, you can quickly define and display scenarios on a worksheet. You can also use the Scenarios command on the Tools menu, which provides additional functionality for working with scenarios.

Note You can also use a data table if you want to see the results of changing one or two variables in a worksheet formula. For information about creating and using a data table, see "Projecting Figures Using a Data Table" in Chapter 27.

What You Can Do with Scenarios

Scenarios are useful when you have a what-if model with uncertain variables. For example, you might create a budget for next year, but you're not certain what your revenue will be. Using the Scenario Manager, you can define different scenarios, switch among them to do what-if analysis, and save the scenarios with your model.

When you create a scenario, you specify the changing cells—the cells in your worksheet model that you want modified—and the values that you want used in those cells. Normally, the changing cells for a scenario are cells on which a key formula depends, but the changing cells themselves should not contain formulas. For example, cells B6 and B13 in the following figure contain key formulas that depend on cells B3 and B4, the changing cells.

	A	B
1	Budget	
2		FY 1993
3	Gross Revenue	$75,000.00
4	Cost of Goods Sold	$17,710.00
5		
6	Gross Profit	$57,290.00
7		
8	Rent	$12,000.00
9	Utilities	$1,000.00
10	General Administrative	$2,500.00
11	Expenses	$15,500.00
12		
13	Operating Income	$41,790.00
14		
15		

These cells are the primary changing cells.

Another scenario might use another set of changing cells.

When you create a scenario, you define and name a set of input values for the changing cells. For example, for the preceding worksheet, you might create the following scenarios:

- A scenario named "Best Case" that includes a Gross Revenue value of $150,000 and a Cost of Goods Sold value of $26,565.

- A scenario named "Worst Case" that includes a Gross Revenue value of $50,000 and a Cost of Goods Sold value of $13,282.

- A scenario named "Most Likely" or "Projected" that includes the Gross Revenue and Cost of Goods Sold values you started with (as shown in the figure).

After you create these scenarios, you can switch among them to see what effect they have on other aspects of your model. The larger the model, the more useful this becomes.

Tip   While you can refer to any cell containing data as an input cell for a scenario, it is helpful to create a separate input area and define names for all cells with data that varies. If you define a name for a changing cell, that name appears in the Scenario Manager dialog boxes and in reports, where appropriate. For information about defining and using names as references, see "Names Make References Easier to Use" in Chapter 10.

Scenario Manager's Automatic Change Tracking

When you create a scenario, the Scenario Manager automatically records the user name and the date the scenario was created in the Scenario Manager dialog box Comment area. In addition, if you or someone else edits the scenario, this information is also recorded, as shown in the following illustration.

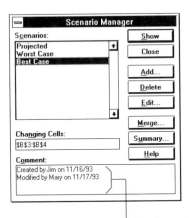

The Scenario Manager records the user name
and date each time a scenario is created or modified.

The Scenario Manager adds information to the Comment box using the current date and the user name as entered in the Options dialog box. (To edit the user name, choose Options from the Tools menu, select the General tab, and type a name in the User Name box. These changes do not take effect until you restart Microsoft Excel.) This tracking feature is especially useful if you plan to route your scenarios to other people in your group.

Merge Scenarios from Other Sheets

Each sheet in a workbook can have its own set of scenarios. Suppose you want to construct a what-if model that includes scenarios for several different parts of the model. You can distribute copies of your model to individuals who can supply data on costs, sales projections, plant and equipment expense, and so on. Then each of them can add a scenario in their specific area of expertise.

Scenario Summary Reports

You can create a report that lists the scenarios you created with their input values and *result cells*. (A result cell is any cell on your worksheet that is recalculated when you apply a new scenario.) Normally, a result cell contains a formula that refers to either the changing cells or cells that depend on the changing cells.

Microsoft Excel creates the summary report on a separate sheet in the current workbook, which you can save and print. For information about printing a sheet, see Chapter 14, "Printing."

For example, three scenarios were created for the budget worksheet discussed earlier in this section. The scenarios specify projected, best-case, and worst-case values for the changing cells named Gross_Revenue and Cost_of_Goods_Sold (cells B3 and B4 on the worksheet). The following summary report provides the input values and results for the cells named Gross_Profit and Operating_Income.

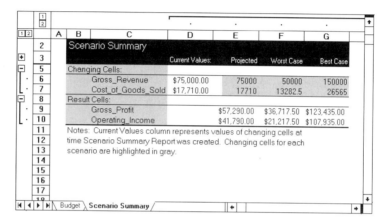

Notice that the report is automatically outlined and formatted for you. Also notice that in columns E, F, and G, the cells containing the changing cell values are shaded. This indicates that these values are included in the scenario. For example, if the "Projected" scenario in column E includes the Gross_Revenue cell but not the Cost_Of_Goods_Sold cell, cell E7 in the report would appear without shading, indicating that the Cost_Of_Goods_Sold cell is not involved in that scenario.

You can also create a pivot table report of your scenarios. Pivot table reports let you mix and match scenarios and view the effects of various scenario combinations on result cells. For example, you can see the effect on Gross Profit when you combine the Best Case scenario for sales and the Worst Case scenario for costs.

For more information about pivot tables, see Chapter 24, "Creating a Pivot Table."

Using the Scenario Manager and Microsoft Excel Solver Together

If you define changing cells on your worksheet using the Scenario Manager, the changing cells are displayed automatically as the changing cells in Microsoft Excel Solver if you have not yet defined a Solver problem. You can also save changing cell values used in Solver as a named scenario.

For more information about Microsoft Excel Solver, see Chapter 29, "Using Solver to Analyze Multiple-Variable Problems."

Using the Scenarios Box on the Workgroup Toolbar

Using the Scenarios box is the easiest way to add, display, and edit scenarios in Microsoft Excel. When you first display the Workgroup toolbar, the Scenarios box is empty, as shown in the following illustration.

Adding a Scenario

First, enter the values you want to use into the changing cells that are to be included in the scenario. Then select all the changing cells you want in your scenario (up to a total of 32), and type a scenario name (up to 255 characters) in the Scenarios box, as shown in the following illustration.

System	To select nonadjacent cell ranges
Windows	Hold down CTRL while you select the cells or cell ranges.
Macintosh	Hold down COMMAND while you select the cells or cell ranges.

To add another scenario, select the changing cells you want to use, and enter the values you want in the changing cells. Then click the Scenarios box, and type a name for the new scenario. Each scenario can use a different set of changing cells.

Displaying a Scenario

Once defined, you can display scenarios by clicking the arrow to the right of the Scenarios box and selecting the scenario name from the list. When you do this, the values that you entered into the changing cells when you defined the scenario reappear in the changing cells.

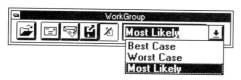

Caution If a scenario name is displayed in the Scenarios box, and you select the same scenario name again, a dialog box appears, asking if you want to redefine the existing scenario. If you choose Yes, the scenario is redefined. Be sure that you do not modify the changing cells before choosing Yes.

Editing a Scenario

To redefine a scenario, first select the scenario you want to redefine in the Scenarios box. Microsoft Excel displays the changing cell values on the sheet. Next, edit the changing cell values. Finally, select or type the scenario name again in the Scenarios box and press ENTER. A dialog box appears asking if you are sure you want to redefine the scenario. Choose the Yes button.

Step By Step

For step-by-step instructions and related information, double-click the ⓀⓀ button to display the Search dialog box in Help, and then:

Type this keyword and choose Show Topics	Select a topic and choose Go To
scenarios, creating	Creating a scenario
scenarios, displaying	Displaying a scenario
scenarios, editing	Editing a scenario
scenarios, Solver	Saving Solver's changing cell values as a scenario
summary reports	Creating a summary report

Using the Scenarios Command on the Tools Menu

Creating a Scenario

From the Tools menu, choose Scenarios, and click the Add button. Type a name for the scenario (such as "Best Case" or "Mary's Assumptions"). In the Changing Cells box, enter the references or the names for the cells that you want to change. If you enter more than one reference, separate each reference with a comma. You can either type references or select cells directly on the sheet.

System	To select nonadjacent cell ranges
Windows	Hold down CTRL while you select the cells or cell ranges.
Macintosh	Hold down COMMAND while you select the cells or cell ranges.

You can also type a comment for each scenario in the Comment box. When you are finished naming, adding references, and adding comments, choose the OK button. The Scenario Values dialog box appears, displaying the current input values for the changing cells you specified.

If your model contains more than five changing cells, a scroll bar appears to the right of the edit boxes. You can include as many as 32 changing cells.

Tip Be sure to name and save the initial input values as a scenario if you want to restore these values later.

Enter the values you want to save in your scenario. When you're finished, choose the Add button if you want to return to the Add Scenario dialog box and create additional scenarios. If you choose the OK button, you return to the Scenario Manager dialog box, where your new scenario is added to the scenarios list.

Displaying a Scenario

From the Tools menu, choose Scenarios. In the Scenario Manager dialog box, select the name of the scenario that you want to use, and choose the Show button. The input values for the selected scenario appear in the changing cells on the worksheet. The worksheet recalculates to reflect the new values.

Tip Double-clicking the name of the scenario displayed in the Scenarios box is the same as selecting the name and choosing the Show button.

Making Changes to a Scenario

Use this procedure to specify different changing cells or different values for the changing cells in an existing scenario.

From the Tools menu, choose Scenarios. In the Scenario Manager dialog box, select the scenario that you want to edit, and choose the Edit button. In the Edit Scenario dialog box, make any desired changes to the references for the changing cells, add comments in the Comments box, and then choose the OK button. In the Scenario Values dialog box, modify the values for the changing cells, and then choose the OK button.

Deleting a Scenario

Caution   Deletions cannot be canceled or undone.

From the Tools menu, choose Scenarios. In the Scenario Manager dialog box, select the scenario that you want to delete, and choose the Delete button.

Protecting Scenarios

The Add Scenario and Edit Scenario dialog boxes contain two protection options: Prevent Changes and Hide. If you select Prevent Changes and then activate sheet protection, the scenarios you define cannot be edited. However, this does not prevent you from editing the values in the changing cells directly on the sheet (unless the cells themselves are locked). Rather, the scenarios themselves are protected from modification when the Prevent Changes check box is selected. In addition, selecting the Hide check box removes a scenario name from the list of defined scenarios, preventing its display.

Once you select protection options in the Add Scenario or Edit Scenario dialog box, you must activate sheet protection. To do this, use the Protection command on the Tools menu, and then choose Protect Sheet. For more information about protecting cells, sheets, and workbooks, see Chapter 39, "Protecting a Workbook."

Note   When sheet protection is activated, you can still add scenarios. However, you cannot edit or delete them unless the Prevent Changes check box is cleared.

Merging Scenarios

Before merging scenarios, make sure all workbooks containing scenarios you want to merge are open. You can also merge scenarios from separate sheets in the same workbook.

Tip   It is easier to merge scenarios if all the what-if models in the workbooks or sheets you want to merge are identical. All the changing cells defined in the merged scenarios should refer to appropriate changing cells on the sheet into which you are merging them.

From the Tools menu, choose Scenarios, and click the Merge button. The Merge
Scenarios dialog box appears. In the Book box, select the workbook name; in the
Sheet box, select the sheet names that contain the scenarios you want to merge.
After you choose the OK button, all the scenarios defined on the source sheet are
copied to the active sheet.

Scenario Name Conflicts It is possible that when you merge scenarios, some of the
scenario names added by others in your group will be duplicates. "Best Case" and
"Worst Case" are common examples. You can even create duplicate scenarios
yourself on duplicate sheets. When you merge, Microsoft Excel appends identifying
information to duplicate scenario names. For example:

- If you create and merge two scenarios named "Best Case," Microsoft Excel
  appends the date to the merged scenario name, as in "Best Case 7/15/93."

- If you create and merge two scenarios named "Best Case" with the same
  creation date, a number is added, as in "Best Case 7/15/93 1."

- If you merge scenarios from other members of your group that duplicate existing
  scenario names, the creator's name is added as well, as in "Best Case Jim
  7/15/93."

- If you merge scenarios from other members of your group that duplicate existing
  scenario names and have the same creation date, a number is added, as in "Best
  Case Jim 7/15/93 1."

After merging, you can rename scenarios using the Edit button in the Scenario
Manager dialog box.

Creating a Summary Report

From the Tools menu, choose Scenarios, and then choose the Summary button. The
Scenario Summary dialog box appears. (The Summary button is unavailable if there
are no scenarios defined for the current worksheet.) In the Result Cells box, enter
the references or the names for the result cells that you want to appear in the report.
If you enter more than one reference, separate each reference with a comma.

Note Result cells are optional for summary reports, but they are required for pivot
table reports.

When you are finished, choose the OK button. Microsoft Excel creates a report on
a separate sheet in the same workbook and names it "Scenario Summary" or
"Scenario PivotTable."

Special Considerations for Pivot Table Reports   With pivot tables, you get instant what-if analyses of different scenario combinations. For this reason, pivot table reports have advantages primarily when you have multiple sets of changing cells provided by several users. If a model consists of a single set of changing cells from a single user, create a scenario summary report instead.

Step By Step

For step-by-step instructions and related information, double-click the 🔲 button to display the Search dialog box in Help, and then:

Type this keyword and choose Show Topics	Select a topic and choose Go To
scenarios, creating	Creating a scenario
scenarios, deleting	Deleting a scenario
scenarios, displaying	Displaying a scenario
scenarios, editing	Editing a scenario
scenarios, merging	Merging scenarios
scenarios, protecting	Protecting scenarios

C H A P T E R   2 9

Using Solver to Analyze Multiple-Variable Problems

For command, keyboard, and toolbar button information, see online Help.

In This Chapter

Answer Complex What-If Questions Using Microsoft Excel Solver

Microsoft Excel Solver is a powerful optimization and resource allocation tool. It can help you to determine the best uses of scarce resources so that desired goals such as profit can be maximized, or undesired goals such as cost can be minimized. Microsoft Excel Solver answers questions such as:

- What product price or promotion mix will maximize profit?
- How can I live within the budget?
- How fast can we grow without running out of cash?

Instead of guessing over and over, you can use Microsoft Excel Solver to find the best answers.

When to Use Solver

Use Solver when you need to find the optimum value for a particular cell by adjusting the values of several cells, or when you want to apply specific limitations to one or more of the values involved in the calculation.

If you want to find a specific value for a particular cell by adjusting the value of only one other cell, you can also use the Goal Seek command. For information about the Goal Seek command, see Chapter 27, "Solving What-If Problems."

Identifying Key Cells in Your Worksheet

To use Microsoft Excel Solver with your worksheet model, you define a problem that needs to be solved by identifying a target cell, the changing cells, and the constraints that you want used in the analysis.

After you define the problem and start the solution process, Solver finds values that satisfy the constraints and produce the desired value for the target cell. Solver then displays the resulting values on your worksheet.

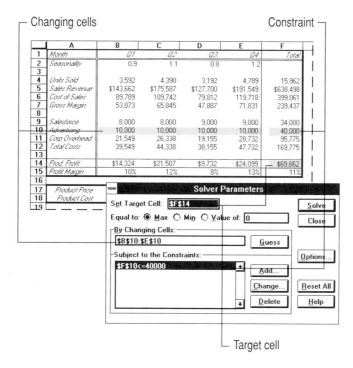

Changing cells   Constraint

	A	B	C	D	E	F
1	Month	Q1	Q2	Q3	Q4	Total
2	Seasonality	0.9	1.1	0.8	1.2	
3						
4	Units Sold	3,592	4,390	3,192	4,789	15,962
5	Sales Revenue	$143,662	$175,587	$127,700	$191,549	$638,498
6	Cost of Sales	89,789	109,742	79,812	119,718	399,061
7	Gross Margin	53,873	65,845	47,887	71,831	239,437
8						
9	Salesforce	8,000	8,000	9,000	9,000	34,000
10	Advertising	10,000	10,000	10,000	10,000	40,000
11	Corp Overhead	21,549	26,338	19,155	28,732	95,775
12	Total Costs	39,549	44,338	38,155	47,732	169,775
13						
14	Prod. Profit	$14,324	$21,507	$9,732	$24,099	$69,662
15	Profit Margin	10%	12%	8%	13%	11%
16						
17	Product Price					
18	Product Cost					
19						

Solver Parameters

Set Target Cell: $F$14

Equal to: ⦿ Max ○ Min ○ Value of: 0

By Changing Cells:
$B$10:$E$10   Guess

Subject to the Constraints:
$F$10<=40000   Add...
                                               Change...   Reset All
                                               Delete   Help

Solve
Close
Options...

Target cell

- The *target cell* (also called the *objective* or *objective function*) is the cell in your worksheet model that you want to minimize, maximize, or set to a certain value.

- The *changing cells* (also called *decision variables*) are cells that affect the value of the target cell. Solver adjusts the values of the changing cells until a solution is found.

- A *constraint* is a cell value that must fall within certain limits or satisfy target values. Constraints may be applied to the target cell and the changing cells.

Once these items are specified, you are ready to solve the problem. You can optionally adjust other parameters that control the reporting options, precision, and mathematical approach used to arrive at a solution.

Solver Settings Are Persistent

After you define a problem, Solver retains the settings you entered in the Solver Parameters and Solver Options dialog boxes. In a workbook, you can define separate problems on different sheets, and Solver retains the settings you made for each sheet individually. The next time you open the workbook and start Solver, the settings for each sheet appear automatically. You can also try different settings for a problem on a sheet and save each different group of settings as a *model*.

Saving a Model or Scenario

After a solution is found, you can choose to save the current settings as a model using the Save Model button in the Solver Options dialog box.

Saving a model saves the target cell, changing cells, constraints, and Solver Option settings in a range of cells on the worksheet. Each sheet in a workbook can contain a different Solver problem, with as many different models as you want for each problem. Once saved, you can easily load a model by specifying the cell range where it was saved in the Load Model dialog box.

If you use multiple models, you may want to use the Scenario Manager. The changing cells you specify with the Scenario Manager will be suggested automatically as the changing cells in Solver. You can save multiple scenarios for each worksheet using the Save Scenario button in the Solver Results dialog box. For more information about the Scenario Manager, see Chapter 28, "Managing What-If Scenarios."

Types of Problems Solver Can Analyze

The three types of optimization problems that the Solver can analyze are:

- Linear
- Nonlinear
- Integer

Linear and nonlinear optimization problems reflect the nature of the relationships between elements of the problem as expressed in formulas on your worksheet. If you know that the problem you are trying to solve is a linear programming problem or a linear system of equations and inequalities, you can greatly speed up the solution process by selecting the Assume Linear Model check box in the Solver Options dialog box. This is particularly important if your worksheet is large and takes a long time to recalculate.

Integer problems are created by applying an integer constraint to any element of the problem using the Solver. Use integer constraints when a value used in the problem, or the result, must be yes or no (1 or 0), or when decimal values are not desired (calculating number of employees, for example). Keep in mind that using the integer method can greatly increase the time necessary for Solver to reach a solution.

The Difference Between Linear and Nonlinear Problems

A majority of optimization problems involve *linear* relationships between variables. A linear problem would be represented by a straight line on a graph. These include problems using simple arithmetic operations such as:

- Addition and subtraction.
- Built-in functions such as SUM(), TREND(), FORECAST().

A problem becomes *nonlinear* when one or more elements share a disproportional relationship to one another. A nonlinear problem would be represented by a curved line on a graph. This can happen when:

- Pairs of changing cells are divided or multiplied by one another.
- Exponentiation is used in the problem.
- You use built-in functions such as GROWTH(), SQRT(), and all logarithmic functions.

Working with Microsoft Excel Solver

Solver Installation

The Solver command is an add-in. If the Solver command appears on the Tools menu, it is already installed. If the Solver command doesn't appear, choose the Add-ins command from the Tools menu to see the list of add-ins currently available. If Solver appears there, make sure that its adjacent check box is selected. If Solver does not appear, you need to run the Microsoft Excel Setup program to install the Solver add-in. For more information, see Chapter 1, "Installing and Starting Microsoft Excel," or the Step By Step table at the end of this section.

Start Solver

Start by opening the worksheet model you want to use, and then choose Solver from the Tools menu.

Specify the Target Cell (Objective Function)

In the Set Target Cell box, enter the reference or name of the cell you want to minimize, maximize, or set to a certain value.

- The target cell should contain a formula that depends, directly or indirectly, on the changing cells you specify in the By Changing Cells box.

- If the target cell does not contain a formula, it must also be a changing cell.

- If you don't specify a target cell, Solver seeks a solution (adjusts values for the changing cells) that satisfies all of the constraints.

Specify the Changing Cells (Decision Variables)

Changing cells normally contain the key variables of your model, such as product prices and interest rates. Enter in the By Changing Cells box the references or names of the cells you want changed by Solver until the constraints in the problem are satisfied and the target cell reaches its goal.

- If you want Solver to propose the changing cells based on the target cell, choose the Guess button. If you use the Guess button, you must specify a target cell.

- You can specify up to 200 changing cells.

- Entries in the Changing Cells box usually consist of a reference to a range of cells, or references of several nonadjacent cells separated by commas.

Caution If your changing cells contain formulas, Solver will replace them with constant values if you choose to keep the solution.

Specify the Constraints

Using the Add, Change, and Delete buttons in the Solver Parameters dialog box, build your list of constraints in the Subject To The Constraints box.

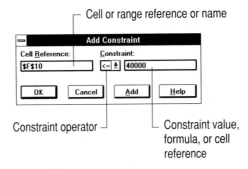

Cell or range reference or name

Constraint operator

Constraint value, formula, or cell reference

- Constraints can include upper and lower bounds for any cell in your model, including the target cell and the changing cells.

- The cell referred to in the Cell Reference box usually contains a formula that depends, directly or indirectly, on one or more of the cells you specify as changing cells.

- When you use the "int" operator, the constrained value is limited to whole numbers (integers) only. When using integer constraints, you can use the Tolerance setting in the Solver Options dialog box to adjust the allowable margin of error.

- Only changing cells can be restricted to integer values.

- For each problem, you can specify two constraints for each changing cell (one upper-limit and one lower-limit constraint), plus up to 100 additional constraints.

For more information about integer constraints and the Tolerance setting, see "Microsoft Excel Solver Tips and Troubleshooting" later in this chapter.

Solve the Problem

Choosing the Solve button initiates the problem-solving process.

Problem solution time depends on:

- The number of changing cells.

- The size and complexity of the worksheet.

- The intrinsic difficulty of the problem.

Microsoft Excel Solver's solution process involves successive trials, or *iterations*. During each iteration, Solver uses a new set of changing cell values to recalculate the worksheet, and examines the constraints and optimum cell values. The process stops when a solution is found to acceptable precision, no further progress is possible, or the maximum time allowed or the maximum number of iterations is reached.

What to Do with the Solver Results

When the problem-solving process ends, a dialog box displays several choices. You can:

- Keep the solution Solver found, or restore the original values in your worksheet.

- Save the solution as a named scenario using the Scenario Manager.

- View any of Solver's built-in reports.

For more information about Solver reports, see the following section, "Microsoft Excel Solver Solutions and Special Reports." For more information about the Scenario Manager, see Chapter 28, "Managing What-If Scenarios."

Save the Model

You can save your model's settings (cell selections, constraints, and options) by choosing the Save Model button in the Solver Options dialog box. When you save a model, Microsoft Excel stores its settings as a range of cells containing formulas. While the latest Solver settings are automatically displayed the next time you open the worksheet, you can save many different models using the Save Model button.

	A	B	C	D	E	F	G	H
1	Month	Q1	Q2	Q3	Q4	Total		
2	Seasonality	0.9	1.1	0.8	1.2			
3								
4	Units Sold	3,592	4,390	3,192	4,789	15,962		
5	Sales Revenue	$143,662	$175,587	$127,700	$191,549	$638,498		
6	Cost of Sales	89,789	109,742	79,812	119,718	399,061		$69,662
7	Gross Margin	53,873	65,845	47,887	71,831	239,437		4
8								TRUE
9	Salesforce	8,000	8,000	9,000	9,000	34,000		100
10	Advertising	10,000	10,000	10,000	10,000	40,000		
11	Corp Overhead	21,549	26,338	19,155	28,732	95,775		
12	Total Costs	39,549	44,338	38,155	47,732	169,775		
13								
14	Prod. Profit	$14,324	$21,507	$9,732	$24,099	$69,662		
15	Profit Margin	10%	12%	8%	13%	11%		
16								

Model saved on worksheet

Solver saves a model in a range starting with the cell you specify in the Save Model dialog box. The size of the range depends on the number of constraints you specify.

Tip Naming each model range that you save makes it easier to remember your models and load them later.

Loading Solver Models

To replace the current Solver settings with a set of saved settings, choose the Load Model button and enter the name or reference of the range containing the settings you want to load.

Resetting the Solver

If you apply Solver to a problem previously undefined in Solver on a new sheet, the settings of the Solver Parameters dialog box appear in their default state. However, for the Solver Options dialog box, any settings you used during your current Microsoft Excel session remain in effect. You can easily reset them using the Reset All button in the Solver Parameters dialog box.

Step By Step

For step-by-step instructions and related information, double-click the [▶?] button to display the Search dialog box in Help, and then:

Type this keyword and choose Show Topics	Select a topic and choose Go To
add-ins	Installing or removing an add-in
adding, constraints	Adding, changing, or deleting constraints in Solver
scenarios, Solver	Solving a problem using Solver
settings, Solver	Adjusting the Solver settings
	Saving and loading a problem model using Solver
Solver	Defining a problem using Solver
Solver reports	Creating a report using Solver

Microsoft Excel Solver Solutions and Special Reports

Using Microsoft Excel Solver, you can create three types of reports that summarize the results of the successful solution process.

Microsoft Excel creates each report on a separate sheet in the current workbook. To print the report, switch to the sheet containing the report, and choose the Print command from the File menu.

The Sensitivity Report

The Sensitivity report contains information demonstrating how sensitive a solution is to changes in the formulas used in the problem. There are two versions of this report, depending on whether you selected the Assume Linear Model option in the Solver Options dialog box.

```
Microsoft Excel 5.0 Sensitivity Report
Worksheet: [SOLVER.XLS] Product Mix
Report Created: 2/23/93 16:21


Changing Cells
                                      Final    Reduced
      Cell          Name             Value     Gradient
      $D$9   Number to Build-> TV set    160        0
      $E$9   Number to Build-> Stereo    200        0
      $F$9   Number to Build-> Speaker    80        0


Constraints
                                      Final    Lagrange
      Cell          Name             Value     Multiplier
      $C$11   Chassis No. Used          360        0
      $C$12   Picture Tube No. Used     160        0
      $C$13   Speaker Cone No. Used     800        6
      $C$14   Power Supply No. Used     360        0
      $C$15   Electronics No. Used      600       14
```

Sensitivity report for nonlinear problems

- **Reduced Gradient**   Measures the increase in the target cell per unit increase in the changing cell.

- **Lagrange Multiplier**   Measures the increase in the target cell per unit increase of the corresponding constraint.

A different version of the Sensitivity report is generated if you select the Assume Linear Model check box in the Solver Options dialog box.

```
Microsoft Excel 5.0 Sensitivity Report
Worksheet: [SOLVER.XLS] Product Mix
Report Created: 2/23/93 16:25


Changing Cells
                                   Final   Reduced  Objective   Allowable  Allowable
      Cell          Name          Value    Cost     Coefficient Increase   Decrease
      $D$9   Number to Build-> TV set   200     0        75          25         5
      $E$9   Number to Build-> Stereo   200     0        50          25        12.5
      $F$9   Number to Build-> Speaker    0    -2        35          2.5      1E+30


Constraints
                                   Final   Shadow   Constraint  Allowable  Allowable
      Cell          Name          Value    Price    R.H. Side   Increase   Decrease
      $C$11   Chassis No. Used         400     0        450        1E+30       50
      $C$12   Picture Tube No. Used    200     0        250        1E+30       50
      $C$13   Speaker Cone No. Used    800    13        800         100       100
      $C$14   Power Supply No. Used    400     0        450        1E+30       50
      $C$15   Electronics No. Used     600    25        600          50       200
```

Sensitivity report for linear problems

This version of the Sensitivity report adds the following information for each changing cell:

- **Reduced Cost**   Replaces Reduced Gradient, and measures the increase in the target cell per unit increase in the changing cell.
- **Objective Coefficient**   Measures the relative relationship between a changing cell and the target cell (objective function).
- **Allowable Increase**   Shows the change in the objective coefficient before there would be an increase in the optimal value of any of the changing cells.
- **Allowable Decrease**   Shows the change in the objective coefficient before there would be a decrease in the optimal value of any of the changing cells.

Note   When solving a linear problem, if the allowable increase or allowable decrease column contains extremely high values (such as 1E+30), and this result appears incorrect, add constraints indicating that the corresponding changing cells must be greater than or equal to zero.

The following information is added for each constraint cell:

- **Shadow Price**   Replaces Lagrange multiplier, and measures the increase in the objective per unit increase in the right side of the constraint equation.
- **Constraint RH Side (right-hand side)**   Lists the constraint values you specify.
- **Allowable Increase**   Shows the change in the Constraint RH Side value before there would be an increase in the optimal value of any of the changing cells.
- **Allowable Decrease**   Shows the change in the Constraint RH Side value before there would be a decrease in the optimal value of any of the changing cells.

The Answer Report

This report shows:

- The target cell (entered in the Set Target Cell box in the Solver Parameters dialog box).
- The changing cells, with their original and final values.
- The constraints and information about them.

```
Microsoft Excel 5.0 Answer Report
Worksheet: [SOLVER.XLS] Product Mix
Report Created: 2/23/93 16:21
```

Target Cell (Max)

Cell	Name	Original Value	Final Value
$D$18	Total Profits:	$10,095	$14,917

Adjustable Cells

Cell	Name	Original Value	Final Value
$D$9	Number to Build-> TV set	100	160
$E$9	Number to Build-> Stereo	100	200
$F$9	Number to Build-> Speaker	100	80

Constraints

Cell	Name	Cell Value	Formula	Status	Slack
$C$11	Chassis No. Used	360	$C$11<=$B$11	Not Binding	90
$C$12	Picture Tube No. Used	160	$C$12<=$B$12	Not Binding	90
$C$13	Speaker Cone No. Used	800	$C$13<=$B$13	Binding	0
$C$14	Power Supply No. Used	360	$C$14<=$B$14	Not Binding	90
$C$15	Electronics No. Used	600	$C$15<=$B$15	Binding	0
$D$9	Number to Build-> TV set	160	$D$9>=0	Not Binding	160
$E$9	Number to Build-> Stereo	200	$E$9>=0	Not Binding	200
$F$9	Number to Build-> Speaker	80	$F$9>=0	Not Binding	80

Information about constraints appears in the Status and Slack columns. These columns tell you how well each constraint was met.

In the Status column, one of the following values is displayed.

- **Binding**   The final cell value equals the constraint value. For example, if the constraint is C11<=400 and the status is Binding, the final cell value would be 400.

- **Not Binding**   The constraint is met but does not equal the constraint value. For example, if C11 contains 350 and the constraint is C11<=400, the status would be Not Binding.

The Slack column tells you the difference between the value displayed in the cell at solution time and the value of the original constraint for that cell. For example, if the constraint is C11<=400 and cell C11 contains 350, the slack would be 50. When the status is binding, the slack value is zero.

The Limits Report

The Limits report lists the target cell and the changing cells, with their values, lower and upper limits, and target results.

Microsoft Excel 5.0 Limits Report
Worksheet: [SOLVER.XLS] Product Mix
Report Created: 2/23/93 16:22

Cell	Target Name	Value
$D$18	Total Profits:	$14,917

Cell	Adjustable Name	Value	Lower Limit	Target Result	Upper Limit	Target Result
$D$9	Number to Build-> TV set	160	0	7698	160	14917
$E$9	Number to Build-> Stereo	200	0	9030	200	14917
$F$9	Number to Build-> Speaker	80	0	13107	80	14917

- **Lower Limit**   The smallest value that a changing cell can take while holding all the other changing cells fixed and still satisfying the constraints.

- **Upper Limit**   The greatest value that a changing cell can take while holding all the other changing cells fixed and still satisfying the constraints.

- **Target Result**   The value of the target cell when the changing cell is at its lower or upper limit.

Step By Step

For step-by-step instructions and related information, double-click the [?] button to display the Search dialog box in Help, and then:

Type this keyword and choose Show Topics	Select a topic and choose Go To
Solver reports	Creating a report using Solver

Microsoft Excel Solver Tips and Troubleshooting

When Changing Cells and the Target Cell Differ in Magnitude

To find a solution to a problem involving changing cells that differ from the target cell by more than one order of magnitude, select the Use Automatic Scaling check box in the Solver Options dialog box. For example, you would select this option if you were planning to invest $10,000,000 in five different stocks and were trying to find the best return on the investment. The changing cells would be in the tens of millions, and the target cell would be a percentage value, eight or nine orders of magnitude smaller than the changing cells.

If you select the Use Automatic Scaling check box, make sure that the initial values of the changing cells are the same order of magnitude as the final values you expect for the changing cells, before selecting the Solve button.

Mathematical Approaches Used by Solver

You can use the boxes at the bottom of the Solver Options dialog box to choose among alternative technical approaches used by Solver at various points in the solution process. The default settings for these options are suitable for nearly all problems. Use of these options is primarily for those experienced in mathematical programming methods; if you're having difficulty reaching the optimal solution you want, you can experiment with these options in an effort to obtain better results.

When Solver Finds a Solution

Solver will display one of the following messages when it has found a solution to your problem.

- **Solver found a solution**   All constraints and optimality conditions are satisfied. All constraints are satisfied to within the precision and integer tolerance settings, and, if appropriate, a maximum, minimum, or target value has been found for the cell in the Set Target Cell box.

- **Solver has converged to the current solution**   All constraints are satisfied. The value in the cell named in the Set Target Cell box is virtually unchanged for the last five trial solutions. A solution may have been found, but it is also possible that the iterative solution process is making very slow progress and is far from a solution, that the Precision setting (set with the Precision box in the Solver Options dialog box) is too low, or that the initial values for the changing cells were too far from the solution.

When Solver Stops Before a Solution Is Found

While solving a problem, Solver may stop before an optimal solution or even a feasible solution has been found. If this happens, a dialog box with one of the Solver completion messages will appear, and you'll have the choice of keeping the latest values of the changing cells or restoring their former contents.

Some of the reasons this may happen:

- You interrupted the solution process.
- You chose the Stop button while stepping through iterations.
- You chose the Stop button when the maximum time or maximum number of iterations was reached.
- The Set Target Cell value is increasing or decreasing without limit.
- The Assume Linear Model option is selected when the problem is nonlinear.

- You have a complex model containing integer constraints, and you need to adjust the Tolerance setting to a higher percentage or increase the Max Time or Iterations setting.

- You need to select the Automatic Scaling option because some input values are several orders of magnitude apart, or input values are different from output values by several orders of magnitude.

Starting from Different Initial Solutions

The ultimate solution can depend on the initial values you supply for the changing cells. Setting the changing cells to values that you suspect are close to optimal can often reduce the solution time. This is especially important if you select the Use Automatic Scaling option or if you have applied integer constraints. If Solver finds a solution that is very different from what you expected, try rerunning Solver with different starting values for the changing cells.

C H A P T E R   3 0

Examples of Using Solver

For command,
keyboard, and
toolbar button
information, see
online Help.

In This Chapter

A Case Study Using Microsoft Excel Solver

This section takes you on a quick tour of Microsoft Excel Solver's features. The sample worksheet used in this section is available in the following location, within the directory or folder where Microsoft Excel is located.

System	Sample worksheet location
Windows	Directory: EXAMPLES\SOLVER
	Workbook: SOLVEREX.XLS
Macintosh	Folder: EXAMPLES:SOLVER
	Workbook: SOLVER EXAMPLE

You can open the workbook and solve several problems by following the examples in this section. In the process, you'll learn how to:

- Solve for one value or several values to maximize or minimize another value.
- Enter and change constraints.
- Save a problem model.

The following illustration shows the Solver sample worksheet.

	A	B	C	D	E	F
1	Month	Q1	Q2	Q3	Q4	Total
2	Seasonality	0.9	1.1	0.8	1.2	
3						
4	Units Sold	3,592	4,390	3,192	4,789	15,962
5	Sales Revenue	$143,662	$175,587	$127,700	$191,549	$638,498
6	Cost of Sales	89,789	109,742	79,812	119,718	399,061
7	Gross Margin	53,873	65,845	47,887	71,831	239,437
8						
9	Salesforce	8,000	8,000	9,000	9,000	34,000
10	Advertising	10,000	10,000	10,000	10,000	40,000
11	Corp Overhead	21,549	26,338	19,155	28,732	95,775
12	Total Costs	39,549	44,338	38,155	47,732	169,775
13						
14	Prod. Profit	$14,324	$21,507	$9,732	$24,099	$69,662
15	Profit Margin	10%	12%	8%	13%	11%
16						
17	Product Price	$40.00				
18	Product Cost	$25.00				
19						

Row	Contains	Explanation
2	Fixed values	Seasonality factor: sales are higher in quarters 2 and 4, and lower in quarters 1 and 3
4	=35*B2*(B10+3000)^0.5	Forecast for units sold each quarter: row 2 contains the seasonality factor; row 10 contains the cost of advertising
5	=B4*$B$17	Sales revenue: forecast for units sold (row 4) times price (cell B17)
6	=B4*$B$18	Cost of sales: forecast for units sold (row 4) times product cost (cell B18)

Row	Contains	Explanation
7	=B5-B6	Gross margin: sales revenues (row 5) minus cost of sales (row 6)
9	Fixed values	Sales personnel expenses
10	Fixed values	Advertising budget (about 6.3% of sales)
11	=0.15*B5	Corporate overhead expenses: sales revenues (row 5) time 15%
12	=SUM(B9:B11)	Total costs: sales personnel expenses (row 9) plus advertising (row 10) plus overhead (row 11)
14	=B7-B12	Product profit: gross margin (row 7) minus total costs (row 12)
15	=B14/B5	Profit margin: profit (row 14) divided by sales revenue (row 5)
17	Fixed values	Product price
18	Fixed values	Product cost

This is a typical marketing model that shows sales rising from a base figure (perhaps due to the sales personnel) along with increases in advertising, but with diminishing returns. For example, the first $5000 of advertising in Q1 yields about 1092 incremental units sold, but the next $5000 yields only about 775 units more.

You can use Solver to find out whether the advertising budget is too low, and whether advertising should be allocated differently over time to take advantage of the changing seasonality factor.

Solving for a Value to Maximize Another Value

One way you can use Solver is to determine the maximum value of a cell by changing another cell. The two cells must be related through the formulas on the worksheet. If they are not, changing the value in one cell will not change the value in the other cell.

For example, in the sample worksheet, you want to know how much you need to spend on advertising to generate the maximum profit for the first quarter. You are interested in maximizing profit by changing advertising expenditures.

- From the Tools menu, choose Solver. In the Set Target Cell box , type **b14** or select cell B14 (first-quarter profits) on the worksheet. Select the Max option button. In the By Changing Cells box, type **b10** or select cell B10 (first-quarter advertising) on the worksheet. Choose the Solve button.

You will see messages in the status bar as the problem is set up and Solver starts working. After a moment, you'll see a message that Solver has found a solution. Solver finds that Q1 advertising of $17,093 yields the maximum profit $15,093.

- After you examine the results, select the Restore Original Values option button and choose the OK button to discard the results and return cell B10 to its former value.

Resetting the Solver Options

If you want to return the options in the Solver Parameters dialog box to their original settings so that you can start a new problem, you can use the Reset All button.

Solving for a Value by Changing Several Values

You can also use Solver to solve for several values at once to maximize or minimize another value. For example, in the sample worksheet, you can solve for the advertising budget for each quarter that will result in the best profits for the entire year. Since the seasonality factor in row 2 enters into the calculation of unit sales in row 4 as a multiplier, it seems logical that you should spend more of your advertising budget in Q4 when the sales response is highest, and less in Q3 when the sales response is lowest. Use Solver to determine the best quarterly allocation.

- From the Tools menu, choose Solver. In the Set Target Cell box, type **f14** or select cell F14 (total profits for the year) on the worksheet. Make sure the Max option button is selected. In the By Changing Cells box, type **b10:e10** or select cells B10:E10 (the advertising budget for each of the four quarters) on the worksheet. Choose the Solve button.

- After you examine the results, select the Restore Original Values option button and choose the OK button to discard the results and return all cells to their former values.

You've just asked Solver to solve a moderately complex nonlinear optimization problem—that is, to find values for the four unknowns in cells B10 through E10 that will maximize profits. (This is a nonlinear problem because of the exponentiation that occurs in the formulas in row 4.) The results of this unconstrained optimization show that you can increase profits for the year to $79,706 if you spend $89,706 in advertising for the full year.

However, most realistic modeling problems have limiting factors that you will want to apply to certain values. These constraints may be applied to the target cell, the changing cells, or any other value that is related to the formulas in these cells.

Adding a Constraint

So far, the budget recovers the advertising cost and generates additional profit, but you're reaching a point of diminishing returns. Since you can never be sure that your model of sales response to advertising will be valid next year (especially at greatly increased spending levels), it doesn't seem prudent to allow unrestricted spending on advertising.

Suppose you want to maintain your original advertising budget of $40,000. Add the constraint to the problem that limits the sum of advertising during the four quarters to $40,000.

- From the Tools menu, choose Solver. Choose the Add button. The Add Constraint dialog box appears. In the Cell Reference box, type **f10** or select cell F10 (advertising total) on the worksheet. Cell F10 must be less than or equal to $40,000. The relationship in the Constraint box is "<=" (less than or equal to) by default, so you don't have to change it. In the box next to the relationship, type **40000**. Choose the OK button. Choose the Solve button.

- After you examine the results, select the Restore Original Values option button and choose the OK button to discard the results and return the cells to their former values.

The solution found by Solver allocates amounts ranging from $5117 in Q3 to $15,263 in Q4. Total Profit has increased from $69,662 in the original budget to $71,447, without any increase in the advertising budget.

Changing a Constraint

When you use Microsoft Excel Solver, you can experiment with slightly different parameters to decide the best solution to a problem. For example, you can change a constraint to see whether the results are better or worse than before. In the sample worksheet, try changing the constraint on advertising dollars to $50,000 to see what that does to total profits.

- From the Tools menu, choose Solver. The constraint, $F$10<=40000, should already be selected in the Subject To The Constraints box. Choose the Change button. In the Constraint box, change 40000 to 50000. Choose the OK button. Choose the Solve button. Select the Keep Solver Solution option button and choose the OK button to keep the results that are displayed on the worksheet.

Solver finds an optimal solution that yields a total profit of $74,817. That's an improvement of $3,370 over the last figure of $71,447. In most firms, it's not too difficult to justify an incremental investment of $10,000 that yields an additional $3,370 in profit, or a 33.7% return on investment. This solution also results in profits of $4,889 less than the unconstrained result, but you spend $39,706 less to get there.

Saving a Problem Model

When you choose Save from the File menu, the last selections made in the Solver Parameters dialog box are attached to the worksheet and retained when you save the workbook. However, you can define more than one problem for a worksheet by saving them individually using the Save Model button in the Solver Options dialog box. Each problem model consists of cells and constraints that you entered in the Solver Parameters dialog box.

When you choose the Save Model button, the Save Model dialog box appears with a default selection, based on the active cell, as the area for saving the model. The suggested range includes a cell for each constraint plus three additional cells. Make sure that this cell range is an empty range on the worksheet.

- From the Tools menu, choose Solver. Choose the Options button. Choose the Save Model button. In the Select Model Area box, type **c17:c20** or select cells C17:C20 on the worksheet. Choose the OK button.

Note You can also enter a reference to a single cell in the Select Model Area box. Solver will use this reference as the upper-left corner of the range into which it will copy the problem specifications.

To load these problem specifications later, choose the Load Model button in the Solver Options dialog box, then type **c17:c20** in the Model Area box or select cells C17:C20 on the sample worksheet, and choose the OK button. Solver displays a message asking if you want to reset the current Solver option settings with the settings for the model you are loading. Choose the OK button to proceed.

Microsoft Excel Solver Sample Worksheets

This section gives brief introductory information about the six sample worksheets included for use with Solver.

The sample worksheets are available in the following location, within the directory or folder where Microsoft Excel is located.

System	Sample workbook location
Windows	Directory: EXAMPLES\SOLVER
	Workbook: SOLVSAMP.XLS
Macintosh	Folder: EXAMPLES:SOLVER
	Workbook: SOLVER SAMPLES

When you open this workbook, and then switch to one of the worksheets and choose the Solver command, you will see that the target cell, changing cells, and constraints are already specified for that worksheet.

The Most Profitable Product Mix

The sample worksheet named Product Mix provides data for several products using common parts, each with a different profit margin per unit. Parts are limited, so your problem is to determine the number of each product to build from the inventory on hand in order to maximize profits.

Problem Specifications

Target cell	D18	Goal is to maximize profit
Changing cells	D9:F9	Units of each product to build
Constraints	C11:C15<=B11:B15	Number of parts used must be less than or equal to the number of parts in inventory
	D9:F9>=0	Number to build value must be greater than or equal to 0

The formulas for profit per product in cells D17:F17 include the factor ^H15 to show that profit per unit diminishes with volume. H15 contains 0.9, which makes the problem nonlinear. If you change H15 to 1.0 to indicate that profit per unit remains constant with volume, and then choose the Solve button again, the optimal solution will change. This change also makes the problem linear.

The Least Costly Shipping Routes

The problem presented on the sample worksheet named Shipping Routes involves the shipment of goods from three plants to five regional warehouses. Goods can be shipped from any plant to any warehouse, but it obviously costs more to ship goods over long distances than over short distances. The problem is to determine the amounts to ship from each plant to each warehouse at minimum shipping cost in order to meet the regional demand, while not exceeding the plant supplies.

Problem Specifications

Target cell	B20	Goal is to minimize total shipping cost
Changing cells	C8:G10	Amount to ship from each plant to each warehouse

Problem Specifications

Constraints	B8:B10<=B16:B18	Total shipped must be less than or equal to supply at plant
	C12:G12>=C14:G14	Totals shipped to warehouses must be greater than or equal to demand at warehouses
	C8:G10>=0	Number to ship must be greater than or equal to 0

You can solve this problem faster by selecting the Assume Linear Model check box in the Solver Options dialog box before choosing the Solve button. A problem of this type has an optimum solution at which amounts to ship are integers, if all of the supply and demand constraints are integers.

Staff Scheduling at Minimum Cost

The goal for the sample worksheet named Staff Scheduling is to schedule employees so that you have sufficient staff at the lowest cost. In this example, all employees are paid at the same rate, so by minimizing the number of employees working each day, you also minimize costs. Each employee works five consecutive days, followed by two days off.

Problem Specifications

Target cell	D20	Goal is to minimize payroll cost
Changing cells	D7:D13	Employees on each schedule
Constraints	D7:D13>=0	Number of employees must be greater than or equal to 0
	D7:D13=Integer	Number of employees must be an integer
	F15:L15>=F17:L17	Employees working each day must be greater than or equal to the demand
Possible schedules	Rows 7-13	1 means employee on that schedule works that day

In this example, you use an integer constraint so that your solutions do not result in fractional numbers of employees on each schedule. Selecting the Assume Linear Model check box in the Solver Options dialog box before you choose the Solve button will greatly speed up the solution process.

Maximizing Income from Working Capital

If you're a financial officer or a manager, one of your tasks is to manage cash and short-term investments in a way that maximizes interest income, while keeping funds available to meet expenditures. You must trade off the higher interest rates available from longer-term investments against the flexibility provided by keeping funds in short-term investments.

The sample worksheet named Maximizing Income calculates ending cash based on initial cash (from the previous month), inflows from maturing certificates of deposit (CDs), outflows for new CDs, and cash needed for company operations for each month.

You have a total of nine decisions to make: the amounts to invest in one-month CDs in months 1 through 6; the amounts to invest in three-month CDs in months 1 and 4; and the amount to invest in six-month CDs in month 1.

Problem Specifications

Target cell	H8	Goal is to maximize interest earned
Changing cells	B14:G14 B15, E15 B16	Dollars invested in each type of CD
Constraints	B14:G14>=0 B15:B16>=0 E15>=0	Investment in each type of CD must be greater than or equal to 0
	B18:H18>=100000	Ending cash must be greater than or equal to $100,000
Amount to invest	B11	$400,000
Cash use aside from investments	Row 17	

The optimal solution determined by Solver earns a total interest income of $16,531 by investing as much as possible in six-month and three-month CDs and then turns to one-month CDs. This solution satisfies all of the constraints.

Suppose, however, that you want to guarantee that you have enough cash in month 5 for an equipment payment. Add a constraint that the average maturity of the investments held in month 1 should not be more than four months.

The formula in cell B20 computes a total of the amounts invested in month 1 (B14, B15, and B16), weighted by the maturities (1, 3, and 6 months), and then it subtracts from this amount the total investment, weighted by 4. If this quantity is zero or less, the average maturity will not exceed four months. To add this constraint, restore the original values and then choose Solver from the Tools menu. Choose the Add button. Type **b20** in the Cell Reference box, type **0** in the Constraint box, and then choose the OK button. To solve the problem, choose the Solve button.

To satisfy the four-month maturity constraint, Solver shifts funds from six-month CDs to three-month CDs. The shifted funds now mature in month 4 and, according to the present plan, are reinvested in new three-month CDs. If you need the funds, however, you can keep the cash instead of reinvesting. The $56,896 turning over in month 4 is more than sufficient for the equipment payment in month 5. You've traded about $460 in interest income to gain this flexibility.

An Efficient Portfolio of Securities

One of the basic principles of investment management is diversification. By holding a portfolio of several stocks, for example, you can earn a rate of return that represents the average of the returns from the individual stocks, while reducing your risk that any one stock will perform poorly.

Using the sample worksheet named Portfolio of Securities, you can use Solver to find the allocation of funds to stocks that minimizes the portfolio risk for a given rate of return, or that maximizes the rate of return for a given level of risk.

This worksheet contains figures for beta (market-related risk) and residual variance for four stocks. In addition, your portfolio includes investments in Treasury bills (T-bills), assumed to have a risk-free rate of return and a variance of zero. Initially, equal amounts (20 percent of the portfolio) are invested in each security.

Use Solver to try different allocations of funds to stocks and T-bills to either maximize the portfolio rate of return for a specified level of risk or minimize the risk for a given rate of return. With the initial allocation of 20 percent across the board, the portfolio return is 16.4 percent and the variance is 7.1 percent.

Problem Specifications

Target cell	E18	Goal is to maximize portfolio return
Changing cells	E10:E14	Weight of each stock
Constraints	E10:E14>=0	Weights must be greater than or equal to 0
	E16=1	Weights must equal 1
	G18<=0.071	Variance must be less than or equal to 0.071
Beta for each stock	B10:B13	
Variance for each stock	C10:C13	

Cells D21:D29 contain the problem specifications to minimize risk for a required rate of return of 16.4 percent. To load these problem specifications into Solver, choose Solver from the Tools menu, choose the Options button, choose the Load Model button, select cells D21:D29 on the worksheet, and then choose the OK button until the Solver Parameters dialog box is displayed. Choose the Solve button. As you can see, Solver finds portfolio allocations in both cases that surpass the rule of 20 percent across the board.

You can earn a higher rate of return (17.1 percent) for the same risk, or you can reduce your risk without giving up any return. These two allocations both represent efficient portfolios.

Cells A21:A29 contain the original problem model. To reload this problem, choose Solver from the Tools menu, choose the Options button, choose the Load Model button, select cells A21:A29 on the worksheet, and then choose the OK button. Solver displays a message asking if you want to reset the current Solver option settings with the settings for the model you are loading. Choose the OK button to proceed.

An Engineering Design Problem

The sample worksheet named Engineering Design depicts an electrical circuit containing a battery, switch, capacitor, resistor, and inductor. With the switch in the left position, the battery charges the capacitor. When the switch is thrown to the right, the capacitor discharges through the inductor and the resistor, both of which dissipate electrical energy.

Using Kirchhoff's second law, you can formulate and solve a differential equation to determine how the charge on the capacitor varies over time. The formula relates the charge q[t] at time t to the inductance L, resistance R, and capacitance C of the circuit elements.

Use Solver to pick an appropriate value for the resistor R (given values for the inductor L and the capacitor C) that will dissipate the charge to one percent of its initial value within one-twentieth of a second after the time the switch is thrown.

Problem Specifications

Target cell	G15	Goal is to set to value of 0.09
Changing cells	G12	Resistor
Constraints	D15:D20	Algebraic solution to Kirchhoff's law

This problem and solution are appropriate for a narrow range of values; the function represented by the charge on the capacitor over time is actually a damped sine wave.

C H A P T E R   3 1

Statistical Analysis of Data

For command, keyboard, and toolbar button information, see online Help.

In This Chapter

Data Analysis Tools Make Statistical or Engineering Analysis Easier

Microsoft Excel provides a set of special analysis tools called the Analysis ToolPak. These tools include statistical analyses you can apply to many types of data as well as analyses specifically designed for engineering applications.

Use these tools to save steps in developing complex analysis scenarios. You interact with the tool by providing the data and parameters for each analysis; the tool then uses the appropriate statistical or engineering worksheet functions, performs the necessary calculations, and displays the results.

The Analysis ToolPak includes the following tools.

Type	Tool name
Statistical	Anova: Single-Factor
	Anova: Two-Factor with Replication
	Anova: Two-Factor Without Replication
	Covariance
	Correlation
	Descriptive Statistics
	Exponential Smoothing
	F-Test: Two-Sample for Variances
	Histogram
	Moving Average
	Random Number Generation
	Rank and Percentile
	Regression
	t-Test: Paired Two-Sample for Means
	t-Test: Two-Sample Assuming Equal Variances
	t-Test: Two-Sample Assuming Unequal Variances
	z-Test: Two-Sample for Means
Engineering	Fourier Analysis
	Sampling

A general description of each analysis tool appears later in this chapter. More specific details about options and dialog box settings are available in Help.

The documentation assumes that you are familiar with the specific area of statistical or engineering analysis you want to use.

Note In addition to the analysis tools described in this section, Microsoft Excel provides many additional statistical, financial, and engineering worksheet functions. For descriptions of all the functions available for use with worksheets, click the Function Wizard button on the Standard toolbar or see online Help.

Using a Data Analysis Tool

Before you use an analysis tool, you must enter and organize the data you want to analyze into columns or rows on your worksheet. This is your input range. You can also include a text label in the first cell of a row or column to identify your variables.

When you use an analysis tool to analyze data in an input range, Microsoft Excel creates an output table of the results. The contents of the output table depend on the analysis tool you are using. If you included labels in the input range, Microsoft Excel uses them to label data in the output table. If you did not include labels in the input range, Microsoft Excel automatically generates data labels for the results in the output table.

You can choose to save the output table on the same sheet as the input range, on a separate sheet in the same workbook, or in a new workbook. If you attempt to save your output table in a location where data already exists, Microsoft Excel warns you and gives you the opportunity to specify a new location.

Caution You cannot use the Undo command on the Edit menu to reverse the creation of an output table if you choose to overwrite existing data.

Where to Find the Data Analysis Tools

To use an analysis tool, choose Data Analysis from the Tools menu. In the Analysis Tools box, select the name of the tool you want to use. Then specify the input and output ranges and any other options you want.

Note If the Data Analysis command does not appear on the Tools menu, run the Setup program to install the Analysis ToolPak. For more information about adding or removing add-in macros, see Chapter 37, "Installing Add-in Features."

You can enter cell ranges in the Input Range and Output Range boxes by typing a cell reference in the box or by selecting the contents of each box and then selecting the cell range on the worksheet.

You can also enter references to other sheets or to other workbooks in the Input Range and Output Range boxes. For information about entering a reference to another sheet, see "References Make Formulas More Powerful" in Chapter 10. For information about entering a reference to a sheet in another workbook, see "Linking Microsoft Excel Workbooks" in Chapter 10.

Step By Step

For step-by-step instructions and related information, double-click the ⟨k?⟩ button to display the Search dialog box in Help, and then:

Type this keyword and choose Show Topics	Select a topic and choose Go To
anova	Anova: Two-Factor with Replication
	Anova: Two-Factor Without Replication
	Anova: Single-Factor
Correlation tool	Correlation
Covariance tool	Covariance
Descriptive Statistics tool	Descriptive Statistics
equal-variances t-tests	t-Test: Two-Sample Assuming Equal Variances
Exponential Smoothing tool	Exponential Smoothing
F-tests	F-Test: Two-Sample for Variances
Fourier Analysis tool	Fourier Analysis
histogramsl	Histogram
Moving Average tool	Moving Average
random numbers	Random Number Generation
Rank and Percentile tool	Rank and Percentile
Regression tool	Regression
Sampling tool	Sampling
two-sample t-tests	t-Test: Paired Two-Sample for Means
unequal variances t-tests	t-Test: Two-Sample Assuming Unequal Variances
z-Test	z-Test: Two-Sample for Means

Anova

Generally, analysis of variance, or *anova*, is a statistical procedure used to determine whether means from two or more samples are drawn from populations with the same mean. This technique expands on the tests for two means, such as the t-test.

Anova: Single-Factor

The single-factor Anova tool performs a simple analysis of variance, which tests the hypothesis that means from several samples are equal.

In the following illustration, you'll find a group of test scores arranged in columns in an input range. Labels are included in the first cell in each column of the input range.

	A	B	C
1	Group 1	Group 2	Group 3
2	75	58	61
3	68	56	63
4	71	61	65
5	75	60	64
6	66	62	61
7	70	60	68
8	68	59	63
9	68	68	61
10	69	60	64
11			

Note   You can also use samples that contain different number of values with the single-factor Anova tool.

Anova: Two-Factor with Replication

The two-factor with replication Anova tool performs an extension of the single-factor anova that includes more than one sample for each group of data.

The following illustration shows how to organize your input range.

	A	B	C	D
1		Group 1	Group 2	Group 3
2	Trial 1	75	58	61
3		68	56	63
4		71	61	65
5		75	60	64
6	Trial 2	66	62	61
7		70	60	68
8		68	59	63
9		68	68	61
10				

Data in the preceding input range includes test scores for three different groups of students. The test was administered to each group in two trials. The data for the test includes four rows per sample.

Anova: Two-Factor Without Replication

The two-factor without replication Anova tool performs two-factor anova that does not include more than one sampling per group.

The data in the following input range includes temperature readings, in Celsius, taken from a lake at different depths. The depth variable is measured in feet. The readings were taken on four different dates.

	A	B	C	D	E
1	Depth	Date 1	Date 2	Date 3	Date 4
2	1	23	24.2	24.8	25.2
3	2	22.2	23	24	24.5
4	3	22	22.5	22.8	23
5	4	21.2	22	22.3	22.5
6	5	18.4	20	21	22
7	6	13.5	15	17	18
8	7	9.7	10	13	15
9	8	5.9	6.5	8	9
10	9	5.7	5.9	6.5	7
11	12	5.5	5.7	6.1	6.5
12	15.5	5.3	5.5	5.9	6.2
13					

Covariance and Correlation

The following illustration shows an input range that could be used in either a covariance or a correlation problem. The data is arranged in columns.

	A	B	C
1	Sample 1	Sample 2	Sample 3
2	1.2	4.2	120
3	2.5	8.7	40
4	3.6	11.4	40
5	2.8	9.1	130
6	4.8	4.2	120
7	1.8	6.6	20
8	2.2	7.9	40
9	5.1	12.2	40
10			

Covariance

The Covariance tool returns the average of the product of deviations of data points from their respective means. Covariance is a measure of the relationship between two ranges of data.

$$cov(X,Y) = \frac{1}{n}\sum(x_i - \mu_x)(y_i - \mu_y)$$

Use the Covariance tool to determine whether two ranges of data move together; that is, whether large values of one set are associated with large values of the other (positive covariance), whether small values of one set are associated with large values of the other (negative covariance), or whether the values in the two sets are unrelated.

Note If large values of Y tend to accompany large values of X, their products tend to be positive and yield a positive covariance. Similarly, if large values of Y tend to accompany small values of X, the result is a negative covariance. If there is a weak relationship between X and Y data sets, the covariance tends toward zero.

Covariance is sensitive to the unit of measure for X and Y. Two pairs of similarly related ranges of data yield different covariance values if the magnitudes of the data points vary. The correlation statistic overcomes this liability by adjusting covariance by the standard deviation of each range of data.

Correlation

The Correlation tool measures the relationship between two data sets that are scaled to be independent of the unit of measure. The population correlation calculation returns the covariance of two data sets divided by the product of their standard deviations.

$$\rho_{X,Y} = \frac{cov(X,Y)}{\sigma_X \cdot \sigma_Y}$$

where

$$\sigma_x^2 = \frac{1}{n}\sum (X_i - \mu_x)^2$$

and

$$\sigma_y^2 = \frac{1}{n}\sum (Y_i - \mu_y)^2$$

You can use the Correlation tool to determine whether two data sets move together; that is, whether large values of one set are associated with large values of the other (positive correlation), whether small values of one set are associated with large values of the other (negative correlation), or whether the values in the two sets are unrelated.

Note When correlation is high, large values of Y tend to accompany large values of X. The products of X and Y tend to be positive and yield a positive correlation. If large values of Y tend to accompany small values of X, the result is a negative correlation. If there is a weak relationship between X and Y data sets, the correlation tends toward zero.

Unlike covariance, correlation is independent of the units of measure. Similarly related pairs of data sets yield similar correlations even if their magnitudes differ. This is because correlation is covariance adjusted by the correlation for standard deviations of the ranges of data.

For More Information

For more information, click the Function Wizard button on the Standard toolbar or see the CORREL and COVAR functions in online Help.

Descriptive Statistics

The Descriptive Statistics tool generates a report of univariate statistics for data in the input range. This procedure provides information about the central tendency and variability of your data. The statistics in this table are a common starting point for further analysis and can indicate which tests are appropriate to explore next.

Outputs Among the output values generated by the Descriptive Statistics tool are: standard deviation of sample (sample variance), kurtosis, and skewness. These outputs are derived using the same algorithms used by the built-in Microsoft Excel functions STDEV, VAR, KURT, and SKEW, respectively. For more information about these functions, see online Help.

Forecasting

Exponential Smoothing

The Exponential Smoothing tool predicts a value based on the forecast for the prior period, adjusted for the error in that prior forecast. This tool uses a smoothing constant, a, the magnitude of which determines how strongly forecasts respond to errors in the prior forecast.

$$F_{t+1} = F_t + a(A_t - F_t) = F_t + (1 - dampFact)(A_t - F_t)$$

You can use exponential smoothing to forecast sales, inventory, or other trends.

Note Values of 0.2 to 0.3 are reasonable smoothing constants. These values indicate that the current forecast should be adjusted 20 to 30 percent for error in the prior forecast. Larger constants yield a faster response but can produce erratic projections. Small constants can result in long lags for forecast values behind actual ones.

Another method, *regression*, involves a series of procedures that predict values based on relationships in existing data. *Linear regression* seeks to fit a linear function to a data set. The *least squares* linear regression technique finds the relationship that minimizes the sum of the squared deviations of data points from the regression function. For more information about using the Regression tool, see "Regression" later in this section.

Note If you are interested in charting an exponential smoothing problem, you can use the Chart Output option in the Exponential Smoothing dialog box, or you can use the Microsoft Excel built-in charting features to create a smoothed line or an xy (scatter) chart. For more information, see "Formatting Data Markers and Data Labels" in Chapter 18.

Moving Average

The Moving Average tool projects values in the forecast period, based on the average value of the variable over a specific number of preceding periods. Each forecast value is based on the following formula:

$$F_{(t+1)} = \frac{1}{N} \sum_{i=1}^{N} A_{t-i+1}$$

where N is the number of prior periods to include in the moving average. A_j is the actual value at time j, and F_j is the forecasted value at time j. You can use this procedure to forecast sales, inventory, or other trends.

A moving average provides trend information that a simple average of all historic data masks. The following input range displays the seasonal ticket sales for Blue Sky Air for the past eight quarters.

	A	B
1		Actual Sales
2	Year 1 Qtr 1	420
3	Year 1 Qtr 2	650
4	Year 1 Qtr 3	800
5	Year 1 Qtr 4	1420
6	Year 2 Qtr 1	1360
7	Year 2 Qtr 2	1600
8	Year 2 Qtr 3	2110
9	Year 2 Qtr 4	2400

If you try to project first-quarter sales in the coming year using a simple arithmetic average of the past eight quarters, the prediction is 1345. This prediction gives equal weight to all sales figures and clearly fails to recognize the rising trend. A moving average simply weighs recent values equally and ignores older values.

The predictions based on moving averages reflect the prevailing trend but lag slightly behind. As the number of periods in the moving average interval increases, the predictions are less susceptible to short-term fluctuations and slower to reflect recent trends. A short moving average interval is strongly affected by the most recent trends; this greater responsiveness comes at the expense of increased volatility.

You can supplement projections with several other calculations. For example, the standard error measures the relative accuracy of projected values.

$$S(k+1) = \left\{ \sum_{i=1}^{N} \left[\frac{\left(A_{k-i+1} - F_{k-i+1} \right)^2}{N} \right] \right\}^{\frac{1}{2}}$$

Microsoft Excel places standard error values in the second column.

Another method, the weighted moving average forecast, includes a large interval and allows you to assign various nonnegative weights to observations over time.

$$F_{(t+1)} = \sum_{i=1}^{N} W_i A_{t-i+1}$$

In the preceding equation, $W1$, $W2$, ..., W_N are nonnegative weights that sum to 1. W_i is the weight at interval i; A_j is the actual value at time j; and F_t is the forecasted value at time t. To calculate a weighted average, use the SUMPRODUCT function.

Another method, *regression*, involves a series of procedures that predict values based on relationships in existing data. Linear regression seeks to fit a linear function to a data set. The least squares linear regression technique finds the relationship that minimizes the sum of the squared deviations of data points from the regression function.

Regression

The Regression tool performs linear regression analysis. Regression fits a line through a set of observations using the least squares method. Regression is used in a wide variety of applications that seek to analyze how a single dependent variable is affected by the values of one or more independent variables. For example, several factors contribute to an athlete's performance, including age, sex, height, and weight. Regression apportions shares in the performance measure to each of these four factors based on a set of performance data. Regression results can then be used to predict the performance of a new, untested athlete. In general, regression arrives at an equation for performance based on each of the inputs.

Depending on the options you choose when using the Regression tool, Microsoft Excel generates the following output:

- A summary output table, including an Anova table, a standard error of y estimate, coefficients, standard error of coefficients, r^2 values, and the number of observations

- A residuals output table that can include residuals, standardized residuals, and predicted values

- A residual plot for each independent variable versus the residual

- A line fit plot of the predicted values with the observed values

- A normal probability plot

- A two-column probability data output table displaying the dependent variable values and percentiles used to generate the normal probability plot

---

Important   When choosing options, you can tell Microsoft Excel where you want your output tables to appear by entering output ranges—one cell reference for each output table indicating the position of the upper-left corner of the output table. Because the size of an output table varies depending on the amount and type of input data, follow these guidelines when specifying output ranges so that your output tables do not overlap.

- Arrange output ranges side by side on your worksheet. In general, output tables vary in length rather than width.

- Allow at least four columns for the residuals output table.

- Allow at least two columns for the probability data output table.

When you enter data in the input y range or the input x range, you can include or exclude report labels. The following input ranges include report labels. To use this type of input range, select the Labels check box before generating the output table.

	A	B	C	D	E
1					
2	Weight	Height	Age		Seconds to complete
3	165	64	25		15
4	175	68	40		25
5	180	68	30		17
6	200	72	42		30
7	195	70	28		25
8	183	68	45		32
9					

Input x range   Input y range

Microsoft Excel orders independent variables in ascending order from left to right and uses x1, x2, and x3 for the variable names in the output table.

The output that Microsoft Excel might generate using the preceding input ranges depends on the options you select in the Regression dialog box. For example, if you select the Residuals check box, the Residual Plots check box, the Line Fit Plot check box, and the Normal Probability Plot check box, and you fill in the appropriate output range boxes, Microsoft Excel generates the following output:

- An Anova table and summary data
- A residuals output table showing residuals and predicted values
- Three residual plots
- One line fit plot
- One normal probability plot
- A probability data output table

Note If you are interested in charting trendlines, you can use the Microsoft Excel built-in charting features to create trendlines on charts automatically. For more information, see "Formatting Trendlines and Error Bars" in Chapter 18. You can also use the Fill command on the Edit menu to generate numeric trend and growth series automatically on a sheet. For more information, see "Filling Adjacent Cells and Creating Series" in Chapter 9.

For More Information

For more information, click the Function Wizard on the Standard toolbar or see the EXPONDIST, FORECAST, GROWTH, LINEST, LOGEST, SUMPRODUCT, and TREND functions in online Help.

Histogram

The Histogram tool calculates individual and cumulative frequencies for a cell range of data and data bins. The Histogram tool also generates data for the number of occurrences of a value in a data set. For example, in a class of 20 students, you are interested in the distribution of scores in letter-grade categories. A histogram table presents the letter-grade boundaries and the number of scores between the lower bound and the current bound. The single most frequent score is the mode of the cell range of data.

For More Information

For more information, click the Function Wizard button on the Standard toolbar or see the FREQUENCY and MODE functions in online Help.

Random Number Generation

The Random Number Generation tool fills a range with independent random numbers drawn from one of several distributions. Random variables have a variety of applications in statistical simulations. One application of this procedure characterizes subjects in a population with a probability distribution. For example, you can use a normal distribution to characterize the population of individuals' heights, or you can use a Bernoulli distribution of two possible outcomes to characterize the population of coin-flip results.

The following output table shows four columns of data randomly generated using a normal distribution with a mean of 25 and a standard deviation of 5.

	A	B	C	D
1	20.04104	42.81737	33.99099	29.07465
2	19.76846	16.73349	24.67025	21.15821
3	20.65659	22.4749	23.34647	35.84845
4	19.82108	30.23485	35.24782	31.77304
5	26.5312	19.45326	27.90549	34.32882
6				

You can use the Histogram tool with the data generated by the Random Number Generation tool to show the distribution of your data.

For more information, see the RAND and RANDBETWEEN functions in online Help.

Rank and Percentile

The Rank and Percentile tool produces a table that contains the ordinal and percentage rank of each value in a data set. You can use this procedure to analyze the relative standing of values in a data set.

For More Information

For more information, click the Function Wizard button on the Standard toolbar or see the PERCENTILE and PERCENTRANK functions in online Help.

Tests for Variances and Means

F-Test: Two-Sample for Variances

The two-sample for variances F-Test tool performs a two-sample F-test. An F-test is a method for comparing two population variances. For example, you can use an F-test to determine whether the time scores in a swimming meet have a difference in variance between samples from two teams.

In the following illustration, two sets of test scores are compared in the input range in cells A1:B10.

	A	B
1	Group 1	Group 2
2	64	26
3	52	35
4	48	34
5	52	32
6	43	34
7	44	28
8	46	29
9	58	28
10	45	33
11		

T-Test: Paired Two-Sample for Means

The paired two-sample for means t-Test tool performs a paired two-sample student's t-test. This form of the t-test tests whether a sample's means are distinct. It does not assume that the variances of both populations from which the data sets are drawn are equal. A paired test is appropriate whenever there is a natural pairing of observations in the samples, such as when a sample group is tested twice, before and after an experiment. For example, the same subjects could be tested after a treatment to see whether the treatment produces any effects.

Because this is a paired test, the two input ranges of data must contain the same number of data points.

Outputs   Among the output values generated by this analysis tool is Pearson Correlation. This value is derived using the formula

COVAR(indrng1,indrng2)*((df+1)/df)

where df is the degree of freedom. Another output value generated by this analysis tool is Pooled Variance. This value is derived using the formula

$$S^2 = \frac{n_1 S_1^2 + n_2 S_2^2}{n_1 + n_2 - 2}$$

where S^2 is pooled variance.

T-Test: Two-Sample Assuming Equal Variances

The two-sample assuming equal variances t-Test tool performs a two-sample student's t-test. This form of the t-test assumes that the means of both data sets are equal and is referred to as a homoscedastic t-test. You use t-tests to determine whether the two samples' means are equal.

T-Test: Two-Sample Assuming Unequal Variances

The two-sample assuming unequal variances t-Test tool performs a two-sample student's t-test. This form of the test assumes that the variances of both ranges of data are unequal and is referred to as a heteroscedastic t-test. You use t-tests to determine whether two sample means are equal. Use this test when the groups under study are distinct. Use a paired test when there is one group before and after a treatment.

The formula used to determine the test statistic value t is

$$t' = \frac{\bar{x} - \bar{y} - \Delta_0}{\sqrt{\dfrac{S_1^2}{m} + \dfrac{S_2^2}{n}}}$$

The formula below is used to approximate the degrees of freedom. The result of the calculation is usually not an integer. The nearest integer is used to obtain a critical value from the t table.

$$df = \frac{\left(\dfrac{S_1^2}{m} + \dfrac{S_2^2}{n}\right)^2}{\dfrac{\left(S_1^2/m\right)^2}{m-1} + \dfrac{\left(S_2^2/n\right)^2}{n-1}}$$

Z-Test: Two-Sample for Means

The two-sample for means z-Test tool performs a two-sample z-test for means with known variances. This procedure is commonly used to test hypotheses about the difference between two population means. For example, we can use this test for differences between the performance of two car models.

For More Information

For more information, click the Function Wizard button on the Standard toolbar or see the COVAR, FDIST, FINV, FTEST, NORMDIST, NORMSDIST, NORMINV, NORMSINV, STANDARDIZE, TDIST, TTEST, and ZTEST functions in online Help.

Engineering Functions

Fourier Analysis

Fourier Analysis is a technique for solving problems in linear systems and for analyzing periodic data. The Fourier Analysis tool transforms data using the Fast Fourier Transform (FFT) method. The procedure also supports inverse transformations in which the inverse of transformed data returns the original data.

Note The number of input values used must be a power of 2; that is, the number of input values must be 2, 4, 8, 16, 32, and so on.

The following illustration shows an example input range and the resulting output table.

	A	B	C
1	Time Domain Data	Frequency Domain Output	
2	1	3	
3	1	1.707106769-1.707106769i	
4	1	-i	
5	0	0.292893231+0.292893231i	
6	0	1	
7	0	0.292893231-0.292893231i	
8	0	i	
9	0	1.707106769+1.707106769i	
10			

Note As the preceding figure illustrates, the Fourier Analysis tool generates an output range containing complex numbers. The numbers in rows 3, 5, 7, and 9 in the illustration are actually text entries. You can use the IMARGUMENT function in the Analysis ToolPak to compute the argument (phase) of complex numbers. You can also use the IMABS function to return the absolute value (amplitude) of complex numbers.

Sampling

The Sampling tool creates a sample from a population by treating the input range as a population. You might use a sample rather than the entire population when the population is too large to process or chart. In addition, if you believe the input data is periodic, you can create a sample that contains only values from a particular part of a cycle. For example, if the input range contains quarterly sales figures, sampling with a periodic rate of 4 places values from the same quarter in the output table.

> **Note** If the input range contains the values 1, 2, 3, 4, 5, 6, 7, 8, 9, and 10, a periodic sampling rate of 3 places the values 3, 6, and 9 in the output column. A random sample of 3 might produce the values 2, 8, and 4.

The following illustration shows an example input range.

	A	B	C	D
1	13	26	22	28
2	26	25	23	30
3	29	28	22	29
4	28	25	23	16
5	20	24	21	21
6	24	24	22	15
7	16	24	25	26
8	46	26	21	27
9	25	24	19	26
10	28	28	25	23
11				

For More Information

For more information, click the Function Wizard button on the Standard toolbar or see the IMABS, IMAGINARY, and IMARGUMENT functions in Help.

Additional References

For detailed information about the algorithms used to create the Microsoft Excel engineering tools or functions, see the following book.

- Strum, Robert D., and Donald E. Kirk. *First Principles of Discrete Systems and Digital Signal Processing*. Reading, Mass.: Addison-Wesley Publishing Company, 1988.

For detailed information about statistical methods or the algorithms used to create the Microsoft Excel statistical tools or functions, see the following books.

- Abramowitz, Milton, and Irene A. Stegun, eds. *Handbook of Mathematical Functions with Formulas, Graphs, and Mathematical Tables*. Washington, D.C.: U.S. Government Printing Office, 1972.

- Box, George E.P., William G. Hunter, and J. Stuart Hunter. *Statistics for Experimenters*. New York: John Wiley and Sons, 1978.

- Devore, Jay L. *Probability and Statistics for Engineering and the Sciences*. 3d ed. Pacific Grove, California: Brooks/Cole Publishing Company, 1991.

- McCall, Robert B. *Fundamental Statistics for the Behavioral Sciences*. 5th ed. New York: Harcourt Brace Jovanovich, 1990.

- Press, W.H., B.P. Flannery, S.A. Teukolsky, and W.T. Wetterling. *Numerical Recipes in C: The Art of Scientific Computing*. New York: Cambridge University Press, 1988.

- Sokal, Robert R., and F. James Rohlf. Biometry: *The Principles and Practice of Statistics in Biological Research*. 2d ed. New York: W.H. Freeman and Company, 1981.

Customizing Microsoft Excel

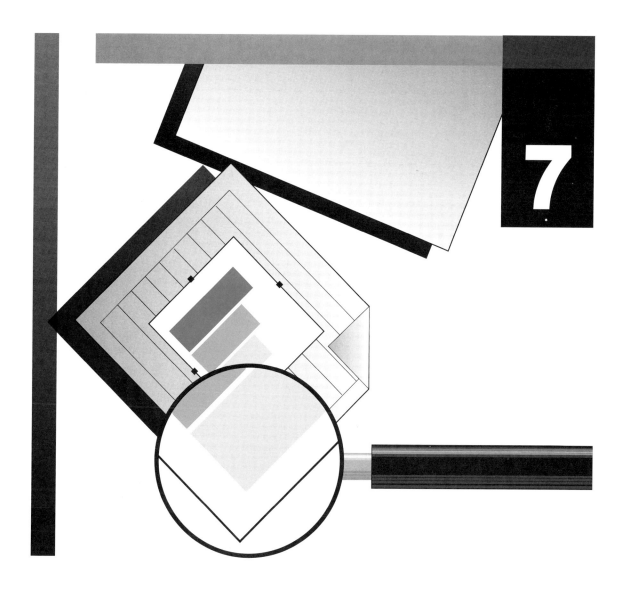

C H A P T E R   3 2

Changing How You View Your Worksheet

For command, keyboard, and toolbar button information, see online Help.

In This Chapter

Splitting Worksheets and Freezing Titles

When you want to scroll your worksheet and still be able to see your titles for the columns or rows, you can split the worksheet into panes. Then you can scroll the worksheet in one pane, while your titles remain visible in another pane. Splitting a worksheet is especially useful for viewing large lists or tables of data.

Both the Split command and the Freeze Panes command on the Window menu split the window into panes at the active cell. If an entire row or column is selected, the window is split above the row or to the left of the column. The Freeze Panes command also automatically freezes the panes, preventing scrolling in the upper or left pane.

The following illustration shows split panes.

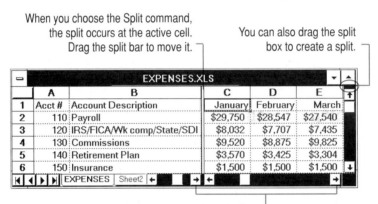

When you choose the Split command, the split occurs at the active cell. Drag the split bar to move it.

You can also drag the split box to create a split.

Scroll each pane individually.

The following illustration shows frozen panes.

Columns A and B and row 1 stay on the screen as you scroll through your data.

The Freeze Panes command splits the window at the active cell and freezes the panes. Panes are frozen at these lines.

You can also display two sections of your worksheet by creating a new window with the New Window command on the Window menu. For more information about working with windows, see "Opening, Arranging, and Closing Workbook Windows" in Chapter 7.

Tip   Split or frozen panes do not affect printing. To freeze rows or titles on a printed document, specify print titles on the Sheet tab in the Page Setup dialog box. For more information about print titles, see "Setting Up What You Want to Print" in Chapter 14.

Unfreezing Panes and Removing Splits

To	Do this
Unfreeze frozen panes	Choose the Unfreeze Panes command from the Window menu.
Remove a window split	Double-click the split bar or split box, or choose the Remove Split command from the Window menu.

Step By Step

For step-by-step instructions and related information, double-click the button to display the Search dialog box in Help, and then:

Type this keyword and choose Show Topics	Select a topic and choose Go To
freezing, panes	Freezing and unfreezing worksheet titles and panes
windows, splitting	Splitting a window into panes
workbook windows	Arranging workbook windows
	Displaying and closing new windows of a workbook

Zooming In or Out on a Worksheet

Zoom Control box

Use the Zoom command on the View menu or the Zoom Control box to make the display of your worksheet, macro sheet, or chart sheet larger or smaller.

L39		=SUM(L33:L37)

With the worksheet zoomed to 25 percent, you can see more rows and columns of data.

Worksheets can be displayed at different scales for:

- Navigating.

- Arranging and placing objects and blocks of data.

- Setting print options.

- Getting an overview of the worksheet's contents.

- Enlarging a section of the worksheet for easier viewing.

When used with the model auditing tools, zooming the worksheet helps you see relationships between formulas and data. For more information about auditing tools, see "Auditing Your Worksheets Visually" in Chapter 38.

Another way to see more of your data on the screen is to hide certain screen elements such as the toolbars, status bar, and so on with the Full Screen command on the View menu. When you want to unhide the hidden screen elements, click the Full Screen button or choose the Full Screen command again.

Guidelines for Zooming a Worksheet

- You can use all normal editing and formatting procedures on a zoomed sheet.

- Zooming affects only the selected sheets in a workbook.

- Zoomed sheets are printed at 100-percent size. To print a reduced or enlarged view of a sheet, adjust the scaling of the sheet in the Page Setup dialog box. For more information, see "Setting Up What You Want to Print" in Chapter 14.

- The magnified or reduced state of a sheet is saved when the workbook is saved.

Step By Step

For step-by-step instructions and related information, double-click the ⟨?⟩ button to display the Search dialog box in Help, and then:

Type this keyword and choose Show Topics	Select a topic and choose Go To
error tracers	Using the error tracer to find error values visually
page size	Setting page orientation and size
screens	Displaying the full screen
zooming	Zooming in or out on a worksheet

Hiding and Unhiding Rows and Columns

You can hide and unhide rows and columns to view or print only the data you want. For example, you might want to hide columns containing monthly detail in a sales report and display just quarterly and annual totals.

	A	B	C	D	E	F	G	H	I	J
1	*BUDGET FORECAST*									
2										
3	Site	Operating Exp	Jun	Jul	Aug	Q1	Sep	Oct	Nov	Q2
4	Albany, NY									
5		Salaries	10,000	10,000	10,000	30,000	10,000	10,000	13,000	33,000
6		Supplies	3,000	2,500	3,000	8,500	2,500	3,000	2,500	8,000
7		Equipment	4,575	4,575	4,575	13,725	4,575	4,575	4,575	13,725
8		Lease Pmts	9,600	9,600	9,600	28,800	9,600	9,600	9,600	28,800
9		Advertising	1,500	1,500	1,500	4,500	2,000	2,400	2,200	6,600
10		Total	$28,675	$28,175	$28,675	$85,525	$28,675	$29,575	$31,875	$90,125

This worksheet contains monthly detail in columns, and line item detail in rows.

	A	B	F	J
1	*BUDGET FORECAST*			
2				
3	Site	Operating Exp	Q1	Q2
4	Albany, NY			
10		Total	$85,525	$90,125
11	Memphis, TN			
17		Total	$84,600	$77,500

Hide the detail columns and rows to view just the totals.

Hiding rows or columns does not delete them from the worksheet; it just puts them out of sight.

You can also use worksheet outlining to automatically hide rows and columns of data. For more information about outlining, see Chapter 33, "Outlining a Worksheet."

By creating views for a worksheet, you can save the different arrangements of hidden or visible rows and columns, and then easily display or print the different views. For more information, see "Creating Different Views of a Worksheet" later in this chapter.

For information about hiding entire workbooks or sheets, see "Hiding and Unhiding Workbooks and Sheets" in Chapter 39.

Hiding Rows and Columns

You can hide selected rows or columns by choosing the Row command or the Column command from the Format menu, and then choosing the Hide command.

You can also point to row or column heading borders and drag to the edge of the row above or the column to the left.

Unhiding Rows and Columns

To unhide rows or columns, select a range that includes the hidden row or column. Then, from the Format menu, choose Row or Column, and then choose Unhide.

Tip To unhide all rows or columns at once, select the entire worksheet by clicking the Select All button to the left of the column headings. Then, from the Format menu, choose Row or Column, and then choose Unhide.

To unhide specific rows or columns, choose Go To from the Edit menu and enter a range of cells that includes the hidden rows or columns. Then, from the Format menu, choose Row or Column, and then choose Unhide.

Step By Step

For step-by-step instructions and related information, double-click the [?] button to display the Search dialog box in Help, and then:

Type this keyword and choose Show Topics	Select a topic and choose Go To
hiding, columns	Hiding and unhiding a row or column
hiding, sheets	Hiding and unhiding a sheet
hiding, workbooks	Hiding and unhiding a workbook

Creating Different Views of a Worksheet

Using the View Manager command on the View menu, you can save different sets of worksheet display and print settings as a *view*. Then you can switch to any of the views whenever you want to display or print information in a different way.

	A	B	C	D	E
1	NORTHWIND TRADERS SALES				
2		Jan	Feb	Mar	1st Qtr.
3	*Mike Jones*				
4	Greenville	$7,128	$8,135	$12,200	$27,463
5	Hempton	$5,675	$5,919	$6,295	$17,889
6	S. Minton	$7,750	$13,982	$17,055	$38,787
7	*Totals*	$20,553	$28,036	$35,550	$84,139
8					
9	*Pam Coburn*				
10	Metro Area	$7,005	$8,106	$7,877	$22,988
11	East End	$2,172	$2,124	$2,103	$6,399
12	*Totals*	$9,177	$10,230	$9,980	$29,387
13					
14	*Janis Kincaid*				
15	Clear Spring	$7,328	$13,054	$13,981	$34,363
16	Lakewater	$13,175	$21,075	$22,092	$56,342
17	Riverton	$3,285	$3,165	$3,385	$9,835
18	*Totals*	$23,788	$37,294	$39,458	$100,540

Your worksheet data may look like this.

	A	B	C	D	E
1	NORTHWIND TRADERS SALES				
2		Jan	Feb	Mar	1st Qtr.
3	*Mike Jones*				
7	*Totals*	$20,553	$28,036	$35,550	$84,139
8					
9	*Pam Coburn*				
12	*Totals*	$9,177	$10,230	$9,980	$29,387
13					
14	*Janis Kincaid*				
18	*Totals*	$23,788	$37,294	$39,458	$100,540
19					
20	TOTALS	$53,518	$75,560	$84,988	$214,066

You can quickly switch to a previously defined view that displays only subtotals and no gridlines.

```
NORTHWIND TRADERS SALES
               1st Qtr.
   Mike Jones
       Totals   $84,139

   Pam Coburn
       Totals   $29,387

Janis Kincaid
       Totals  $100,540

TOTALS     $214,066
```

Another view may eliminate row and column headings and present only the titles and the column for quarterly totals.

Installing the View Manager Add-in

If the View Manager command appears on the View menu, it is already installed. If not, choose the Add-ins command from the Tools menu to see if View Manager is in the list of add-ins currently installed. If View Manager appears there, make sure that its adjacent check box is selected. If View Manager does not appear, see Chapter 1, "Installing and Starting Microsoft Excel" or the Step By Step table at the end of this section for information about installing add-ins.

Creating, Displaying, and Deleting Views

To	From the View menu, choose View Manager and then
Create a view	Choose the Add button.
Display a view	Select the view you want and choose the Show button.
Delete a view	Select the view you want and choose the Delete button.

Using Views to Create Reports

You can use the Report Manager to print a number of different views of a worksheet as a single report. Be sure to define a print area for each view you want to print separately. For more information about using the Report Manager, see "Creating and Printing Custom Reports" in Chapter 14.

Step By Step

For step-by-step instructions and related information, double-click the 🔼? button to display the Search dialog box in Help, and then:

Type this keyword and choose Show Topics	Select a topic and choose Go To
add-ins	Installing or removing an add-in
reports, creating	Creating a report
worksheet views	Creating or deleting a view of a worksheet
	Displaying a view of a worksheet
	Printing a view of a worksheet

C H A P T E R   3 3

Outlining a Worksheet

For command,
keyboard, and
toolbar button
information, see
online Help.

In This Chapter

How Worksheet Outlines Work

You can outline your worksheet data to create summary reports. With summary reports, you can show or hide as much detail as you want.

Worksheet outlining is especially useful when you want to share your summary reports with others. Other people can change the view of the outline to show or hide as much detail as they need.

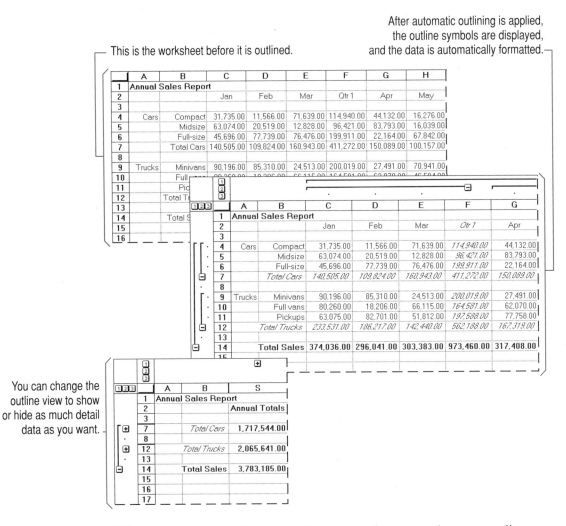

This is the worksheet before it is outlined.

After automatic outlining is applied, the outline symbols are displayed, and the data is automatically formatted.

You can change the outline view to show or hide as much detail data as you want.

When you create an outline, you define ranges of rows or columns as outline groups. Each group consists of detail data in rows and columns and summary data in an adjacent row or column. The outline can contain up to eight levels of vertical groups and eight levels of horizontal groups. You can create one outline per worksheet.

You use the outline symbols to change the view of the outline.

What the Outline Symbols Do

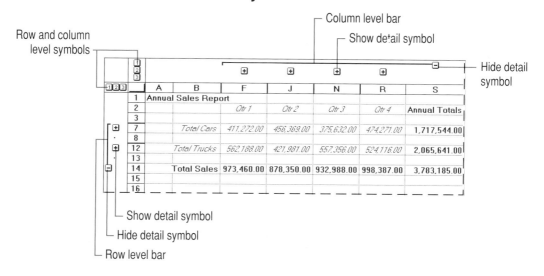

This symbol	Does this
Row or column level symbol	Shows specific levels of data in an outline.
Row or column level bar	Hides the detail rows or columns.
Hide detail symbol	Hides the rows or columns marked by the column or row level bar.
Show detail symbol	Shows hidden detail rows or columns. This symbol marks a summary row or column with adjacent detail rows or columns that are hidden.

Creating and Removing an Outline

There are three ways to create an outline.

- Use automatic outlining when worksheet data is organized in detail and summary rows or columns and the summary formulas refer to the detail data directly above or to the left of the summary data.

- Use manual outlining when summary data is not directly below or to the right of detail data or does not contain summary formulas that refer to detail data.

- Summarize lists when data is in list form and you want to automatically subtotal the data. For more information about summarizing lists, see "Displaying Automatic Subtotals in a List" in Chapter 22.

Automatic Outlining

Microsoft Excel can automatically outline selected worksheet data. Automatic outlining relies on formulas and direction of reference.

To group rows and columns into outline levels, Microsoft Excel looks for references to ranges of cells directly adjacent to the cell containing the formula, especially ranges above and to the left. Microsoft Excel examines which direction references point when grouping rows and columns in an outline. If the references point up or down, Microsoft Excel groups the rows. If the references point to the left or right, Microsoft Excel groups the columns.

	A	B	C
1	Annual Sales Report		
2			Jan
3			
4	Cars	Compact	31,735.00
5		Midsize	63,074.00
6		Full-size	45,696.00
7		*Total Cars*	*140,505.00*
8			
9	Trucks	Minivans	90,196.00
10		Full vans	80,260.00
11		Pickups	63,075.00
12		*Total Trucks*	*233,531.00*
13			
14			

These cells contain formulas that refer to ranges directly above them, so Microsoft Excel puts the rows into two groups.

To create an outline automatically, select the data you want to outline, choose the Group And Outline command from the Data menu, and then choose the Auto Outline command.

Styles in Outlines

Microsoft Excel includes built-in cell styles for the levels of an outline. You can automatically apply these styles to rows and columns in your outline. Then, if you want to change the formatting for a level in an outline, you can change the style for that level, and all of the cells that have that style assigned will be reformatted.

Before you automatically create the outline, you need to select the Automatic Styles option. To do this, choose the Group And Outline command from the Data menu, choose the Settings command, and then select the Automatic Styles check box. The styles that Microsoft Excel applies are named RowLevel_1, ColLevel_1, and so forth.

Manual Outlining

If your data is not organized for automatic outlining, you can create an outline manually.

To group	Do this
Detail data that is arranged in rows	Select the rows of detail data, choose the Group And Outline command from the Data Menu, and then choose the Group command.
Detail data that is arranged in columns	Select the columns of detail data, choose the Group And Outline command from the Data Menu, and then choose the Group command.

Removing an Outline

You can remove a portion of an outline or an entire outline from your worksheet.

To remove	Do this
A portion of an outline	Select the rows or columns from which you want the outline removed, choose the Group And Outline command from the Data menu, and then choose the Clear Outline command.
The entire outline	Select the entire outlined range, choose the Group And Outline command from the Data menu, and then choose the Clear Outline command.

Note   Instead of removing an outline, you can hide the outlining symbols and preserve the outline structure on the worksheet. To do this, choose the Options command from the Tools menu, select the View tab, and then clear the Outline Symbols check box. You can later display the outlining symbols when you need them.

Step By Step

For step-by-step instructions and related information, double-click the ⟨?⟩ button to display the Search dialog box in Help, and then:

Type this keyword and choose Show Topics	Select a topic and choose Go To
creating, outlines	Creating an outline automatically
	Creating an outline manually
removing, outlines	Removing an outline

Showing and Hiding Details in an Outline

You can change how a summary report is displayed. Showing or hiding detail in an outline does not change either the data on the worksheet or the structure of the outline. You can show or hide detail by using the outline symbols or the menu commands.

- The outline symbols provide a quick way to change the display of outlined data. Use the outline symbols to display or hide several outline levels at once.

- Use the menu commands to show or hide details when you do not want to view the outline symbols on the worksheet.

Using the Outline Symbols to Show or Hide Detail

By clicking the outline symbols on this summary report...

...you can hide
as much detail
data as you want.

To	Do this
Display the outline symbols on the worksheet	From the Tools menu, choose the Options command. Select the View tab, and then select the Outline Symbols check box.
Show a specific level of the outline	Click a row or column level symbol (①②③).
Show the detail within a group	Click the show detail symbol (⊞).
Hide the detail within a group	Click the hide detail symbol (⊟).

Using the Menu Commands to Show or Hide Detail

After selecting a summary data cell within a group...

	A	B	F	J	N	R	S
1	Annual Sales Report						
2			*Qtr 1*	*Qtr 2*	*Qtr 3*	*Qtr 4*	Annual Totals
3							
7		*Total Cars*	*411,272.00*	*456,369.00*	*375,632.00*	*474,271.00*	1,717,544.00
8							
12		*Total Trucks*	562,188.00	*421,981.00*	*557,356.00*	*524,116.00*	2,065,641.00
13							
14		Total S					
15							
16							

...you can use the Show Detail and Hide Detail commands to show or hide detail data on the worksheet.

	A	B	F	J	N	R	S
1	Annual Sales Report						
2			*Qtr 1*	*Qtr 2*	*Qtr 3*	*Qtr 4*	Annual Totals
3							
7		*Total Cars*	*411,272.00*	*456,369.00*	*375,632.00*	*474,271.00*	1,717,544.00
8							
9	Trucks	Minivans	*200,019.00*	*128,240.00*	*200,375.00*	*181,959.00*	710,593.00
10		Full vans	*164,581.00*	*125,146.00*	*148,991.00*	*186,743.00*	625,461.00
11		Pickups	*197,588.00*	*168,595.00*	*207,990.00*	*155,414.00*	729,587.00
12		*Total Trucks*	562,188.00	*421,981.00*	*557,356.00*	*524,116.00*	2,065,641.00
13							
14		Total Sales	973,460.00	878,350.00	932,988.00	998,387.00	3,783,185.00
15							
16							

To	Do this
Hide the outline symbols on the worksheet	From the Tools menu, choose the Options command. Select the View tab, and clear the Outline Symbols check box.
Show the detail within a group	Select any summary data cell within the group, choose the Group And Outline command from the Data menu, and then choose the Show Detail command.
Hide the detail within a group	Select any summary data cell within the group, choose the Group And Outline command from the Data menu, and then choose the Hide Detail command.

Step By Step

For step-by-step instructions and related information, double-click the [?] button to display the Search dialog box in Help, and then:

Type this keyword and choose Show Topics	Select a topic and choose Go To
levels, outline	Displaying a different outline level
showing detail data	Showing or hiding detail data

Changing an Outline's Organization

After creating an outline, you may want to change its structure. You change an outline's structure by grouping or ungrouping rows or columns.

To	Do this
Display or hide the outline symbols on the worksheet	From the Tools menu, choose the Options command. Select the View tab, and then select the Outline Symbols check box.
Define rows or columns as a group	Select the rows or columns you want to group. Choose the Group And Outline command from the Data menu, and then choose the Group command. You can also click the Group button on the Query And Pivot toolbar.
Remove rows or columns from the current group	Select the rows or columns you want to remove from the group. Choose the Group And Outline command from the Data menu, and then choose the Ungroup command. You can also click the Ungroup button on the Query And Pivot toolbar.

Here's a sample worksheet with automatic outlining applied. It was not set up quite right to produce the desired results.

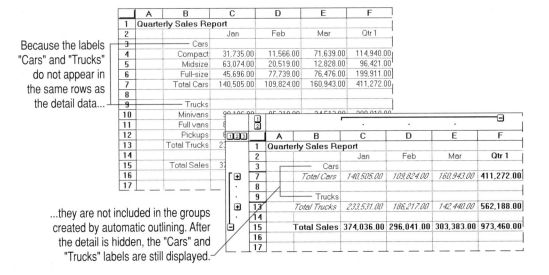

Because the labels "Cars" and "Trucks" do not appear in the same rows as the detail data...

...they are not included in the groups created by automatic outlining. After the detail is hidden, the "Cars" and "Trucks" labels are still displayed.

To correct this problem, add the rows that contain the "Cars" and "Trucks" labels (rows 3 and 9) to the existing groups. Select the row, choose the Group And Outline command from the Data menu, and then choose the Group command.

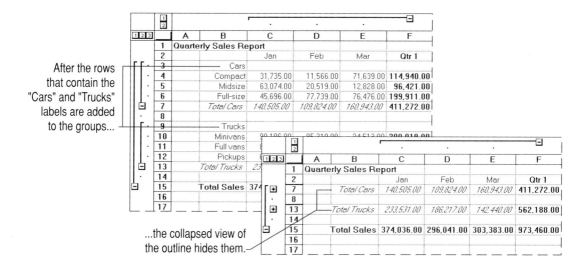

After the rows that contain the "Cars" and "Trucks" labels are added to the groups...

...the collapsed view of the outline hides them.

Step By Step

For step-by-step instructions and related information, double-click the [?] button to display the Search dialog box in Help, and then:

Type this keyword and choose Show Topics	Select a topic and choose Go To
grouping	Grouping or ungrouping rows or columns
levels, outline	Selecting a section of an outline
styles, outline	Applying styles to an outline
symbols, outline	Displaying or hiding the outline symbols
visible cells	Selecting visible cells in an outline

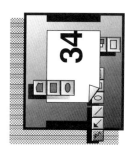

C H A P T E R   3 4

Customizing Your Workspace

For command, keyboard, and toolbar button information, see online Help.

In This Chapter

Changing Defaults and Settings

You can change most of the elements of the Microsoft Excel workbook, sheet, workspace, and window display. You can also turn many features of Microsoft Excel on or off, or change the way they work to best suit your working style.

Options You Can Change

You use the tabs in the Options dialog box to change Microsoft Excel defaults and settings. Choose the Options command from the Tools menu to display the dialog box.

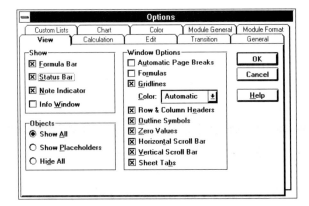

- **View Tab**   Change the way workbooks, sheets, objects, and windows are displayed.

- **Calculation Tab**   Change how and when Microsoft Excel recalculates data, how it manages links to data on other sheets, and the date system it uses.

- **Edit Tab**   Change how you enter, edit, copy, and move data.

- **Transition Tab**   Choose options that help you switch from another spreadsheet to Microsoft Excel. For more information about switching to Microsoft Excel, see Chapter 3, "If You're Switching from Another Spreadsheet."

- **General Tab**   Change options such as the number of sheets in a new workbook, the standard font, and the worksheet reference style.

- **Custom Lists Tab**   Create custom lists that can be used with the AutoFill feature and with custom sort orders. For more information about custom lists, see "Customizing AutoFill" in Chapter 9. For more information about custom sort orders, see "Sorting Data in a List" in Chapter 21.

- **Chart Tab**   Define how empty and hidden cells are plotted for line charts and how charts are sized with windows, and specify a default chart format for creating new charts.

- **Color Tab**   Change the default color palette, including the colors that are used for chart fills and lines, and copy color palettes from other workbooks.

- **Module General Tab**   Specify various options for how Visual Basic procedures are run, and how they are displayed when entered. You can also specify the international settings for the procedures you're writing.

- **Module Format Tab**   Specify the font, font size, and color of various types of code you write and record in Visual Basic.

For more information about the choices in the Options dialog box, you can click the Help button on any of the tabs.

Switching Between Tabs in a Dialog Box

To switch between tabs in a dialog box, click the name of the tab you want to view, or press CTRL+TAB.

Step By Step

For step-by-step instructions and related information, double-click the ⟨?⟩ button to display the Search dialog box in Help, and then:

Type this keyword and choose Show Topics	Select a topic and choose Go To
chart settings	Changing chart settings
display options	Changing what Microsoft Excel displays
editing, options for	Changing the way you enter and edit data
options, general	Changing general Microsoft Excel settings
switching to Microsoft Excel	Using features that help you switch to Microsoft Excel

Saving a Workspace File

You can open a group of workbooks in one step if you first save them as a workspace file. The workspace file does not contain the workbooks themselves. Instead, it contains information about which workbooks were open, their locations, and their size and position on the screen. When you open the workspace file, all of the workbooks are opened and positioned as you had them.

In many cases, you can accomplish what you need by including all your sheets within a single workbook. You can also create and save different views of a worksheet that display different sets of display and print settings for the same data. For more information, see "Creating Different Views of a Worksheet" in Chapter 32. By saving templates, you can create workbooks and sheets that are already set up as you want them. For more information, see Chapter 36, "Using Templates to Create Your Own Default Workbooks."

Creating and Saving a Workspace File

To create a workspace file, open all the workbooks you want to include in your workspace. Size and position them as you want them to appear the next time you open the file.

Note In Windows, the size and position of the application window is saved every time you quit Microsoft Excel.

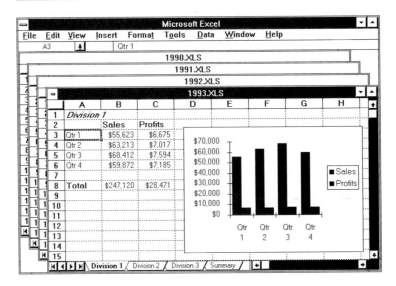

When you open a workspace, the workbooks are opened and arranged just as you saved them.

To save a workspace file, choose the Save Workspace command from the File menu. Microsoft Excel suggests the filename listed in the following table.

System	Suggested filename
Windows	RESUME.XLW
Macintosh	RESUME

To save your workspace with another name, type a name in the File Name box in the Save Workspace dialog box.

Opening a Workspace File

To open a workspace file, choose the Open command from the File menu and open the workspace file just as you would any other file.

Note The workbook names and directory or folder locations are saved with the workspace file. If you move your files to another location, Microsoft Excel will not be able to find them.

When you are done working, save and close your individual workbooks, just as you normally would.

Tip If you repositioned your workbooks on the screen and you want the new positions remembered, save your workspace file again.

Opening a Workspace Automatically

To have your workspace file open automatically each time you start Microsoft Excel, move or copy it into the startup directory or folder or alternate startup directory or folder. For more information about startup directories or folders, see Chapter 35, "Controlling What Happens When You Start Microsoft Excel."

Note You should not place the workbook files themselves in the startup directory or folder, only the workspace file.

Step By Step

For step-by-step instructions and related information, double-click the ▶? button to display the Search dialog box in Help, and then:

Type this keyword and choose Show Topics	Select a topic and choose Go To
workspace files	Creating and saving a workspace file
	Opening a workspace file

Customizing Toolbars

You can display any of the Microsoft Excel built-in toolbars, and you can customize them to include the buttons that you use the most. You can also create entirely new custom toolbars and custom buttons that perform actions that you program them to do.

Microsoft Excel automatically saves any changes you make to toolbars, so they are available the next time you open Microsoft Excel.

Displaying and Hiding Toolbars

Microsoft Excel initially displays two toolbars, the Standard toolbar and the Formatting toolbar.

Standard toolbar

Formatting toolbar

In addition, Microsoft Excel automatically displays the Chart toolbar when you are working on a chart and the Visual Basic toolbar when you are working in a module. Other toolbars, such as the Query And Pivot toolbar, automatically appear when you are working with Microsoft Excel features.

To display other toolbars, choose a toolbar from the toolbar shortcut menu.

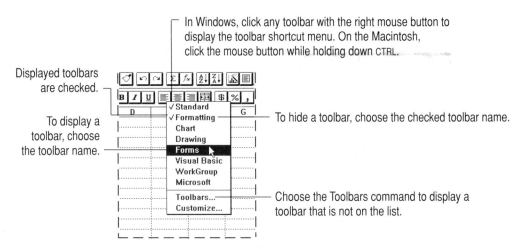

In Windows, click any toolbar with the right mouse button to display the toolbar shortcut menu. On the Macintosh, click the mouse button while holding down CTRL.

Displayed toolbars are checked.

To display a toolbar, choose the toolbar name.

To hide a toolbar, choose the checked toolbar name.

Choose the Toolbars command to display a toolbar that is not on the list.

If a toolbar is not displayed, choose the Toolbars command from the View menu, and select the toolbar you want to display.

Microsoft Excel Version 5.0 Toolbars

Toolbar	Used for
Standard	Basic workbook tasks
Formatting	Formatting characters, numbers, and cells
Query And Pivot	Working with pivot tables and Microsoft Query add-ins
Chart	Creating and modifying charts
Drawing	Creating graphic objects

Toolbar	Used for
TipWizard	Displaying tips while using Microsoft Excel
Stop Recording	Stopping the recording of a macro
Full Screen	Returning to normal view after displaying the full screen
Forms	Creating Visual Basic dialog boxes
Visual Basic	Working in Visual Basic modules
Auditing	Tracing precedents, dependents, and errors within formulas
Workgroup	Finding, routing, and sending files
Microsoft	Switching to other Microsoft applications

Moving Toolbars

Toolbars can be displayed as floating toolbars or docked along the edges of the application window.

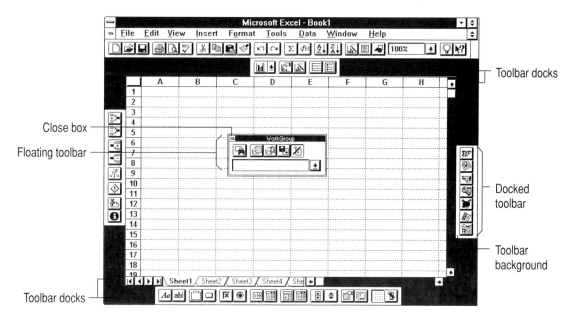

Floating toolbars can be sized the same way as a window. You can hide floating toolbars by clicking the close box.

To move a toolbar, drag the toolbar background. If the toolbar is floating, you can also drag the title bar. As you move the toolbar around the workspace, it will stick to the sides of the application window. If you release the mouse in this position, the toolbar will dock along the edge.

Note A toolbar that contains a drop-down list box or a palette, such as the Font box or the Color button, cannot be docked along the left or right sides of the application window.

Tip If you double-click a toolbar background, it will switch between a floating toolbar and a docked toolbar. If you double-click the background of a toolbar dock, the Toolbars dialog box is displayed.

Creating Custom Toolbars

To create a custom toolbar, choose the Toolbars command from the View menu or the toolbar shortcut menu. Type a name in the Toolbar Name box, and then choose the New button. A new blank toolbar with your title will appear along with the Customize dialog box. You can then drag the buttons you want onto the new toolbar.

You can also create a custom toolbar by dragging a button from the Customize dialog box anywhere except onto an existing toolbar. Microsoft Excel creates a new custom toolbar and names it Toolbar 1. Other toolbars created this way will be named Toolbar 2, Toolbar 3, and so on.

Note You cannot rename a toolbar.

To delete a custom toolbar, choose the Toolbars command from the View menu or the toolbar shortcut menu. Select the toolbar you want to delete, and then choose the Delete button.

Note You cannot delete the built-in toolbars.

Adding and Deleting Toolbar Buttons

You can customize toolbars to display any of the buttons included with Microsoft Excel or any custom buttons that you create.

To add an existing button to a toolbar, choose the Customize command from the toolbar shortcut menu. Drag the button from the Customize dialog box to the toolbar.

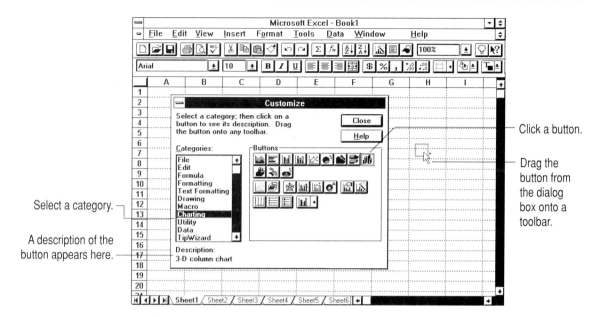

Select a category.

A description of the
button appears here.

Click a button.

Drag the
button from
the dialog
box onto a
toolbar.

To delete a button from a toolbar, choose the Customize command from the toolbar shortcut menu. With the dialog box open, drag the button you want to delete off the toolbar, anywhere except onto another toolbar.

Moving and Sizing Toolbar Buttons

You can move buttons around on toolbars. First choose the Customize command from the toolbar shortcut menu. With the dialog box open, drag the button to its new position on the toolbar. You can also regroup buttons by dragging them slightly to add spacing or close up spaces on a toolbar.

You can size any of the drop-down list boxes that appear on a toolbar—the Font box, Font Size box, Zoom Control box, Style box, and Scenarios box. With the Customize dialog box open, select the list box, position the mouse over the right or left side of the box, and drag to resize it.

Using Tear-off Palettes

The Borders, Pattern, Color, Font Color, Drawing, and Chart Type buttons feature movable tear-off palettes. If a toolbar contains one of these buttons, you cannot dock the toolbar on the left or right side of the application window.

Click the arrow to display the palette.

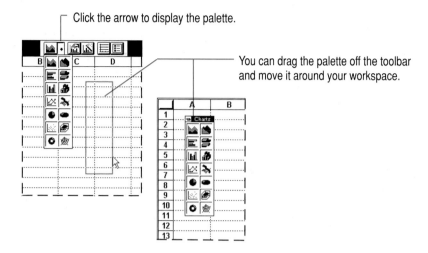

You can drag the palette off the toolbar and move it around your workspace.

The last button you choose from the palette is displayed on the toolbar button for quick access.

Changing a Button Image

You can change the button image by copying an existing button image to another button. To do this, choose the Customize command from the toolbar shortcut menu. With the dialog box open, select a button whose image you want to copy. Then choose the Copy Button Image and Paste Button Image commands from the Edit menu to copy and paste any button image.

You can also create your own custom button image using the Button Editor. To do this, choose the Customize command from the toolbar shortcut menu. On the toolbar, click the button you want to change, and then choose the Edit Button Image command from the button shortcut menu. Use the options in the dialog box to change the button image.

Select the color you want to use. If you select Erase, foreground colors are erased.

Click the pixels to use the selected color.

Click an arrow to move the entire image in that direction.

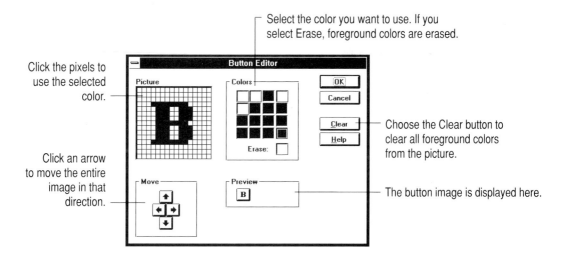

Choose the Clear button to clear all foreground colors from the picture.

The button image is displayed here.

Creating Custom Buttons

You can create custom buttons by assigning or recording a macro to a button. For information about assigning or recording macros to buttons, see Chapter 1, "Automating Repeated Tasks," in the *Microsoft Excel Visual Basic User's Guide*.

Resetting Toolbars

You can easily reset any of the built-in toolbars provided with Microsoft Excel to their original configuration. From the View menu or the toolbar shortcut menu, choose the Toolbars command. In the Toolbars list, select the toolbar you want to reset, and then choose the Reset button.

Note   You cannot reset custom toolbars, but you can delete them.

Saving Custom Toolbars

Your toolbars and their arrangement are saved in the file listed in the following table every time you quit Microsoft Excel.

System	File and location
Windows	EXCEL5.XLB in the Windows directory
Macintosh	EXCEL TOOLBARS (5) in the PREFERENCES folder in the SYSTEM folder

Tip If you want to save a particular toolbar configuration, customize and arrange your toolbars as you want them and then quit Microsoft Excel. Make a copy of the toolbar file, and then save it with a different name. Use the .XLB extension when naming toolbar files in Windows. When you want to display your saved toolbar configuration, open your toolbar file using the Open command on the File menu. The original toolbar file will continue to contain your most recently used toolbar configuration.

Attaching Custom Toolbars to a Workbook

You can attach custom toolbars to a workbook. To do this, insert a module into your workbook, or select a module you already have inserted. From the Tools menu, choose the Attach Toolbars command. Use the dialog box to copy any of your custom toolbars into the current workbook. Now each time you open that workbook, your custom toolbars are available.

For more information, see "Managing Toolbars and Toolbar Buttons with Visual Basic" in Chapter 12 of the *Microsoft Excel Visual Basic User's Guide*.

Step By Step

For step-by-step instructions and related information, double-click the  button to display the Search dialog box in Help, and then:

Type this keyword and choose Show Topics	Select a topic and choose Go To
button images	Changing the image on a toolbar button
buttons	Using Toolbar Buttons
buttons, adding to toolbar	Adding or deleting a toolbar button
buttons, moving	Moving and copying toolbar buttons
buttons, spacing	Spacing buttons on a toolbar
custom toolbars	Creating and deleting a custom toolbar
	Saving custom toolbars
list boxes	Changing the width of a drop-down list box on a toolbar

Type this keyword and choose Show Topics	Select a topic and choose Go To
toolbars	Displaying or hiding toolbars
	Moving and resizing toolbars
	Restoring a built-in toolbar

Using Custom Color Palettes

Each Microsoft Excel workbook has a palette of 56 colors that you can apply to cells, fonts, individual characters, gridlines, graphic objects, and fills and lines in a chart. If you are using a color monitor, you can customize the shade and intensity of the colors in the color palette for each workbook.

To use the same custom color scheme in a set of workbooks, you can copy the color palette from one workbook to another. For example, you can create a custom color palette that matches your company's logo and image and then copy it into all the workbooks used in company presentations. You can use a workbook with a custom color palette saved as a template to replace the default color palette Microsoft Excel uses when it creates a new workbook.

Changing a Color Palette

You can change individual colors in workbooks using the color palette. To change a default color, choose the Options command from the Tools menu, select the Color tab, and then double-click the color you want to change. You can also click a color to select it and then choose the Modify button. The dialog box your operating system uses to control colors is displayed. When you change a color in a color palette, that color is changed for all of the sheets in the workbook. Anything formatted with the color you changed will change as well.

You can also change the default color palette that Microsoft Excel uses whenever a new workbook is created. To change the default palette, save the workbook containing a custom color palette as a template, and then place the template in Microsoft Excel's startup directory or folder. For information about templates, see Chapter 36, "Using Templates to Create Your Own Default Workbooks." For information about changing how Microsoft Excel starts, see "Opening Workbooks Automatically with a Startup Directory or Folder" in Chapter 35.

Restoring the Default Color Palette

You can restore the color palette to the original 56 colors. To do this, choose the Options command from the Tools menu, select the Color tab, and then choose the Reset button.

Copying a Color Palette from Another Workbook

Custom color palettes you've created for one workbook can be used in other workbooks. Open the workbook you want to copy a color palette from and then choose the Options command from the Tools menu. Select the Color tab and then select a workbook in the Copy Colors From list. The color palette from the workbook you selected is copied into the active workbook, replacing the existing palette.

Note When you copy an object or cell containing a custom color from one workbook to another, the custom color is copied with it and replaces one of the colors on the default palette.

Using Custom Colors in Custom Number Formats

You can use custom colors in custom number formats by typing **[color***n***]** in the custom format, where *n* is the number of the color from the color palette. (You must type the brackets.) The colors in the color palette are numbered 1 through 56 by row, starting with the upper-left color. For example, to format numbers with the General Number format and the color in the upper-right corner of the Color Palette box, create the following custom number format:

[Color8]General

You can also use the color names black, white, red, green, blue, yellow, magenta and cyan within brackets in a custom number format. If you use a color name in a format, text or numbers in that format will always have that color. If you use a number from the color palette in a format, text and numbers in that format will change whenever the corresponding color is changed in the palette.

Step By Step

For step-by-step instructions and related information, double-click the [?] button to display the Search dialog box in Help, and then:

Type this keyword and choose Show Topics	Select a topic and choose Go To
custom number formats	Creating and deleting custom number formats
color palettes	Copying color palettes between workbooks
	Customizing colors in a color palette
default startup workbook	Changing the appearance and contents of the default startup workbook
templates, workbook	Saving a workbook as a template

CHAPTER 35

Controlling What Happens When You Start Microsoft Excel

For command, keyboard, and toolbar button information, see online Help.

In This Chapter

- Opening Workbooks Automatically with a Startup Directory or Folder   642

- Setting the Working Directory or Folder   646

- Controlling How Microsoft Excel for Windows Starts Using Startup Switches   646

Note This chapter provides information about opening workbooks automatically at startup and changing your working directory. For information about changing workspace elements such as standard font and default toolbars, see Chapter 34, "Customizing Your Workspace."

Opening Workbooks Automatically with a Startup Directory or Folder

If you want to open a workbook automatically when you start Microsoft Excel, move or copy the workbook to the *startup directory* or *startup folder*. When you start Microsoft Excel, it checks the contents of the startup directory or folder and:

- Opens all workbooks, charts, and workspace files it finds there. If you have not placed your own workbooks in the startup directory or folder, Microsoft Excel opens a new, unsaved workbook.

- Lists all workbook templates it finds there in the New dialog box so you can use them to create new workbooks. For more information about templates, see Chapter 36, "Using Templates to Create Your Own Default Workbooks."

For more information about starting Microsoft Excel, see "Starting and Quitting Microsoft Excel" in Chapter 1.

Where to Find the Startup Directory or Folder

System	Name of startup directory or folder	Location of startup directory or folder
Microsoft Windows	XLSTART	C:\EXCEL or the directory in which you installed Microsoft Excel
Apple Macintosh	EXCEL STARTUP FOLDER (5)	PREFERENCES folder in SYSTEM FOLDER

Making a Workbook Open Automatically

To make a workbook open automatically, move or copy it into the startup directory or folder. If you do not want a workbook to display at startup, move it out of the startup directory or folder.

Note   Microsoft Excel does not automatically open workbooks placed in subdirectories of the startup directory or in folders located within the startup folder.

You can also control which workbooks open on startup by placing a *workspace file* in your startup directory. Use a workspace file if you want to open multiple workbooks in a customized workspace. For more information about creating and saving workspace files, see "Saving a Workspace File" in Chapter 34.

In Microsoft Excel for Windows, you can also open a workbook automatically using a command line option called a *startup switch* with the Microsoft Excel icon in the Windows Program Manager. For more information, see "Controlling How Microsoft Excel for Windows Starts Using Startup Switches" later in this chapter.

Using an Additional Startup Directory or Folder

After opening workbooks in the startup directory or folder, Microsoft Excel opens workbooks located in the *alternate startup directory* or *alternate startup folder,* if you have specified one. Use an alternate startup directory or folder if you want to automatically open workbooks that are not stored in the primary startup directory or folder.

For example, use an alternate startup directory or folder to open workbooks or templates that reside on a shared network drive.

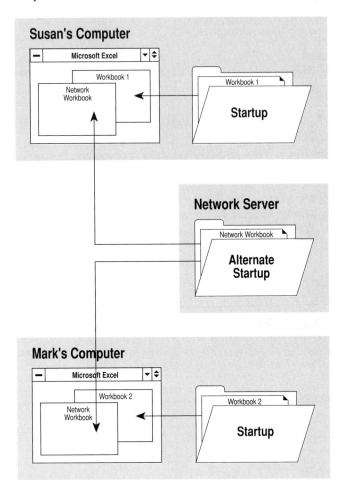

If two or more users want to open the same workbook when they start Microsoft Excel, they can place that workbook in a network directory or folder and then specify the network directory or folder as an alternate startup directory or folder.

For more information about sharing workbooks, see "Creating or Opening Workbooks" in Chapter 6.

You specify an alternate startup directory or folder using the Alternate Startup File Location box on the General tab in the Options dialog box. To display the Options dialog box, choose the Options command from the Tools menu. You can specify only one additional startup directory or folder.

Changing the Appearance and Contents of the Default Startup Workbook

If you do not specify a startup workbook, Microsoft Excel displays a new, unsaved workbook when you start Microsoft Excel. You can change the format and contents of all future default workbooks by saving a workbook with your preferences as a template in a startup directory or folder. You can also use this *autotemplate* to determine the format for any new workbook you display by using the New command on the File menu.

System	Template name and location
Windows	BOOK.XLT in the startup or alternate startup directory
Macintosh	WORKBOOK in the startup or alternate startup folder

You can also place sheet autotemplates in the startup directory or folder. Sheet autotemplates enable you to change the default contents or format for any new worksheet, chart, module sheet, dialog sheet, or Microsoft Excel version 4.0 macro sheet you insert in your workbooks using the commands on the Insert menu.

For more information about creating and saving autotemplates, see Chapter 36, "Using Templates to Create Your Own Default Workbooks."

Changing the Standard Font   You do not have to create a special template if you want to change only the standard font for your workbooks. Choose the Options command from the Tools menu, and select the General tab. Then select the font you want in the Standard Font box. This will change the standard font for the startup workbook or any new workbook once you restart Microsoft Excel.

For more information about changing the standard font or Normal style, see "Changing Defaults and Settings" in Chapter 34.

Step By Step

For step-by-step instructions and related information, double-click the  button to display the Search dialog box in Help, and then:

Type this keyword and choose Show Topics	Select a topic and choose Go To
default startup workbook	Changing the appearance and contents of the default startup workbook
startup directory	Specifying an additional startup directory (Windows)
startup folder	Specifying an additional startup folder (Macintosh)
workbooks, opening	Opening a workbook automatically
workspace files	Overview of Saving Workspace Files

Setting the Working Directory or Folder

The working directory or folder is the directory or folder that Microsoft Excel first makes available to you when you choose the Save As or Open command from the File menu. Unless you specify otherwise, Microsoft Excel assumes that the working directory or folder is the directory or folder where you installed Microsoft Excel. If you routinely store and access your documents in another directory or folder, you may want to specify a different working directory or folder.

You set the working directory or folder using the Default File Location box on the General tab in the Options dialog box. To display the Options dialog box, choose the Options command from the Tools menu.

In Microsoft Excel for Windows, you can also set the working directory by changing the properties of the Microsoft Excel icon in Program Manager. If you add a working directory setting to the Microsoft Excel icon, make sure you have not entered a working directory path in the General tab because the General tab overrides any working directory setting you make in Program Manager. For more information, see the following section, "Controlling How Microsoft Excel for Windows Starts Using Startup Switches."

Step By Step

For step-by-step instructions and related information, double-click the [▶?] button to display the Search dialog box in Help, and then:

Type this keyword and choose Show Topics	Select a topic and choose Go To
working directory	Setting the working directory (Windows)
working folder	Setting the working folder (Macintosh)

Controlling How Microsoft Excel for Windows Starts Using Startup Switches

If you want to set options such as the startup workbook or the working directory for the current session in Microsoft Excel for Windows, you can use command line options called *startup switches* in the Properties dialog box for the Microsoft Excel icon.

To change the properties of the Microsoft Excel icon, click the Microsoft Excel icon in the Program Manager window, then choose Properties from the File menu. Enter the Microsoft Excel startup command and the startup switch in the Command Line box.

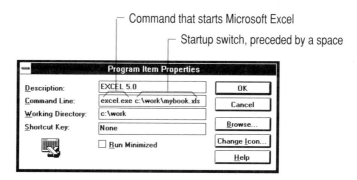

If you add a switch to the Microsoft Excel icon's properties, it stays in effect until you remove it. If you want to specify more than one switch, separate each switch with a space.

You can also enter a startup switch when you start Microsoft Excel using the Run command on the File menu in either the Windows Program Manager or File Manager. Startup switches used with the Run command are in effect only for the current session.

Startup Switches

If you want to	Type	Example
Open a specific file	**excel.exe** *filename* in the Command Line box	**excel.exe c:\mywork\mybook.xls** Opens the file MYBOOK.XLS in the MYWORK directory.
Open a specific file as read only	**excel.exe /r** *filename* in the Command Line box	**excel.exe /r c:\mywork\mybook.xls** Opens the file MYBOOK.XLS in the MYWORK directory as read only.

If you want to	Type	Example
Specify a working directory in the Properties dialog box	*directory path* in the Working Directory box	**c:\mywork** Makes the MYWORK directory the working directory.
Specify a working directory in the Run dialog box	**excel.exe /p** *directory path* in the Command Line box	**excel.exe /p c:\mywork** Makes the MYWORK directory the working directory for the current session.
Start Microsoft Excel without a new, unsaved workbook	**excel.exe /e** in the Command Line box	Prevents Microsoft Excel from opening BOOK1.

Note If you want to set the working directory using a startup switch or the Working Directory box, make sure that you have not entered a working directory path in the Default File Location box on the General tab in the Options dialog box. The General tab setting overrides any working directory setting you make in Program Manager. For more information about the General tab, see "Setting the Working Directory or Folder" earlier in this chapter.

Creating Multiple Startup Options

If you use Microsoft Excel to work on several different sets of documents, you can use Program Manager to create different Microsoft Excel icons that open different workbooks or that use different working directories. For example, you might use Microsoft Excel some days to view order records stored on a server and on other days to create sales reports or review budgets. By using separate icons, you can set up one icon that displays your order workbooks on startup, and others that display your report templates and budget worksheets.

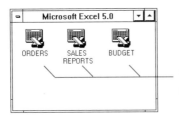

You can specify a different startup workbook and working directory for each icon.

To create multiple startup icons, copy the Microsoft Excel icon in the Microsoft Office program group or the group in which you installed Microsoft Excel. Then customize the startup options for each icon using the Properties command on the Program Manager File menu. For more information about creating and customizing icons in Program Manager, see your Microsoft Windows documentation.

Step By Step

For step-by-step instructions and related information, double-click the ⬛?️ button to display the Search dialog box in Help, and then:

Type this keyword and choose Show Topics	Select a topic and choose Go To
startup switches	Controlling how Microsoft Excel starts using startup switches (Windows)

C H A P T E R   3 6

Using Templates to Create Your Own Default Workbooks

For command, keyboard, and toolbar button information, see online Help.

In This Chapter

What Is a Template?

A *template* is a special workbook you can use as a pattern to create other workbooks of the same type. For example, you can create a sales report workbook, save it as a template, and then create weekly sales reports based on the template. In addition to creating new workbooks based on templates, you can insert sheets from templates into your workbooks.

Templates can contain:

- Text and graphics, such as a company name and logo.
- Formatting and page layout, such as styles and custom headers and footers.
- Formulas and macros.

This sales report template contains the formatting and formulas—but not the data—for a monthly sales report.

	A	B	C	D	E	F
1		Northwind Traders				
2		Daily Average Sales Report				
3						
4	Sales Office:					
5	Month, Year:					
6						
7		Week 1	Week 2	Week 3	Week 4	
8	Monday	$0	$0	$0	$0	
9	Tuesday	$0	$0	$0	$0	
10	Wednesday	$0	$0	$0	$0	
11	Thursday	$0	$0	$0	$0	
12	Friday	$0	$0	$0	$0	
13	Saturday	$0	$0	$0	$0	
14	Sunday	$0	$0	$0	$0	
15						
16	DAILY AVERAGE	$0				
17						
18						

These two completed sales reports for October and November are based on the sales report template. Note that no additional formatting or formulas were needed—just the monthly sales numbers.

Northwind Traders
Daily Average Sales Report

| Sales Office: | Western Division |
| Month, Year: | October, 1993 |

	Week 1
Monday	$408,657
Tuesday	$386,860
Wednesday	$395,308
Thursday	$363,681
Friday	$348,464
Saturday	$310,997
Sunday	$340,899
DAILY AVERAGE	$377,979

Northwind Traders
Daily Average Sales Report

| Sales Office: | Western Division |
| Month, Year: | November, 1993 |

	Week 1	Week 2	Week 3	Week 4
Monday	$473,272	$375,673	$324,492	$477,345
Tuesday	$476,811	$451,904	$394,526	$483,644
Wednesday	$401,630	$308,109	$383,455	$355,317
Thursday	$453,456	$409,089	$306,531	$483,936
Friday	$429,315	$374,428	$303,997	$399,351
Saturday	$342,372	$469,582	$406,087	$427,467
Sunday	$482,561	$399,306	$425,106	$408,007
DAILY AVERAGE	$408,099			

When you open a template, Microsoft Excel creates a copy of the template for you to work with. This leaves the original template intact the next time you need it.

In Microsoft Excel for the Macintosh, a template works the same way as a System 7 stationery pad. Templates created with Microsoft Excel are automatically recognized by the Finder as stationery pads. For information about stationery pads, see your Macintosh system documentation.

Creating New Workbooks and Inserting New Sheets with Autotemplates

You can create special templates, called *autotemplates*, in your startup or alternate startup directory or folder. You can then use autotemplates as the basis for all new workbooks and all new sheets you insert into your workbooks. Autotemplates are just templates saved with a specific name, in a specific location.

Creating and Editing Templates

Saving a Workbook as a Template

You can save any workbook as a template. To create a template, first create the workbook that includes any text, formats, and formulas you want, and then choose the Save As command from the File menu. Enter the filename and select the directory or folder and drive you want. Under Save File As Type, select Template.

You can also create autotemplates in your startup or alternate startup directory or folder to change the default workbook or sheet. When you create autotemplates, you can use them as the basis for all new workbooks you create and all new sheets you insert into workbooks. For information about creating autotemplates, see the following sections, "Creating New Workbooks from Templates" and "Inserting New Sheets from Templates into Workbooks."

Opening and Editing the Original Template

You can open the original template workbook to edit it. You can identify a template by its filename and description.

System	Template identifier
Windows	.XLT filename extension, for example SALES.XLT
Macintosh	Microsoft Excel Stationery Pad file type (System 7) and icon in the Finder

Open

To open the original template, click the Open button, select the template you want to edit, and do the following.

System	Do this
Windows	Hold down SHIFT and choose the OK button.
Macintosh	Hold down SHIFT and choose the Open button.

Save

When you're ready to save the template, click the Save button. Microsoft Excel saves the template using the template format.

Step By Step

For step-by-step instructions and related information, double-click the 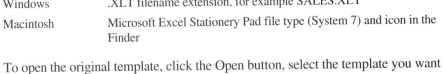 button to display the Search dialog box in Help, and then:

Type this keyword and choose Show Topics	Select a topic and choose Go To
templates, opening	Opening and editing the original template
templates, workbook	Saving a workbook as a template

Creating New Workbooks from Templates

Open

To create a new workbook based on a template, just open the template. Click the Open File button, and then choose the template filename. Microsoft Excel creates a copy of the template, leaving the original template intact.

Tip You can quickly open templates by saving them in your startup or alternate startup directory or folder and then choosing the New command from the File menu to select the template you want. For information about the startup and alternate startup directory or folder, see "Opening Workbooks Automatically with a Startup Directory or Folder" in Chapter 35.

Caution When linking workbooks, do not use the original template as a source workbook. Because you always work with a copy created from a template, you will break the links from the original template. However, you can create formulas that reference other sheets in the same template.

Using an Autotemplate to Create Your Own Default Workbooks

You can specify the default font, formatting, and other options for new workbooks by creating a default workbook template, called an *autotemplate*. For example, you can create a workbook autotemplate that includes customized headers and footers and your company name or any text, formatting, formulas, and macros you can enter in a regular workbook.

When you create a workbook autotemplate, you can use it as the basis for all new workbooks you create. If there are other templates in the startup or alternate startup directory or folder, you can also create new workbooks based on them.

To create a workbook autotemplate, create or open the workbook you want to use as the autotemplate. Choose the Save As command from the File menu and save the workbook in the template file format using the filename and location listed in the following table, or in your alternate startup directory or folder.

System	Workbook autotemplate name and location
Windows	BOOK.XLT in the XLSTART startup directory
Macintosh	WORKBOOK in the EXCEL STARTUP FOLDER (5)

New Workbook

When you choose New from the File menu and select Workbook, or when you click the New Workbook button, Microsoft Excel creates a new workbook based on the autotemplate.

For information about the startup directory or folder, see "Opening Workbooks Automatically with a Startup Directory or Folder" in Chapter 35.

> ## Changing the Font for All New Workbooks
> Have you ever wanted to use a different default font in your workbooks? You could format each new workbook to use the font you want, but there's a better way. Choose the Options command from the Tools menu, and select the General tab. Then select the font you want in the Standard Font box. This will change the standard font for any new workbook once you restart Microsoft Excel.

Step By Step

For step-by-step instructions and related information, double-click the [?] button to display the Search dialog box in Help, and then:

Type this keyword and choose Show Topics	Select a topic and choose Go To
autotemplates	Changing the default new workbook using an autotemplate
templates	Getting quick access to your templates
templates, workbook	Creating a new workbook based on a template

Inserting New Sheets from Templates into Workbooks

You can insert sheets from your templates into your workbooks. To create a template, create or open the workbook you want to use as a template. Choose the Save As command from the File menu and save the workbook using the template file format in the startup directory or folder listed in the following table, or in your alternate startup directory or folder.

System	Template location
Windows	XLSTART startup directory
Macintosh	EXCEL STARTUP FOLDER (5)

From the sheet tab shortcut menu, choose the Insert command, and then select the template whose sheet you want to insert.

To insert a new sheet, choose Insert from the sheet tab shortcut menu.

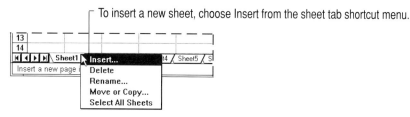

A list of sheet types appears. This includes all of the templates in your startup directory or folder. In this case, Calendar and Sales are templates.

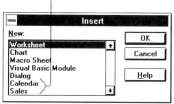

After selecting the Sales template, its single worksheet is inserted into the workbook.

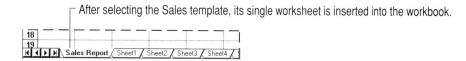

The new sheet is inserted to the left of the active sheet.

Using an Autotemplate to Insert Your Own Default Sheets

By creating sheet autotemplates, you can change the default for most new sheets you insert into your workbooks using the commands on the Insert menu (autotemplates for modules are not supported). For example, you can add your company name and logo to a worksheet autotemplate, or you can add code structure to a Visual Basic module autotemplate.

To create a sheet autotemplate, edit a sheet to include the formatting, text, and other options you want. Choose the Save As command from the File menu and save it as a template in your startup or alternate startup directory or folder using the filename listed in the following table. Because you want only a single sheet inserted, the workbook template you save should contain only a single sheet.

Sheet type	Save in Windows XLSTART startup directory	Save in Macintosh EXCEL STARTUP FOLDER (5)
Worksheet	SHEET.XLT	WORKSHEET
Chart	CHART.XLT	CHART
Dialog	DIALOG.XLT	DIALOG
MS Excel 4.0 macro	MACRO.XLT	MACRO

Once you've created autotemplates, you can use them as the basis of new sheets you insert into your workbooks.

To insert this sheet type	Choose this command from the Insert menu
Worksheet	Worksheet
Chart	Chart, and then As New Sheet
Dialog	Macro, and then Dialog
MS Excel 4.0 macro	Macro, and then MS Excel 4.0 Macro

Note You may find chart autoformats easier to use than chart templates. Microsoft Excel will use chart templates only if your default chart autoformat is a built-in format. For information about chart autoformats, see Chapter 16, "Working with Chart Types and Autoformats."

Step By Step

For step-by-step instructions and related information, double-click the ⟨?⟩ button to display the Search dialog box in Help, and then:

Type this keyword and choose Show Topics	Select a topic and choose Go To
autotemplates	Creating an autotemplate for new sheets
chart sheets, autotemplates	Inserting a new sheet based on an autotemplate
templates, new sheets based on	Inserting a new sheet based on a template

CHAPTER 37

Installing Add-in Features

For command, keyboard, and toolbar button information, see online Help.

In This Chapter

Installing Add-ins

Add-ins are commands or functions that add special capabilities to Microsoft Excel.

To install an add-in in Microsoft Excel, choose the Add-ins command from the Tools menu, and then select the check box next to the add-in you want. If the add-in you want is not listed, choose the Browse button to locate it. If you can't locate the add-in on your hard disk or network drive, you can select the Macro Library option or another add-in option in the Microsoft Excel Setup program to install these add-ins. For information, see Chapter 1, "Installing and Starting Microsoft Excel," or the Step By Step table at the end of this section.

Once an add-in is installed...

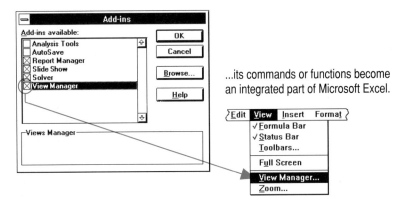

...its commands or functions become an integrated part of Microsoft Excel.

You can also create your own add-ins with Visual Basic. For more information, see Chapter 13 , "Creating Automatic Procedures and Add-in Applications" in the *Microsoft Excel Visual Basic User's Guide.*

Step By Step

For step-by-step instructions and related information, double-click the ⮕? button to display the Search dialog box in Help, and then:

Type this keyword and choose Show Topics	Select a topic and choose Go To
add-ins	Add-ins Included with Microsoft Excel
	Installing or removing an add-in

Add-ins Included with Microsoft Excel

System	Add-in location
Windows	LIBRARY directory or one of its subdirectories
Macintosh	MACRO LIBRARY folder or one of its subfolders

The following table describes the add-ins included with Microsoft Excel and tells you where to find more information about them.

Add-in	Description	For more information, see
Analysis ToolPak	Adds financial and engineering functions, and provides tools for performing statistical and engineering analysis.	"Data Analysis Tools Make Statistical or Engineering Analysis Easier" in Chapter 31.
AutoSave	Saves workbooks automatically as you work.	"Saving and Closing Workbooks" in Chapter 6.
Microsoft ODBC	Adds worksheet and macro functions for retrieving data from external sources with Microsoft Open Database Connectivity (ODBC).	Chapter 23, "Retrieving Data with Microsoft Query."
Microsoft Query Add-in	Retrieves data from external database files and tables using Microsoft Query.	Chapter 23, "Retrieving Data with Microsoft Query."
Report Manager	Prints reports that consist of views and scenarios.	"Creating and Printing Custom Reports" in Chapter 14.
Slide Show	Works with the Slide Show template workbook to create a slide show from Microsoft Excel worksheets and charts.	Appendix A, "Producing a Slide Show."

Add-in	Description	For more information, see
Solver	Calculates solutions to what-if scenarios based on adjustable cells, constraint cells, and, optionally, cells that must be maximized or minimized. You must select the Solver option during Setup if you want to use Solver.	Chapter 29, "Using Solver to Analyze Multiple-Variable Problems."
View Manager	Saves the current window display as a view and lets you apply your saved views to see your worksheet in different formats.	"Creating Different Views of a Worksheet" in Chapter 32.

PART 8

Reviewing and Sharing
Workbooks

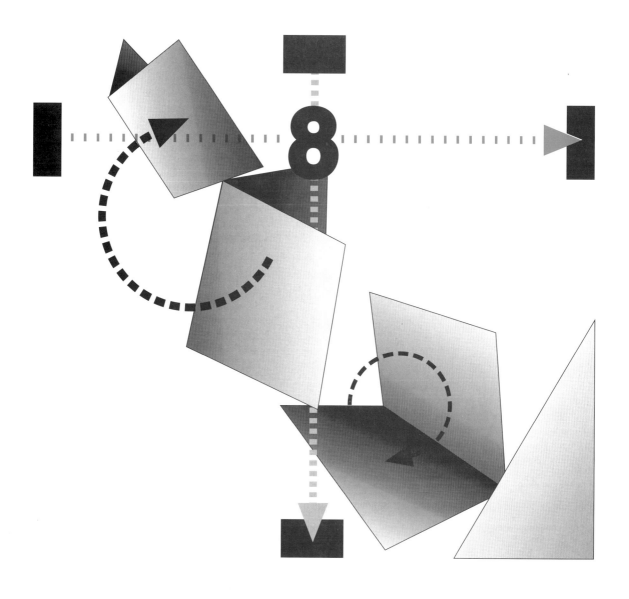

C H A P T E R   3 8

Troubleshooting and Annotating a Worksheet

For command, keyboard, and toolbar button information, see online Help.

In This Chapter

Understanding the Auditing Features

Microsoft Excel provides features that help you track down problems on your worksheets. Most are available either as menu commands or on the Auditing toolbar.

Auditing Toolbar   The eight buttons on this toolbar give you an easier way to conduct a troubleshooting session using tracers and the other auditing features. (The rest of this chapter assumes you'll be using this method.) To display the Auditing toolbar, choose Auditing from the Tools menu, and then choose Show Auditing Toolbar.

Tracers   The precedent, dependent, and error tracers display a graphic representation of the flow of computations on your worksheet. You can quickly see the cells that a selected formula uses in its calculations (precedents) or see all the formulas that use the value contained in a selected cell (dependents). The error tracer helps you identify the source of any error value on your worksheet. To use the tracer menu commands, choose Auditing from the Tools menu, or click one of the tracer buttons on the Auditing toolbar.

Notes   You can attach text or an audio message to a cell containing a value that needs explanation, or to a cell containing a complex formula that you want to document for future reference. From the Insert menu, choose Note, or click the Attach Note button on the Auditing toolbar.

Info Window   You can display selected data about the active cell. You can configure the Info window to display the active cell's formula, the value that the formula produces, the cell's format, protection status, precedents and dependents, and more. You use the Options command on the Tools menu or the Show Info Window button on the Auditing toolbar to display the Info window.

Go To Special   This dialog box enables you to select all the cells with specified types of contents. For instance, it can select only those cells that contain formulas, constants, text, or cell notes. To display the Go To Special dialog box, choose Go To from the Edit menu, and then choose the Special button.

About Cell Precedents and Dependents

Precedents are cells that are referred to by a formula. *Dependents* are cells containing formulas that refer to other cells. Precedents and dependents can be further described as *direct* or *indirect*.

A direct precedent is a cell that is referred to by the formula in the active cell. An indirect precedent is a cell referred to by a formula in a direct precedent cell or another indirect precedent cell.

A direct dependent is a cell containing a formula that refers to the active cell. An indirect dependent is a cell that contains a formula that refers to a direct dependent cell or another indirect dependent cell.

There are three ways to identify precedents and dependents:

- Display them visually using the tracers.
- Select them with the Go To Special feature.
- List them in the Info window.

You can see all of a cell's precedents or dependents or only direct precedents or dependents using any of these methods.

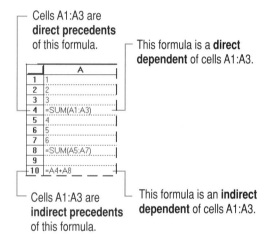

Cells A1:A3 are **direct precedents** of this formula.

This formula is a **direct dependent** of cells A1:A3.

Cells A1:A3 are **indirect precedents** of this formula.

This formula is an **indirect dependent** of cells A1:A3.

The Auditing Toolbar

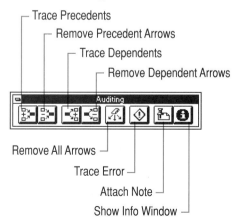

Trace Precedents

Remove Precedent Arrows

Trace Dependents

Remove Dependent Arrows

Remove All Arrows

Trace Error

Attach Note

Show Info Window

Clicking this button	Does this
Trace Precedents	Draws tracer arrows to the cells directly referred to by the selected formula. Subsequent clicks of the button add tracer arrows to additional levels of indirect precedents.
Remove Precedent Arrows	Removes tracer arrows from one level of precedents. Subsequent clicks remove the next level of arrows.
Trace Dependents	Draws tracer arrows to the formulas that directly refer to the active cell. Subsequent clicks of the button add additional levels of indirect dependents.
Remove Dependent Arrows	Removes tracer arrows from one level of dependents. Subsequent clicks remove the next level of arrows.
Remove All Arrows	Removes all the tracer arrows from the worksheet.
Trace Error	Draws tracer arrows to the source of an active cell containing an error value.
Attach Note	Displays the Cell Note dialog box.
Show Info Window	Displays the Info window.

Note Pressing SHIFT while clicking either Trace Precedents or Trace Dependents is the same as clicking the corresponding remove-arrows button, and vice versa.

Auditing Your Worksheets Visually

Using the tracers is the fastest and easiest way to track the flow of computations on your worksheet. Use the tracers when you want to:

- Find all the cells that have a direct or indirect relationship to a formula (precedents).
- See all the formulas that are directly or indirectly affected by changes in a particular cell (dependents).
- Track down the source of error values.

About Tracer Arrows

The tracers track data flow by drawing arrows connecting the active cell with related cells on your worksheet. Tracer arrows point in the direction of data flow. Because data always flows into formulas, whether you are tracing precedents or dependents, tracer arrows always point toward the formula.

Cell A5 is the active cell. Click the Trace Precedents button and an arrow appears, pointing to A5. The dot at the end of the arrow, in cell A3, shows A5's direct precedent.

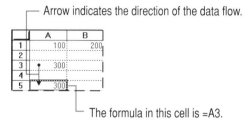

Arrow indicates the direction of the data flow.

The formula in this cell is =A3.

Note   Tracer arrows do not appear if objects are hidden. To display hidden objects, choose Options from the Tools menu and select the View tab. Then select Show All or Show Placeholders in the Objects group. Choose the OK button.

Click the Trace Precedents button again to display the next level of cell precedents. Cells A1 and B1 are indirect precedents of the active cell, A5.

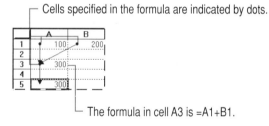

Cells specified in the formula are indicated by dots.

The formula in cell A3 is =A1+B1.

Similarly, when you trace cell dependents, all formulas that directly use the value in the active cell are indicated by arrows and dots.

The tracers produce three types of arrows.

Tracer type	Arrow type on color screens	Arrow type on black and white screens
Formula	Solid blue	——————▶
Error	Solid red	- - - - - -▶
External reference or reference to another sheet in the same workbook	Dashed black with icon	▦ —— ▶

If you want to go to the precedents once you've drawn arrows, you can navigate the tracer arrows by double-clicking.

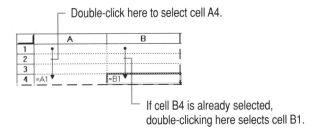

Double-click here to select cell A4.

If cell B4 is already selected,
double-clicking here selects cell B1.

Double-clicking an arrow selects the cell or range at either end.

Removing Tracer Arrows   You can perform any number of tracer actions on a worksheet. New tracer arrows do not replace existing tracer arrows. If you select a cell for which tracing isn't an appropriate action, Microsoft Excel beeps and no tracer arrows appear. All existing tracer arrows continue to be displayed unless one of the following actions occurs:

- You click the Remove All Arrows button.

- You edit a formula in a tracer path. Arrows showing precedents disappear from an edited formula because editing a formula might change its precedents.

- You perform an editing action that changes the overall worksheet. Actions such as inserting or deleting rows or columns, deleting cells, or moving cells cause all tracer arrows on the worksheet to disappear.

- You close the workbook. Tracer arrows are not saved with their worksheet.

What Not to Trace   The following types of references and other linking relationships are not traced:

- Macintosh Publishers and Subscribers

- References to objects, including drawn objects, text boxes, embedded charts, and worksheet pictures created with the Camera button

- Microsoft Visual Basic controls on sheets

- Pivot tables

- References to named constants

Tip   To get a wider view of how tracer arrows appear on a large worksheet, use the Zoom command on the View menu to display the entire worksheet on your screen. For information about the Zoom command, see "Zooming In or Out on a Worksheet" in Chapter 32.

Tracing Cell Data

Use the Auditing commands on the Tools menu or the tracer buttons on the Auditing toolbar to get a quick display of the precedents, dependents, and data flow path for a particular cell.

Tip   You can see the arrows better if you turn off the gridlines on your worksheet. To do this, choose Options from the Tools menu. Next, select the View tab in the Options dialog box. Then clear the Gridlines check box. Choose the OK button.

- You can trace selected single cells only. The tracers trace only the active cell of selected cell ranges or multiple selections.
- The tracers can be used only on worksheets.
- The Trace Precedents button works only when the active cell contains a formula.

Finding Cells Referred to by a Selected Formula

Trace Precedents

To find precedent cells, select the cell you want to trace and click the Trace Precedents button.

The formula in B4 is = SUM (F9:F11). The heavy box and arrow show that this precedent is a range.

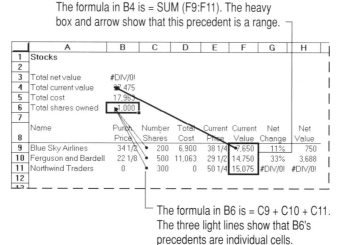

The formula in B6 is = C9 + C10 + C11. The three light lines show that B6's precedents are individual cells.

- To add more precedent levels to the trace path, click the Trace Precedents button once for each level you want to add.

Remove Precedent
Arrows

Remove All Arrows

- To remove the arrows farthest from the active cell (or least directly related to it), click the Remove Precedent Arrows button. Click it again to delete the next-farthest level of arrows.

- To clear all the arrows from the worksheet, click the Remove All Arrows button.

A Quicker Way to Trace Precedents You can double-click a formula cell to select its direct precedents if you turn off editing in cells. To turn off editing in cells, choose the Options command from the Tools menu and select the Edit tab. Then turn off the Edit Directly In Cell option. For more information about editing in cells, see Chapter 11, "Editing a Worksheet."

Error Values in the Chain Cause Red Arrows to Appear Selecting cell B3 in the preceding illustration and clicking the Trace Precedents button draws a heavy red arrow from cell H9 to cell B3, with a red border indicating the entire Net Value range, which contains an error value. Click the Trace Error button to pinpoint the source of the error. For more information about the Trace Error button, see "Tracking Down Errors with the Error Tracer" later in this chapter.

Checking References to Other Sheets (Precedents) When you click the Trace Precedents button, special tracer arrows appear indicating references to cells on other sheets in the current workbook or in other workbooks.

Cell E9's direct precedents
are on a different sheet or
in another document.

	A	B	C	D	E	F	G	H
1	Stocks							
2								
3	Total net value	#DIV/0!						
4	Total current value	37,475						
5	Total cost	17,963						
6	Total shares owned	1,000						
7								
8	Name	Purch. Price	Number Shares	Total Cost	Current Price	Current Value	Net Change	Net Value
9	Blue Sky Airlines	34 1/2	200	6,900	38 1/4	7,650	11%	750
10	Ferguson and Bardell	22 1/8	500	11,063	29 1/2	14,750	33%	3,688
11	Northwind Traders	0	300	0	50 1/4	15,075	#DIV/0!	#DIV/0!
12								

When you double-click the arrow shown in the preceding illustration, the Go To dialog box appears, showing you the workbook name, sheet name, and cell reference of the precedent. If the reference resides in the same workbook or in another open workbook, select the reference from the list and choose the OK button to switch to the sheet. If the reference resides in a workbook that is not open, you must first open it.

Finding Formulas That Refer to a Selected Cell

Trace Dependents

To find dependent cells, select the cell you want to trace and click the Trace Dependents button.

- To add more dependent levels to the trace path, click the Trace Dependents button once for each level you want to add.

Remove Dependent Arrows

- To remove the most remote level of dependent tracer arrows, click the Remove Dependent Arrows button.

- To clear all the arrows from the worksheet, click the Remove All Arrows Button.

	A	B	C	D	E	F	G	H
1	Stocks							
2								
3	Total net value	#DIV/0!						
4	Total current value	32,475						
5	Total cost	7,963						
6	Total shares owned	1,000						
7								
8	Name	Purch. Price	Number Shares	Total Cost	Current Price	Current Value	Net Change	Net Value
9	Blue Sky Airlines	34 1/2	200	6,900	30 1/4	7,650	11%	750
10	Ferguson and Bardell	22 1/8	500	11,063	29 1/2	14,750	33%	3,688
11	Northwind Traders	0	300	0	50 1/4	15,075	#DIV/0!	#DIV/0!
12								

Two levels of cell A9's dependents are traced here.

You can use the Trace Dependents button when the active cell is referred to by:

- A formula on the active sheet.
- Another sheet in the active workbook.
- A sheet in an external workbook that is currently open.

You can't use the Trace Dependents button when the active cell is referred to by:

- A formula located in an external workbook that is currently closed.
- A formula located on a macro sheet.

Tracking Down Errors with the Error Tracer

Trace Error

Often a single error in a formula on a worksheet can cause a proliferation of error values. You can use the Trace Error command on the Tools menu, Auditing submenu or the Trace Error button on the Auditing toolbar to discover which error value is at the root of the problem. The Trace Error command works only when the active cell contains an error.

The error in B3 originates in G11.

	A	B	C	D	E	F	G	H
1	Stocks							
2								
3	Total net value	#DIV/0!						
4	Total current value	37,475						
5	Total cost	17,963						
6	Total shares owned	1,000						
7								
8	Name	Purch. Price	Number Shares	Total Cost	Current Price	Current Value	Net Change	Net Value
9	Blue Sky Airlines	34 1/2	200	6,900	38 1/4	7,650	11%	750
10	Ferguson and Bardell	22 1/8	500	11,063	29 1/2	14,750	33%	3,688
11	Northwind Traders	0	300	0	50 1/4	15,075	#DIV/0!	#DIV/0!
12								

Here's the 0 value that's causing the error.

If you select cell B3 in the preceding illustration, and then click the Trace Error button, red or dotted arrows point from the source of the first error value. Blue or solid arrows trace the precedents farther back to the possibly erroneous values that feed the first formula in the chain of errors. Also, the error tracer automatically selects the cell where the error and formula arrows converge, so you can see the formula it contains.

What Happens When You Trace an Error The error tracer finds errors along the trace path until it:

- Finds the source of the error.
- Comes to a branch point with two or more error sources and cannot determine the correct path to continue.
- Encounters existing tracer arrows.
- Encounters a circular reference.

What Happens with Multiple Trace Paths If the worksheet contains multiple trace paths, the error tracer follows the path that leads to the error—unless there is more than one error path. In that case, the error tracer stops at the branch point, enabling you to select the path along which you want to continue.

If the worksheet contains other tracer arrows along the error tracer's current path, the error tracer stops. This is because existing arrows might indicate a circular reference. To avoid this, click the Remove All Arrows button on the Auditing toolbar before tracing an error. For more information about circular references, see "Solving Circular Reference Formulas Using Iteration" in Chapter 10.

What Happens When You Fix an Error   Fixing constant values that cause errors changes error tracer arrows to solid black tracer arrows. Fixing formulas causes any precedent arrows to disappear.

Tip   If you find errors that originate in a complex formula, you can use the Function Wizard to help you analyze the problem formula. For information about the Function Wizard, see "Using the Function Wizard" in Chapter 10.

Step By Step

For step-by-step instructions and related information, double-click the ⓀⓉ button to display the Search dialog box in Help, and then:

Type this keyword and choose Show Topics	Select a topic and choose Go To
arrows, tracer	Tracing dependent formulas
	Tracing precedent data and formulas
	Using the error tracer to find error values visually

Adding Comments to a Worksheet

Annotating your sheets is a good idea if:

- You share your sheets with others.
- The worksheet is large and complex.
- The sheet contains complex formulas that will be hard to decipher later.
- Certain values on the worksheet are not in line with expectations or reflect inconsistencies that demand explanation.

Annotating a Cell

Use text notes when you don't want to display comments on your worksheet or when you want to print comments on a separate sheet. You can attach sound notes to a cell by recording a message or importing a prerecorded sound that can be played back later. You can attach notes to worksheets.

Important   To record sounds, you must have recording hardware and sound driver software installed in your computer.

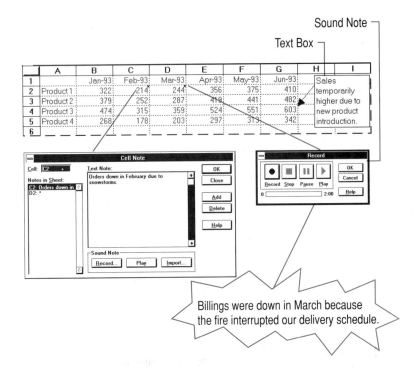

You can attach a text note or an audio comment to a cell on your worksheet.

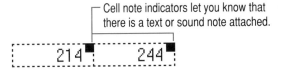

You can easily add a note to a cell by choosing the Note command from the Insert menu or by clicking the Attach Note button on the Auditing toolbar.

Attach Note

Checking the Spelling in Notes

You can use the Spelling command on the Tools menu to check the spelling of all text on a worksheet, including the text in cell notes. For information about checking spelling on a worksheet, see "Checking Spelling" in Chapter 11.

Printing Cell Notes

You can print text notes. On the Sheet tab in the Page Setup dialog box, select the Notes check box. To print the cell references with the notes, select the Row And Column Headings option. Choose the Print button. The Print dialog box enables you to print all the notes on your worksheet or only the notes you select.

Turning Off the Note Indicators

You can control the display of note indicators on your workspace. From the Tools menu, choose the Options command. Select the View tab. Then select or clear the Note Indicator check box to turn note indicators on or off.

Deleting All Notes from a Worksheet

To delete all the notes from a worksheet, you can use the Go To command on the Edit menu to select all the cells that contain notes. Then you can use the Clear command on the Edit menu to clear the notes. For more information about selecting all the cells with notes attached, see "Selecting Cells with Common Types of Contents" later in this chapter.

Step By Step

For step-by-step instructions and related information, double-click the [?] button to display the Search dialog box in Help, and then:

Type this keyword and choose Show Topics	Select a topic and choose Go To
sound notes	Adding an imported sound note
	Playing a sound note
	Recording a sound note
sound notes, deleting	Erasing a sound note
text notes	Copying a text or sound note to another cell
	Creating text notes
	Deleting text or sound notes from a cell
	Displaying a text note
	Displaying or hiding cell note indicators
	Printing text notes

Getting Information About a Cell

You can see detailed information about the active cell in the Info window. You can also specify exactly which categories of data you want displayed.

Displaying the Info Window

Show Info Window

To open the Info window, choose the Options command from the Tools menu. In the Options dialog box, View tab, select the Info Window check box. Or, you can click the Show Info Window button on the Auditing toolbar.

In the following illustration, the Info window in Microsoft Excel for Windows is set up to display all the available categories of information. You can also display this information in Microsoft Excel for the Macintosh, but it looks slightly different.

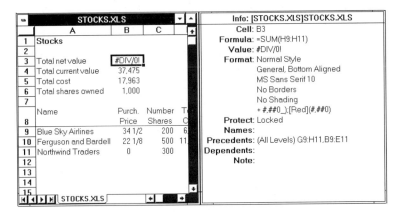

You can arrange the Info window and your workbook window so both are visible in the workspace.

When you select a cell, the Info window changes to display the characteristics of that cell. To display the Info window and your workbook window together, choose Arrange from the Window menu and select the Tiled option.

When the Info window is active, the Info menu appears on the menu bar. The Info menu contains the commands you use to display different categories of information in the Info window.

Printing the Contents of the Info Window

You can print the Info window statistics for one or more selected cells. With the workbook window and the Info window displayed, click in the workbook window to switch to it. Select the cell or range of cells you want printed information about. Then select the Info window. Finally, from the File menu, choose Print.

An Info window printout can contain any or all of the categories of data the Info window displays for each cell. You can print information about several cells on one piece of paper.

Finding Specific Characters in a Formula or Note

You can use the Find command on the Edit menu and the Info window together to find specific characters or text quickly in a formula or note. Make sure both the Info and workbook windows are visible. Then, switch to the workbook window and use the Find command to find formulas, notes, or values. The Find command selects the cell, and the Info window displays the information. For information about using the Find command, see "Finding and Replacing Text, Numbers, or Cells" in Chapter 11.

Closing the Info Window

You can close the Info window just as you close any window.

System	Action
Windows	Double-click the window control button in the upper-left corner.
Macintosh	Click the close box in the upper-left corner.

You can also choose Options from the Tools menu, select the View tab, and clear the Info Window check box.

Step By Step

For step-by-step instructions and related information, double-click the [k?] button to display the Search dialog box in Help, and then:

Type this keyword and choose Show Topics	Select a topic and choose Go To
Info window, categories	Displaying or removing information in the Info window
Info window, displaying	Opening and closing the Info window
	Viewing specific cells with the Info window
	Working with the Info window displayed
Info window, printing	Printing Info window information for a range of cells

Selecting Cells with Common Types of Contents

The Go To Special feature enables you to select cells with specific properties or contents. Use it to select cells that match the types of contents you specify in the Go To Special dialog box.

Selecting Specific Cells

To select specific cells on only part of the worksheet, first select that area. Otherwise, Go To Special searches the entire worksheet. To display the Go To Special dialog box, choose the Go To command from the Edit menu and choose the Special button. The Go To Special dialog box lists the cell types you can choose from. Go To Special selects all cells that meet the criteria you specify. If more than one cell is selected, you can move from cell to cell by pressing TAB and SHIFT+TAB.

Finding Formulas That Do Not Fit the Pattern

Often a worksheet contains many rows and columns with formulas that are essentially the same except for relative references. If you are unsure whether the formulas in a group share the same form—that is, refer to the same relative rows or columns and use the same functions and operators—the Row Differences and Column Differences options can quickly find any formulas that don't fit. Using these options, you can select cells whose contents differ from the contents of another cell, called a *comparison cell*, in the same row or column.

- Row Differences searches each selected row for cells different from the comparison cell in the same row.

- Column Differences searches each selected column for cells different from the comparison cell in the same column.

With the range F2:F6 selected, Select Special Column Differences finds this cell, because the formula refers to columns C through E, while the other selected formulas refer to columns B through E.

	A	B	C	D	E	F
1		Qtr 1	Qtr 2	Qtr 3	Qtr 4	Total
2	Item 1	1	6	11	16	=SUM(B2:E2)
3	Item 2	2	7	12	17	=SUM(B3:E3)
4	Item 3	3	8	13	18	=SUM(C4:E4)
5	Item 4	4	9	14	19	=SUM(B5:E5)
6	Item 5	5	10	15	20	=SUM(B6:E6)
7	Total	=SUM(B2:B6)	=SUM(C3:C6)	=SUM(D2:D6)	=SUM(E2:E6)	

With the range B7:E7 selected, Select Special Row Differences finds this cell, because the formula refers to rows 3 through 6, while the other selected formulas refer to rows 2 through 6.

How the Comparison Cells Are Determined   Which cells Microsoft Excel uses as the comparison cells depends upon the following factors:

- The position of the active cell determines which column or row contains the comparison cells.

    If you are searching for row differences, the comparison cells are the cells in the same column as the active cell. If you are searching for column differences, the comparison cells are the cells in the same row as the active cell.

- The current selection minus the comparison cells is the area Microsoft Excel searches for differences.

The search range can include nonadjacent selections. After searching all the selected cells, Microsoft Excel makes nonadjacent selections of all cells that differ from their corresponding comparison cells.

Choosing Comparison Cells Outside the Search Range   You can use cells outside the current selection as the comparison cells. Select the area or areas you want searched, then hold down the key indicated in the following table and select any cell in the column or row containing the comparison cells.

System	Key
Windows	CTRL
Macintosh	COMMAND

About Reference Styles   Microsoft Excel compares formulas based on the R1C1 reference style. Therefore, if your workbook's reference style is set to A1, the Row or Column Differences option might not produce the desired results. For more information about reference styles, see "Use Formulas to Analyze Your Data" in Chapter 10.

Step By Step

For step-by-step instructions and related information, double-click the [?] button to display the Search dialog box in Help, and then:

Type this keyword and choose Show Topics	Select a topic and choose Go To
finding, cells	Selecting cells with common types of contents
finding, dependents	Finding cells with formulas that refer to selected cells (dependents)
finding, differences,	Finding cells that don't fit the pattern in a row or column
finding, precedents	Finding cells referred to by formulas in selected cells (precedents)

CHAPTER 39

Protecting a Workbook

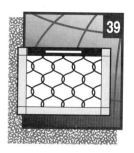

For command, keyboard, and toolbar button information, see online Help.

In This Chapter

Protecting Workbooks, Sheets, and Their Contents

Once you create a workbook, you can restrict the way others can access the workbook or its contents. Microsoft Excel gives you several options for restricting access and changes at the workbook level, at the sheet level, and even at the cell or graphic object level. You can:

- Prevent other people from opening a workbook or accessing its contents.

- Enable other people to open a workbook and enter changes to its contents, but prevent them from replacing the original copy.

- Enable people to open a workbook, but not change its contents or the way it's organized and displayed.

- Prevent other people from entering changes to some or all of the items on a sheet (for example, cell ranges and embedded charts on worksheets, graphic objects on worksheets or chart sheets, or code in a Visual Basic module).

- Hide a workbook so other people can open or access it, but not see it (for example, so they can run macros on the workbook).

- Hide selected sheets in an open workbook.

- Hide some or all items on a sheet so other people can't see them or accidentally change them.

- Prevent worksheet formulas from appearing in the formula bar.

Using passwords, you can mix different levels of protection for the same workbook so that different groups of people have different levels of access. For example, suppose your company's personnel department has a workbook containing sensitive information about employees. You can use three separate passwords to provide different levels of protection for different groups. You can have:

- One password so that only managers who know the password can see the information.

- Another password so that only people in the personnel department who know that password can save changes to information in the workbook.

- Another password to protect some information about each employee—birth date, for example—from being changed, even by those who have the password needed to save changes to the workbook.

Preventing Workbooks from Being Opened or Saved

You can protect workbook files with a password so that only those who know the password can open the workbook, save changes to it, or access its data through links. You can also arrange it so that when people open a workbook, Microsoft Excel recommends they open it as read only.

Passwords in Microsoft Excel are case sensitive. A password can contain any combination of letters, numbers, and symbols, and it can be up to 15 characters long.

Requiring a Password When a Workbook File Is Opened or Accessed

You can require people to type a password to open a workbook or access its data through links from a sheet in another workbook. To assign this level of protection, choose the Save As command from the File menu, choose the Options button, and then type a password in the Protection Password box.

Caution If you forget the protection password, you cannot open the workbook, remove protection from the workbook, or recover data from the workbook. It's a good idea to keep a list of your passwords and their corresponding workbook and sheet names in a safe place. (Remember that passwords are case sensitive.)

Requiring a Password When a Workbook File Is Saved

By assigning a write-reservation password to a workbook, you can protect it so other people can't save changes to it. This enables people to change the contents of the workbook, but they can't replace the original copy unless they know the password. They have to save the workbook under another name.

To assign this level of protection, choose the Save As command from the File menu, choose the Options button, and then type a password in the Write-Reservation Password box.

Making a Workbook File Read-Only Recommended

You can assign Read-Only Recommended protection to a workbook so when people open it, Microsoft Excel displays a dialog box that recommends they open it as a read-only workbook. That way, they know they shouldn't be changing the workbook unless it's necessary. To save changes to a read-only workbook, they have to use the Save As command on the File menu and then save the workbook under a new name. The original workbook remains unchanged.

To assign Read-Only Recommended protection to the workbook, choose Save As from the File menu, choose the Options button, and then select the Read-Only Recommended check box.

Removing Password Protection

To remove a password, you have to know the password. First, open the workbook and supply the password. Then choose the Save As command from the File menu, choose the Options button, and press the DEL key to remove the password from one or both of the Password boxes.

Step By Step

For step-by-step instructions and related information, double-click the [?] button to display the Search dialog box in Help, and then:

Type this keyword and choose Show Topics	Select a topic and choose Go To
passwords	Requiring a password when a workbook file is opened or accessed
	Requiring a password when a workbook file is saved
passwords, removing	Removing password protection for a workbook file
workbooks, read-only	Making a workbook file read-only recommended

Controlling Changes to Workbooks That Are Open

There are several ways you can limit other people's ability to see and change a workbook after it is opened. You can prevent changes to the way a workbook is displayed and arranged, and you can prevent changes to all or part of the contents of a sheet.

Protecting and Unprotecting Workbook Windows

You can protect a workbook's windows so they can't be moved, resized, hidden, unhidden, or closed. Protect windows when you want to make sure a workbook's windows are always sized and positioned the same way each time the workbook is opened.

To protect a workbook's windows, choose the Protection command from the Tools menu, choose the Protect Workbook command, and then select the Windows check box. Type a password if you want to restrict other people's ability to unprotect the workbook.

When you protect workbook windows in Microsoft Excel for Windows, the maximize and minimize icons, the Control-menu box, and the window sizing borders are hidden. In Microsoft Excel for the Macintosh, protected workbook windows don't display the close box or the zoom box, and the size box is disabled.

To unprotect a workbook's windows, choose the Protection command from the Tools menu, and then choose the Unprotect Workbook command. If a password was assigned, type the password.

Caution   If you forget the password, you cannot remove protection from the workbook. It's a good idea to keep a list of your passwords and their corresponding workbook and sheet names in a safe place. (Remember that passwords are case sensitive.)

Protecting and Unprotecting Workbook Structure

You can protect the structure of a workbook so that sheets in the workbook can't be deleted, moved, hidden, unhidden, or renamed, and so that new sheets can't be inserted. This level of protection prevents any operation that results in the addition of a new sheet, including:

- Adding a new chart sheet. (You can still add an embedded chart to an existing sheet by using the ChartWizard.)

- Recording a macro on a new sheet in your workbook.

- Moving or copying a sheet from within the workbook or from another workbook.

- Displaying source data for a cell in the data area of a pivot table.

- Using the Scenario Manager to create a summary report for a scenario.

- Creating a report from an Analysis ToolPak function.

To protect a workbook's structure, choose the Protection command from the Tools menu, choose the Protect Workbook command and then select the Structure check box. Assign a password if you want to restrict other people's ability to unprotect the workbook.

To unprotect a workbook's structure, choose the Protection command from the Tools menu and then choose the Unprotect Workbook command. If a password was assigned, type the password.

Caution   If you forget the password, you cannot remove protection from the workbook. It's a good idea to keep a list of your passwords and their corresponding workbook and sheet names in a safe place. (Remember that passwords are case sensitive.)

Protecting and Unprotecting a Sheet

You can protect a sheet to prevent other people from changing its contents. For example, you can prevent changes to cells on worksheets, items in a chart, graphic objects on a worksheet or chart sheet, code on a module sheet, or items on a dialog sheet.

To protect a sheet, first activate it, choose the Protection command from the Tools menu, and then choose the Protect Sheet command. A dialog box appears in which you can assign a password, if you want password protection for the sheet. For worksheets, Microsoft Excel 4.0 macro sheets, and chart sheets, check boxes are displayed so you can customize the level of protection applied to the sheet.

- Select the Contents check box to prevent changes to cells on worksheets or Microsoft Excel 4.0 macro sheets, or to prevent changes to items on a chart sheet.

- Select the Objects check box to prevent other people from deleting, moving, editing, or resizing graphic objects on a worksheet, Microsoft Excel 4.0 macro sheet, or chart sheet.

- Select the Scenarios check box to prevent changes to the definition of a scenario on a worksheet.

To unprotect a sheet, choose the Protection command from the Tools menu, and then choose the Unprotect Sheet command. If the sheet is protected by a password, you have to type the password to unprotect the sheet.

Caution If you forget the password, you cannot remove protection from the sheet. It's a good idea to keep a list of your passwords and their corresponding workbook and sheet names in a safe place. (Remember that passwords are case sensitive.)

Locking and Unlocking Individual Cell Ranges on a Worksheet

Unless you specify otherwise, when you use the Protection command on the Tools menu to protect a worksheet, all cells on the worksheet are locked automatically. Often, you might want to prevent changes to some cells on a worksheet and leave other cells unlocked. For example, if you use a worksheet as a form, you need to have cells containing labels and instructions locked, and you want entry fields to be unlocked. To do this, before choosing the Protect Sheet command to protect the worksheet, specify that some cell ranges remain unlocked.

To specify that a cell range is to remain unlocked, select the range, choose the Cells command from the Format menu, select the Protection tab, and then clear the Locked check box. You have to do this before you protect the sheet; you can't unlock cells on a protected sheet.

To activate protection, choose the Protection command from the Tools menu, and then choose the Protect Sheet command and set the Contents check box. For more information, see "Protecting and Unprotecting a Sheet" earlier in this section.

You can use the TAB key to move between unlocked cells on a protected worksheet.

Locking and Unlocking Graphic Objects on a Worksheet or Chart Sheet

When you use the Protection command on the Tools menu to protect objects on a worksheet or chart sheet, all graphic objects on the sheet are automatically locked. To unlock a graphic object, unprotect the sheet first. Then select the object, choose the Object command from the Format menu, select the Protection tab, and then clear the Locked check box. If the selected object is a text box, you can lock or unlock the text box by selecting or clearing the Lock Text check box. You can also use the Lock Cell button to lock or unlock objects.

To activate object protection, choose Protection from the Tools menu, choose Protect Sheet, and then select the Objects check box. For more information, see "Protecting and Unprotecting a Sheet" earlier in this section.

Hiding Formulas

In addition to locking a cell to prevent changes, you can hide its formula so it doesn't show in the formula bar when the cell is selected. To hide formulas, select the cells that contain the formulas, choose the Cells command from the Format menu, select the Protection tab, and then select the Hidden check box.

After you specify which formulas to hide, activate the hiding of formulas by choosing the Protection command from the Tools menu, choosing the Protect Sheet command, and then selecting the Contents check box.

Step By Step

For step-by-step instructions and related information, double-click the [?] button to display the Search dialog box in Help, and then:

Type this keyword and choose Show Topics	Select a topic and choose Go To
formulas, hiding	Hiding formulas
sheets, locking and unlocking	Locking and unlocking graphic objects on a worksheet or chart sheet
	Locking and unlocking individual cell ranges on a worksheet
sheets, protecting	Protecting and unprotecting a sheet
workbooks, protecting	Protecting and unprotecting workbook windows or structure

Hiding and Unhiding Workbooks and Sheets

Hiding workbooks and sheets within workbooks reduces the number of windows and sheets on your screen and helps prevent unwanted changes. Sheets containing macros or critical data can be open and accessible to other sheets, but not readily available for editing.

Hiding and Unhiding Workbooks and Sheets

- You can hide an entire workbook with the Hide command on the Window menu.
- You can hide an individual sheet of a workbook by choosing the Sheet command from the Format menu and then choosing the Hide command. The workbook containing the sheet you want to hide has to have other sheets in it; you can't hide the last visible sheet in a workbook.

The hidden workbook or sheet remains open, and all the sheets in the workbook are available to be referenced from other documents.

- You can unhide workbooks by choosing the Unhide command from the Window menu and then selecting the workbook you want to unhide.
- You can unhide sheets by choosing the Sheet command from the Format menu and then choosing the Unhide command.

Tip By using a Visual Basic statement, you can hide a sheet so that people can't use the Unhide command to display it. Once a sheet has been hidden in this way, the only way it can be displayed is by using a Visual Basic statement to unhide it. For more information, see "Visible Property" in the online *Visual Basic Reference*.

For information about hiding rows and columns in worksheets, see "Hiding and Unhiding Rows and Columns" in Chapter 32.

Saving Workbooks as Hidden

Suppose you create a workbook, modify it, and then decide to hide it. You can save the workbook after it is hidden. After choosing the Exit command from the File menu, a message box appears asking you if you want to save changes to the workbook. Choose the Yes button. The changes are saved, and the workbook will be hidden the next time it is opened.

Step By Step

For step-by-step instructions and related information, double-click the [⬚?] button to display the Search dialog box in Help, and then:

Type this keyword and choose Show Topics	Select a topic and choose Go To
sheets, hiding and unhiding	Hiding and unhiding a sheet
workbooks, hiding and unhiding	Hiding and unhiding a workbook

CHAPTER 40

Routing Workbooks with Electronic Mail

For command, keyboard, and toolbar button information, see online Help.

In This Chapter

How Microsoft Excel and Electronic Mail Work Together

The Difference Between Mailing and Routing a Workbook

Microsoft Excel and your electronic mail system work together so that you can share your work with others in two ways:

- Mailing a workbook attaches a copy of the workbook to an electronic mail message. Mailing a workbook is a one-way trip.

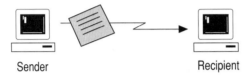

Sender   Recipient

- Routing a workbook among a workgroup sends a copy of a workbook sequentially among recipients, or to all recipients simultaneously. Routing a workbook can be a round trip.

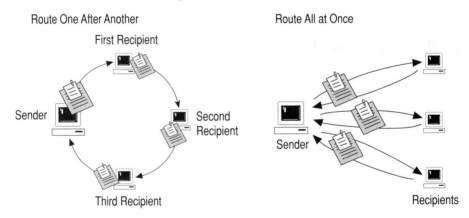

Route One After Another   Route All at Once

First Recipient

Sender   Second
                      Recipient

Third Recipient   Recipients

Sender

Caution   When you mail or route a workbook, you send only a copy of the workbook. The original remains open in Microsoft Excel. Microsoft Excel does not link the original workbook and its copy or copies in any way. You can protect portions of the workbook copies that you do not want recipients to change. For information about protecting workbooks, see Chapter 39, "Protecting a Workbook."

What You Need to Use Workbook Mailing and Routing

System	What you need
Windows	Microsoft Mail (or other mail system compliant with Messaging Application Programming Interface [MAPI]), or Lotus cc:Mail™ (or other mail systems compliant with Vendor Independent Messaging [VIM]).
Macintosh	Microsoft Mail (or other mail system compliant with Messaging Application Programming Interface [MAPI] mail system).
All	Recipients of a mailed or routed workbook need Microsoft Excel version 5.0 to open the workbook.

Workbook mailing and routing may not work across electronic mail gateways.

Note In Microsoft Excel for the Macintosh, the PowerTalk system extension replaces the workbook mailing and routing features described here. For information about PowerTalk, see your electronic mail administrator, online Help, or your PowerTalk system extension documentation.

Mailing a Workbook

Mailing a workbook is an easy way to distribute a workbook to others in your workgroup. Mail a workbook when you do not need to send it to recipients in any particular order, and do not want it automatically returned to you.

System	To mail a workbook
Windows	Choose the Send command from the File menu.
Macintosh	Choose the Mail command from the File menu, and then choose the Send command.

Microsoft Excel and your mail program will create an electronic mail message with a copy of the workbook attached. Enter the recipients and message text, and then send the message.

Even if a workbook has a routing slip attached, you can mail the workbook without sending it to the recipients listed on the routing slip. For information about routing slips, see the following section, "Routing a Workbook."

Step By Step

For step-by-step instructions and related information, double-click the ⟨▶?⟩ button to display the Search dialog box in Help, and then:

Type this keyword and choose Show Topics	Select a topic and choose Go To
mailing workbooks, PowerTalk	Using Microsoft Excel with PowerTalk (Microsoft Excel for the Macintosh only)
workbooks, mailing	Mailing a workbook

Routing a Workbook

Routing a workbook instead of mailing it gives you greater control over the workbook's journey. You can:

- Automatically receive an electronic mail routing status message as each recipient forwards the workbook.

- Ensure that each recipient is automatically reminded that they should forward the workbook on to the next recipient.

- Automatically receive the workbook back after the recipients have had it.

When you route a workbook, you either send it to one recipient after another, or to all recipients at once.

One after another	All at once
Useful when each recipient must add to the workbook, or approve a portion of it. An expense report workbook, for example, may require the approval of your manager before it goes to the accounting department. In this case, each recipient adds something to the workbook in a specific order.	Useful when you want to solicit comments on a workbook. A sales manager, for example, may send a sales report workbook to all salespeople to complete and return. In this case, all recipients add something to the workbooks independently of one another.

Creating the Routing Slip

The routing slip contains the routing instructions that the workbook will follow. The routing slip information is saved with the workbook file, and travels with the workbook when you route it. You can create one routing slip per workbook.

System	To create a routing slip
Windows	Choose the Add Routing Slip command from the File menu.
Macintosh	Choose the Mail command from the File menu, and then choose the Add Routing Slip command.

After you create a routing slip, you can edit it.

System	To edit a routing slip
Windows	Choose the Edit Routing Slip command from the File menu.
Macintosh	Choose the Mail command from the File menu, and then choose the Edit Routing Slip command.

Routing the Workbook

Once you've created a routing slip, you can send the workbook.

- To route the workbook as soon as you've created the routing slip, choose the Route button in the Routing Slip dialog box.
- To route the workbook any time after creating the routing slip, follow the instructions in the following table.

System	To route a workbook
Windows	Choose the Send command from the File menu.
Macintosh	Choose the Mail command from the File menu, and then choose the Send command.

Use Workbook Routing and Smart Forms

You can combine the calculating and formatting features of Microsoft Excel to create smart forms. For example, you can create an expense report that automatically totals items. You could then use workbook routing to send it to the correct recipients via electronic mail. Route an expense report, for example, to your manager for approval, and then to your accounting department for processing.

To build more intelligence into your smart forms, use Visual Basic. For example, you may want to route your expense report workbook to one person if some value in the workbook is above a certain amount, and to another person if it's below that amount. For more information, see the *Microsoft Excel Visual Basic User's Guide.*

Step By Step

For step-by-step instructions and related information, double-click the [?] button to display the Search dialog box in Help, and then:

Type this keyword and choose Show Topics	Select a topic and choose Go To
mailing workbooks, PowerTalk	Using Microsoft Excel with PowerTalk (Microsoft Excel for the Macintosh only)
routing slips	Creating and editing a routing slip
routing workbooks	Routing a workbook

Routing a Workbook to the Next Recipient

If you are a recipient of a routed workbook, you will receive a workbook attached to an electronic mail message. Follow the instructions of your electronic mail program to open the attached workbook in Microsoft Excel.

When you have finished with the workbook in Microsoft Excel, route the workbook to the next recipient.

System	To route a workbook to the next recipient
Windows	Choose the Send command from the File menu.
Macintosh	Choose the Mail command from the File menu, and then choose the Send command.

Microsoft Excel will prompt you to route the workbook on to the next recipient. You can also choose to mail the workbook to another person independently of the routing slip.

Editing the Routing Slip

Any recipient of a routed workbook can edit the subject, message text, and recipient list on the routing slip. You can change the recipients subsequent to yourself, but not the prior recipients.

System	To edit the routing slip
Windows	Choose the Edit Routing Slip command from the File menu.
Macintosh	Choose the Mail command from the File menu, and then choose the Edit Routing Slip command.

Step By Step

For step-by-step instructions and related information, double-click the ⬚?⬚ button to display the Search dialog box in Help, and then:

Type this keyword and choose Show Topics	Select a topic and choose Go To
mailing workbooks, PowerTalk	Using Microsoft Excel with PowerTalk (Microsoft Excel for the Macintosh only)
routing slips	Editing the routing slip
routing workbooks	Opening a routed workbook
	Routing a workbook to the next recipient

Exchanging Data with Other Applications

C H A P T E R   4 1

Sharing Data and Graphics with Other Applications

For command, keyboard, and toolbar button information, see online Help.

In This Chapter

Understanding Linking and Embedding

With the linking and embedding features available in Microsoft Excel, you can include information, or *objects,* created in other applications. The main difference between linking and embedding is where the data is stored.

- *Embedding* means inserting information—such as a chart, a graphic, or data copied from a word processor document—into a Microsoft Excel workbook. Embedded objects become part of the workbook itself.

- *Linking* means inserting into a workbook information that retains a connection to the source document. Linked data is updated when the data in the source document changes. Linked data is stored in the source file; the workbook stores only the location of the source but displays a representation of the linked data.

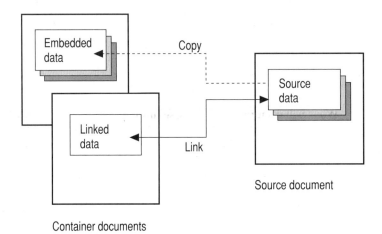

Container documents

Important To use embedding, the source application must support object linking and embedding (OLE). To create links, the source application must support dynamic data exchange (DDE) or OLE.

If you are using Microsoft Excel for the Macintosh with System 7 or later, you can also use the Publish and Subscribe features to create links to other files. For more information, see "Creating Publishers and Subscribers in Microsoft Excel for the Macintosh" later in this chapter.

When to Use Linking and Embedding

- Embed data or graphics that are fairly stable, when you don't need to have the most current versions in your document, when the embedded data does not need to be included in more than one document, or when the source documents would not be available for updating if they were linked.

- Create links when data or graphics are likely to change, when it is essential that your document includes the latest versions available, when the source documents are available on your computer or across a network whenever they need to be updated, or when the source data needs to be shared with more than one document.

Suppose you are putting together a summary spreadsheet to use as part of a presentation. You can assemble a presentation-quality document using formatted Microsoft Excel data along with embedded graphic elements (such as company logos and clip art) as well as linked information from sources such as word processing documents and databases.

Use the following guidelines in determining whether to embed information or to link it.

When you want to	Use this method	Comment
Create a document that you can use on other computers or edit even if the source files are not present.	Embed the objects from another application in a workbook.	To edit the objects, all relevant applications must be installed on the computer.
Include data that may not always be available, such as data stored on a server.	Embed the data from another application in a workbook.	All the necessary information is included with the embedded object.
Include a very large file, such as a video clip or sound clip.	Create a link in the workbook to the source file.	Microsoft Excel stores only the link, keeping the size of the workbook manageable.
Include data that is maintained separately in its source application.	Create a link in the workbook to the source file.	The workbook reflects any changes made to the source file.

Commands You Can Use with Objects

The most commonly used commands available for working with an object are readily accessible through the shortcut menu. When you use the shortcut menu, the valid commands for that object type are assembled in one place, allowing easy access. The commands displayed can vary, depending on the object type. To display the shortcut menu, move the mouse pointer over an object and then do the following.

System	To display the shortcut menu
Windows	Click the right mouse button.
Macintosh	Press CONTROL (or OPTION+COMMAND) and click the mouse button.

Switching to Other Microsoft Applications

Microsoft Excel includes buttons that you can use to switch to other Microsoft applications quickly and easily. These buttons are on the Microsoft toolbar. To display the Microsoft toolbar, choose Microsoft from the toolbar shortcut menu.

The Microsoft toolbar includes the following buttons, from left to right:

- Microsoft Word button
- Microsoft PowerPoint® button
- Microsoft Mail button
- Microsoft Access button (Windows only)
- Microsoft FoxPro button (FoxBASE+ button on the Macintosh)
- Microsoft Project button
- Microsoft Schedule+ button

If the application is running, clicking its button activates it. If the application is not running, clicking its button opens it. You must have installed an application properly before you can use its button.

Exchanging Data Using the Clipboard

When you cut or copy data, Microsoft Excel temporarily stores the data on the *Clipboard.* You can then paste the data into another location in the same document, into another document created with the same application, or into a document created with another application. You can also paste data, graphic objects, or pictures into your Microsoft Excel worksheets from documents created with other applications, such as Microsoft Word.

If you have Microsoft Excel for the Macintosh running with system software versions earlier than Macintosh System 7, the Clipboard is your primary means of exchanging data with other applications. For more information about Clipboard operations, see your Windows or Macintosh documentation. For more information about copying and pasting data within Microsoft Excel, see Chapter 11, "Editing a Worksheet."

Pasting Graphics   When you copy a graphic object from another application and paste it into Microsoft Excel, it is embedded as an object.

Pasting Text   When you copy text from another application and paste it into Microsoft Excel, different things happen depending on what is selected at the time you paste.

- If a cell is selected, Microsoft Excel chooses an appropriate format—object, graphic, or text—for the pasted text, depending on its source.
- If the formula bar is active, all copied text is pasted into it.
- If an object is selected, copied text is embedded as an object.
- If the selected object is a text box, copied text is pasted into the text box.

If you paste text and the results are not what you expect, choose Undo from the Edit menu. Then choose Paste Special from the Edit menu, and select an option that meets your needs.

Dragging Information Between Applications

Some applications allow you to select data or graphics and drag them to another active application window. However, both applications must be running and visible on your screen.

Important   Both applications must support object linking and embedding version 2 (OLE 2) to drag and drop information between applications.

There are several options available to drag data between applications.

- Dragging data is the same as cutting and pasting, which removes the data from the source document and pastes it into the destination document. The data is permanently removed from the source document.
- Pressing SHIFT while dragging inserts the data at the location of the cursor or the active cell, if appropriate in the destination document.
- Pressing CTRL or CONTROL while dragging is the same as copying and pasting, which creates a duplicate in the destination document.

Caution   Error messages might not appear when you're copying data between applications, so be sure not to overwrite important data in the destination area.

Using the Paste Special Command

If you are working in the source application, you can copy the material to be embedded, switch to Microsoft Excel, and then use the Paste Special command on the Edit menu.

The formats available for pasting the copied material are listed in the As box. You can choose to display the pasted material as an icon or to create a link to the material. For more information, see "Linking to Other Applications" later in this chapter. For information about displaying an embedded object as an icon, see "Embedding Objects" later in this chapter.

The Paste Special dialog box that appears when you copy data from another application is different from the normal Paste Special dialog box. For more information about the Paste Special command, see "Copying and Pasting Cells for Special Results" in Chapter 11.

Exchanging Pictures with Other Applications

If you want to copy data as a picture or object to another application that does not have a Paste Special command, use the Copy Picture command. The Copy Picture and Paste Picture commands replace the Copy and Paste commands on the Edit menu when you hold down SHIFT before displaying the menu. For more information, see "Pictures of Charts and Worksheets" in Chapter 13.

- In Microsoft Excel for Windows, you can export pictures to any application that supports the picture or bitmap formats used by the Clipboard.

- In Microsoft Excel for the Macintosh, you can export pictures to any application that supports the PICT format on the Clipboard.

Step By Step

For step-by-step instructions and related information, double-click the [?] button to display the Search dialog box in Help, and then:

Type this keyword and choose Show Topics	Select a topic and choose Go To
copying, from other appplications	Copying data from another application to Microsoft Excel
	Dragging data between applications
copying, pictures	Copying a linked picture of cells
	Copying a picture of a chart, cells, or an object
	Copying a picture to another application
copying, to other applications	Copying data from Microsoft Excel to another application

Embedding Objects

Without leaving Microsoft Excel, you can embed an existing file or create and embed a new object. An embedded object increases the file size of a workbook because all the object's native data is stored there. For example, if you embed a Microsoft Word document in a workbook, the file size of the workbook increases by approximately the file size of the Word document. The file size increases even if you display the object as an icon because Microsoft Excel still stores all the information about the embedded document.

Embedding a New Object

Select the cell where you want to position the upper-left corner of the embedded object. From the Insert menu, choose Object. To create and embed a new object, select the Create New tab; select the type of object you want, and then choose the OK button.

When you create a new object, the appropriate application opens, and you can begin working on the object you want to add to your workbook. Suppose you want to add a graphic to a workbook. If you select MS WordArt in the Object Type box and choose the OK button, Microsoft Excel opens Microsoft WordArt, in which you can create a graphic. When you quit Microsoft WordArt, the graphic is displayed in your workbook.

Note The applications you use to create embedded objects must have been properly installed using their original installation programs; otherwise, they are not listed in the Object dialog box.

In-Place Activation In some applications, an embedded Microsoft Excel object remains in place when you double-click it, and the other document remains visible surrounding it. This is called *in-place activation.*

If the application in which you choose to create a new object also supports in-place activation, the object is inserted into your workbook, which remains visible surrounding the object. When you embed an object from one of these applications in a workbook:

- A hatched border appears, surrounding the embedded object.

- The application name in the title bar changes from "Microsoft Excel" to the name of the object's source application.

- All the menus except the File and Window menus change to those of the object's source application.
- The toolbars change to those of the object's source application.
- You return to Microsoft Excel by clicking anywhere outside the embedded object.

Important In-place activation requires that an application support object linking and embedding version 2 (OLE 2).

Activation in a Separate Window When you create new embedded objects in a workbook using applications that do not support in-place activation, a separate window is displayed, allowing you to create the object in that application. You return to Microsoft Excel by choosing either Exit And Return or Quit And Return from the application's File menu.

Important To open Microsoft Excel objects embedded in other applications by double-clicking, the other application must support dynamic data exchange (DDE) or object linking and embedding (OLE).

Creating Embedded Objects From Existing Files

When you embed an existing file, Microsoft Excel stores an independent copy of the file in the workbook. The original file remains unchanged, even if you change the embedded file. To embed an entire existing document, choose Object from the Insert menu. On the Create From File tab, select the filename, and then choose the OK button.

In Microsoft Excel for Windows, you can also insert pictures into your workbooks using the Insert Picture command, which is discussed later in this section.

Displaying Embedded Objects as Icons

You can display an embedded object as an icon when the workbook will be used primarily on-screen and when the embedded object contains supplementary information. To do this, select the Display As Icon check box in the Object dialog box. You can then change the icon by choosing the Change Icon button.

For example, if the workbook contains financial statements, you can embed a Microsoft Word document containing lengthy explanatory notes as an icon on the first sheet in the workbook. To see the contents of the document, online readers can double-click the icon to open the Word document.

Note Some objects created from a file (for example, from an ASCII text file) are always displayed as icons.

Printing Embedded Objects

If you print a workbook containing embedded objects, the objects or icons are printed at their on-screen locations. You can control whether or not objects are printed. First, select the object or objects, then choose Object from the Format menu, and select the Properties tab. Finally, select or clear the Print Object check box. For more information about printing, see Chapter 14, "Printing."

Editing an Embedded Object

In most cases, double-clicking an embedded object opens the application in which it was created. However, some embedded objects, such as video and sound clips, play when you double-click them, instead of opening an application for editing.

You can also open an embedded object for editing using a menu command. First, select the object, and then choose Object from the Edit menu. Then choose Open or Edit from the submenu. When an object is selected, the Object command appears with the name of the object type included in the command name—for example, "Microsoft Word Object."

- If you choose Open, the object is opened in a separate window for editing by its source application.

- If you choose Edit, the object is activated in place in the workbook, if the source application supports in-place activation; otherwise, the object is opened in a separate window.

Note The commands available on the submenu of the Object command (Edit menu) can vary, depending on the type of object selected.

Editing Documents in Place   In some applications, an embedded object remains in place when you double-click it, and the Microsoft Excel workbook remains visible surrounding the object.

Editing Documents in a Separate Window   When you double-click an embedded object created in an application that does not support in-place activation, a separate window is displayed, and the object is opened in its original application. In this case, you return to Microsoft Excel by choosing either Exit And Return or Quit And Return from the application's File menu.

Object Formatting and Placement

The Object and Placement commands on the Format menu are available to use with embedded objects. With these commands, you can control properties, including graphic patterns, protection, and positioning relative to cells. For more information, see Chapter 13, "Creating Graphic Objects on Worksheets and Charts."

Inserting Pictures

In Microsoft Excel for Windows, you can use the Picture command on the Insert menu to add graphics to your workbooks without first opening the graphic in its own application to copy it. The Picture command recognizes many additional types of graphics files, including those created in applications that are not installed on your computer.

When you choose the Picture command, the Picture dialog box appears. You can then select a graphics file that is stored on disk. When you choose the OK button, Microsoft Excel embeds an object based on the selected file.

Note   In Microsoft Excel for the Macintosh, use the Clipboard to insert graphics. For more information, see "Exchanging Data Using the Clipboard" earlier in this chapter.

Converting an Embedded Object to a Different Format

Suppose you receive a Microsoft Excel workbook with a Word document embedded in it. Microsoft Word is not installed on your computer, but you do have another word-processing application. When you double-click the Microsoft Word object to edit it, Microsoft Excel displays the Convert dialog box. You can then specify which application you'll use to edit the object. The applications displayed in the list are those installed on your computer that can convert the object to the correct file format.

You can also display the Convert dialog box using the Links command on the Edit menu, which is displayed with the name of the selected object (for example, "Microsoft Word Link"), and then choosing Convert from the submenu.

- If you select the Convert To option button, Microsoft Excel converts the embedded object to the format you specify in the Object Type box. The object remains in this format unless you specifically convert it to another format.

- If you select the Activate As option button, Microsoft Excel opens all embedded objects in the proper application for the format you specify in the Object Type box. You can edit the objects in the application you specify, but Microsoft Excel saves changes to the objects in their original file format.

Note If you upgrade to a more recent version of an application after creating an embedded object with that application and then want to edit the object, you must first convert the object to match the current version of the application.

Many application Setup programs convert existing files to the new format when you install an updated version of the application. With some applications, you can run the Setup program at any time to convert existing files to the new format.

Converting an Embedded Object to a Simple Graphic   All embedded objects are represented in workbooks as graphics. Think of one of these graphics as a facade with information behind it. For example, a Microsoft Word document embedded in a workbook looks like an ordinary Word document, but it is actually a graphic, or picture, of the original document. Behind the graphic is all the information necessary to open and edit the file in Microsoft Word. When you convert the Microsoft Word object to a simple graphic, you remove the information behind the facade—that is, the information that enables Microsoft Excel to open the object in Microsoft Word for editing.

To convert an embedded object to a simple graphic, choose Convert from the shortcut menu. In the Object Type box, select Picture, and then choose the OK button.

Converting an embedded object to a graphic reduces the file size of the workbook. You cannot convert the graphic back to an embedded object. For information about graphics in Microsoft Excel, see Chapter 13, "Creating Graphic Objects on Worksheets and Charts."

Step By Step

For step-by-step instructions and related information, double-click the 💡? button to display the Search dialog box in Help, and then:

Type this keyword and choose Show Topics	Select a topic and choose Go To
changing, embedded objects	Converting an embedded object to a different format
	Editing a Microsoft Excel object embedded in another application

Type this keyword and choose Show Topics	Select a topic and choose Go To
deleting, embedded objects	Deleting an embedded object from Microsoft Excel
	Editing an object embedded in a Microsoft Excel document
embedding	Embedding a Microsoft Excel object in another application
	Embedding existing information in a Microsoft Excel document
	Embedding new information in a Microsoft Excel document

Using Microsoft Excel Data in Other Applications

You can use Microsoft Excel workbooks as source documents for data you link or embed in documents created in other applications. These are called *container* documents. In this case, Microsoft Excel is the source, or *object,* application.

Embedded Microsoft Excel Objects Activated in Place Within Container Documents

In some applications, an embedded Microsoft Excel object remains in place when you double-click it, and the container document remains visible surrounding it. This is called *in-place activation.*

Important   In-place activation requires that an application support object linking and embedding version 2 (OLE 2).

Microsoft Excel provides specific elements that become available when you work in a container document. When you double-click a Microsoft Excel object contained in a document created in an application that supports in-place activation:

- A gray hatched border appears, surrounding the Microsoft Excel object.
- The Microsoft Excel scroll bars, row and column headings, and workbook tabs appear and are active.
- In Microsoft Windows, the application name in the title bar changes from the name of the container application to "Microsoft Excel."
- All the menus except the File and Window menus change to those of Microsoft Excel.
- The toolbars change to those of Microsoft Excel.

- You return to the container application by clicking anywhere outside the Microsoft Excel object.

- The Open, Edit, and Convert commands are made available to the container application for editing embedded Microsoft Excel objects. Choosing Edit activates the object in place; choosing Open activates the object in a separate Microsoft Excel window.

Embedded Microsoft Excel Objects Activated in a Separate Microsoft Excel Window

Double-clicking a Microsoft Excel object in another application often starts Microsoft Excel in a separate window and opens the object for editing. In this case, you return to the container application by choosing either Exit And Return or Quit And Return from the Microsoft Excel File menu.

Important To open Microsoft Excel objects embedded in other applications by double-clicking, the container application must support dynamic data exchange (DDE) or object linking and embedding (OLE).

Linking to Other Applications

In addition to creating links to other Microsoft Excel workbooks, as described in Chapter 10, you can also create *remote* links when you want to incorporate data from a file created in another application. Microsoft Excel uses object linking and embedding (OLE) and dynamic data exchange (DDE) to establish these kinds of links.

Creating a Link

Creating a link is as easy as copying and pasting. You copy a selection from a file (the source) and paste it into your workbook (the destination) using the Paste Special command on the Edit menu. Select the Paste Link option button, select the type of linked object in the As box, and then choose the OK button. Before you can establish a link, however, the source file must be saved on disk.

Important To create a link between a workbook and a document from another application, the other application must support dynamic data exchange (DDE) or object linking and embedding (OLE).

Pasting a Linked Picture   The Paste Link button in the Paste Special dialog box is not available when a picture is on the Clipboard. To link a picture, you must first select the cell or range you want to copy using the Copy command. Then choose the Paste Picture Link command on the Edit menu. The Paste Picture Link command replaces the Paste Special command when you hold down SHIFT and open the Edit menu. For more information about the Paste Picture command, see "Pictures of Charts and Worksheets" in Chapter 13.

Editing Linked Information

To edit linked information, you can either double-click the linked object, or you can select it and then choose the object's name from the Edit menu. For example, if you link an object to a Microsoft Word document, the Edit menu displays the command "Microsoft Word Link." When you choose this command, the source application opens the document for editing.

Editing Links

Microsoft Excel provides a way to control each link in your workbooks individually. The Links dialog box displays every link that exists on the currently active sheet in the workbook. To display the Links dialog box, use the Links command on the Edit menu.

Updating Links   In the Links dialog box, you can specify either manual or automatic updating for each link in your workbook. By default, newly created links are set to automatic updating, but you can easily change this to manual updating.

- Microsoft Excel updates automatic links when you open the workbook and when the source document is changed while the workbook is open.

- Microsoft Excel updates manual links only when you choose Links from the Edit menu and then choose the Update Now button.

If you want Microsoft Excel to update links automatically, choose Options from the Tools menu, select the Calculation tab, and then select the Update Remote References check box. If this check box is cleared, Microsoft Excel uses the last values received from the other application to calculate the formulas. This option affects only the active workbook. Clearing this check box overrides automatic updating set for individual links in the Links dialog box.

Note   You can also choose to have Microsoft Excel display a message before opening a document containing automatic links. In the Options dialog box, select the Edit tab, and then select the Ask To Update Automatic Links check box.

You can apply formatting, such as fonts or pattern formats, to linked material. Microsoft Excel retains such formatting and reapplies it when the link is updated.

Reconnecting or Changing a Link   You may lose a link if you rename or move the source file. If this happens, you must reconnect the link to the original source file or redirect the link to a different file. To edit a link, choose Links from the Edit menu. The dialog box shows all the links for the currently active workbook sheet, including links—or *external references*—to other Microsoft Excel workbooks. For information about linking between workbooks, see "Linking Microsoft Excel Workbooks" in Chapter 10.

Creating DDE Remote Reference Formulas

In addition to the other methods described in this chapter, you can also construct dynamic data exchange (DDE) links to source documents created in other applications by entering *remote reference* formulas. A remote reference formula contains one or more references to cells, cell ranges, values, or fields of data in a document from another application.

The following illustration shows the parts of a remote reference formula.

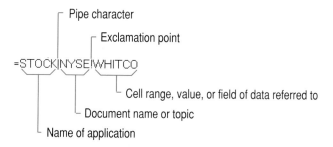

In the preceding illustration, NYSE is the name of a document that contains New York Stock Exchange data. Some applications, such as certain servers, do not manage data as documents but rather as topics. For information about how an application manages data, see the documentation for that application.

If the application name, document or topic, or data is not a valid Microsoft Excel name, or if it resembles a cell reference, enclose it in single quotation marks (for example, if the application name contains a space character or exclamation point, or if the data is a letter and number combination, such as A1). For information about characters you can use in Microsoft Excel names, see "Names Make References Easier to Use" in Chapter 10.

You can also link your Microsoft Excel for the Macintosh worksheet to an open document in a program that is currently running on another Macintosh on the network using the following syntax in the remote reference formula.

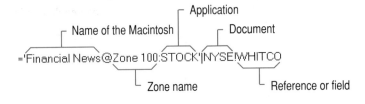

To link to an application on another Macintosh, you need access privileges to that Macintosh. For information about access privileges, see your Macintosh System 7 documentation.

For information about programming with linked and embedded objects, see Chapter 10, "Controlling and Communicating with Other Applications," in the *Microsoft Excel Visual Basic User's Guide*.

Step By Step

For step-by-step instructions and related information, double-click the ⓀⓀ button to display the Search dialog box in Help, and then:

Type this keyword and choose Show Topics	Select a topic and choose Go To
remote links	Linking a Microsoft Excel document to a document from another application
	Redirecting links to source documents
remote links, updating	Controlling whether a DDE or OLE link is updated automatically
	Disabling updating of all links to other applications on a worksheet
	Opening and updating data from a list of source documents
	Suppressing the updating of all remote references in a worksheet
	Updating a DDE or OLE link manually
remote references	Controlling remote requests
	Freezing the remote reference portion of a larger formula
	Linking a document from another application to a Microsoft Excel worksheet
	Replacing an entire remote reference with its value

Creating Publishers and Subscribers in Microsoft Excel for the Macintosh

With Microsoft Excel for the Macintosh, you can exchange information between documents in different applications or on different computers connected by a network. To make part of a document available for use with other applications or for other users on a network, you can create a *publisher* for that portion of the document. A publisher contains the part of the document you want to share—text, graphics, spreadsheet data, and so forth.

When you create a publisher, Microsoft Excel automatically creates an intermediate file called an *edition,* which contains a copy of the information that is in the publisher. An edition is a separate file that can be saved on a hard disk or on a network server. When you change information in the publisher, these changes are reflected in the edition and in all documents *subscribing* (similar to linking) to the edition. You can specify how often Microsoft Excel sends updated information from the publisher to the edition. You can also specify how often subscribers receive updated information from the edition.

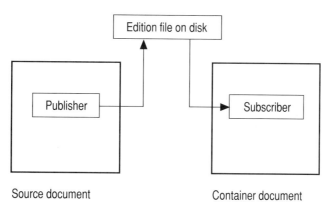

You can name and move an edition just as you would do with any other file. The connection is maintained even if you change the name of the edition. However, if you want Microsoft Excel to maintain the connection to all publishers and subscribers, you cannot move the edition off the file server or the hard disk.

Creating a Publisher and an Edition

To publish information from a Microsoft Excel document, use the Create Publisher command (Edit menu, Publishing submenu). You can edit a publisher the same way you edit other parts of a document. When you create a publisher, Microsoft Excel creates an edition file that is linked to the contents of the selected publisher range.

Note If you want to make editions available to other computers on a network, you can store them on a network file server. If you must store the editions on your hard disk and use the file-sharing option, make sure to share the folder that contains the editions. To share files on the Macintosh, choose Control Panel from the Apple menu, double-click the Sharing Startup icon, and then choose the Start button under File Sharing. For more information, see your Macintosh documentation.

Updating an Edition

Once you have created a publisher and its corresponding edition file, you can specify how frequently you want to update the edition with changes you make to the publisher. Unless you specify otherwise, Microsoft Excel updates the edition as soon as you save changes to the publisher. To specify alternatives to this method, choose Links from the Edit menu. In the Link Type box, select Publishers. Select the edition name in the Links box, and then choose the Options button. There are three update options in the Publisher Options dialog box: On Save, Manually, and Send Edition Now.

In the Send Editions box, do one of the following.

To update the edition	Do this
Whenever you save the publisher	Select the On Save option button.
Only when you choose the Send Edition Now button	Select the Manually option button.

Canceling a Publisher

If you decide that you no longer want to publish information in your document, choose the Cancel Publisher button in the Publisher Options dialog box. The contents of the publisher remain in your document. The data also remains in other documents that subscribed to the edition. However, the edition is gone, and the subscriber can no longer be updated. To remove the edition entirely, delete it in the Finder just as you would delete any other file.

Subscribing to an Edition

To subscribe to an edition file, use the Subscribe To command (Edit menu, Publishing submenu). When you subscribe to an edition, you insert a copy of the edition into your workbook. This copy is called the *subscriber*. Once you have inserted a subscriber into the workbook, updates received by the edition are sent to the subscriber. As long as the edition remains on the same file server or hard disk, Microsoft Excel maintains the connection between the edition and the subscriber, even if you change the name of either one.

When you create a subscriber, Microsoft Excel enters a formula in the cells that contain the subscriber. You cannot enter or edit this formula yourself.

Note If an edition contains both data and a picture, Microsoft Excel subscribes only to the data if you select a worksheet range, and only to the picture if you select an object. If you want to subscribe to both the data and the picture portion of an edition, hold down SHIFT while you choose the Subscribe button. The subscriber is then placed on your worksheet as a graphic object.

Updating a Subscriber

When you've subscribed to an edition, you can specify how frequently you want to receive updated information from the edition. Unless you choose another option, Microsoft Excel updates the subscriber automatically as soon as a new edition is available—that is, any time the publisher sends new information to the edition. To specify alternatives, choose Links from the Edit menu. In the Link Type box, select Subscribers. Select the subscriber name in the Links box, and then choose the Options button.

To update the subscriber	Choose
Whenever a change is made in the edition	The Automatically button
Only when you choose the Get Edition Now button	The Manually button

Switching from a Subscriber to Its Publisher

If you need to change the contents or formatting of a subscriber, you must make the changes in the publisher itself. This way, the changes are reflected in the subscriber and in any other subscribers that use the same edition file. If you are connected to a network, you must have access to the publisher to perform this procedure.

To open a subscriber's publisher, choose Links from the Edit menu. In the Link Type box, select Subscribers. Select the subscriber name in the Links box, and then choose the Options button. In the Subscriber Options dialog box, choose the Open Publisher button. Microsoft Excel opens the document that contains the publisher you want, allowing you to make the changes in the publisher.

Canceling a Subscriber

If you do not have access to the publisher to make changes and you do not need to receive any more updates from the edition, you can cancel the subscriber. You can then edit the information as you would edit any other text without losing any changes when updates are sent. The contents of the subscriber remain in the document.

To cancel a subscriber, choose Links from the Edit menu. In the Link Type box, select Subscribers. Select the subscriber name in the list box, and then choose the Options button. In the Subscriber Options dialog box, choose the Cancel Subscriber button.

Step By Step

For step-by-step instructions and related information, double-click the [?] button to display the Search dialog box in Help, and then:

Type this keyword and choose Show Topics	Select a topic and choose Go To
canceling	Canceling a subscriber or publisher
editions	Changing the format of an edition created from a chart
	Changing the format of an edition created from a worksheet
	Controlling when an edition is updated
	Subscribing to an edition
	Updating a Microsoft Excel edition
publishers	Creating a publisher
subscribers	Controlling when a subscriber is updated
	Switching from a subscriber to its publisher

C H A P T E R   4 2

Importing and Exporting Documents

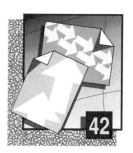

For command, keyboard, and toolbar button information, see online Help.

In This Chapter

Opening and Saving Documents in Different File Formats

With the Open command on the File menu, you can open documents created by many other applications, including Lotus 1-2-3, Borland® Quattro Pro, and dBASE. You can also save documents—using the Save As command on the File menu—in file formats readable by many other applications. The list of supported file formats appears in the Open dialog box under List Files Of Type, and in the Save As dialog box under Save File As Type.

If the file type you select cannot save multiple sheets, a message appears to inform you that only the active sheet will be saved.

You can also open and save text files. When you open a text file, the TextWizard opens so you can specify how you want the text distributed across columns.

To copy just part of a Microsoft Excel file to or from another application, see Chapter 41, "Sharing Data and Graphics with Other Applications."

Step By Step

For step-by-step instructions and related information, double-click the [?] button to display the Search dialog box in Help, and then:

Type this keyword and choose Show Topics	Select a topic and choose Go To
applications, external	Saving a document for use in another application
file formats, defined	File Formats
other applications	Opening a document created by another application

Converting Text to Columns

If you copy into Microsoft Excel data from a document created by another application, you might find that several columns of data are condensed into a single column. This also happens if you open a text file and choose not to delimit it or specify column boundaries. You can use the Text To Columns command on the Data menu to distribute the fields of each record into separate columns. The Text To Columns command opens the TextWizard, a series of dialog boxes that guide you through the steps necessary to convert the text.

The range you convert can be any number of rows high, but you can convert only one column of data at a time. The converted data typically begins in the column you are converting and then fills cells to the right. If you prefer, you can specify a different upper-left cell in the Destination box.

Make sure you have enough blank cells to the right of the column you are converting to accommodate the data. If there is already data in the destination range, a message appears asking if you want the converted data to overwrite the existing data.

For information about copying data from another application into Microsoft Excel, see Chapter 41, "Sharing Data and Graphics with Other Applications."

Step By Step

For step-by-step instructions and related information, double-click the [?] button to display the Search dialog box in Help, and then:

Type this keyword and choose Show Topics	Select a topic and choose Go To
Clipboard	Overview of Exchanging Data Using the Clipboard
converting, text to columns	Converting text to columns

Moving Microsoft Excel Files Between Windows and the Macintosh

All versions of Microsoft Excel can read files created by earlier versions of Microsoft Excel, but they can't read files created by later versions unless you first save the file in the format for the earlier version. For example, to read a Microsoft Excel version 5.0 for Windows file in Microsoft Excel version 4.0 for the Macintosh, use the Save As command on the File menu in Microsoft Excel for Windows to save the file in Microsoft Excel version 4.0 for the Macintosh format before moving the file.

Methods for Moving Microsoft Excel Files

The file formats of Microsoft Excel version 2.0 and later for Windows and for the Macintosh are the same for each version. There are several tools for reading files directly from one platform to the other, including:

- Apple File Exchange (comes with Macintosh System software).
- Third-party programs, such as DOS Mounter, Access PC, and PC Exchange, that enable the Macintosh to read MS-DOS formatted floppy disks.
- Mail systems, such as Microsoft Mail.
- Servers that can be accessed by both Macintosh and Windows-based computers —for example, MS LAN Manager or Novell® NetWare®.

- A modem or null modem cable and communication software.
- Special third-party hardware that enables either the Macintosh or the Windows-based computer to read floppy disks from the other platform.

Using Apple File Exchange

The Apple File Exchange program enables an Apple 3.5-inch floppy disk, high-density (FDHD) drive to read and write to MS-DOS disks and translate Microsoft Excel files to and from MS-DOS disks. Apple File Exchange is supplied with all Apple Computer operating systems. Apple floppy disk high-density drives can read disks in the following formats:

- MS-DOS (720 kilobytes and 1.44 megabytes)
- Apple 400K, 800K, and 1.44 MB

The names of Macintosh files might be truncated in Windows. This can cause filename conflicts. If conflicts do occur, Apple File Exchange enables you to edit the filenames before translation. For easiest translation, make sure that the files you will transfer to Windows have names that follow the MS-DOS file-naming convention: up to eight characters followed by a period (.) and the XLS extension (for Microsoft Excel workbooks).

Note Apple File Exchange is on the Utilities 2 disk in Apple Macintosh System 6, and the Tidbits disk in System 7.

Step By Step

For step-by-step instructions and related information, double-click the 🅿️ button to display the Search dialog box in Help, and then:

Type this keyword and choose Show Topics	Select a topic and choose Go To
Windows and Macintosh	Moving files between Windows and the Macintosh
	Overview of Moving Microsoft Excel Files Between Windows and the Macintosh

Appendixes

APPENDIX A

Producing a Slide Show

You can create a slide show with Microsoft Excel to present data, charts, and graphics created in Microsoft Excel or imported from other applications. Slide shows are created on a special template included with Microsoft Excel. You can include a variety of graphics in a slide show and apply a number of video and audio transition effects between slides. Slide shows can be saved in a workbook and can be viewed on other computers.

Slide shows can be run only on a computer screen or on another display device attached to your computer; they cannot be printed.

To create and display slide shows, the Slide Show add-in must be installed.

For complete information about slide shows and how they work, see Help.

Step By Step

For step-by-step instructions and related information, double-click the [k?] button to display the Search dialog box in Help, and then:

Type this keyword and choose Show Topics	Select a topic and choose Go To
add-ins	Installing or removing an add-in
slide shows	Producing a slide show

APPENDIX B

Accessibility for People with Disabilities

Microsoft is committed to making its products and services easier for everyone to use. This appendix provides information about the following products and services, which make Microsoft Windows and Microsoft Excel more accessible for people with disabilities:

- Microsoft Excel accessibility
- Microsoft services for people who are deaf or hard-of-hearing
- Access Pack for Microsoft Windows
- Keyboard layouts designed for people who type with one hand or a wand
- Microsoft software documentation on audiocassettes and floppy disks
- Products for people who are blind or have low vision
- Hints for customizing Microsoft Windows
- Other products and services for people with disabilities

Note The information in this section applies only to users who purchased Windows in the United States. If you purchased Windows outside the United States, your Windows package contains a subsidiary information card that lists Microsoft support services telephone numbers and addresses. You can contact your subsidiary to find out whether the products and services described in this appendix are available in your area.

Microsoft Excel Accessibility

In addition to Microsoft and Microsoft Windows accessibility products and services, the following features make Microsoft Excel more accessible for people with disabilities.

Zooming to Magnify the View   You can view your worksheets at any magnification from 10 to 400 percent. By default, Microsoft Excel displays worksheets at 100 percent, but you can magnify the view up to 400 percent. At 400-percent magnification, 12-point type is almost 1 inch high on the screen. You can zoom worksheets, macro sheets, and charts. From the View menu, choose the Zoom command, or select the magnification you want in the Zoom Control box on the Standard toolbar. For more information about zooming in or out on a worksheet, see Chapter 32, "Changing How You View Your Worksheet."

Enlarging Toolbar Buttons   To view enlarged toolbar buttons, choose the Toolbars command from the View menu and then select the Large Buttons check box.

Enlarging Text in Column and Row Headings and in the Formula and Status Bars
To view enlarged text in row and column headings and in the formula bar and the status bar, choose the Options command from the Tools menu. Select the General tab, and then set the font and size you want.

Customizing the Keyboard   Microsoft Excel for Windows supports Dvorak keyboard layouts, which make the most frequently typed characters more accessible. For more information about Dvorak keyboard layouts, see "Keyboard Layouts for Single-Handed Users" later in this appendix.

Customizing the Toolbars   You can add, delete, and move buttons on toolbars to best suit the way you work. You can also create entirely new toolbars that contain buttons for the commands, formats, and macros that you use most frequently. For information about customizing toolbars, see "Customizing Toolbars" in Chapter 34. For more information about assigning macros to buttons, see Chapter 1, "Automating Repeated Tasks," in the *Microsoft Excel Visual Basic User's Guide*.

Customizing the Menus   You can add new menus, delete existing menus, and customize menus so that they contain the commands, formats, and macros that you commonly use. For information about customizing menus, see Chapter 12, "Menus and Toolbars," in the *Microsoft Excel Visual Basic User's Guide*.

Automating Tasks with Macros   A macro is a series of Microsoft Excel commands that you can group together as a single command. Macros can automate complex tasks and reduce the number of steps required to complete tasks that you perform frequently. You can assign a macro to a toolbar button, menu command, or shortcut key, making the macro as convenient to use as any standard Microsoft Excel command. For more information about creating and assigning macros, see Chapter 1, "Automating Repeated Tasks," in the *Microsoft Excel Visual Basic User's Guide*.

Applying Built-in Format Combinations Using Autoformat The Autoformat feature automatically changes the look of your worksheet or chart. You can use built-in autoformats or create your own. For more information, see Chapter 12, "Formatting a Worksheet, " and Chapter 16, "Working with Chart Types and Autoformats."

Step By Step

For step-by-step instructions and related information, double-click the ⟦▸?⟧ button to display the Search dialog box in Help, and then:

Type this keyword and choose Show Topics	Select a topic and choose Go To
autoformats, applying	Applying an autoformat to a chart
	Applying an autoformat to a range
custom toolbars	Overview of Assigning a Macro to the Tools Menu, a Button, or a Graphic Object
	Overview of Customizing Toolbars
recording macros	Recording a macro
running macros	Running a macro
writing macros	Writing a macro
zooming	Zooming in or out on a worksheet

Microsoft Services for People Who Are Deaf or Hard-of-Hearing

Through a text telephone (TT/TDD) service, Microsoft provides people who are deaf or hard-of-hearing with complete access to Microsoft product and customer services.

You can contact Microsoft Sales and Service on a text telephone by dialing 800-892-5234 between 6:30 A.M. and 5:30 P.M. Pacific time. For technical assistance, you can contact Microsoft Product Support Services on a text telephone at 206-635-4948 between 6:00 A.M. and 6:00 P.M. Pacific time. Microsoft support services are subject to Microsoft prices, terms, and conditions in place at the time the service is used.

Access Pack for Microsoft Windows

Microsoft distributes Access Pack for Microsoft Windows, which provides people
with motion or hearing disabilities better access to computers that are running
Microsoft Windows. Access Pack for Microsoft Windows contains several features
that:

- Allow single-finger typing of SHIFT, CTRL, and ALT key combinations.
- Ignore accidental keystrokes.
- Adjust the rate at which a character is repeated when you hold down a key, or
  turn off character repeating entirely.
- Prevent extra characters if you unintentionally press a key more than once.
- Enable you to control the cursor by using the keyboard.
- Enable you to control the computer keyboard and the mouse by using an
  alternate input device.
- Provide a visual cue when the computer beeps or makes other sounds.

Access Pack for Microsoft Windows is included in the Microsoft Windows Driver
Library in the file ACCESS.EXE. If you have a modem, you can download
Microsoft Windows Driver Library components, including the following, from
network services:

- CompuServe.
- GEnie™.
- Microsoft OnLine.
- Microsoft Download Service (MSDL), which you can reach by calling
  206-936-MSDL (936-6735) any time except between 1:00 A.M. and 2:30 A.M.
  Pacific time. Use the following communications settings.

For this setting	Specify
Baud rate	1200, 2400, or 9600
Parity	None
Data bits	8
Stop bits	1

- Various user-group bulletin boards (such as the bulletin board services on the
  Association of PC User Groups network).

People within the United States who do not have a modem can order Access Pack
for Microsoft Windows on floppy disks by calling Microsoft Product Support
Services at 206-637-7098 or 206-635-4948 (text telephone).

Keyboard Layouts for Single-Handed Users of Microsoft Windows

Microsoft distributes Dvorak keyboard layouts that make the most frequently typed characters on a keyboard more accessible to people who have difficulty using the standard "QWERTY" layout. There are three Dvorak layouts: one for two-handed users, one for people who type with their left hand only, and one for people who type with their right hand only. The left-handed and right-handed keyboard layouts can also be used by people who type with a single finger or a wand. You do not need to purchase any special equipment to use these features.

Microsoft Windows already supports the two-handed Dvorak layout, which can be useful for coping with or avoiding certain types of repetitive-motion injuries associated with typing. To get this layout, choose International in the Windows Control Panel. The two layouts for people who type with one hand are distributed as Microsoft Application Note GA0650. They are also contained in file GA0650.ZIP on most network services or GA0650.EXE on the Microsoft Download Service. For instructions on obtaining this application note, see the preceding section, "Access Pack for Microsoft Windows."

Microsoft Documentation on Audiocassettes and Floppy Disks

People who have difficulty reading or handling printed documentation can obtain most Microsoft publications from Recording for the Blind, Inc. Recording for the Blind distributes these documents to registered members of their distribution service either on audiocassettes or on floppy disks. The Recording for the Blind collection contains more than 80,000 titles, including Microsoft product documentation and books from Microsoft Press. You can contact Recording for the Blind at the following address or phone numbers:

Recording for the Blind, Inc.   Phone: 800-221-4792
20 Roszel Road   Outside the United States: 609-452-0606
Princeton, NJ 08540   Fax: 609-987-8116

Products for People Who Are Blind or Have Low Vision

There are numerous products available to help people who are blind or have low vision use Microsoft Windows or the Macintosh. For people with low vision, there are screen-enlargement utilities, and for people who cannot use visual information, there are screen readers that provide alternative output by means of synthesized voice or refreshable Braille displays. In addition, people with low vision can customize the Microsoft Windows or Macintosh display to suit their needs.

For more information about the various products that are available, see "Getting More Information" later in this appendix. For more information about customizing Microsoft Windows for people with low vision, see the following section.

Customizing Microsoft Windows

There are many ways you can adjust the appearance and behavior of Microsoft Windows to suit varying vision and motor abilities without requiring any additional hardware or software. These include ways to adjust both the appearance and behavior of the mouse and keyboard. The specific methods available depend on which operating system you are using. Application notes are available that describe the specific methods available for each operating system.

For information relating to customizing Windows version 3.0 for people with disabilities, see Application Note WW0786; for Windows version 3.1, see Application Note WW0787; for Windows NT version 3.1 for Workgroups, see Application Note WG0788; for Windows NT version 3.1, see Application Note WN0789. For information about obtaining application notes, see "Access Pack for Microsoft Windows" earlier in this appendix.

Getting More Information

For more information about Microsoft products and services for people with disabilities, contact Microsoft Sales and Service at 800-426-9400 (voice) or 800-892-5234 (text telephone).

The Trace R&D Center at the University of Wisconsin–Madison produces a book and a compact disc that describe products that help people with disabilities use computers. The book, titled *Trace Resource Book,* provides descriptions and photographs of about 2000 products. The compact disc, titled *CO-NET CD,* provides a database of more than 17,000 products and other information for people with disabilities. It is issued twice a year.

You can contact the Trace R&D Center by using the following address or telephone numbers:

Trace R&D Center   Phone: 608-263-2309
S-151 Waisman Center   Text telephone: 608-263-5408
1500 Highland Avenue   Fax: 608-262-8848
Madison, WI 53705-2280

For general information and recommendations about how computers can help specific people, you should consult a trained evaluator who can best match the individual's needs with the available solutions.

If you are in the United States, you can obtain information about resources in your area by calling the National Information System, an information and referral center for people with disabilities, at the following address:

National Information System (NIS)
Center for Developmental Disabilities
University of South Carolina, Benson Bldg.
Columbia, SC 29208

Phone or text telephone: 800-922-9234 (outside South Carolina)
                           800-922-1107 (in South Carolina)
                           803-777-6222 (outside the United States)
Fax: 800-777-6058

This service is available only in the English language.

Index

Symbols

: (colon), range operator 29, 133
, (comma)
    number formats
        applying 209–211
        symbols, codes for 215–216
    permitted in numbers 110, 111
    union operator 133
! (exclamation point), reference operator 135, 144
^ (exponentiation operator) 127
> (greater-than operator) 128
>= (greater-than, equal-to operator) 128
< (less-than operator) 128
<= (less-than, equal-to operator) 128
<> (not-equal-to operator) 128
error 108, 131
#DIV/0! error 109, 131
#N/A error 109, 131
#NAME? error 109, 131, 147
#NULL! error 109, 131
#NUM! error 109, 131
#REF! error 109, 131
#VALUE! error 109, 130–131
() (parentheses)
    as numeric characters 110
    in formulas 111, 129
% (percent sign)
    as numeric character 110
    in formulas 111
    percentage operator 127, 209
. (period)
    as decimal point 110, 216
    denoting cell ranges 29
.. range operator, Lotus 1-2-3 29
1-2-3, Lotus *See* Lotus 1-2-3
1900 date system 30, 109, 168–169
1904 date system 30, 109, 168–169
3-D charts
    adjusting data marker spacing 339
    adjusting depth 339
    area 295
    auto scaling 339
    bar 295
    column
        illustrated 280
        types of 296

3-D charts *(continued)*
    elevation, changing 338–339
    error bars 354
    formatting 336–339
    graphic objects in 340
    gridlines 337
    height of base 339
    line 296, 328
    multicategory 264
    parts of 271
    perspective 336, 338–339
    pie 297, 336
    right angle axes 339
    rotation 338–339
    series axis 336
    simple 336
    surface 297, 329, 333
    types of 336
    viewing while dragging 339
3-D references
    described 135–137
    effects on deleted and inserted sheets 141
    in Microsoft Excel vs. Lotus 1-2-3 29
    names, defining as 144

A

A1 reference style 132
About command (Help menu) xiii–xiv
absolute references
    See also cell references
    described 132–133
absolute value of complex numbers 604
Access (Microsoft application), activating with toolbar button 706
Access Pack for Microsoft Windows 734
access, controlling *See* protecting workbooks and sheets
ACCESS.EXE 734
accessibility for users with disabilities
    Access Pack for Microsoft Windows 735–736
    products and services listed 731

accessing external data
    files, drivers 446
    in other formats 443
    macros for 442
    methods, components 438
accidental keystrokes, ignoring 734
accounting formats
    applying 209–211
    symbols, codes for 215–218
across-then-down page numbering 249
actions, repeating and undoing 101
activating
    charts 268
    Data Access macro 447
    embedded charts 269
    embedded objects 709–715
    linked objects 715
    other applications 706
    Q+E add-in 447
active cell
    changing 14
    defined 14
    illustrated 13–14
    moving within selections 95–96
    splitting windows at 610
    updating query 445
active sheet 78
add-in macros, Microsoft Query add-in 439
Add-in menu commands, Lotus 1-2-3 39
add-ins
    See also specific add-in
    Analysis ToolPak 661
        See also Analysis ToolPak
    AutoSave 67, 661
    converting from earlier versions 42
    described 67, 660–661
    included with Microsoft Excel 661
    installing
        individual add-ins 448, 660
        on hard disk 661
    location 661
    Microsoft ODBC Support 661
        See also ODBC
    Microsoft Query add-in 661
        See also Microsoft Query add-in